Ex Libris

Professor Steve Murdoch

THE SOCIETY OF JESUS
IN IRELAND, SCOTLAND, AND
ENGLAND 1541–1588

STUDIES IN MEDIEVAL AND REFORMATION THOUGHT

EDITED BY

HEIKO A. OBERMAN, Tucson, Arizona

IN COOPERATION WITH

THOMAS A. BRADY, Jr., Berkeley, California
E. JANE DEMPSEY DOUGLASS, Princeton, New Jersey
JÜRGEN MIETHKE, Heidelberg
M. E. H. NICOLETTE MOUT, Leiden
ANDREW PETTEGREE, St. Andrews
MANFRED SCHULZE, Wuppertal
DAVID C. STEINMETZ, Durham, North Carolina

VOLUME LX

THOMAS M. McCOOG SJ

THE SOCIETY OF JESUS
IN IRELAND, SCOTLAND, AND
ENGLAND 1541–1588

THE SOCIETY OF JESUS IN IRELAND, SCOTLAND, AND ENGLAND 1541–1588

'Our Way of Proceeding?'

BY

THOMAS M. McCOOG SJ

E.J. BRILL
LEIDEN · NEW YORK · KÖLN
1996

The paper in this book meets the guidelines for permanence and durability of the Committee on Production Guidelines for Book Longevity of the Council on Library Resources.

Library of Congress Cataloging-in-Publication Data

McCoog, Thomas M.
　The society of Jesus in Ireland, Scotland, and England 1541-1588 : "our way of proceeding" / by Thomas M. McCoog.
　　　p. cm. — (Studies in medieval and Reformation thought, ISSN 0585-6914 ; v. 60)
　Includes bibliographical references and index.
　ISBN 9004104828 (cloth : alk. paper)
　1. Jesuits—Ireland—History—16th century. 2. Jesuits—Scotland--History—16th century. 3. Jesuits—England—History—16th century. 4. Ireland—Church history—16th century. 5. Scotland—Church history—16th century. 6. England—Church history—16th century. I. Series.
BX3719.M33　　1996
271'.53041'09031—dc20　　　　　　　　　　　　　　　　　　96–2790
　　　　　　　　　　　　　　　　　　　　　　　　　　　　　　CIP

Die Deutsche Bibliothek - CIP-Einheitsaufnahme

McCoog, Thomas M.:
The Society of Jesus in Ireland, Scotland, and England 1541 - 1588 / by Thomas M. McCoog. – Leiden ; New York ; Köln : Brill, 1996
　(Studies in medieval and reformation thought ; Vol. 60)
　ISBN 90–04–10482–2
NE: GT

ISSN　0585-6914
ISBN　90 04 10482 8

© *Copyright 1996 by E.J. Brill, Leiden, The Netherlands*

All rights reserved. No part of this publication may be reproduced, translated, stored in a retrieval system, or transmitted in any form or by any means, electronic, mechanical, photocopying, recording or otherwise, without prior written permission from the publisher.

Authorization to photocopy items for internal or personal use is granted by E.J. Brill provided that the appropriate fees are paid directly to The Copyright Clearance Center, 222 Rosewood Drive, Suite 910 Danvers MA 01923, USA. Fees are subject to change.

PRINTED IN THE NETHERLANDS

To My Mother, Elizabeth Cole McCoog,
and the Memory of My Father, James Clarence McCoog

TABLE OF CONTENTS

Acknowledgements ix

Abbreviations xi

Illustrations xiii

Introduction: "Lewdly Cal Jebusites" 1

Chapter One: "The Open Door" 11

Chapter Two: "The Hour of Satan" 43

Chapter Three: "According to the Spirit of the Society" 80

Chapter Four: "The Enterprise is Begun" 129

Chapter Five: "On the Conversion of Scotland" 178

Chapter Six: "The Winter in the Soul" 224

Conclusion: "Our Way of Proceeding" 265

Bibliography 281

Index of Names, Places, and Subjects 299

ACKNOWLEDGEMENTS

Of Francis Bacon's many observations none rings more true to a scholar than "I hold every man a debtor to his profession." I have accumulated many debts in writing this book; some have been outstanding for so long that they may have been written off.

My interest in English Jesuits began in 1971 at the Jesuit novitiate in Wernersville, Pennsylvania when I was given Evelyn Waugh's *Edmund Campion* for spiritual reading. The late William V. Bangert, S.J., fostered my enthusiasm during visits to the novitiate, and throughout our subsequent friendship. Professors John C. Olin and Albert J. Loomie, S.J., of Fordham University, John W. Padberg, S.J., then of Weston School of Theology, and John E. Booty, then of Episcopal Divinity School, sponsored my initiation into the mysteries of Catholic Reformation, Tudor England, Jesuit historiography, and Elizabethan recusant controversies when I should have been concentrating on philosophy and theology. Professor J.J. Scarisbrick supervised my doctoral research at the University of Warwick. His direction was steady and gentle despite my periodic change of topic. It was he who recommended that I centre on the Society's Institute and its implementation in England after he had read the institutional analysis intended as introduction to a history of the English province from 1678 to 1688.

During the years of research old ideas were resuscitated and new ones debated in tearooms and pubs through southern England, and cafes in Rome. I am indebted to Father Thomas E. Clancy, S.J., the late Dr. David Rogers, Dr. Nancy Pollard Brown, Dr. Christopher Haigh, and Father John LaRocca, S.J. More recently Dr. Thomas Mayer, Dr. A. Lynn Martin, Dr. Michael Questier, and Father Philip Endean, S.J., have been formidable sparring partners. Fathers George E. Ganss, S.J., and Ladislas Örsy, S.J., clarified many arcane canonical matters. The late Father Michael Kyne, S.J., Dom Sebastian Leonard, O.S.B., Father Anthony O'Sullivan, and the parishioners of the Church of St. Mary Immaculate, Warwick, and Farm Street, London, prevented my preoccupation with Jesuits and recusants from becoming a myopia. The late Antony Allison's assistance has been enormous. For fifteen years we discussed recusant matters with costly regularity at the same table in the Pizza Express near the British Museum. He listened patiently to my ideas, theories, and schemes; his subsequent comments saved others from a similar fate. From him I learned much. I am sorry that he did not see the finished product.

ACKNOWLEDGEMENTS

Throughout the research I have benefited from the kindness and generosity of three different Jesuit communities. Fathers Joseph A. Sobierajski and James P. Bradley, rectors during my sojourn in the Jesuit community at Loyola College, Baltimore, did all they could spiritually and financially to facilitate my research. Dr. Jack Breihan, Dr. Chuck Cheape, and Dr. Steven Hughes deftly balanced my research interests with departmental requirements.

The Jesuit Historical Institute, Rome provided stimulating discussions and easy, privileged access to the Jesuit archives. Among the many who aided transcriptions of difficult manuscripts and translations of that odd mixture of Spanish-Latin-Italian found in many Jesuit letters are László Lukács, co-editor of future volumes of *Monumenta Angliae*, Mario Zanardi, Mario Zanfredini, Antonio Maldonado, Antonio Queralt, Francesco de Borja de Medina, Charles Libois, Hugo Storni, and László Polgár. I am especially indebted to Charles E. O'Neill and László Szilas, past and current director of the Institute, and to Wiktor Gramatowski, and Jozef de Cock, past and current archivist.

At the Jesuit residence in Farm Street, London, Fathers Francis Edwards and Geoffrey Holt, my predecessors as archivist, provided much needed advice and encouragement, even when we do not agree. Father John Edwards, S.J., Ms Patricia McHugh, and Ms Audrey Marcheselli cautioned me against too many Americanisms. Mr. Pedro Zanatti came to my assistance by translating Portuguese documents. Father Frederick Turner, S.J., and Mr. Anthony Symondson, S.J., at Stonyhurst College are exemplary archivists with quick and gracious replies to all queries. Father Stephen Redmond, S.J., then archivist of the Irish Jesuit province, guided me through the unfamiliar terrain of Irish Jesuit history.

I acknowledge with tremendous gratitude the help of Fathers James A.P. Byrne, S.J. of Georgetown Preparatory School, North Bethesda, Maryland, and William M. Davish, S.J. of Loyola College, Baltimore. Father Byrne is always ready to abandon the ethereal world of Ciceronian Latin for the more mundane Latin of Jesuit correspondence when I needed his assistance. Father Davish amiably accepted the unenviable task of translating my convoluted English into something more comprehensible and grammatically correct. Both are so self-effacing that they give the impression that I am doing them a favour with my requests. They "toiled without asking any reward." To them, to all, I tip my hat and proclaim my appreciation. Without them this volume would never have been completed.

Finally I thank Professor H.A. Oberman for his kind assessment of this manuscript and for including it in the series *Studies in Medieval and Reformation Thought*.

London, 1 March 1996   Thomas M. McCoog SJ

ABBREVIATIONS

AAW	Archives of the Archdiocese of Westminster
ABSI	Archivum Britannicum Societatis Iesu (Farm Street)
AH	*Archivium Hibernicum*
AHSI	*Archivum Historicum Societatis Iesu*
ARCR	A.F. Allison and D.M. Rogers, eds., *The Contemporary Printed Literature of the English Counter-Reformation between 1558 and 1640*, 2 vols. Aldershot, 1989-94.
ARSI	Archivum Romanum Societatis Iesu
CHR	*Catholic Historical Review*
Cons.	Ignatius Loyola, *The Constitutions of the Society of Jesus*, ed. George E. Ganss, S.J. St. Louis, 1970.
CRS	Catholic Record Society
CSP Domestic	Robert Lemon et al., eds., *Calendar of State Papers, Domestic Series of the Reigns of Edward VI. . .*, 12 vols. London, 1856-72.
CSP Foreign	Joseph Stevenson et al., eds., *Calendar of State Papers Foreign Series of the Reign of Elizabeth*, 23 vols. in 26. London, 1863-1950.
CSP Rome	J.M. Rigg, ed., *Calendar of State Papers relating to English Affairs, preserved principally at Rome*, 2 vols. London, 1916-26.
CSP Scotland	Joseph Bain, William K. Boyd, et al., eds., *Calendar of State Papers Relating to Scotland and Mary, Queen of Scots, 1547-1603*, 13 vols. in 14 parts, London, 1898-1969.
CSP Simancas	Martin A.S. Hume, ed., *Calendar of letters and papers... preserved principally in the archives of Simancas*, 4 vols. London, 1892-99.
CSP Spain	Royall Tyler et al., eds., *Calendar of State Papers Spanish*, 15 vols. in 20. London, 1862-1954.
CSP Venice	Rawdon Brown et al., eds., *Calendar of State Papers and Manuscripts, Relating to English Affairs in the Archives and Collections of Venice*, 38 vols. in 40. London, 1864-1947.
EHR	*English Historical Review*
Epp. Bobad.	D. Restrepo, S.J., ed., *Bobadillae Monumenta*. Madrid, 1913. MHSI 46.

Epp. Borgia	I. Rodriguez, S.J., V. Agustí, S.J., and F. Cervós, S.J., eds., *Sanctus Franciscus Borgia*, 5 vols. Madrid, 1894-1911. MHSI 2, 23, 35, 38, 41.
Epp. Broet	F. Cervós, S.J., ed., *Epistolae P.P. Paschasii Broëti, Claudii Jayi, Joannis Codurii et Simonis Rodericii, S.I.* Madrid, 1903. MHSI 24.
Epp. Laínez	E. Astudillo, S.J., ed., *Epistolae et Acta patris Iacobi Lainii secundi praepositi generalis Societatis Iesu*, 8 vols. Madrid, 1912-16. MHSI 44, 45, 47, 49, 50, 51, 53, 55.
Epp. Nadal	F. Cervós, S.J. and M. Nicolau, S.J., eds., *Epistolae et Monumenta P. Hieronymi Nadal*. 5 vols. Madrid-Rome, 1898-1964. MHSI 13, 15, 21, 27, 90.
Epp. Ribadeneira	D. Restrepo, S.J. and Joannes Vilar, S.J., eds., *Patris Petri de Ribadeneira, Societatis Iesu sacerdotis, confessiones, epistolae aliaque scripta inedita*, 2 vols. Madrid, 1920-23. MHSI 58, 60.
Epp. Sal.	Raimundus Vidaurre, S.J. and F. Cervós, S.J., eds., *Epistolae P. Alphonsi Salmeronis, Societatis Iesu*, 2 vols. Madrid, 1906-7. MHSI 30, 32.
HMC	Historical Manuscripts Commission
IR	*Innes Review*
JEH	*Journal of Ecclesiastical History*
MHSI	Monumenta Historica Societatis Iesu
MI *Epp. Ign.*	M. Lecina, S.J., V. Agustí, S.J., and D. Restrepo, S.J., eds., *Sancti Ignatii de Loyola Societatis Iesu Fundatoris Epistolae et Instructiones*, 12 vols. Madrid, 1903-11. MHSI 22, 26, 28, 29, 31, 33, 34, 36, 37, 39, 40, 42.
Mon. Ang.	Thomas M. McCoog, S.J., ed., *Monumenta Angliae*, 2 vols. Rome, 1992. MHSI 142, 143.
Pol. Chron.	J.M. Velez, S.J. and V. Agustí, S.J., eds., *Vita Ignatii Loiolae et rerum Societatis Iesu historia auctore Joanne Alphonso de Polanco*, 6 vols. Madrid, 1894-98. MHSI 1, 3, 5, 7, 9, 11.
PRO	London, Public Record Office
RH	*Recusant History*
SC	Stonyhurst College
SCJ	*Sixteenth Century Journal*
SP	State Papers
STC	A.W. Pollard & G.R. Redgrave, eds., *A Short Title Catalogue of Books Printed in England, Scotland, & Ireland and of English Books Printed Abroad, 1475-1640*, 2nd edn. 3 vols. London, 1976-91.

ILLUSTRATIONS

Everard Mercurian, engraving by Arnoldo van Westherhout from *Imagines praepositorum generalium Societatis Iesu* (Rome, 1748).

Claudio Acquaviva, engraving by van Westherhout from *Imagines*.

Robert Parsons, engraving by Jan Valdor (fl. 1620), Stonyhurst College. Reproduced by kind permission of the Rector.

Jasper Heywood, pencil drawing by Charles Weld (1844-1927), of Chideock, Dorset, from an original painting in Rome. Weld donated his of drawings of the English martyrs and others who suffered for their faith to Stonyhurst College. I was unable to locate the original. Reproduced by kind permission of the Rector.

Edmund Campion, Alexander Briant, and Ralph Sherwin on the hurdle, engraving by G.B. Cavalleri from the frescoes by Niccolò Circignano in the English College, Rome, in *Ecclesiae Anglicanae Trophaea* (Rome, 1584) ARCR, II, nos. 944-946.

"Popish Plots and Treasons, From the Beginning of the Reign of Queen Elizabeth. Illustrated with Emblems and explain'd in Verse," engraving by Cornelius Danckerts (1561-c. 1634). The scenes illustrate the Northern Rebellion, the practises of Don Juan, the crusade of Sir Thomas Stucley, the murder of Henry Davells and Arthur Carter, the arrival of Campion and Parsons, the Sommerville Plot, the Throckmorton Plot, the capture of William Crichton, S.J., the Parry Plot, the Babington Plot, William Stafford's clearing himself in 1587, the Armada, the Lopez Plot (1592), and the rebellion of the Earl of Tyrone. Two others refer to events in the reign of James I and VI: Watson Plot and Gunpowder Plot. Copyright British Museum.

Everard Mercurian.

Claudio Acquaviva.

Robert Parsons.

P . GASPER HAYEWOOD ANGLUS ROMANUN TIROCINIUM
INGRESSUS 21Maii 1562 FRO FIDE CARCERE ET EXILIO MULTATUS
OBIIT NEAPOLI 19 FEBR 1598 Æ T. 63.

Jasper Heywood.

Qui Summi Pontificis primatum Reginæ in Anglia negant tribui posse, tanquam Læsæ Maiestatis rei damnantur, et ad suppilicij locum, Cratibus impositi, ministris interim hæreticis ad fidem Catholicam deserendam adhortantibus, per mediam Vrbem ignominiosè raptantur. Sic Edmundus Campianus cum socijs, alijque Catholici tum Sacerdotes tum laici ad mortem tracti sunt. Anno Domini 1581. 1582. 1583.

Edmund Campion, Alexander Briant,
and Ralph Sherwin on the hurdle.

POPISH PLOTS
AND
TREASONS

From the beginning of the Reign of Queen Elizabeth. Illustrated with Emblems and explain'd in Verse.

Figure 1.

The *Pope* aloft on Armed Shoulders Rides,
And in vain Hopes the English spoils divides;
His *Leaden Bull* 'gainst good *Eliza*. roares,
And scatters dire Rebellion round our shoars.
The Priest *Blesses* the Villians, Chears them on,
And promises Heav'n Crown, when her Crown's won,
But God doth blast their Troops, their Counsels mock,
And brings bold Traitors to th' deserved *block.*

Figure 3.

Spains King, and *Romes* Triple-Crown'd-Pelate Joyn,
And with them both bold *Stukely* does Combine
Ireland to conquer, And the Pope ha' lent,
For that Blest work, an *Holy Regiment*;
But in their way at *Barbary* they call,
Where at one Blow the *Moors* destroy them All.
See here, what such Ambitious Traitors Gain,
The shame of Christians is by *Pagans* Slain.

Figure 5.

What trusty Janizaries are Monks to *Rome*,
From their dark Cells the blackest Treasons come.
By the Popes Licence horrid Crimes they Act,
And Guild with piety each Treacherous Fact.
A seminary Priest, like Comets Blaze,
Doth always Blood-shed and Rebellion Raise;
But still the fatal Gibbet's ready fixt
For such, where Treason's with Religion mixt.

Figure 7.

Whilst *Spains* Embassador here Leiger lies,
Designs are laid the English to surprize;
Two Catalogues his Secretary had Got
The better to effect the Hellish Plot.
One all our Havens Names, where Foes might Land,
T' other what Papists were to lend an hand.
For this base Trick he's forc'd to pack to *Spain*
Whilst Tyburn greets confederates that remain.

Figure 9.

The Jesuites vile Doctrines do Convince
Parry, Tis Merit for to kill his Prince,
The fatal Dagger he prepares with Art,
And means to sheath it in her Royal Heart.
Oft he Attempts, and is as oft put by,
By the Majestick Terrors of her Eye;
At last his Cursed Intentions he Confest
And So his welcom'd a fit Tyburn Guest;

Figure 11.

Nor was 't with *Spain* alone, Great *Betty*'s Strife;
Now *France* attempts upon her pretious Life;
The Guises cause th' Ambassador to bribe
Moody, and others, of the Roman Tribe;
To Cut her off. To which they soon Consent,
But watchful Heav'n does that Guilt prevent.
Stafford doth to the Councel All disclose,
And Home with shame perfidious, *Mounsieur* goes.

Figure 13.

But now a private horrid Treason view
Hatcht by the Pope, the Devil, and a Jew;
Lopez, a Doctor must by Poison do
What all their Plots have fail'd in hitherto:
What will you give me then, the *Judas* Cries;
Full *fifty thousand Crowns*, t' other replies.
Tis done — but hold, the wretch shall miss his hope,
The Treasons known, and his Reward's the Rope.

Figure 15.

No Sooner *James* had blest the English Throne,
But Traiterous Priests Conspire to pull him down,
Watson the poisonous Maximes does Instill,
And draws some Nobles to Join in the Ill;
But Princes then appear the most divine,
When they with unexpected Mercy Shine.
Just as the Fatal Ax attempts the Stroke,
Pardon steps in and does the Blow Revoke.

And now let us, with chearful Hymns of praise,
And Hearts inflam'd with love *an Altar* raise
Of Gratitude to God, who doth advance
His out-stretched Arm in our Deliverance,
Tis only He, that doth protect his Sheep,
Tis he alone doth this poor Island keep
From Romish *Wolves*, which would us soon devour,
If not Defended by his mighty power.
Tis he that doth our *Church* with freedome Crown,
And beats the Popish *Superstitions* down,
Under her feet, and may they never rise.
Nor in vile *Darkness* Reinvolve our Eyes;
Since Heaven whose mercies ever are most tender
Hath both restor'd our *Faith*, and Faiths Defender.

First are describ'd the Cursed plots they laid.
And on the side their wretched ends display'd.

Figure 2.

Don John, who under Spain did with proud Hand
The then unsever'd *Netherlands* Command,
Contrives for Englands Conquest, and does Hope
To Gain is by Donation from the Pope.
Yet to Amuse our Queen does still pretend
Perpetual peace, and needs will seem a friend;
But Heav'n looks through those Juggles and in's prime,
Grief Cuts off Him and's Hopes All at a time.

Figure 4.

The Priests, with *Crosses* Ensigne-like displaid,
Prompt bloody *Desmond* to those spoiles he made
On Irish Protestants, and from afar
Blow Triumphs to Rebellions Holy War;
But against Providence all Arts are vain,
The Crafty, in their Craft are over-tane;
Behold where kill'd the Stubborn *Traitor* lies,
Whilst to the *Woods* his *Ghostly Father* flies;

Figure 6.

Mad *Sommervil*, by Cruel Priests inspir'd
To do whatever mischiefe they requir'd,
Swears that he instantly will be the death
Of good and Gracious Queen *Elizabeth.*
Assaults her Guards, but Heav'ns protecting pow'r
Defeats his rage makes him a Prisoner:
Where to avoid a just, though shameful Death,
Self-strangling hands do Stop his loathsome breath.

Figure 8.

View here a Miracle —— A Priest Conveys,
In Spanish Bottom o're the path-less Seas,
Close treacherous Notes, whilst a Dutch Ship comes by
And streight Engag'd the well-known Enemy:
The Conscious Priest his Guilty Papers tears,
And over board the scatter'd fragments bears;
But the just winds do force them back o' th' Decks,
And peice-meal all the lurking plot detects.

Figure 10.

Here *Babington* and all his desperate Band,
Ready prepar'd for Royal Murder stand,
His Motto seems to glory in the Deed,
These my Companions are whom dangers lead.
Cowardly Traitors, so many Combine
To Cut off one poor Ladies vital Twine;
In vain, — Heaven's her Guard, and as for you;
Behold, the Hangman gives you all your due.

Figure 12.

Spain's proud *Armado*, whom the Pope did bless,
Attacques our Isle, Confident of success.
But Heav'ns just Blast doth Scatter all their force,
They fly and quite round *Scotland* take their Course:
So many taken, burnt, and Sunk i' th' Main,
Scarce one in Ten did e're get home Again;
Thus *England* like *Noahs* Ark, amidst the Waves
Indulgent providence from Danger saves.

Figure 14.

The Great *Tyrone* that did so oft embrew
Ireland with Blood, and Popish Plots Renew;
Here vanquisht Swears, upon his bended Knee,
To the Queens Deputy fidelity.
Yet breaks that vow, and loaded with the Guilt
Of perjuries and Blood which he had spilt.
Being forc'd at last to fly his Native Land,
Carries in's Breast a sting, a Scourge in's *hand*

Figure 16.

In this Curs'd Powder-plot we plainly see
The Quintessence of Romish Cruelty.
King Lords and Commons at one Hellish Blast
Had been destroy'd, and half our Land laid wast,
See *Faux*, with his dark Lanthorn, ready stands
To Light the fatal Train with desperate hands,
But Heavens All-seeing eye defeats their desire,
And saves us as a Brand snatcht from the fire;

Let us to both a strict Adherence pay,
And for their *preservation* ever pray,
Since thus *Truths* happy *Bark* hath reach'd our shore
O may it *never, never* Leaves us more.

Sold by *John Garret* at his Shop, at the *Exchange-Staires* in *Cornhill* where you may have choice of all Sorts of Large and Small Maps: Drawing Books Coppy books, and Pictures for Gentlewomens works: and also very good originals of French and Dutch Prints.

"Popish Plots and Treasons."

"Popish Plots and Treasons."

INTRODUCTION

"LEWDLY CAL JEBUSITES"

In 1567 Thomas Stapleton concluded his attack on Robert Horne, newly appointed Bishop of Winchester, with a defence of the Society of Jesus. While much of Europe was being "carried away with errours and heresies," God opened new worlds for the proclamation of the true Gospel. Of the apostles sent to these faraway lands, the most important were Jesuits "whom you so lewdly cal Jebusites." Far from being cursed descendants of Cham as Horne suggested, Protestants are the real Jebusites, and Jesuits

> good gracious children. . . . Who worthely beare that name also, their workes being correspondent to theire name, which doth signifie a Saviour. For they, by their preaching have saved, and brought from damnation many an hundred thousand of souls, to the everlasting bliss of heaven, the which God of his goodness and mercie graunt unto us.[1]

The Society of Jesus was founded in 1540. A few Jesuits passed through England on their way to Ireland or Scotland; one returned to his homeland for reasons of health. There was no permanent Jesuit mission. Yet, as a Society, they were already known and derided. Well before the fabled Jesuit invasion of England in 1580, the Society of Jesus was attacked—and defended.

Throughout the Elizabethan period, the myth of the evil Jesuit developed, often as a subsidiary of the anti-Spanish "Black Legend" because of the Society's Spanish founder and its strong base in Spain.[2] The mythical Jesuit's plots were real, his malice infamous, his powers and exploits almost superhuman. The perfidious activities and the uncanny powers of the Society of Jesus became a favourite theme with English authors. One of the classic *bêtes noires* of English literature was born.[3]

---

[1] *A counterblast to M. Hornes vayne blaste against M. Fekenham* (Louvain, 1567) STC 23231, ARCR, II, no. 729, ff. 533ᵛ [*vere* 541ᵛ], 542ʳ. In his old age Stapleton entered a Jesuit novitiate, but did not remain. See Thomas M. McCoog, S.J., ed., *Monumenta Angliae*, 2 vols. (Rome, 1992) [henceforth *Mon. Ang.*] II, 489.

[2] On the role played by the myth in Elizabethan England see Arnold Pritchard, *Catholic Loyalism in Elizabethan England* (London, 1979) pp. 175-91. For the myth in general see Jean Lacouture, *Jesuits: A Multibiography* (Washington, D.C., 1995) pp. 348-77.

[3] See e.g. John Donne, *Ignatius His Conclave*, ed. T.S. Healy (Oxford, 1969).

An interesting feature on the literary, political, and religious landscape, the myth of the evil Jesuit must not be confused with reality. The literature and the polemics of the period reveal a stereotypical image created and nurtured by years of propaganda and fed occasionally on selectively interpreted facts.[4] The myth provided a handy hermeneutic with convenient scapegoats for any misfortune or malady; it should be appreciated for the literary creation that it is, and for the powerful role that it played in the nation's politics.[5] But what is the reality behind the myth? Who were the English Jesuits? How many were there? Where were they? How did they live? How were they organized? How were their activities financed? The myth provided its answer to these questions: they were too numerous to count; they lurked in shadows and hid behind many masks; they filled their coffers with money from Spain and Rome; they plotted and schemed to overthrow laws and governments in order to establish their own kingdom dependent on Rome. So answered the myth. But what do the records say?

In a recent comparison of how historians have assessed Martin Luther and Ignatius Loyola, Professor Heiko A. Oberman admitted that "the history of the investigation of the life and works of a religious leader, particularly one living in the sixteenth century, generally goes through a hagiographical phase." Noting that in the case of Loyola this phase has not ended, Oberman contrasted the "sophistication and scholarly 'distance'" that characterized the more non-confessional investigations of Martin Luther with the "gratitude and loyalty" that were found in Ignatian studies, still primarily a Jesuit preserve.[6]

---

[4] In an explanation of the myth, David Mathew was extremely kind to the Jesuits: "In any discussion of Catholicism in England it is essential not to shirk the question of the profound unpopularity of the Jesuits. It is very difficult to explain it completely. The governmental propaganda, the mass of hostile legend, the false charges of equivocation, the efficiency of the Jesuit organization, the perjury of such witnesses as Titus Oates, the effects of Pascal's writings in educated circles all these are admitted. The complete self-sacrifice of the Jesuits, the intense devotion with which they were regarded by their friends, their personal humility and magnificent corporate solidarity were always remarkable. How is it that they gained an unpopularity in non-Catholic England which the Benedictines, Dominicans and secular clergy have never shared? In regard to the seventeenth century one small point may, perhaps, serve as an indication. The contemporary records give us for the first time an adequate picture of the entire English priesthood. We can see that while the old crusty testy Benedictine sat in his skull-cap over the fire in the chaplain's room making no bones about his dislikes, and the robust secular clergy quarrelled loudly, honestly and frankly, the Jesuit repressed his irritations" (*Catholicism in England 1535-1935: Portrait of a Minority: Its Culture and Tradition* [London, 1936] pp. 69-70).

[5] The evil Jesuit is one aspect of the near-hysterical, apocalyptic anti-Catholicism often encountered in Elizabethan writings. On this theme see Carol Z. Wiener, "The Beleaguered Isle. A Study of Elizabethan and Early Jacobean Anti-Catholicism," *Past and Present* 51 (1971) 27-62.

[6] "Ignatius of Loyola and the Reformation: The Case of John Calvin," *Ignacio de Loyola y su Tiempo*, ed. Juan Plazaola (Bilbao, n.d. [1992]) p. 809.

Professor Oberman's evaluation of Ignatian studies can be extended to Jesuit history in general, and English Jesuit history in particular. The first historians of the Society of Jesus in England were Jesuits whose interests stemmed largely from confessional or hagiographical concerns. They were attracted to the piety of the English martyrs and the sufferings they endured. Pedro de Ribadeneira, who, as we shall see, was in England briefly during the early months of Queen Elizabeth's reign, wrote in 1588 *Historia ecclesiastica del scisma del reyno de Inglaterra*, a translation and adaption of Nicholas Sander's *De origine et progressu schismatis anglicani*.[7]

Ten years later, in a letter of 26 September 1598 addressed to all provincials, Father General Claudio Acquaviva asked each to make sure that the history of his province was written. That history was to be edifying, and among the suggested topics were noteworthy vocations, conversions, and benefactors; piety and sanctity of deceased members of the province; graces that have accrued to the Society's friends, and calamities that have befallen its foes and deserters.[8] Around this time, and probably as a consequence of the directive, individual English Jesuits (e.g. William Weston and John Gerard) were asked to write their autobiographies.

There was a longer wait for general histories of the province, but when these appeared they usually conformed to the General's directions. English Jesuit Henry More published his still important *Historia Provinciae Anglicanae Societatis Iesu* (St. Omers, 1660). As second Provincial of the English Jesuits, he played an influential role in many of the affairs he relates. Thus his *Historia* is an important primary source. Italian Jesuit Daniello Bartoli based his *Dell'Istoria della Compagnia di Giesu. L'Inghilterra* (Rome, 1667) on manuscripts of Robert Parsons and documents collected by English Jesuit Christopher Grene.

In the early 18th century the General suggested that someone be designated to collect material for a history of the province. Henry Sheldon, then professor of theology at Liège, was not enthusiastic about the proposal."[9] He replied: "The more I explore our archives [then in Ghent], the more I am convinced that there are really very few records of our achievements that have not been published many years ago in the excellent

---

[7] (Madrid, 1588) ARCR, I, no. 993. Sander's *De origine ac progressu schismatis Anglicani* ([Cologne, 1585] ARCR, I, no. 972) was edited posthumously by Edward Rishton. There were a number of subsequent editions. For more information see Peter Milward, *Religious Controversies of the Elizabethan Age* (London, 1977) pp. 70-72, and ARCR, I, nos. #973-1011.

[8] ARSI, Instit. 121, ff. 174^r-175^v. For an early controversy concerning a history more critical than edifying see James Brodrick, S.J., *The Progress of the Jesuits* (London, 1946) pp. 309-21.

[9] "Littera P. Henrici Sheldon de annuis et aptis ad Historiam Soc. 1700," SC, Glover Transcripts II, B.I.16, pp. 202-07.

histories of Father Henry More written in Latin and Father Bartoli in Italian." Fortunately most of the manuscripts that Sheldon described survived the Suppression and remain in the archives of the province, either in London or in Stonyhurst. His lack of enthusiasm, however, may explain the absence of any study until Brother Henry Foley's monumental *Records of the English Province of the Society of Jesus* in the 1880s.[10] Although it remains the foundation on which all subsequent investigations have been built,[11] Foley's *Records* need a thorough revision in light of recent scholarship.

The turn of the century saw the publication of Ethelred Taunton's *The History of the Jesuits in England*, the first study by a non-Jesuit. Behind its claim to be an examination of the Society's role in the Roman Catholic Church lay an extensive polemic against the English Jesuits insofar as they had followed the example set by Robert Parsons.[12] The book is in fact a continuation of the Jesuit/secular battles of the 16th and 17th centuries, battles that originated, as we shall see, in the conflict between William Allen and Robert Parsons, on the one hand, and Thomas Morgan and Charles Paget on the other. Two years later, an equally hostile and biased account appeared. In *The Jesuits in Great Britain*, Walter Walsh claimed that his book would "certainly differ from every other book on the Jesuits written by a Protestant, inasmuch as the great majority of my authorities are either Jesuits or ordinary Roman Catholics." The author's intention was to leave no doubt in the reader's mind that "during the sixteenth and seventeenth centuries the Jesuits were a thoroughly disloyal body of men, and the ringleaders in sedition and rebellion." For events that he did not cover, Walsh recommended that the reader consult the aforementioned volume by Taunton.[13] John H. Pollen, S.J., severely criticised Taunton's history, along with his other works, in articles in *The Month*.[14]

In 1892 the fathers assembled at the 24th General Congregation of the Society of Jesus asked the General to promote the writing of the histories of

---

[10] *Records of the English Province of the Society of Jesus*, 7 vols. in 8 (Roehampton/London, 1877-84).
[11] An often neglected series of articles by Louis Delplace, S.J., presented many of the fruits of Foley's endeavours to a French-speaking audience. Although Delplace added the results of his own research, his interest was restricted to the Society's involvement in England before the arrival of Campion and Parsons in 1580. See "L'Angleterre et la Compagnie de Jésus avant le martyre du B. Edmond Campion," *Précis Historiques* 39 (1890) 269-88, 329-48, 417-35, 492-508.
[12] (London, 1901).
[13] (London, 1903) vi.
[14] "The Rise of the Anglo-Benedictine Congregation," *The Month* 90 (1897) 581-600; "A Curious and Original History of the Jesuits in England," *The Month* 97 (1901) 502-18; 98 (1901) 315-18; "The Portrait of Father Robert Parsons," *The Month* 98 (1901) 113-26.

individual provinces.[15] As a result, Jesuit historians were soon at work on histories of their provinces and assistancies.[16] Pollen prepared a detailed history of the English province in response to the congregational decree and as a reply to the tendentious works of Taunton and Walsh. His *The English Catholics in the Reign of Queen Elizabeth: A Study of Their Politics Civil Life and Government* was to serve as an introduction, but his death in 1925 prevented the completion of the task.[17]

Bernard Basset, S.J., made the next attempt at a provincial history with *The English Jesuits*.[18] As the title suggests, he was more concerned with stories of individual Jesuits than with the history of the Society in England. Like Foley's *Records*, Basset's history contains wonderful anecdotes about the lives and mores of members of the Society, but avoids larger issues and historiographical problems.

Since 1980 Francis Edwards, S.J., has contributed two works to the field. The first is his translation and edition of Henry More's *Historia Provinciae Anglicanae Societatis Iesu, The Elizabethan Jesuits*. Edwards's edition, however, translated only half of More's work—indeed, the half in which More played no significant role—and consciously omitted "pious anecdote[s] and passages of devotional rather than historical interest."[19] Edwards's second contribution is *The Jesuits in England*. Although it was written at the same time as Basset's, publication of Basset's book delayed this volume's appearance for nearly twenty years. It is now offered as a supplement to Basset's history in that "it treats of the English Jesuit Province rather in terms of an institution than of its individual members." Edwards proposed his work as the first study of the province as a corporate institution, with the hope that the book would "provide a useful handbook of dates and data

---

[15] John W. Padberg, S.J., Martin D. O'Keefe, S.J., and John L. McCarthy, S.J., eds., *For Matters of Greater Moment: The First Thirty Jesuit General Congregations* (St. Louis, 1994) decree 21, p. 487.

[16] For administrative reasons the Society of Jesus is divided into geographical provinces subject to a major superior called provincial. The Jesuit Father General has the authority to establish, modify, or divide provinces. See Thomas M. McCoog, S.J., "The Establishment of the English Province of the Society of Jesus," *RH* 17 (1984) 124. Assistancies are collections of provinces, often along linguistic lines. An assistant is an advisor to Father General, normally elected by a general congregation. He does not exercise any jurisdiction, but provides the General with information about the provinces within his assistancy.

[17] (London, 1920). The manuscript for the uncompleted volume is in ABSI, 46/5A/1. From the literary remains, one can see that this would have been an exceptional history. David G. Schultenover, S.J., in *A View from Rome On the Eve of the Modernist Crisis* (New York, 1993), a study of Roman perceptions of the Anglo-Saxon world, argues that Father General Luis Martín did not want a history of the English province written because he feared that it would arouse controversy and would have harmful effects on the Society in general (pp. 10 n. 4, 77-78, 120 n. 44).

[18] (London, 1967).

[19] (London, 1981) xi.

concerning primarily, houses, work and problems involved in the Society's work in England."[20] Unfortunately the history includes little written since Edwards completed the first draft, and reflects few of the developments in the field over the past two decades. Moreover, too little is said about the Society's *Constitutions* and "way of proceeding" for an analysis of the English province as an institution. A history of the province must investigate the origins and growth of the mission within the institutional and legal context of the Society, and within the political and ecclesiastical conditions of England.

Until recently interest in martyrs dominated the field. Their biographies, e.g. of Edmund Campion, Robert Southwell, Henry Garnet, were written but important men such as Robert Parsons[21] and Richard Blount, first Provincial in England, were ignored. Often, however, these biographies were criticized because of their general neglect of political context. Hugh Trevor-Roper's *caveat*, although at times exaggerated, pressed the point. In "Twice Martyred: The English Jesuits and Their Historians," Trevor-Roper complained that Elizabethan Jesuits were being martyred once again "not by Protestants but . . . by those more comfortable co-religionists who push them forth, *perinde ac cadavera*, to maintain an unreal position in a real world."[22] In the rush to establish individual credentials for martyrdom and sanctification, Trevor-Roper reminds Catholic authors that they must not forget that England and Spain were at war, and that many priests were educated at seminaries located in and financed by their country's enemy. The instructions given to Campion and Parsons in 1580 clearly stated that they were not to involve themselves in politics and that their ministry was among the English Catholics. But the temporal proximity of the mission to the unsuccessful Papal-Spanish invasion of Ireland must be discussed if one is to understand the Elizabethan reluctance to accept "the olive branch" carried by the Jesuits. It must also be recalled that throughout Elizabeth's reign, besides the plots concocted for political reasons by William Cecil, there were—and this is too often ignored in Catholic investigations of plots—real conspiracies involving Catholic powers to liberate the imprisoned Mary Queen of Scots and to place her on the throne occupied by her heretical cousin. Jesuits played more than a small role in some of these conspiracies. The Elizabethan world was not as black and white as many hagiographers would like us to believe. A credible history must consider the English Jesuits not simply as harmless victims of a cruel oppressive

---

[20] (London, 1985) p. 9.
[21] Francis Edwards's biography has finally appeared: *Robert Persons: The Biography of an Elizabethan Jesuit 1546-1610* (St. Louis, 1995). I had finished this volume before its publication. Nonetheless I tried to incorporate Edwards's study as much as I could.
[22] *Historical Essays* (London, 1957) pp. 113-18.

government, but as agents whose actions had some bearing on the formation of official policy. It is not the historian's role to proclaim martyrs but to explain events. The following chapters will reveal how extensive Jesuit involvement was in divers political and diplomatic negotiations. In so doing we shall see the historical roots of the myth of the evil Jesuits and how easily they became, if not the "stuff of dreams," at least the stuff of legends.

Twice the focus of this volume was modified. The first was a result of Trevor-Roper's attack. Heeding his admonition, I wanted to locate Jesuit activity clearly within the context of political, military, and religious events in France, Spain, Italy, Portugal, and the Low Countries. In so doing I, like many other English historians, realized that events, especially religious events, in 16th and 17th century England cannot be analyzed in isolation, but must be considered in the context of developments in Scotland and Ireland. Thus I widened my focus to include both countries. England, Scotland, and Ireland were distinct Jesuit missions before the Suppression of the Society in 1773. Nonetheless events in one affected developments in another.

Unfortunately the Scots and Irish missions have suffered even more historical neglect than the English, and I have wandered into strange terrain without a secure guide. There is no history of the Jesuit mission to Scotland. William Forbes-Leith, S.J., and John H. Pollen, S.J., edited important collections of documents in *Narratives of Scottish Catholics under Mary Stuart and James VI*[23] and *Papal Negotiations with Mary Queen of Scots*[24] respectively, but an extensive serious study is needed. The Irish mission has fared somewhat better. Edmund Hogan, S.J., prepared a documentary history of the Society's involvement in Ireland from 1540 until 1609.[25] A few years later he used much of this material in *Distinguished Irishmen of the Sixteenth Century*.[26]

At least two theses have investigated the Society of Jesus in Ireland in the 16th and 17th centuries. The first, "'Archdevil' and Jesuit: The Background, Life, and Times of James Archer from 1550 to 1604" by Thomas J. Morrissey, S.J., surveyed the first two Jesuit missions in Ireland as background for a detailed study of Archer.[27] Building on the research of Morrissey, Fergus O'Donoghue, S.J., concentrated on the early Stuart

---

[23] (Edinburgh, 1885).
[24] (Edinburgh, 1901).
[25] *Ibernia Ignatiana* (Dublin, 1880).
[26] (London, 1894).
[27] (Unpublished M.A. thesis: University College, Dublin, 1968). Unfortunately the history of the first and second missions was not included in the shorter published version of this thesis (*James Archer of Kilkenny: An Elizabethan Jesuit* [Dublin, 1979]).

period in his thesis, "The Jesuit Mission in Ireland 1598-1651."[28] Louis McRedmond's *To the Greater Glory: A History of the Irish Jesuits*, the first published history of the Irish mission and province, is a general overview that occasionally confuses (e.g. the insistence that Edmund Daniel and Edmund O'Donnell are two different Jesuits) rather than clarifies.[29]

My account does not pretend to be an in-depth study of Jesuit activity in Ireland and Scotland; I lack the expertise for that. Ireland and Scotland serve more as a setting in which I explore the activities of the English Jesuits, whose history I sought to relate along conventional, narrative lines. Perhaps my brief expositions of Jesuit work in Ireland and Scotland will stir others to write the detailed histories that these missions deserve.

The appearance of John W. O'Malley's *The First Jesuits* in 1993 occasioned the second change. In the Introduction, the author echoes Professor Oberman:

> Most popular writing on the Society of Jesus, whether favorable or unfavorable, has been woefully inadequate. Scholarly articles and monographs of reliable quality appear each year, although perhaps not in the quantity one might expect. Until relatively recently practically all the scholarship came from Jesuits. Generally characterized by technical accuracy, it tended to take up familiar and even familial issues and was relatively unaffected by the new historiography. Even today this scholarship is not always free of hagiographical vestiges, especially when dealing with Ignatius, for whom we still await a biography that satisfies sophisticated canons of scholarship.[30]

Well versed in the historiography of early modern Europe, John O'Malley heralds the arrival in the English-speaking world of a more critical Jesuit history with an analysis of the foundation and early growth of the Society of Jesus. Reflecting a current shift of interest from major figures to their influence on their followers, O'Malley is concerned with the early Society's understanding of Ignatius and its attempt to translate his principles into practice. Throughout his work O'Malley examines concrete implementation of the spiritual principles enshrined in *The Spiritual Exercises* of Ignatius Loyola, the *Constitutions* and congregational decrees, and the other documents that together comprise the Society's Institute.[31] By "Institute," Jesuits mean "the way they lived and worked, and they thus include in the term all the official documents of the order."[32] Another cherished expression practically synonymous with Institute is "our way of proceeding" (*noster*

---

[28] (Unpublished Ph.D. thesis: The Catholic University of America, 1981).
[29] (Dublin, 1991).
[30] *The First Jesuits* (Cambridge, Mass., 1993) p. 2.
[31] For a brief survey of these documents see the introduction to O'Malley's volume.
[32] O'Malley, *The First Jesuits*, p. 8.

modus procedendi, nuestro modo de proceder). According to Jerónimo Nadal, generally acknowledged to be the authoritative interpreter of the mind of Ignatius, the expression originated with Loyola. Through a study of Jesuit activity O'Malley ascertained the self-understanding of the early Society.

John Bossy in "The Character of Elizabethan Catholicism" juxtaposed the crises faced by secular priests because of the absence of a hierarchical structure, and those encountered by the Jesuits, who because of "the support of a religious order whose organization could without great change be adapted to the conditions of work in England," were "relatively immune" from such difficulties.[33] Was the organization that flexible? English Jesuits were members of an international order and bound by its constitutions, rules, and decrees. How harmonious the life, practices, and structures of the English Jesuits were with those presented in and mandated by their Institute is an area that has never been explored. Could the Institute be adapted to meet the exigencies of England, as Bossy stated, or was England so singular that the number of dispensations and special permissions left the Jesuits there scarcely recognizable as members of the same Society by their continental brothers? O'Malley's monograph and Bossy's contrast prompted me to include many of the institutional issues that I treated in my doctoral thesis.[34]

With Trevor-Roper nipping at my heels and O'Malley and Bossy leading me on, I embark on a critical—and not apologetic—account of Jesuit activities between the first mission to Ireland (1541) and the collapse of the Armada (1588). Throughout I stress two aspects of the Institute: relations between religion and politics, and style of religious life in an "underground" Church. There is more information on the former than on the latter and it can be more easily interwoven into the narrative. Despite initial protests that its work was solely spiritual, the Society gradually realised the political implications of its ministry and sought to define what was proper and what was alien to its Institute. Religious life will be discussed in the conclusion.

Although I have relied primarily on material drawn from Jesuit archives in Rome,[35] in London, and at Stonyhurst College, I have also consulted major manuscript collections in the Bodleian Library, Oxford, British Library, Public Record Office, and Westminster Archdiocesan Archives. By no means has that exhausted the archival material.

---

[33] *Past and Present* 21 (1962) 52.
[34] "The Society of Jesus in England, 1623-1688: An Institutional Study" (unpublished Ph.D. thesis: University of Warwick, 1984).
[35] Future volumes of the *Monumenta Angliae* will include documents cited in this monograph. Volume 3 (1541-65) is scheduled for publication in 1997 and volume 4 (1565-72) a few years later.

CHAPTER ONE

"THE OPEN DOOR"

In the summer of 1529, prospects that King Henry VIII's "Great Matter" would be resolved in his favour were good. Despite the appeal of Queen Catherine of Aragon to the papacy, Thomas Cardinal Wolsey had induced Pope Clement VII to send a cardinal to London to hear the case. From Henry's and Wolsey's point of view, the designated Cardinal, Lorenzo Campeggio, was an excellent choice. Since 1524 the titular Bishop of Salisbury, who enjoyed the fruits of his office without shouldering its burdens, Campeggio had worked successfully with Wolsey in 1518-19 when he was legate *a latere* in England. Moreover he was one of the few cardinals who sought English assistance in 1527 when imperial troops occupied Rome. The hearings opened on 21 June and continued until 23 July when, to the astonishment of all, Campeggio announced that the court would honour the Roman practice of adjourning for the summer holidays. But even before Campeggio's unsettling announcement, the Pope had already decided to call the case to Rome. That was, after all, what Catherine's nephew, the Emperor Charles V, wanted. In an Italy totally dominated by Charles, the imperial wishes could not be ignored. With the departure of Campeggio in August, Wolsey's strategy for obtaining the divorce was destroyed and his future was in jeopardy.[1]

Threats to withdraw England from papal allegiance were put into practice in January of 1531. Anxious to secure a clergy loyal to the crown in the event of a confrontation with the Pope, Henry charged the prelates and abbots assembled in Convocation with *Praemunire*.[2] The clergy had not only to pay the exorbitant fine of £100,000 but also to acknowledge Henry as the "Supreme Head" of the Church in England "in so far as the law of Christ allow." Each member of the Convocation had, in some way, to raise his share of the fine. John Stokesley, Bishop of London, sought to obtain his

---

[1] Richard Marius, *Thomas More* (New York, 1984) pp. 357-60. For Wolsey's relations with Campeggio and for a revisionist interpretation of his downfall see Peter Gwyn, *The King's Cardinal: The Rise and Fall of Thomas Wolsey* (London, 1990).
[2] The three statutes of *Praemunire* (1353, 1365, and 1393) were directed against perceived papal attempts to undermine the crown's role in the government of the English Church. See A.G. Dickens, *The English Reformation*, 2nd edition (London, 1989) pp. 109-10, for a short presentation of the origins of these laws.

portion from the clergy of his diocese. His intention and his methods caused considerable discontent among both the taxed lower clergy and the laity onto whom the burden would eventually be passed. Their anger erupted in a riot on 30 August 1531. The mob, composed of clergy and laity, attacked the bishop's palace and the chapter house of St. Paul's. After the crowd was quelled, Lord Chancellor Sir Thomas More issued warrants for the arrest of five laymen and fifteen priests.[3] Into the religious cauldron that was England wandered a poor Basque student from the University of Paris.

Ignatius Loyola had arrived in Paris in February of 1528. For his studies he chose the College of Montaigu, a bastion of traditionalism, which was the butt of many Erasmian and Rabelaisian satires. At Montaigu Ignatius enrolled as a *martinet*, a student who lodged outside the college. What money Ignatius had went quickly, and he was soon obliged to beg alms. An unnamed Spanish friar recommended that he travel to Flanders every summer to beg assistance from the affluent Spanish merchants in Bruges and Antwerp. He made that trip three times. The first was in 1529; the second and third were in August and September of 1530 and 1531. On the first of these trips he met at Bruges the Spanish humanist Juan Luis Vives, who had recently returned from his post in England.[4] He suggested that Ignatius expand his begging tour to include England. In 1531 Ignatius crossed the channel to England and possibly visited London.[5] Regarding that trip, Ignatius made only one brief remark in his laconic autobiography: "Once he even went to England and brought back more alms than he usually did in

---

[3] Marius, *More*, p. 402. For a vivid discussion of the religious atmosphere of London see Susan Brigden, *London and the Reformation* (Oxford, 1989).

[4] There is some confusion about the date of the first trip. Juan de Polanco in his life of Ignatius places the trip and the dinner in Lent. According to Polanco, Ignatius was angered by Vives's views on the Lenten fast and so he later forbade the reading of all his books in the Society. James Brodrick points out the absurdity of this claim: because of the class schedule at Paris it is unlikely that Ignatius would have visited Bruges during Lent; it is hard to believe that Ignatius, while a guest at Vives's table, would have argued in such a way; finally, Ignatius did not ban the reading of Vives in the Society. See *Saint Ignatius Loyola, The Pilgrim Years* (London, 1956) p. 227. For the reasons behind Polanco's redaction of the event see John C. Olin, "Erasmus and St. Ignatius Loyola," in *Six Essays on Erasmus* (New York, 1979) pp. 75-92. The later redaction of Ignatius's relations with Vives is part of the larger question, currently being reexamined by historians, of Ignatius's relations with humanism. On this topic see two articles by John W. O'Malley, S.J., "Renaissance Humanism and the Religious Culture of the First Jesuits," *Heythrop Journal* 31 (1990) 471-87 (reprinted in John W. O'Malley, S.J., *Religious Culture in the Sixteenth Century* [Aldershot, 1993] article X) and "Renaissance Humanism and the First Jesuits," in *Ignacio de Loyola y su Tiempo*, ed. Juan Plazaola (Bilbao, n.d. [1992]) 381-403; and his *The First Jesuits* (Cambridge, Mass., 1993).

[5] Cándido de Dalmases, S.J., *Ignatius of Loyola* (St. Louis, 1985) pp. 108-10. Jerónimo Nadal and Juan de Polanco were the first to specify Ignatius's destination as London in Nadal's "Dialogi pro Societate contra haereticos" (1563) and Polanco's "De Vita P. Ignatii" (1574) in Dionysius Fernández Zapico, S.J., and Cándido de Dalmases, S.J., eds., *Fontes Narrativi de S. Ignatio de Loyola et de Societatis Iesu initiis*, 4 vols. (Rome, 1943-65) II, 251, 556.

other years.[6] If Ignatius visited the capital, Stokesley's enforced donations apparently had not destroyed the charity of the Londoners.

We search Ignatius's writings in vain for any account of his English sojourn to supplement the autobiography. To fill this gap, some earlier biographers attempted to deduce the pilgrim's movements. It could be taken for granted that Ignatius would have spent his time with the Spanish merchants who clustered around the monastery of Austin Friars. It was "well-nigh certain" that he visited the shrine of St. Thomas of Canterbury and "more certain still" that he prayed at Edward the Confessor's tomb in Westminster Abbey. Finally, according to Stewart Rose, it was "probable" that the Carthusians received Ignatius at the Charterhouse.[7] John H. Pollen, S.J., even surmised that Loyola may have visited Sir Thomas More in Chelsea and benefitted from his well-known liberality.[8] Basing his claim on some striking similarities between passages in Ignatius's *Spiritual Exercises* and sections of the works of Richard Whitford, an English cleric who had forsaken a good ecclesiastical career and retired to the monastery, Willem A.M. Peters, S.J., has asserted that Ignatius spent most of his visit at the Syon monastery near Isleworth.[9] Fascinating as these similarities are, without concrete evidence Ignatius's English itinerary remains subject to conjecture. But, no matter where he went, because of the generosity he found there, he returned to Paris with more money than he had ever collected in Flanders.

---

[6] A good edition of the autobiography is Joseph N. Tylenda, S.J., ed., *A Pilgrim's Journey: The Autobiography of Ignatius of Loyola* (Wilmington, 1985) p. 87.

[7] *Saint Ignatius Loyola and the Early Jesuits*, 2nd edition (London, 1871) pp. 124-25. In a style more typical of hagiography than of biography, Rose also conjectures: "And, peradventure, as he [Loyola] knelt in prayer before Our Lady's picture near the Tower, or traversed deep in meditation the long line of road that led to Tyburne [sic], the veil of the future may have been lifted for a moment, and his prescient eye have foreseen the day, and his soul gloried in the thought, that his heroic sons, with others as brave and good, would encounter the ignominy and all the frightful horrors of a traitor's death, rather than stoop to acknowledge, by word or sign, a supremacy as much opposed to the rightful liberties of a Christian man as to the inalienable prerogatives of the Vicar of Jesus Christ" (p. 124). Brodrick has tempered Rose's enthusiasm: "It would not be straining the possibilities too outrageously to imagine him [Loyola] visiting the London Charterhouse and being given hospitality by the monks soon to be martyrs" (see *Saint Ignatius Loyola*, p. 229). *Ignatius Loyola: A Biography of the Founder of the Jesuits* by Philip Caraman, S.J. (San Francisco, 1990) pp. 82-83, re-instates the earlier approach. Such traditional biographies have been criticized as lacking in a sound sense of method. Many of the criticisms levelled by Philip Endean, S.J. and Heiko A. Oberman are valid. See Endean's "Who Do You Say Ignatius Is? Jesuit Fundamentalism and Beyond," *Studies in the Spirituality of Jesuits* 19/5 (1987) 1-53; and Oberman's "Ignatius of Loyola and the Reformation: The Case of John Calvin," in *Ignacio de Loyola y su Tiempo*, ed. Juan Plazaola (Bilbao, n.d. [1992]) 809.

[8] "The First Jesuits in Great Britain," *The Month* 102 (1903) 647.

[9] "Richard Whitford and St. Ignatius' Visit to England," *AHSI* 25 (1956) 328-50.

Over the next few years Ignatius attracted a number of followers in Paris: Pierre Favre, Diego Laínez, Francis Xavier, Alfonso Salmerón, Simão Rodrigues, and Nicolás Bobadilla. On 15 August 1534 this band vowed to make a pilgrimage to Jerusalem—if this were not possible, they would place themselves at the disposal of the pope—in order to strengthen their bond of unity.[10] Shortly thereafter they were joined by Claude Jay, Paschase Broët, and Jean Codure.[11] By November of 1538 they had abandoned all hope of going to Jerusalem and approached Pope Paul III. In 1540, the Pope constituted these "friends in the Lord" as the Society of Jesus in the bull *Regimini militantis Ecclesiae*.[12]

II

At the University of Paris many of the followers of Loyola were instructed by the Scot Robert Wauchope, who became an early supporter of their aspirations. Although a priest of the diocese of St. Andrews, Wauchope was appointed by Pope Paul III administrator of the Irish archdiocese of Armagh in 1539.[13] The appointment resulted from the suspension of Archbishop George Cromer on suspicion of heresy. Much involved in the religious affairs on the continent, Wauchope could not travel to Ireland immediately.[14] In March of 1540 Wauchope sought papal permission to send two of

---

[10] The precise formula of the vow is not known. We know its contents from the testimonies of the individuals who pronounced it. See Dalmases, *Ignatius of Loyola*, pp. 120-22.

[11] Short biographies of the nine original followers can be found in a special number of *AHSI* 59 (1990) 185-344, prepared as part of the 500th anniversary of the birth of Ignatius Loyola (1491) and the 450th anniversary of the foundation of the Society. See also *Mon. Ang.*, II, 546-48; Thomas M. McCoog, S.J., ed., *English and Welsh Jesuits 1555-1650*, 2 vols. (London, 1994-95) I, 126, II, 287, 342. Henceforth, to avoid needless repetition, I shall simply cite the *Mon. Ang.* volumes. The same information can also be found in the CRS volumes under the Jesuit's name.

[12] In a recent article Elisabeth G. Gleason argues that Paul should be classified as the first Counter-Reformation pope because he was the first to admit that "the split in Western Christianity was final, and that instead of the one Church several churches actually co-existed." Only after such recognition, Professor Gleason contends, can we talk of a Counter-Reformation. See "Who Was the First Counter-Reformation Pope?" *CHR* 81 (1995) 173-84.

[13] For possible explanations why a Scottish priest was appointed to an Irish see, see John Durkan, "Robert Wauchope, Archbishop of Armagh," *IR* 1 (1950) 50.

[14] Durkan, "Wauchope," 50-51. Brendan Bradshaw, in *The Dissolution of the Religious Orders in Ireland under Henry VIII* (Cambridge, 1974) p. 213, claims that Wauchope's appointment "effectively killed papal influence in the diocese of Armagh" because of his overinvolvement on the continent. He was unable to travel to Ireland until 1550, and even then he did not reach Armagh. He died in France in 1551. As a result it was the King's appointee George Dowdall that governed. Wauchope had been a teacher of Reginald Pole, who may have suggested his name to the Pope. But Wauchope also enjoyed the favour of David Beaton, Archbishop of St. Andrews and the "Cardinal of Scotland," and it may have been he that proposed Wauchope (Margaret H.B. Sanderson, *Cardinal of Scotland: David Beaton, c. 1494-1564* [Edinburgh, 1986] p. 114).

Ignatius's followers, Jean Codure and Alfonso Salmerón, to Ireland to survey the situation. Because of many demands for assistance and the small number of priests, the men could not be dispatched immediately.[15] A year later the mission was launched. In a letter written to the Irish bishops and princes on 15 May 1541, Pope Paul III explained how he had heard of the hardships and disasters that they suffered because of the English King Henry VIII. In order to sustain their faith, to report on the damage, and to reconcile the lapsed, the Pope had decided to send the two Jesuits.[16] Originally a secular priest, Francesco Marsupino, a doctor both of canon law and civil law, was to accompany Codure but, for reasons unknown, Salmerón replaced Marsupino. Departure was again delayed, and during the wait Paschase Broët replaced the seriously ill Codure, who died shortly thereafter on 29 August 1541. Accompanied by Francesco Zapata, an aspirant to the Society, Broët and Salmerón, armed with the powers of papal legates, left for Ireland on 10 September.[17]

The two Jesuits were conceded extensive faculties for their mission. Each was granted authority to preach, hear confessions, celebrate Mass, and commute any vows of overseas pilgrimages. They were commissioned to admonish any negligent rector and, if necessary, to punish him with censures and ecclesiastical penalties. They could absolve the laity from heresy. The two Jesuits were granted considerable authority for dealing with marital difficulties and ecclesiastical problems.[18]

To the papal faculties Ignatius added his own very specific instructions.[19] Indeed the precision and number of instructions reveal how seriously Loyola

---

[15] Ignatius was slightly hesitant about this mission. On 20 March 1540 he wrote to Beltrán Loyola that he was under extreme pressure to send some men to the Indies, to Ireland, and to parts of Italy, and that he really did not have the resources to fulfil the requests (*Letters of St. Ignatius of Loyola*, ed. William J. Young, S.J. [Chicago, 1959] p. 42).

[16] F. Cervós, S.J., ed., *Epistolae P.P. Paschasii Broeti, Claudii Jayi, Joannis Codurii et Simonis Rodericii, S.I.* (henceforth *Epp. Broet*) (Madrid, 1903) pp. 204-05.

[17] Georg Schurhammer, S.J., *Francis Xavier: His Life, His Times*, trans. M. Joseph Costelloe, S.J., 4 vols. (Rome, 1973-82) I, 248, 499, 548; Edmund Hogan, S.J., *Ibernia Ignatiana* (Dublin, 1880); Aubrey Gwynn, *The Medieval Province of Armagh 1470-1545* (Dundalk, 1946) pp. 248-53. Both Broët and Salmerón wrote detailed accounts of their expedition upon their return to the continent. Broët's can be found in *Epp. Broet*, pp. 23-31 and Salmerón's in Raimundus Vidaurre, S.J. and F. Cervós, S.J., eds., *Epistolae P. Alphonsi Salmeronis, Societatis Iesu* (henceforth *Epp. Sal.*) 2 vols. (Madrid, 1906-07) I, 2-10.

[18] Rome 3 July 1541, *Epp. Broet*, pp. 206-12. The papal faculties granted earlier to Codure and Salmerón are in *Epp. Broet*, pp. 421-27.

[19] Ignatius's instructions to the missionaries can be found in M. Lecina, S.J., V. Agustí, S.J., and D. Restrepo, S.J., eds., *Sancti Ignatii de Loyola Societatis Iesu Fundatoris Epistolae et Instructiones* (henceforth MI *Epp. Ign.*) 12 vols. (Madrid, 1903-11) I, 174-81, 727-31; and English translations in *Letters and Instructions of St. Ignatius Loyola*, ed. Alban Goodier, S.J. (London, 1914) pp. 50-64. One wonders whether Loyola consciously modelled his instructions on the diplomatic practice of the time. See Garrett Mattingly, *Renaissance Diplomacy* (London, 1955) pp. 39-41 for a discussion of said practices.

took the mission. In Edinburgh, as they awaited an audience with the Scottish King, they were instructed to preach and hear confessions. Salmerón was specifically told to "give the Exercises." Important throughout was spiritual conversation.[20] Among the guidelines for writing was the admonition that they were to relate the news "without any sermonizing, taking account of the fact that the letter will be shown to shrewd persons who look for substantial work done." Means of travel and the style of life were to reflect their poverty. Mules and horses were forbidden; they were to spend between a third and a half of the money allotted. What was left was to be distributed to the poor. Periodically they should beg from door to door "for the love of Our Lord, if Our Lord shall give the opportunity." They were neither to handle money nor to have it in their possession and were to "let others provide for you as they think best for the service of God."

In the third set of instructions Loyola reminded Broët and Salmerón that the purpose of the mission was to provide spiritual assistance. To accomplish their tasks more effectively, Loyola advised the two to visit the major Catholic leaders and to encourage resistance to alteration in religion. Bishops and priests were to be exhorted to fidelity and perseverance and their sacramental and religious activities supervised. If possible the nuncios should establish grammar schools and *monti della pietà*. Although the nuncios were to proceed with discretion and caution, if "the glory of God and the common good" demanded that they risk their lives, the two were not to avoid the danger.

The first Jesuit mission to the British Isles was a spiritual enterprise but, in common with later ones, this spiritual work had political repercussions: the obverse side to confirmation of the faith of the Irish was resistance to the pretensions of the English crown. In the first mission we note certain Jesuit characteristics that will recur: the importance of education, preaching, spiritual conversation, the *Spiritual Exercises*, and the support of elites.

Ireland, according to the historians D.B. Quinn and K.W. Nicholls, was "considerably more than a geographical expression and much less than a political entity" in 1534. King Henry VIII was Lord of Ireland even though most of the island was outside his effective control, despite his attempts to extend his authority beyond the Pale. In 1534 Thomas FitzGerald, Lord Offaly, son of Gerald FitzGerald, Earl of Kildare and Lord Deputy of Ireland, was appointed Vice-Deputy during his father's absence in London. "Silken Thomas," as Lord Offaly was known, believing that his father had been executed and that the Kildare dynasty was doomed, raised the standard of rebellion in June. Named as Kildare's replacement as Lord Deputy, Sir

---

[20] On the role of "spiritual conversation" in the early Society see Thomas H. Clancy, S.J., *The Conversational Word of God* (St. Louis, 1978) and O'Malley, *The First Jesuits*, pp. 110-15.

William Skeffington arrived in Ireland with English troops in October, and the rebellion was effectively suppressed with the capture of Maynooth castle on 23 March 1535. The English administration in Dublin under Skeffington's governance now expanded the power of the Tudor King through conquest or conciliation. This was a fateful step, and Quinn and Nicholls see it as the beginning of Ireland's early modern history.[21]

The collapse of the rebellion resulted in the surrender of "Silken Thomas" in August of 1535. He and five of his uncles were executed at Tyburn on 3 February 1537 in an attempt to eliminate the Kildares as potential opponents to English plans in Ireland. But one son, Gerald, child of the ninth Earl's second marriage (to Lady Elizabeth Grey) and half-brother of "Silken Thomas", survived. Despite attempts by the English to capture him, he was protected and hidden by family and supporters until 1542 when he left Ireland, first for France and then for Italy.[22]

Gerald FitzGerald's uncle, Leonard, Lord Grey, was appointed Lord Deputy on 1 January 1536 after the death of Skeffington the previous day. With a small but efficient militia Grey succeeded in controlling or destroying any opposition generated by the presence of his nephew. In May of 1539 Grey's campaign extended to Armagh. There he tried to persuade two local lords, Conn Bacach O'Neill and Manus O'Donnell, traditional rivals but now allied in their support of FitzGerald, to hand over the fugitive. Grey failed and the subsequent struggle between English forces and the Ulster lords became more violent. O'Neill and O'Donnell successfully evaded capture and sought assistance from England's enemies abroad.[23] As a result of his failure to capture FitzGerald, Grey was summoned to London in April of 1540. With the fall of his patron Thomas Cromwell in June of 1540, he was charged with treason and executed in June of 1541. His successor as Lord Deputy was Sir Anthony St. Leger, who continued the policies of his predecessors and demonstrated that his military forays were not parades to impress the people but were meant to ensure the fidelity of the local lords.[24]

To bolster English authority St. Leger summoned the Irish Parliament in 1541. On 18 June this Parliament altered the King's claim to Ireland and

---

[21] "Ireland in 1534," in *A New History of Ireland: III Early Modern Ireland 1534-1691*, eds. T.W. Moody, F.X. Martin, and F.J. Byrne (Oxford, 1991) p. 1. See also G.A. Hayes-McCoy's article "The royal supremacy and ecclesiastical revolution, 1534-47" in the same volume, pp. 40-42; and Colm Lennon, *Sixteenth Century Ireland: The Incomplete Conquest* (Dublin, 1994) pp. 104-11.
[22] Hayes-McCoy, "Royal Supremacy," p. 43.
[23] On 31 October 1540 O'Neill sent a courier, the priest Redmond O'Gallagher, to Rome with a message for the Pope. In it he explained the damage done by Henry and what he himself was doing to preserve Catholicism on the island. Broët and Salmerón carried the papal response of 24 April 1541 (*Epp. Broet*, pp. 431-32).
[24] Hayes-McCoy, "Royal Supremacy," pp. 44-46; Lennon, *Ireland*, pp. 145-52.

declared that henceforth the kings of England would always be kings of Ireland.²⁵ St. Leger also reached agreements with various lords whereby they would receive English titles personally conferred in Westminster by the King to replace their renounced traditional ones.²⁶ Manus O'Donnell recognized the King as his Liege Lord on 6 August 1541. The Lord Deputy, in turn, promised to defend the O'Donnells against their enemies. Conn O'Neill was forced to capitulate on 28 December 1541. Obliged to abandon the name of O'Neill, he was created Earl of Tyrone after Henry VIII refused to grant him the earldom of Ulster.²⁷ After the defection of his two chief supporters, Gerald FitzGerald fled Ireland.

Contemporaneous with Henry's efforts to establish his authority over the secular lords in Ireland were similar endeavours in the ecclesiastical field. The Irish Parliament that sat in May of 1536 enacted legislation comparable to that passed by the English Parliament. Throughout 1536 and 1537 various laws affected the political and ecclesiastical life of the country. The Act of Succession (28 Henry VIII c. 2) decreed that the title would pass to the heirs of Henry and Anne Boleyn. The Act of Supremacy (28 Henry VIII c. 5) proclaimed Henry and his heirs "the only supreme head on earth of the whole church of Ireland" and imposed an oath of allegiance to Henry and his heirs as designated. The Act of Slander (28 Henry VIII c. 7) declared anyone labelling Henry a heretic, schismatic, or usurper guilty of high treason. The recognition of papal authority was forbidden by the Act against the Authority of the Bishop of Rome (28 Henry VIII c. 13). The Act of Appeals (28 Henry VIII c. 6) prescribed that all appeals in spiritual matters formerly addressed to Rome were now to be directed to the King. The Act of Faculties (28 Henry VIII c. 19) decreed that all dispensations and licences formerly issued by Rome were to be granted by the Archbishop of Canterbury or the King.²⁸ Implementation of this legislation began in 1538.

---

²⁵ St. Leger advised Henry to assume this title because "the Irish have a foolish notion that the bishop of Rome is the King of Ireland" (cited in William Palmer, *The Problem of Ireland in Tudor Foreign Policy 1485-1603* [Woodbridge, 1994] p. 58). Pope Paul IV implicitly recognized this claim when he elevated Ireland to the status of a kingdom on 16 September 1555. This declaration can be found in J. Hagan, "Miscellanea Vaticano-Hibernica, 1420-1631," *AH* 4 (1915) 217.

²⁶ The declaration that Henry was King of Ireland altered relations between the English monarch and the Irish lords. Through their renunciation of Irish titles in favour of English ones, the lords recognized, according to Ciaran Brady, "that the new Irish King was no mere distant overlord, demanding occasional homage, but the personal sovereign of a new Irish nobility" (*The Chief Governors: The Rise and Fall of Reform Government in Tudor Ireland 1536-1588* [Cambridge, 1994] p. 30).

²⁷ Hayes-McCoy, "Royal Supremacy," pp. 46-51; Lennon, *Ireland*, pp. 152-58; Steven G. Ellis, *Tudor Ireland: Crown, Community and the Conflict of Cultures 1470-1603* (London, 1985) p. 141.

²⁸ Robert Dudley Edwards, *Church and State in Tudor Ireland* (London, 1935) pp. 11-15; Lennon, *Ireland*, pp. 134-43.

The monasteries, at least those within the area fully controlled by the English, were suppressed. Pressure on bishops to recognize royal authority was strong. George Cromer, Archbishop of Armagh, acknowledged Henry as Supreme Head in 1536 and consequently was suspended by the papacy in July of 1537. Wauchope was appointed administrator in 1539. Papal suspensions and refusals to acknowledge royal appointments resulted in the establishment of two parallel ecclesiastical systems, often with the royal appointee in control of the diocese and its finances, and the papal appointee relatively penniless.[29] Ireland, the destination of the Jesuit missionaries, was in the throes of radical changes both political and ecclesiastical.

On their journey, the Jesuits sought advice from those who might know more about Irish affairs.[30] At Viterbo they spoke with Reginald, Cardinal Pole, who warned them of the dangers they would face and recommended that they should leave the island at the first sign of trouble. At Lyon they met David, Cardinal Beaton, Archbishop of St. Andrews and Primate of Scotland. He too tried to dissuade them from their task. Of all peoples, he explained, the Irish were the most rude, the most barbarous, and most incapable of any discipline. Moreover, the English King controlled the cities, forts, and castles. In Paris the Jesuits received some encouragement from the Archbishop of Reims, Charles Guise, Cardinal of Lorraine, who entrusted them with a letter for his sister, the Scottish Queen, Mary of Guise. Despite the warnings, the band continued and sailed from Flanders to Scotland in December of 1541. Because of high winds and turbulent seas, the voyage lasted twenty days and the ship was twice driven into English ports. In order to quell any suspicions aroused by their foreign dress and their ignorance of English, the Jesuits simply claimed to be Spanish travellers. Because England and Spain were negotiating a treaty directed against France, this was a successful gambit. The Jesuits finally reached Edinburgh on 31 December.

At Edinburgh the Jesuits were received by King James V and Queen Mary of Guise. During their stay almost everyone at the Scottish court tried to convince the priests that they must cancel their expedition. Informants as diverse as Gavin Dunbar, Archbishop of Glasgow; Jean de Morviller, French ambassador to Scotland; and three unnamed Irish priests on their way to Rome, decried the conditions in Ireland and warned the Jesuits that their lives would be in danger there. Undaunted by the reports, the Jesuits sought more specific and, it was hoped, more optimistic information about Ireland.

---

[29] Hayes-McCoy, "Royal Supremacy," pp. 56-66; Prionsias Ó Fionnagáin, S.J., *The Jesuit Missions to Ireland* (n.p. n.d. [privately printed]) p. 1.

[30] The best and the most recent account of the expedition (and one on which I am extremely dependent) is William V. Bangert, S.J., *Claude Jay and Alfonso Salmerón* (Chicago, 1985) pp. 167-71. See also Ó Fionnagáin, *Jesuit Missions to Ireland*, p. 4.

While Salmerón stayed in Edinburgh where, in an unspecified fashion, he followed Ignatius's instructions and gave the Spiritual Exercises, Broët journeyed to Glasgow in the hope of learning something from Irish merchants. There he had no success and so, clad in a kilt, he continued to Irvine, a port about fifteen miles from Glasgow. Because the news that Broët gathered was not as devastating as stories heard from the Scots, the Jesuits decided to continue their mission.

With letters of recommendation from James V to the Irish chieftains,[31] the men set out for Ireland. They landed in Ulster on 23 February 1542 and remained on the island for thirty-four rather hectic days. The more they investigated, explored, and learned, the more they realized that the state of Ireland was as bad as or worse than they had heard in Scotland. Everything that they had been warned about, Broët lamented, they saw in Ireland. Politically the island was in turmoil. As we have seen, the local lords were capitulating to the English Lord Deputy. Manus O'Donnell and Conn O'Neill, the latter addressed by Pope Paul III as a champion of "the Catholic faith," now recognized Henry Tudor as supreme ruler in Ireland of all things temporal and spiritual. As a demonstration of their good faith these lords promised to hand over to the King's Deputy any apostolic legate from Rome. Shortly after this agreement, through the mediation of the Abbot of Derry, O'Donnell proposed a secret meeting with the Jesuits. Fearful for their safety, the missionaries rejected the invitation. Suspicion of treachery thus destroyed any reliance on Ireland's traditional leaders.

From the perspective of the Jesuits the defection of the lords confirmed the sorry state of Ireland's Catholicism. Few monasteries still stood; most had been destroyed and their inhabitants had fled either from the island or to a safe refuge on it. To consolidate their hold over the island the English were building houses and fortresses where the religious houses once stood. The few bishops who remained faithful to Rome, such as the Archbishop of Tuam, Arthur O'Friel, and the Bishop of Kildare, Thady Reynolds, were forced to abandon their sees and hide in the woods. There they awaited the news of the King's death, hoping then to return to their offices.

According to their instructions from Ignatius, the Jesuits were urged to establish peaceful relations among the Irish chieftains and lords. This unity was an absolute prerequisite for resistance to the King. The "disease of internal strife," however, they found to be irremediable. No peace among the lords had ever lasted in Ireland. The Irish thrived too much on plunder, theft, and destruction. Indeed, the Jesuits concluded that the only justice in

---

[31] Because of various rumours that France and Scotland planned to support the Irish chieftains militarily, the English would have been even more suspicious of the Jesuits' mission if they had known about such letters (Palmer, *Problem of Ireland*, p. 60).

the land was meted to piracy. Robbers, murderers, even the incestuous escaped without punishment. Prelates claimed that they were unable to do anything to halt the spread of crime because of their lack of secular power. But, the Jesuits wondered whether even if the bishops had the authority, there would be any change since ecclesiastical and civil leaders were infected with the same disease.[32]

Even among the Irish who retained their affection for the Holy See and had not capitulated to Henry, there was little that the missionaries could do. The fathers heard confessions (whose we do not know because neither Broët nor Salmerón could speak either English or Irish),[33] offered Mass, and imparted indulgences permitted in their bull. They also granted dispensations from illegitimacy and incest. The latter was especially common.[34] Any money received from indulgences and dispensations, although meagre because of the general poverty of the country, was distributed among the poor and used for pious works. After thirty-four days of stress and disappointment, Broët and Salmerón decided to withdraw because of the lack of support from the chieftains, the inability to arrange a sound peace between the leaders, the lack of a strong city or fort where they could reside safely, and "because it was not to the honour of the Apostolic See for them to hide in forests and in secret places." They then returned to Scotland. Once Pope Paul III heard that the Jesuits had returned to Scotland, he granted the same faculties for that country that they had held in Ireland. Apparently they left Scotland before the arrival of the brief.[35]

After his exposition of the mission of Broët and Salmerón, William V. Bangert, S.J. concludes that their report was misleading: "It lacked completeness, balance, and integrality."[36] Because the two missionaries

---

[32] For a short survey of the state of the Irish Church on the eve of the Reformation see Ellis, *Tudor Ireland*, pp. 183-227.

[33] Fergus O'Donoghue asserts that the common language was Latin, "which was widely spoken in Ireland" ("The Jesuits Come to Ireland," *Studies* 80 [1991] 18); Ó Fionnagáin furnishes evidence to substantiate this claim (*Jesuit Missions to Ireland*, pp. 6-7).

[34] Quinn and Nicholls note that "the majority of Irish clergy were at least technically illegitimate, either as sons of clerics themselves or because their parents were within the wide degrees of consanguinity and affinity within which marriage was forbidden by medieval canon law—and cousin marriage remained the norm in Gaelic Ireland throughout the later middle ages as in the pre-Norman period . . . " ("Ireland in 1534," p. 30). This was probably true throughout the island and would explain the charge of incest: marriage within prescribed degrees of consanguinity.

[35] Paul III to Broët and Salmerón, Rome 27 March 1542, *Epp. Broet*, pp. 215-16; Bangert, *Jay and Salmerón*, p. 172.

[36] *Jay and Salmerón*, p. 171. Bangert is not the first historian to argue that Broët and Salmerón failed to notice the latent loyalty of the Irish people. Thirty years earlier James Brodrick concluded that the two Jesuits "were not prophets but bewildered foreigners who saw and noted the blatant evil while missing the hidden, intensely active leaven of good" (see *The Origin of the Jesuits* [London, 1940] p. 110). Brodrick questioned their depiction of the moral

failed to get beyond mid-Ulster, they were, he continued, unable to perceive the undercurrents of religious loyalty that persisted among the Irish people despite the capitulations of Catholic leaders. Any chance that Henry had of gaining the popular support of the Irish had been lost because of the spoliation of the monasteries.[37] This loyalty, Bangert notes, nurtured by the friars who retained their Roman allegiance, grew "into, first, a mild obstructionism, then into violent opposition." Because the Jesuits did not perceive this loyalty, their report was excessively pessimistic.

One wonders, however, how realistic it is to expect them to perceive—indeed, to be interested in—popular religious sentiment. The Jesuits were sent to reconcile the Irish leaders and to organize their resistance. Their mission was to the Irish leaders and not the Irish people. Moreover, such concern for social elites was consistent with the practices and policies of the young Society.

The collection of testimonials was a common Ignatian reaction to criticism and accusation. Urging silence on members of the Society, Ignatius considered the statements of non-Jesuits, especially influential friends, an adequate response. In 1540 he solicited recommendations from important and well-connected persons, religious and lay, to overcome the opposition of Bartholomeo, Cardinal Guidiccioni to the Society's establishment.[38] Social elites were carefully cultivated. On 24 September 1549, Loyola advised the fathers who were sent to Germany: "You must try to be on good terms with those in government positions and be kindly disposed toward them. It will help to this if the Duke [William IV of Bavaria] and the members of his household who have a wider influence confess to Ours, and insofar as their duties permit, make the Spiritual Exercises. You should win over the doctors

---

state of the country because the missionaries could "only have learned these things from hearsay, and Ireland is well known to be a place where tall stories have ever abounded for the quizzing of earnest-minded foreigners" (p. 111). Presumably Broët and Salmerón drew their conclusions on the morals of the Irish from observations that they made and the dispensations that they granted—evidence far stronger than hearsay. On the other hand, the Irish Jesuit John MacErlean asserted that their report gave a full and accurate picture of the state of Ireland (see "The Society of Jesus in Ireland [1540-1773]," *Irish Jesuit Directory* [1928] 168).

[37] Edwards, *Church and State in Tudor Ireland*, pp. 97, 117-18.

[38] Dalmases, *Ignatius of Loyola*, p. 171. See James Brodrick, S.J., *The Progress of the Jesuits* (London, 1946) p. 46; André Ravier, S.J., *Ignatius of Loyola and the Founding of the Society of Jesus* (San Francisco, 1987) p. 375; Schurhammer, *Francis Xavier*, I, 671; John W. Padberg, S.J. "Ignatius and the Popes," in *Ignacio de Loyola y su Tiempo*, ed. Juan Plazaola (Bilbao, n.d. [1992]), 683-99; John W. Padberg, S.J., "Ignatius, the Popes, and Realistic Reverence," *Studies in the Spirituality of Jesuits* 25/3 (1993) 19. Occasionally Loyola is attacked for his pursuit of elites. It is important to note that in this regard for elites, Loyola was guided not by worldly values but by a concern for the greater glory of God. See William V. Bangert, S.J., *Jerome Nadal, S.J. (1507-1580): Tracking the First Generation of Jesuits*, ed. Thomas M. McCoog, S.J. (Chicago, 1992), p. 102; and Clancy, *Conversational Word of God*, pp. 20-25.

of the university [Ingolstadt] and other persons of authority by your humility, modesty, and obliging services."[39] Years later, in 1552, Ignatius formulated this concern into a principle that was included in his general instructions for missionaries:

> With regard to the neighbor, we must be careful with whom we deal. They should be persons from whom we can expect greater fruit, since they [the missionaries] cannot deal with all. They should be such as are in greater need, and those in high position who exert such influence because of their learning or their possessions . . . and, generally speaking, all those who if helped will be better able to help others for God's glory.[40]

The *Constitutions* made this policy even stronger:

> The more universal the good is, the more it is divine. Therefore preference ought to be given to those persons and places which through their own improvement, become a cause which can spread the good accomplished to many others who are under their guidance or take guidance from them.
> For that reason, the spiritual aid which is given to important and public persons ought to be regarded as more important, since it is a more universal good.[41]

Ignatius accepted the hierarchically organized society of his time and assumed, in the words of historian W.R. Trimble, that "the ingrained habits of obedience and respect of the lower classes for those above them . . . inclined acceptance of the decision of creed determined by the powerful, the wealthy, and the educated."[42] Since it was the will and the example of the elites that governed the state, decided the religion, and moved the people, it is little wonder that the Ignatian instructions consistently insist on the Society's involvement with them: the Jesuits needed their support if their ventures were to bear fruit. It is hardly surprising, therefore, that the evaluations of Broët and Salmerón were so bleak. Everything that the Jesuits had been told about Ireland proved to be true. The last faint glimmer of

---

[39] Young, *Letters of Ignatius Loyola*, p. 213. See also his letter to Jean Pelletier on 13 June 1551, p. 248.

[40] Young, *Letters of Ignatius Loyola*, p. 268.

[41] *The Constitutions of the Society of Jesus*, ed. George E. Ganss, S.J. (St. Louis, 1970) [henceforth *Cons.*] no. 622d, e. See also nos. 823, 824. John O'Malley does not give proper recognition to this point, and thus refashions the early policy of the Society with claims such as "Striking in the early years of the Society is how consistently indiscriminate the Jesuits were regarding the socio-economic status of their 'clientele'. Although some documentation insisted on the value of ministry to leaders in society, it was perhaps more insistent that Jesuit ministries were meant for all classes, for the rich and the poor, with a preference for those who were in greater spiritual, moral, or physical need" ("Renaissance Humanism and the First Jesuits," p. 398).

[42] *The Catholic Laity in Elizabethan England 1558-1603* (Cambridge, Mass., 1964) p. 4.

hope vanished with the desertion of the leaders. Without the support of those leaders, in the eyes of the Jesuits, Roman Catholicism in Ireland was doomed.

According to the Annual Letter for 1551, Archbishop Wauchope sought the Jesuit Giambattista Viola's assistance as the Archbishop prepared to go to Ireland. Viola informed him that such a decision was not his to make but must be referred to Loyola. Wauchope lamented that he had never been able to persuade Loyola to grant him any Jesuits, but he hoped that through the intercession of Marcello, Cardinal Cervini he would have some success with this request. How many earlier requests had been made by Wauchope we do not know.[43] But all had been refused by Loyola because he did not deem them advantageous (*nunquam enim existimavit P. Ignatius expedire*) even though Wauchope was a great friend of the Society. This request too was denied in Rome because Ignatius did not think the mission would benefit the Society.[44] Loyola may have decided on the basis of Broët's and Salmerón's earlier experience that, in light of the current political and religious conditions, Ireland was no place for Jesuits.

III

Despite Ignatius's profitable visit to England as a student, he initiated no mission to that country during the religious upheavals under Kings Henry VIII and Edward VI. Unlike Ireland England had no papal commission to aid the Catholics, only a fleeting suggestion that Reginald Pole, with Nicolás Bobadilla as his assistant, return to England in 1549 at the time of the Western Rising against the new Prayer Book.[45] Interest was kindled, however, when the Catholic Mary Tudor succeeded her step-brother Edward in 1553. Edward had died on 6 July and Mary ascended the throne on the

---

[43] Wauchope had asked for the assistance of André des Freux in 1547. See Durkan, "Wauchope," 63.

[44] J.M. Vélez, S.J. and V. Agustí, S.J., eds., *Vita Ignatii Loiolae et rerum Societatis Iesu historia auctore Joanne Alphonso de Polanco* [henceforth *Pol. Chron.*], 6 vols. (Madrid, 1894-98) II, 298-99.

[45] *Pol. Chron.*, I, 392. In the spring of 1549, Pole had asked for Bobadilla's assistance in the reformation of a congregation in Pisa (Loyola to Bobadilla, Rome 13 April 1549, MI *Epp. Ign.*, II, 379-80). This association may have been the basis for the proposal. Bobadilla was one of the most colourful and controversial of the early followers of Ignatius. Too often dismissed as mad by later Jesuit historians, Bobadilla had a number of important and influential friends. Besides Pole, Bobadilla was highly esteemed by Pole's nemesis Gian Pietro Carafa, later Pope Paul IV. Unfortunately we lack a close study of Bobadilla. Until its appearance see Arthur L. Fisher, "A Study in Early Jesuit Government: The Nature and Origins of the Dissent of Nicolás Bobadilla," *Viator* 10 (1979) 397-431; Ravier, *Loyola and the Founding of the Society*, *passim*; and Bangert, *Nadal*, *passim*. Bobadilla, interestingly, was one of the two Jesuits chosen by Loyola for the first mission to India in 1540. Because he was ill, Francis Xavier was chosen as his replacement.

19th after a foiled attempt by the John Dudley, Duke of Northumberland, to secure the crown for his daughter-in-law Jane Grey. By 5 August word of Edward's death had reached Rome, but there was still some uncertainty about Mary's success.[46] Her accession was confirmed a few days later, and on 19 August Ignatius enthusiastically reported that Mary was liberating those who had been imprisoned for religious reasons, including Bishop Stephen Gardiner.[47]

Once Ignatius was certain of religious developments in England, he wrote to Cardinal Pole, a man described by Nicholas Sander as the "hope of England, glory of the Roman Church, and light of Christendom,"[48] and thanked God that the kingdom had been restored "to the bosom of our holy Church and the purity of our Catholic faith." Jesuits had earlier been instructed to pray for England's return, and Ignatius promised that they would continue to do so.[49] Almost immediately Loyola began to seek more active involvement. Well aware of England's key position in the Protestantism of northern Europe and hoping that its return could mark the beginning of the complete reunification of Christendom, Ignatius wanted his young Society to do more than pray at a distance. Jesuits were already involved in the ecclesiastical and religious affairs of the Empire and had been successful in the reestablishment of Catholicism there. It was, therefore, only natural, "almost inevitable" according to Thomas H. Clancy, S.J., that he expected to be invited to England eventually, especially since he and other early Jesuits knew Cardinal Pole.[50]

It is not known when or how Ignatius and Pole first met. It could have been through the English priest John Helyar, who perhaps made the Spiritual Exercises in Paris under the direction of either Ignatius himself or Pierre Favre between 1534 and 1537. Helyar had been vicar of Warblington in Hampshire, the parish of the family of Reginald Pole.[51] For religious reasons

---

[46] Loyola to Martín de Olave, Rome 5 August 1553, MI *Epp. Ign.*, V, 288.
[47] Loyola to Martín de Olave, Rome 19 August 1553, MI *Epp. Ign.*, V, 353.
[48] *Rise and Growth of the Anglican Schism*, trans. and ed. David Lewis (London, 1877) p. 202.
[49] Rome 7 August 1553, MI *Epp. Ign.*, V, 304-05 (translated in Young, *Letters of Ignatius Loyola*, pp. 304-05); Loyola to the Universal Society, Rome 25 July and 7 August 1553, MI *Epp. Ign.*, V, 221 (translated in Young, *Letters of Ignatius Loyola*, p. 301). See MI *Epp. Ign.*, V, 164, 281, 288 for other letters in which prayers for England were requested.
[50] "The First Generation of English Jesuits 1555-1585," *AHSI* 57 (1988) 137. The first study of Ignatius and Pole was that of Joseph Crehan, S.J., "Saint Ignatius and Cardinal Pole," *AHSI* 25 (1956) 72-98.
[51] For clarification of the relation between Pole and Helyar, I am grateful to Professor Thomas F. Mayer for his assistance. For a short synopsis of that relation see his *Thomas Starkey and the Commonweal: Humanist Politics and Religion in the Reign of Henry VIII* (Cambridge, 1989) p. 273. Mayer doubts that Helyar ever made the Spiritual Exercises. We do know, however, that he was sufficiently impressed with Loyola to copy the *Exercises* into his notebook.

he fled to the continent in 1536, joined Pole in Rome in 1537 and, probably through the Cardinal's assistance, became the penitentiary of the English Hospice there in 1538.

A second possibility, and a more likely one, is that Loyola and Pole met through their mutual friends Bishop Gian Matteo Giberti, Gasparo, Cardinal Contarini, Vittoria Colonna, and those other Catholic reformers,[52] the humanistic and conciliatory *spirituali*, who had enthusiastically welcomed Ignatius and his companions in Italy in the late 1530s and early 1540s.[53]

Regardless of the date of the initial meeting, by 1541 Pole was involved with the Society. In August of that year Pole was appointed Governor of the Papal States, and his new residence at Viterbo quickly became a centre for the Italian *spirituali*.[54] As we have seen, Fathers Broët and Salmerón called on him on their way to Ireland in September of 1541 in order to consult him about certain apparent defects in their papal bulls. In that same month Pole asked Pope Paul III to send Nicolás Bobadilla, another of Ignatius's first companions, to Viterbo to help in the administration of the Patrimony of St. Peter. Because of other commitments, Bobadilla could only remain with Pole a few months, and the Cardinal was much disappointed when he lost the Jesuit's services.[55]

Nonetheless Pole continued to assist the Society when asked to do so. In his correspondence Ignatius referred to Pole as a patron of the Society throughout 1550; in June Pole assisted the Society in having its Institute and privileges confirmed by Pope Julius III in *Exposcit debitum* of 21 July 1550.[56]

---

[52] Paul Dudon suggests a third possibility: the Basque Martín de Zornoza, who was Spanish consul in Venice (*St. Ignatius of Loyola* [Milwaukee, 1949] p. 183). In the most recent study of Contarini (*Gasparo Contarini: Venice, Rome and Reform* [Berkeley, 1993]), Elisabeth G. Gleason notes both Contarini's friendship with Pole and his admiration "of the methodical spirituality" of Loyola (pp. 92, 141) but does not shed any new light on this question.

[53] For a general discussion of the *spirituali* see Elisabeth G. Gleason, "On the Nature of Sixteenth-Century Italian Evangelism: Scholarship, 1953-1978," *SCJ* 9 (1978) 3-25, and *Contarini*, pp. 260-76; and William V. Hudon, *Marcello Cervini and Ecclesiastical Government in Tridentine Italy* (DeKalb, 1992) pp. 3-17. On relations between Ignatius and the *spirituali* see John O'Malley, S.J., "The Jesuits, St. Ignatius, and the Counter-Reformation," *Studies in the Spirituality of Jesuits* 14/1 (1982) 19-21 and *The First Jesuits*, pp. 315-17.

[54] See Dermot Fenlon, *Heresy and Obedience in Tridentine Italy: Cardinal Pole and the Counter Reformation* (Cambridge, 1972) for the Viterbo circle.

[55] Pole to Loyola, Viterbo 22 December 1541, ARSI, Epp. Ext. 7/II, f. 43^r (published in A.M. Quirini, ed., *Epistolarum Reginaldi Poli S.R.E. Cardinalis et Aliorum ad Ipsum*, 5 vols. [Brescia, 1744-57] V, 115-16).

[56] D. Restrepo, S.J., ed., *Monumenta Bobadillae* (henceforth *Epp. Bobad.*) (Madrid, 1913) pp. 29-30, 620; Loyola to Broët, Rome 29 March 1550, MI *Epp. Ign.*, II, 725; Broët to Loyola, Bologna 12 April 1550, *Mon. Broet*, pp. 45-46; Loyola to Broët, Rome 26 April 1550, MI *Epp. Ign.*, III, 25; same to Simão Rodrigues, Rome 12 January 1550, MI *Epp. Ign.*, II, 643; same to Superiors of the Society, Rome 6 February 1550, MI *Epp. Ign.*, II, 674; same to Pole, Rome 16 June 1550, MI *Epp. Ign.*, III, 89-90.

As the Cardinal prepared to return to England, Ignatius, as was noted earlier, informed Pole of the Society's prayers. In his reflections, Ignatius was certain that the English people had been seduced by their leaders and princes. As papal legate, Pole would be able to deal with those leaders, correct the problem and restore the popularly favoured Catholicism.[57] Unfortunately the situation did not develop as Ignatius hoped.

Pole's legatine mission from Pope Julius III in August of 1553 was part of a general mission to northern Europe. Among his duties, he was specifically charged with mediation of a peace between Emperor Charles V and the French King Henry II. Pole's progress to England, however, was halted at Dillingen in Bavaria by a cautious Charles. Fearful of Pole's opposition to a marriage between the spinster Mary and her cousin Philip of Spain, the Emperor would not allow Pole to enter England.[58] He was only allowed to continue to Brussels after the negotiations were successfully concluded.

The Emperor's fears were justified: Pole was not in favour of the Spanish marriage. Because of the Queen's age, the legate believed that she should not marry at all but, for political and ecclesiastical reasons, he considered a Spanish marriage especially unfortunate. Politically Pole did not relish the possibility "that my country should pass into the hands of a stranger." Equally important was his fear that the Queen's marriage to a foreigner, a marriage opposed by the English people, would impede the restoration of Catholicism. After Julius III endorsed the match, Pole accepted the decision.[59]

---

[57] Rome 7 August 1553, MI *Epp. Ign.*, V, 304-05 (translated in Young, *Letters of Ignatius Loyola*, pp. 304-05).

[58] Writing in 1610 a brief account of the reign of Queen Mary, Robert Parsons blamed William Paget for preventing Pole's entrance. Lord Paget convinced the Emperor that Pole would disrupt the plans for a marital alliance either by siding with Stephen Gardiner's faction or by offering himself as an alternative candidate. Pole, although a Cardinal, had not yet been ordained ("A Storie of Domesticall Difficulties," ed. John Hungerford Pollen, S.J., in *Miscellanea II* [London, 1906] p. 57). Geoffrey Woodward reminds us that this marriage "was not made in heaven but in Brussels by Charles V's councillors" (*Philip II* [London, 1992] p. 81).

[59] For Pole's diplomatic activities at this time see Heinrich Lutz, "Cardinal Reginald Pole and the Path to Anglo-Papal Mediation at the Peace Conference of Marcq, 1553-55," in *Politics and Society in Reformation Europe*, eds. E.I. Kouri and Tom Scott (New York, 1987) pp. 329-52. Pole's opposition to the Spanish marriage is discussed on p. 334. Because of the unclear relation between a queen regnant and her husband the English opposed a marriage with any foreigner and not specifically with a Spaniard (see Jennifer Loach, *Parliament and the Crown in the Reign of Mary Tudor* [Oxford, 1986] pp. 190-91, 234). Nonetheless, anti-Spanish propaganda circulated in England before and after the marriage (see M.J. Rodríguez-Salgado, *The Changing Face of Empire: Charles V, Philip II and Habsburg Authority, 1551-1559* [Cambridge, 1988] p. 91). Although all the ingredients of the "Black Legend" are present in Mary's reign (see, e.g. the anonymous *A Warning for Englande Conteyning the horrible practises of the King of Spain in the Kingdom of Naples and the miseries whereunto that noble*

Further political concerns kept Pole waiting in Brussels until November of 1554. The Emperor wanted the restoration of Catholicism to follow the Spanish marriage so that the Habsburgs could receive the credit and prestige.[60]

For years Ignatius had sought to gain admission for his men into Flanders. For the reestablishment of Catholicism in northern Europe, it was essential that the Society gain a foothold at Louvain, the intellectual centre. As early as 1550 Ignatius favoured establishing a Jesuit college at the University of Louvain. His proposals, however, came to naught because of the opposition of Mary of Hungary, the younger sister of the Emperor Charles V and the Governess of the Netherlands. Advised by Antoine Perrenot de Granvelle, Bishop of Arras, and Viglius van Aytta, her secretary,[61] Mary refused permission for such an establishment despite a favourable decision on the proposal by the University's theological faculty. All subsequent attempts to persuade Mary to lift her ban failed. While Pole was in Brussels, he threw his influence on the side of the Society but this too left Mary unmoved.[62] Permission for a Jesuit college did not come until the abdication of Charles V in October of 1555. Mary then relinquished control and left Flanders.. The new ruler, Philip of Spain, granted the required permission the following summer.[63]

Realme is brought [n.p. n.d.], two editions of which were published probably in Strasbourg and Emden in 1555 [STC 10023.7, 10024]) the legend itself did not flower until the reign of her sister Elizabeth. See William S. Maltby, *The Black Legend in England: The Development of anti-Spanish Sentiment, 1558-1660* (Durham, N.C., 1971). Although the English had always been notoriously xenophobic, it was during the reign of Mary that the identification of English nationalism and Protestantism was forged (see David Loades, "The Origins of English Protestant Nationalism," in *Religion and National Identity*, ed. Stuart Mews [Oxford, 1982] pp. 297-317. Of the Queen's advisers only William, Lord Paget strongly supported the Spanish marriage. The rest pleaded that she marry an Englishman (G.W. Bernard, *The Power of the Early Tudor Nobility: A Study of the Fourth and Fifth Earls of Shrewsbury* [Brighton, 1985] pp. 78-79). See also pp. 86-87 for illustrations of anti-Spanish sentiment.

[60] R.H. Pogson, "Reginald Pole and the Priorities of Government," *Historical Journal* 18 (1975) 3-20; R.H. Pogson, "The Legacy of the Schism: Confusion, Continuity and Change in the Marian Clergy," in *The Mid-Tudor Polity c 1540-1560*, eds. Jennifer Loach and Robert Tittler (London, 1980) pp. 116-36; and D.M. Loades, *The Reign of Mary Tudor* (London, 1979) pp. 118, 170-76, 220.

[61] It seems that the secretary regarded the Jesuits suspiciously ever since Nicolás Bobadilla attacked Charles V's efforts to reconcile the Catholics and the Protestants by the *Interim* of Augsburg in 1548. See Bangert, *Jay and Salmerón*, p. 216.

[62] Ignatius Loyola to Adrian Adriaenssens, Rome 27 February 1554, MI *Epp. Ign.*, VI, 391. At the same time Pole intervened on the behalf of the Society in a dispute between a few Jesuits and the Bishops of Cambrai and Tournai (Pole to Loyola, Brussels 27 April 1554, ARSI, Epp. Ext. 7/II, f. 414ʳ [printed in Quirini, *Epistolarum Poli*, V, 116-17]). See the Annual Letter for 1554 (*Pol. Chron.*, IV, 285-88, 295-96] for an account of Pole's intercession.

[63] Charles transferred authority to his son in stages. Philip did not assume the Spanish crowns until January of 1556; Charles did not hand Franche-Comté over until April. See Hugo Rahner, S.J., ed., *Saint Ignatius Loyola: Letters to Women* (Edinburgh, 1960) pp. 38-44.

The announcement of the engagement of Mary Tudor to Philip of Spain in October of 1553 increased Loyola's hopes. Through Dona Leonor Mascarenhas, the Prince's governess, Ignatius had met Philip when the Prince was eight years old.[64] Loyola had not been successful in his dealings with Philip's father Charles V, but he hoped for better cooperation with the prince.[65] One acquaintance was King, another a papal legate. Loyola's expectation of a request for Jesuit assistance was therefore not unrealistic. So confident was he that such a request would be forthcoming, that he planned to create a new administrative unit within the Society (a province) to include the Jesuits working in England, Lower Germany, and the Low Countries.[66]

Not knowing how long Pole would be kept waiting in Brussels, Ignatius prepared Jesuits in the Low Countries and in Spain for an English mission. On 1 May 1554 Loyola told Bernard Olivier to ready himself for the assignment, presumably in the company of Cardinal Pole.[67] In a letter to Jerónimo Nadal two days later, Ignatius suggested sending his nephew Antonio Araoz into England with the Prince.[68] Araoz was considered presumably because of his friendship with Philip's advisor Rui Gómez de Silva, Prince of Éboli. But Araoz was not included in the retinue. Informed of this, Nadal was more than slightly annoyed and concluded that Araoz had not been persistent enough. Nadal wanted Jesuits in England in one way or another despite the Society's secretary Juan de Polanco's protestation that the

---

[64] Dona Leonor yearned to join the Society. In a letter to Pierre Favre, she confessed "But as I am only a woman and a worthless sinner, I have no right to dream or speak of holy things, more especially the things of Inigo's Company" (Brodrick, *Saint Ignatius Loyola*, p. 313).

[65] Rahner, *Saint Ignatius Loyola*, pp. 31-35. Loyola was much more successful with the Habsburg women—with the exception of Mary of Hungary. In fact the Infanta Juana, daughter of Emperor Charles V and Regent of the Spanish kingdoms, was actually a member of the Society of Jesus. For an exposition of Loyola's relations with royal women see Rahner's introduction, "The Courtier of Heaven," in the above-cited work, pp. 29-37. Charmarie J. Blaisdell makes a fascinating comparison between Loyola's and John Calvin's relations with women in "Calvin's and Loyola's Letters to Women: Politics and Spiritual Counsel in the Sixteenth Century," in *Calviniana: Ideas and Influence of Jean Calvin*, ed. Robert V. Schnucker (Kirksville, 1988) pp. 235-53.

[66] *Pol. Chron.*, IV, 310-11. One wonders whether Ignatius's decision reflects one of the most important aspects of the marriage treaty between Mary Tudor and Philip of Spain: the creation of a new northern state out of England and the Spanish Netherlands in order to contain the growing power of France. Their heir would inherit not only England and its dominions but also the Low Countries and Franche-Comté. Don Carlos, Philip's son by a previous marriage, would inherit Spain and its dominions. If Don Carlos died without heirs, his inheritance would pass to the children of Philip and Mary (John Lynch, *Spain 1516-1598: From Nation State to World Empire* [Oxford, 1991] p. 134).

[67] Rome 1 May 1554, MI *Epp. Ign.*, VI, 651.

[68] Araoz had long been an exceptionally large thorn in the side of Nadal as the latter travelled through Spain as the General's Vicar. Disputes and confrontations were relatively common. See Bangert, *Nadal, passim*.

Society was already over-committed and that there were enough problems with finding men for the current projects. Nadal next approached Francis Borgia and asked him to intercede with Philip.⁶⁹ This time Philip deferred the decision to Mary.⁷⁰ By the end of June of 1554, however, it was decided to keep Araoz out of England and maybe even send him to Rome.⁷¹ In later letters Ignatius explained that the English mission had been postponed. Queen Mary did not want the Jesuits to enter her country.⁷² Thus Philip decided that the time was not ripe for their arrival and asked that they not be included in his retinue.⁷³ Because of the inclusion of Dominicans and

---

⁶⁹ This was a delicate move because Philip was seeking to elevate Borgia to the cardinalate despite the opposition of Nadal, Loyola, and the Society. Borgia eventually persuaded Infanta Juana, Regent in Spain while Philip was in England, to write to her father Charles V and her brother Philip to urge them to drop their proposal. See Bangert, *Nadal*, pp. 130-33 and Padberg, "Ignatius, the Popes, and Realistic Reverence," 24-26. On Borgia see Cándido de Dalmases, S.J. *Francis Borgia: Grandee of Spain, Jesuit, Saint* (St. Louis, 1991) p. 111, and Mario Scaduto, S.J., *L'Opera di Francesco Borgia (1565-1572)* (Rome, 1992) p. 34.

⁷⁰ Loyola to Nadal, Rome 3 May 1554, MI *Epp. Ign.*, VI, 675 same to same, Rome 15 May 1554, *ibid.*, 713; same to same, Rome 14 June 1554, MI *Epp. Ign.*, VII, 102; same to same, Rome 21 June 1554, *ibid.*, 142-43; *Pol. Chron.*, IV, 435; Nadal to Loyola, Valladolid 14 May 1554, F. Cervós, S.J. and M. Nicolau, S.J., eds., *Epistolae et Monumenta P. Hieronymi Nadal* (henceforth *Epp. Nadal*) 6 vols. (Madrid/Rome, 1898-1964) I, 261; Borgia to Loyola, Ascalone 26 February 1556, I. Rodriguez, S.J., V. Agustí, S.J., and F. Cervós, S.J., eds., *Sanctus Franciscus Borgia* (henceforth *Epp. Borgia*) 5 vols. (Madrid, 1894-1911) III, 256; Antonio Astraín, S.J., *Historia de la Compañia de Jésus en la Asistencia de España*, 7 vols. (Madrid, 1902-25) I, 405-06.

⁷¹ Ignatius Loyola to Jerónimo Nadal, Rome 21 June 1554, MI *Epp. Ign.*, VII, 142-43. Infanta Juana was much upset at the prospect of either Araoz or Borgia leaving Spain for the Low Countries or England. Her opposition may explain the change (*Pol. Chron.*, VI, 628). So adamant was the Princess that, after she had been received into the Society in 1555, she asked Loyola that she be named the superior of both Borgia and Araoz to make sure that they did not leave Spain (Thomas H. Clancy, S.J., "Ignatius as Fund-Raiser," *Studies in the Spirituality of Jesuits* 25/1 [1993] 24).

⁷² Mary's reasons for forbidding the Society's entry into England are unknown. Some historians suspect the Emperor's involvement in the decision. It seems more likely, however, that Mary acted on the advice of Mary of Hungary, Bishop Granvelle, and Viglius van Aytta. These three worked out the marital negotiations. Charles V was too ill to play a major role. See Rodríguez-Salgado, *Changing Face of Empire*, p. 81.

⁷³ Loyola to Salmerón, Rome 26 August 1554, MI *Epp. Ign.*, VII, 472; same to Adrian Adriaenssens, Rome 27 September 1554, *ibid.*, 576; same to Olivier, Rome 27 September 1554, *ibid.*, 573; *Pol. Chron.*, IV, 296. The marriage treaty stipulated "That Philip shall have none in his service but the queen's natural born subjects. That he shall not bring Foreigners into England, to make the English uneasy, and that he shall punish the contraveners. That he shall make no Alteration in the laws and customs of England" (*Acta Regia: or An account of the Treaties, Letters, and Instruments Between Monarchs of England and Foreign Powers* [London, 1728] III, 407-8). Philip's vacillation over the Society is but one example of his uncertainty regarding the composition of his retinue. In response to advice from his father, the Spanish ambassador, and his councillors, Philip changed his mind several times (*Reign of Mary Tudor*, p. 134). Approximately a dozen clerics journeyed to England with Philip (Rodríguez-Salgado, *Changing Face of Empire*, p. 199). To many in Philip's retinue, England was an extremely strange country. One of his companions wrote that the English "are white and pink and quarrelsome, inclined to cruel dissensions, but not so much now that they have realized the evil

Franciscans in Philip's entourage, both Nadal and Borgia judged the absence of Jesuits to reflect poorly on the Society. Eager to secure official recognition and confident in the support of a friend, Ignatius was extremely disappointed in the Society's exclusion. Only Philip's promise that, once he had studied the situation, he would invite the Society into England, moderated Loyola's grief. The setback was only temporary, and Ignatius was sure that the need for Jesuit assistance remained. He was confident that within a short time one of his men would accompany Pole or be summoned by Philip.[74]

Mary and Philip married on 25 July 1554 at Winchester. Because the position of a king consort was unprecedented in English law, Philip's position was carefully regulated by the marriage treaty and was codified in a statute of the realm in order to quell the fears of the English. Philip, however, was not satisfied either with his status or with his role as it had been defined.[75]

With the marriage and the Spanish treaty safely concluded, Pole was finally permitted to enter the country the following November. He arrived at Westminster on the 27th. Work on a religious reconciliation with Rome began immediately. The issue of confiscated ecclesiastical property was the hardest to resolve. Many of the gentry and the nobility had raised this thorny question and wanted some guarantees that the papal legate would not attempt to restore confiscated property. But in that, as in other areas, Pole moved slowly. "My commission," he told both Houses of Parliament, "is not to pull down but to build; to reconcile, not to censure; to invite but without compulsion. My business is not to proceed by way of retrospection, or to question things already settled. . ."[76] Once that had been treated adequately, other topics followed nicely and a final settlement was reached on Christmas

---

that comes from them. . . . They are a ferocious, barbarous and restless people. Their celebration consists in eating and drinking and they think of nothing else. They drink more beer than there is water in the river at Valladolid," cited in Henry Kamen, "Toleration and Dissent in Sixteenth-Century Spain: The Alternative Tradition," *SCJ* 19 (1988) 13 n. 46. For examples of anti-Spanish behaviour see James M. Boyden, *The Courtier and the King: Ruy Gómez de Silva, Philip II, and the Court of Spain* ((Berkeley, 1995) pp. 40-43.

[74] Ignatius Loyola to the Jesuits at Louvain, Cologne, and Tournai, Rome 21 August 1554, MI *Epp. Ign.*, VII, 427; *Pol. Chron.*, IV, 435, 492-93.

[75] For Philip's role in the government of England see David Loades, "Philip II and the Government of England," in *Law and Government under the Tudors*, eds Claire Cross, David Loades, and J.J. Scarisbrick (Cambridge, 1988) pp. 177-94. Constance Jordan addresses "the anomalous character of a female prince" and the various attempts either to justify or to repudiate such a prince in "Woman's Rule in Sixteenth-Century Political Thought," *Renaissance Quarterly* 40 (1987) 421-51. Similarly Carole Levin contrasts how traditional religious practices such as touching to cure the king's evil were used by Mary and by Elizabeth to justify their possession of the English throne ("'Would I Could Give You Help and Succour': Elizabeth I and the Politics of Touch," *Albion* 21 [1989] 191-205).

[76] Quoted in Loades, *Reign of Mary Tudor*, p. 325.

Eve of 1554.[77] Less than a month later, on 23 January 1555, after he heard the news about the reconciliation, Ignatius conveyed his enthusiastic response in a letter to Philip. The following day, a more important letter was sent to Cardinal Pole.[78] After he repeated his joy at the return of England to allegiance with Rome, Ignatius was eager to bring Pole uptodate on affairs of the Roman College and the German College because Pole had often expressed interest in both.[79] In the latter there were now an Englishman "of talent and character" and an Irishman "of who we have great hopes," both of whom might be of some use to the Cardinal. Ignatius included accounts of many and diverse missions, including the important mission to Ethiopia, on which individual Jesuits were sent. These accounts seem to be little more than thinly disguised hints at the Society's availability.

---

[77] For a discussion of the significance of the restoration of confiscated ecclesiastical property see J.H. Crehan, S.J., "The Return to Obedience: New Judgment on Cardinal Pole," *The Month* 200 (1955) 221-29. Loades notes that Philip consistently sided with the lay aristocracy and suggests that he may well have been responsible for the papal bull *Praeclara* promulgated on 20 June 1555. This bull settled the problem by officially suppressing the former religious houses. See "Philip II and the Government of England," 189. Interestingly the issue of ecclesiastical property was resurrected frequently over the next century as a strong reason against a Catholic king. In fact Gilbert Burnet explained Pole's refusal to invite the Jesuits because of an indiscreet suggestion by some unnamed Jesuit that monastic property be given to the Society to endow colleges (Nicholas Pocock, ed., *The History of the Reformation of the Church of England by Gilbert Burnet*, 7 vols. [Oxford, 1865] II, 525-26. Thomas Mayer finds this explanation more credible than I do. Compare Thomas M. McCoog, S.J., "Ignatius Loyola and Reginald Pole: A Reconsideration," *JEH* (forthcoming) and Thomas F. Mayer, "A Test of Wills: Cardinal Pole, Ignatius Loyola, and the Jesuits in England," in *The Reckoned Expense: Edmund Campion and the Early English Jesuits. Essays in Celebration of the First Centenary of Campion Hall, Oxford (1896-1996)*, ed. Thomas M. McCoog, S.J. (Woodbridge, 1996) pp. 21-37.

[78] Loyola to Philip, Rome 23 January 1555, MI *Epp. Ign.*, VIII, 305-06; same to Pole, Rome 24 January 1555, *ibid.*, 308-10 (translated in Young, *Letters of Ignatius Loyola*, pp. 361-62).

[79] The Roman College was opened in 1551 and the German in August of 1552. Much of the credit for the latter is due to Cardinal Morone. A former Nuncio in Germany, Morone worked for the establishment of a seminary in Rome where German students could be educated in their faith. This was essential for the confirmation of the Church in Germany. Loyola offered his assistance and Morone obtained the full consent of Pope Julius III. See O'Malley, *The First Jesuits*, p. 234; Philip Caraman, S.J, *University of the Nations* (New York, 1981) pp. 9-10. On the foundation of the German College see Peter Schmidt, *Das Collegium Germanicum in Rom und die Germaniker* (Tübingen, 1984) and Oskar Garstein, *Rome and the Counter-Reformation in Scandinavia: Jesuit Educational Strategy 1553-1622* (Leiden, 1992) pp. 103-29. On the relationship between the German College and Loyola's educational policy see Francesco C. Cesareo, "The Collegium Germanicum and the Ignatian Vision of Education," *SCJ* 24 (1993) 829-41. On the effectiveness of the training see István Bitskey, "The Collegium Germanicum Hungaricum in Rome and the Beginning of the Counter-Reformation in Hungary," in *Crown, Church and Estates: Central European Politics in the Sixteenth and Seventeenth Centuries*, eds. R.J.W. Evans and T.V. Thomas (London, 1991) pp. 110-22. Cardinal Pole had promised 500 aurei annually to assist the German College (ARSI, Rom. 157/I, f. 13r).

Pole's illness throughout the spring of 1555 prevented him from attending the conclave that elected as pope first Marcellus II in April and then Paul IV in May. Upon his recovery the Cardinal replied to Ignatius. The letter, although polite, made no mention of Loyola's offer and simply asked that the Society continue to remember England in its prayers.[80] In England for more than six months Pole had re-established communion with Rome and was embarking on a true reformation of the English Church—but without the Jesuits.[81]

Even before Pole's polite reply, Ignatius tried a new tactic. He had decided to ask a mutual friend, Giovanni, Cardinal Morone, to intercede. Morone, Vice-Protector of England, was a close personal friend and confidant of Pole.[82] As early as 19 March, Loyola was confiding to Nadal that he planned to solicit Morone's assistance,[83] and references to Morone's intervention appear periodically in the Ignatian correspondence over the next year. Morone's letter, Ignatius believed, would have the desired effect on Pole. Again Loyola's expectations were high: Pole would finally invite the Society to England for some specific and important task. But again disappointment set in. By March of 1556, after nearly a year of promise, Ignatius reluctantly admitted that Morone's letter had not borne the desired results.[84]

Loyola's persistence in the face of Pole's indifference was remarkable. So convinced was he of the need for the Society's involvement that in the summer of 1555 he finally abandoned subtlety and offered the few English- and Irish-speaking Jesuits to Pole. In the same letter, he again expressed his willingness to accept Pole's candidates for the priesthood at either the

---

[80] Richmond 8 May 1555, MI *Epp. Ign.*, VIII, 311-12 and *Epp. Ign.*, XII, 508-09.

[81] David Loades contends that Pole's reformation was a "distinctive hybrid," an "uneasy mixture of late medieval formalism and humanist intelligence" more dependent on Erasmus and Cranmer than on Luther and Loyola. See "The Spirituality of the Restored Catholic Church (1553-1558) in the Context of the Counter Reformation," in *The Reckoned Expense: Edmund Campion and the Early English Jesuits. Essays in Celebration of the First Centenary of Campion Hall, Oxford (1896-1996)*, ed. Thomas M. McCoog, S.J. (Woodbridge, 1996) pp. 3-20.

[82] In his doctoral thesis "Cardinal Pole—Papal Legate to England in Mary Tudor's Reign" (unpublished D.Phil. thesis: Cambridge University, 1972), Rex Pogson demonstrates Pole's reliance on Morone, whose friendship and advice Pole valued (121).

[83] Loyola to Nadal, Rome 19 March 1555, MI *Epp. Ign.*, VIII, 574. The Diet of Augsburg was scheduled to open on 5 February 1555, and Pope Julius III had appointed Cardinal Morone to head the papal delegation. Both the Pope and the Cardinal asked Loyola for two Jesuit theologians. Although Alfonso Salmerón was an obvious candidate, Nadal was selected perhaps because of an earlier clash between Salmerón and Morone over justification. See Bangert, *Nadal*, pp. 139-41.

[84] Loyola to Francis Borgia, Rome 14 November 1555, MI *Epp. Ign.*, X, 132; same to Olivier, Rome 3 December 1555, *ibid.*, 247; same to Nadal, Rome 5 December 1555, *ibid.*, 259; same to Ribadeneira, Rome 31 March 1556, MI *Epp. Ign.*, XI, 195; *Pol. Chron.*, VI, 445-46.

Roman College or the German College. But again Pole did not accept the proffered assistance.[85]

In the pursuit of Pole, the Society's other acquaintance in England, King Philip, was not forgotten. A year had expired since Philip's promise to introduce Jesuits into England after his careful study of the situation and, presumably, his persuading the Queen of their importance. Ignatius renewed his appeal to Philip in the summer of 1555 around the same time that he offered the English- and Irish-speaking Jesuits to Pole. The chosen emissary was again Bernard Olivier. In July he was in Flanders and was given instructions for a mission to England. His mission was to Philip, and among the various items of business that he was to transact with the King were the establishment of the Society in Louvain; financial support for the Roman College; the scandalous life of the Bishop of Limerick, John Quinn, O.P.;[86] the application of Juan de Mendoza, custodian of Castel Nuovo in Naples, for admission into the Society; and the encouragement of a Jesuit mission to England through the establishment of a college in England. Father Adrian Candidus (*vere* de Witte), who was to preach in Flemish and hear confessions in Italian, was to accompany him. Although Olivier could not speak English, he hoped to preach in French, "a language known to many Englishmen," and to hear confessions in French and Italian. Loyola hoped that the two would be able to gather more spiritual fruit in the court and in the country than originally expected, but he insisted that Olivier approach directly the King and the Cardinal and not wait for them to contact him.[87]

Olivier never sailed. He was ready to depart when he received word of Philip's imminent return to Flanders for the abdication of his father Charles V at Brussels on 25 October. To assist in Olivier's task Loyola sent Pedro de Ribadeneira to Brussels.[88] Despite everything, Loyola was confident of success. He considered carefully possible candidates for this sensitive venture. In a letter to Francis Borgia he finally proposed Pedro Tablares, Francisco Rojas, and Antonio Araoz as candidates for the mission. While the King was in Brussels, it seems likely that he received Olivier there and

---

[85] Rome 2 July 1555, MI *Epp. Ign.*, IX, 273-75.

[86] The Irish Jesuit David Wolfe was the source of information about Quinn. Before he entered the Society, Wolfe had been dean of Limerick cathedral and was very familiar with Quinn's style of life. For this see Olivier was to propose Richard Creagh to Philip and Mary. Creagh, however, was not eager to accept the burden (Loyola to Olivier, Rome 27 July 1555, MI *Epp. Ign.*, IX, 378-79). Wolfe suggested the establishment of a Jesuit college in Limerick (Loyola to Wolfe, Rome 28 December 1555, MI *Epp. Ign.*, X, 389). Perhaps this was a reason for Loyola's interest in the reigning Bishop.

[87] Loyola to Olivier, Rome 4 and 8 July 1555, MI *Epp. Ign.*, IX, 299-300; same to same, Rome 6 July 1555, *ibid.*, 277-78; same to Alexis Fontana, Rome 8 July 1555, *ibid.*, 302-05. The various instructions given to Olivier can be found in MI *Epp. Ign.*, IX, 278-86; *Pol. Chron.*, V, 26-27, 291, 312.

[88] On Ribadeneira see *Mon. Ang.*, II, 452.

granted some of his petitions. As we have seen, Philip granted the Society permission to found a college at the University of Louvain.[89] Yet he was still hesitant about allowing the Society to send some men into England.[90] That matter, he claimed, should be in the hands of Cardinal Pole.[91] He did, however, agree to include one Spanish Jesuit in his entourage upon his return to England. The Ignatian dream was on the brink of realization. Ignatius quickly informed Cardinal Pole that Ribadeneira would accompany Philip.[92] After he arrived in England, Ribadeneira could bring Pole uptodate on the Society, supply him with information about its missions and projects, and answer any questions that he might have. Ignatius hoped that such a conversation would result in an invitation for more Jesuit involvement. Aside from a polite willingness to receive the Spanish Jesuit, Pole's response, written in the midst of his synod of London, was again noncommittal.[93]

The Society expected great things from Ribadeneira's mission. Because of his ignorance of English, he planned to preach in Latin.[94] Although he was being sent with only one companion, others would certainly follow, once a convenient way was established. To prepare for their arrival, Ignatius hoped to establish colleges in England with Spanish financial assistance, perhaps through the assignment of fixed rents from estates in Flanders. To gain Spanish financial support, the Society turned towards the well-connected Araoz, who was to travel to Flanders to meet King Philip.[95] But nothing happened. Philip did not return to England until May of 1557 and then for only a few months. For some unknown reason, perhaps the intervention of Pole, Philip again changed his mind.

---

[89] Loyola to Olivier, Rome 10 September 1555, MI *Epp. Ign.*, IX, 581-83; same to Adrian Adriaenssens, Rome 8 October 1555, *ibid.*, 691-93; same to Olivier, Rome 8 October 1555, *ibid.*, 694-95; same to Philip, Rome 23 October 1555, MI *Epp. Ign.*, X, 32-35; same to Borgia, Rome 14 November 1555, *ibid.*, 132; same to Ribadeneira, Rome 4 December 1555, *ibid.*, 251-52; same to Nadal, Rome 5 December 1555, *ibid.*, 259; *Pol. Chron.*, V, 555.

[90] Loyola suggested to Nicolaus de Lanoy, rector of the Jesuit college in Vienna, that he ask Ferdinand, King of the Romans and eventually Holy Roman Emperor, to write to Philip to recommend the foundation of Jesuit colleges in his realms (Rome 24 January 1556, MI *Epp. Ign.*, X, 567).

[91] *Pol. Chron.*, V, 555-56.

[92] Loyola to Nicolaus de Lanoy, Rome 21 March 1556, MI *Epp. Ign.*, XI, 154; same to Ribadeneira, Rome 9 June 1556, *ibid.*, 551. Loyola's first candidate was Pedro Tablares but Borgia's doubts resulted in the change. See *Pol. Chron.*, V, 555-56.

[93] Loyola to Pole, Rome 25 October 1555, MI *Epp. Ign.*, X, 38-39; Pole to Loyola, London 15 December 1555, *ibid.*, 39-40.

[94] Laínez believed that Latin sermons would be especially fruitful in Oxford (Laínez to Ribadeneira, Rome 16 September 1556, E. Astudillo, S.J., ed., *Epistolae et Acta patris Iacobi Lainii secundi praepositi generalis Societatis Iesu* [henceforth *Epp. Laínez*] 8 vols. [Madrid, 1912-16] I, 366).

[95] Loyola to Borgia, Rome 14 September 1555, MI *Epp. Ign.*, IX, 616; same to Nadal, Rome 21 November 1555, MI *Epp. Ign.*, X, 179; same to Lanoy, Rome 24 January 1556, *ibid.*, 567.

When Loyola died on 31 July 1556, no member of his Society had yet entered England. Pole expressed his tremendous sorrow at the death of Loyola and his deep admiration for him. Yet for England all he asked of the Society was prayer.[96] Nevertheless Ribadeneira prepared to visit England, and it was decided that Bernard Olivier would accompany him as a French preacher. Olivier's death on 22 August 1556 altered those plans and postponed Ribadeneira's departure.[97] The consequent constitutional crisis within the Society after the death of Loyola made the delay even longer.[98]

Although the quest to send Jesuits into England continued, Loyola's successor, Diego Laínez, did not pursue it as fervently. Without Loyola it seemed even less likely that the Society would work in England.

The reformation of the English Church continued without Jesuit assistance, but the reestablishment of Catholicism was seriously disrupted in the spring of 1557. On 9 April the fiercely anti-Spanish Pope Paul IV recalled all his agents in Spanish territories and by name revoked Pole's legatine authority.[99] On 31 May Cardinal Morone was arrested and on 12 June the Inquisition initiated its investigation of him as a suspected Lutheran. As Cardinal, Carafa had opposed the *spirituali*; as Pope, he was taking action against them.[100] It was commonly believed that Pole would join Morone in prison if he returned to Rome as the Pope requested. In October the Pope sent his nephew Carlo Carafa to Flanders to seek Pole's extradition. The Queen refused the Cardinal permission to leave the realm and the consequent stalemate paralysed serious religious reform within the kingdom for the last year of the Queen's reign.[101]

Preoccupied with his problems with Rome, Pole still ignored any suggestion that he invite the Society into England. The refusal continued despite the assistance that the Society provided in defence of Morone and

---

[96] Pole to Laínez, London 15 November 1556, ARSI, Epp. Ext. 7/II, ff. 52ʳ-53ᵛ (printed in Quirini, *Epistolarum Poli*, V, 120-21); *Pol. Chron.*, VI, 452.

[97] Ribadeneira considered Olivier's death a great setback for the project. Without him Ribadeneira did not have a suitable Jesuit who could preach in French. See Ribadeneira to Loyola, Ghent 26 August 1556, D. Restrepo, S.J. and Johannes Vilar, S.J., eds., *Patris petri de Ribadeneira, Societatis Iesu sacerdotis, confessiones, epistolae aliaque scripta inedita* (henceforth *Epp. Ribadeneira*) 2 vols. (Madrid, 1920-23) I, 189-90; *Pol. Chron.*, VI, 445-46.

[98] On this crisis see Bangert, *Nadal*, chapters 11, 12, and 13.

[99] For the effect of the Pope's anti-Spanish position on the Society of Jesus see Bangert, *Nadal, passim*.

[100] An early biographer, Luis Gonçalves da Câmara, wrote "On receiving this news [of Carafa's election], the Father showed a notable change and disturbance in his countenance and, as I came to know later (whether from his own lips or from the Fathers to whom he told this, I do not know), all his bones were shaken within him" (quoted in Dalmases, *Ignatius of Loyola*, p. 286). See also Peter A. Quinn, "Ignatius Loyola and Gian Pietro Carafa: Catholic Reformers at Odds," *CHR* 67 (1981) 386-400.

[101] See Fenlon, *Heresy and Obedience*, pp. 251-81, and Loades, *Reign of Mary Tudor*, pp. 428-57.

Pole in their problems with the papacy throughout the winter and spring of 1558.[102] Sometime in early 1558 Gómez Suárez de Figueroa, Duke of Feria, petitioned the General for the services of Ribadeneira, who had returned to Flanders from Rome the preceding November. The Duke, it seems, wanted the Society to establish a seminary in England like the German College in Rome. Thrice he had written to Pole about his plans, but neither the King nor the Cardinal approved. In a letter written from Greenwich to Ribadeneira on 22 March 1558, the Duke of Feria laid the blame for his failure at the feet of the Cardinal:

> I have written to my brother [Antonio de Córdoba] that I have so far been unable to move the Queen or the Cardinal towards letting members of the Company come here, advantageous though it would be to this kingdom. But they would have no standing or protection here unless they entered by the Cardinal's door. I will keep at the matter until we see how it turns out. The Cardinal is a good man, but very lukewarm; and I do not believe that the lukewarm go to Paradise, even if they are called moderates.[103]

Feria advised that the matter be left in his hands. Nothing could be done until the time was ripe. Meanwhile he cautioned Ribadeneira that he must not leave Brussels for England until the Duke summoned him. Laínez also favoured such caution because of Cardinal Pole's reluctance. Laínez confessed, however, that he did not understand Pole's actions. But he knew that Pole would not be able "when the time comes, to hinder the Divine will; this will of God is leading us on gently in hope, as I think, until it has supplied to our Society sufficient strength and numbers to enable it to extend further in the service of God, and then it will open the doors which at present remain closed, even as we have seen to happen up to the present."[104]

With or without Pole's permission—indeed without that of the General—Ribadeneira sailed for England and arrived in London in November of 1558, shortly before the deaths of Queen Mary and Cardinal Pole. There he remained until 20 March 1559. From the Duke of Feria's London residence, Ribadeneira watched the vacillation in faith after the Queen's death and the final destruction of any hope for Jesuit involvement. In his letters to Father

---

[102] For the support the Society provided see Mario Scaduto, *L'Epoca di Giacomo Laínez: Il Governo 1556-1565* (Rome, 1964) pp. 82-83; and Paolo Simoncelli, *Il Caso Reginald Pole: Eresia e Santità nelle Polemiche Religiose del Cinquecento* (Rome, 1977) pp. 187-91. On Salmerón's testimony during the proceedings against Morone see Bangert, *Jay and Salmerón*, pp. 239-40, and O'Malley, *The First Jesuits*, pp. 315-17.

[103] CSP Spain (1554-58) 370-71. See also Ribadeneira to Laínez, Brussels 4 April 1558, *Epp. Ribadeneira*, I, 293.

[104] Antonio de Córdoba to Laínez, Montilla 3 March 1558, *Epp. Laínez*, III, 172; Laínez to Duke of Feria, Rome 17 September 1558, *ibid.*, 539 (see also the note on 539-40); *Epp. Ribadeneira*, I, 70-71.

General, he complained that he was unable to do anything. Dispirited, he returned to Brussels.[105]

Ignatius's plans to involve his new Society in the restoration of English Catholicism were never accepted by either Reginald Pole or King Philip. Juan de Polanco, the Society's first chronicler, sadly noted that the Society had no chance to work in England, even though the kingdom needed good workers and the Jesuits were on good terms with Cardinal Pole. The Cardinal often asked the Society for prayers but nothing else.[106] All ventures were either rejected or ignored because Cardinal Pole did not want the Jesuits in his realm.

In his memoirs Robert Parsons discussed the religious history of England prior to his arrival with Edmund Campion in 1580. Aware of the friendship between Pole and the Society, Parsons asserted that this friendship made "some mervaile why he had not called in some fathers of ye Soc^y in those days to help to sett forward Cath: Religion."[107] According to Parsons there were two reasons. There was "little leisure to think upon men from abroad" because the Cardinal's arrival in England was delayed by the marital negotiations, and once he arrived the major concern was the establishment of Roman Catholicism and the settlement of the succession. The second reason was the conviction that older religious orders should be reestablished because they "had more right to be respected then [sic] Jesuits that were strangers."[108] Parsons's explanation touches the core of the problem. The exclusion of the Society from England resulted from more concrete causes: the programme for reform, the absence of appropriate Jesuits, and the Society's Institute.[109]

The novelty of the Society of Jesus provided no place in Pole's reform. His primary concern was the restoration of Catholic discipline and worship. John Guy has noted that both Mary and Pole "saw the future in terms of the past."[110] They wanted restoration of normality.[111] Within this framework

---

[105] 6 January 1559, 20 January 1559, 1 April 1559, *Epp. Ribadeneira*, I, 308-10, 310-14, 320-23; Joannes Marie Prat, *Histoire du Pére Ribadeneyra* (Paris, 1862) p. 143. Ribadeneira was ill for much of his stay and was not fully recovered until the middle of January. Laínez now hoped that he would be able to do something in England even though it was "a sterile vineyard." The Jesuits in Rome were praying that England would not again separate from the Catholic Church (Laínez to Ribadeneira, Rome 4 March 1559, ARSI, Epp. N.N. 51, ff. 252^v-253^r [printed in *Epp. Ribadeneira*, I, 318-20]).
[106] *Pol. Chron.*, V, 316.
[107] "The First Entrance of the Fathers of the Society into England," ed. John Hungerford Pollen, S.J., in *Miscellanea II* (London, 1906) p. 189.
[108] Parsons, "Entrance of the First Jesuits," p. 189.
[109] For a more detailed historiographical discussion of proposed explanations see McCoog, "Loyola and Pole." For a different interpretation see Mayer, "A Test of Wills."
[110] *Tudor England* (Oxford, 1988) p. 227.

there was no place for a new religious order that had not been part of the religious tradition disrupted by Henry VIII and now so conscientiously restored by his daughter. Moreover, what the new religious order offered was not what Pole wanted or needed. Despite his earlier encouragement of the new orders noted for preaching, the Cardinal was no longer enthusiastic about its role in the restoration of Catholicism. Strong leaders and not preachers were required. And these the Society could not provide because its *Constitutions* forbade the acceptance of curacies and episcopacies.[112] At least in England Pole preferred visual ceremonies to theological discourse for the reestablishment of Catholicism. Here too the Society could offer little because its *Constitutions* restricted elaborate liturgical ceremonies and its "way of proceeding" freed Jesuits from the monastic pattern of choral office.[113]

In a letter to Pole in January of 1555 Loyola told of an Englishman and an Irishman who could assist in the restoration of English Catholicism. He mentioned neither name but he praised both men. The first was a Thomas Anglus who entered the German College in 1554. He was probably the Thomas Natale who then entered the Society in 1556.[114] The Irishman was David Wolfe, who entered the Society in Rome in 1554.[115] Neither man, so praised by Loyola, died within the Society. But they were the only non-foreigners Ignatius could offer. Spanish Jesuits were abundant, but there was already enough Spanish involvement in England. As the seeds of the "Black Legend" germinated, Pole was eager to avoid an identification of Spain and Roman Catholicism. As Laínez commented in 1558, the doors would remain closed until the Society had sufficient strength and numbers.

---

[111] Ronald Hutton has noted that "the reign of Mary Tudor was beyond any doubt a period in which the seasonal activities of early Tudor England reappeared upon a grand scale" (*The Rise and Fall of Merry England: The Ritual Year 1400-1700* [Oxford, 1994] p. 101). Could their restoration be but another sign of the same mentality?

[112] *Cons.* nos. 588, 817. On the question of bishoprics see Padberg, "Ignatius, the Popes," 20-28.

[113] Antonio de Córdoba, the Duke of Feria's Jesuit brother, relayed to Laínez reports that he received from Fernando Álvarez de Toledo, Count of Oropesa and later Duke of Alba, who claimed to have received the news from Pedro de Soto. According to de Soto, Pole's refusal to admit the Jesuits stemmed from two causes: they did not have choir and they were forbidden to accept bishoprics (Montilla 3 March 1558, *Epp. Laínez*, III, 172).

[114] Schmidt, *Collegium Germanicum*, p. 219; *Mon. Ang.*, II, 415.

[115] We do not know the precise date of his admission, but he pronounced simple vows in Rome on 22 February 1554 (ARSI, Ital. 58, f. 294ʳ).

* * * * *

The mission to Ireland pre-dated papal approval of the Society of Jesus. In the original instructions from Pope Paul III in March of 1540, Jean Codure and Alfonso Salmerón were identified not as members of the Society of Jesus but as priests of their dioceses. By the time they embarked, the Society had been recognized. But after the initial contact with Ireland, the Society showed no interest in later efforts by its friend Robert Wauchope to engage a few Jesuits to assist him in his return. Aside from a passing reference to sending Bobadilla to England in Reginald Pole's entourage during the rebellion of 1549, there was a similar disinterest in England. After the return of Salmerón and Broët, there was no mention of Scotland. A few years later Loyola realized the religious importance of England. This realization may have been based solely on the fact that there were new opportunities now that a Catholic monarch had ascended the throne. On the other hand, his interest in England and his persistent attempts to have his men involved there are, I think, evidence of a development within the Society.

Recent Jesuit historiography, most notably the works of John W. O'Malley, S.J., has stressed the anachronistic depiction of Loyola's founding the Society of Jesus as a Counter-Reformation order.[116] Basing their argument on an analysis of the Society's foundational documents, writers contend that the Society's origins must be seen in the context of a movement for Catholic reform that predates Protestantism, and not as an order established to combat Protestantism. Yet Protestantism did have an effect of the early Society. In 1550 "for the defense and propagation of the faith" was added to the Society's "Formula of the Institute" when changes within the order were approved by Pope Julius III in the bull *Exposcit debitum* of 21 July.[117] As the Society became more involved in the reinforcement of Catholicism

---

[116] *The First Jesuits, passim.* His views are briefly summarized in his "The Society of Jesus," in Richard L. DeMolen, ed., *Religious Orders of the Catholic Reformation: In Honor of John C. Olin on His Seventy-Fifth Birthday* (New York, 1994) pp. 152-54.

[117] Compare *Regimini militantis Ecclesiae* (1540) with *Exposcit debitum* (1550). The major differences are in italics. The first states: "Whoever desires to serve as a soldier of God beneath the banner of the Cross in our Society, which we desire to be designated by the name of Jesus, and to serve the Lord alone and the Roman Pontiff, His vicar on earth, should, after a solemn vow of perpetual chastity, keep what follows in mind. He is a member of a Society founded chiefly for this purpose: to strive especially for the progress of souls in Christian life and doctrine and for the propagation of the faith. . . ." The second reads; "Whoever desires to serve as a soldier of God beneath the banner of the Cross in our Society, which we desire to be designated by the name of Jesus, and to serve the Lord alone *and the Church, His spouse, under* the Roman Pontiff, the vicar of Christ on earth, should, after a solemn vow of perpetual chastity, *poverty, and obedience,* keep what follows in mind. He is a member of a Society founded chiefly for this purpose: to strive especially *for the defense and propagation of the faith* for the progress of souls in Christian life and doctrine. . . ."

in the Holy Roman Empire, Jesuit alarm at the success of Protestantism confirmed this development. The foundation of the German College in Rome in 1552 and the establishment of a chair of controversial theology at the Roman College a year or two later are evidence of intensified involvement.

In 1555 Jerónimo Nadal was sent as official Visitor[118] to the Society's houses in the Empire. From Vienna he wrote to Ignatius on 8 May 1555:

> The truth is this: ever since I arrived in Germany, I have been charged with a dream so aglow and a hope so fervid in the Society's ability to succor these peoples that the thought of staying here gives a lift to my spirit. No question, this conviction grips me: in no part of the world is the Society, supported of course by God's grace, more needed; in no part of the world would the Society be more helpful. It is more than a matter of opposing, with God's grace, the heretics. There is the very grave danger that if the remnant of Catholics here are not helped, in two years there will be not one in Germany. Everybody says this, even the Catholic leaders. What stirs me most is the awareness that practically everyone has lost hope that Germany can be salvaged. . . . I think that the task of helping Germany in its religious life is reserved to the Society.[119]

Nadal not only exhorted the Society to become more actively involved in the salvation of Germany; he reinterpreted the Society's origins as a providential response to the Protestant threat. Henceforth a favourite Nadalian image was that of the Society as a large bird whose two wings were Germany and the Indies, the two parts of the world whose spiritual needs were the most severe.[120]

England presented another opportunity for the Society to work for the restoration of Catholicism and the destruction of heresy. In the Empire, with the financial support of the nobles and the ecclesiastical hierarchy, the Society was perfecting a missionary strategy that focused on colleges that served not just as educational institutions but as spiritual centres for the evangelization and re-Catholicization of the area.[121] Loyola hoped to do

---

[118] With specific powers delegated by the General, a Visitor travelled from house to house within a given province or region, examining all aspects of communal and individual religious life. Because he was the General's Vicar, his powers exceeded those of the provincial. Because he was a Vicar, his authority ceased with the death of the General.

[119] Quoted in Bangert, *Nadal*, p. 147.

[120] On Nadal and the Counter-Reformation see Jos E. Vercruysse, S.J., "Nadal et la Contre-Réforme," *Gregorianum* 72 (1991) 289-315.

[121] According Louis Châtellier, Jesuit colleges were "very active centres of apostleship, from which preachers, catechists and missionaries left in a steady stream for the various parts of the town and for the neighbouring countryside" (*The Europe of the Devout: The Catholic Reformation and the Formation of a New Society* [Cambridge, 1989] p. 1). For examples see Bangert, *Nadal*, pp. 62-63; A. Lynn Martin, *The Jesuit Mind: The Mentality of an Elite in Early Modern France* (Ithaca, N.Y., 1988) pp. 68-69; David Gentilcore, *From Bishop to Witch: The System of the Sacred in Early Modern Terra d'Otranto* (Manchester, 1992) p. 71.

something similar in England. He assumed that he had the support of the hierarchy (Pole) and the nobility (Philip). He talked of colleges; he formulated his plans. But he was foiled. Laínez clearly—and Loyola presumably—believed that it was God's will that the Society work in England. The setback therefore was temporary. Once the Society had sufficient resources, no one would be able to prevent the doors now closed from being opened.

CHAPTER TWO

"THE HOUR OF SATAN"

When Elizabeth ascended the English throne in 1558, in the words of Nicholas Sander, "the hour of Satan" had come "and the power of darkness took possession of the whole of England."[1] During her first year, the major issue was the religious settlement. The Protestants generally and rightly believed that Elizabeth, as the daughter of Anne Boleyn, would dismantle the Roman Church as reestablished by her step-sister and would introduce a truly reformed one. The role of Parliament in the establishment of the distinctive Elizabethan settlement has long been a focus of historical research.

The traditional interpretation, as expounded by J.E. Neale,[2] argued that a personally conservative Elizabeth was obliged to enact more radical reforms by a Puritan House of Commons. More recently Norman Jones has shown that resistance to the Elizabethan settlement came not from a radical House of Commons but from a conservative House of Lords that deleted or amended the legislation.[3] This resistance was broken by the imprisonment of recalcitrant bishops after a craftily staged disputation at Westminster in March 1559,[4] a few royal concessions on the *Book of Common Prayer*, and the sheer accidents of death and illness. The Act of Supremacy (1 Eliz. c. 1) left Elizabeth as the "Supreme Governor" and not the head of the Church. Such an alteration may have consoled the theologically sensitive,

---

[1] *Rise and Growth of the Anglican Schism*, trans. and ed. David Lewis (London, 1877) p. 233. Also see his 1561 report to Cardinal Morone on the change of religion in England. The report was edited by John H. Pollen, S.J., in *Miscellanea I* (London, 1905) pp. 1-47.

[2] *Elizabeth I and Her Parliaments*, 2 vols. (London, 1953, 1957).

[3] *Faith by Statute: Parliament and the Settlement of Religion, 1559* (London, 1982). For a short historiographical exposition on the topic see Michael A.R. Graves, *The Tudor Parliaments: Crown, Lords and Commons, 1485-1603* (London, 1985) pp. 115-30.

[4] During the parliamentary recess over Easter 1559, the Westminster disputation between eight or nine representatives from the Protestant and the Roman Catholic camps "was staged as a public show to win support for the program of religious change by putting the Marian bishops on the defensive, discrediting their arguments, and thus eroding their support and possibly silencing them" (Winthrop S. Hudson, *The Cambridge Connection and the Elizabethan Settlement of 1559* [Durham, N.C., 1980] p. 122). This is but one example of the government's use of public debate to discredit its religious opponents. For discussions of the disputes see Henry Norbert Birt, O.S.B., *The Elizabethan Religious Settlement* (London, 1907) pp. 98-119; and Jones, *Faith By Statute*, pp. 123-27.

but it had little effect on the jurisdiction claimed by the Queen. The Act of Uniformity (1 Eliz. c. 2) imposed the second Edwardian *Prayer Book* with some revisions: the rite had been altered to allow a Catholic understanding of the Eucharist; abuse of the pope was removed; and ecclesiastical vestments and ornaments were to remain those from the reign of Henry VIII.[5]

Many Protestants saw this as just the first step towards an authentic reformation and they agitated for greater changes throughout Elizabeth's reign. Aware, however, that the apparent successor to the English throne was the Catholic Mary Stuart, Protestants realized that the survival of a reformed Church required a Protestant heir. Because Elizabeth frequently tempered the Protestantism of her bishops by injunctions that tended in a Catholic direction, conservatives hoped that marriage with a Catholic would result in the restoration of Catholicism.[6] For both groups marriage was essential, but a request from the Commons in February of 1559 that the Queen marry received a polite but evasive reply from Elizabeth.[7]

The promulgation of new legislation that created the Elizabethan settlement was much simpler than the conversion of the populace to that settlement. The Benedictine Henry Norbert Birt put it well: "The parliamentary power that put them in possession of a great public trust could not transfer the allegiance of their nominal spiritual subjects from their predecessors to themselves as land passes from hand to hand by a stroke of the pen."[8] Recent historical studies have stressed the overwhelming devotion of the populace to the old religion.[9] For reasons of conviction and for

---

[5] For important speeches from both houses see T.E. Hartley, ed., *Proceedings in the Parliaments of Elizabeth I* (Leicester, 1981) I, 1-51.

[6] For some of these alterations see Christopher Haigh, *Elizabeth I* (London, 1988) pp. 31-33. On the enforcement of early anti-Catholic legislation see Leslie Ward, "The Treason Act of 1563: A Study of the Enforcement of Anti-Catholic Legislation," *Parliamentary History* 8 (1989) 289-308.

[7] Her reply is printed in Hartley, *Proceedings*, I, 44-45.

[8] *Elizabethan Religious Settlement*, p. 297.

[9] The clearest statement of this emphasis comes from J.J. Scarisbrick: "I am not saying that all was well. I am not claiming that pre-Reformation England was a land of zealous, God-fearing Christians (although I suspect that there were many more of them than some recent historians would admit). I *am* saying that, however imperfect the old order, and however imperfect the Christianity of the average man or woman in the street, there is no evidence of loss of confidence in the old ways, no mass disenchantment" (*The Reformation and the English People* [Oxford, 1984] p. 12). Christopher Haigh has been advocating the same conclusion since the publication of his doctoral thesis *Reformation and Resistance in Tudor Lancashire* (Cambridge, 1975) and more recently in articles such as "The Continuity of Catholicism in the English Reformation," in Christopher Haigh, ed., *The English Reformation Revised* (Cambridge, 1987) pp. 176-208 and *English Reformations: Religion, Politics, and Society under the Tudors* (Oxford, 1993). Recent studies by R.N. Swanson, *Church and Society in Late Medieval England* (Oxford, 1989), and Eamon Duffy, *The Stripping of the Altars: Traditional Religion in England c. 1400-c. 1580* (New Haven, 1992) have argued similarly. For local studies that tend to the

reasons of custom, they preferred traditional Catholicism. The reformers often complained of the obstinacy of the people. "Oh! if we were not wanting in our exertions," wrote John Jewel, the Elizabethan Bishop of Salisbury, "there might yet be good hopes of religion. But it is no easy matter to drag the chariot without horses, especially uphill."[10]

So few supported the settlement that Catholic critics, such as the future Jesuit John Rastall,[11] claimed that practically anyone, "cobblers, weavers, tinkers, tanners, cardmakers, tapsters, fiddlers, gaolers," could climb into the pulpit because of the dearth of clergy.[12] Again, according to Jewel, the universities were in ruin because there were so few there who believed in the reformed religion. He confessed to Peter Martyr that ignorance and obstinacy had increased at Oxford since Martyr's departure and that "religion, and all hope of good learning and talent is altogether abandoned."[13]

Winning the people required the full thrust of the Tudor government. The implications of the Acts of Supremacy and Uniformity were many. Recognition of any foreign religious authority, a recognition that would deny the Queen's claim to spiritual jurisdiction, could be punished by the loss of office, property, and, for the third offence, life. Alternatives to the established worship were forbidden, and clerics who attempted to use other services could be deprived of their office and imprisoned. Anyone who treated the new service with scorn or disdain could be fined 100 marks or given life imprisonment for the third offence. Absentees from church had to pay a fine of a shilling per Sunday. Episcopal visitations ensured that the new *Prayer Book* was followed with no popish overtones. Sermons instilled

---

Scarisbrick/Haigh interpretation see Robert Whiting, *The Blind Devotion of the People: Popular Religion and the English Reformation* (Cambridge, 1989). Leo Hicks's earlier analysis of the Catholic exiles' rejection of the Elizabethan settlement primarily because it was a "state-made religion" makes similar claims ("The Catholic Exiles and the Elizabethan Religious Settlement," *CHR* 22 [1936] 129-48). Opposed to this view, A.G. Dickens stresses the importance of Lollardy, the impact of Lutheran and Calvinist theologies during the reign of Edward VI, and the effect of anti-clericalism on popular religious sentiments. England was more Protestant at the accession of Elizabeth than Haigh and Scarisbrick believe: "Few religious revolutions have been more dramatic and momentous than that of 1558-9, yet none has encountered more feeble opposition" (*The English Reformation*, 2nd edition [London, 1989] p. 349). A short exposition of Dickens's views can be found in "The Reformation in England," in A.G. Dickens, *Reformation Studies* (London, 1982) pp. 443-56. On the discussion whether the English Reformation was an official one imposed on a reluctant people or whether the people had been eager for it because of important Protestant ideas and domestic Lollardy see Rosemary O'Day, *The Debate on the English Reformation* (London, 1986) especially chapters 5 and 6, pp. 102-65. Diarmaid MacCulloch's article "The Myth of the English Reformation," *Journal of British Studies* 30 (1991) 1-19 sets this current debate in a wider context.

[10] Quoted in Birt, *Elizabethan Religious Settlement*, p. 178.
[11] See *Mon. Ang.*, II, 450-51.
[12] Quoted in Birt, *Elizabethan Religious Settlement*, p. 440.
[13] Quoted in Birt, *Elizabethan Religious Settlement*, pp. 506-07.

the new theology, emphasized the virtue of obedience to rightful authority—obedience manifested by attending church—and abominated the vice of rebellion. Obliged to attend and listen to lengthy sermons, the laity would be won through a combination of attrition and indoctrination.[14]

A concerted effort to captivate the minds of Englishmen began on 26 November 1559 when John Jewel challenged Roman Catholics to prove specific doctrines on the authority of scripture, the fathers of the Church, and the early Church councils. Jewel sought to provide the historical, canonical, and theological foundations for the settlement and to confirm his Church's intellectual credentials. He would demonstrate that the religion as currently established was not a recent innovation but the traditional religion of England purified of all popish emendations. If any Catholic could prove that specific doctrines that the established Church had eliminated were actually maintained by the early Church, Jewel promised that he would forsake the established Church and become a Roman Catholic.[15]

The challenge was immediately taken up by Thomas Harding, a Catholic refugee in Louvain, with a prolonged and bitter "battle of the books" as the result, the first between the Catholics and the established Church.[16] Later Edmund Campion and Robert Parsons would again raise this challenge, but by then debates had been forbidden: "the queen's majesty being most desirous of all other earthly things, that her people should live in charity towards God and man, and therein abound in good works, wills and straitly commands all manner her subjects to forbear all vain and contentious disputations in matters of religion."[17]

The theological debates between scholars in Louvain and those in England, and the persuasive powers of the Elizabethan clergy would probably not have effected a true reformation among the people without the

---

[14] Elizabeth apparently believed that adherence to the traditional religion would die out eventually, and this conviction dominated her policy towards the recusants in the first fifteen years of her reign. See John LaRocca, S.J., "Time, Death and the Next Generation: The Early Elizabethan Recusancy Policy," *Albion* 14 (1982) 103-17.

[15] See John E. Booty, *John Jewel as Apologist of the Church of England* (London, 1963) pp. 27-35.

[16] See Peter Milward, *Religious Controversies of the Elizabethan Age* (London, 1977) pp. 1-6 for an index of books published during this controversy.

[17] The Royal Injunctions of 1559, in Henry Gee, *The Elizabethan Clergy and the Settlement of Religion* (Oxford, 1898) p. 60. Ten years later, on 1 March 1569, a royal proclamation forbade imported books "containing sundry matters repugnant to truth, derogatory to the sovereign estate of her majesty, and stirring and nourishing sedition in this realm," whose authors intended "to draw them [her majesty's subjects] to error and to withdraw them seditiously from their duties and allegiance due to her majesty as their only sovereign" (Paul L. Hughes and James F. Larkin, C.S.V., eds., *Tudor Royal Proclamations*, 3 vols. [New Haven, 1964-69] II, 312). Similar proclamations were issued 1 July 1570, 14 November 1570, 28 September 1573, 26 March 1576, and 12 October 1584 (*Tudor Royal Proclamations*, II, 341-43, 347-48, 376-79, 400-01, 506-08).

assistance of the English parliamentary and legal system. Then progress was still slow because, even if Elizabeth wanted it, strict enforcement would be difficult. The Queen herself hesitated to enforce the laws because she did not wish to drive her Catholic subjects to despair, a despair that could result in rebellion. Enforcement was difficult because local bonds of kinship proved stronger than those that tied justices of the peace to a distant Queen.

The new legislation did not drive Catholicism out of the parish churches. The investigations of Haigh and Scarisbrick abound with references to ministers and parishes that sought to maintain as many Catholic practices as possible. Despite the law, services were adapted to reflect the familiar Mass. Ministers were known to celebrate both the Roman Catholic Mass and the reformed service on the same day. Many who opposed the changes attended services in obedience to their monarch but spent the time in private prayer or casual conversation. There was no need for recusancy because of the continuation of so many traditional practices.[18] The English had lived through so many religious changes that few believed that this was permanent. Consequently the liturgical furnishings and devotional ornaments of Roman Catholicism were hidden away for eventual restoration.[19]

The Queen's close brush with death from smallpox in October of 1562 demonstrated how vulnerable the settlement still was. When Parliament met again the following January, the question of the succession to the crown was more urgently discussed. This time speeches on the importance of a royal marriage and on the urgency of the succession question,[20] and petitions from the Commons, prompted the Queen to promise that she would marry. The same Parliament passed a bill (5 Eliz. c. 1) that sought to ensure the religious conformity of the justices of the peace, to reduce their role in the

---

[18] The question of occasional conformity was one that would haunt the English Catholic community for years. During the early years of Elizabeth's reign, there was no official ruling. As we shall see, recusancy *per se*, that is the refusal to attend the parish church, began only after the condemnation of occasional conformity by the Pope and the more vigorous enforcement of the religious legislation, an enforcement that eliminated Catholic practices. Thereafter many Catholic theologians attacked occasional conformity as vigorously as the Protestants repudiated "Nicodemism." On occasional conformity see Alexandra Walsham, *Church Papists: Catholicism, Conformity, and Confessional Polemic in Early Modern England* (London, 1993).

[19] Susan Doran and Christopher Durston argue that the continuation of these "residual" Catholic practices resulted from the "failure of Elizabeth's government to purge the ranks of the lower clergy of these residual Catholic elements . . . [because] in 1558 there was an insufficient number of Protestant ministers to put in their place. The early years of Elizabeth's reign experienced an acute shortage of clerical manpower; this had been partly caused by the influenza epidemic of 1556, but also a legacy of the long-term slump in ordinations which had begun with the religious upheavals of the 1530s." (*Princes, Pastors and People: The Church and Religion in England 1529-1689* [London, 1991] p. 147). See also pp. 144-61.

[20] On various tracts proposing different candidates at this time see Geoffrey de C. Parmiter, "Edmund Plowden as Advocate for Mary Queen of Scots: Some Remarks upon Certain Elizabethan Succession Tracts," *IR* 30 (1970) 35-53.

enforcement of the religious laws, and to make conformity more attractive to Catholic heirs. John LaRocca, S.J., concludes from this new law "that the first five years of the reign had shown the Queen and Council that it could not trust local officials to enforce conformity."[21] With this law the crown may have found more reliable officials, but enforcement nonetheless was still variable and inconsistent.[22]

The religious changes were cautiously observed by the continental powers. Spain, England's ally in a war against France and the papacy, feared papal condemnation of the illegitimate daughter of Henry VIII and her possible replacement by the Franco-Scottish Mary Stuart, currently married to the French dauphin.[23] Even after King Philip's own proposal to move from brother-in-law to husband was rejected and the suits of his Austrian cousins discarded,[24] the Spanish King continued to shield Elizabeth from the Pope, out of a desire to maintain the Anglo-Spanish alliance. Philip was worried that the accession of a pro-French Queen would jeopardize Spain's control over the Netherlands. Therefore he was eager to do all he could to protect Elizabeth from papal wrath. The death of the Hispanophobe Pope Paul IV on 18 August 1559 and his replacement by the more moderate Pius IV on 25 December aided the Spanish King.[25]

---

[21] "English Catholics and the Recusancy Laws 1558-1625: A Study in Religion and Politics," (unpublished Ph.D. thesis: Rutgers University, 1977) 23.

[22] For an account of the session see Neale, *Elizabeth I and Her Parliaments*, I, 85-128; Hartley, *Proceedings*, I, 53-115. For a discussion of various attempts to arrange a marriage for Elizabeth in the 1560s see Norman Jones, *The Birth of the Elizabethan Age: England in the 1560s* (Oxford, 1993) pp. 119-55 and Susan Doran, *Monarchy and Matrimony: The Courtships of Elizabeth I* (London, 1996) pp. 13-98.

[23] Pedro de Ribadeneira witnessed the religious developments. Writing from London on 20 January 1559, he informed Diego Laínez that Elizabeth "has not made any great change, but that she had made a start from which one augurs nothing less than a disastrous end." Nonetheless Ribadeneira advised that Rome do nothing. A hasty move by the Pope would destroy the little hope that remained (*Epp. Ribadeneira*, I, 310-14). Initial reports about Elizabeth were wrong. On 21 January 1559, Diego Laínez informed Nicolás Bobadilla that he had heard that Elizabeth would not alter anything regarding religion (ARSI, Ital. 61, f. 382^r).

[24] See Susan Doran, "Religion and Politics at the Court of Elizabeth I: the Habsburg marriage negotiations of 1559-1567," *EHR* 104 (1989) 908-26, and *Monarchy and Matrimony*, pp. 21-39; and Carole Levin, *The Heart and Stomach of a King: Elizabeth I and the Politics of Sex and Power* (Philadelphia, 1994) pp. 39-54. By March, the Jesuit Peter Canisius was writing about the possibility of a marriage between one of the Emperor's sons and Elizabeth. The first reaction of the General was to ask Canisius to do what he could to make sure that a Jesuit was included in any embassy to England to discuss the matter (Canisius to Laínez, Augsburg 28 March 1559, in Otto Braunsberger, ed., *Beati Petri Canisii, Societatis Iesu, Epistulae et Acta*, 8 vols. [Friburg, 1896-1923] II, 381; Juan de Polanco to Canisius, Rome 15 April 1559, *ibid.*, II, 388).

[25] According to J.N.D. Kelly, as opposed to Paul IV, Pius IV was "affable and convivial, with a private life which intrigued gossips; but he was also politically astute. He at once reversed Paul's repressive measures. . . " (*The Oxford Dictionary of Popes* [Oxford, 1986] p. 266 col. 2).

The French King Henry II, naturally, advanced the claims of his daughter-in-law in an attempt to destroy the Anglo-Spanish coalition. Because the Catholic Church had not recognized the marriage of Henry VIII and Anne Boleyn, Elizabeth was considered illegitimate according to both canon and civil law. Since Elizabeth could not succeed to the English throne, Henry encouraged his daughter-in-law to emblazon the arms of England on her shield as soon as Mary Tudor died. Henry's sudden death on 10 July 1559, during the celebrations that surrounded the Treaty of Câteau-Cambrésis (2 April 1559) ending the war, brought Mary to the French throne as the Queen Consort of Francis II and brought her ambitious uncles, Charles Guise, Cardinal of Lorraine, and Francis, Duke of Guise, into power.

Even after the treaty, the international situation remained tense because many Protestants feared that Spain and France, either jointly or independently, would redirect their combined military power on the reformed Churches. Of the reformed Churches the most vulnerable was in Scotland.

On 3 December 1557 supporters of the Scottish reformer John Knox, then in Geneva, met and bound themselves to do everything they could to maintain the Protestant cause, to support ministers who agreed with them, and to renounce and destroy all things associated with popery. Despite initial attempts at compromise by Catholic leaders, the power and influence of the Lords of the Congregation increased. At the insistence of her Guise brothers, the Regent Mary of Guise resorted to force in the spring of 1559. Shortly thereafter, on 2 May 1559, John Knox arrived back in Scotland.[26] On the 10th an assembly of followers of the Lords met at Perth. Inflamed by the fiery rhetoric of Knox, the crowd lashed out in iconoclastic furore. To prevent further outbursts and to control the Protestants, a body of French troops was dispatched to Scotland that summer. Because of Mary's Guise connections, it was understood that this was an attempt by the Guise faction to strengthen French influence in Scotland as a prelude to gaining the English throne for Mary. Not only did the French troops met stiff Protestant resistance, but their very presence increased tension between England and Scotland by aggravating the consistent English fear of a French invasion from the north. Hence Elizabeth first clandestinely and then openly assisted the Lords of the Congregation, by sending an English army north and besieging Leith in March of 1560.

---

[26] Knox had been invited to return to Scotland in the autumn of 1557, but after he arrived at Dieppe the invitation was withdrawn. During the two months that he remained in Dieppe, he began his most famous work, *The first blast of the trumpet against the monstruous regiment of women* ([Geneva], 1558) STC 15070. This was directed against the reigns of Mary Tudor and Mary of Guise, and the two countries that had accepted them. On this work see Robert M. Healey, "Waiting for Deborah: John Knox and Four Ruling Queens," *SCJ* 25 (1994) 371-86.

The Queen Regent died on 10 June. As a result of direct English intervention the Treaty of Edinburgh was signed on 6 July 1560. It demanded evacuation of all foreign troops from Scotland, the establishment of the Protestant Lords as the provisional government, and a convening of the Estates on 1 August. The Reformation Parliament duly met. The Lords drafted their "Confession of Faith professed and believed by the Protestants within the Realm of Scotland" and presented to the Parliament. On 17 August it was approved. On the 24th further acts abolished the jurisdiction of the pope, repealed all laws that favoured the Catholic faith, and decreed that henceforth all who either said or attended Mass should be punished for the first offence by the confiscation of all goods, for the second by banishment, and for the third by death.[27] From France Mary denounced the parliamentary acts and refused to ratify them. Without a French army, however, protests and threats from a distant monarch were of little avail.[28]

Barely had Pius IV been crowned when he began to work for the reconvention of the Council of Trent, suspended in 1552. In the hope of obtaining English, Scottish, and Irish participation, the Pope wanted to send nuncios to the three kingdoms; the men chosen for Scotland and Ireland were Jesuits. The man chosen to reestablish relations with England was Vincenzo Parpaglia, Abbot of S. Solutor, Turin, a former secretary of Cardinal Pole and widely reputed to be a friend of France, especially of the Guise family, who were, at the time, sending troops into Scotland. C.G. Bayne summed up the Abbot's career with the statement that "he was a friend, perhaps a spy, of France, odious to Elizabeth, and an object of suspicion to Philip."[29] He was obviously not an ideal choice for the mission. Parpaglia left Rome on 25 May 1560 and, after visiting the French court, he travelled to Flanders, where he awaited permission from the English government to cross the channel. It was hoped that the Spanish ambassador in England, Alvaro de la Quadra, Bishop of Aquila,[30] would obtain this for him. The Spanish government, however, was in no way eager to assist a man whose mission would most probably profit the French. Spain feared a papal ultimatum that Elizabeth's refusal to restore Catholicism would result in her deposition and a French invasion. Thus the abbot's journey ended in Flanders.[31]

---

[27] Alphons Bellesheim, *History of the Catholic Church of Scotland*, 4 vols. (Edinburgh/London, 1887-90) II, 187-310.

[28] On events leading to the Parliament and on the Parliament itself, and the development of the Kirk see Jenny Wormald, *Court, Kirk and Community: Scotland 1470-1625* (Edinburgh, 1981) pp. 108-39.

[29] C.G. Bayne, *Anglo-Roman Relations 1558-1565* (Oxford, 1913) p. 47.

[30] On 11 October 1562 Pius IV granted de la Quadra the power to absolve heretics after abjuration and proper penance (CSP Rome [1558-71], 106).

[31] Bayne, *Anglo-Roman Relations*, pp. 40-72.

There was a second attempt to establish contact with England when Abbot Martinengo was sent from Rome on 14 March 1561. Elizabeth and her Council had debated sending representatives to Trent after its reconvention was announced in 1560. More important, however, in the decision regarding the reception of the papal envoy was the relation between the Queen and Robert, Lord Dudley. Conveniently widowed on 8 September 1560, Dudley applied to Spain for assistance with his hope to marry the Queen. Reconciliation with Rome was the price that Dudley would pay for Philip II's support.[32] Hopes that Martinengo would be admitted were shattered, however, when William Cecil discovered the first of many plots to overthrow the Protestant establishment and restore Catholicism. The fears raised by Cecil's discoveries were made more acute by the missionary activities of the Jesuit David Wolfe in Ireland and the outbreak of Shane O'Neill's rebellion in early 1561 (we shall return to this shortly). The envoy was not admitted, and Pius abandoned any hope of direct communication with Elizabeth but not of restoration of Catholicism in England.[33]

The rejection of two—albeit not ideal—envoys reduced the papal options in dealing with England. The death of Francis II in December of 1560 and the ascendancy of Catherine de Medici as the Regent for her son Charles IX removed the Guises from power and left Mary with little influence and no alternative but to return to Scotland. There she still refused to ratify the Treaty of Edinburgh and continued to bear the English arms on her shield. Throughout this interlude Philip supported his English sister-in-law. Politically he preferred a heretical ally to an orthodox enemy on the throne of England and accordingly resisted any attempt to unseat Elizabeth. After

---

[32] Kenneth Bartlett has recently reexamined these clandestine negotiations ("Papal Policy and the English Crown, 1563-1565: The Bertano Correspondence," *SCJ* 23 [1992] 643-59) and concluded that they "provide further support for the assessment of Dudley as a cynical, ambitious opportunist" but Elizabeth emerged "as the most subtle player in the intrigue, using her religious convictions much as she used her marriageability to increase her flexibility and multiply her options in both foreign and domestic policy" (658-59). See also Jones, *Birth of the Elizabethan Age*, pp. 35-47 and Doran, *Monarchy and Matrimony*, pp. 40-72.

[33] Did the collapse of negotiations lead Rome to consider seriously other possibilities? Bayne published in his work (*Anglo-Roman Relations*, p. 274) "Proposals for depriving Elizabeth and transferring the English crown to Mary Queen of Scots" from late 1561. According to the anonymous author, Catholicism could be restored in England if Elizabeth were deposed. To do this, he suggested that all English and Irish be absolved of obedience to Elizabeth and that this absolution be published in England, Ireland, and Scotland; that the Queen of Scotland's claim to the English throne be published as soon as possible and confirmed by the Pope; and that the most influential English exiles be sent to Scotland to pledge their allegiance. It was believed that many of the nobles in northern England would then cross into Scotland to offer their assistance. Everything, the author concluded, depended on the Holy See: "It has been sufficiently demonstrated that silence and toleration under the Sovereign Pontiff Paul III have been of no profit; further, the daughter is far more wicked than her father. Good fruit is not to be looked for from a tree so bad."

Mary lost the support of her brother-in-law Charles IX, whose Regent Catherine de Medici was now seeking a Huguenot counterweight to the power of the Guises,[34] and with the construction of an Anglo-Franco-Scottish alliance no longer likely, Philip's support of Elizabeth diminished. Thus the death of Francis II and Mary's return to Scotland strongly affected the international balance by destroying the common interest that held England and Spain together.

England's support of the Protestant Scottish Lords had resulted in a settlement very favourable to English interests. Now the English feared the effect that the arrival of the Scottish Queen might have on the arrangement. The death of Mary's husband not only removed a major objection to her succession to the English throne but also established her as the most eligible widow in Christendom, one whose hand could be used to further the interests of the Habsburgs. It is no wonder that Elizabeth indulged in secret intrigues with the papacy designed to prevent a coalition of Catholic powers centring on Mary Queen of Scots.

II

During the early years of Elizabeth's reign, Ireland remained extremely volatile. The most powerful man in Ulster, Conn Bacach O'Neill, created Earl of Tyrone in 1542 when, as we have seen, he was obliged to abandon the name of O'Neill in favour of the English title, was often suspected of treasonous dealings with the Scots and the French. His death in July of 1559 removed one problem for Elizabeth but created another: a disputed succession. Conn O'Neill had nominated as his successor not Shane O'Neill, who was the more powerful and who claimed to be the oldest legitimate son, but the illegitimate Matthew. The issue was complicated even more when Matthew died in 1558, a year before his father. Brian, Matthew's son, was therefore claiming the title. Shane O'Neill continued to resist the pretensions of such claimants and in so doing he, like his father, found willing allies in the Scots and the French. As long as Elizabeth refused to acknowledge Shane's claim to the earldom, she risked pushing him totally into an alliance

---

[34] According to R.J. Knecht, Catherine's preoccupation was "to preserve the independence of the throne, and in order to achieve this she strove to maintain a fine, if uneasy balance between the two families, favouring each in turn. Because the Guises had dominated the realm in the recent past and still had a majority on the council, she turned first to the Bourbons to establish equilibrium" (*The French Wars of Religion 1559-1598* [London, 1989], p. 29). Catherine's preference for the Bourbons resulted in her taking the King to a Huguenot service. This behaviour so antagonized many of the nobles that on Easter Sunday (6 April) 1561, Anne de Montmorency, Constable of France, Francis, Duke of Guise, and Jacques d'Albon, Marshal Saint-André, the so-called Triumvirate, pledged themselves to defend Roman Catholicism with Spanish assistance (p. 30).

with the French.[35] To prevent this, a politically astute policy then dictated that Shane O'Neill's claims be recognized. After the treaties of Câteau-Cambrésis (1559) and Edinburgh (1560), however, Shane O'Neill became less a threat and Elizabeth's position shifted to support for his rival, Brian O'Neill. Aware that he could not now depend on either French or Spanish support, Shane hoped to negotiate an acceptable compromise to avoid a major military confrontation. Having obtained a pardon, a promise of safe conduct, and money to cover his expenses, Shane went to London in December of 1561 to argue his case. No decision was made regarding the earldom, but Shane O'Neill's authority as head of the O'Neills was recognized, even if the recognition was not well defined. In turn Shane O'Neill acknowledged the Queen's overlordship.[36]

In Munster there was a comparable dispute between traditional rivals the Earls of Ormond, the Butlers, and the Earls of Desmond, the FitzGeralds. Both sides had their English partisans: Thomas Radcliffe, Earl of Sussex and Lord Deputy since 1556, supported Ormond; Robert, Lord Dudley (Earl of Leicester after 1564), supported Desmond (and Shane O'Neill). Leicester moreover worked for Sussex's dismissal and the appointment of his own *protégé*, Sir Henry Sidney, as Lord Deputy.[37] In this contest the Queen preferred the Earl of Ormond, and both sides were ordered to abide by her orders. Ormond did, but Desmond's resistance eventually flared into open rebellion.[38] The second attempt of the Society of Jesus to penetrate Tudor Ireland occurred in this context.

In January and February of 1560 the Irish Parliament enacted legislation that established the Elizabethan reformation in that country.[39] The Irish Act of Supremacy (2 Eliz. c. 1) declared Elizabeth "Supreme Governor" of the Church in Ireland with clauses and penalties comparable to the English act. The Act of Uniformity (2 Eliz. c. 2) prescribed the second Edwardian *Book of Common Prayer* with the same changes as in England and the same penalties for non-use, effective from the feast of St. John the Baptist, 24 June 1560, one year after the English version went into effect. Other acts

---

[35] Shane O'Neill considered it a matter of honour that he regain his rightful inheritance. On the role that honour played in the Anglo-Irish conflicts of the 16th century see William Palmer, "That 'Insolent Liberty': Honour, Rites of Power and Persuasion in Sixteenth Century Ireland," *Renaissance Quarterly* 46 (1993) 308-27.

[36] G.A. Hayes-McCoy, "Conciliation, Coercion, and the Protestant Reformation, 1547-71," in *A New History of Ireland: III Early Modern Ireland 1534-1691*, eds. T.W. Moody, F.X. Martin, and F.J. Byrne (Oxford, 1991) pp. 69-83; Colm Lennon, *Sixteenth Century Ireland: The Incomplete Conquest* (Dublin, 1994) pp. 266-70.

[37] Ciaran Brady, *The Chief Governors: The Rise and Fall of Reform Government in Tudor Ireland 1536-1588* (Cambridge, 1994) p. 102.

[38] Hayes-McCoy, "Conciliation, Coercion," pp. 86-88.

[39] Robert Dudley Edwards, *Church and State in Tudor Ireland* (London, 1935) pp. 181-86.

recognized Elizabeth's right to the throne (2 Eliz. c. 5) and restored first fruits to the crown (2 Eliz. c. 3). Fortunately for the Catholic cause, the English authorities made one serious mistake: they did not take into account the fact that Irish was the language spoken by the vast majority of the population, and an Irish *Book of Common Prayer* was not published until after the death of Elizabeth.[40] Even though there was little consistent effort to implement the laws during the first decade, a few Irish chieftains, fearful that many would succumb to Protestantism, appealed to Pope Pius IV for assistance. Even before the new laws were known in Rome, the Pope asked for two Jesuits to go to Ireland as nuncios.[41] One was sent.

David Wolfe was a priest and had been dean of the chapter in Limerick, a position he resigned in 1555, after he entered the Society in 1554. Appointed rector of the college in Modena in 1558, Wolfe remained interested in the ecclesiastical affairs of Ireland. On 12 July 1559 he wrote to Father General Diego Laínez from Modena that he was astonished at the poor quality of bishops appointed for Ireland. Some newly appointed bishops had just passed through Modena. According to Wolfe one was a "public sinner and murderer" and others "are not satisfied with having wives and children publicly, but wish to have them by force of arms in spite of their husbands." He urged the General to use his influence so that such men were not promoted.[42] Not surprisingly Wolfe was recommended to Giovanni, Cardinal Morone, Cardinal Protector of Ireland, by Laínez. At Morone's suggestion, Pope Pius IV named Wolfe Apostolic Nuncio in August of 1560 and sent him to Ireland around the same time that Abbot Parpaglia was sent to England. Wolfe was instructed to contact the Catholic leaders in Ireland and to urge them to maintain their fidelity. He was commissioned to examine the quality of the Irish clergy and the state of the Irish Church, to dispense from all censures and matrimonial impediments, to reform monasteries, to establish *montes pietatis* for the relief of the poor, and, if possible, to establish schools. The second task was predominately religious, but the first, because it could stiffen the resistance of Shane O'Neill and the Earl of Desmond had political implications.[43]

---

[40] According to Edwards, "the excuse for not using Irish was that few could read it, and that it was very difficult to provide Irish type." If the minister were ignorant of English, the Act of Uniformity allowed him to use the Latin version (*Church and State in Tudor Ireland*, p. 184).

[41] Prionsias Ó Fionnagáin, *The Jesuit Missions to Ireland in the Sixteenth Century* (n.p. n.d. [privately printed]) pp. 13-14.

[42] ARSI, Ital. 115, ff. 23ʳ-24ᵛ. It will be recalled that Wolfe had earlier complained about the scandalous life of the Bishop of Limerick, John Quinn.

[43] Pius IV to David Wolfe, 2 August 1560, CSP Rome (1558-71) 25; Louis McRedmond, *To The Greater Glory: A History of the Irish Jesuits* (Dublin, 1991) pp. 18-19; Fergus O'Donoghue, "The Jesuit Mission in Ireland 1598-1651," (unpublished Ph.D. thesis: The Catholic University of America, 1981) 13; Ó Fionnagáin, *Jesuit Missions to Ireland*, p. 15.

According to Wolfe's testimony to Laínez, he was warmly received in Cork by the Catholics and the Earl of Desmond on the feast of St. Sebastian, 20 January 1561. From Cork Wolfe continued to his native Limerick, where the mayor was an old friend. Again the popular reception was so great that the mayor feared an English reaction. In light of his reception the Jesuit was convinced that few had been affected by the new doctrines. Unfortunately, Wolfe continued, the welcome received from the Irish ecclesiastics was not as warm. Whereas the people rejoiced that they were able to receive matrimonial dispensations *gratis*, a number of the religious leaders objected to the innovation and sought to restrict his powers. Others were annoyed that the papal Nuncio was a mere priest and not a bishop or cardinal. These leaders were not uninfected with heresy: many had wives or concubines and thus gave scandal to the faithful, while others sought to turn the people against the Pope.

A revival of Catholic liturgical practices was apparently triggered by Wolfe's arrival. In Limerick, Cork, Youghal, and Kilmallock, Masses were offered publicly. Wolfe's friend, the mayor of Limerick, was aware of his responsibilities and wrote to Lord Deputy Sussex about the arrival of the Jesuit and the public celebration of Mass. The Deputy forwarded the matter of the Mass to the Queen and ordered the immediate arrest of Wolfe, who thus was forced into hiding.

The Society was so esteemed that many, according to Wolfe, wanted the Jesuits to establish a school in Limerick. Indeed some suggested specific monastic sites. One possibility was a former Dominican priory at Kilmallock, about twelve miles from Limerick, known as Peter's Cell, which had been abandoned. Now, hopeful for the future, the Prior wanted to restore it, and the Jesuits were invited to establish a college there.[44] There were already three candidates for the Society, and more would apply if the Jesuits established this college.[45]

Around the same time as Wolfe's expedition to Ireland, the Society initiated a mission to Scotland. Despite the fanatical anti-popery of John Knox and his followers, the Society expected great things because of the presence of Mary in the kingdom. But Mary was isolated religiously: even a private Mass in her own chapel at Holyrood was greeted with strident denunciation by Knox. And that chapel was practically all that was left of the Scottish Catholic Church. Everything else had quickly collapsed under the Protestant attack as a result of internal corruption and external associ-

---

[44] Interestingly Thomas S. Flynn, O.P., says nothing about this in his *The Irish Dominicans 1536-1641* (Dublin, 1993).

[45] Wolfe to Laínez, Limerick 29 June 1561, ARSI, Germ. 143, ff. 80^r-82^r. See also McRedmond, *To The Greater Glory*, pp. 19-20 and Ó Fionnagáin, *Jesuit Missions to Ireland*, pp. 16-17.

ation with the French policies of the dowager Queen Mary of Guise. By the time Mary Stuart returned to her native Scotland in 1561, Catholicism was on the verge of disappearing.

Because information on the state of the Scottish Church was so scanty, Pope Pius IV in December of 1561 decided to send an envoy to investigate. He was ordered to ascertain the exact condition of the Church, to comfort the Queen and encourage her both to be steadfast in her faith and to send ecclesiastical representations to the reconvened Council of Trent. Despite the Society's attempt to shun this "honour," the Pope wanted a Jesuit for the mission. Diego Laínez, the Jesuit General, was in France at the Colloquy of Poissy on papal business.[46] The Vicar-General during his absence was Alfonso Salmerón, who had been sent on a similar mission to Ireland twenty years earlier. Armed with memories of his expedition, he tried to dissuade the Pope from this venture. Pius, however, was adamant.

Of the available men, Salmerón selected the Dutchman Nicholas Floris or, as he is more commonly known, Nicholas Goudanus or de Gouda. De Gouda had worked with Peter Canisius throughout the Holy Roman Empire and he had appeared with Canisius at the Conference of Worms in 1557.[47] Although de Gouda had been ill, exhausted from his work, news of his recovery reached Salmerón as the Vicar-General sought to meet the Pope's request. The Dutchman was advised to "accept the hard mission with a brave heart for the honour of God our Lord, for the general good of the Church, and particularly for the good of the Kingdom of Scotland." Salmerón confessed rather bluntly that "we could not fail the Pope and there was nobody but yourself available." Under separate cover Salmerón sent to Everard Mercurian, Provincial of Flanders, a bill of exchange for two hundred scudi to subsidize the expedition. If that was not enough for the required wardrobe, de Gouda could borrow more money on the Pope's security. "Because nobody here in Rome has knowledge of the entire nobility of that Kingdom, nor of those who can help the case of religion," Salmerón advised de Gouda to choose his own companion and to address the papal letters to whomever he considered suitable.[48]

---

[46] For an analysis of the Colloquy, its significance, and Laínez's role in it see Donald Nugent, *Ecumenism in the Age of the Reformation: The Colloquy of Poissy* (Cambridge, Mass., 1974).

[47] On de Gouda's work with Canisius see James Brodrick, S.J., *Saint Peter Canisius, S.J. 1521-1597* (London, 1935) *passim*.

[48] Rome 16 December 1561, ARSI, Germ. 105, ff. 31^v, 32^r (translated in J.H. Pollen, S.J., ed., *Papal Negotiations with Mary Queen of Scots* [Edinburgh, 1901] pp. 75-78). Monsignor, later Cardinal, Gian Francesco Commendone suggested that Mercurian be sent with de Gouda. The latter, Commendone argued, was so caught up in his prayers that he would not notice many things in Scotland. The former, because he had held so many posts of authority, would perceive the broader picture (lii, p. 92).

Salmerón's choice of de Gouda surprised many, including the General. On 31 December 1561 Laínez wrote to Salmerón about the projected mission:

> I can understand your reluctance to despoil the colleges of a useful man for this mission, but I fail to see how the mission is going to profit from the choice you have made. Why, Dr. Goudanus knows no French and is besides a sick man, so much so that I doubt whether he will return from Scotland alive. Surely it would be better to send Master Ponce Cogordan[49] who is an adept at all languages? .... If this advice reaches you too late, God will protect and direct Dr. Goudanus.[50]

Laínez's letter did arrive too late: the papal brief had already been sent to de Gouda. To protect a still weak de Gouda from the rigors and demands of Scotland, Mercurian did his best to postpone the mission, but his efforts only succeeded in arousing the ire of Salmerón. On 6 June 1562, de Gouda wrote to the Vicar-General that he was about ready to depart for Scotland.[51] As companions, he had chosen a French Jesuit Jean Rivat and a Scottish priest "of good family," Edmund Hay. Another Scot, William Crichton, had crossed ahead of the party in order to make necessary arrangements. Between Rivat and Hay, the problem with languages seemed to be solved. The Dutchman promised "to take all possible pains with the help of Christ to carry through the business committed to us most carefully." Before his departure, de Gouda returned the papal bill of exchange because he could not obtain anything on the basis of its security. To pay for his travelling expenses he accepted some money from Father Leonard Kessel, Jesuit rector

---

[49] It is interesting that Laínez would recommend this man as papal envoy, because Cogordan, along with Nicolás Bobadilla, had been the General's most severe critic and opponent in the Society's institutional crisis of 1556-1558. For the full story of this important conflict see André Ravier, S.J., *Ignatius of Loyola and the Founding of the Society of Jesus* (San Francisco, 1987) pp. 282-314, and William V. Bangert, S.J., *Jerome Nadal, S.J. (1507-1580): Tracking the First Generation of Jesuits*, ed. Thomas M. McCoog, S.J. (Chicago, 1992) pp. 173-207. Cogordan was the subject of one of the most famous Ignatian anecdotes. Notorious for his parsimony, Cogordan was the Society's procurator. In that capacity he had become friendly with a number of cardinals, one of whom feasted him on lampreys. After Ignatius was informed of that dinner, he chided his procurator: "So you dine on lampreys, do you? I have nothing against that, but you do not buy the brethren even decent sardines. Go now, and in the future buy them lampreys." The expense of such a meal horrified Cogordan, but Ignatius was adamant and ordered him to find the money for the meal. As a result, the procurator was cured of his stinginess (*The Origin of the Jesuits* [London, 1940] p. 253).

[50] *Epp. Laínez*, VI, 188 (translated in James Brodrick, *The Progress of the Jesuits* [London, 1946] p. 188).

[51] Aware of de Gouda's bad health, Pius IV wrote to Mary Queen of Scots on 3 June 1562 that the Dutch Jesuit would not be able to complete this mission and that Pius had sent Everard Mercurian instead. On the following day he informed Mercurian of this decision (CSP Rome [1558-71] 91). Apparently de Gouda had already departed by the time the news reached the Low Countries.

in Cologne.⁵² On the 10th they sailed from Antwerp. The boat docked at Leith ten days later.

Shortly after their arrival Stephen Wilson, a servant of the Queen, contacted the Nuncio at the house of a relative of Hay where the Nuncio lodged. Wilson relayed the news of their arrival to the Queen. Unfortunately Wilson told others and so news of the arrival of a papal Nuncio quickly spread through Edinburgh. Although Mary did consent to a meeting with the Nuncio, she could not and would not permit the public reading of any papal letter. Indeed rumours of the arrival of a papal Nuncio so antagonized citizens of Edinburgh and public officials that Mary scheduled her meeting for 24 July "at an hour when the courtiers were attending the great preacher's [John Knox's] sermon, and could not therefore know of the interview."⁵³

Although the Queen understood the Nuncio's Latin, her inability to reply in that tongue resulted in the use of Edmund Hay as translator. Through him Mary explained her plight and told how she had been compelled to do many things of which she did not approve. Indeed, she could not even shelter her co-religionists from the force of the anti-papist legislation. And, because of her precarious position, she doubted that she would be able to send bishops to the Council of Trent. Before she gave a definitive answer to that question, however, she wanted to consult her bishops. As for the letters from the Pope and addressed to individual Scottish bishops, the Queen feared a "great tumult" if it became know that a Nuncio was attempting to deliver them. Indeed so hostile was the general population to anything or anyone from Rome that Mary could not even guarantee the envoy's safety during his stay. She advised him to spend most of his time indoors. Apparently frustrated and dismayed, de Gouda advised her to follow the example of many Catholic princes and "establish a college where she could always have pious and learned priests at hand, and where the young men, on whom the hopes of the country depended, could be trained in the Catholic religion." At the moment that was, she thought, rather impractical.

De Gouda did not see the Queen again during his stay; all subsequent dealings were through her secretary. Nonetheless the envoy sought to confirm the Queen in her faith and to assure her of the papal affection. For

---

⁵² Louvain 6 June 1562, ARSI, Germ. 144, ff. 21ʳ-23ᵛ (translated in Pollen, *Papal Negotiations*, pp. 103-05).
⁵³ De Gouda to Diego Laínez, Mainz 30 September 1562, ARSI, Germ. 144, ff. 32ʳ-37ᵛ (printed in William Forbes-Leith, S.J., ed., *Narratives of Scottish Catholics under Mary Stuart and James VI* [Edinburgh, 1885] pp. 63-79). This is the nuncio's official report to his Jesuit superior. With John Hungerford Pollen, S.J., *The Counter-Reformation in Scotland* (London, 1921) pp. 19-21 and Brodrick, *Progress of the Jesuits*, pp. 185-206, it provides the basis for this account.

the Queen's part, she tried to persuade Henry Sinclair, Bishop of Ross, to meet de Gouda. The Bishop refused despite the Queen's expressed wish and the Nuncio's insistence. Such a visit, the Bishop claimed, "would bring about the sacking and plundering of his house within twenty-four hours, and would involve himself and his household in the peril of their lives." De Gouda next tried to contact William Chisholm, Bishop of Dunblane, who happened to be in Edinburgh. Eight days later, probably because of de Gouda's approach, the Bishop returned to his episcopal city.[54] Undaunted, de Gouda, at times dressed as one of the Bishop's servants, followed him. For the second time, de Gouda's persistence failed to gain him an audience. After the second refusal such attempts to gain private meetings with members of the hierarchy were abandoned as hopeless.

De Gouda next wrote to all the orthodox Catholic bishops in Scotland. Only two replied immediately; a third, William Gordon, Bishop of Aberdeen, answered later.[55] Of the first two John Hamilton, Archbishop of St. Andrews, wrote directly to de Gouda, and Robert Crichton, Bishop of Dunkeld, wrote to the Pope. Crichton consented to a meeting with de Gouda. The Nuncio shortly thereafter visited the Bishop at his island residence in the disguise of a bank clerk. So terrified was the Bishop that the Nuncio's true identity would be revealed that he even insisted that the dinner conversation be restricted to financial matters.[56] Thus, even the one successful attempt to arrange a meeting bore no fruit. De Gouda concluded this section of his report with an ironic judgement: "Your Reverence will be at no loss to gather from these particulars, how far the cause of religion is likely to be advanced by negotiations with these good men. So much then for the Bishops."

The bishops were not an anomaly: the general state of Catholicism within the country was bleak. Statues had been destroyed and altars torn down. No Masses could be publicly celebrated. Indeed, except in the Queen's private chapel, there were no Masses. As Catholicism declined, Protestantism

---

[54] Two successive bishops were named William Chisholm. The first was consecrated on 14 April 1527 and died sometime before 14 December 1564. His nephew was named his coadjutor on 2 June 1561. The Chisholm that tried to avoid de Gouda by leaving Edinburgh was the uncle.

[55] Interestingly the two bishops who replied to de Gouda's letter, the Archbishop of St. Andrews and the Bishop of Dunkeld, were two of the three bishops (the third was the Bishop of Dunblane who had refused to grant the Nuncio an audience) who had opposed the *Confessio Scoticana* in 1560. See W. Ian P. Hazlett, "The Scots Confession 1560: Context, Complexion and Critique," *Archiv für Reformationsgeschichte* 78 (1987) 287-320, especially n. 11 on 290.

[56] Recent historical investigations have shown that the Bishop's fervour for Catholicism was not as muted as the Nuncio suggested. See John Durkan, "William Murdoch and the Early Jesuit Mission in Scotland," *IR* 35 (1984) 3-11; Michael J. Yellowlees, "The Ecclesiastical Establishment of the Diocese of Dunkeld at the Reformation," *IR* 36 (1985) 74-85; and "Dunkeld and Nicholas de Gouda's Mission to Scotland, 1562," *IR* 44 (1993) 48-57.

thrived: "One day, close to the place where I lodged, three priests publicly abjured the Catholic faith. . . ." As more and more Catholics abandoned their traditional religion, de Gouda saw little hope for a remedy. The Queen was helpless. She lacked any Catholic advisors, and the Protestants who surrounded her "prevent[ed] her exercising any of the rights of sovereignty" ; whenever she attempted to do so against their advice, they frightened her with threats of an English invasion. In the face of the total destruction of Catholicism, the bishops stayed "quietly at home, and in truth are for the most part destitute of all personal qualifications requisite for taking any lead in such stormy times." The Bishop of Dunblane, presumably William Chisholm (II), was the only prelate excluded from this condemnation.

The envoy passed over the style in which the prelates lived. His comment was brief but powerful: "it is hardly surprising if God's flock is eaten by wolves, while such shepherds as these have charge of it." Of the lower clergy few priests remained, in appearance indistinguishable from laymen. Occasionally one of them offered a clandestine Mass in the home of one of the nobility. As for the Catholic commoners, "they are so trampled in the dust by the tyranny of their opponents, that they can only sigh and groan, waiting for the deliverance of Israel."

De Gouda ended his report with a few recommendations for the survival of Catholicism and its eventual restoration. For the sake of the religion it was essential that the Queen marry a Catholic prince strong enough to restrain and control the Scottish Protestants. In her government the Queen must have good Catholic advisors. For the good of the Church Scotland must be provided with "faithful bishops and prelates." To bring all this about, the Pope should send legates with full canonical authority to remove unworthy prelates and replace them with true shepherds. For the better education of the lower clergy a college should be established. Finally, in order to neutralize the threats of an English invasion and the intimidations by Protestants, the Queen should receive the military protection of the King of Spain.[57]

Because of the many threats against his life, de Gouda assumed the disguise of a sailor when he left Scotland on 3 September. He reached Antwerp on the 13th. The first Jesuit mission to Scotland had lasted three

---

[57] In a letter to Father Laínez from Rome on 2 January 1563, Edmund Hay agreed with de Gouda's evaluation: "Father de Gouda has described in great part, what no letter could describe fully, the miseries with which Scotland is afflicted (the particulars of which he has collected with great diligence, and recorded with great accuracy), as well as the causes which produced these evils, and the best way of remedying them. On these heads I have nothing to add, unless I were to describe still more in detail the tyranny exercised towards the Catholics by the heretical party now in power, under pretence of carrying out the laws, of which the effect is exactly that of a sword placed in the hands of a madman" (ARSI, Ital. 122, ff. 170^r-171^v [translated in Forbes-Leith, *Narratives of Scottish Catholics*, p. 80]).

months, nearly thrice as long as the first mission to Ireland, but it was just as fruitless. De Gouda's report on the state of the Church in Scotland was just as pessimistic as the Irish account of Broët and Salmerón, who held no hope for the Church in Ireland because of the capitulation of the chieftains. According to de Gouda, the only remedy for Scotland's plight was consolidation of the Queen's power through marriage to a powerful Catholic prince.[58] Only then would Mary be able to vanquish the heretics and reform the Scottish Church.

The situation continued to deteriorate. In 1563, as Catholics tried to celebrate the Easter feast with appropriate dignity, the Archbishop of St. Andrews, along with a number of priests, was arrested and charged with the crime of saying Mass. On 19 May 1563 he and forty-seven others were tried in Edinburgh on charges of hearing confessions and either saying or assisting at Mass. They were found guilty and imprisoned. Fearful that the Pope would interpret their apprehension incorrectly, Mary dispatched William Chisholm, Bishop of Dunblane, to Rome.[59] At an audience with Pius IV in September, the Bishop assured the Pope not only of Mary's loyalty, but also of the fidelity of the Earls of Lennox [Matthew Stuart], Atholl [John Stuart], Huntly [George Gordon], Montrose [William Graham], Eglinton [Hugh Montgomery], Cassilis [Gilbert Kennedy], Erroll [George Hay], and Caithness [George Sinclair]. Pius wrote to each to exhort them to steadfastness. The following June Pius sent Mary copies of the acts of the Council of Trent, which had finished its sessions in December of 1563. Pius pleaded with Mary to ensure that these were implemented and to dismiss all heretics from positions of authority. In October of 1564 Mary promised to do all she could to execute the decrees. But she could expect no assistance from her two metropolitans: the Archbishop John Hamilton of St. Andrews was still in prison and Archbishop James Beaton of Glasgow was in Paris.[60]

De Gouda's mission to Scotland lasted three months but that of David Wolfe in Ireland continued.[61] As Nuncio, Wolfe had the authority to open

---

[58] Of candidates for her hand, Mary was most interested in Don Carlos, son of King Philip II of Spain. Serious negotiations began in the summer of 1563, but Philip aborted them in early 1564 because he questioned the emotional stability of his son. See Simon Adams, "The Release of Lord Darnley and the Failure of Amity," *IR* 38 (1987) 125. A comparative study of the marital diplomacy of Elizabeth and Mary at this time would be interesting.

[59] This is William Chisholm (II), coadjutor Bishop of Dunblane. According to de Gouda, he once wanted to join the Jesuits (Forbes-Leith, *Narratives of Scottish Catholics*, p. 71).

[60] Bellesheim, *Catholic Church of Scotland*, III, 72-81.

[61] G.A. Hayes-McCoy, "The Completion of the Tudor Conquest and the Advance of the Counter-reformation, 1571-1603," in *A New History of Ireland: III Early Modern Ireland 1534-1691*, eds. T.W. Moody, F.X. Martin, and F.J. Byrne (Oxford: Clarendon Press, 1991) p. 138; McRedmond, *To The Greater Glory*, pp. 20-21; Ó Fionnagáin, *Jesuit Missions to Ireland*, pp. 17-18. Regarding Wolfe's nominees for episcopal sees, Ó Fionnagáin concluded: "With these appointments to the hierarchy, a page was now definitely turned in the history of the Church

schools —and even to consider the erection of colleges throughout Ireland, to nominate bishops, and to reform the religious houses. Within a few years of his arrival, he opened schools in a number of Munster towns.and, despite the persistent opposition of many Irish bishops, he succeeded in encouraging numerous vocations and in sending the men to the continent for their education.

But episcopal opposition and increased English vigilance took their toll. In a letter to Francis Borgia on 29 July 1563 Wolfe complained of loneliness and spiritual poverty. He must have written something similar to Everard Mercurian because the latter, in a letter to Laínez on 28 May 1564, relayed specific details about Wolfe's mission and spiritual state. Wolfe had been disconsolate since his departure from Rome, and he feared for his life and his soul. Because of opposition and frustration, he doubted that he would ever be able to carry out his assignment, and he wanted to be recalled.[62] Laínez's response was both practical and exhortatory. He understood Wolfe's problems and promised, if the Nuncio truly wanted to be recalled, that he would do all he could to bring this about. But, since Wolfe had been sent by the Pope, the General could not act on his own authority. The Pope had appointed Richard Creagh, who earlier resisted Jesuit efforts to have him nominated as Bishop of Limerick, Archbishop of Armagh on 22 March 1564. He would be embarking shortly for Ireland, and Laínez suggested that Wolfe discuss the situation with him after his arrival.[63] The General also suggested that Wolfe's spirits would improve if he resided in a less dangerous area. Therefore he recommended that Wolfe consider moving to Ulster. Because of the increase in Irish vocations, Wolfe should investigate the establishment of a novitiate, preferably in O'Neill's territory, or in some other part of the island where the novices would not be molested by the English. Finally, he promised that a few Jesuits would be sent to assist him.[64]

At his departure from Rome, the Archbishop of Armagh was given a letter of introduction for Everard Mercurian. In it Laínez explained that the

---

in Ireland. For the future, only such men of known worth and loyalty to the Holy See would be chosen to govern the Church. The day of temporizing bishops was over and the Church in Ireland could be said to have entered into the mainstream of Tridentine discipline and the counter-reform that were destined to undo much of the damage caused by the religious revolt a generation earlier" (p. 18).

[62] David Wolfe to Francis Borgia, Limerick 29 July 1563, ARSI, Germ. 144, ff. 142^r-143^v; Everard Mercurian to Diego Laínez, Tournai 28 May 1564, ARSI, Germ. 145, ff. 104^r-105^v.

[63] There is an undated set of instructions for Wolfe in Creagh's handwriting in ARSI, Instit. 187, ff. 219^{r-v}. These were drafted presumably before Creagh's departure.

[64] Laínez to Wolfe, Rome 27 July 1564, ARSI, Ital. 65, ff. 110^v-111^r (published in *Epp. Laínez*, VIII, 114-16). See also Laínez to Mercurian, Rome 22 July 1564, ARSI, Germ. 105, ff. 138^v-139^r.

Archbishop was returning to Ireland with ample faculties for himself and Wolfe, one of which concerned the establishment of a university.[65] Because the Archbishop—and the Pope—sincerely hoped that a university would be opened, the Archbishop wanted a few Jesuits to assist him. It was especially important that one of the Jesuits sent to Ireland have the authority, in conjunction with Wolfe, to accept candidates into the Society. The choice of Jesuits the General left to Mercurian, but he wanted at least one good Irish, English, or Scottish Jesuit assigned to Ireland.[66] From the limited field of candidates, William Good was selected; he and the Archbishop departed in early autumn.

Bad weather forced Good and the Archbishop to disembark in England. Fearful of remaining too long on English soil, the Archbishop left Good in Dover and departed for Chester, where he hoped to find a ship crossing to Ireland. Good remained in Dover for three weeks before he set off on foot for London and then for Chester. Good arrived in Dublin on 18 December, a few days after the Archbishop. Again on foot, he set out for Armagh, where he hoped to meet the Archbishop. The Archbishop, however, had been arrested near Drogheda a few days after Christmas.[67] Unaware of the capture, Good continued his pursuit.

Good arrived in Armagh around 4 January 1565 and called on Shane O'Neill. O'Neill's position in Ulster was even stronger after his visit to the English court in late 1561. Throughout 1562 and 1563 he consolidated his position in the north despite attempts by Lord Deputy Sussex to curb his power. In September of 1563 O'Neill was granted almost all his demands in a treaty in which the Queen acknowledged him as "O'Neill," although his claim to the earldom was still under review, and the English garrison at Armagh was withdrawn. In 1564 Sussex resigned his commission.[68]

O'Neill knew nothing about the Archbishop and so Good headed south to meet Wolfe and the recently arrived Irish scholastic Edmund Daniel. He arrived in Limerick on 1 February, where he and Daniel opened a school a

---

[65] On 31 May 1564 Pius IV gave Creagh and Wolfe new faculties for the establishment of a university in Ireland similar to Paris and Louvain. The bull was published in Patrick Francis Moran, *Spicilegium Ossoriense* (Dublin, 1874) pp. 32-38. Another set of faculties dated 13 July 1564 can be found in CSP Rome (1558-71) 166-68.

[66] Laínez to Mercurian, Rome 22 July 1564, ARSI, Germ. 105, ff. 138^v-139^r; same to same, Rome 4 September 1564, ARSI, Germ. 105, ff. 174^v-176^r.

[67] Everard Mercurian to Diego Laínez, Louvain 24 December 1564, ARSI, Germ. 145, ff. 275^r-276^v. Years later, in 1580, William Good wrote a long account of his Irish sojourn. The original can be found in Archivio di Stato di Roma, Paesi Stranieri, busta 28, fasc. 1. I have used a more legible transcript in ABSI, 46/23/8.

[68] Hayes-McCoy, "Conciliation, Coercion," pp. 84-85; Lennon, *Ireland*, pp. 270-72. Sir Thomas Cusacke attributed O'Neill's docility to his English wife. See William Palmer's fascinating study of English hostility towards Irish women, "Gender, Violence, and Rebellion in Tudor and Early Stuart Ireland," *SCJ* 23 (1992) 704.

week later. Meanwhile the Archbishop of Armagh was transferred to the Tower of London. Committed to it on 18 January, he escaped to Antwerp on 29 March. There he wrote, perhaps out of despair, to Francis Borgia that he wanted to enter the Franciscans. The situation in Ireland was so dangerous that he advised Borgia that Wolfe should be recalled.[69]

The school in Limerick functioned openly with little difficulty for six months. On Saturday 13 October 1565, the mayor and a small company of soldiers entered the school and ordered Good and nearly 100 students to leave the building.[70] They did so without protest and went into the church for vespers. Good was informed that he had nothing to fear if he answered a few questions. After the examination, Sir Thomas Cusacke, Lord Chancellor of Ireland,[71] said that he would listen to Good's sermon the following day. So impressed was Cusacke with the sermon that he ordered Good to preach again the following Sunday and promised that he would secure the Lord Deputy's permission for Good to preach openly. Whether he ever did so we do not know. Around 24 October Cusacke summoned Wolfe for an examination. When the Jesuit failed to appear, Cusacke condemned him as guilty of treason. Wolfe fled north; the school was sacked and looted. And Good, perhaps from his travels and labours, became extremely ill.[72]

After the devastation in Limerick and after Daniel had nursed Good back to health, the two Jesuits reopened their school in Kilmallock. Daniel and Good remained there for three months before returning to Limerick by the beginning of April of 1566. In a letter to the General on 8 April 1566, Good explained that, although they expected to be expelled from Limerick by the

---

[69] "Good's Memorial," ABSI, 46/23/8, pp. 11-14; Richard Creagh to Francis Borgia, Antwerp 23 May 1564 [sic=1565], ARSI, Epp. Ext. 10, ff. 167ʳ-171ᵛ (published in *Epp. Borgia*, III, 703-14). An autobiographical account of his escape from the Tower can be found in Moran, *Spicilegium Ossoriense*, pp. 40-42. Creagh was arrested a second time in 1567; after six months in prison in Dublin he escaped a second time. He was arrested a third time before the end of the year. He was returned to the Tower of London, where he remained until his death on 14 October 1585. For more information see Moran, *Spicilegium Ossoriense*, pp. 38-58.

[70] This increased vigilance probably resulted from Elizabeth's anxiety over the recruitment and teaching of candidates for priesthood, whose subsequent activity would nurture Irish Roman Catholicism (Steven G. Ellis, *Tudor Ireland: Crown, Community and the Conflict of Cultures 1470-1603* [London, 1985] p. 222).

[71] Ciaran Brady referred to Cusacke as "that weather-vane of Anglo-Irish politics" (*Chief Governors*, pp. 21-22). Cusacke was instrumental in the conciliatory 1563 treaty with O'Neill (pp. 105-06).

[72] "Good's Relation for 1565," ABSI, 46/23/8, pp. 11-14. See also Good's letter to Diego Laínez, Limerick [30 September] 1565. I have not been able to locate the original and have relied on a transcript in ABSI, 46/23/8, pp. 100-01. Writing in the mid-17th century, the English Jesuit Henry More claimed that Good spent four years in Ireland "with no apparent result. But his efforts were incessant" (Francis Edwards, S.J., ed., *The Elizabethan Jesuits* [London, 1981] p. 14). Father Brodrick claimed that Good spent his six years on the mission maligning his Irish brethren (*Progress of the Jesuits*, p. 235 the continuation of n. 2).

English, they returned to that city because the citizens of Kilmallock had not fulfilled their promises of providing financial support for the school.[73] A return to Limerick improved neither the spiritual nor the material state of the Jesuits. By 8 June Good admitted to the General that the Jesuits could not teach in the cities unless they received the approval of the Queen's officials, and that this could be obtained only if the Jesuits agreed to two conditions: that they promised to have no contact with Wolfe and that they would not celebrate Mass publicly. Good wanted to leave and had argued with Wolfe that it was not the "mind of the Society" to expose them to such peril. Wolfe, however, remained optimistic. Regardless of the fruits of their labours, Wolfe reminded Good that the Apostolic Nuncio had not the authority either to leave Ireland or to send the Jesuits back to the continent.[74]

Depending as it did on O'Neill's power, Wolfe's optimism was brief. Leicester's *protégé*, Sir Henry Sidney, returned to Ireland in January of 1566 as the Earl of Sussex's successor as Lord Deputy. Unlike Sussex, who was satisfied with defending the Pale, Sidney wanted to extend effective English rule over the island.[75] Government policy towards Shane O'Neill changed almost immediately. Sidney argued that O'Neill was the greatest obstacle to the anglicization of Ulster. He therefore must be opposed and not pacified. Sidney worked for the restoration of the power of O'Neill's rivals, the O'Donnells. By March the destruction of O'Neill became official policy. Shane O'Neill, meanwhile, looked for support in both Scotland and France. Claiming that he was a champion of the faith, O'Neill offered the Irish crown to the French King Charles IX in return for his assistance in the struggle. Archibald Campbell, Earl of Argyll, received an emissary from O'Neill. There were fears in the English court of an alliance. Mary Queen of Scots was also susceptible to O'Neill's pleas since he could be used in her struggle with Elizabeth and it was believed that she would stir up trouble in Ireland.[76]

In late 1566 an English army marched through Ulster and restored Calvagh O'Donnell, who had been O'Neill's prisoner; nonetheless, Ulster

---

[73] ARSI, Angl. 41, ff. 01^r-02^v. The school later moved to Clonmel and finally settled in Youghal. For an account of the school's activities see "Good's Relation for 1568," ABSI, 46/23/8, pp. 56-57.

[74] ARSI, Angl. 41, ff. 04^r-05^v. See also Wolfe's letter to Juan de Polanco, June 1566, ARSI, Ital. 131, ff. 382^{r-v}. For a description of the curriculum of these schools see Ó Fionnagáin, *Jesuit Missions to Ireland*, pp. 21-23.

[75] Colm Lennon argues that Edmund Campion's history of Ireland was an *apologia* for his friend Sir Henry Sidney. See "Edmund Campion's *Histories of Ireland* and Reform in Tudor Ireland," in *The Reckoned Expense: Edmund Campion and the Early English Jesuits. Essays in Celebration of the First Centenary of Campion Hall, Oxford (1896-1996)*, ed. Thomas M. McCoog, S.J. (Woodbridge, 1996) pp. 67-83.

[76] Ellis, *Tudor Ireland*, p. 254; William Palmer, *The Problem of Ireland in Tudor Foreign Policy 1485-1603* (Woodbridge, 1994) p. 85.

remained beyond effective English control. The return of Calvagh O'Donnell, even though he died shortly thereafter, revived the friction between the O'Neills and the O'Donnells. In May of 1567 Shane O'Neill moved against Hugh O'Donnell shortly after Hugh succeeded his brother as O'Donnell. O'Neill was defeated on 8 May, escaped, crossed Tyrone, and entrusted himself to the Scots at Cushendun. O'Neill negotiated with Alexander Óg MacDonnell for Scottish assistance. MacDonnell may have been made a better offer by Sidney: on 2 June the Scots assassinated O'Neill and his closest followers. His pickled head was later impaled outside Dublin Castle. Sidney's success over O'Neill was unexpected but nonetheless acclaimed.[77]

The loss of a powerful protector affected the entire Irish Catholic community. Wolfe, however, encountered more personal reasons for regret. By April of 1566, as the tide was turning against O'Neill, the Archbishop of Armagh, having abandoned his desire to enter the Franciscans, prepared to return to Ireland. On 17 April he wrote to Francis Borgia that he had recently heard several rumours about Wolfe that led him to conclude that it would be in everyone's best interest if he were withdrawn either from Ireland altogether or at least from his native district. Although the Archbishop did not specify the content of the rumours, he did say that several important persons were no longer inclined to assist Wolfe.[78] In light of Wolfe's later political involvement, one wonders whether his association, real or suspected, with Shane O'Neill was behind the Jesuit's increased unpopularity.

Good's pleas and the rumours about Wolfe led to the General's decision to recall the Jesuits. Because Wolfe's status as Apostolic Nuncio expired with the death of Pius IV on 9 December 1565, Borgia did not anticipate any difficulty with the recall. The General was slightly more hesitant about Good, because he had been promised as assistant to the Archbishop who was on his way back to Ireland. It was decided, therefore, that Good would remain until Creagh's return. They would then discuss the possibility of Good's departure. From the Society's perspective it seemed foolish to expose priests to such dangers with so little apparent fruit. The situation deteriorated with the Archbishop Creagh's recapture on 30 March 1567 and Wolfe's apprehension in the same year. Good meanwhile continued to

---

[77] Hayes-McCoy, "Conciliation, Coercion," pp. 85-86; Lennon, *Ireland*, pp. 272-74; Brady, *Chief Governors*, pp. 113-25.
[78] Madrid 17 April 1566, ARSI, Epp. Ext. 10, ff. 290^{r-v}. William Good in his letter of 8 June 1566 to Laínez explained that Wolfe's attempt to found a religious Institute for women had not turned out well (ARSI, Angl. 41, ff. 04^r-05^v). Around 1563 Wolfe drew up a rule for some women in Limerick known as the "Menabochta" who continued to live in their own homes. One of the purposes of the group was to win back fallen women. Not all, however, continued on the path of virtue. See Ó Fionnagáin, *Jesuit Missions to Ireland*, pp. 18-19. One wonders if Wolfe's association with these women was a reason for the rumours.

preach, and his success apparently dispelled his desire to abandon the mission.[79] Frans De Costere forwarded to the General a report from Good himself that his sermons so moved a congregation in Youghal to tears that they begged him to remain in Ireland. Because of the congregation's insistence, and because Daniel was in the country, the two Jesuits missed their ship to the continent. Such popularity did not move the General, and through Juan de Polanco he repeated his insistence that De Costere recall them.[80] The Society's mission to Ireland was to be aborted: the two Jesuits outside prison were to return to the continent.[81] As attempts were made to get them out of the country, Ireland again erupted.

The absence of Gerald FitzJames FitzGerald, Earl of Desmond, and of Thomas Butler, Earl of Ormond—and possibly the destruction of Shane O'Neill—fuelled rumours that the English authorities in Dublin were planning to dismantle the traditional Irish power structure in Munster. Faced with this possibility, FitzGeralds and Butlers abandoned their rivalry and united against a common foe. By 1569 most of Munster was in revolt under the leadership of James FitzMaurice FitzGerald, cousin of the Earl of Desmond. FitzMaurice, according to Colm Lennon, "adopted the rhetoric of the Counter-Reformation" and consistently asserted that the rebellion was prompted by the English Queen's attempts to impose Protestantism upon the Irish. Through the embassy of Maurice MacGibbon, Archbishop of Cashel, he sought Spanish and papal support for his crusade and even suggested that Philip II appoint a new king for Ireland in order to save the country from heresy. By August of 1569, however, the rebellion was effectively over; only FitzMaurice continued the struggle.[82]

---

[79] Borgia to Frans De Costere, Rome 23 July 1566, ARSI, Germ. 106, f. 154^r; De Costere to Borgia, Louvain 31 August 1566, ARSI, Germ. 147, ff. 201^r-202^v; Juan de Polanco to De Costere, Rome 15 October 1566, ARSI, Germ. 106, f. 185^v; De Costere to Borgia, 30 October 1566, ARSI, Germ. 147, ff. 255^r-256^v; Polanco to Archbishop of Armagh, Rome 19 December 1566, ARSI, Germ. 106, ff. 209^r-210^v; Polanco to either Good or Wolfe, Rome 19 December 1566, ARSI, Germ. 106, f. 210^r; Polanco to De Costere, Rome 8 January 1567, ARSI, Hisp. 68, ff. 1^{r-v}; De Costere to Borgia, Ghent 30 November 1567, ARSI, Germ. 148, ff. 295^r-296^v; Wolfe to [?], 13 October 1568, ABSI, 46/23/8, pp. 59-73.

[80] De Costere to Borgia, Louvain 31 August 1568, ARSI, Germ. 149, ff. 174^r-175^v; Polanco to De Costere, Rome 19 October 1568, Germ. 107, ff. 182^r-183^r; De Costere to Borgia, Tournai 31 July 1569, Germ. 150, ff. 209^{r-v}, 211^{r-v}.

[81] Edmund Tanner, an Irish Jesuit and later Bishop of Cork, consistently pleaded to be allowed to return to work in Ireland. The authorities, preparing to close the mission, dissuaded him. On 23 September 1569 Father General Francis Borgia informed him that little could be done in Ireland at that time but, once peace had been restored in France and Philip II had successfully suppressed the rebellion in Granada, there were hopes that he would direct his attention to the religious situation of northern Europe. Once these hopes were realized, the Society would be among the first to aid Ireland with Irish Jesuits (Father General to Tanner, Frascati, ARSI, Germ. 108, ff. 9^{r-v}).

[82] Hayes-McCoy, "Conciliation, Coercion," pp. 86-91; Lennon, *Ireland*, pp. 212-15; Palmer, *Problem of Ireland*, p. 90.

III

When de Gouda returned to the continent after his mission to Scotland, in his entourage were a few candidates for the Society.[83] As a result the Society retained an interest in Scottish affairs and followed closely the political and religious events of Mary's reign even though no Jesuits were actively involved.

Because Mary was the most eligible bride in the Catholic world, Catholic leaders argued among themselves as to the best candidate for her hand. Pope Pius V was ready to recognize her claim to the English throne if she married one of the European Catholic nobility.[84] Philip II was eager to find a suitable husband for Mary, perhaps among the very suitors rejected by Elizabeth. Fearful that an inappropriate suitor would result in a hostile Scotland, Elizabeth herself sought a suitable spouse for Mary. Her candidate was Robert Dudley, raised to the peerage with the title Earl of Leicester in 1564. Such a marriage would neutralize the traditional Scottish-French alliance.

All these intrigues ended abruptly when, impatient and smitten, Mary married her cousin Henry Stuart, Lord Darnley, in July of 1565, to the evident displeasure of Elizabeth and without a papal dispensation from the impediment of consanguinity. Their marriage began well. Aided by the Catholic lords, the King and the Queen defeated their Protestant enemies, whose leaders sought sanctuary across the border in England.[85] Although Darnley was not the King the Catholics desired, he seemed to possess the strength the Catholics needed. Catholic expectations were such that some Scots requested the return of William Crichton and of Edmund Hay, who had joined the Society after he accompanied de Gouda to Scotland in 1561.[86] The General, however, did not think that the time would be ripe "until arms have done their work."[87]

---

[83] De Gouda was accompanied by Mary's confessor Ninian Winzet, her chaplain René Benoist, and William Crichton. Edmund Hay followed with Robert Abercrombie, William Murdoch, James Tyrie, John Hay, and possibly James Gordon. All but Winzet and Benoist became Jesuits (Yellowlees, "Dunkeld and de Gouda," 52-53).

[84] One suggestion made at Trent concerned Mary's title. If Elizabeth were excommunicated, the English crown should be offered to a Catholic prince who, with the approval of the other Catholic rules and the Pope, would marry Mary (F.B. von Bucholtz, *Geschichte der Regierung Ferdinand des Ersten*, 9 vols. [Vienna, 1831-38] IX, 699-703).

[85] In order to destabilize each other's authority, Elizabeth protected Mary's Protestant foes and Mary encouraged Elizabeth's Irish rebels.

[86] On Crichton and Hay see *Mon. Ang.*, II, 280; and Thomas M. McCoog, S.J., ed., *English and Welsh Jesuits 1555-1650*, 2 vols. (London, 1994-95) II, 205.

[87] Father General to William Crichton, Rome 26 November 1565, ARSI, Germ. 106, f. 42^v (translated in Pollen, *Papal Negotiations*, p. 489). On the reforms introduced in Scotland during this period of Catholic ascendancy see Julian Goodare, "Queen Mary's Catholic Interlude," *IR* 38 (1987) 154-70.

To maintain a superior military position against the English-backed nobles, Mary needed considerable financial support. In 1566, she sent William Chisholm, Bishop of Dunblane, to Rome to obtain a papal subsidy for her army and a papal dispensation for her marriage. Pope Pius V, keenly interested in affairs of the British Isles, was delighted by the news of a Catholic restoration in Scotland and proposed to send Vincenzo Laureo, Bishop of Mondovì, to counsel the Queen on the best method for treating the Protestants.[88] The Bishop favoured a generally repressive treatment of the Protestants, with exceptionally harsh methods directed against the rebellious lords, especially after the assassination of the Queen's secretary David Rizzio.[89]

The Scottish Jesuit Edmund Hay was chosen to carry this proposal to Mary. Oliver Mannaerts, the General's Visitor to France and thus Hay's Jesuit superior, feared for his subject's safety and opposed this new Scottish venture, an opposition that he clearly expressed to Rome. He reminded Francis Borgia that "the Queen of Scotland has great need of advice and consequently of grave prudent and God-fearing men about her, men of the country rather than foreigners sent by that See which the heretical Scots hate more than the Devil." He suggested that James Beaton, Archbishop of Glasgow and Mary's ambassador to the French court, be returned to Scotland for this purpose. Hay and others could then go as members of his household.[90] Mannaerts's objections had no effect: Hay was sent to Queen Mary to advise her to receive the Italian Bishop with his vindictive solution to the country's religious problems. Hay went off, in the words of Mannaerts, "as it were to martyrdom."

After a delay of a month because of the baptism of Mary's son and heir James, who secured the Stuart dynasty and, unless Elizabeth married, made Catholic succession to the English throne more probable, Hay was received by the Queen on 14 January 1567. Mary absolutely refused to recognize the mission of the Bishop of Mondovì. Even though some of her subjects were traitors, she could not permit their legalized slaughter. The rejection of the

---

[88] In the name of the General, Juan de Polanco wrote to Edmund Hay from Rome on 18 February 1566 that the Pope "was more pleased with that news [the restoration of the Mass in Scotland] than with his election to the Papacy" (ARSI, Germ. 106, f. 68^v, [translated in Pollen, *Papal Negotiations*, p. 492]). Father Pollen also published an undated letter to Father Everard Mercurian, apparently from the Bishop of Dunblane in an attempt to secure the latter's support for increased involvement in Scotland (pp. 257-61).

[89] J.N.D. Kelly described Pius V as "single-minded, devout to the point of bigotry, relentless in his persecution of heresy" (*Dictionary of Popes*, p. 269, col. 2). In the Bishop of Mondovì the Pope found a man with similar views.

[90] Paris 26 June 1566, ARSI, Gal. 81, ff. 77^r-78^v (translated in Pollen, *Papal Negotiations*, p. 499). See Ian B. Cowan, "The Roman Connection: Prospects for Counter-Reformation during the Personal Reign of Mary, Queen of Scots," *IR* 38 (1987) 105-22 for the most recent investigation of Laureo's mission.

Bishop presumably meant the loss of a papal subsidy. Hay's mission had failed. He remained in Edinburgh for a month after his audience.[91] A few nights before his departure, on 10 February 1567, the nocturnal calm of the city was shattered by an explosion in Kirk o' Field: Darnley had been murdered.

Three months later the Queen married James Hepburn, Earl of Bothwell, before a Protestant minister. Shortly thereafter, Hay wrote about the religious defection of the Queen and the subsequent destruction of all Catholic hope: "I shall only beg of you of your wonted charity towards the Queen to be sure that she is remembered in the Sacrifices and the prayers of the Society. It may be that someday all things will co-operate for the good of that sinful woman, and that she will become the doer of great deeds who formerly would not consent to sound counsel."[92]

After Mary's marriage there was a new revolt against her rule. She was captured and imprisoned in Loch Leven in July of 1567. The government of the kingdom was entrusted to an illegitimate son of James V, James Stuart, Earl of Moray, who acted as Regent for Mary's infant son. Mary escaped from her island prison in May of 1568, but the forces that rallied to her support were no match for the superior strength of the Regent. After their defeat at Langside, Mary fled into England and arrived at Workington on 16 May 1568. She remained Elizabeth's prisoner for the rest of her life. Shortly after her incarceration, Mary was reconciled with the Catholic Church. On 30 November 1568 she wrote to the Pope to ask his pardon for her participation in Protestant services and to give satisfaction for any scandal she might have caused. On 9 January 1570 Pope Pius V consoled Mary:

> Mighty is God. He who freed David from the hand of Saul, and the Apostle Paul from the mouth of the lion, He can also snatch you from your many misfortunes, and set you again on your own throne. In order that this may be accomplished, we on our part stand ready to help, in such matters as we can, and in the way we have done previously. We will take good care that both the Kings be approached in your name, as you request. We will urgently commend to them your safety, and the integrity of your realm. We are ever prepared to show all those manifestations of paternal affection which are deserved by that strong, unconquered heart of yours, and your burning zeal for the Catholic faith.[93]

---

[91] On his return, Hay stopped in London. There, according to the Annual Letter of Paris for 1567, "he animated and consoled many, both men and women. He did the same good office in writing letters for the Bishop of that city [Edmund Bonner], who is detained in prison" (Pollen, *Papal Negotiations*, p. 507).

[92] Hay to Father General, Paris 21 January 1569, ARSI, Gal. 82, ff. 16^r-18^v (translated in Pollen, *Papal Negotiations*, p. 508).

[93] Quoted in John H. Pollen, S.J., "Mary Stuart and the Opinions of her Catholic Contemporaries," *The Month* 91 (1898) 591.

On 28 February Pius V promulgated *Regnans in Excelsis*, which excommunicated Elizabeth and declared her deposed. We shall treat other "manifestations of paternal affection" in later chapters. Mary was not forgotten by the Society of Jesus and she continued to play a role in the missionary strategies of the English and Scots Jesuits. Her involvement in these schemes will be discussed later.

IV

After two unsuccessful attempts to reestablish contact with England and after the failure of secret negotiations regarding the marriage of Dudley and Elizabeth, papal policy towards England hardened. Pius IV, with the advice of a growing number of English religious exiles, considered urging the Council of Trent to take the drastic step of excommunication in June of 1563. An anonymous proposal, rumoured to be from Louvain, proposed that Elizabeth be excommunicated. After various ambassadors at Trent had examined the proposal, they concluded that Elizabeth deserved to be excommunicated but that the time was not opportune. The date should be designated either by the current Pope or his successors.[94] Holy Roman Emperor Ferdinand opposed the measure. Although he deplored Elizabeth's conduct, he deemed it totally inappropriate for an ecumenical council to decree a sentence that could not be implemented. In this he received the support of his Spanish cousin Philip and so the project was abandoned. Not unrelated were the intercessions made by both branches of the Habsburg family to Elizabeth for kinder treatment of the imprisoned Catholic bishops. Both rulers feared that the implementation of a decree that held guilty of high treason all persons who refused to acknowledge the Queen's title as supreme governor of the Church in England would result in the execution of the bishops. Their appeals may have had something to do with the law's not being fully enforced. Little concessions continued to keep Pius IV hopeful that careful negotiations would result in England's conversion. He continued to pursue any lead until his death on 9 December 1565. Hopes of a peaceful reconciliation died with him.[95]

By the time that Elizabeth's second Parliament reconvened in September of 1566, the issue of the succession was hotly debated in books and pamphlets. The Catholics had the clearest contender in Mary Queen of Scots, and her rights were openly championed: she had an impeccable pedigree, an heir, and, at the time, secure possession of the Scottish throne.

---

[94] See Bucholtz, *Geschichte der Regierung Ferdinand des Ersten*, IX, 699-703. On the difficulties raised by the Emperor see also Bangert, *Nadal*, pp. 306-07.
[95] Bayne, *Anglo-Roman Relations*, pp. 158-217.

The time was ripe for broaching the subject again in Parliament. Despite efforts by Privy Councillors to convince members of Parliament that they must avoid the issue, Parliament persisted because of fear of a civil war if the succession were not settled and because of concern about the survival of Protestantism, not just in England but throughout Europe, if a Catholic ascended the English throne. Nonetheless Elizabeth did not wish the subject to be discussed, and the session ended with no resolution of the problem, aside from another promise to marry and some more evasive words about settling the succession.[96]

Lacking strong leadership from Rome, the English Catholics, under the leadership of the much-neglected Marian priests,[97] were left to fend for themselves. Occasional conformity in order to avoid the financial consequences of the penal laws was common. Indeed, Edward Rishton was exceptionally tolerant of occasional conformers in his continuation of Sander's *Rise and Growth*: many were "Catholic at heart, nevertheless they thought they might to some extent outwardly obey the law, and yield to the will of the queen; if in so doing there was any sin, that must be laid at the queen's door, not at theirs, for they were of the opinion that the straits they were in somehow or other might be held to excuse them."[98] Even after the condemnation of the practice by Rome in mid-1564, the priests, during their training in the continental seminaries, were still instructed to be tolerant and understanding.[99] Occasional conformity, although not the ideal, protected the Catholic gentry and nobility and in many ways contributed to the survival of Catholicism.[100]

The 1560s were years of crisis for Elizabeth and the English Catholics. The massacre of Huguenots by followers of Francis, Duke of Guise at Vassy on 1 March 1562 shattered French religious peace and led eventually to English support for the Huguenots at Newhaven.[101] A treaty was finalized with Louis, Prince of Condé by early October whereby English troops occupied Le Havre and fought in the defence of Rouen. By the following March, after the Prince of Condé was captured and the Duke of Guise

---

[96] See Neale, *Elizabeth I and Her Parliaments*, I, 129-76; Hartley, *Proceedings*, I, 117-75.

[97] Until a fuller study of the Marian priests is available see the sympathetic accounts in Scarisbrick, *Reformation*, pp. 136-45; Patrick McGrath and Joy Rowe, "The Marian Priests under Elizabeth I," *RH* 17 (1984) 103-20. McGrath justifiably includes as Marian priests "those who conformed outwardly and kept their livings but who endeavoured to retain inside the new settlement something of the old religion."

[98] *Rise and Growth of the Anglican Schism*, p. 265.

[99] See John Guy, *Tudor England* (Oxford, 1988) pp. 299-301; Walsham, *Church Papists*, pp. 5-49. We will return to this question in a later chapter.

[100] A sympathetic treatment can be found in Walsham, *Church Papists*, pp. 73-99.

[101] On this intervention see Wallace MacCaffrey, *The Shaping of the Elizabethan Regime: Elizabethan Politics 1558-72* (London, 1969) pp. 86-101.

assassinated, Catherine de Medici established a truce. Protestant and Catholic forces then united against the English. On 29 July 1563 Le Havre was surrendered.[102] Around the time that the treaty with the Huguenots was being negotiated, the Queen nearly died from smallpox. This close brush with death again raised the spectre of a Catholic heir firmly ensconced in Scotland and related to the hated Guises, and introduced the urgent issue of succession.

The religious wars in France, and especially Catholic successes, intensified English fears. In 1566 Sir Ralph Sadler contended in Parliament that England was surrounded by wars all rooted in religion. Although England remained at peace, a secret conspiracy of the French King with the Pope and his allies plotted to overthrow Elizabeth after the Huguenots were destroyed. Their agenda included an attack on England, where they expected to be assisted by the native Catholics.[103] A Catholic monarch in Scotland related to the Guises, and rebellious Irish chieftains seeking continental support, would provide ideal bases for an invasion.

The solution to Elizabeth's dilemma was the revival of earlier hopes for a marriage alliance with either the Austrian Archduke Charles or, after the Treaty of Troyes in April of 1564 normalized Anglo-French relations, with the French royal family.[104] Neither venture was successful despite the encouragement to further negotiation provided by the birth of a Scottish heir. Religion remained the stumbling block. Fortunately for Elizabeth, events in Scotland unseated Mary. Although the establishment of a Protestant government in Scotland eliminated the possibility of a foreign coalition using that country for an invasion of England, the overthrow of a legitimate monarch disturbed Elizabeth by providing a possible precedent for comparable action in England.[105] Mary remained not only the most widely accepted candidate as Elizabeth's successor but, for many Catholics, an ideal replacement. Her presence in England, especially in the north, whose loyalty Elizabeth was not sure of, was destabilizing. Had Mary simply exchanged the Scottish throne for the English one?

---

[102] In the treaty of 12 April 1564 Elizabeth ceded Calais to France in return for a cash settlement (Knecht, *French Wars of Religion*, p. 39). On the truce see pp. 38-39.

[103] For this speech see Hartley, *Proceedings*, I, 141-44. For a discussion of the role played by these and similar fears in Elizabeth's quest for funds see Wallace MacCaffrey, "Parliament and Foreign Policy," in *The Parliaments of Elizabethan England*, eds. D.M. Dean and N.L. Jones (Oxford, 1990) pp. 65-90.

[104] See Doran, *Monarchy and Matrimony*, pp. 73-129.

[105] Elizabeth found a way out of this dilemma through her insistence on a hearing to absolve Mary of any involvement in her husband's death. MacCaffrey noted that "the device of a semi-judicial hearing, which the Queen may originally have intended to be an instrument for reconciling Mary and her rebellious subjects, had become a powerful weapon for crippling the Queen of Scots" (*Shaping of the Elizabethan Regime*, p. 180).

In the same year 1568 Dr. William Allen founded a seminary at Douai to train English priests to work in their country for the preservation of Catholicism.[106] Their arrival was but the first sign that Elizabeth's policy of attrition was failing. With a new generation of clergy to strengthen the resolve of English Catholics, the old religion would not pass away with the current generation.[107]

Technically, religious peace had been restored within France; nonetheless Protestant fears had not been quelled completely. In June of 1565 Queen Regent Catherine met her daughter Elizabeth, Queen of Spain, at Bayonne. During her stay Catherine also met Philip II's chief minister, Fernando Álvarez de Toledo, Duke of Alba. Officially the meeting was to arrange marriages between Charles IX and the Emperor's daughter, Anna, and between Catherine's daughter Marguerite and Philip's son Don Carlos. The Spanish, however, were more interested in persuading the French into revoking their edicts of toleration and embarking on a joint campaign against the heretics in France and the Netherlands. Nothing concrete came of the meeting but rumours circulated. The rumours became more credible two years later, in April of 1567, when the Duke of Alba marched along the Spanish Road at the head of an army of 10,000 soldiers designed to pacify the Netherlands after the Calvinist iconoclastic riots in the summer of 1566.[108]

The arrival of a strong Spanish army heightened fear throughout Protestant Europe. Would the army be used to support Mary Queen of Scots in her struggle against the Protestant lords? Would it be directed at the restoration of Catholicism in England by supporting an Irish and/or English rebellion? Had a secret agreement been made at Bayonne to coordinate efforts against the Huguenots? Even the French government was uneasy about the presence of so many troops so near its borders. French efforts to

---

[106] For an exposition of the religious formation in the seminary see Allen's letter to John Vendeville, 16 September 1578 (or 1580), in Thomas Francis Knox, ed., *The Letters and Memorials of William Cardinal Allen (1532-1594)* (London, 1882) pp. 52-68. A new biography of Allen is needed. Until it appears see Michael Williams, "William Allen: The Sixteenth Century Spanish Connection," *RH* 22 (1994) 123-40; and Eamon Duffy, "William, Cardinal Allen, 1532-1594," *RH* 22 (1995) 265-90.

[107] William Cecil argued that the foundation of the seminary must be linked with *Regnans in Excelsis* and the Northern Rising. For him this was another act of aggression. Because of the failure of the rebellion, the leaders fled abroad and established seminaries whose products would infiltrate the kingdom and cause future trouble (*The Execution of Justice in England* [London, 1584/5], ed. Robert M. Kingdon [Ithaca, N.Y., 1965] p. 6). For a discussion of Cecil's rejection of the papal deposing power see Thomas H. Clancy, S.J., "English Catholics and the Papal Deposing Power, 1570-1640," *RH* 6 (1961) 117-19.

[108] Henry Kamen, *Spain 1469-1714: A Society of Conflict*, 2nd edition (London, 1991) pp. 130-31; Knecht, *French Wars of Religion*, pp. 39-40; Peter Limm, *The Dutch Revolt 1559-1648* (London, 1989) pp. 24-32.

strengthen defences against a possible Spanish attack led to a second religious war in mid-1567. The Huguenots interpreted the preparations as a feint to disguise a Franco-Spanish alliance. The second war lasted until the Peace of Longjumeau, signed on 23 March 1568. The peace held for approximately six months. Over the next two years a third religious war raged as the French King received reinforcements from the Pope, Florence, and Spain, and the Huguenots, from England and from the German Protestants. This war ended with the Peace of St. Germain-en-Laye on 29 July 1570. Although Protestantism was still banned at court and in Paris, the Huguenots were given liberty of conscience throughout the kingdom and freedom to practice their religion in the cities where it had been permitted before the recent war. As guarantees the Huguenots were given certain towns as security, e.g. La Rochelle.[109]

The presence of Alba's army in Brussels in late summer of 1567 threatened to turn the cold war between Elizabeth and Philip into something much more violent. Alba moved quickly, striking at the opposition through the establishment of the Council of Troubles, better known as the Council of Blood. Two of the rebel leaders, Lamoral, Count of Egmont and Philip, Count of Hornes, were arrested in September; the third leader, William (the Silent) of Orange, escaped into Germany, where he recruited an army for his return. His attack on the Spanish forces failed to win wide support and was easily defeated by Alba in the spring of 1568. On 5 June the two imprisoned counts were executed in Brussels.[110] Alba later celebrated his victory by forcing Antwerp to erect a statue in his honour on which was inscribed that he "extirpated sedition, reduced rebellion, restored religion, secured justice and established peace."[111] The area was now secure enough for Philip II to make his proposed visit. Two tragedies, however, prevented the trip: the death of his son and heir Don Carlos on 24 July 1568, and the death of the Queen in childbirth the following October.

Although Philip did not make the trip, the Duke and his army remained. And their presence was expensive. Philip II borrowed heavily from Genovese bankers to pay for the Spanish troops. The gold never reached them. Queen Elizabeth "borrowed" the Genovese gold from the Spanish ships that had taken refuge in Plymouth and Southampton from bad weather and pirates in November of 1568. Alba retaliated with an embargo on all English property in the Netherlands and with the arrest of English merchants. To raise money the Duke levied new unpopular taxes. Loss of the

---

[109] Knecht, *French Wars of Religion*, pp. 41-42; MacCaffrey, *Shaping of the Elizabethan Regime*, p. 169.
[110] John Lynch, *Spain 1516-1598: From Nation State to World Empire* (Oxford, 1991) pp. 398-400.
[111] Cited in Limm, *Dutch Revolt*, p. 33.

gold transformed Philip from a protector into a threatening foe with a powerful invasion force under the Duke of Alba less than two hundred miles from London. Plans were gradually formulated for the army's use in England.

On 3 November 1569 Pope Pius V urged the Duke of Alba to do all he could to aid the English Catholics and to free the imprisoned Queen.[112] A month later, on 16 December 1569, Philip wrote to the Duke that Elizabeth would have to be taught a lesson because of what she had done. She would not listen to reason, and so the King suggested that the northern Catholics be encouraged to rise in rebellion, that the Irish lords be supported, and that arrangements be made to transfer the English crown to Mary Stuart.[113] From London on 18 January 1570 Spanish ambassador Don Guerau de Spes notified Philip that English Catholics would rebel if they received foreign assistance, especially if a papal bull absolved them from their oath of allegiance to the Queen. Guerau de Spes argued that this bull was desirable and would bestow prestige on Catholic efforts.[114]

William Cecil was responsible for the seizure of the Spanish gold in 1568 and was indirectly responsible for the Northern Rising of the following year. An anti-Cecil faction composed of conservative peers such as Thomas Howard, Duke of Norfolk, and Henry FitzAlan, Earl of Arundel, William Herbert, Earl of Pembroke, Thomas Percy, Earl of Northumberland, and Charles Nevill, Earl of Westmorland, with nebulous support from the Earl of Leicester, sought to conciliate Philip II and improve the state of Mary Stuart with no harm to Elizabeth. Their goal was a marriage of Mary with Norfolk that would secure her succession to the English throne and the replacement of Cecil as chief minister. Many, especially the northern earls, were distressed at the exclusion of the old nobility, the traditional advisors of the monarch, and their replacement by "new men" such as Cecil. By confiscation of the gold Cecil hoped to deprive the Duke of Alba of money needed to pay his troops and thus to weaken his military position (to counter the pro-Spanish faction Cecil had consistently exaggerated the dangers that a powerful Alba posed to England). Cecil aimed to undermine the credibility of his political opponents.[115]

The anti-Cecil coalition collapsed completely when Elizabeth learned of Norfolk's marital scheme. Norfolk, Arundel, Pembroke, and their supporters quickly capitulated to the Queen. After Norfolk was committed to the Tower, a royal summons called Westmorland and Northumberland to court.

---

[112] CSP Rome (1558-71) 314.
[113] CSP Simancas (1568-79) 217-18.
[114] CSP Simancas (1568-79) 228-30.
[115] See William S. Maltby, *Alba* (Berkeley, 1983) pp. 190-92 for an analysis of this crisis.

Fearful of a similar fate, they proceeded with their plans and raised their retainers in November of 1569. The rebellion was brief and unsuccessful.

In February of 1570, before Pius knew of the unsuccessful rebellion, he was still exhorting Alba to provide the English Catholics with "whatever strength you may, to protect, reenforce or assist their own forces." At the same time the Pope urged the Earls of Northumberland and Westmorland to renew the ancient bond between England and Rome and to liberate "their kingdom from a most vile servitude to a woman's lust."[116] But Alba resisted the overtures of Philip and Pius because he considered such a venture at this time mere folly.[117] Without assistance from Mary Stuart's faction in Scotland or from Alba, the revolt collapsed. Westmorland escaped to the Netherlands and would reappear in various intrigues against the Crown. Northumberland was captured by the Scots and returned to Elizabeth in 1572 for £2,000. Cecil lost no opportunity to subdue the north after the destruction of the two traditional magnates. In the evaluation of John Guy, Elizabeth and Cecil "enforce[d] compliance, acting with a degree of severity that reflected their sense of insecurity in the region."[118] The anti-Cecil faction was apparently destroyed; the traditional leaders of the north were in exile; Mary Stuart's party was weakened; and sound Protestantism was promoted throughout the north.

* * * * *

Of the three legates selected by Pope Pius IV for missions to the British Isles in the early 1560s, two were Jesuits. That should not be surprising, because Pius consistently demonstrated a marked preference for the Society and often employed Jesuits on papal missions, e.g. Diego Laínez at Poissy. The choice of David Wolfe is understandable: he had been a secular priest and dean of the chapter in Limerick. Moreover he retained an interest in Irish ecclesiastical affairs and protested Rome's ignorance in its choice of bishops. There was no equally obvious candidate for Scotland. Perhaps that was the reason for Salmerón's attempt to "shun" the honour. Nonetheless his selection of Nicholas de Gouda, given his physical state and linguistic limitations, surprised Everard Mercurian and Diego Laínez. The choice in 1566 of Edward Hay, now a member of the Society, made much more sense. But, given Pius's fondness for the Society, perhaps a more interesting mystery is why the third envoy was not a Jesuit. As we shall see in the next chapter,

---

[116] Pius V to Duke of Alba, Rome 4 February 1570, CSP Rome (1558-71) 324-25; same to Thomas, Earl of Northumberland and Charles, Earl of Westmorland, Rome 20 February 1570, *ibid.*, 326-27.
[117] Lynch, *Spain 1516-1598*, p. 379.
[118] *Tudor England*, p. 275.

there were English Jesuits in Flanders and Rome familiar with developments in their native land. One of them, Thomas Darbyshire, was considered as a companion for Hay in 1566. Perhaps we shall never know why Pius passed over the Society for this position. As a result the only Jesuits directly involved in England were William Good as he travelled to Ireland, Hay on his return from Scotland, and Thomas King, who worked there for nearly a year before his death in 1565.[119]

The Scottish missions were brief. De Gouda and Hay were sent for specific purposes, and once their goals were achieved they returned to the continent. The mission to Ireland was more stable. Wolfe received two Jesuit assistants, Good and the scholastic Edmund Daniel. Under their direction a school was established. Wolfe had papal authorization for erection of a university, and he and the General discussed the possibility of opening a novitiate in Ulster. It looked as if the Society intended to remain. But subsequent developments led superiors on the continent to reconsider.

The Irish mission raised issues that will recur throughout the Society's history in the British Isles. The first was the danger of political involvement. Preaching the gospel and reenforcing popular Catholicism may not *in se* be political acts, but they had political ramifications when they went counter to official governmental policy. The Society was able to work much more effectively in areas beyond the Pale, beyond English control. Although William Good seems to have won over the conciliatory Sir Thomas Cusacke, official approval for public teaching would be granted only if the Jesuits promised that they would not celebrate Mass publicly and that they would have nothing to do with Wolfe. Cusacke had proclaimed Wolfe a traitor. Although the sources give no reason for the accusation, it seems clear that he was associating with the Irish chieftains. It would have been impossible for him to ignore the struggle of the Lord Deputy against the O'Neills and the FitzGeralds, especially when the Irish waved the papal banner and proclaimed their rebellion a crusade. The Society's future in Ireland depended on their success; their defeat and the consequent English supremacy could result in a thorough destruction of Catholicism and the establishment of Protestantism. Did a Jesuit's desire to "save souls" include supporting the chieftains? Were there limits to the type of assistance a religious could provide?

Spiritually the mission made excessive demands on the men. From the beginning Wolfe complained of loneliness and depression. Good wailed about conditions. The rumours about Wolfe and his women testified to the difficulty in living religious life without proper supports. The rumours may not have been true but they were so strong that they aroused the suspicions

---

[119] What little we know of King's activities will be discussed in the next chapter.

of the Society's friend the Archbishop of Armagh. Would it be possible to pursue the Jesuit "way of proceeding," the Jesuit style of religious life, in such conditions? Good insisted that it was not the "mind of the Society" to expose its men to such dangers. Apparently the General and De Costere agreed: they ordered the Jesuits to leave Ireland. But it was too late for Wolfe—he was already in prison.

CHAPTER THREE

"ACCORDING TO THE SPIRIT OF THE SOCIETY"

On 25 February 1570 the rupture between Elizabeth and the Catholic Church was completed with the promulgation of Pope Pius V's *Regnans in Excelsis*.[1] In virtue of his office as Peter's successor, the Pope complained that "the number of the ungodly has grown so strong in power" that there was no place in the world still free from their corruption. The "pretended Queen of England," because she gave sanctuary to the most notorious offenders, played a significant role in this growth. After a litany of her offences, which range from the promotion of "obscure heretical men" to the persecution of the faithful, Pius V confessed that he was obliged to act and thus "out of the plenitude of our apostolic power we declare the aforesaid Elizabeth to be heretic and an abetter of heretics, and we declare her, together with her supporters in the above-said matters, to have incurred the sentence of excommunication and to be cut off from the unity of the Body of Christ." Elizabeth was deprived of her claim to the crown, and all her subjects were absolved from any oath of allegiance or fealty that they may have sworn. The final blow was the command that her subjects must not obey her and the threat that those who persisted in their loyalty would be similarly excommunicated.[2] Thomas H. Clancy, S.J., has argued that "It would be a mistake to think that this papal Bull had a great impact in England." Although it is true that the majority of the people were unaware of its existence, it would be a mistake to underestimate its impact. Because of the bull, the government's qualms about the allegiance of Catholics were reinforced. The result

---

[1] In the Jesuit archives in Rome there is a copy of a petition to the Pope from unnamed English Catholics that dates from this period. It mentions that Elizabeth has held the throne for ten years and that the time is now ripe for the formation of a coalition to depose her and to arrange the marriage of the Duke of Norfolk and the imprisoned Mary Stuart. To assist this proposal the petition asks the Pope to excommunicate the Queen (ARSI, Fondo Gesuitico 651/598). Is there a connection between this petition and Pius V's letter to the Duke of Alba, cited in the last chapter and written without the knowledge of Philip II a few months before the promulgation of the bull, that urged an attack on England (CSP Rome [1558-71] 314). As we have seen, Alba rejected the proposal as unfeasible because it would require three armies: one for the conquest of England, the second to protect the enterprise from the King of France, and the third to defend the Netherlands against the Germans. See William S. Maltby, *Alba* (Berkeley, 1983) pp. 194-96.

[2] An English translation of the papal bull can be found in Sidney Z. Ehler and John B. Morrall, eds., *Church and State Through the Centuries* (Westminster, Md., 1954) pp. 181-83.

was the introduction of new penal legislation and the formulation of the "Bloody Questions." The bull also encouraged foreign coalitions against Elizabeth.[3]

Official reaction was swift. John Felton posted the bull on the door of the palace of the Bishop of London in May, an offence for which he was executed on 8 August 1570. On 1 July 1570 a royal proclamation ordered the arrest of anyone who circulated seditious books and bulls "as it were from Rome, thereby with untruths and falsehoods, yea, with divers monstrous absurdities to the slander of the nobility and council of the realm, and not sparing also in the same to utter high treasons against the estate and royal dignity of her majesty, to engender in the heads of the simple ignorant multitude a misliking or murmuring against the quiet government of the realm."[4] Although the Northern Revolt had collapsed by the time the bull appeared, its contents and the rebellion were linked by the Elizabethan government in subsequent propaganda as cause and effect. The equation was a simple one for the government: Protestants were loyal to their Queen; Catholics were traitors.[5]

Most of the attention of Elizabeth's third Parliament (April and May of 1571) was focused on the effects of the Northern Revolt and the need to counter the papal bull.[6] Thus legislation aimed at protection of the government and control of the Catholics was passed. Reconciliation with the Church of Rome and recognition of the pope's spiritual jurisdiction were forbidden (13 Eliz. c. 2). Anyone who brought a papal bull into the kingdom, sought absolution from a papal representative, or granted said absolution was guilty of high treason. A second law (13 Eliz. c. 3) dealt with religious exiles, whom the government blamed for the Northern Revolt, by seeking to deprive them of their estates in England. Surprisingly, however, an attempt to extend the Act of Uniformity to demand reception of communion was defeated. The sensitive subject of the Queen's marriage

---

[3] The best treatment of the papal deposing power remains Thomas H. Clancy, S.J., "English Catholics and the Papal Deposing Power 1570-1640," *RH* 6 (1961) 114-40, 205-27; 7 (1963) 2-10. The citation comes from 115.

[4] Paul L. Hughes and James F. Larkin, C.S.V., eds., *Tudor Royal Proclamations*, 3 vols. (New Haven, 1964-69) II, 341. A subsequent proclamation (*ibid.*, 347-48) commanded all good subjects "to employ their uttermost diligence in the apprehension of such secret persuaders of disobedience and breaking of laws, and of the sowers and stirrers of sedition, and specially of such as do or shall bring into the realm any seditious books, writings, or such like traitorous devices against the laws and government of the realm or any wise prejudicial to the royal estate of her majesty."

[5] On the identification of Protestantism and patriotism during Elizabeth's reign see Gillian E. Brennan, "Papists and Patriotism in Elizabethan England," *RH* 19 (1988) 1-15; and Geoffrey de C. Parmiter, "The Imprisonment of Papists in Private Castles," *RH* 19 (1988) 16-38.

[6] J.E. Neale, *Elizabeth I and Her Parliaments*, 2 vols. (London, 1953, 1957) I, 177-240; T.E. Hartley, ed., *Proceedings in the Parliaments of Elizabeth I* (Leicester, 1981) pp. 179-258.

was not raised, and the issue of succession was dealt with only indirectly in the treatment of Mary Queen of Scots.

II

An unnamed English petitioner, probably a fugitive after the Northern Revolt, drafted a series of reflections on the state of England in the autumn of 1570. The kingdom's condition was truly deplorable, not simply because of the persecution endured by the faithful, but also "because Catholic Princes, who with slight exertion might make a riddance of all this evil" do nothing. The English had expected some assistance from abroad and they received nothing. If the foreign powers were not going to aid the persecuted English, they should at least refrain from assisting their common enemy. The author suggested that the Catholic kings recall their ambassadors and forbid all commerce with England. This could be done without any risk or loss on the part of the Catholic powers. But the author wanted more: because of the old alliance between the French and the Scots, the French should send some soldiers to aid the Catholic lords to expel the English army and open Scotland for Catholicism.[7] After the excommunication of Elizabeth, schemes and plots directed towards her deposition proliferated. Although most remained unfulfilled wishes and unrealised projects, their circulation rendered the Queen's position extremely precarious.

English pirates in the Caribbean and the seizure of the money intended for Alba's troops had antagonized Philip. He had contemplated providing some assistance for the Northern Revolt; even after its failure, he still considered some type of attack against Elizabeth either directly or through Ireland. On the other hand, Philip opposed the Queen's excommunication, issued without consulting him, because it "will embitter feelings in England and drive the Queen and her friends to oppress and persecute the few good Catholics who still remain there."[8] Another objection to the excommunication of Elizabeth was the fear that her deposition would indirectly benefit the French by encouraging all to consider Mary Queen of Scots not just as the heir but as the rightful monarch. We have already noted how the Duke of Alba had prevented any expedition against England because he realized that

---

[7] CSP Rome (1572-78) 549-54. There follows immediately another memorial written to encourage Philip II to assist Mary Queen of Scots and to show him how this assistance will not ultimately benefit the French (554-55).

[8] Philip II to Duke of Alba, Madrid 16 December 1569, CSP Simancas (1568-79) 217-18; Guerau de Spes to Philip II, London 18 January 1570, *ibid.*, 228-30; same to same, London 13 May 1570, *ibid.*, 244-45; same to same, London 12 June 1570, *ibid.*, 245-46; Philip II to Guerau de Spes, The Escorial 30 June 1570, *ibid.* 254-55; John Lynch, *Spain 1516-1598: From Nation State to World Empire* (Oxford, 1991) pp. 378-79.

Spain's resources were already overstretched and could not endure a war on another front. The revolt of the Moriscos in Granada and the resurgence of Ottoman strength in the western Mediterranean were more immediate concerns and threats. Until the victory of the Holy League of Venice, the papacy, and Spain at the battle of Lepanto on 7 October 1571, Philip could sacrifice few troops for further involvement in northern Europe.

The Dutch too were aware that Spanish military power was overextended and took full advantage of Spanish preoccupation with the Turks. Because of the naval battles in the Mediterranean, the powerful Spanish army in the Netherlands was without sufficient naval support. Thus it was unable to deal adequately with the Sea-Beggars. In an attempt to reduce tension, Elizabeth expelled them from English ports in February of 1572. The expulsion only aggravated the problem. The Beggars seized the city of Brill on 1 April and from that base expanded to other towns. Their success encouraged others to renew the rebellion. With the resources at hand, however, Alba was more worried about his southern border with France than with the immediate gains of the rebels in the north. Since the end of the most recent religious war in September of 1570, Huguenot influence over King Charles IX increased. By the summer of 1572 the King was almost persuaded to intervene actively in the Dutch revolt. In return for his support France would receive the Flemish coast and much of the southern Netherlands. Anxious not to commit himself totally to a war with Spain, Charles only allowed a French army of 6000 men to advance into the Low Countries to aid the rebels at Mons. The army, however, was ambushed and defeated at St. Ghislain with the result that Charles IX was no longer sure of the wisdom of intervention. Without French assistance the rebels were pushed back by Alba's forces. The subsequent fighting frequently resulted in atrocities committed by both sides. Despite these successes Philip decided to replace Alba in 1573. His successor, Don Luis de Requesens, Governor of Lombardy, arrived in Brussels on 17 November and was sworn in as Alba's successor on the 29th.[9] According to John Lynch, Philip realized that a change was needed because Alba's methods were failing. Advocate of a more moderate approach, Requesens abolished the Council of Troubles and issued a general pardon on 5 June 1574. But the change occasioned no concessions on the part of the rebels, and Requesens was obliged to turn to the army to implement his policies. Unfortunately for the Spanish cause, the army, although victorious, turned mutinous because of the lack of supplies and pay. Antwerp was occupied, and Requesens had to negotiate to prevent the destruction of the city. This was but one of a series of mutinies caused by the crown's failure to pay the soldiers. Throughout 1574 the estimated cost

---

[9] Peter Limm, *The Dutch Revolt 1559-1648* (London, 1989) pp. 36-40.

of maintaining the army in Flanders was 1.2 million florins a month, a sum greater than the King's income from the Indies and Castile combined. In 1575 Philip declared bankruptcy for the second time and repudiated his debts. But before he took this drastic step he sought to end the war in the Netherlands through diplomacy. In November of 1574 he instructed Requesens to initiate a peace conference with William (the Silent) of Orange, Prince of Nassau. The conference was held in Breda in March of 1575. Because of Philip's refusal to grant religious toleration to the Calvinists, the talks solved nothing. The Prince then renounced his allegiance to Philip and offered sovereignty to Elizabeth and to Henry, Duke of Anjou. Since neither was eager to accept the offer, William had to continue the war alone.[10]

III

Spain was too involved in wars against the Dutch and the Ottoman empire to take advantage of any opportunity against England. Nonetheless England remained vulnerable to attack from Scotland and from Ireland. After the collapse of the latest Irish rebellion in 1570, James FitzMaurice FitzGerald remained free. His military campaign continued until he finally submitted to Sir John Perrot, president of Munster, in early 1573. A few years later FitzMaurice fled to France to seek foreign assistance in his attempt to prevent the English from reducing the entire island to submission.[11]

After the collapse of the rebellion, attempts were made at the Irish Parliament in 1569 to introduce legislation against the recusants as severe as the laws in England. These, however, failed even though the government had packed the house. Not all the Irish supported the rebellion, but few were in favour of more repressive legislation.[12]

Even without FitzMaurice, Ireland remained volatile. Walter Devereux, created Earl of Essex in 1572, was granted almost all of Antrim by Elizabeth. His attempts to colonize the area met fierce opposition from the Scots and the Irish. His major foe was, of course, an O'Neill: Turlough Luineach, Lord of Tyrone and successor to Shane O'Neill. Although he had renounced the name of O'Neill and accepted the terms of Shane O'Neill's forfeiture when he (Turlough Luineach) submitted to Sir Henry Sidney in

---

[10] Lynch, *Spain 1516-1598*, pp. 403-04; Limm, *Dutch Revolt*, 40-43.
[11] G.A. Hayes-McCoy, "Conciliation, Coercion, and the Protestant Reformation, 1547-71," in *A New History of Ireland: III Early Modern Ireland 1534-1691*, eds. T.W. Moody, F.X. Martin, and F.J. Byrne (Oxford, 1991) pp. 90-93; Colm Lennon, *Sixteenth Century Ireland: The Incomplete Conquest* (Dublin, 1994) pp. 215-16.
[12] Robert Dudley Edwards, *Church and State in Tudor Ireland* (London, 1935) pp. 199-200.

1567, his marriage to the Scot Agnes Campbell, widow of James MacDonald, in 1569 aroused English suspicions. The powerful Earl of Argyll, a supporter of Mary Queen of Scots and the dominant force in the western Highlands, was Agnes's brother. Fears of an alliance between strong Scots and Irish chieftains were strengthened when Agnes's daughter Finola, known as the "Dark Daughter," married the other Ulster chief Hugh O'Donnell. Mother and daughter schemed to use Scottish forces to defend Ulster's independence from the English authorities in Dublin. But the English were apprehensive that this network of alliances would affect more than the government of Ireland, especially in light of various rumours of French assistance.[13]

Scotland remained quiet as the pro-English Protestant Regent tightly controlled the kingdom's affairs. James Stuart, Earl of Moray, was a powerful Regent strongly opposed to Mary Queen of Scots. He and the English thus worked well together as they fought to frustrate all attempts by Mary and the Queen's party to regain the reins of power. His assassination on 23 January 1570 shocked England and encouraged the Queen's party to reassert themselves by proclaiming that they were the legitimate government because they had a commission from the Queen. Without the Earl of Moray there was no one to prevent the fugitive northern rebels, the Earl of Westmorland and Leonard, Lord Dacre, from reorganizing their forces with the assistance of sympathetic supporters along the borders.

The Queen's party was also encouraged by the renewed interest that King Charles IX took in Mary. Because France was more tranquil internally, he could turn his attention to foreign affairs (we have noted how the Huguenots tried to persuade him to intervene in the Netherlands) and he was afraid that Spain would use the Scottish Queen to its own advantage. Hence the French ambassador began to encourage the Duke of Norfolk as an alternative to a Spanish suitor. French concerns were especially aroused when an English army under the direction of Thomas Radcliffe, Earl of Sussex, crossed the border to deal with the Scottish lords who were still aiding the English rebels. In March of 1570 the French envoy to Scotland let it be known that Charles IX was raising an army to be sent to Dumbarton. A month later Charles IX demanded the withdrawal of the English army. The French threats were real, and Queen Elizabeth feared that the situation would

---

[13] G.A. Hayes-McCoy, "The Completion of the Tudor Conquest and the Advance of the Counter-reformation, 1571-1603," in *A New History of Ireland: III Early Modern Ireland 1534-1691*, eds. T.W. Moody, F.X. Martin, and F.J. Byrne (Oxford, 1991) pp. 94-99. On the roles played by Agnes and Finola Campbell see William Palmer, "Gender, Violence, and Rebellion in Tudor and Early Stuart Ireland," *SCJ* 23 (1992) 701-03. Regarding French assistance see the discussion of Cormac O'Fergus's confessions in Thomas S. Flynn, O.P., *The Irish Dominicans 1536-1641* (Dublin, 1993) pp. 53-57.

deteriorate further, especially if Spain supported the French position. Despite the Queen's hesitation Sussex continued his military campaign even to the extent of providing strong support for the King's party. The Queen, however, drew the line and forbade him to assist the attack on Dumbarton, with the injunction that assistance of that type would of necessity result in a war with Charles IX. Because of French threats Elizabeth offered to withdraw English forces from Scotland and to open diplomatic negotiations with Mary if the French promised to send no troops. Charles IX accepted the conditions.[14]

In July of 1570 the King's supporters elected a new Regent: Matthew Stuart, Earl of Lennox. Not surprisingly the Queen's party would not accept this decision. As both sides prepared for the negotiations regarding Mary Stuart that were to be held in England, the remaining leaders of the northern rebellion slipped out of Scotland to Flanders.

Under Moray and Lennox, new legislation was introduced against the Catholics. The Parliament summoned in December of 1567 by Moray renewed the earlier edicts against saying Mass etc. The first Parliament convoked by Lennox at Stirling in 1571 ordered the removal of all popish decorations from the Chapel Royal in Stirling. Although there were no Jesuits in the kingdom, the Society became involved in a theological dispute with John Knox. The brother of the Scottish Jesuit James Tyrie abandoned Catholicism for Knox's Protestantism. To win back his brother, Tyrie addressed a long letter to him in which the Jesuit defended the traditional doctrines of Catholicism against the novelties of Protestantism. The letter achieved its aim: Tyrie's brother returned to Catholicism. Its success, however, prompted Knox to write a rejoinder, *An Answer to a Letter of a Jesuit named Tyrie*. Tyrie's reply *The refutation of ane answer made be schir Iohne Knox, to ane letter, send be Iames Tyrie, to his umquhyle brother* appeared in 1573.[15] Any possibility of the debate's continuing died with Knox on 24 November 1572.[16]

Throughout the last half of 1570 Mary's prospects were auspicious. Among the Privy Councillors the anti-Cecil faction remained favourably disposed to Mary and the Duke of Norfolk despite events of the previous year, and strove to achieve a peaceful settlement with France regarding Scotland, and with Spain regarding the Low Countries. This party was

---

[14] Wallace MacCaffrey, *The Shaping of the Elizabethan Regime: Elizabethan Politics 1558-1572* (London, 1969) pp. 247-50.
[15] (Paris, 1573) STC 24476, ARCR, II, no. 746 (sections were published in Thomas Graves Law, ed., *Catholic Tractates of the Sixteenth Century (1573-1600)* [Edinburgh/London, 1901] xxx-xxxv, Scottish Text Society 45).
[16] Alphons Bellesheim, *History of the Catholic Church of Scotland*, 4 vols. (Edinburgh/London, 1887-90) III, 225-38.

strengthened by the public support of the Earl of Leicester. Debate between the two factions was often bitter. The Cecil faction raised all the traditional fears of an anti-Protestant crusade against Elizabeth, the existence of which, they claimed, was witnessed in Pope Pius V's bull of excommunication. The anti-Protestant crusade would be even more powerful with a restored Mary in Scotland as heir to the English throne. The anti-Cecil faction contended that the French were not hostile towards England and that their grievances were just. The conclusion of the religious wars with the peace of St. Germain in August and the crushing defeat of the revolt of the Moriscos, along with a temporary lull in the conflict in the Low Countries, left France and Spain free to deal with England if the problems were not settled diplomatically. Cecil's position ironically could have caused the very crusade that he feared.

The negotiations regarding Mary started at Chatsworth in the autumn and continued throughout the winter. Cecil and the King's party delayed and blocked the proceedings at every opportunity. Cecil demanded apparently unacceptable conditions for Mary's release and return to Scotland. Regardless of how strict the conditions were, the King's party feared that Mary's return would destroy their future. Both prolonged the discussions and raised difficulties whenever possible. The entire issue was postponed in March of 1571 when the King's party claimed that it could not continue without authorization from the Scottish Parliament. On the 23rd Elizabeth decreed that further discussion would be postponed until May. Ultimately more damaging to Mary's cause than the postponement was the initiation of a marital alliance between Elizabeth and the Duke of Anjou, a possibility that made French pursuit of England more attractive than support of Scotland.[17] If Mary retained any hope of restoration it was destroyed by the discovery of the Ridolfi Plot.

In the spring of 1571 the government seized the baggage of Charles Bailly, a Scotsman living in France, as he entered the country through Dover. Within were found a number of letters. Through his use of spies and agents and through careful monitoring of the correspondence, Cecil "discovered" the Ridolfi Plot, in which Mary Stuart and Norfolk were again the chief actors. Financed and supported by Spain and the Pope, the plot concerned the deposition of Elizabeth and her replacement with Mary, safely married to Norfolk. Norfolk was tried and convicted of treason in January of 1572, but Elizabeth hesitated over his execution and over the fate of Mary. Demands that Mary be attainted were ignored by Elizabeth, who

---

[17] MacCaffrey, *Shaping of the Elizabethan Regime*, pp. 251-60; Robert Ashton, *Reformation and Revolution 1558-1660* (London, 1985) pp. 112-13; Susan Doran, *Monarchy and Matrimony: The Courtships of Elizabeth I* (London, 1996) pp. 99-129.

feared taking such action against a rightful monarch. Ultimately Elizabeth did nothing against Mary, but Norfolk was executed in June. Although Cecil had not succeeded in eliminating Mary as heir to the throne, he had removed his last major opponent.[18] Mary, however, deprived of her most powerful supporter within England and of any possible French support, because of the discussion of a marriage treaty between the Duke of Anjou and Queen Elizabeth, had no alternative but to continue to hope for Spanish assistance. Since that assistance was not forthcoming, her supporters in Scotland lost ground. Even though the pro-English Earl of Lennox was assassinated on 4 September 1571, the King's party continued to control the regency. John Erskine, Earl of Mar, acted as Regent until his death by natural causes on 28 October 1572. The fourth Regent, James Douglas, Earl of Morton, held the position until he was toppled in 1578.[19] Elizabeth consistently backed the Scottish regents. As long as they remained in power, Elizabeth had nothing to fear from an attack from the north.

Elizabeth's fourth Parliament met in May of 1572 as Norfolk sat in the Tower of London, awaiting execution. Understandably the major topic was Mary Queen of Scots and the need to take action against her. In order to preserve Queen, country, and the established religion, her execution was demanded. Sir Thomas Scott argued that popery was the root cause of all the country's problems. Indeed the continued presence of Papists in all levels of the kingdom's government simply encouraged the Pope, the King of Spain, and Catholic rebels. His solution was execution of the Scottish Queen and the English Duke, denial of right of succession to Mary's heirs, and settlement of the succession on a more worthy candidate.[20]

Attacks on Norfolk[21] and Mary Stuart, and their denunciations as traitors, resulted in the appearance of the first Catholic political pamphlet, *Treatise of Treasons*, in 1572.[22] In the *Aeneid* Virgil tells the story of the deceitful

---

[18] Although most historians would agree that Cecil carefully exploited the plot and used it for the destruction of his political enemies, Francis Edwards, S.J., would like to move a step further. He sees the plot as a Cecilian concoction to destroy Mary and the Catholic faction. See *The Dangerous Queen* (London, 1964) and *The Marvellous Chance* (London, 1968).

[19] Jenny Wormald, *Court, Kirk, and Community: Scotland 1470-1625* (Edinburgh, 1981) pp. 145-46.

[20] Neale, *Elizabeth I and Her Parliaments*, I, 241-312; Hartley, *Proceedings*, I, 259-418.

[21] Norfolk had been maligned in the anonymous *Salutem in Christo. Good men and evill delite in contraryes* ([London], 1571) STC 11504. The pamphlet lacks a title page but was signed R.G. It is generally believed that William Cecil was the author.

[22] *A Treatise of Treasons against Q. Elizabeth, and the Croune of England* ([Louvain], 1572) STC 7601, ARCR, II, no. 502. On authorship of this work see Thomas H. Clancy, S.J., "A Political Pamphlet: *The Treatise of Treasons* (1572)," in *Loyola Studies in the Humanities*, ed. G. Eberle (New Orleans, 1962) pp. 15-30; and Peter Holmes, *Resistance and Compromise: The Political Thought of the English Catholics* (Cambridge, 1982) pp. 23-26. A much shorter summary, *A Table gathered owt of a Booke named A Treatise of treasons* ([n.p.n.d.] STC 23617.5, ARCR, II, no. 742) appeared the following year.

but eloquent Sinon, who persuaded the Trojans to open their gates and receive the horse left by the departing Greeks. There were two Sinons in England: William Cecil and Nicholas Bacon. They were the true traitors, said the pamphlet, not those attacked in Parliament. Cecil and Bacon were responsible for the religious changes and for the failure to settle the question of succession. Their motives for doing nothing about the second were totally selfish. On 28 September 1573 the government retaliated with a proclamation ordering the confiscation and destruction of this work.[23]

Cecil was apparently much more affected by the appearance of *Treatise of Treasons* than Bacon. Perhaps it cut a little too close to the bone. What effect the pamphlet had on Elizabeth, we do not know. But she could not be induced either to judge the imprisoned Mary or to exclude her from succession because of her involvement in the plots. Elizabeth had no qualms about Norfolk, who was executed. None of the other remedies proposed in Parliament were used.

Attempts to conclude a marriage alliance between France and England foundered. From an English perspective the negotiations served their purpose: they diverted French support from Mary through the allure of a dynastic marriage. The Duke of Anjou, to the distress of his mother, provided the English with good grounds for abandoning negotiations by his insistence on religious concessions. Both countries were apprehensive of Spain so they were reluctant to abandon a treaty totally. When France proposed a different treaty, with Francis, Duke of Alençon, youngest son of Catherine de Medici, as the husband, negotiations were renewed. The defensive Treaty of Blois was signed on 19 April 1572, but without a marriage clause. The treaty benefitted England: the new alliance would discourage any Spanish threat.

The cordial relations between France and England, however, were not long-lived. The St. Bartholomew's Day massacres of some three thousand Huguenots in Paris between 24 and 30 August, and of some ten thousand others throughout the kingdom in the following week, substantiated Elizabethan fears of an international conspiracy to end Protestantism. Englishmen were warned of the fate that awaited them if Catholicism were restored through the succession of Mary Stuart. As a result of the massacres, the Guises returned to power and the religious wars were renewed.[24] The

---

[23] Hughes and Larkin, *Tudor Royal Proclamations*, II, 376-79.
[24] On events in Paris that led to the massacres see Barbara B. Diefendorf, *Beneath the Cross: Catholics and Huguenots in Sixteenth Century Paris* (Oxford, 1991). On the massacres see A.G. Dickens, "The Elizabethans and St. Bartholomew," in *Reformation Studies* (London, 1982) pp. 471-89; Robert M. Kingdon, "Reactions to the St. Bartholomew Massacres in Geneva and Rome," in *The Massacre of St. Bartholomew*, ed. Alfred Soman (The Hague, 1975) pp. 25-49; A. Lynn Martin, "The Jesuit Emond Auger and The Saint Bartholomew's Massacre at

death of Charles IX on 30 May 1574 and the accession of the Duke of Anjou as Henry III consolidated the Guises' control over the country.[25] So afraid was Elizabeth that France would finally act in favour of Mary that she began to make overtures to Philip in the hope of ending their hostility.[26] These overtures lost their urgency when Henry, influenced by his brother the Duke of Alençon, adopted more moderate religious policies. On 5 May 1576 Henry issued the Edict of Beaulieu, also known as the Peace of Monsieur because of Alençon's influence, that allowed the Huguenots free public exercise of their religion for the first time.[27]

Despite Philip's involvement in military campaigns on many fronts, and his deteriorating finances, English and Irish Catholic exiles continued to look towards him as the one ruler who could restore Catholicism in their kingdoms.[28] Any possibility that France would defend the rights of Catholics and work for the deposition of Elizabeth had been abandoned because of the French quest for a marriage alliance with England, and later because of its own internal religious policies. On 10 August 1572 a number of English Catholic exiles, including William Allen, Thomas Stapleton, and Thomas Harding, drafted a memorial to Pope Gregory XIII, who had been elected Pope on 14 May. In a covering letter addressed to Giovanni, Cardinal Morone, they mourned:

> Alas, most illustrious Cardinal, anguish is to be found in the sacrilegious pestilence of schism and heresy, and with the sad loss of many souls and its calamitous disturbance of the whole Christian world, the kingdom of England, once mighty and noble, and certainly pre-eminent and glorious among those lands which gave their allegiance to Christ, has now long lain sick.

The authors, however, did not abandon hope because

Bordeaux: The Final Word?," in *Regnum, Religio et Ratio: Essays presented to Robert M. Kingdon*, ed. Jerome Friedman (Kirksville, 1987) pp. 117-24; N.M. Sutherland, *The Massacre of St. Bartholomew and the European Conflict 1559-1572* (London, 1973); and Robert M. Kingdon, *Myths about the St. Bartholomew's Day Massacres, 1572-1576* (Cambridge, Mass., 1988). In "Reactions," Kingdon interprets papal approval of what had taken place in France as a sign of the new militancy of the Counter-Reformation and of "a heightened conviction in Rome that violence is an effective way to handle Protestant opposition, that war, massacre, and assassination are justifiable tools for advancing Christian truth." The success of the massacres was proof that "God was truly on their side and that violence works" (43).

[25] On Henry's religious policies see A. Lynn Martin, *Henry III and the Jesuit Politicians* (Geneva, 1973).

[26] A sign of the thaw between England and Spain was Alba's negotiation of the Convention of Nijmegen for restoration of trade between the two countries and of property seized (Lynch, *Spain 1516-1598*, p. 416).

[27] R.J. Knecht, *The French Wars of Religion 1559-1598* (London, 1989) pp. 54-56.

[28] On Irish Catholic attempts to arouse Philip's interest in their state see Patrick Francis Moran, *Spicilegium Ossoriense* (Dublin, 1874) pp. 59-70.

there may be found among those who, for the zeal of God's house grieve and lament with us such a great kingdom, and for such a deplorable loss of souls in it, and are willing as far as in them lies to come to its aid. God grant this as quickly as possible, so that even in all those who have been cut off and fallen away from it, the Apostolic see may inspire fear and terror, for otherwise it will be contemned and derided by them in their folly. . . .

In the memorial they begged that the Pope be mindful of the miseries and anguish of the Catholics in England. Through the efforts of his illustrious predecessor Pope Gregory the Great, the people of England received the Catholic faith. Now "those relapsed into heresy, [could] be brought back to the same faith, to the great rejoicing of the whole world, through the care, prudence and zeal of Gregory XIII." Although it appeared that many embraced heresy, the overwhelming majority were motivated by fear: "There are there infinite numbers of people, who through fear of loss of their possessions, and of imprisonment, even of death, frequent their impious communions, preachings and schismatical rites, although in their hearts, however, they execrate all heresy." Among the few Protestants were "certain obscure men" who advised the Queen. The exiles implored the Pope that "the outstanding work" began by his predecessor be completed: the excommunication of Elizabeth must be followed up by some military action.[29] Around the same time, another exile in Louvain, a former pirate and later a veteran of the battle of Lepanto, Sir Thomas Stucley,[30] drafted a memorial to King Philip in which he encouraged an invasion of Ireland timed to coincide with an insurrection led by Lord Dacre in the north of England. This invasion would result, according to Stucley, in the withdrawal of English and French forces from the Low Countries in order to face the new threat.[31]

The new Pope did in fact continue his predecessor's support for militant Counter-Reformation zeal. In the future he would encourage Philip to military action against the Calvinists in the Netherlands and in England. In the summer after his election he celebrated news of the St. Bartholomew's massacres with a *Te Deum* and other thanksgiving services for the victory of faith over infidelity. Gregory's secretary of state and closest advisor, Tolomeo Galli, Cardinal of Como, established contact with various Catholic causes throughout Europe. In late winter of 1573 Galli investigated another Spanish crusade against Elizabeth. There was no doubt that such action

---

[29] In Penelope Renold, ed., *Letters of William Allen and Richard Barret 1572-1598* (London, 1967) pp. 275-84. On Allen's involvement in schemes for the reconversion of England see Eamon Duffy, "William, Cardinal Allen, 1532-1594," *RH* 22 (1995) 280-88.

[30] For more on his intrigues see Anthony Kenny, "From Hospice to College," *The Venerabile* 20 (1960-1962) 3-11, 89-103, 171.

[31] [July 1572] CSP Rome (1572-78) 19-20. See also 20-25.

would be justified, but he feared that Spain would not act without France, which was then preoccupied with its own religious problems.[32] A few months later he suggested to Louis, Cardinal of Guise the Pope's recommendation that the Cardinal and his brother Charles, Cardinal of Lorraine should arrange for the kidnapping of James Stuart out of Scotland into the safe hands of the Guises in France. It is not clear from the sources whether proposals for an attack on England and for kidnapping James were related or distinct.[33] In the summer of 1573 Nicholas Sander gave his support.[34]

Sander had been involved with the English Catholic refugees in Louvain from 1564 to 1572 before he departed for Rome in January of 1572. There he remained until the late summer of 1573 when he was sent to Philip's court in Spain as accredited agent of the English exiles in Flanders.[35] Before his departure he received letters of recommendation from the Jesuit General Everard Mercurian and from the Pope. Galli informed the Spanish Nuncio that Sander was being sent to discuss with Philip matters that related to the service of God and the Church. Whatever those matters were, as Galli heard from Ormanetto in his reply, the King was interested.[36] Meanwhile other Englishmen, e.g. Sir Thomas Stucley, urged the King not to delay.[37]

---

[32] Father Hagan published much of the relevant correspondence concerning papal support for the Irish rebellion in "Miscellanea Vaticano-Hibernica, 1420-1631," *AH* 4 (1915) 219-22 and "Miscellanea Vaticano-Hibernica (1572-1585)," *AH* 7 (1918-22) 67-356. On the basis of his investigations he concluded: "But if the plans of Gregory XIII and his great Secretary of State, known to history as the Cardinal of Como, came to naught from the military point of view in Ireland, they were far from being utter failures. Estimating the events of that Pontificate in the light of the documentary evidence here presented, one can hardly fail to draw the conclusion that if the policy of Gregory XIII left England definitely Protestant and anti-papal, it lined up Ireland once for all on the side of Rome and banished effectually from the hearts of clerk and chief the wavering and uncertainty that had been so much in evidence throughout the whole generation that went before" (69).

[33] Galli to Nicholas Ormanetto, Apostolic Nuncio in Spain, [Rome February-March 1573], CSP Rome (1572-78) 94-95; same to Louis, Cardinal of Lorraine, Rome 7 September 1573, *ibid.*, 127-28.

[34] For more on Sander see Thomas McNevin Veech, *Dr. Nicholas Sanders and the English Reformation* (Louvain, 1935).

[35] Veech, *Sanders*, p. 202.

[36] Gregory XIII to Philip II, Rome 4 September 1573, CSP Rome (1572-78) 126; Tolomeo Galli to Nicholas Ormanetto, Rome 4 September 1573, *ibid.*, 126-27; Ormanetto to Galli, Madrid 26 November 1573, *ibid.*, 135; letter of commendation to Nicholas Sander, [c. end of August] 1573, ARSI, Hist. Soc. 61, f. 2^r. Mercurian, usually a prudent and cautious man, was enthusiastic in his support of Sander. In a letter written on 29 August 1573 to Father Francesco de Porres, Sander is called a true pillar of the Church. Because he has deserved well of the Society, Mercurian asked that all the Jesuits at Philip's court assist him (ARSI, Tolet. 1, f. 6^r). To Sander, Mercurian wrote on 8 February 1574 that he hoped Sander's hopes for England would be successful and that he and the other Jesuits would assist him in whatever way they could (ARSI, Tolet. 1, ff. 9^{r-v}). Sander's letter to Mercurian from Madrid on 25 December 1574, thanked him for his assistance and commended him on his great affection for England (ARSI, Hisp. 122, ff. 277^r-278^v).

[37] CSP Rome (1572-78) 138-40.

The exact nature of the enterprise had not yet been determined. The Nuncio in Spain suggested that the enterprise centre on Mary Queen of Scots, who would be married either to the Duke of Savoy or to Don Juan of Austria. According to the same source, the King was undecided as to the destination of the invasion. One possibility was Ireland. To expedite a decision, Ormanetto reminded Philip that England and Ireland were different kingdoms and that the bull of excommunication deprived Elizabeth of the crown of England but said nothing about her Irish title.[38]

The former Spanish ambassador in England supported an invasion of Ireland. Expelled from England because of his part in the Ridolfi Plot, Guerau de Spes returned to Spain in 1572 convinced that Ireland could be taken with a force of three or four thousand men and a competent fleet.[39] Once Ireland had been secured, it would provide an ideal base for conquering England. The conquest would even be easier if the Duke of Alba could be persuaded to join the venture. With Elizabeth deposed, Mary would be put forward as the legitimate Queen with the object of marrying her to a member of the Habsburg family.[40] All eyes were focused on Don Juan, who was imminently expected in Spain.[41] Among the proposals for an enterprise against England was one submitted by David Wolfe.

IV

The Jesuit mission to Ireland had been aborted. Although Edmund Daniel and William Good had been ordered to leave the island, only Good arrived in Belgium, sometime before 3 April 1570. In a letter to Francis Borgia, the Provincial Frans De Costere reported that Edmund Daniel had decided against travelling to Belgium because of the climate. He would, however, leave Ireland for Spain. Apparently there was some question regarding Daniel's continued membership in the Society, because De Costere argued that if he remained in the Society he must be removed from Ireland.[42] Daniel arrived in Lisbon by the following July. In his travels throughout the Iberian peninsula, he solicited money to ransom Wolfe, still imprisoned in Dublin

---

[38] Ormanetto to Galli, Madrid 25 October 1574, CSP Rome (1572-78) 187-89.

[39] His successor Bernardino de Mendoza arrived in England in March of 1578. He was instructed to inform the Queen that Philip had no intention of doing anything that would harm her, and he asked in return that she not aid his enemies (CSP Rome [1572-78] 179; Wallace T. MacCaffrey, *Elizabeth and the Making of Policy, 1572-1588* [Princeton, 1981] p. 315).

[40] CSP Simancas (1568-79) 386-88.

[41] Sander in a letter to Mercurian from Madrid on 31 March 1575 explained that hopes for an enterprise were now very high because of the arrival of Don Juan. He again thanked Mercurian for the Society's assistance and claimed that God was using the Society as his instrument in this matter (ARSI, Ital. 146, ff. 330^{r-v}, 331^v).

[42] De Costere to Borgia, Antwerp, 3 April 1570, ARSI, Germ. 151, ff. 93^r-94^v.

Castle. It is not known whether Daniel had the General's approval for his efforts at raising ransom. It seems rather unlikely that Borgia, who had ordered Daniel out of Ireland, would permit him to become involved in a task that resulted in his return to Ireland by the end of the month.[43] Apparently the amount collected was not sufficient, and within two years Daniel was back on the continent in quest of more money. Sometime after his return to Ireland in 1572 he was arrested and charged with bringing apostolic letters addressed to FitzMaurice. More important was the accusation that Daniel carried into Ireland a copy of Pius V's bull of excommunication. The copy was addressed to FitzMaurice, presumably to encourage him to continue his resistance. Daniel was arrested in Limerick but tried in Cork, where he was hanged, drawn, and quartered on 25 October 1572.[44]

Daniel's second attempt to secure Wolfe's release was partially successful.[45] To supplement the money collected, Wolfe borrowed more from a merchant and promised to reimburse him in Lisbon. He was released from prison in September of 1572. He remained in Ireland a year and, according to the Irish Jesuit historian Prionsias Ó Fionnagáin, abandoned his allegiance to the English Queen. Having concluded that the only way to preserve the Catholic faith in Ireland was by repudiating English rule, he cast his lot with James FitzMaurice FitzGerald. On 17 September 1573 Wolfe and a young child, accompanied by his bailsman, boarded a Portuguese ship. On the 29th the ship docked at Bayonne.[46] What happened to Wolfe thereafter is still somewhat mysterious and controversial.

After a pilgrimage to Santiago de Compostela, Wolfe separated from his bailsman and proceeded to Lisbon. Before their separation, however, Wolfe

---

[43] Leo Henriques to Francis Borgia, Lisbon 30 July 1570, ARSI, Lus. 64, ff. 79^r-81^v. On the collection of ransom money see Prionsias Ó Fionnagáin, *The Jesuit Missions to Ireland in the Sixteenth Century* (n.p. n.d. [privately printed]) pp. 27-29.

[44] Ó Fionnagáin, *Jesuit Missions to Ireland*, p. 29; Louis McRedmond, *To The Greater Glory: A History of the Irish Jesuits* (Dublin, 1991) p. 23.

[45] There were rumours that Wolfe had caused scandal in Ireland because he escaped from prison after giving his word that he would not (Pedro Trigoso to Juan de Polanco, Antwerp 1573, in D. Restrepo, S.J., and Dionysius Fernández [Zapico], *Polanci complementa, epistolae et commentaria P. Joannis Alphonsi de Polanco e Societate Jesu*, 2 vols. [Madrid, 1916-17] II, 300-01). According to Ó Fionnagáin, the rumours lacked foundation (*Jesuit Missions to Ireland*, p. 30).

[46] Ó Fionnagáin, *Jesuit Missions to Ireland*, pp. 29-30. See also Manuel da Costa, S.J., "The Last Years of a Confessor of the Faith: Father David Wolf," *AHSI* 15 (1946) 127-43. This article is the source of much of Ó Fionnagáin's analysis of Wolfe's release from prison and subsequent activities on the continent. Ó Fionnagáin states that there were no Jesuits in Ireland from the departure of Wolfe until the arrival of Charles Lee, who arrived with the former Jesuit Bishop Edmund Tanner in November of 1576. However, William Good wrote to Borgia from Louvain on 1 November 1572 that Robert Rochford had crossed to Ireland from France and had opened a small school in Wexford (ARSI, Germ. 141, ff. 1^r-4^v).

had to swear in the presence of the Jesuit superior in Oporto that he would not flee Portugal or seek to avoid paying the money owed. On 11 November 1573 Wolfe arrived at São Roque, the Jesuit professed house in Lisbon. Shortly thereafter he asked the Portuguese Provincial and the rector of the college in Lisbon for money to repay the Irish merchant. They replied that they were unable to give him anything until they had received the approval of Father General. Thus Wolfe had nothing to give the bailsman when he arrived in Lisbon at the end of November. Angered that there was no money, the merchant complained loudly and publicly that he had been deceived by the Jesuits and he demanded that Wolfe return to Ireland with him. Wolfe pleaded with the Provincial and argued that he would be exposed to considerable dangers if he were forced to return to Ireland as he had promised. On the advice of some Jesuits in Lisbon, Wolfe begged for money throughout the city. Upon his return to Lisbon, the Provincial decided that it was better to pay the merchant some money than to permit Wolfe to beg. The merchant received approximately half the amount due him and was promised the rest once the Provincial received approval from Father General.[47]

Subsequent payment was delayed by two disturbing reports. An Irishman at the University of Coimbra informed the Jesuit rector of rumours received from Ireland that Wolfe had been guilty of serious violations against faith and morals: "It is commonly reported in Ireland that Father David had carnal knowledge of a niece and from this there had been offspring and that when he served as Nuncio he took bribes and he secured his release by swearing to obey the Queen's laws." The second report related a growing conviction that the money was not meant to pay Wolfe's ransom but to purchase arms for FitzMaurice's rebellion.[48]

Juan Borgia, son of the late Jesuit General Francis Borgia, was Spanish ambassador to Portugal. Wolfe met him a few times, and it was he who persuaded Philip II to support FitzMaurice's son at the Jesuit college in Lisbon. This son was the young boy who accompanied Wolfe to the continent, although the same rumours that accused Wolfe of religious and moral laxity suggested that the child was in fact his son. In March of 1574

---

[47] Wolfe's account of his departure from Ireland and his first months on the continent are found in his letter to Everard Mercurian, Lisbon 12 December 1573, ARSI, Lus. 65, ff. 286ʳ-88ᵛ. A Portuguese translation of this letter can be found in M. Gonçalves da Costa, ed., *Fontes inéditas Portuguesas para a história de Irlanda* (Braga, 1981) pp. 161-65. Further details on Wolfe and his need for money can be found in Provincial Jorge Serrão's letters to the General from Almerino on 6 December 1573, Lisbon on 9 December 1573, and Lisbon on 4 March 1574, ARSI, Lus. 65, f. 269ʳ⁻ᵛ; 277ʳ⁻ᵛ; Lus. 66, ff. 76ʳ⁻ᵛ. In the second the Provincial suggested that the Pope, since Wolfe was on a papal mission, and other provinces be approached for aid in paying Wolfe's debt.

[48] Quoted in Ó Fionnagáin, *Jesuit Missions to Ireland*, p. 32.

a new problem developed. Alexandro Vallareggio, Portuguese Jesuit procurator for the missions, urged Father General Mercurian to order Wolfe to leave Portugal because of a book that he was writing. Vallareggio had been informed of the book's existence by the Spanish ambassador. According to Juan Borgia the book demonstrated how easily Philip II could conquer Ireland.[49] When he heard about the book's contents, Vallareggio called on Wolfe and pleaded that he abandon the work. Meddling in matters of war and politics was alien to our profession, the procurator explained, but Wolfe was unwilling to listen. Thus, Vallareggio concluded, the General must order Wolfe to leave Portugal to prevent a scandal.[50]

In Portugal Wolfe continued seeking money to pay the persistent merchant. In May he wrote again to the General about the money and complained that the heretics would rejoice if they discovered that Catholics did not keep their word. The merchant's persistence meanwhile angered the Portuguese Provincial, who called the merchant's agent a "New Christian" and threatened to have him banished from the kingdom if he continued to plague the Society. Such tactics alarmed Wolfe: the merchant was an honest man simply seeking what was rightly his, and abuse would not reflect well on the name of the Society.[51]

Wolfe was understandably upset. Vallareggio reported to the General that he had often heard Wolfe say that he would rather be in chains again than suffer such treatment from his Portuguese brothers. Again the procurator implored the General to summon Wolfe from Portugal.[52]

In his reply of 11 August 1574 Mercurian requested specific information to clarify what was becoming an extremely confused situation.[53] He asked Wolfe to answer certain questions. Had Wolfe in any way acted against the Catholic faith by conforming to the established Church? If so, was the motivation to save his life? Was he a public sinner? Whose son was the young man that he brought to Portugal? What was the true amount of the ransom? Was anything to be diverted to support the child or to buy arms?

---

[49] This was probably Wolfe's description of Ireland, written at the insistence of Don Juan Borgia.

[50] Vallareggio to Mercurian, Lisbon 23 March 1574, ARSI Lus. 66, ff. 91^r-93^v.

[51] Lisbon 7 May 1574, ARSI Lus. 66, ff. 119^r-122^v (Portuguese translation in da Costa, *Fontes inéditas*, pp. 167-69).

[52] Vallareggio to Father General, Lisbon 1 June 1574, ARSI, Lus. 66, ff. 154^r-156^v. In his reply from Rome on 25 July 1574, Mercurian asked Vallareggio to do all he could to console Wolfe (ARSI, Epp. N.N. 1, ff. 4^v-5^r). Others complained of Wolfe's treatment. Francisco de Varia wrote to the General from Lisbon on 17 October 1574 that the treatment of Wolfe grieved many. When he was in Ireland the fathers venerated him; now they treat him in a way unbecoming to one who has so suffered. No wonder few foreign Jesuits come to the province! And those who do leave disedified and dejected (ARSI, Lus. 66, ff. 281^{r-v}).

[53] Mercurian to Wolfe, Rome 11 August 1574, ARSI, Epp. N.N. 1, ff. 6^v-7^r. See also Mercurian's letter to Jorge Serrão, Rome 14 August 1574, *ibid.*, ff. 7^{r-v}.

Wolfe replied through the Portuguese Provincial Jorge Serrão on 31 October. In his covering letter the Provincial explained that Wolfe had just departed for Sanlúcar de Barrameda.[54] In light of the gravity of the questions addressed to him by the General, Wolfe wanted to go to Rome to speak with the General personally, but Serrão dissuaded him. Regarding the issues raised, Wolfe asserted that he had never denied the faith, either interiorly or exteriorly. Once, he admitted, he had suggested to the jailers that torture was not an effective way to convert him. If they were able to demonstrate through reason and the doctors of the Church that their Church was the true Church, he would be willing to conform. Neither had he committed any sins of the flesh, and thus he had no children. Finally, the true amount of the ransom was as he had specified; Wolfe had not inflated it for any reason. Assured by these answers, the Provincial gave most of the ransom to the merchant and promised to pay the remaining 166 ducats within three months.[55]

Shortly after his departure from Lisbon, Wolfe changed directions. Instead of heading for Sanlúcar de Barrameda he went to Madrid. On 20 December 1574 the Apostolic Nuncio to Spain, Nicholas Ormanetto, wrote from Madrid to Tolomeo Galli, Cardinal of Como, that Wolfe had just arrived at court to ask Philip II to aid FitzMaurice in his revolt against Elizabeth. FitzMaurice had even offered his son as a hostage. The Nuncio suggested that the boy had been left in Portugal because his transfer to Spain would arouse English suspicions. Wolfe wished to continue his journey, presumably to Sanlúcar de Barrameda, but Ormanetto persuaded him to remain in Madrid. Philip was interested in the proposals and had promised some assistance. If the Cardinal could persuade the Pope to contribute something, Ormanetto was confident that an expedition would be launched.[56] Meanwhile Wolfe remained at court.

Wolfe's report was the book that he had written in March of 1574, to the chagrin of Vallareggio. Confident that Philip was not eager to extend his empire, Wolfe suggested that he should appoint Don Juan king. Because Ireland was a papal fief bestowed upon the English king by the Pope, the Pope could present it to Philip. As a result any expedition must be carried out with the consent of the Holy See. As king Don Juan could undertake the

---

[54] On 2 May 1574 Mercurian had informed Pedro Bernal that a priest who spoke French, English, and Flemish was needed to work in Sanlúcar de Barrameda. He intended to ask the Portuguese Provincial to send Wolfe because he knew Irish, Scots, English, Italian, and Latin and would continue to look for someone who knew French and Flemish. Mercurian recommended Wolfe as a man of virtue (ARSI, Baet. 1a, ff. 13^v-14^v).

[55] Jorge Serrão to Mercurian, Lisbon 31 October 1574, ARSI, Lus. 66, ff. 296^r-297^v; Ó Fionnagáin, *Jesuit Missions to Ireland*, pp. 31-33.

[56] CSP Rome (1572-78) 191-92.

98   CHAPTER THREE

necessary reform of the Irish Church. Regardless of whether the kingdom were given to Don Juan or retained by Philip, Wolfe urged that the services of two men be properly utilized: the Irishman James FitzMaurice FitzGerald and the Englishman Sir Thomas Stucley. Wolfe thought that 12,000 men "that fear God and are of good character, for in truth the sins of the Spaniards and their insolence and pride do great mischief, making the submissive rebellious, the kindly cruel and the friendly hostile" would be sufficient even though FitzMaurice and Stucley had lower estimates. Once Ireland was conquered, attention could be turned to England.[57]

Instead of travelling to Sanlúcar de Barrameda as instructed by the General, Wolfe remained in Madrid and became involved in various schemes for the invasion of Ireland. Wolfe consistently received the support of the Spanish Jesuits at court, who perhaps thought that in so doing they were following the General's instructions to assist Nicholas Sander. On 14 March 1575 Gonzalo Meléndez, Jesuit procurator at Philip's court, reported to the General that he had supported Wolfe's report and had helped him gain admission to the King. Philip had been impressed with what he heard. After the audience the King suggested that Wolfe return to Portugal to work for the enterprise. The procurator concurred.[58] The Portuguese Jesuits, however, were not enthusiastic at Wolfe's return.

V

On the eve of the Northern Revolt, English Catholicism was a curious spectrum ranging from zealous exiles in Louvain and Rome to inconspicuous Church Papists throughout England. During the 1560s many theologians in Louvain wrote tracts to instruct their co-religionists within the kingdom and to dispute doctrinal points with leaders of the established Church. But not all priests with Catholic sentiments had fled. Many remained with their flock, doing what they could to adapt the prayerbook service to satisfy the desires and standards of Catholics. Some conducted Protestant services and offered the Mass. Among the laity many attended required services but used the time to read their own prayerbooks or to disturb the minister. Throughout the period, as we noted in a previous chapter, attempts to dissuade the Catholics from even passive conformity gained strength.

Sometime in the early 1570s the imprisoned Abbot of Westminster John Feckenham explained his reasons for refusing to attend Protestant services:

---

[57] 24 March 1574, CSP Rome (1572-78) 151-68.
[58] Mercurian to Meléndez, Rome 15 March 1575, ARSI, Tolet. 1, ff. 40^v, 44^r; Meléndez to Mercurian, Madrid 14 March 1575, ARSI, Hisp. 123, f. 206^r; Francesco de Porres to Mercurian, Madrid 30 March 1575, ARSI, Hisp. 123, f. 261^r.

"Certaine considerations and causes, movying me not to bee presente at, nor to receive, neither use the service of the new booke, otherwise called the Common boke of praiers." His work circulated widely in manuscript among Catholics and was first printed in *A confutation of a popishe and sclaunderous libelle, in forme of an apologie*, an attack by William Fulke.[59] A few years earlier Nicholas Sander had addressed the same subject in the preface to his *A treatise of the images of Christ, and of his saints*. Attendance at Protestant services was forbidden and "Christ can never take him to be his faithful frind or servant, who useth to frequent such a Congregation, as is purposelie erected against his owne wife and Spouse, which I have shewed to be the Societie of Catholickes." Those who attend such services "for feare of a small temporal losse, they can be content to put in hasard their everlasting salvation."[60] The fullest attack on occasional conformity was Gregory Martin's *A Treatise of Schisme*. On the basis of his examination of Scripture, especially the account of the leper Naaman in 2 Kings 5, the fathers of the Church and other ecclesiastical histories, the author insisted that Catholics refrain from attending Protestant services.[61]

Christopher Haigh has showed that *Regnans in Excelsis* did not initiate a movement towards recusancy—that movement was already evident in the writings of Feckenham and Sander and the practices of many Catholics in England—but it did resolve the doubts of many, and works such as that of Gregory Martin were intended to strengthen their new resolution. It is true that statistically recusancy was more pronounced after the bull. But, according to Haigh, that increase can be explained thus: the papal bull so frightened the government that it devised better ways to identify recusants.[62]

After the Northern Revolt and the Queen's excommunication, persecution of Catholics intensified. Their loyalty was suspect; the kingdom was surrounded by potential enemies who could take advantage of the Queen's excommunication to gain Catholic support. Scotland was for the moment secure, but because of Mary its future was always uncertain. Ireland was a boiling kettle always liable to bubble over if its pleas for foreign assistance were ever heard. Spain and France, although currently occupied with greater problems, would eventually conclude their wars and settle their rebellions. The papacy of Gregory XIII promised to be as militant as that of Pius V—if not more so. Thus the government could not risk doing nothing about the

---

[59] (London, 1571) STC 11426.
[60] (Louvain, 1567) STC 21696, ARCR, II, no. 696, A^v, Aiiii^v.
[61] (Douai, 1578) STC 17508, ARCR, II, no. 524.
[62] *English Reformations: Religion, Politics, and Society under the Tudors* (Oxford, 1993) pp. 251-61. See also his *Reformation and Resistance in Tudor Lancashire* (Cambridge, 1975) pp. 247-68; and "The Continuity of Catholicism in the English Reformation," in Christopher Haigh, ed., *The English Reformation Revised* (Cambridge, 1987) pp. 192-99.

Catholic menace within the kingdom. A consequence of potential foreign intrigues, the revitalized persecution was a sign that Elizabeth's policy of attrition was failing: Catholicism would not die with the last of the Marian clergy; they were quickly replaced by new graduates from the seminary in Douai, priests less tolerant of occasional conformity. Catholics within the kingdom were left to ponder the implications of Elizabeth's deposition and the limits of their own co-operation with her government. Because the bull had not been properly promulgated, could they continue to obey the Queen in civil matters with a clean conscience?[63]

Among the papers in Rome is an anonymous document, entitled in the calendar "Questions Touching the Bull of Pope Pius V against the Queen of England." Though no date is given, it was composed most likely in the early 1570s by some Catholic in exile, possibly Sir Thomas Stucley, trying to resolve doubts about the validity of *Regnans in Excelsis*. The bull, on the one hand, could not bind English Catholics because it failed in its purpose. Instead of fulfilling its aim of assisting the Catholic cause, it had damaged that cause and "a law that has proved futile is no longer binding." On the other hand, no one alleged defective publication against the bull. The author concluded that Catholics could continue to obey the Queen, acknowledge her as head of the Church "with a mental reservation," and defend her against unlawful attack. They could not, however, defend her against those who attacked the Queen with reasonable hope of victory "*vi bullae* or *studio religionis*." Presumably this did not constitute "unlawful attack." On the contrary, Catholics were obliged to assist such lawful invasions because the Queen "though the bull had not been published, might lawfully be dethroned as a perturber of the universal Church."[64] If foreign powers hoped to elicit support from Catholics within the kingdom, the validity of the bull urgently needed resolution.

Throughout the 1560s and 1570s the Jesuits played no significant role in the life of English Catholicism. At least one historian interprets their absence as aversion. In a discussion of the relations between Robert Parsons and William Allen, J.C.H. Aveling wondered "Why were the English so reluctant to become Jesuits?"[65] The context makes it clear that Aveling agrees with a traditional explanation that the blame rests firmly on the shoulders of Parsons. Regardless of Parsons's role in recruitment of Englishmen into the Society, the question as raised by Aveling is badly phrased. A more important question asks why there were any recruits and why they were not serving in England. By Pole's prohibition the Society of

---

[63] Allen had no doubt about the bull's validity. See Duffy, "Allen," 281.
[64] CSP Rome (1572-78) 140-41.
[65] *The Handle and the Axe* (London, 1976) p. 57.

Jesus was prevented from establishing itself in England during the reign of Mary Tudor. As we have seen, a few Jesuits passed through the kingdom on their way to or from Ireland and Scotland.

The first English Jesuit to return to his native land was Thomas King, who did so for reasons of health in the spring of 1564. Given full faculties, he worked zealously among the Catholics for nearly a year before he died in May of 1565.[66] William Good, after his return to Flanders from Ireland, hoped to work in England or in Scotland but he was not sent.[67]

For reasons unknown, the Society's fame spread throughout the country despite its absence. The Society was esteemed highly enough for the imprisoned Thomas Woodhouse, a Marian priest, to petition the French Provincial for admission shortly before his martyrdom in 1573. Thomas Pounde, an imprisoned layman, petitioned for admission in 1578.[68]

Even though there were no Jesuits in England, they were known and feared. In 1561 Everard Mercurian relayed to Diego Laínez a rumour that the Society had been the subject of sermons in England. Protestant preachers warned their congregations that the Jesuits were eager to enter the country and that, once in, they would do terrible harm. "May the name of the Lord always be a terror to heretics" was Mercurian's judgement on the report![69]

The Englishmen who joined tried to keep abreast of developments in their homeland. In 1564 Simon Belost, an English recruit and probable source of the above story, asked Juan de Polanco to assign someone in Rome to relay news about England to him. He had previously received such information from Thomas Darbyshire and Jasper Heywood, but both were now stationed in Germany.[70] Someone, perhaps through the English Hospice, could retain contact with England. Belost was the first Jesuit assigned to work among the English. As early as 1562, he was given faculties, including those for reconciliation of heretics, for the English in Flanders.

---

[66] John Hungerford Pollen, S.J., *The English Catholics in the Reign of Queen Elizabeth: A Study of Their Politics Civil Life and Government* (London, 1920) p. 106. There may have been a few other Jesuits who had briefly returned to their country. See Thomas H. Clancy, S.J., "The First Generation of English Jesuits 1555-1585," *AHSI* 57 (1988) 152. On 26 April 1566 Frans De Costere wrote to Francis Borgia from Tournai that he had just received a letter from King. In it the Jesuit reported that religious matters were still unsettled in England and that he continued to take care of his health while working among the Catholics (ARSI, Germ. 147, ff. 97^r-98^v). This letter must have taken considerable time to reach De Costere, because King had died on 30 May 1565 (ARSI, Angl. 14, f. 74^v, Hist. Soc. 42, f. 121^r). Unfortunately we know nothing about King's work in England.

[67] William Good to Everard Mercurian, Louvain 4 February 1573, ARSI, Germ. 152, ff. 308^{r-v}.

[68] *Mon. Ang.*, II, 444, 537; Clancy, "First Generation," 140.

[69] Cologne 16 April 1561, in *Epp. Laínez*, V, 482. In the introduction to this volume we noted Thomas Stapleton's defence of the Society in 1567.

[70] Louvain 19 December 1564, ARSI, Germ. 145, ff. 270^{r-v}.

Contrary to Aveling's assertion, many Englishmen were attracted to the Society. Henry More claimed that there were some sixty-nine Englishmen in the Society between 1556 and 1580. Clancy has showed that some 140 English and Welsh men entered the Society between 1555 and 1585.[71] For most, we have no idea why they were attracted to the Society. We do know, however, that their talents were put to varied uses by the Society. Some worked in Poland and Lithuania; most in western Europe. A few, e.g. Thomas Stephens, who travelled to India, worked in the missions. As their numbers increased, so did their agitation for a mission to England.

In a letter to William Good some time after 19 March 1579, Robert Parsons mentioned the difficulties involved in a mission to England:

> You know what great difficulties are in the enterprise, which many men do not consider; untill therefore that I see myselfe in my owne opinion able to resolve the same, and until a way might be laid downe how the Company might beginne and go through with the matter: when I was somewhat satisfied in that poynt, I begane the assault and it had such successe, as I think you would marvell to understand the particulars which I dare not heere wryte to you, but the impediment you shal understand by that which I wryte here under: now it is enough for F. Darbyshire and me if we can keep our Englishe men of the Company togeather, and from other Missions, which also we shall not be able to do long, for albeit our Superiours do not gladly grant any Englishe man to any other Mission, for desire they have to reserve them for England, yet the multitude of us dayly encreasing (for there hath entered at Rome 8 or 9 this yeare, besides divers in other places) and also many Englishe men dayly for the greate zeale and desire they have to suffer somewhat for Christ, demanding instantly underhand and privily (for in this thing they will not lett us be of their councell, whome they know will lett them) to be sent in other Missions, seeing England is shutt from them.

By the spring of 1579 Parsons had settled his own doubts about the value of initiating a Jesuit mission to England. Unfortunately he was not able to convince the General and had been excluded from the discussions. Meanwhile he was doing his best to keep the English Jesuits together and ready for a possible mission. If permission were not granted soon, Parsons feared, there would be "a diminishment of fit labourers when the tyme of harvest shall come."[72]

---

[71] Francis Edwards, S.J., ed., *The Elizabethan Jesuits* (London, 1981) p. 38; Clancy, "First Generation," 138. My own research on the Society's catalogues confirms their conclusions if not their precise numbers.

[72] Parsons to William Good, Rome [after 19 March 1579], in Leo Hicks, S.J., ed., *Letters and Memorials of Father Robert Persons, S.J.* (London, 1942) p. 7.

VI

On a visit to Rome during the winter of 1575/6, William Allen arranged a meeting with Everard Mercurian. The two knew each other, having met years earlier through the Jesuits in Louvain after the former had left England and while the latter was Provincial of Flanders. Because of Mercurian's consistent kindness to the English exiles, Allen was confident as he prepared for the conference. In June of 1575 Allen had written to Mercurian that his election as General on 23 April 1573 made him optimistic about the Society's future involvement in the English mission.[73] Hoping to take advantage of Mercurian's interest, Allen explained the state of England and pleaded for Jesuit assistance.[74]

Catholicism remained strong throughout the north of England and in Wales. Because of "the greater number of merchants and intercourse with heretics," the towns were more infected "but we reckon less on the cities than on the rest of the people." Of the two universities, Oxford was more sympathetic to the ancient faith. The Inns of Court in London were especially fruitful vineyards. London, because of its size, provided a safe haven for the priests. They were secure in the estates of many gentle and noble families who remained faithful and whose estates were scattered throughout the country. Allen estimated that the seminary founded at Douai could produce ten priests a year for work in England. If the seminary had stronger financial resources it would educate even more. It was in conclusion that Allen finally came to the point of the meeting. Within the Society there were certain Englishmen, e.g. the Heywood brothers, Jasper and Elizeus, and Edmund Campion, who would be "very well qualified" for work in England.[75] England needed more priests, and the seminary was unable to provide them. Because the Society had men qualified for the work, Allen wished the Jesuits would become involved in the endeavour. Although

---

[73] Allen to Mercurian, Douai 13 June 1575, in Renold, *Letters of Allen and Barret*, pp. 1-3.

[74] See Leo Hicks, S.J., "Cardinal Allen and the Society," *The Month* 160 (1932) 342-53 for Allen's dealings with Mercurian.

[75] "Some Correspondence of Cardinal Allen, 1579-85," ed. Patrick Ryan, S.J., in *Miscellanea VII* (London, 1911) pp. 62-69. Dennis Flynn in "The English Mission of Jasper Heywood, S.J.," *AHSI* 54 (1985) 49-50, draws attention to a rumour circulating among the English Catholics in the Netherlands in 1574. According to it, a petition was to be addressed to Elizabeth, through the mediation of Philip of Spain, that sought permission for William Allen, Nicholas Sander, and Jasper Heywood to preach freely in England. Flynn suggests that this rumour may be behind Allen's request for specific Jesuits noted in England for their learning. See also Flynn's "'Out of Step:' Six Supplementary Notes on Jasper Heywood," in *The Reckoned Expense: Edmund Campion and the Early English Jesuits. Essays in Celebration of the First Centenary of Campion Hall, Oxford (1896-1996)*, ed. Thomas M. McCoog, S.J. (Woodbridge, 1996) pp. 179-92.

there is no record of the General's reaction to this meeting, he denied the petition. Allen had lost the first battle, but he was not ready to abandon the war.

The English College in Rome began as a hospice for pilgrims in 1362. By the beginning of the 15th century it had become the spiritual centre for the English in Rome. By the end of the same century the crown directly controlled the hospice and appointed the warden. Temporarily after Henry VIII's break with Rome and permanently after the Elizabethan settlement, the hospice became a sanctuary for religious exiles. In order to ensure the continuing fidelity of the warden, the papacy assumed right of appointment. After the accession of Elizabeth an odd assortment of clerics gathered there. Most were exiled pluralists looking for sinecures. "Some of them," Anthony Kenny concluded, "had been imprisoned for their religion; but few, if any of them appear to have been saintly men."[76] The most distinguished resident was the Welshmen Morys Clynnog. An Oxford D.D., Clynnog had studied law at Louvain, Bologna, and Padua. A *confidante* of Cardinal Pole, to whom he was confessor in Italy and in England, he had held responsible positions in the English Church during the Marian restoration of Catholicism. Shortly before Mary's death Clynnog was nominated Bishop of Bangor but was never consecrated. He was appointed warden of the hospice in 1565, an appointment probably not unrelated to his friendship with Cardinal Morone,[77] Protector of England.

In many ways the lives of the clerics at the English Hospice retained the characteristics of a collegiate senior common room. The liturgical demands were not excessive. Many residents devoted too much time to drinking, gambling, quarrelling, and associating with rather dubious female companions. Clynnog was one of the exceptions. He did, however, share one interest with his less industrious colleagues: the reconversion of England. On this issue he was extremely fervent. As early as 1561 Clynnog, in a letter to Morone, argued that Elizabeth should be deposed through the military might of Philip II, and Mary Stuart installed in her stead. Dr. Owen Lewis,

---

[76] In an exceptional series of articles, Anthony Kenny traced the early history of the college ("From Hospice to College," *The Venerabile* 19 [1958-60] 477-85; 20 [1960-62] 1-11, 89-103, 170-96). Unfortunately *The Venerabile*, the alumni magazine of the English College, is not readily available. The more accessible *The Venerable English College Rome* (London, 1979) by Michael E. Williams, summarizes the fruits of Kenny's research on pp. 1-24. An undated memorial regarding the English Hospice testifies to the sad state (see Ryan, "Correspondence of Allen," pp. 46-63).

[77] By this time Morone seems to have been more ambivalent in his dealings with the Society. Although he still gave his support to various Jesuit projects, including the proposal that the Society take over the direction of the new Roman seminary, his relations with Laínez and Salmerón had cooled. See William V. Bangert, S.J., *Claude Jay and Alfonso Salmerón* (Chicago, 1985) pp. 246, 285.

another Welshman, arrived in Rome in 1574 and immediately joined Clynnog in his crusade against Elizabeth.[78] Sir Thomas Stucley joined the conspiracy in 1575. Various English Catholics with similar desires, but occasionally with different proposals, gathered in Rome during the winter of 1575/6: William Allen and Sir Francis Englefield, a Privy Councillor under Mary and an attainted fugitive under Elizabeth, arrived in February of 1576. Nicholas Sander was invited but remained in Spain; Sir Richard Shelley, Lord Prior of England, attended.[79] During this meeting Allen fruitlessly sought Jesuit assistance from Mercurian. The General was a cautious man and, at the time of Allen's request, was dealing with the urgent problem of David Wolfe. Perhaps it was his fear that an English mission, especially in the context of the political and military matters being discussed in Rome, would result in other Jesuits becoming involved in such affairs that caused him to say no.

Pope Pius V's excommunication of Elizabeth and his pronouncement that she was "to be deprived of her pretended claim to the aforesaid kingdom [England] and of all lordships, dignity and privileges whatsoever" legitimated the efforts of the exiles. The factions at the summit conference could not agree on an invasion project but, by the time Allen returned to Douai in June, tentative plans had been formulated for a joint Papal-Spanish invasion for the spring of 1577.[80] Before the group disbanded they agreed on one significant, non-military proposal: the conversion of the English hospice into a college for the education of clergy. Thrice before similar proposals had been made. This time the proposal was successful because Stucley was able to win Pope Gregory XIII's support.

---

[78] For a brief biography of Lewis see Godfrey Anstruther, O.P., "Owen Lewis," *The Venerabile* 21 (1962) 274-94.

[79] See Albert J. Loomie, S.J., *The Spanish Elizabethans: The English Exiles at the Court of Philip II* (New York, 1963) pp. 14-51 for a life of Englefield. Allen's involvement in this scheme is quite evident and can be seen in a letter written from Douai to Owen Lewis before November of 1576 (see Ryan, "Correspondence of Allen," pp. 44-47) and in a memorial drafted at this time (Renold, *Letters of Allen and Barret*, pp. 284-92). In a passage that could have substantiated many of the worst fears of the English government, the authors wrote "There can easily be found some Englishmen, men of trust and prudent, chiefly priests, who will cross over into England secretly from Flanders, and covertly prepare certain gentlemen in England, useful in this affair, whose names, of course, will only be given to them by word of mouth, when all these plans are mature. No reply, however, is to be expected from those thus sent into England, but meanwhile let the fleet proceed in God's name towards that country" (p. 289). While Parsons was still studying theology, Allen had embarked on his political schemes. For Parsons's account of the meeting see "A Storie of Domesticall Difficulties," in *Miscellanea II*, ed. John Hungerford Pollen, S.J. (London, 1906) p. 64.

[80] For an exposition of Clynnog's plans see J.M. Cleary, "Dr. Morys Clynnog's Invasion Projects of 1575-1576," *RH* 8 (1966) 300-22. One proposal urged that the estates of heretical nobles and the illegally confiscated ecclesiastical properties be used "for establishing seminaries for the English clergy, and setting up colleges of the Fathers of the Society of Jesus and of other religious orders" (305).

The first students arrived from Douai in late 1576. and there was immediate tension. Many resident clergy resisted change and resented the introduction of students into their comfortable style of life. Their hostility was directed at the two men who had championed the changes, Morys Clynnog and Owen Lewis. Nationalist animosities were aggravated by the selection of students. Lewis and Clynnog were suspected of partiality when they admitted two older Welshmen after rejecting two slightly younger Englishmen for reasons of age a year earlier. The anger surfaced in May of 1578 when Clynnog's term as warden expired. Cardinal Morone had already permitted Clynnog to extend his term an extra year because of the establishment of the college. In the election, however, the resident clergy did not choose Clynnog. Instead they voted for an Englishman, Henry Henshaw, sometime rector of Lincoln College, Oxford. Cardinal Morone quickly intervened on behalf of Clynnog. The Cardinal separated the administration of the hospice from the government of the college. To the latter he reappointed Clynnog as rector. The division, however, was only temporary. Around Christmas of 1578 Morone reunited the offices and gave Henshaw and the other residents fifteen days to leave the hospice. Cardinal Morone and Pope Gregory XIII turned to the Society for assistance in weathering the storm. Their request was simple: the loan of two fathers for two months. Mercurian's consent clearly noted that the term was two months. Giovanni Paolo Novarola was named spiritual father and Ferdinando Capeci prefect of studies. Both fathers remained after their term expired. Mercurian reluctantly allowed the men to stay because of petitions from students and because of Lewis's influence at the papal court.[81] Mercurian's decision was more significant than anyone involved would have realized: it was the first commitment that the Society had to England.

The addition of two Jesuits did not improve relations between Welsh and English students. Suspicions and recriminations were common. As more and more seminarians progressed from Douai to Rome, the difference between their missionary zeal and the relative complacency of their English administrators occasioned a new outburst. The new arrivals considered Clynnog a problem. By January of 1579 students complained that Clynnog's governance impeded their missionary aspirations. In a memorial prepared for Cardinal Morone, these students asserted that they came to Rome to acquire sufficient knowledge for their future work in England. Clynnog, they claimed, admitted students who had no desire to return to England. Moreover, the memorial concluded, the Welsh and the English are so naturally hostile to each other that only a third party could establish peace.[82]

---

[81] Pollen, *English Catholics in the Reign of Queen Elizabeth*, pp. 274-75.
[82] The memorials are printed in Parsons, "Domesticall Difficulties," pp. 102-17.

Beneath these claims lurked considerably different understandings of the current state of English religious affairs. Almost accustomed to swings of the English religious pendulum, older men such as Clynnog and Lewis considered the Elizabethan settlement a temporary setback. England would change again. A Catholic would ascend the throne as a result of the Queen's death or her deposition. Until then the English College would provide employment for scholars and education for a clergy ready to serve once Catholicism had been restored. The younger men regarded England as a mission country as dangerous and difficult as the Indies. The Catholics in England needed priests now; they could not wait for a restoration. The students demanded that Clynnog be removed and that the administration of the college be put in the hands of the Society of Jesus.[83] Why the students favoured the Society was not explained. Presumably the Society's work in the missions, its increasing Counter-Reformation zeal in Europe, and the example provided by the German College were factors.

Cardinal Morone continued to support Clynnog in the struggle. In a move that must have surprised everyone including Morone, the Pope decided to meet representatives of the students. After the audience a shocked Morone was ordered to accept Clynnog's resignation. The students were then told to elect an Englishman as Clynnog's successor. Claiming that there was no qualified Englishman, the students repeated their request for Jesuits. Their reasons were varied: the Society trained men for missionary enterprises and not ecclesiastical comforts; the Society was experienced in the administration of seminaries; Jesuits would be able to reconcile the English and the Welsh; and finally, the experience would provide the basis for a better working relation between Jesuits and seculars once the re-conversion of England was accomplished. Despite Morone's final attempt to reimpose Clynnog, the students' wishes were granted. Mercurian's reluctance to involve the Society further in this imbroglio was overcome. On 19 March 1579, Cardinal Morone, in the Pope's name, commanded Mercurian to take charge of the college. The General's plea that the Society was already overcommitted in Rome was dismissed, and Mercurian had no choice but to submit.[84] Against Mercurian's better judgement the Society was being pulled deeper and deeper into English affairs. Later that spring the first Jesuit rector, the Italian Alfonso Agazzari, was installed. On 23 April the changes in administration were publicly demonstrated by the introduction of the

---

[83] Kenny, "From Hospice to College," 177-78.

[84] Not all the secular clergy enthusiastically welcomed the Society's involvement. In a letter to Owen Lewis from Paris on 12 May 1579, Allen relayed a report from a certain Hughes that "the Jesuits have no skill nor experience of our country's state nor of our mens nature, and that their trade of syllogizing there is not fit for the use of our people" (Thomas Francis Knox, ed., *The Letters and Memorials of William Cardinal Allen (1532-1594)* [London, 1882] p. 82).

missionary oath. Henceforth each student pronounced an oath that he was willing to embark for England whenever his superiors saw fit.[85]

VII

Many Catholics continued to look to Spain as the only solution to their problems. Nicholas Sander and David Wolfe actively sought Spanish assistance. Others, such as Sir Thomas Stucley and Morys Clynnog, drafted memorials demonstrating the feasibility of intervention. On 13 June 1575 Stucley received papal support for one of his proposals when Gregory XIII presented him with a number of crucifixes. Among the graces and indulgences attached were two especially important ones:

> 2. For each time that prayer is made before any one of them for the prosperity of Holy Mother Church, and the exaltation of the Holy Catholic Faith, and the preservation and liberation of Mary, Queen of Scotland, and the reduction of the realms of England, Scotland and Ireland, and the extirpation of the heretics, other 50 days', and on feasts, 100 days' indulgences.
> 3. For taking part in any warfare against the foes of our holy faith, seven years and seven quarantines of indulgence, and in case of death therein, for such as have at least confessed and communicated at the beginning of the said conflict, and are in a state of contrition for their sins, and invoke the most holy name of Jesus with their mouths or with their hearts, a plenary indulgence and remission of all their sins.[86]

Preparations for a crusade were afoot, but nothing happened. By the end of the year the Apostolic Nuncio confessed to Tolomeo Galli that he did not foresee an invasion of England within the near future because of developments in the conflicts in the Mediterranean and in Flanders.[87] Philip was too distracted by events on these fronts to consider an invasion seriously. The Nuncio could have added Philip's financial straits as another reason. Although, contrary to Ormanetto's fears, the Mediterranean remained tranquil, the rebellion continued in Flanders.

---

[85] According to the bull of foundation, *Quoniam Divinae Bonitati*, the seminarians were "to be instructed in the Catholic religion in which they were born, with the aim primarily of assuring their own salvation, but also so that once instructed in the knowledge of theology they might return to England to enlighten others who had fallen away from the truth." The same bull forbade the prior clerical residents of the Hospice "to intervene in the aforesaid [collegiate] buildings, church, houses, shops, rents, produce and other property, rights and privileges, neither directly nor indirectly on any pretext whatsoever. Nor shall they presume to molest or disturb the College, its Rector, Students and Staff now and subsequently" (Williams, *Venerable English College*, pp. 212, 214). The Pope had approved the foundation on 10 December 1578 in *Exigit saepenumero* (Antonio de Aldama, S.J., ed., *Litterae Apostolicae ad Societatem Iesu pertinentes* [unpublished compilation: Rome, 1953] 25).

[86] CSP Rome (1572-78) 208-09.

[87] Ormanetto to Galli, Madrid 19 December 1575, CSP Rome (1572-78) 240-42.

Bankruptcy and the death of Requesens in March of 1576 continued to disrupt Spanish policy in Flanders. In the same month troops mutinied more violently than ever. The subsequent violence was so extreme that many moderates shifted to the side of the rebels. Anti-Spanish Catholic nobles in the southern provinces united for mutual defence. On 7 October 1576 Catholic delegates met at Ghent with representatives of the Prince of Nassau and of the Protestant states. The agreement reached called for expulsion of all Spanish and foreign troops from the Netherlands and recognition of the religious *status quo*. After the expulsion the Estates General would determine the religious and political structures that would govern the country. Support for the new agreement, the Pacification of Ghent, increased after the "Spanish Fury" (the army) attacked Antwerp and killed 8000 citizens on 4 November. The agreement was rapidly ratified and was published on the 8th. Around the same time the new Governor Don Juan of Austria arrived with a royal command to make some concessions.[88]

Although Don Juan was not eager to become involved in the deteriorating military situation in the Netherlands, he thought he could use his position and authority to achieve what he earnestly desired: a kingdom of his own, specifically England as King-Consort of the legitimate Queen, Mary Stuart. The Estates General would acknowledge his authority only if he ratified the Pacification of Ghent. He did so on 12 February 1577 with the Perpetual Edict. The Spanish troops began to leave shortly thereafter. Don Juan wanted to evacuate the troops by sea and in so doing to employ them in his personal enterprise against England. Philip and the Dutch rebels, albeit for different reasons, insisted that the troops return to Spain by land. Without his troops Don Juan was left without power in the Netherlands and without any hope of attacking England.

The Perpetual Edict did not usher in a period of peace. Don Juan's negotiations with William (the Silent) of Orange collapsed because William refused to accept a clause in the Perpetual Edict that the Catholic religion would be upheld. Frustrated in his negotiations with William, Don Juan resorted to the tactics that he knew best: he seized Namur on 24 July in an attempt to restore his authority. His failure to take Antwerp on 1 August led to the recall of the Spanish troops. Fearful of their return, the Estates General looked for foreign allies and transferred their allegiance from Don Juan to another Habsburg, Archduke Matthias. The Prince of Nassau was appointed the new Governor's deputy and *de facto* ruler of the country.[89]

---

[88] Lynch, *Spain 1516-1598*, pp. 404-06; Limm, *Dutch Revolt*, pp. 44-45. According to MacCaffrey there were secret instructions that concerned the invasion of England after a solid peace was established in the Netherlands, assurances were received of French neutrality, and a precise agreement with the English Catholics was made (*Making of Policy*, pp. 219-20).

[89] Lynch, *Spain 1516-1598*, pp. 406-08; Limm, *Dutch Revolt*, pp. 46-52.

Deterioration of Spanish control in the Netherlands did not prevent new intrigues regarding a Spanish attack on the British Isles. Ormanetto wrote to Galli about the gathering of English exiles scheduled for Rome in January of 1576. He hoped for a concrete proposal. In fact he had heard it rumoured that all future negotiations regarding the enterprise had been transferred to Rome. Presumably the reasons for this were the King's bankruptcy and the Pope's dissatisfaction with Philip's failure to act. Whenever the possibility was discussed with a member of the royal council, Ormanetto wrote, the reply was the same: the King was unable to embark on such a project because he lacked sufficient financial resources and troops. Ormanetto nonetheless found the King well disposed towards the enterprise whenever they spoke. Yet he was not inclined to act. If, however, he did launch an expedition directed towards Ireland, Ormanetto reminded Galli in March, the Pope must prepare the way by depriving Elizabeth of that kingdom.[90]

In April the King's secretary Antonio Pérez informed Ormanetto that Philip had finally decided to move against England. To launch the enterprise he would contribute 100,000 crowns, but it was too late, he argued, to organize an attack for the summer. He contended that the invasion must be delayed until autumn. No decision had been made regarding the enterprise's leader, but Philip did not want anyone to suspect Spanish involvement. Lest the presence of a legate antagonize the English even more, Philip recommended that a nuncio be sent. Finally, the King suggested that a decision be postponed on installing a brother of the Earl of Huntingdon as king[91] if

---

[90] Ormanetto to Galli, [Madrid] 18 January 1576, CSP Rome (1572-78) 246-47; same to same, [Madrid] 29 March 1576, *ibid.*, 256-57.

[91] Henry Hastings, Earl of Huntingdon, joint custodian of Mary Queen of Scots and Lord President of the North, was a fervent persecutor of Catholics. His father, Francis Hastings, had married Lady Catherine Pole, elder daughter and co-heir of Henry Pole, Lord Montague. Through her the Hastings family inherited the Yorkist claim to the English throne. The family was divided religiously. Henry, a favourite candidate for the throne among the Puritans, and his brothers Francis and Edward were Protestants; his mother and his brothers George and Walter were Catholics in fact or in sympathy. George married Dorothy Porte, a relative of the Jesuit John Gerard. Some Catholics advocated George's claim to the throne before he conformed and succeeded his brother as Earl in 1595. Walter remained a Catholic. See Claire Cross, *The Puritan Earl: The Life of Henry Hastings Third Earl of Huntingdon 1536-1595* (London, 1966) pp. 16-17, 31, 34-35; and *The Letters of Sir Francis Hastings 1574-1609* (Frome, 1969) xvi. According to "a Yorkshire recusant's relation," Henry Hastings was such a persecutor of Catholics that "the right honourable Countess, his mother, seeing his barbarous and bloody mind, and fearing against herself his cruelty, many times would pray to God and wish she might end this mortal life before he could come to the supreme authority he aspired to. Neither did this great lady, his own mother, without great cause, fear herself to feel the smart of this her son Nero his knife, whose nature and inclination she knew to be infected with heretical fury, when also himself would often gloriously vaunt and say, that if the day should [come] he hoped for, when he might have authority and controlment, he would begin with them of his own kindred and root out of them as many as were Catholics" (John Morris, S.J., ed., *The Troubles of Our Catholic Forefathers Related by Themselves*, 3 vols. [London, 1872-77] III, 66).

anything happened to Mary Stuart.⁹² Despite Philip's consent the enterprise was not launched in the autumn, probably because of the Flemish troubles that led to the Pacification of Ghent. The Pope meanwhile continued to remind Philip that he had received assurances from numerous Irishmen, including Patrick O'Healy, O.F.M., Bishop of Mayo, that the time was right for a military expedition to Ireland. Gregory exhorted Philip to deliver England from Jezebel.⁹³

As was mentioned earlier, the departure of the Spanish troops provided an excellent opportunity to invade England. Philip assured Ormanetto of his continued interest in such an enterprise, but the departing Spanish troops could not be used for it. According to the agreement the troops had to depart immediately, and Spain did not have the means for transporting these troops to England. Moreover their departure could not be delayed until sufficient preparations were made. A week later the Cardinal of Como wrote to Don Juan of his and the Pope's disappointment that he had not been able to take advantage of this heaven-sent opportunity to transport the Spanish troops by sea. This setback, the Cardinal hoped, would not abate Don Juan's enthusiasm for the enterprise. In fact, Como added, he had been informed that the Pope wanted Don Juan to head the attack. Until Don Juan was able to arrange something, the Pope had directed James FitzMaurice FitzGerald, who had been on the continent seeking support since April of 1575, first to Portugal and then to Ireland to join the rebellion against Elizabeth.⁹⁴

David Wolfe returned to Portugal after his stay at the Spanish court in Madrid. Mercurian was still sceptical about Wolfe's activities. In a letter from Rome on 29 April 1575 Mercurian warned Wolfe to conduct himself "according to the spirit of the Society." Hopeful that Wolfe's eventual return to Ireland would bring tremendous benefits, he nonetheless exhorted the Irishman to be circumspect in everything, to attend to his vocation, and not to meddle in affairs that were alien to the Society's Institute.⁹⁵

Apparently the General's fears were justified. The new Portuguese Provincial Manuel Rodrigues described Wolfe's return. When Wolfe arrived in Évora, few recognized him in his newly acquired beard. More important than his facial hair was his disturbing insistence that he was going to Lisbon, where he would dress as a layman and negotiate for the Spanish King even

---

[92] Ormanetto to Galli, [Madrid] 17 April 1576, CSP Rome (1572-78) 260-64. See also the summary of the King's letter, 264-65.
[93] Gregory XIII to Philip II, Rome 10 November 1576, CSP Rome (1572-78) 287. See also the petitions on behalf of Ireland on pp. 286-87.
[94] Ormanetto to Galli, Madrid 25 March 1577, CSP Rome (1572-78) 296; Galli to Don Juan, Rome 2 April 1577, *ibid.*, 297-99; Filippo Sega, Bishop of Riga and Nuncio in Spain, to Galli, Madrid 13 September 1577, *ibid.*, 334-35.
[95] ARSI, Tolet. 1, ff. 45ᵛ-46ʳ.

without the General's permission. The topic of these negotiations, it seems, was the purchase of arms for the rebels and arrangements for their transport to Ireland. Rodrigues did not think that Jesuit involvement in such matters was appropriate. Consequently he and his consultors tried to dissuade Wolfe from his course. They feared that if the affair ended badly it would alienate Philip from the Society. Because the Provincial was concerned that Wolfe's appearance in Lisbon, where he was well known, would cause scandal, he instructed the Jesuit rector in Évora to detain Wolfe. If such gentle tactics failed, the Provincial would employ harsher ones in order to curtail Wolfe's involvement.

After the provincial consultation, Alexandro Vallareggio was dispatched to Philip's court to dissuade the King from sending Wolfe on this assignment to Ireland. He hoped to convince the Spanish Jesuits that their encouragement of Wolfe's negotiations was detrimental to the honour of God and of the Society: Jesuits should not be involved in matters of war and rebellion. Such involvement, Vallareggio feared, would arouse suspicion among Catholic and heretical princes that Jesuit zeal was false, and that they were in fact spies.[96]

The Wolfe affair quickly turned into a Spanish/Portuguese conflict. The Portuguese were indignant at Wolfe's involvement in military matters and at his efforts to raise money in Portugal for an attack on Ireland. Portugal was at peace with England. On the other hand, Spanish Jesuits were angry that the Portuguese risked Philip's displeasure for obstructing his plans. Moreover Philip was already angry because the complaints of the Portuguese were so loud that they threatened to make public extremely sensitive plans; this would have deleterious consequences.

Others became implicated in this family quarrel. The Nuncio in Lisbon, Giovanni Andrea Caligari, complained to the Cardinal of Como about the antics of the Portuguese Jesuits.[97] Como must have relayed the information to Pope Gregory, who then informed Mercurian of his annoyance with the Portuguese.[98]

---

[96] Rodrigues to Mercurian, Lisbon 13 April 1575, ARSI, Lus. 67, ff. 83^{r-v}; Vallareggio to [Mercurian], Toledo n.d. [c. May 1575], ARSI, Hisp. 124, ff. 190^{r-v}. See also Vallareggio to Mercurian, Madrid 4 May 1575, ARSI, Hisp. 124, ff. 11^{r}-13^{v}; Manuel López to Mercurian, Toledo 4 May 1575, Hisp. 124, ff. 14^{r-v}; Ó Fionnagáin, *Jesuit Missions to Ireland*, pp. 33-34.

[97] Caligari to Galli, Évora 21 March 1575, CSP Rome (1572-78) 198-99. The criticisms centred on the Society's influence over the Portuguese King.

[98] Gonzalo Meléndez to Francesco de Porres, Granada 12 May 1575, (a copy of this letter was forwarded to the General on 1 June, ARSI, Hisp. 124, f. 106^{r}); Vallareggio to Mercurian, Madrid 22 May 1575, ARSI, Hisp. 124, ff. 48^{r}-49^{v}; Meléndez to Mercurian, Madrid 15 June 1575, ARSI, Hisp. 124, f. 145^{v}; Vallareggio to Mercurian, np [Lisbon?] 20 June 1575, ARSI, Lus. 67, f. 102^{v}; Rodrigues to Mercurian, Coimbra 21 June 1575, ARSI, Lus. 67, f. 108^{v}; da Costa, "Last Years," 136-37. Full, though not objective, accounts of the whole affair can be found in de Porres's letter to Mercurian, Madrid 1 June 1575, ARSI, Hisp. 124, ff. 98^{r-v} and

Meanwhile Wolfe again altered his plans after he received a letter from FitzMaurice, who had arrived in France in early April. Since he was at St. Malo, there was no longer any need for Wolfe to go to Ireland to consult him.[99] Wolfe therefore headed for France. After their rendezvous the Jesuit hoped to travel to Rome with FitzMaurice in October. The Portuguese Jesuits were relieved once Wolfe left their country; he was no longer their problem.[100] One happy consequence of the whole affair was a papal order to the Nuncio in Spain that he not use Jesuits in any business that was alien to their Institute.[101]

After Wolfe's meeting with FitzMaurice the two did not go to Rome as the Jesuit had hoped. Instead Wolfe proceeded on his own. To the dismay of the Portuguese fathers, the road from St. Malo to Rome passed through Lisbon. Father Ó Fionnagáin suggests that he returned in order to bring a message to Don Juan Borgia from FitzMaurice. Whatever the business, it was concluded by the end of October when Wolfe sailed to Rome.[102] FitzMaurice remained in St. Malo and on 31 January 1576 wrote to Mercurian to ask for the services of a Jesuit priest, presumably expecting the priest to be Wolfe. Probably apprehensive that the required services would be alien to the Society's Institute, Mercurian sadly declined the request.[103] Despite this, Wolfe and FitzMaurice met in Rome in late 1576 and apparently left together in February of 1577. Subsequently—and probably consequently—Wolfe was dismissed from the Society. Wolfe continued to assist FitzMaurice until Wolfe's death sometime after June of 1578.[104]

With or without Wolfe various plots were concocted and schemes devised. The return of Spanish troops to the Netherlands in the summer and autumn of 1577 rekindled English Catholic hopes. With them came

---

Manuel Rodrigues's letter to Mercurian, Coimbra 5 August 1575, ARSI, Lus. 67, ff. 150ʳ-151ᵛ (published in da Costa, *Fontes inéditas*, pp. 173-75).

[99] Over the next few years FitzMaurice travelled between France, Italy, and Spain as he sought foreign aid. On the role that his wife played in his diplomatic dealings see Palmer, "Gender, Violence, Rebellion," 703.

[100] Wolfe to Mercurian, Cascais 21 May 1575, ARSI, Hisp. 124, ff. 41ʳ⁻ᵛ; Vallareggio to Mercurian, Lisbon 22 July 1575, ARSI, Lus. 67, f. 138ʳ (printed in da Costa, *Fontes inéditas*, pp. 172-73).

[101] Mercurian to Meléndez, Rome 6 August 1575, ARSI, Tolet. 1, ff. 51ᵛ-52ʳ.

[102] *Jesuit Missions to Ireland*, pp. 34-35.

[103] FitzMaurice to Mercurian, St. Malo 31 January 1576, (I was unable to locate the original and have relied on a transcript in ABSI, 46/23/8, pp. 251-52); Mercurian to FitzMaurice, Rome 16 April 1576, ARSI, Franc. 1/I, f. 52ᵛ.

[104] We do not know the exact date of his dismissal but the *terminus ad quem* is 18 March 1577 (Mercurian to Jean Harlem, Rome 18 March 1577, ARSI, Fl. Belg. 2, p. 105). Apparently FitzMaurice had not been informed because as late as October he still considered Wolfe a Jesuit (FitzMaurice to Mercurian, Lisbon 1 October 1577, ARSI, Lus. 68, f. 18ʳ [printed in da Costa, *Fontes inéditas*, pp. 178-79]); Ó Fionnagáin, *Jesuit Missions to Ireland*, pp. 34-35. On his dismissal see Ó Fionnagáin, pp. 37-41.

Alessandro Farnese, Prince and later Duke of Parma, as Don Juan's aide and eventual successor after Don Juan died of plague on 1 October 1578. The Spanish forces quickly took the initiative; on 31 January 1578 they defeated the army of the Estates General at Gembloux. They followed this victory by taking Louvain in February. A month later William (the Silent) of Orange, Archduke Matthias, and all the members of the Estates General fled to safety in Antwerp.

Desperate for aid, the Estates General appealed to the French Duke of Alençon and to the English Queen. In July Alençon (now Duke of Anjou but herein called by his more familiar title) entered Mons with an army of 12,000 men.[105] The Catholic members of the Estates General hoped that his presence would undermine the growing influence of the Prince of Nassau. Although Elizabeth was still reluctant to enter the war, she did encourage John Casimir, administrator of the Rhine Palatinate, to raise an army of mercenaries. Under command of this stalwart Protestant, the army, a counterweight to the French Catholic forces, entered Brabant six weeks after the arrival of Alençon in Mons. The presence of two large foreign forces aggravated the religious differences that always threatened to divide the rebels, differences that were cleverly exploited by Parma.

By the autumn of 1578 the southern provinces refused to contribute further towards the war effort. In January of 1579 representatives from the northern provinces met in Utrecht, endorsed the rebellion, and signed an agreement of alliance and union, the Union of Utrecht. In the same month the Catholic provinces signed an alliance at Arras. Unlike their northern countrymen, they did not endorse the rebellion but initiated negotiations with Parma. A formal treaty was signed at Arras on 17 May 1579. In return for their obedience, Parma ratified the rights and privileges of the provinces and confirmed the Pacification of Ghent and the Perpetual Edict. The Treaty of Arras ended any lingering hope that William could reconcile Catholic and Protestant provinces, and so he signed the Union of Utrecht. With the southern provinces secure, Parma's steady reconquest of the northern ones began.[106]

Concern about the Netherlands might explain Philip's failure to do anything to satisfy the aspirations of the English exiles and their zealous

---

[105] The Apostolic legate in France, Fabio Mirto Frangipani, Archbishop of Nazareth, informed the Cardinal of Como that he had strongly advised the French King and the Queen Mother to avoid any military involvement in the Netherlands and had complained to both that Alençon "while he professes himself a Catholic, . . . has made common cause with heretics, rebels against God and their natural prince, with [John] Casimir, who, besides being a heretic, makes it his profession to hire himself out to all rebels against God . . . " (Paris 31 August 1578, CSP Rome [1572-78] 501-03).

[106] Lynch, *Spain 1516-1598*, pp. 407-11; Limm, *Dutch Revolt*, pp. 49-52.

Roman comrades. The Cardinal of Como complained to Filippo Sega that the Spanish ambassador in Rome had begged the Pope not to put any more pressure on the King to do something about Elizabeth. Such supplications, however, would not silence Rome, and the Nuncio was instructed to continue to raise the matter at any opportunity. Because of Philip's refusal to act, Como feared that the King had abandoned FitzMaurice, who left Lisbon for Ireland "*sine armis, sine classe et sine hominibus.*" The Pope had done all he could for FitzMaurice's enterprise by sending Sir Thomas Stucley with 40,000 crowns. If the King was reluctant to send soldiers, Rome contended, he could still provide financial assistance and military materials, which could be sent secretly from Portugal.

Whether it was Sega's prodding or the success of Parma's army in Flanders we know not, but by the end of March of 1579 Philip was again eager to do all he could for the enterprise. The King, however, still wanted his involvement to remain a secret and preferred that Sega, the Nuncio in Spain, do all the public work. Sega pulled together the various strands. Divers English and Irish gentlemen left Madrid to rendezvous with Stucley in Lisbon. FitzMaurice and Stucley were instructed to work together. Sega wrote to the Italian soldiers and to the Irish bishops. The latter were charged to assist the enterprise. Nicholas Sander wrote a manifesto to justify the venture. All seemed ready. Haste was even more important now because the Spanish ambassador in Paris reported that the English ambassador there, Sir Amias Paulet, Stucley's uncle, had relayed to Elizabeth rumours of Stucley's departure. Even if this report were true, the English would not be able to prevent a landing in Ireland. But Stucley never reached Ireland. After his departure from Italy, Stucley diverted his forces to join the armies of the Portuguese King Sebastian in a crusade against the Moslems in North Africa. The Portuguese were defeated at Alcazar-Kebir on 4 August 1578.[107] Portugal lost a King; the Irish enterprise lost much of its force. The remnant of the enterprise embarked from Portugal, but the Spanish King was now more interested in the Portuguese succession.

Sebastian's immediate successor was his great-uncle Cardinal Henry, last legitimate son of King Manuel I. The Cardinal was old and epileptic; all believed that his reign would be brief. Among other claimants were the Duchess of Braganza; Catherine de Medici; Antonio, Prior of Crato and a illegitimate son of Manuel I; and, through Empress Isabella, eldest daughter of Manuel, Philip II. The Spanish King had the strongest claim and the best

---

[107] Galli to [Sega], Rome 18 January 1578, CSP Rome (1572-78) 369-70; Nicholas Sander to [Galli], Madrid 20 March 1578, *ibid.*, 389; [Sega] to [Galli], [Madrid] 22 March 1578, *ibid.*, 389-91. One of the criticisms levelled against the Portuguese Jesuits by the Nuncio Caligari was their nurturing the young King's unrealistic dream of conquering Africa (*ibid.*, 198-99).

means for ensuring that his right was recognized. Through a twofold campaign of diplomacy and propaganda Philip demonstrated the legitimacy of his claim. In case such reasonable approaches failed, his army studied the border defence and prepared for an attack. Cardinal Henry died in February of 1580 and a council of regents was to settle the succession. But Philip did not await judicial decree. He recalled the Duke of Alba in February and placed him at the head of an army that crossed the Portuguese frontier in June. Meanwhile the Spanish fleet under the Marquis of Santa Cruz sat at the mouth of the Tagus. Don Antonio, Prior of Crato and Philip's only rival, escaped to northern Portugal in August and eventually fled abroad. Philip was officially recognized as King in April of 1581.[108] Philip's acquisition of the only other world empire fuelled the fears of France and England.

The Portuguese fiasco at Alcazar-Kebir gained Philip another throne and deprived the Irish enterprise of one of its leaders and many of its forces. Yet it did not deter the organizers. Sega encouraged FitzMaurice to embark alone and suggested to Galli that an Italian nuncio accompany the invaders. Sega preferred that a Jesuit be appointed.[109] Before Galli learned of the defeat at Alcazar-Kebir, he advised Sega to continue his campaign for the enterprise "and now that we are in the dance we must needs lead it as far as we may, and disguise certain shortcomings, which, affairs being as they are, cannot be helped: therefore it will be well that you walk warily, and not only make no display of dissatisfaction, but encourage and embolden them by exhortations to make their deeds substantiate the Pope's expectation and their own promises . . . ."[110]

FitzMaurice finally sailed for Ireland with 700 men, arms, and money. He landed at Smerwick in County Kerry on 17 July 1579. Flanked by Sander as papal Nuncio, a bishop and a few friars, FitzMaurice unfurled a papal banner, issued a proclamation written by Sander, and invited the Irish lords to join him in a rebellion against the heretical pretended Queen of England, for the glory of God and the restoration of Catholicism.[111] Initial response was very disappointing. Nicholas Sander promised the Irish that additional support could be expected from the continent and that the

---

[108] Lynch, *Spain 1516-1598*, pp. 429-35.

[109] We do not know if the papacy requested a Jesuit from Mercurian. I would assume that Gregory XIII did not, since I have found no reference to any request among the manuscripts in the archives. If the request had been made, Mercurian would of necessity have granted it. The man selected for this role was Nicholas Sander.

[110] [Sega] to [Galli], Madrid 26 August 1578, CSP Rome (1572-78) 496-98; [Galli] to [Sega], Rome 27 August 1578, *ibid.*, 499. In a later letter Galli complained of the amount of money the Pope spent on this enterprise, but he did not deem this the time to demand compensation from Portugal for the men and arms lost in Africa ([Galli] to [Sega], [Rome] 2 October 1578, *ibid.*, 511-12).

[111] On Sander's involvement see Veech, *Sanders*, pp. 259-92.

Catholics in England and Scotland were poised for rebellion. FitzMaurice tried to enlist the support of the Earls of Desmond and Kildare and the various lords in Munster. Most, however, e.g. Turlough Luineach O'Neill, refused to commit themselves. Gerald FitzJames FitzGerald, Earl of Desmond, had no more success as he attempted to rally his forces to resist the invaders. On 1 August two of the Earl's brothers, Sir John and Sir James FitzGerald, assassinated Henry Davells, sent by the Lord Deputy to work with the Earl of Desmond. Many from the Geraldine clan flocked to support the two brothers. Sir John and FitzMaurice tried to work together. Fewer than three weeks later, on 18 August, FitzMaurice was killed in a skirmish while crossing the Shannon near Castleconnell, after some of his men tried to steal horses belonging to the Burkes of Clanwilliam.[112]

The struggle continued under Sir John FitzGerald. Because the Earl of Desmond was unable to restrain his family and supporters, Sir William Pelham, Lord Justice of Ireland, proclaimed him a traitor on 2 November 1579. Even though the Earl had notified the English government of the arrival of FitzMaurice, aided in the capture of Bishop O'Healy of Mayo, and provided provisions for the English troops, he was accused of supporting the rebellion, condoning the murder committed by his brothers, and protecting the rebels, especially Nicholas Sander. Desmond now actively joined the rebellion. He had popular sympathy but little practical support.

In July of 1580 the rebellion was on the brink of extinction when unexpectedly James Eustace, Viscount Baltinglass, rebelled in Leinster. The English had not expected trouble within the Pale and were clearly worried by the support Eustace received. Once again the papal banner was displayed, and Baltinglass complained that a woman could never be supreme governor of the Church and that Ireland had never suffered as much as under Elizabeth. The defence of Catholicism against such transgression provided a rallying cry that transcended petty tribal conflicts. It was commonly believed that O'Neill would soon follow; he did not. In September reinforcements arrived from the continent, but this small force of Italians and Spaniards was massacred at Smerwick on 10 November. With no more hope of outside assistance and with many Irish lords refusing to participate in a conflict beyond their counties, the English slowly eradicated the last vestiges of the rebellion. Nicholas Sander died of dysentery in April of 1581 in the woods of Cleanglaise; in July Baltinglass escaped to the continent. The Earl of Desmond was tracked down and eventually slaughtered near Tralee on 11

---

[112] Edwards, *Church and State in Tudor Ireland*, p. 253; Lennon, *Ireland*, pp. 223-24; Steven G. Ellis, *Tudor Ireland: Crown, Community and the Conflict of Cultures 1470-1603* (London, 1985) pp. 279-80. One of the Italian or Spanish soldiers who came with FitzMaurice left an interesting account of Irish life. See Reginald Walsh, O.P., "Irish Manners and Customs in the Sixteenth Century," *AH* 5 (1916) 17-19.

November 1583.[113] With them died the first enterprise against Elizabeth. Regardless of the ease with which the English took care of the rebellion, many exiles remained hopeful that a second attempt would be more successful—especially if it avoided Ireland.[114]

Mercurian's problem with Wolfe made him cautious in his subsequent dealings with Ireland. Robert Rochford remained the only Jesuit on the island, but little is known about his work. In June of 1575 two other Irish Jesuits were sent home: Charles Lee and David Irish.[115] The reason was restoration of health in their native air. Lee, appointed superior for the journey and in Ireland, warned that no one was to meddle in matters alien to the Society's Institute. They accompanied Edmund Tanner, former Jesuit and newly appointed Bishop of Cork and Cloyne.[116] According to plans, Tanner would ordain Rochford once he arrived in Ireland. Although personally he would have preferred to go to India, Lee acknowledged the instructions and prepared for departure. The two Jesuits caught up with Bishop Tanner in Madrid at the end of August and left for Ireland in early 1576. Lee and Rochford ran a school in Youghal where they instructed their students in Christian doctrine, good morals, and fervent devotion. We know nothing about Dymus's activities. A fourth Jesuit, David Stackpole, returned to Ireland in April of 1577 to take care of an inheritance.[117]

On 6 June 1578 FitzMaurice wrote to Tolomeo Galli and to Everard Mercurian that he would like two or three learned Jesuits to be sent to

---

[113] Hayes-McCoy, "Completion of the Tudor Conquest," pp. 99-109; Edwards, *Church and State in Tudor Ireland*, pp. 254-61; Lennon, *Ireland*, pp. 224-28; Ellis, *Tudor Ireland*, pp. 280-84.

[114] Father Ó Fionnagáin claims that Baltinglass entered the Society of Jesus in Spain and died a few months later (*Jesuit Missions to Ireland*, p. 42). His brother Richard entered the Society in Rome in 1585.

[115] There is some confusion about the identity of this David. There are two possibilities: David Dymus or David Stackpole. Because of Stackpole's later departure for Ireland, this is more than likely Dymus.

[116] Tanner was named the new papal commissary in 1577. During his two years in Ireland he travelled throughout most of the country. He died on 4 June 1579 (Thomas J. Morrissey, S.J., "'Archdevil' and Jesuit: The Background, Life, and Times of James Archer from 1550 to 1604" [unpublished M.A. thesis: University College, Dublin, 1968] 54-55).

[117] Instructions to Charles Lee and David Irish, Rome 25 June 1575, ARSI, Rom. 12/I, ff. 34^{r-v}; Charles Lee to Mercurian, Loreto 30 June 1575, ARSI, Ital. 148, ff. 19^r-20^v; Tanner to Mercurian, Madrid 31 August 1575, transcript in ABSI, 46/23/8, pp. 247-48; Charles Lee to Claudio Acquaviva, Alvero 1 January 1576, transcript in ABSI, 46/23/8, p. 251; Mercurian to Charles Lee and Robert Rochford, Rome 29 April 1577, ARSI, Gal. 45, f. 10^r; Tanner to Mercurian, Ross 11 October 1577, transcript in ABSI, 46/23/8, p. 265. There is nothing in the letters about either David Stackpole or David Dymus so we do not know how long the former remained in Ireland nor do we know when the latter returned to the continent. In a letter to Bishop Tanner, Mercurian grieved at the defection of David and hoped that he would soon return to his senses and persevere in his vocation (Rome 18 August 1578, ARSI, Gal. 45, f. 29^r). This was probably Dymus, who according to Ó Fionnagáin left the Society in 1577 (*Jesuit Missions to Ireland*, p. 42).

Ireland and Scotland. Their task would be to arouse the Catholics to join FitzMaurice's crusade. Mercurian discreetly denied the request. Although the General assured FitzMaurice that he had the good of Ireland and Scotland very much at heart, he did not think the time ripe for establishing the Society there. Two years later Mercurian was still hesitant about sending Jesuits to Ireland.[118] Of the two Jesuits there, Rochford escaped from Ireland in late 1581 after the Baltinglass rebellion, which he strongly supported, was suppressed; Lee was captured and imprisoned in Dublin Castle, presumably accused of involvement in the revolt.[119]

VIII

Hope that Scottish Catholics would provide some assistance during FitzMaurice's rebellion was one of many frustrations suffered by the Irish during that misadventure. Under the guiding hand of James Douglas, Earl of Morton, Scotland did little that would have aroused the fears of Queen Elizabeth. The government was Protestant, pro-English and, as a result of the capture of Edinburgh Castle in May of 1572, with little organized opposition. French influence was minimal. Nonetheless the Guises were still interested in Scotland. In September of 1577 Antonio Maria Salviati, Nuncio in France, wrote to Cardinal Galli that the Scottish ambassador and Louis, Cardinal of Guise had resurrected a proposal to abduct Prince (King) James and to transport him to France, where he would be reared as a Catholic. Nothing came of the scheme. By March of 1578 news of a confederacy against the Earl of Morton aroused fear for James's safety. Mary Stuart's ambassador in Paris, James Beaton, Archbishop of Glasgow, urged the French King to take James under his protection and to safeguard his interests.[120] A coalition overthrew Morton in the spring of 1578, but he later regained his power. The recovery, however, was temporary. Morton's fate was sealed in September of 1579 with the arrival of Esmé Stuart.

A Lennox cousin, Esmé Stuart, Sieur D'Aubigny, born and educated in France, was escorted to his ship by Henry, Duke of Guise when he embarked for Scotland. D'Aubigny rose rapidly in James's affection: in March of 1580 he was elevated to Earl and then Duke of Lennox and made

---

[118] FitzMaurice to the Cardinal of Como, Paris 6 June 1578, CSP Rome (1572-78) 452; same to Mercurian, Paris 6 June 1578, ARSI, Gal. 90, ff. 58^r-59^v; Mercurian to FitzMaurice, Rome 28 June 1578, ARSI, Gal. 45, ff. 27^{r-v}; same to William Murdoch, Rome 7 February 1580, ARSI, Franc. 1/I, f. 71^v.

[119] Claudio Acquaviva to Robert Rochford, Rome 19 January 1582, ARSI, Franc. 1/I, f. 117^r.

[120] Salviati to Galli, Poitiers 12 September 1577, CSP Rome (1572-78) 332-33; same to same, Paris 17 March 1578, ibid., 388; Bellesheim, *Catholic Church of Scotland*, III, 245-46.

custodian of the important fortress of Dumbarton. Fearful that the Duke of Lennox was an agent of the Guise family, the English government tried to counteract his growing influence. That effort ended when the Earl of Morton was arrested on 31 December 1580. Lennox's triumph was complete when Morton was executed in June of 1581.[121]

The Scottish candidates for the Society who had crossed to the continent either with or shortly after de Gouda were distributed among various Jesuit provinces. Many, however, retained contact with their homeland and dreamed one day of initiating a Jesuit mission there. In January of 1579 the first Jesuit returned to Scotland for reasons of health. In a subsequent letter to the General, John Hay recounted his adventures. Stories about Jesuits circulated wildly: "The word Jesuit was in everybody's mouth, and nothing else was heard at table, among the higher classes, in taverns, in the market, or in sermons delivered in the church." The ministers were distressed, and despaired of maintaining their hold over the people: "the Jesuits (they said) were a new race of persons, far worse than the Papists (as they call the Catholics), and so skilled in the use of controversial weapons, that wherever they go they easily lead the minds of men astray." Upon Hay's return to France he asked to be sent back to Scotland "to cultivate that neglected vineyard of our Lord," and he had no doubt that every other Scot would volunteer for the same mission if the General approved.[122]

For reasons unknown, Robert Abercrombie, another Scotsman who crossed to the continent with de Gouda, returned to Scotland for a month in late spring/early summer of 1580."[123] Although there is no evidence that Abercrombie was sent on a reconnaissance mission, his report explained, among other topics, how long it took to get to Scotland, the number of Catholic bishops and clergy within the kingdom, and how favourably disposed the nobles were to Catholicism. The last was especially important. According to Abercrombie, many nobles were Catholic, at least in sympathy; many others could be won over "with presents, offices, and services." Regarding the King, he was "educated in Calvinism, and will not

---

[121] MacCaffrey, *Making of Policy*, pp. 402-12; Wormald, *Court, Kirk, and Community*, p. 146.

[122] Hay to Everard Mercurian, Paris 9 November 1579, in William Forbes-Leith, S.J., ed., *Narratives of Scottish Catholics under Mary Stuart and James VI* (London, 1889) pp. 141-65. Shortly after his return to the continent and probably as a challenge to Scottish Protestant ministers, Hay published *Certaine demandes concerning the Christian religion and discipline, proponed to the ministers of the new pretended kirk of Scotland* (Paris, 1580) STC 12969, ARCR, II, no. 410 (reprinted in Law, ed., *Catholic Tractates*, pp. 31-70).

[123] In his report he specified that he was in Scotland for a month and that it took him two weeks to return to Danzig (now Gdansk). He was back in Danzig by 20 August. His report was edited by William James Anderson, "Narratives of the Scottish Reformation, I: Report of Father Robert Abercrombie, S.J. in the Year 1580," *IR* 7 (1956) 27-59 with a correction in *IR* 8 (1957) 69.

lightly accept any other religion, as he is so strictly watched that no books of Catholic writers can come into his hands. Lord D'Aubigny (Duke of Lennox) was the only Catholic who could talk to the King in private. None of the suggestions made by Abercrombie after his sojourn said anything about further involvement of the Society of Jesus. William Good, however, annotated the report, presumably for Roman authorities. He suggested that a Jesuit be sent to James in the company of the next ambassador. The Jesuit, preferably Italian or French, should be given detailed instructions. Good was uncertain whether the Jesuit should go dressed as a servant or not.

Hay's and Abercrombie's reports fuelled the hopes of the Scottish Jesuits. They and the Archbishop of Glasgow, James Beaton, pleaded with Mercurian to establish a Jesuit mission in Scotland. Cautious as always, Mercurian postponed a decision. Just as the time was not ripe for establishment of the Society in Ireland, neither was it ripe for Scotland.[124] Since neither Mary Queen of Scots nor Pope Gregory XIII was in favour of the proposal, the issue remained in abeyance until the election of a new Jesuit General, Claudio Acquaviva, in February of 1581, and the execution of Morton the following June.[125] As we shall see, it was Acquaviva's support that launched the Jesuit mission to England and a subsequent one to Scotland.

IX

In the late 1570s Spain's power and influence were waxing. Parma's army had secured a peace with the southern provinces in the Netherlands and was successfully subduing the rebellious northern ones. The Ottoman Empire wanted peace with Philip II so that it could deal with the Persians. Rebellions within Spain had been quashed and with the death of King Sebastian, Philip was heir to the Portuguese throne. France and England needed each other, and proposals for the marriage of Elizabeth and Alençon were re-introduced.

The second session of Elizabeth's fourth Parliament (February and March 1576) was no more successful than the first in forcing the Queen to address the problem of Mary Stuart and the question of the succession. Another petition for the Queen to marry prompted the reply that, although she was a private person and not inclined to marriage, she would enter into that state for the good of the kingdom provided certain unspecified conditions were

---

[124] At the time, there were approximately 15 Irish and 20 Scottish Jesuits.
[125] Martin, *Henry III and the Jesuit Politicians*, pp. 67-69; William James Anderson, "Narratives of the Scottish Reformation, II. Thomas Innes on Catholicism in Scotland 1560-1653," *IR* 7 (1956) 120.

met "some touching the estate of her most royall person, some the person of him whom God shall ioyne, some touching the estate of the whole realme. . . ."[126] The last serious marriage negotiations of Elizabeth's reign followed.

According to Wallace MacCaffrey, the diplomatic and marital "flirtation" with Alençon was a turning point in English foreign policy: it marked the kingdom's emergence from traditional quasi-isolationism to active intervention. For years Elizabeth had been urged by her more Protestant Councillors to support the rebels in the Netherlands. But she preferred to undertake such action in alliance with France. Parma's military successes in 1578 brought the issue to a head: unless the Dutch received some foreign assistance their rebellion appeared doomed. As we have seen, Alençon and a small French force came to their assistance. Unless Elizabeth were careful, the long-standing desire that the Habsburgs be evicted from the Low Countries would result in their replacement by the French. A marital treaty with France would allow the two countries to work together against Spain—and prevent France from assuming sovereignty. Elizabeth could accept the role of protector of the Huguenots while assuring Henry III of their loyalty.[127] An alliance with France would end French intrigues with English Catholics and Mary Stuart. The death of the Portuguese King Sebastian and the probability of Philip II's eventual succession further highlighted the importance of an alliance. Nonetheless English domestic opposition led to the abandonment of a marriage proposal in 1579. Alençon sought to renew the marriage plans in 1581 when he made his second visit to England. No treaty was ever signed, however, even though the two countries continued to provide some assistance to the Dutch rebels and arranged the installation of Alençon as sovereign of any of the seventeen Dutch provinces that wished to acknowledge him. They shared efforts to make the Portuguese pretender Don Antonio a viable candidate to oppose Philip II. The second venture ended in the summer of 1582 when Philip expelled the supporters of Don Antonio from the Azores.[128]

---

[126] Hartley, *Proceedings*, p. 464. See also pp. 421-96 and Neale, *Elizabeth I and Her Parliaments*, I, 313-68.

[127] At this time France was relatively free of religious disturbances. Henry III and the Huguenots signed the Peace of Bergerac on 25 September 1577, confirmed by the Edict of Poitiers. The edict forbade leagues and associations throughout the realm, and the treaty restricted Huguenot freedom of worship to the towns already held by them. A further treaty was signed in Nérac in February of 1579. Despite the treaties a seventh war, the "Lovers' War," began in November of 1579 when Henry, Prince of Condé seized a border town. Not all Huguenots, however, supported the war. The Duke of Alençon opposed it because it interfered with his marital negotiations in England and plans for the Netherlands (Knecht, *French Wars of Religion*, pp. 57-58).

[128] MacCaffrey, *Making of Policy*, pp. 243-82; Lynch, *Spain 1516-1598*, p. 438; Doran, *Monarchy and Matrimony*, pp. 130-53.

During the last half of the 1570s Catholics in general and recusancy in particular were increasing within England. Years later when Parsons wrote about this period, he remarked on the boldness of secret Catholics who were "not content with one private Mass, but caused two High Masses to be sung in his house, with all ornaments and inferior ministers, as though he had been in the middle of Rome and not in England." Bishops complained that not enough was being done to stamp out Catholicism. Although the period saw the execution of the first seminary priests, Cuthbert Mayne in 1577 and John Nelson in 1578,[129] the government generally proceeded cautiously. Catholics who had begun to re-appear at court were cultivated by the French ambassador Castelnau de Mauvissière to support the French marriage, a marriage earlier disdained by many because of their adherence to Spain. Now, however, they pressed the marriage upon the Queen with the hope that it would result in an improvement of their situation. Whether the ambassador in his quest for allies encouraged false hopes we do not know, but there was never an official representation to the Queen that the Catholic question be addressed in the marital negotiations.[130]

X

Shortly after the problems at the English College began, William Allen made another attempt to gain Mercurian's support for Jesuit involvement in England. From Reims on 26 October 1578 he reminded the General of their former associations:

> For you will recall that even from the beginnings of our desolation, many were saved from that perdition, either received into your own order, or restored to Mother Church by the zeal and efforts of your men, or then in subsequent years, first at Louvain, then at Douai, finally also at Rome, they were saved by your counsel and charity, by your consolation and especially by your authority.

The kindnesses continued. Only a short time ago the Society granted a few men to the English College even though "the Society [was] otherwise completely occupied with numerous works of charity." In the near future, once the Pope has officially established the college in Rome, the Society's favour will again be seen in its assumption of the administration of the college. "But most approachable father," Allen continued,

---

[129] Nelson entered the Society before his execution (Edwards, *Elizabethan Jesuits*, p. 41; *Mon. Ang.*, II, 415).
[130] Parsons, "Domesticall Difficulties," p. 78; Haigh, *English Reformations*, pp. 262-63; John Bossy, "English Catholics and the French Marriage, 1577-81," *RH* 5 (1959) 2-16.

> Allen in all the responsibilities of his life, son and servant to you and yours, and sincere admirer in Christ, asks, or rather the nation and our native land asks, and suppliantly requests some part of the charity and concern which you bestow upon all nations, Christian and barbarous. Father, do not repel us as we ask for justice. And you who go about collecting sheep for the flock of Christ in the far-off Indies, do not be disdainful of seeking with us the lost British lamb.[131]

In January of 1579 Mercurian explained his unwavering veto: demands on the Society were too great and its men all too few. Although the Society was eager to help all people, "and especially your country of England," the lack of men prevented it. Until the Society had sufficient resources for a mission, Mercurian assured Allen, the Jesuits "will not cease, by the only way we can—namely by our own prayers and masses and those of our subjects—from commending that intention to our Lord God."[132]

Despite Mercurian's position, Allen continued to press for greater cooperation with the Society. Immediately after Agazzari's installation as rector of the English College in Rome, Allen proposed that the affairs of the colleges in Douai and in Rome be placed under control of Agazzari for more efficient regulation. That arrangement appealed to Mercurian and won his approval. He therefore suggested that the proposal be placed before the Pope on some fitting occasion.[133] Nothing more is heard about the recommendation. Did the Pope disapprove? Or was the scheme abandoned in favour of the Society's more direct involvement in England? With hindsight we know that implementation of this proposal would have curtailed—if not prevented—later disturbances at the English College in Rome.

Mercurian's steady unwillingness to embark on a mission discouraged not only Allen but Parsons. In a letter to William Good, Parsons anticipated Good's complaint that there "are Missions for all Contryes but only for England which seemeth to be abandoned above all others." Parsons went so far as to blame Good for the omission because he had not actively pursued that mission while he was in Rome, even though he had more influence than Parsons. Until an English mission was initiated, Parsons and Thomas Darbyshire were doing their best to keep the Englishmen within the Society organized. That task was not easy, because the increasing number of English were assigned to many provinces in various capacities. Recently Parsons had been hopeful. Had not "the enimy cast in an impediment which no man loked for," Good would have been the recipient of good news. Indeed, he

---

[131] Knox, *Letters of Allen*, pp. 68-69.

[132] Mercurian to Allen, Rome 5 January 1579, in Ryan, "Correspondence of Allen," p. 69.

[133] Allen to Agazzari, Reims 28 June 1579, in Ryan, "Correspondence of Allen," p. 17; Mercurian to Allen, Rome 3 June 1579, *ibid.*, p. 71.

probably would have been "pulled . . . out of your furres in Suetia" and assigned.[134]

If only the General would grant the required permission! Parsons assured Good "not only of the Englishmen, but also of all others that abid in the English Colledg, so great and marvellous is the affection they beare to England, and to English Catholics that if our Superiours would but once give a signe of consent to sett open the Colledge gates towards the enterprise of England, they would all runne out, even from the Rector himselfe to the lowest scholer in the Colledge." Although no one knew anything definite, rumours were circulating through Rome that Parsons was petitioning the General to start a Jesuit mission. Many "and they were of the best" now pleaded with Parsons that they be included in any enterprise. The likelihood of such a venture, Parsons sadly concluded, was now low. Any possibility that Mercurian would lift his embargo vanished once the troublesome nature of the English again manifested itself in the nationalistic conflicts at the English College.[135]

* * * * *

In *An Introduction to Jesuit Life*, Thomas H. Clancy, S.J., summarized Everard Mercurian thus:

> He enjoyed several distinctions: the oldest man elected [General], the first man who had entered the Society as a priest to be elected, and the first non-Spaniard. Mercurian is famous for his promulgation of the *Summary of the Constitutions* and various Rules, his decree on spiritual authors "not suitable for Ours," and for his work on the *Ratio Studiorum*. He was a consolidator and rather cautious.[136]

Joseph de Guibert, S.J., a historian of the Society's spirituality, states similarly: Mercurian "feared more than anything else to see his religious no longer understanding the original end and form of life which had been established for them by their founder. . . ."[137] Twice he took decisive action against two highly esteemed and holy Spaniards, Antonio Cordeses in 1574 and Baltasar Álvarez in 1578, because he considered the type of prayer they

---

[134] Parsons, alas, does not explain the impediment but it is likely that disturbances at the English College were to blame. The English Jesuits in Rome were opposed to sending two Jesuits to work at the English College in the summer of 1578 because they "were loth that our Fathers should go thither to se the nakedness of our Nation, and the impossibility to redresse it."

[135] Parsons to Good, Rome [after 19 March 1579], in Hicks, *Letters of Persons*, pp. 5-28.

[136] (St. Louis, 1976) p. 120.

[137] *The Jesuits: Their Spiritual Doctrine and Practice* (St. Louis, 1964) p. 227. See pp. 221-29 for the context.

advocated too contemplative, rigoristic and contrary to the Society's Institute. A desire to prevent further problems, e.g. a movement away from the activist spirituality understood by Mercurian as the only truly Ignatian form, towards a contemplative, quasi-monastic spirituality that smacked of the *alumbrados*,[138] was the motivation of his prohibition of certain authors, including many medieval mystics, e.g. Jan van Ruysbroeck, Henry Suso, and John Tauler.[139] Ignatian prayer—Jesuit prayer—must remain rooted in three questions from the *Spiritual Exercises*: "What have I done for Christ? What am I doing for Christ? What ought I to do for Christ?"[140] Jesuit prayer must lead to work for the *magis*, the "greater glory of God."

Mercurian's preoccupation with fidelity to the Society's Institute appears frequently in his dealings with David Wolfe. Mercurian had inherited the Jesuit mission to Ireland. Besides the religious problems that surfaced during Borgia's tenure, Mercurian had to deal with a gradual movement towards political involvement. Unlike Cordeses and Álvarez, Wolfe went to the other extreme: his work for the *magis* involved him in diplomatic and political affairs. Commenting on Antonio Possevino's mission to Sweden where, with the connivance of the King, he established what was ostensibly a Lutheran seminary for the training of Catholic missionaries, John Bossy astutely noted that "the boundaries between Jesuit missioning and Jesuit politics were, in Europe at least, rather thin. . . ."[141] Mercurian sought to make this line more visible.

---

[138] Implicit approval of Mercurian's interpretation can be found in Robert E. McNally, S.J., "The Council of Trent, the 'Spiritual Exercises,' and the Catholic Reform," *Church History* 34 (1965) 36-49. Reprinted as Facet Book Historical Series—15 (Philadelphia, 1970) p. 15: "The revolutionary cast of mind, which is characteristic of Ignatius is expressed in the society's Constitutions. Here the master idea of the *Exercises*—the Christian as God's perfect servant—is concretely embodied. The whole juridical structure of his order is inspired by the conviction that it is to produce perfect servants of God. It has been well remarked [by Joseph de Guibert, S.J.]; 'Service is the operative word in the Foundation text and in all Ignatian spirituality'. In terms of the apostolate of service, Ignatius broke ruthlessly with the monastic and mendicant tradition of the medieval Church."

[139] John O'Malley argues that Mercurian's understanding of Ignatian spirituality was too narrow. His approach was "cautious and soberly ascetical, favourable almost exclusively to a methodical and even moralistic style of prayer, suspicious of contemplation and other higher forms of prayer as inimical to the active ministry to which the order was committed." Under the generalate of his successor, Claudio Acquaviva, a second strain, "more expansive, more syncretistic within the broad tradition of Christian spirituality, and intent on developing the implications of the affective and even mystical elements" developed. See "Early Jesuit Spirituality: Spain and Italy," in *Christian Spirituality: Post-Reformation and Modern*, eds. Louis Dupré and Don E. Saliers (New York, 1989) pp. 15-17. Reprinted in John W. O'Malley, S.J., *Religious Culture in the Sixteenth Century* (Aldershot, 1993), article IX.

[140] Ignatius Loyola, *The Spiritual Exercises of St. Ignatius*, ed. Louis J. Puhl, S.J. (Chicago, 1951) no. 53

[141] "The Jesuits and the Reformation," in *Reconciliation: Essays in Honour of Michael Hurley*, ed. Oliver Rafferty, S.J. (Dublin, 1993) p. 224. On Possevino's Swedish mission see Oskar Garstein, *Rome and the Counter-Reformation in Scandinavia* (Bergen, 1963) *passim*.

In the Jesuit *Constitutions* Loyola was rather ambiguous about political involvement. In his discussion of works proper to the Society, Ignatius wrote: "That the Society may be able to devote itself more entirely to the spiritual pursuits pertaining to its profession, it should abstain *as far as possible* [italics mine] from all secular employments. . . ."[142] Later, in the delineation of criteria to be employed in decisions about missions, he wrote: "First of all, the members of the Society may occupy themselves in undertakings directed toward benefits for the soul, and also *in those directed toward benefits for the body through the practice of mercy and charity* [italics mine]. . . . In all these cases, if both things cannot be done simultaneously and the other considerations are equal, the spiritual goods ought to be preferred to the bodily. . . ."[143] There was room for considerable interpretation in each restriction. The second General Congregation (1565), addressing a request for a Jesuit theologian to reside in a cardinal's court and to travel in his entourage, decreed that "no one of our religious ought to be assigned to princes or other lords, secular or ecclesiastical, to attach themselves to their courts or dwell . . . *except occasionally and for a very brief period of one or two months* [italics mine]."[144] Prompted by Portuguese Jesuits, Mercurian interpreted such aspects of the Institute very narrowly in the case of Wolfe. The Irishman had attached himself to the court of a secular prince, and his activities were works of mercy directed towards the alleviation of suffering in Ireland. But Mercurian admonished Wolfe to follow the Institute as interpreted by the General; Wolfe's failure to withdraw from political and diplomatic involvement resulted in his dismissal from the Society. Other Jesuits in Ireland apparently followed Wolfe's lead. As a result Edmund Daniel was executed in 1572; Charles Lee was imprisoned and Robert Rochford forced to flee in 1581. As a result Mercurian was not eager to send more Jesuits to Ireland or to approve a new mission to England that could evolve in the same direction.

Mercurian's efforts to ensure that Jesuits stayed away from political affairs were made more difficult by the zealous Counter-Reformation activities of Gregory XIII. According to Tolomeo, Cardinal Galli, of all the orders Gregory XIII preferred the Society of Jesus. He was a generous benefactor whose financial assistance furthered Jesuit educational enterprises throughout Europe. Moreover he often employed individual Jesuits in sensitive diplomatic roles, e.g. Possevino's mission to Sweden in 1577 and Tommaso Raggio's and Giambattista Eliano's mission to the Maronites in

---

[142] *Cons.* no. 591. See also nos. 793, 794.
[143] *Cons.* no. 623b.
[144] John W. Padberg, S.J., Martin D. O'Keefe, S.J., and John L. McCarthy, S.J., eds., *For Matters of Greater Moment: The First Thirty Jesuit General Congregations* (St. Louis, 1994) decree 40, p. 122.

1578.[145] But some missions entrusted to the Society could involve Jesuits in activities that Mercurian would rather avoid.

Professor Elisabeth G. Gleason may well be right in her selection of Paul III as the first Counter-Reformation pope,[146] but few popes typify the military spirit of the Counter-Reformation as well as Gregory XIII. Through his nuncios Gregory stayed abreast of developments throughout Europe and did all he could to further a more forward policy against Protestants wherever they were to be found. Gregory provided military subsidies and encouraged intrigues. To the dismay of Mercurian, David Wolfe was pulled more and more into the whirlpool. In 1575 Mercurian finally—we do not know how—secured Gregory's instruction to the Nuncio in Spain that Jesuits were not to be employed in any matter alien to their Institute.

The Irish experience left Mercurian averse to any Jesuit mission to England or to Scotland. The latter could be postponed because neither the ruler, Mary Stuart, nor the Pope asked for Jesuit assistance. A mission to England was pressed upon him periodically. But the same men, e.g. William Allen, who requested Jesuit involvement in England were intricately involved in papal and Spanish schemes for the invasion of the isles. A mission to England would introduce Jesuits into these circles. Everard Mercurian would extol Nicholas Sander and provide him with the Society's assistance, but he would not want a Jesuit in that role. He had learned from David Wolfe that such activities were not according to the spirit of the Institute.

---

[145] William V. Bangert, S.J., *A History of the Society of Jesus* (St. Louis, 1972) pp. 79-83; Ludwig Freiherr von Pastor, *The History of the Popes From the Close of the Middle Ages*, vol. XIX (London, 1930) pp. 234-58.

[146] "Who Was the First Counter-Reformation Pope?," *CHR* 81 (1995) 173-84.

CHAPTER FOUR

"THE ENTERPRISE IS BEGUN"

Friction between English and Welsh at the English College in Rome did not end with the arrival of the Jesuits. Robert Parsons therefore suggested to William Allen that he return to use his personal influence to quell the national strife. While in Rome he could negotiate a larger papal subsidy for the English colleges. A third reason—and indeed the most important—was "the right informing also of F. Generall of the Society in our English affayres, where perhaps you may induce him to joyne some of his also (seeing God hath sent so many now of our nation into the Society) with our other Priests to go into England." Mercurian might be more sympathetic since Allen and others had written that many in England desired Jesuit involvement. Parsons did not doubt that "there wanteth not desire in divers to adventure there bloud in that mission, among whome I dare put myselfe for one, if Holy Obedience imploy me therein." His personal involvement, however, was not important as was "the combination of other Fathers of the Society with our Priests of the seminary is so importing a thing and of so great consequence": it alone would justify Allen's trip.[1]

How oddly roles were reversed! At every opportunity Ignatius Loyola had sought to send a few Jesuits into Marian England only to have his offers refused by a hesitant Cardinal Pole. Twenty-five years later Allen, Pole's successor—not yet in rank but in influence—actively sought from a reluctant Everard Mercurian, Loyola's successor, Jesuit assistance in the reconversion of England. Pole resisted all Loyola's offers of men with a mere request for prayers; Mercurian offered prayers when Allen wanted men. In both cases the Englishman won. During his visit to Rome, Allen had an audience with Mercurian and his consultors.[2] The petition that he addressed to them was better organized and more detailed than the earlier ones. Probably with the

---

[1] Rome 30 March 1579, in Leo Hicks, S.J., ed., *Letters and Memorials of Father Robert Persons, S.J.* (London, 1942) pp. 3-4.

[2] In his autobiography Parsons states that he gained the Pope's approval of Allen's visit to Rome through the mediation of Father Alfonso Agazzari. Allen arrived in October of 1579 and remained until February of 1580 (Robert Parsons, "Father Persons' Autobiography," ed. John H. Pollen, S.J., in *Miscellanea II* [London, 1906] p. 26). An enthusiastic supporter of Allen, Parsons hoped that he would become the organizer of the English mission (Parsons to William Good, Rome [after 19 March 1579], in Hicks, *Letters of Persons*, p. 27).

advice and assistance of Parsons, Allen cunningly modelled his plea on the guidelines for the choice of ministries established in the *Constitutions*.

Since Loyola assumed that there would be more requests for the Society's assistance than it had manpower to provide, he exhorted superiors to consider carefully the location of the mission and its duration, the availability of qualified men, and the conditions under which the men would live and work. The superior should investigate "the disposition of the people." Although a favourable disposition towards the Society by the general population was important, Loyola was especially concerned with elites, a concern already noted in this monograph. Were "important and public" persons agreeable? Loyola was also aware that the Society had certain obligations to areas that produced vocations. Finally, preference should be given to the more important countries and to those places "where the enemy of Christ our Lord has sown cockle," where heresy was undermining the Church.[3]

Allen's reconstructed petition followed these criteria. He repeated his claim that influential lay Catholics sought Jesuit assistance.[4] To their request were now added the needs of seminary priests. Priests already engaged in the dangerous but essential English mission sought the Society's solace and assistance. Because the Society, Allen continued, had been especially raised

---

[3] *Cons.* nos. 603-32.

[4] One of the reasons given by the discontented English students at the college in Rome for Jesuit assistance was: "there is such great esteem for the Fathers of the Society of Jesus in the remote areas of England and the surrounding kingdoms, that many people seem to be retained to the faith by the very name of Jesuits, or are restrained from attacking that name. For since they have nothing nor have ever heard anything which either heretics or catholics object to in these men or in their morals or writings, they are compelled to hesitate about heresy which these men so vehemently oppose. Hence it happens that because of the highest opinion that our people have of these Fathers, our own approach to them would be more acceptable and of greater authority if they understood that we had been educated under the discipline of such men" (Parsons, "A Storie of Domesticall Difficulties," ed. John H. Pollen, S.J., in *Miscellanea II* [London, 1906] p. 115). In the first Annual Letter of the English Mission, the anonymous author, probably Parsons, repeated this assertion: "To share in these dangers [the persecutions] and merits, our Fathers are invited by the English themselves, with most pressing entreaties and by constant letters; they desire to have some of the Society to whom they can fly for advice and assistance amidst the innumerable dangers which every moment threaten them" (*Annuae Litterae Societatis Iesu anni 1581* [Rome, 1583] pp. 205-11, translated in Henry Foley, S.J., *Records of the English Province of the Society of Jesus*, 7 vols. in 8 [Roehampton/London, 1877-84] III, 38). Edward Rishton echoed the esteem in which many English held the Society: "There was much talk at this time among the Catholics of the admirable training, order, and learning of the Fathers of the Society of Jesus, how much they were in favour with God and man. There was also a very great desire on the part of the English to profit by their labours. Earnest representations were therefore made to the superiors of the society—the Pope himself exerted his authority to the same end—that they should send some of their own subjects, especially the most distinguished Englishmen who were in the order, to labour in the British harvest; for many men of great piety and learning had during their exile entered the society" (Nicholas Sander, *Rise and Growth of the Anglican Schism*, trans. and ed. David Lewis [London, 1877] p. 309).

by God at this time to fight heresy,[5] it could execute that role in England, a country nearer and needier than India. The preservation of the unity of Christendom was more important than its expansion, he thought. God had already made his choice very clear: the presence of so many Englishmen in the order was a sure sign that the Society should be in England.

The Society's recent undertaking in the English College was advanced as another reason: the fathers could continue their instruction by their example in the mission. The Jesuits had a distinct advantage over other orders in regard to England. As a new order, they had no pre-Reformation associations and could not be suspected of self-interest or surreptitious ploys to recover ecclesiastical estates. If the Society were to get involved now, it would reap benefits later. Once Roman Catholicism was restored, the English would remember with gratitude the Society's contribution. Allen concluded his plea with a gratuitous analogy between Benedictines and Jesuits. Nearly a thousand years earlier a Pope Gregory had despatched members of a new religious order to convert Anglo-Saxon England. Now another Gregory wanted to send another new order to reconvert England. With God's grace, the results would be as spectacular.[6]

Mercurian still hesitated. As Provincial he had been wary of the mission of de Gouda into Scotland. As General he was anxious about Wolfe in Ireland and judged his political involvement a violation of the Society's Institute. He had resisted pleas from FitzMaurice for Jesuits and he was denying petitions for more Jesuits in Ireland and for a renewal of a mission in Scotland. Because of the Society's prior experience in the British Isles, Mercurian and his consultors were especially worried about conditions in England, a criterion ignored or forgotten by the future cardinal. Moreover there may have been a fundamental disagreement between Allen and Mercurian over the very nature of the mission.[7]

---

[5] Allen's argument testifies to the prevalence of Jerónimo Nadal's interpretation of the Society's origins.

[6] Comparison between the two Gregories was common and can be found in the bull *Quoniam Divinae Bonitati* that founded the English College in Rome. The bull is printed in Michael Williams, *The Venerable English College Rome* (London, 1979) pp. 210-19. See also Robert Parsons, "The Entrance of the Fathers of the Society into England," ed. John H Pollen, S.J., in *Miscellanea II* (London, 1906) pp. 194-95. A few years later, in *An apologie and true declaration of the institution and endevours of the two English Colleges* (Mons, 1581) STC 369, ARCR II, no. 6, Allen defended the involvement of the Jesuits in the English mission and explained how Mercurian "much moved by the example and profitable endevours of the Priests of both the Colleges, and other learned men at home and in banishment" (f. 83ʳ) finally agreed to the venture. In this book Allen elaborated many of the reasons that he presented to Mercurian (ff. 80ʳ-86ʳ).

[7] On the possibility of a divergence between the mission strategy of Allen and Parsons, on the one hand, and of Mercurian on the other, see Thomas M. McCoog, S.J., "'Playing the Champion': The Role of Disputation in the Jesuit Mission," in *The Reckoned Expense: Edmund Campion and the Early English Jesuits. Essays in Celebration of the First Centenary of Campion*

The dangers of the English mission were too great to be overlooked.[8] Mercurian conceded that the work was necessary and important. But could he knowingly and willingly send his men into such perils? Even if many, perhaps attracted by the dangers and the possibility of martyrdom, would volunteer for the mission, would the good gained by their labours outweigh the loss of these men? Mercurian moreover feared that the English government would depict the missionary expedition as a political enterprise, a fear very understandable because of Papal-Spanish machinations still under consideration. If the government did interpret the Jesuit mission as political, it would make the English Jesuits odious to their countrymen and their actions suspect—perhaps not to the wiser but certainly to the greater part of the people. Moreover, once in England, the General doubted that Jesuits would be able to live an appropriately religious life according to their Institute. The General did not see how they could observe "their religious discipline of prayer, exhortations, meditation, conference and other such like helps." Finally, the absence of a bishop caused further problems. The General worried how so many priests could live in peace and harmony without a hierarchy.[9]

During subsequent conferences, Oliver Mannaerts, German assistant, and Claudio Acquaviva, Roman Provincial, two of the five Jesuits whose advice the General sought on the topic,[10] convinced Mercurian that the English mission was important enough to risk the dangers he feared.[11] Mannaerts's support is interesting because, as we have seen, he earlier had been against sending Edmund Hay into Scotland; later he would side with the English opponents of Parsons. Acquaviva was such an enthusiastic supporter of the endeavour that he himself volunteered for the mission. He was not sent but we shall see how he defended and nurtured the mission despite opposition from different quarters once he became General in 1581 upon the death of

---

Hall, Oxford (1896-1996), ed. Thomas M. McCoog, S.J. (Woodbridge, 1996) pp. 119-39.

[8] In *Roman Catholicism in England* (Oxford, 1985), Edward Norman asserts "The Generals of the Society did not regard England as a particularly fruitful prospect, and gave work there a low priority. . ." (p. 19). This is a far too simplistic explanation of the General's hesitation.

[9] Allen was also concerned about the lack of proper ecclesiastical government. See his letter to Maurice Chauncy, Prior of the English Carthusians at Bruges, Cambrai 10 August 1577, in Thomas Francis Knox, ed., *The Letters and Memorials of William Cardinal Allen (1532-1594)* (London, 1882) pp. 31-37.

[10] Technically the General had only four consultors, each of whom was in charge of a specific geographic area. They were Mannaerts, Benedetto Palmio as Italian assistant, Pedro Fonseca as Portuguese assistant, and Gil González Dávila as Spanish assistant. Acquaviva must have been consulted because the English College in Rome fell within his jurisdiction.

[11] Although the documents do not mention the negotiations for a marital treaty between France and England in 1579, one wonders if the expectation that the plight of Catholics would improve after a marriage, influenced the decision. See Susan Doran, *Monarchy and Matrimony: The Courtships of Elizabeth I* (London, 1996) pp. 154-94, 216-17.

Mercurian the previous year. These two advisors were subsequently appointed the mission's organizers. After Pope Gregory XIII gave approval,[12] Robert Parsons was named superior.[13]

Mercurian's advisors must have been extremely persuasive to have won his approval. But even though the mission was accepted, the General's objections were not ignored. The inclusion of Thomas Goldwell, Bishop of St. Asaph, allayed his concern about clerical discontent and lack of proper ecclesiastical governance. The General's two other anxieties appear in his instructions to Robert Parsons and Edmund Campion, instructions that were required in the *Constitutions* so that all missionaries would know the purpose, methods, and goals of their projects.[14] There Mercurian stressed the religious nature of the mission so as to refute any government claim to the contrary, and urged the implementation of as much of the Society's Institute as possible.

Apparently the decision as to who would be sent on the mission was left to Allen. Parsons was an obvious choice because he had earlier volunteered to return to England and possibly because his influence had tipped the scales in favour of Jesuit involvement. The priest Edmund Campion and the lay brother Ralph Emerson would be his companions.[15] Campion was one of the

---

[12] In his explication of discussions surrounding the foundation of the mission, Francis Edwards concludes "But Pope Gregory wanted the mission and that was that" (*Robert Persons: The Biography of an Elizabethan Jesuit 1546-1610* [St. Louis, 1995] p. 27). The mission, however, was not initiated by the Pope. If it had been, there would have been no need for a consultation because: "In this matter, the Society has placed its own judgment and desire under that of Christ our Lord and His vicar; and neither the superior for himself nor any individual member of the Society will be able for himself or for another to arrange or to try to arrange, directly or indirectly, with the Pope or his ministers to reside in or to be sent rather to one place than another. The individual members will leave this entire concern to the supreme vicar of Christ and to their own superior; and in regard to his own person the superior will in our Lord leave this concern to His Holiness and to the Society" (*Cons.* no. 606). The Society may represent to the Pope specific problems regarding a mission, e.g. de Gouda's assignment to Scotland, but, if the Pope persists, the mission must be accepted.

[13] Parsons, "Entrance of the Jesuits into England," 194-95; Robert Parsons, "Of the Life and Martyrdom of Father Edmond Campian," *Letters and Notices* 11 (1877) 328-32; Bernard Basset, *The English Jesuits* (London, 1967) pp. 33-34.

[14] *Cons.* nos. 612-14. See Ignatius Loyola, *Letters of St. Ignatius Loyola*, ed. William J. Young, S.J. (Chicago, 1959) pp. 51-52, 93-96, 212-14, 267-69, and 365-67 for examples of instructions to other Jesuit missionaries.

[15] Christopher Perkins (or Parkins) was originally selected. Parsons ("Punti per la Missione d'Inghilterra," ed. John H. Pollen, S.J., in *Miscellanea IV* [London, 1907] p. 101) recalled that in 1579 Allen, Parsons, and Mercurian considered Perkins very qualified for the mission. When approached about going, Perkins replied that he was willing but that he wanted dispensations from the Pope to go to Protestant churches and to take the oath of allegiance to the Queen. Parsons and Allen attributed this view to naiveté and kept his name on the list of prospective missionaries. Perkins was later expelled from the Society. See *Mon. Ang.*, II, 431; Thomas H. Clancy, S.J., "The First Generation of English Jesuits 1555-1585," *AHSI* 57 (1988) 149; Patrick McGrath, "Apostate and Naughty Priests in England under Elizabeth I," in *Opening the Scrolls*, ed. Dominic Aidan Bellenger, O.S.B. (Bath, 1987) pp. 53-55.

most important Englishmen to join the Society in the 1570s. A promising Oxford scholar who enjoyed the patronage of Robert Dudley, Earl of Leicester, Campion fled to the continent for religious reasons in 1571. He applied to the Society in Rome in 1573 and was assigned to the Austrian province. While Allen and Parsons were commending the English mission to Mercurian and his advisors, Campion taught at the college in Prague.[16] On 5 December 1579 Allen wrote to Campion from Rome to inform him of his selection as missionary. Allen urged him to hasten from Prague to Rome as soon "as your health allows—I permit no exception for business or other impediment." Confident that Campion did not shrink at the prospect of his mission, Allen informed him that the English harvest was so great that "it calls for men of greater capacity, and for you especially. . . . Reverend Father General has acceded to the prayers of many people. The Pope has approved—he is the true father of our country. God himself, doubtless, in Whose hands is your destiny, has at last permitted that our Campion should be restored to us."[17] Campion left Prague, albeit reluctantly, in early March and arrived in Rome on 9 April 1580.[18] On the 14th Campion and Parsons, with Oliver Mannaerts, had an audience with Pope Gregory XIII at which certain faculties and privileges were granted. The more religious will be discussed presently; here it is sufficient to note the most celebrated: a mitigation of Pope Pius V's pronouncement on Elizabeth.

During the audience eighteen questions were addressed to Gregory XIII; the majority concerned the validity of the bull against Elizabeth.[19] Briefly, Gregory explained that English Catholics were not bound under pain of sin or excommunication to obey the bull. Nonetheless Elizabeth should be

---

[16] Richard Simpson's *Edmund Campion*, 2nd. edition (London, 1896) remains the best biography although it needs to be updated in light of recent research. Evelyn Waugh's *Edmund Campion* (London, 1935) is the best-written but contains a number of historical errors.

[17] Knox, *Letters of Allen*, pp. 84-85 (translated in Francis Edwards, S.J., ed., *The Elizabethan Jesuits* [London, 1981] pp. 72-73).

[18] On Campion's reluctance see McCoog, "'Playing the Champion'."

[19] The document *Ad consolationem et instructionem quorundam Catholicorum angustiis constituorum quaestiones aliquot* lacks specific information regarding authorship and date. The original manuscript can be found in ASV, Arm. 64, vol. 28, ff. 171^{r-v}, 176^{r}-79^{v}. M. Petriburg. [Mandell Creighton] published the document, with the omission of the answers to the final three questions, in "The Excommunication of Queen Elizabeth," *EHR* 7 (1892) 84-88. The questions are numbered from one to nineteen, but inadvertently no. 6 was omitted. Arnold Oskar Meyer (*England and the Catholic Church under Queen Elizabeth* [London, 1916] p. 136 n. 1) places it between 1578 and 1580. John Hungerford Pollen, S.J. (*The English Catholics in the Reign of Queen Elizabeth: A Study of Their Politics Civil Life and Government* [London, 1920] p. 294 and n. 1) considers it a "legal opinion of some Roman jurist, possibly Father Antonio Possevino, S.J." Peter Holmes (*Resistance and Compromise: The Political Thought of the English Catholics* [Cambridge, 1982] pp. 42-43, 228 n. 31) follows Pollen. Father Edwards assumes that the document records questions addressed to the Pope by the Jesuits before their departure (*Robert Persons*, p. 28). I think that he is right.

considered an excommunicated and unlawful queen.[20] Regarding English Catholic subjects' obedience to such a queen, they could "with safe conscience" obey Elizabeth in civil matters. Catholics could not, however, "with safe conscience" defend Elizabeth against any opponent who waged war because of the bull or of zeal for Catholicism. This was further nuanced: Catholics need refrain from assisting the Queen only after hope of victory was certain. Regarding the complex issue of tyrannicide, it was not lawful for a "private person" to kill any tyrant unless that person were to succeed to the throne after her death. It would be lawful for someone to assassinate her if it were certain on accession that he would free the realm from oppression. But, the Pope concluded, things being what they were, it was better not to talk about such matters. In sum, it was lawful to take up arms for the end and by the means carefully explained by the Pope: prudently and not rashly and in order that Catholics might be rescued from harassment.[21]

The final five questions dealt with fasting and attendance at Protestant services. The Pope decided that it was not expedient to dispense Catholics who lived among heretics from the prohibition of meat on days of abstinence. Yet he explained that meat could be eaten "by reason of necessity and for the sake of life" as long as scandal was not given. The question whether a dispensation could be given so that Catholics could be present in Protestant churches during services but without participating in them received the answer *Respondetur ut paulo ante*. Presumably this refers to the response given to the question about fasting. A specific case was cited in yet another question. A Catholic noblewoman recently reconciled to the Church was a lady-in-waiting to the Queen. It was asked whether in order to avoid detection and persecution, she could accompany Elizabeth to a secret chamber from which the Queen observed heretical services, while the noblewoman herself neither by word nor by gesture expressed approval or disapproval. Although such behaviour should be avoided as much as possible for fear of scandal, the Pope permitted her to continue.

The Jesuits left Rome four days after the audience. Besides the three Jesuits the party included the aged Bishop of St. Asaph; Dr. Nicholas Morton, English penitentiary of St. Peter's; four elderly Marian priests from the English Hospice, Dr. Edward Bromberg, William Giblet, Thomas Crane, and William Kemp; three young priests from the English College: Ralph

---

[20] "*Principio videtur expedire declarari autoritate Pontificis Catholicos Regni Angliae non obligari ad peccatum aut excommunicationem ex vi bullae editae a Pio V⁰ ad tollendas multas difficultas quae ex predicta bulla exortae sunt.*"

[21] "*Licuit arma sumere eo fine et mediis quae ante explicata sunt, id est, prudenter et non temere, atque ut Catholici eriperentur iis vexationibus corporis et animi quibus tunc afficiebantur.*"

136   CHAPTER FOUR

Sherwin, Luke Kirby, and Edward Rishton; and two laymen, Thomas Bruscoe and John Pascal. Bishop Goldwell and Dr. Morton later withdrew and were replaced by Dr. Humphrey Ely and Fathers John Hart and Thomas Cottam.[22] The news that awaited them at Reims deflated their optimism: at the time of their departure from Rome Dr. Nicholas Sander had been sent as papal Nuncio with five ships of men and material, to assist the Fitz-Maurice rebellion in Ireland.[23] As a result rumours of the formation of a great army for an invasion of England were circulating throughout the countryside.[24] Because of increased English vigilance, the party broke into small groups. The three Jesuits stayed at the Flemish college in St. Omer. Dressed as a soldier, Robert Parsons crossed to England on 11 June. He was followed by Campion and Emerson on the 24th.[25] The men described by the Jesuit Henry More as the "indomitable defenders of the ancient faith" had arrived.

According to the General's instructions,[26] the English mission had a twofold objective: primarily it was to strengthen Roman Catholics in their faith and, secondarily, to recover those who had left the Church through ignorance or temptation. The General had no illusions about the mission. He knew that it would be especially difficult because the Jesuits would be surrounded by enemies of "outstanding talent, skill and malice." Thus he recommended two tactics for the accomplishment of Jesuit goals despite the competence of their opponents: extraordinary virtue and prudence, which would be best preserved through conscientious observation of the Society's style of life as far as the conditions in England would allow. Since circumstances precluded complete observance of the Jesuit life, "their chief aid will be a right intention, and a combination of distrust in them them-

---

[22] In a letter to the Pope, Goldwell confessed that it would be difficult for him to enter the kingdom without danger. If the Pope wanted him to, he would risk his life. Otherwise he would not cross to England. The letter, written from Reims on 13 July 1580, is printed in Simpson, *Edmund Campion*, pp. 148-49.

[23] About this expedition Parsons later wrote: "it belonged not to us to mislike, yet were we heartily sorry partly for that we had just cause to suspect and fear that which came to pass, that so rare and worthy a man should be lost in that action; and secondly for that we did easily foresee that this would be laid against us and other priests that should be taken in England as though we had been privy or partakers thereof, as in very truth we were not, nor ever heard or suspected the same until this day" ("Of the Life and Martyrdom," 11).

[24] To suppress these rumours, a proclamation was issued on 15 July 1580 (Paul L. Hughes and James F. Larkin, C.S.V., eds. *Tudor Royal Proclamations*, 3 vols. [New Haven, 1964-69] II, 469-71).

[25] Pollen, *English Catholics in the Reign of Elizabeth*, pp. 293, 331.

[26] There are two slightly different versions of the instructions. The first is SC, MS A, V, 1(1); the second is ARSI, Instit. 188, ff. 293^r-94^v. The first was printed in Hicks, *Letters of Persons*, pp. 316-21. See these pages for a discussion of differences between the two manuscripts. Allen discussed the significance of the religious nature of the mission in *An apologie and true declaration of the institution*, ff. 71^r-72^v.

selves with a firm confidence in God to whom alone they can look for grace and light." Loyola always demanded mortified men for his order. He wanted men who placed the greater glory of God before their own plans and proposals. Mercurian wanted the three Englishmen to conform to that ideal. Frequent and fervent prayer and examination of conscience were required for formation of a "right intention."[27]

Examination of conscience has an especially important part in Jesuit spirituality. Twice daily each Jesuit should examine his behaviour to see if he is actually pursuing God's glory or is more interested in his own aspirations.[28] Given the situation in which the men would find themselves, the importance of prudence is obvious. It must be exercised in everything, but especially in any decisions regarding the people, procedures, and issues with which they deal. At all times there was to be temperance in food. The men were to avoid convivial gatherings. Indeed, it would be even better if the Jesuits had their meals in private except "when the guests are such that there is clearly no danger to be feared."[29] Constant circumspection was demanded.

Although the fathers would be forced to dress as laymen, their clothes should be modest and sober.[30] The General urged against even possession of a cassock as worn by the Society. Once the men established permanent residences, if they decided that it was safe, they could wear Jesuit clothes but only "for the purpose of holding services, hearing confessions and carrying out other duties of this kind." Since a communal life was impossible, the men should visit one another as often as possible for advice and

---

[27] It is interesting to compare these instructions with Allen's explanation of missionary tactics in a letter to Maurice Chauncy from Cambrai on 10 August 1577: "and this is certaine that preists there [in England] had nead to pray instantly and fast muche and watche and warde themselves well, lest thee needfull use of sundry entysments to sinne and necessary disimulation in things of them selves indifferent, to be fytt for every company, bring them to offend God, and so whyles they labour to save themselves become reprobate; wherin they must also be more carefull of there wayes, for that every mans eyes be cast upon them as on suche as take upon them to bee guides of other menns lyfes and beleefe, whose faults many a manne spyeth that prayeth not for them; as most men marke there misses, and fewe consider in what feares and daungers they be in and what unspeakable paines they take to serve good menns tornes to there least perill" (Knox, *Letters of Allen*, p. 36).

[28] John O'Malley sets daily examination of conscience within the dynamic of the *Spiritual Exercises*. Through daily examination Jesuits monitored their behaviour to make sure that they remained faithful to the ideals embraced in the Exercises. See *The First Jesuits* (Cambridge, Mass., 1993) p. 40.

[29] Although odd, such concern for food is in keeping with the Jesuit tradition. Loyola appended "Rules with Regard to Eating" to his *Spiritual Exercises*. A combination of spiritual insight and practical wisdom, these rules are intended to free the retreatant from undue attraction to food (*The Spiritual Exercises of St. Ignatius*, ed. Louis J. Puhl, S.J. [Chicago, 1951] nos. 210-17).

[30] For Allen's comments about secular attire see his letter to Maurice Chauncy, Cambrai 10 August 1577, in Knox, *Letters of Allen*, p. 36.

spiritual assistance as was the custom of the Society. When Jesuits had contact with strangers, it should be with the upper classes "rather than with the common people." Not only would the upper classes better able to protect the priests; their conversion would have a far greater effect on the mission. Among Catholics the Jesuits were to prefer the company of the "reconciled" to "schismatics."

The missionaries were forbidden to have direct dealings with "heretics." If any family contained heretics, their conversion should begin with their Catholic relatives. Each Catholic should work for the conversion of his relatives, and the Jesuits should simply provide advice and arguments. Only after heretics "have begun to lose a little of their prejudice and to put away that fury and hatred which they had, so that they are ready to hear the truth with equanimity," should the fathers approach them for fuller instruction. Even then the men should not disclose their identity as Jesuits. In any disputation with Elizabethan ministers, which should be avoided unless necessity forced it, the General advised the men to be temperate with their arguments and to refrain from name-calling and bitter wrangling. Because heretics never concede defeat in arguments, Jesuits should rarely discuss theological matters with them. Only if great profit could be expected should they ignore the prohibition.[31] If there was a discussion, the Jesuits should "produce their strongest arguments first, so as to get the upper hand from the beginning."

Parsons and Campion were told to avoid familiar conversation with women and boys.[32] Indeed, because absolute discretion was essential, they were to avoid garrulity. Equally important, they were to carry none of the religious articles prescribed by law. They were also encouraged to be discreet about revealing their true identity. They were to inform no one that they were priests and Jesuits "unless great hope of profit should demand it in order to give glory to God and gain a notable harvest of souls." To avoid even the slightest suspicion of avarice and greed, the fathers should neither beg nor accept alms. If they needed money, they should ask one or two of their most loyal friends for assistance.[33]

Finally, Campion and Parsons were admonished against any political involvement. Except with the most faithful and trusted friends, they were

---

[31] Allen and Mercurian disagreed on the value of religious disputation. See McCoog, "'Playing the Champion'."

[32] Missionaries were always advised to hear the confessions of women and young boys in open, visible spaces lest there be an occasion for gossip (*Instructiones ad Provinciales et Superiores Societatis* [Antwerp, 1635] p. 62).

[33] For an exposition of the Society's teaching on poverty in general and the practice on the English mission see Thomas M. McCoog, S.J., "The Finances of the English Province of the Society of Jesus in the Seventeenth Century: Introduction," *RH* 18 (1986) 14-33; "'The Slightest Suspicion of Avarice': The Finances of the English Jesuit Mission," 19 *RH* (1988) 103-23.

forbidden to discuss political matters in their letters, to speak against the Queen, or to tolerate such talk in others.[34] Any letter to the Pope should be clearly written and should contain only what is "true and undeniable." Personal matters should be included in a separate letter and not in the reports submitted to the Cardinal Protector or the Pope. Regarding letters, Mercurian asked the men to find safe and secure lines of communication and to create ciphers if necessary.

Robert Parsons was designated superior of the mission.[35] To him the General granted all possible privileges, faculties, and favours "in the internal forum." "In the external forum,"[36] Parsons received all the powers ordinarily bestowed on provincials and rectors.[37] After the missionaries established themselves in England they should advise the General as to what province the mission should be attached.[38] If Campion and Parsons thought that more men were required for the mission, they were to direct their request to the General alone. Here the General sounded an ominous note: he would provide assistance as long as he judged it to be "most conducive to the glory of our Lord."

Faculties granted by Pope Gregory XIII confirmed the spiritual nature of the mission, though within a political context.[39] Most faculties were canonical privileges: permission to celebrate Mass at irregular hours, in any appropriate place, and in the presence of heretics; to alter the divine office when it could not be recited without probable danger; to bless palls, corporals, vestments, indeed anything for which chrism was not required. Jesuits could administer all the sacraments save confirmation and holy

---

[34] The Roman version of the instructions qualified the prohibition. It permitted the fathers to discuss the Queen with those of proven faithfulness and trustworthiness, but only for serious reasons (Hicks, *Letters of Persons*, p. 318, n. 19). For an analysis of the meaning of the prohibition see John Hungerford Pollen, S.J., "The Politics of the English Catholics during the Reign of Elizabeth," *The Month* 99 (1902) 293-94.

[35] According to the directives for missionaries in *Instructiones ad Provinciales et Superiores Societatis* (Antwerp, 1635), the man named first in the letters patent was always the superior.

[36] The "internal forum," or the forum of conscience, pertains to matters pertinent to the spiritual welfare of the individual; the "external forum," concerns activities pertinent to the public good of the Church.

[37] In the Roman version, the phrase *"provincialibus Societatis"* was written in the margin. Thus, according to Hicks, such provincial powers were not originally granted to Parsons but were added later (*Letters of Persons*, p. 317 n. 8).

[38] Ordinarily missions established and administered by the General were brief. Provinces were responsible for permanent missions. If England were to become a permanent mission of the Society, it should be dependent on a given province for financial assistance and for manpower. See Thomas M. McCoog, S.J., "The Establishment of the English Province of the Society of Jesus," *RH* 17 (1984) 122-25.

[39] PRO, SP 12/137/46. The faculties were published as an appendix in Meyer, *England and the Catholic Church*, pp. 486-88. There are other copies simply of Gregory's explanation of the excommunication of Elizabeth (PRO, SP 12/144/131 and 12/153/147).

orders, which required a bishop. Besides authority to grant dispensations from a number of impediments to ordination, the missionaries could reconcile anyone who held confiscated ecclesiastical property. Before reconciliation, however, the current possessors must promise to abide by any decision of ecclesiastical authorities regarding the property once Catholicism had been restored. Meanwhile, they should give alms to the Catholic poor as a reminder "that these goods are in fact church property." The Jesuits could dispense from the vows of poverty and obedience any religious who could not return to their order "provided they secretly wear some habitual garment of their religious institute under their other clothing." Permission to grant dispensations for marriage within the prescribed degrees of affinity was a later addition to the faculties.

Amidst the many canonical and ecclesiastical faculties, four others stand out. Contrary to the decree of the Council of Trent,[40] Jesuits were permitted to publish Catholic books and withhold the names of author, place, and publisher. Although the General's instructions said nothing about publications, printing Catholic books became one of the most important works of the mission.[41] Secondly the faculties summarized Gregory's evaluation of the Queen's excommunication: "it obliges heretics at all times, but does not oblige Catholics under present circumstances, but only when public execution of the same bull becomes possible." Thirdly the Pope blessed an association of pious men working within England for the "salvation of souls and the bringing back of heretics." Gregory approved their zeal and granted them a plenary indulgence four times a year if they confessed and received the Eucharist on the feasts of St. George, St. Martin, St. Gregory the Great, St. Augustine of Canterbury, and St. Thomas of Canterbury. Finally, the Jesuits were permitted to communicate any or all of these faculties to other priests working in England.

According to their instructions and faculties, the Jesuits were in England to work among the Roman Catholics in order to strengthen their faith and to win back the lapsed. Theirs was not a job of conversion. Thus their task was similar to the work done by the Jesuits who preached missions in Europe. In any work of spiritual renewal, even a hint of scandal was to be avoided. In every aspect of their lives the men must give concrete religious witness. That would be even more difficult in England, where they lacked the support of a religious community. Though feigning secular behaviour,

---

[40] Norman P. Tanner, S.J., ed., *Decrees of the Ecumenical Councils*, 2 vols. (London/Washington, D.C., 1990) II, 664-65.

[41] See Nancy Pollard Brown, "Robert Southwell: The Mission of the Written Word," in *The Reckoned Expense: Edmund Campion and the Early English Jesuits. Essays in Celebration of the First Centenary of Campion Hall, Oxford (1896-1996)*, ed. Thomas M. McCoog, S.J. (Woodbridge, 1996) pp. 193-214.

the Jesuits were to observe their Institute as far as possible if the mission was to be successful. The Jesuits of Elizabethan mythology were notorious for their disguises. Dressed as soldiers, merchants, and servants, they moved through Elizabethan England into the world of myth and fable. Only serious prayer, frequent sacraments, and spiritual counselling would prevent the priests from becoming what they appeared to be. Because of the perilous situation, the Jesuits were dispensed from a number of liturgical requirements and restrictions in the hope that it would facilitate work in England.

The absence of a hierarchy resulted in the Jesuits, receiving a number of extraordinary privileges regarding marriage and religious life, privileges which could be shared with other priests on the mission at the Society's discretion. It would be rash to label the association of pious Catholics a sodality, because it was not legally constituted as such, but its efforts were encouraged and blessed and members were bound to the Society through the sacraments. The missionaries, finally, sought to clarify the confused political scene through a clear statement of allegiance: Pope Pius V's deposition of Queen Elizabeth did not oblige Catholics at this time. All Catholics could continue to recognize her as their lawful sovereign. Even though the Pope permitted Catholics to recognize the Queen in all non-religious matters, "the government continued to act as if this gesture of reconciliation had never been made."[42] Did Gregory XIII's elucidation actually solve the problem? One must not forget the explanation's qualifier: "under present circumstances (*rebus sic stantibus*)."[43] Whenever the execution of Pius V's bull of deposition became possible, English Catholics would be obliged to recognize it. Their allegiance to the Queen was then conditional and temporary. Once the Papacy had made the proper arrangements for an enforcement of the bull, the English Catholics would be expected—indeed obliged—to side with the Church. One day the Catholics could repudiate their allegiance: it was simply a question of when. Should anyone then be surprised that the government did not perceive this mission as a peaceful gesture?

II

Before the arrival of the Jesuits the Society was defamed. William Charke, who would later write against Edmund Campion, translated from Latin Christian Francken's *A conference or dialogue discovering the sect of Iesuites: most profitable for all Christendome rightly to know their religion.*

---

[42] Seizing upon this mitigation, Francis Edwards consistently depicts the Jesuit mission as an "olive branch" from the universal Church. See *The Jesuits in England* (London, 1985) p. 18. See also *Robert Persons*, p. 34.
[43] For the role that this phrase played in subsequent controversies see Michael L. Carrafiello, "*Rebus sic stantibus* and English Catholicism, 1606-1610," *RH* 22 (1994) 29-40.

Francken, a Jesuit from 1568 until his apostasy from the Roman Catholic Church in 1579, bitterly attacked the Society and its founder, and contended that only those with a natural tendency towards hypocrisy "either gotten by servile education, or apprehended by some blockishness of mind" could become good Jesuits.[44] This controversial work set the tone for the popular presentation of the Society of Jesus. Within a few years England would not need translations of works of foreigners for attacks on the Jesuits.

Shortly after his arrival Robert Parsons set out for Marshalsea prison.[45] There he contacted Thomas Pounde.[46] Educated at Winchester College and the Inns of Court, Pounde converted to Roman Catholicism around 1570. Arrested three years later as he attempted to leave the country to join the Society of Jesus, he was moved from one prison to another. In 1580 he was confined in the Marshalsea. Before Campion and Parsons departed for England, Father General entrusted them with letters for Pounde, Thomas Metham,[47] and Nicholas Smith.[48] Bearing these letters, Parsons visited each and explained the Society's new mission.[49] Another English Catholic, Edward Brooksby, visiting Pounde when Parsons called, escorted Parsons to the house in Chancery Lane rented by the Catholic George Gilbert from a notorious unnamed pursuivant, whose love of money exceeded his devotion to the established Church. Parsons and Gilbert were old friends. They had met in Rome and, as a result of Parsons's persuasion, Gilbert had returned to England to assist in the maintenance of the Catholic community. To do this effectively, he organized a number of Catholic laymen to care for and protect the priests who were regularly arriving from the continent. Prior to Gilbert's fraternity, each priest had to fend for himself upon arrival. Now

---

[44] (London, 1580) STC 11325, f. iv^v.

[45] In an attempt to correct what they considered an oversight of too many historians, Patrick McGrath and Joy Rowe have studied Catholics imprisoned, but not executed, for their faith. See "The Imprisonment of Catholics for Religion under Elizabeth I," *RH* 20 (1991) 415-35.

[46] Pounde was accepted into the Society by Everard Mercurian on 1 December 1578 through the intercession of the English Jesuit Thomas Stephens (Mercurian to Pounde, Rome 1 December 1578, ARSI, Fl. Belg. 2, pp. 131-32). The General instructed him to reveal his membership in the Society to no one "until better times shall dawn. . . ."

[47] Through the intermediary Thomas Darbyshire, Metham was accepted into the Society on 4 May 1579. He too was told to tell no one (Mercurian to Thomas Metham, Rome 4 May 1579, ARSI, Fl. Belg. 2, p. 142). In ARSI, Fondo Gesuitico 651/593, there is a copy of an anonymous letter written from a London gaol on 14 February 1579. The writer asked to be accepted into the Society. Could he be Metham? See also *Mon. Ang.*, II, 406.

[48] For reasons of health Smith was in and out of the Society a few times. Dismissed on 21 February 1579 he returned to England to recover his health. If he is the Nicholas to whom the General addressed a letter on 15 April 1580 (ARSI, Fl. Belg. 2, p. 158), Mercurian was concerned about him, but Smith was not then a Jesuit. On Smith, *Mon. Ang.*, II, 480.

[49] Mercurian to [Thomas Metham], Rome 15 April 1580, ARSI, Fl. Belg. 2, p. 157; same to Thomas Pounde, Rome 15 April 1580, *ibid.*, p. 158; same to Nicholas [Smith?], Rome 15 April 1580, *ibid.*, p. 158.

he could depend on Gilbert's group for assistance and protection.[50] Presumably Gilbert's association was known to Parsons before his departure from Rome, and the Pope bestowed his blessing on it in the faculties conferred on the missionaries.[51]

Thomas James,[52] probably one of Gilbert's fraternity although not named by Parsons, greeted Campion and Emerson when they reached London. Because rumours of an invasion had intensified the search for priests, Parsons abandoned London after his meeting with Gilbert and before the arrival of the two other Jesuits. Campion's first official act, and a rather foolish one, was to preach on the feast of Saints Peter and Paul (29 June) to a large congregation in the great hall of a house rented by Thomas, Lord Paget in Smithfield. A few days later Campion and Parsons met to discuss missionary strategy. While they were together, the two decided it would be judicious to meet other priests in the London area to calm any fears that the older clergy might have of the new arrivals. Despite the danger of detection, a meeting was called and held in Southwark.

Although Robert Parsons was superior of the small band of Jesuits, he had no authority over the secular clergy; hence he could not command them to attend. Yet many did: the desire to receive the faculties granted to the Jesuits may have been the motivation. During the second week of July the priests abandoned their sanctuaries and gathered in Southwark at a house by the river near St. Mary Overies. At the meeting many questions and issues that would recur and drastically affect relations between Jesuits and seculars would surface for the first time. Some older priests were suspicious and

---

[50] Parsons named the following as members of the association: Henry Vaux and his brother-in-law Mr. Brook [Edward Brooksby], Charles Arundell, Charles Basset, Thomas, Edward, and Francis Throckmorton, William Brooksby, Richard and William Griffen, Arthur [Joseph] Creswell, Edward Fitton, Stephen Brinkley, Gervase Pierrepoint, Nicholas Roscarock, Anthony Babington, Chideock Titchbourne, Charles Tilney, Edward Abingdon, Thomas Salisbury, Jerome Bellamy, William Tresham, Thomas Fitzherbert, John Stonor, James Hall, Richard Stanihurst, and Godfrey Fuljambe ("Of the Life and Martyrdom," *Letters and Notices* 12 [1878] 29). Some were later executed for involvement in the Babington conspiracy; Walter Walsh uses this as proof of the Society's involvement in political affairs (*The Jesuits in Great Britain* [London, 1903] p. 114).

[51] For the narrative, I am following Edwards, *Elizabethan Jesuits*; Pollen, *English Catholics in the Reign of Elizabeth*; E.E. Reynolds, *Campion and Parsons* (London, 1980); Peter Norris, "Robert Parsons, S.J. (1546-1610) and the Counter Reformation in England: A Study of his Actions within the Context of the Political and Religious Situation of the Times" (unpublished Ph.D. thesis: University of Notre Dame, 1984); Robert Parsons, "Of the Life and Martyrdom," *Letters and Notices* 11 (1877) 219-42, 308-39, 1-68; Simpson, *Edmund Campion*; Waugh, *Edmund Campion*; Edwards, *Robert Persons*, pp. 31-46; Thomas M. McCoog, S.J., "Campion's Plea for a Disputation," *The Month* 262 [n.s. 2 vol. 14] (1981) 414-17 and "'Playing the Champion'."

[52] James later played an important role in English Catholic affairs in Spain. See Albert J. Loomie, S.J., "Thomas James: the English Consul of Andalucia (1556-c.1613)," *RH* 11 (1972) 165-78.

perhaps resentful of the newcomers. Not only did the Jesuits possess greater faculties than they, but their imminent arrival had been a cause of renewed persecution. These older priests had heard rumours of an invasion. Was it true, they wondered, that the Jesuits had been sent by Pope Gregory XIII on a political mission? Reading to the assembly his instructions, Parsons explained the spiritual nature of their work. He emphasized that they were not part of the FitzMaurice expedition to Ireland. Indeed, they had not even heard of that expedition until they reached Reims.[53] Even though the Jesuits might be innocent of any political intrigue, one priest suggested that they leave the kingdom anyway because their presence intensified the persecution and made the lives of Catholics ever more difficult. Parsons replied that they could not leave: they were in England at the express order of the Pope and at the request of many leading Catholics.

The second topic discussed was the continuation of England's unique religious customs and ecclesiastical traditions. Until the imposition of the *Book of Common Prayer*, the Sarum use was employed throughout most of the kingdom. It differed from the more common Roman rite in the breviary, in other parts of the liturgy, and in the severity of its fasts and abstinences. Because of their youth and their education at Rome, the new priests were unfamiliar with older traditions and claimed that "it was sufficient for them to observe the fast and dayes of abstinence prescribed by the generall Churche and such as were observed in Rome and other Catholike places."[54] Which should be followed, they asked? Were the older traditions still in force? Parsons's diplomatic reply urged that each priest observe the customs of the area in which he worked.

The third issue was the ever controversial subject of attendance at Protestant services. Although recusancy had been increasing steadily, English Catholics were far from united on the issue. Dr. Alban Langdale, deprived Archdeacon of Chichester and current chaplain to Anthony Browne, Viscount Montague, argued that attendance at services because of obedience to the Queen and fear of persecution was not sinful.[55] According to Langdale, a Catholic who remained seated and did not participate in the

---

[53] Later, in one of his autobiographical writings, Parsons commented that the invasion of Ireland sponsored by the Papacy "made ye whole cause of ye priests that were sent on mission to England more odious" ("First Entrance of the Fathers," p. 199).
[54] Robert Parsons, "Domesticall Difficulties," p. 176. Did this fear apply only to men educated in Rome? Were the seminarians in Douai trained in the English traditions?
[55] On Langdale's argument see Peter Holmes, *Resistance and Compromise: The Political Thought of the English Catholics* (Cambridge, 1982) pp. 90-95, and Alexandra Walsham, *Church Papists: Catholicism, Conformity, and Confessional Polemic in Early Modern England* (Woodbridge, 1993) pp. 50-55. Also see Parsons, "Domesticall Difficulties," pp. 180-81; and Parsons, "Punti," pp. 2-5. Parsons claimed that Langdale's book induced Thomas, Lord Paget and Ralph Sheldon to attend.

service, but was simply present physically, did not scandalize other Catholics and did not demonstrate his support for heresy. Under the direction of Parsons, the Southwark synod agreed that attendance was "the highest iniquity that can be committed" and condemned the practice. Parsons promised to address the issue in a new book.[56]

Other matters were briefly discussed.[57] The issue of the reception and

---

[56] It appears that Parsons may have referred this question to Rome as a "case of conscience." In the Jesuit archives (Angl. 30/I, ff. 175^{r-v}) there is an undated paper regarding attendance at Protestant services. Immediately following is Francisco de Toledo's judgement that the practice was always forbidden because the law is directed against the Catholic religion: "For to be present in assemblies of heretics and in their churches without being distinguished from them but as one of them, is not only to conceal the true faith and religion but is to profess a false sect by an outward act" (f. 176^r). Added to Toledo's decision is an anonymous comment from Paris that Toledo's resolution was not valid: Catholics did not attend the services "as one of them." A third document, again without a date, concerns other disputed matters that needed resolution (ff. 178^{r-v}). Alexandra Walsham rightly notes a discrepancy between the theological attacks on church papists and the understanding shown to them in the cases of conscience (illustrations can be found in P.J. Holmes, ed., *Elizabethan Casuistry* [London, 1981] pp. 20, 50-51, 74-76, 84); but her explanation is not sufficient. According to Walsham, "This superficial inconsistency is not difficult to account for. If recusancy tracts are recognised as confessional polemic designed to outwit and overcome Protestants, as much as the private devotional manuals of a cohesive Catholic 'community,' then the reticence of the Counter Reformation hierarchy becomes explicable. Propagandists who made use of a maturing medium to mount an assault on the mendacity and depravity of a heretical Church could hardly disclose the dissimulation and opportunism upon which their own faith had come to rely" (*Church Papists*, pp. 70-71). The true explanation is the traditional distinction between the preached moral standards towards which all must strive, and confessional, pastoral sympathy for sinners. The tracts condemned the sin in strict, absolute terms; the cases of conscience were designed for counselling the sinner. Perhaps more interesting would be a detailed study of Pope Gregory's explication and Parsons's strident condemnation. Had Parsons taken a stronger line than the Pope?

[57] In Parsons's account of the synod he listed the case of the Jesuit James Bosgrave as a topic discussed. Parsons, however, was mistaken in this regard. For reasons that remain unclear (either for health, for family business, or on a mission from the Jesuit General), Bosgrave returned to England in the fall of 1580. Arrested on arrival, he was confined to the Marshalsea prison and was promised his liberty if he would attend a Protestant service. In Poland, where Bosgrave had been working, many Catholics attended Protestant services to learn the doctrine for the sake of refutation. Unfamiliar with the English prohibition, he did attend a service to the shock of some Catholics. Informed that such an act would scandalize the English Catholics because of religious changes that had transpired since Bosgrave's departure as a babe, he rescinded his promise and declared his Catholicism. This retraction was published as "The satisfaction of M. James Bosgrave the godly confessor of Christ, concerning his going to the Church of the Protestants at his first coming into England," in [William Allen], *A true report of the late apprehension and imprisonnement of Iohn Nicols* (Reims, 1583) STC 18537, ARCR II, no. 13, ff. 32^v-34^v. Sentenced to the Tower and later condemned with Campion, Bosgrave was reprieved through the intercession of Stephen Báthory, King of Poland. In 1585 he was banished (PRO, SP 12/176/9; CSP Foreign [1583] 661-62). Parsons's account of the whole affair can be found in a letter to the German assistant and sponsor of the mission, Oliver Mannaerts, written in London on 20 October 1580 (ARSI, Fondo Gesuitico 651/640). Recent investigations of Paul Skwarczynski ("Elsinore 1580: John Rogers and James Bosgrave," *RH* 16 [1982] 1-16) have shown that Bosgrave had not yet arrived in England when the synod met, and thus could not have been a topic for discussion. See also *Mon. Ang.*, II, 240-41.

distribution of incoming priests was raised. Many thought that this issue, since it involved church discipline, could not be satisfactorily resolved until the clergy had a proper hierarchical structure. Some cases involved personalities. Should Thomas Cottam turn himself in to the government since Dr. Humphrey Ely, who was mistaken for a Protestant and thus given custody of the arrested Cottam, had been apprehended for allowing Cottam to escape? Cottam did surrender himself and was later executed. Ely returned to the continent and became a priest. Another priest, John Hart, arrested upon landing, was allowed to return to his Oxford home on condition that he meet John Rainolds, an Oxford professor of divinity, in theological conferences. Should this be allowed because Hart was not an exceptionally gifted man? The debates were allowed.[58]

In mid-July Campion and Parsons withdrew to a village outside London, probably Hoxton, to escape increased governmental surveillance. There they were visited by Thomas Pounde on leave from prison. Pounde informed them that the government was busily spreading various libels about them and that something must be done lest Catholics believe the stories. Pounde suggested that the two Jesuits ought to reply to these lies, which would only be magnified if they were apprehended. As a precaution, each could draft a brief statement delineating the purpose of their mission. These declarations would be held by a friend, presumably Pounde, and released to the public only after one or both had been captured. Thus they could counteract any propaganda disseminated by the government that would depict the missionaries unfavourably. They agreed: Parsons wrote "A Confession of Faith addressed to the Magistrates of London," and Campion "To the Right Honourable Lords of Her Majestie's Privy Council."[59] Intentionally or not, Campion did not seal his statement. Pounde read it, used its contents in his own debates with Protestant theologians,[60] and made copies for distribution among Catholics.[61] The "Brag," as it came to be known, found its way into the hands of the government. Campion's notoriety was immediate. He became the Catholics' "Champion" and the most wanted priest in England.

---

[58] The debates between Rainolds and Hart were published as *The summe of the conference betwene J. Rainoldes and J. Hart* (London, 1584) STC 20626. Other editions can be found in STC 20627-20631.

[59] Parsons's declaration can be found in Hicks, *Letters of Persons*, pp. 35-41. Campion's has been reproduced often, e.g. in Pollen, *English Catholics in the Reign of Elizabeth*; Waugh, *Edmund Campion*, and Basset, *English Jesuits*.

[60] A manuscript copy of Pounde's "Six Reasons" can be found in PRO, SP 12/142/20.

[61] For information regarding the "Brag's" distribution throughout Hampshire see PRO, SP 12/147/131. By 10 November 1580 Allen had a copy of both statements in Reims and told Agazzari "these written fly-leaves pass from hand to hand everywhere among people in England and are a source of strength to many. . ." (Patrick Ryan, S.J., ed., "Some Correspondence of Cardinal Allen, 1579-85," in *Miscellanea VII* [London, 1911] p. 31).

Parsons's statement is the better of the two. After he recounted the reasons for writing the declaration, for his conversion, and for his entrance into the Society, he explained the mission to England. As a man bound by the vow of obedience, he was at the disposal of the General of the order and could be sent anywhere: he was sent to England. Contrary to the calumnies of the Society's enemies, the Jesuits did not come to stir sedition. In fact, the Society did not accept such involvement in secular affairs and had resisted pressure from Catholic princes to become so. His task was no different from the work of other Jesuits throughout the world: "to teach those Christians who shall receive us, the rudiments of the Catholic faith and to make their habits conform to the most holy commandments of God." Moreover, because "we preach that Princes should be obeyed not merely for fear of punishment or for the sake of avoiding scandal but for conscience's sake as well," the Jesuits inculcated obedience better than the established ministers do.[62] "Greatly encouraged by the very real truth of my cause," Parsons demanded an opportunity to defend his faith. Challenging all Protestant ministers to a public disputation, he faced the possibility of death without fear but warned the government:

> if your intentions are bloodthirsty (from which evil may God defend you) there will be no lack of scope for them. For you are persecuting a corporation that will never die, and sooner will your hearts and hands, sated with blood, fail you, than will there be lacking men, eminent for virtue and learning, who will be sent by this Society and allow their blood to be shed by you for this cause.

About five hundred men in the Society are resolute that this cause will not fail and are prepared to suffer anything for the Catholic faith.

Campion's "Brag" did not differ in its essential message from Parsons's. Yet the "Brag" has an urgency the other lacks:

> And touching our Societie, be it known to you that we have made a league—all the Jesuits in the world, whose succession and multitude must overreach all the practices of England—cheerfully to carry the cross you shall lay on us, and never to despair your recovery, while we have a man left to enjoy your Tyburn, or to be racked with your torments, or consumed with your prisons. The expense is reckoned, the enterprise is begun; it is of God, it cannot be withstood. So the faith was planted, so it must be restored.

It was fruitless to resist. The forces of the Elizabethan government would be helpless against Catholicism, as Marx and Engels, three hundred years later, predicted the forces of Metternich would be against communism.[63]

---

[62] Holmes sees Parsons's profession as an example of "enthusiastic non-resistance" in the vacillation between resistance and compromise (*Resistance and Compromise*, p. 37).

[63] Pollen, *English Catholics in the Reign of Elizabeth*, p. 352.

These declarations share an optimism. If the Jesuits had an opportunity to debate, they would destroy the arguments of the Protestants and firmly reestablish orthodox Catholic doctrine.[64] The appeal for a debate suggests that Campion's and Parsons's understanding of their mission went beyond the instructions they received from Rome. Although the declarations should not have been released until the authors had been arrested, and though the early release of Campion's explanation gave it a challenging tone that it would have lacked if he were in prison, nonetheless that tone was, I think, intentional. The General's instructions insisted the Jesuits have no direct dealings with the heretics, but he allowed them to debate if they were forced to do so. Even then, as we have seen, the General warned them that heretics would never concede defeat. Immediate capture or the premature release of a declaration provided the required necessity. Because debates henceforth play an important role in their strategy, I think it likely that the early release was calculated. Their requests were a delayed response to Bishop John Jewel's earlier challenge. Thomas Harding and others had rebutted Jewel, but these Catholic replies were obviously not easily obtainable in England. Campion and Parsons, therefore, came in person to pick up the thrown gauntlet and to prove the Catholic faith not only on the basis of scripture, the fathers, and the councils, but also by history and by reason.[65]

Protestant reaction to the copies of the "Brag" circulated by Pounde was swift. In a letter presumably to the General in November of 1580, Campion explained the situation:

> I had put in writing in the form of propositions some very reasonable postulates and demands. I admitted that I was a priest of the Society who had come to England with the purpose of spreading Catholic faith, teaching the Gospel and administering the Sacraments. I begged audience with the Queen and the principal men of the kingdom, and I challenged my adversaries to a contest. I decided to keep one copy by me for when I should be taken before the magistrates. The other I gave to a friend, so that if they should lay hold of me and my possessions, the other might be passed around indefinitely. My friend, far from concealing it, had it printed and published.[66]

---

[64] G.R. Evans has studied various disputations in *Problems of Authority in the Reformation Debates* (Cambridge, 1992).

[65] See McCoog, "'Playing the Champion.'" Only Patrick McGrath (*Papists and Puritans under Elizabeth I* [London, 1967] pp. 50-51) has interpreted Campion's "Brag" as a rejoinder to Jewel's "Challenge."

[66] ARSI, Fondo Gesuitico 651/612. Henry More included the letter in his *Historia Provinciae Anglicanae Societatis Iesu* (St. Omers, 1660) pp. 74-76. In Edwards's translation, *Elizabethan Jesuits*, it can be found on pp. 88-91. The new General, Claudio Acquaviva, wrote to Campion on 27 March 1581 that he had not yet received a letter from him; "however, partly because we have received frequent enough letters from your associate and partly because we have had intelligence from elsewhere that you are well and sound and strong, we have been much gladdened" (ARSI, Fl. Belg. 2, p. 172).

According to Campion, many Protestant theologians claimed that they were ready to accept the challenge but that they were unable to do so because the Queen had forbidden further disputations on matters long settled. In the uproar the Jesuits were called "seditious, hypocritical, even heretical." Stories about them circulated widely.[67] Even as Campion wrote this, he held in his hand a letter that claimed he had been captured!

A second anti-Jesuit polemic appeared: *A defence of the olde, and true profession of Christianitie, against the new, and counterfaite secte of Iesuites, or fellowship of Iesus*, by the French Huguenot Pierre Boquin, professor of theology at the University of Heidelberg. Boquin accused the Jesuits of schism by appropriating the name of Jesus to describe their Society. There was no evidence, he continued, that Jesuits deserved this name more than any ordinary Christian. His strongest condemnation was the Jesuit misinterpretation of Scripture in order to please the Pope and to entice the support of secular rulers. Moreover it had been Jesuit policy to arouse the people against the ministers of the Word of God, and to flock to countries where Protestants had been successful.[68]

Regardless of these attacks, no one took up Campion's challenge for a personal debate even though there were written defences of the Protestant settlement.[69] The Puritan William Charke wrote the first response, *An answere to a seditious pamphlet lately cast abroad by a jesuit, with a discoverie of that blasphemous sect*.[70] A more judicious reply came in Meredith Hanmer's *The great bragge and challenge of M. Champion a jesuite*.[71] The latter published the "Brag" in full in order to refute it, and so furthered its distribution. The battle was on.[72]

Official reaction came on 10 January 1581 with the proclamation "Ordering Return of Seminarians, Arrest of Jesuits" with the charge that the Jesuits disturbed the kingdom and stirred up rebellion. The Society's debut in a royal proclamation was ominous and set a tone for subsequent political literature. "Her majesty," the proclamation of 10 January 1581 stated,

---

[67] Parsons confided to Acquaviva that "the talk here is about the Jesuits. About them there are more fables than used to be told about monsters—about their origin, their manner of life, their institute, their teaching—things various and at variance with each other and manifestly false are spread about not only in private conversation and in addresses but also in printed books. The sum of these things is that they are said to be dispatched by the Sovereign Pontiff as traitors and destroyers of states into different provinces" (London 16 June 1581, ARSI, Fondo Gesuitico 651/696).

[68] (London, 1581) STC 3371, pp. 101, 149.

[69] On the orchestration of the government's response see McCoog, "'Playing the Champion.'"

[70] (London, 1580) STC 5005.

[71] (London, 1581) STC 12745.

[72] See Peter Milward, S.J., *Religious Controversies of the Elizabethan Age* (London, 1977) pp. 54-56 for the published works in this debate.

being further given to understand that there are divers of her subjects that have been trained up in the said colleges and seminaries beyond the seas, whereof some of them carry the name of Jesuits under the color of a holy name to deceive and abuse the simpler sort, and are lately repaired into this realm by special direction from the pope and his delegates, with intent not only to corrupt and pervert her good and loving subjects in matter of conscience and religion, but also to draw them from the loyalty and duty of obedience and to provoke them, so much as shall lie in them, to attempt somewhat to the disturbance of the present quiet that through the goodness of Almighty God and her majesty's provident government this realm hath these many years enjoyed.[73]

In the same month, Sir Walter Mildmay warned of dangers:

To confirm them [the Catholics] herein, and to increase their numbers, you see how the Pope hath and doth comfort their hollow hearts with absolutions, dispensations, reconciliations, and such other things of Rome. You see how lately he hath sent hither a sort of hypocrites, naming themselves Jesuits, a rabble of vagrant friars newly sprung up and coming through the world to trouble the Church of God; whose principal errand is, by creeping into the houses and familiarities of men of behaviour and reputation, not only to corrupt the realm with false doctrine, but also, under that pretence, to stir sedition.[74]

The Queen's proclamation and Mildmay's speech made the same accusation: the Jesuits had been sent into England by the Pope to "corrupt" the religion, to "disturb" the government, and perhaps to prepare for a new joint Papal-Spanish venture. To prevent this, new legislation was drafted: the "Act to Retain the Queen's Majesty's Subjects in Their Due Obedience" (23 Eliz. c. 1). If recusants were not willing to abandon their allegiance to a hostile prince as their spiritual leader, they would suffer financial and social ruin and thus be unable to provide any assistance to an invasion or rebellion. Making a distinction between Protestant and Catholic recusancy, the new law prescribed that convicted Catholic recusants could pay fines of £20 for the first month, £40 for the second, £100 for the third, and be imprisoned at the monarch's pleasure, with confiscation of all estates and goods for the fourth. Anyone convicted of having dissuaded any of her majesty's subjects from attending the established Church in favour of the Church of Rome would be guilty of high treason. Anyone reconciled to the Roman Church would suffer the same penalty. To tighten enforcement, the new law promised informers a third of the fines paid by the recusants, and threatened

---

[73] Hughes and Larkin, *Tudor Royal Proclamations*, II, 483.
[74] Quoted in J.E. Neale, *Elizabeth I and Her Parliaments*, 2 vols. (London, 1953, 1957) I, 383-84.

misprision of treason for not revealing information regarding any reconciliations.[75] The old religion would not die the death of attrition. Instead, in the terse summary of Christopher Haigh, "it would have to be murdered."[76]

Having left London in early August, Campion and Parsons were in the countryside when the storm over the "Brag" broke. Furnished with two horses, clothing,[77] vestments, and money by George Gilbert, Parsons travelled through Gloucestershire, Herefordshire, Worcestershire, and Derbyshire, and Campion through Berkshire, Oxfordshire, and Northamptonshire. Both "were escorted in each county by a number of young men of gentle birth, of whom there are quite a few here who volunteer to be our servants (as they themselves term it)."[78] Their escorts took care of all expenses.[79] Presumably the young gentlemen were members of Gilbert's association. The same letter described their journeys throughout the country as Parsons elaborated the nature of his work:

> I think, however, that by the Grace of God I am sufficiently safe from them [pursuivants] owing to the precaution I take, and am going to take, of being in different places from early morning till late at night. After divine service has been performed and sermons preached—I am compelled to preach twice

---

[75] Neale, *Elizabeth I and Her Parliaments*, I, 369-415; T.E. Hartley, ed., *Proceedings in the Parliaments of Elizabeth I* (Leicester, 1981) pp. 499-547; John LaRocca, S.J., "English Catholics and the Recusancy Laws 1558-1625: A Study in Religion and Politics," (unpublished Ph.D. thesis: Rutgers University, 1977) 82-89. In a letter to the General, Parsons explained the new laws: "By these laws not only the property but life itself is entrusted to the hands of the enemies. The first law is that whoever refuses to attend churches of the heretics, which the Catholics do refuse with the greatest constancy, loses 66 gold coins each month. The second is that all priests with authority to absolve should be put to death. The third, that all who welcome such priests in their house, be punished by loss of all property and life imprisonment. They are confident that with these three laws, they will soon annihilate all Catholics. But our hope is in God who is stronger than all" (London 30 August [1581], ARSI, Fondo Gesuitico 651/640).

[76] *Elizabeth I* (London, 1988) p. 38.

[77] Campion confessed that his clothing was very simple and that he changed it—and his name—often. Nonetheless he thought that they could not "hope to escape the hands of the Protestants in the long run; so many eyes, so many mouths, so many traps at the service of the enemy" ([Campion] to [Acquaviva], [England, November 1580], ARSI, Fondo Gesuitico 651/612 (translated in Edwards, *Elizabethan Jesuits*, p. 89). Parsons testified to the same practices: "Wherever they [the Jesuits] go, they enjoy abundant hospitality, and the Catholics welcome them at the risk of their lives. Large throngs of noble youths meet with them; with these they often exchange clothes, horses, and even servants; hence they can with difficulty be distinguished from the rest" ([Parsons] to [Acquaviva], London 16 June 1581, ARSI, Fondo Gesuitico 651/596).

[78] Patrick McGrath and Joy Rowe have given these lay helpers, and others like them, the attention they are due ("The Elizabethan Priests: Their Harbourers and Helpers," *RH* 19 [1989] 209-33).

[79] These guides introduced the Jesuits to their Catholic hosts and conducted them through a still largely roadless country. Joyce Younings notes the absence of roads and remarks that "a good living could be made" leading strangers around the countryside (*Sixteenth-Century England* [London, 1984] p. 92).

on the same day sometimes—I struggle with almost unending business. This consists mainly in solving cases of conscience which occur, in directing other priests to suitable places and occupations, and reconciling schismatics to the Church, in writing letters to those who are tempted at times in the course of the persecution, in trying to arrange financial need for the support of those who are in prison and in want.[80]

The first Annual Letter of the English Mission (1580/1) related the same pattern of missionary life. In the houses of Catholics, the fathers would say an early morning Mass at which they would preach. The time between Mass and dinner was devoted to writing. After dinner, the fathers travelled on different missionary errands and prepared their homilies for the next day. In the evening they heard confessions and solved many difficult cases of conscience.[81]

The two Jesuits returned from their tour of the shires and met again in Uxbridge in October. There they discussed the storm caused by the "Brag." Parsons persuaded Campion to write a reply to his critics. To facilitate its publication they arranged to set up a secret printing press. After the meeting Campion headed north through Nottinghamshire, Derbyshire, Yorkshire, and Lancashire. On the trip he composed his reply, which he entitled *Rationes Decem*, although the original title was to have been the ironic *De Haeresi Desperata*. While Campion travelled, Parsons stayed in London to oversee the new printing press clandestinely set up by Edward and William Brooksby in an unoccupied house in Greenstreet owned by their father Robert. Another friend, Stephen Brinkley, managed the press and looked after the printers.

The first book appeared before 6 November. Under the pseudonym John Howlet, Parsons published *A brief discours contayning certayne reasons why catholiques refuse to go to Church*,[82] the book that he had promised at Southwark. Through a systematic treatment of the theme Parsons sought to strengthen the resolve of Catholics and to explain why such attendance was unlawful. It was neither rebellion nor contempt that prevented Catholics from attending the established services but obligation and an unwillingness to abandon their faith. Among the reasons advanced by the Jesuit were peril of infection, scandal, schism, and loss of the benefits of Catholicism.[83] As

---

[80] Parsons to Father Agazzari, London 17 November 1580, in Hicks, *Letters of Persons*, p. 61.
[81] *Annuae Litterae 1581*, translated in Foley, *Records*, III, 37-41. See also Parsons's letters to Agazzari, 5 August 1580 and August 1581, in Hicks, *Letters of Persons*, pp. 46, 83.
[82] (Doway [*vere* London], 1580) STC 19394, ARCR II, no. 613.
[83] Alban Langdale wrote a brief response to Parsons. This work circulated in manuscript. A copy can be found in PRO, SP 12/144/69. On this response see A.C. Southern, *Elizabethan Recusant Prose 1559-1582* (London, n.d. [1950]) pp. 140-44, 437.

a result, Parsons pleaded to the Queen for toleration and religious liberty. Soon after the book's publication the press was dismantled for reasons of security. But Parsons decided to reassemble it in a different location after he read Charke's and Hanmer's rejoinders to Campion's "Brag." This time the press was set up in the house of Francis Browne, brother of Viscount Montague. *A brief censure uppon two bookes written in answere to M. Edmonde Campions offer of disputation* appeared early in 1581.[84]

Charke's work was Parsons's chief target, and he consistently attacked the former fellow of Peterhouse for a total misrepresentation of Catholic doctrine. A favourite tactic of Puritans such as Charke was, according to Parsons, to arouse the government against the Catholics on grounds of disloyalty. Parsons again dismissed the charge and reminded Charke that the only proper reply to a challenge was an acceptance. In this work Parsons defended Ignatius Loyola and the Society of Jesus against various attacks. A third work produced by this press was a reply to the recent recantation of John Nichols. After a chequered religious career that veered from Protestant minister to seminarian at the English College in Rome, Nichols was arrested upon his return to England and conformed. A highly respected prisoner in the Tower, he delivered an harangue against popery on 5 February 1581, in which he described its many vices. Parsons's rebuttal revealed the fraudulence of the apostate and delineated the true state of religion in Rome.[85]

By the end of March of 1581 Campion completed his work and delivered the manuscript to Parsons. Because of the large number of quotations and citations, Parsons assigned the manuscript to Thomas Fitzherbert, later a Jesuit but now a member of Gilbert's association, to check it for accuracy. While Fitzherbert was confirming sources, the press was moved again, to Stonor Park in Oxfordshire.[86] *Rationes Decem* was secretly distributed in the University Church of St. Mary's in Oxford on 27 June 1581: this church was the site of the "Act," a public disputation at which candidates for a degree had to defend their theses. When the participants arrived they found copies of the small book on their seats.

Rationes Decem was a development of points first raised in the "Brag." Campion repeated his challenge and chided his critics for personal attacks and slanders about the Society instead of actually agreeing to a debate. His confidence in victory, Campion assured his critics, resulted not from pride in his own abilities but from the strong foundations on which his arguments were built. The *Rationes Decem* were the ten reasons for his confidence.

---

[84] (Doway [*vere* London], 1581) STC 19393, ARCR II, no. 612.

[85] *A discoverie of I. Nicols Minister, misreported a Iesuite, latelye recanted in the Tower of London* (n.p. n.d. [*vere* London, 1581]) STC 19402, ARCR II, no. 625.

[86] For more on the perils of publishing these works see Hicks, *Letters of Persons*, xxxi-xxxix and Southern, *Elizabethan Recusant Prose*, pp. 349-59.

The first two concerned scripture. At the hands of the Protestants, Campion claimed, the scriptures had been distorted and misinterpreted. Protestants either had eliminated passages or books that contradicted their doctrines, or they twisted the meaning of these passages to conform to their heresy. Protestants, and this was the third reason, had destroyed the nature of the Church. With them, it had ceased to be a visible, historical entity and had become an invisible community perceived by only a few. Fourthly Campion appealed to the ecumenical councils. If, as John Jewel and other Elizabethan ministers claimed, they accepted the teachings of the early councils, why did they not accept their decrees on the primacy of Rome and the sacrifice of the Mass? The fifth and sixth reasons were the testimonies of the fathers of the Church and their interpretation of the scriptures. The fathers were not the only witnesses to the legitimacy of the Roman Church: seventhly, the entire history of the Church attested to it. The inherent weaknesses in the writings of the Protestants and their fallacious logic were the eighth and ninth reasons. Finally, the truth of the Roman Catholic position had been affirmed by all manners of witnesses throughout the ages: saints and sinners, bishops and heretics, kings and serfs.[87]

On 17 July, less than a month after the books' distribution, he was betrayed by a lapsed Catholic and captured at Lyford Grange in Berkshire.[88] By the 22nd he was in the Tower, imprisoned in the narrow dungeon, Little Ease, and twice tortured.[89] On the 25th he was taken to the house of his former patron Robert Dudley, Earl of Leicester. Special favours and rapid promotions were promised him if only he would disown *Rationes Decem* and conform to the established Church.

Having failed to seduce Campion, the government sought to discredit him. Ostensibly in response to Campion's "Brag," the government staged four separate disputations between the Jesuit and leading Protestant controversialists. Informed of the debates only a few hours before they were scheduled to begin and allowed only a Bible for consultation, Campion was on the defensive from the beginning: he was only allowed to answer the objections raised by his opponents. In the four meetings Campion debated justification by faith, the nature of the Church, the real presence in the Eucharist, and the canon of Scripture with Alexander Nowell, Dean of St.

---

[87] *Rationes Decem* (n.p. n.d. [Stonor Park, 1581]) STC 4536.5, ARCR I, no. 135.1. It was translated and edited by J.H. Pollen and published as *Campion's Ten Reasons* (London, 1914).

[88] See Milward, *Religious Controversies of the Elizabethan Age*, pp. 56-64 for controversial works published about the *Rationes Decem* and Campion's arrest and capture.

[89] Parsons's account of events leading up to Campion's capture and ending with Campion's arrival at the Tower can be found in his letter to Acquaviva, London 30 August [1581], ARSI, Fondo Gesuitico 651/640. On the use of torture to extract "truth" from Campion see Elizabeth Hanson, "Torture and Truth in Renaissance England," *Representations* 34 (1991) 53-84.

Paul's, William Day, Dean of Windsor, John Walker, Archdeacon of Essex, William Fulke, Master of Pembroke College, Cambridge; and William Charke. The crowds quietly dwindled as it became clear that the intention was not the pursuit of truth but the humiliation of the Jesuit. In subsequent literature both sides claimed victory.[90]

Campion was arraigned at Westminster Hall on 14 November. On the 20th he was tried with seven other priests on the charge of treason. It was claimed that they had engaged in treasonable conspiracies regarding the Queen. Paid informers testified to a plot and to Campion's involvement in it. By the Treasons Act of Edward III (1351), he was found guilty and sentenced to death. On 1 December, with two other priests, Alexander Briant and Ralph Sherwin, he was taken from the Tower to Tyburn, where he was hanged, drawn, and quartered.[91]

Parsons was fortunate that he too was not apprehended. Thrice he escaped. The first time he hid in a hayloft to avoid detection while pursuivants searched the house. He eluded capture the second time because he could not find the inn in Holborn where he was scheduled to meet a priest with whom he was to collaborate in the conversion of some schismatics. Sir Francis Walsingham's spies knew of the plans and awaited the arrival of the priests. The other priest, Edward Rishton, was captured.

While in London Parsons used a large room in a house owned by a Protestant and situated at the river bank. In the room was stored everything that the priests needed for their mission: books, vestments, etc. It served as a meeting room for the priests. A bookseller betrayed this information to the government and the house was besieged. Purely by chance a few days earlier Parsons had transferred almost everything to a new location and had gone into the country. Thus he evaded capture a third time; Alexander Briant was not so lucky.[92] After Campion's arrest, the search for Parsons was even more intense, and he fled England for France, never to return. Later Parsons would be accused of cowardice by his enemies and opponents. At the time of his flight he claimed that he went to the continent for four

---

[90] The Protestant account is Alexander Nowell and William Day, *A true report of the Disputation or rather private Conference had in the Tower of London, with Ed. Campion Iesuite, the last of August 1581* and *The three last dayes conferences had in the Tower with Edmund Campion Iesuite, the 18: 23 and 27 of September 1581* published together in London in 1583 (STC 18744). The Catholic accounts can be found in British Library, Harleian MS 422, ff. 132^r-133^r; 136^r-172^v; Add. MS 39828, f. 38 (printed in Historical Manuscripts Commission, *Various Collections*, 8 vols. [London, 1901-14] III, 8-16); Add. MS 11055, ff. 188^r-192^v; Oxford, Bodleian Library, Rawlinson MS D 353, ff. 1-35.

[91] See Thomas M. McCoog, S.J., "'The Flower of Oxford': The Role of Edmund Campion in Early Recusant Polemics," *SCJ* 24 (1993) 899-913 for a discussion of the conflicting portraits of Campion.

[92] [Parsons] to [Acquaviva], London 16 June 1581, ARSI, Fondo Gesuitico 651/640; Parsons, "Punti," pp. 16-17.

reasons: a consultation with William Allen; the setting up of a secure printing press; a meeting with the ambassador of the Queen of Scots regarding a mission to Scotland; and a hope of obtaining the King of France's intercession for the English Catholics with Queen Elizabeth.[93]

The English mission so triumphally proclaimed by Campion and Parsons was in ruins. Of the three Jesuits who crossed to England with such fond hopes in June of 1580, Campion was executed within eighteen months, Parsons fled to France, and Emerson was either still in England or with Parsons on the continent. Thomas Pounde, Thomas Metham, and James Bosgrave remained in prison. Secular priests who had joined the Society in England fared similarly: Alexander Briant, sentenced with Campion, entered the Society shortly before his execution on 1 December 1581;[94] Thomas Cottam, having entered the Jesuit novitiate in Rome as a priest in 1579, returned to England for reasons of health shortly thereafter, was tried with Campion, imprisoned, and later executed in 1582.[95] After the arrival of the Jesuits the persecution was more intense and the laws more stringent. Catholics sought some relief by appealing to Francis, Duke of Alençon in England to negotiate a marriage treaty with Elizabeth. The English Catholics begged the French representatives to use their influence to obtain protection for their co-religionists. The petition was fruitless: the instructions laid down by the marriage commissioners forbade the Duke to interfere in the established religion of England and the laws that protected it. Jean Bodin, when asked to gain some concessions for the Catholics, replied that he was in England to discuss a marriage and not religion. Throughout the summer of 1581 papal pleas to the French King that he intercede for the Catholics were dismissed with polite words.[96] Meanwhile Parsons was on the continent, pursuing other tactics for the restoration of Catholicism. The failure of the challenge to a debate and the execution of Campion affected Parsons seriously. Although we have no clear documentary evidence, he subsequently abandoned his original approach of polite discussion and theological debate in favour of more political and military strategies. After the new legislation of 1581, the language of discourse had changed. No longer was religious orthodoxy the issue; it was now political allegiance. The restoration of Catholicism remained Parsons's most important consideration, but he was

---

[93] Parsons to Acquaviva, [21 October 1581], in Hicks, *Letters of Persons*, p. 107; Parsons, "Autobiography," pp. 30-31.

[94] Briant entered the Society shortly before his execution (*Mon. Ang.*, II, 244).

[95] See *Mon. Ang.*, II, 275-76.

[96] Parsons, "Punti," pp. 22-27; John Bossy, "English Catholics and the French Marriage, 1577-81," *RH* 5 (1959) 8-11. Spain, through its ambassador in England and its embassy in France, tried to bring some pressure on Alençon but with no effect (Mendoza to Philip II, London 7 November 1581, CSP Simancas [1580-86], 209-11).

now willing to discuss more drastic proposals for achieving it: the removal of certain Elizabethan advisors, the liberation of the imprisoned Mary, the use of force to back her title to the English throne, and the overthrow of Elizabeth. As we shall see in the next chapter, his involvement in politics becomes much more pronounced. Both men had warned the authorities that there were hundreds of other Jesuits who were willing to take their places in the English enterprise. It remained to be seen whether others would embark on the mission after the executions at Tyburn.

III

Had the expense been reckoned at such a high price? One Jesuit missionary had been executed, but suffering was not restricted to the Society of Jesus. Fear of arrest compelled George Gilbert and others to flee the country in 1581. For Catholics who remained within the kingdom the persecution intensified.[97] Catholics were kept under even tighter surveillance and, as a result of the papally sponsored enterprise in Ireland and the goals of the Jesuit mission to England, new penal laws were added that increased financial punishment.[98] In the first Annual Letter of the English mission, the author, presumably Robert Parsons, explained to the universal Society of Jesus some conditions within England:

> Many noble citizens, for opposing the ambition of this perverse woman [Elizabeth], suffer in their estates, and moreover by exile, bonds, and death. To such an extent does this insane and cruel disposition of the Queen increase, that in most cities new prisons are built, the old ones being too small to receive the multitudes of the condemned; and into these prisons, which are frightful by reason of their darkness, are thrust crowds of Catholics, who miserably perish in them, laden with fetters, in want and horrid filth; or at least, without exception, are first or last tortured in the rack-chamber. Others she commands to be dragged by horses through the city, and hung, cut down alive, dismembered, disembowelled, their intestines burnt before their eyes, and their bodies afterwards quartered; others are hung up aloft upon the rack

---

[97] In a letter to Father Agazzari written in Reims on 23 June 1581, Dr. Allen reported that persecution against the Catholics, and especially the Jesuits, had escalated. Yet, surprisingly, Parsons testified that there were still a large number of conversions (PRO, SP 12/149/51 and 52 and Knox, *Letters of Allen*, p. 95). The Spanish ambassador informed Philip of increased persecution of the Catholics (Mendoza to Philip, London 6 April 1581, CSP Simancas [1580-86] 97-98; same to same, London 4 July 1581, *ibid.*, 139-40; same to same, London 12 August 1581, *ibid.*, 152-53; same to same, London 1 October 1581, *ibid.*, 175-77).

[98] See John J. LaRocca, S.J., "Popery and Pounds: The Effect of the Jesuit Mission on Penal Legislation," in *The Reckoned Expense: Edmund Campion and the Early English Jesuits. Essays in Celebration of the First Centenary of Campion Hall, Oxford (1896-1996)*, ed. Thomas M. McCoog, S.J. (Woodbridge, 1996) pp. 249-63 for an exposition of the effect of the Jesuit mission on the penal legislation. On the financial aspects, see McCoog, "Finances of the English Province," 29-31.

and so cruelly extended that all their joints are dislocated; others are tortured by having needles thrust beneath their nails and others crushed beneath enormous weights piled upon their bodies."[99]

To rebut the Society's opponents who claimed that the Jesuits were responsible for intensified persecution, the author informed his readers that it was "to share in these dangers and merits" that Jesuits were invited by the English themselves "with most pressing entreaties and by constant letters" so that there would be someone to whom the laity could fly for advice and assistance. Yet, despite the terror, the Society would not desert the mission once undertaken. In fact, the author proclaimed joyously, two new priests had arrived that very year, 1581. Two new men had indeed arrived but the mission's future was not as secure as the author would have liked his audience to believe.

Everard Mercurian, the General under whom the mission was initiated, died on 1 August 1580. His successor Claudio Acquaviva was elected on 19 February 1581. Immediately there was some concern about the mission's future as a result of the capture and execution of Campion. William Allen had some doubts about the intentions of the new General even though Acquaviva had been influential in the mission's establishment. Acquaviva assured Allen on 28 May 1581 that the latter should be "convinced that, as heretofore, so in time to come I shall always be her [England's] champion. . . . I will strive hard, by appointing other labourers who are better and more pleasing to God, to satisfy my duty and also my love towards that nation."[100] Two months earlier, in his first letter to Parsons, the new General promised that he would help Parsons when and in whatever ways he could. Soon he would send some more Jesuits.[101]

The request for more Jesuits was a frequent refrain in letters to Rome. Campion drew the General's attention to the need for more men, especially

---

[99] *Annuae Litterae*, pp. 205-11, translated in Foley, *Records*, III, 37-38.
[100] Ryan, "Correspondence of Allen," p. 79.
[101] Acquaviva to Parsons, Rome 27 March 1581, ARSI, Fl. Belg. 2, p. 172. On 5 August 1580 Parsons wrote to Father Agazzari that "there is a very large field here for useful labour if we had a sufficiency of capable men of our Society. So that above everything else we beg your Reverence to send us as soon as possible a goodly number of competent persons" (*Letters of Persons*, p. 45). On 20 January 1581 Allen petitioned the Cardinal of Como that he seek four or five more Jesuits for immediate posting to England and not wait for the election of a new General (Penelope Renold, ed., *Letters of William Allen and Richard Barret 1572-1598* [London, 1967] p. 26). In 1581 Allen thought that candidates for the English mission must "be eloquent in the Latin tongue and suitable for disputations" (Allen to [Agazzari?], [Reims] 20 April [1581], *ibid.*, p. 30). See also Parsons to Agazzari, 17 November 1580, in Hicks, *Letters of Persons*, pp. 55, 61-62.

those skilled in preaching.¹⁰² In his letter to Oliver Mannaerts, Vicar-General of the Society after the death of Mercurian, Robert Parsons asked that the Jesuits selected for the mission be suitable for the life in England. The English had such a high opinion of the Society that extreme care must be exercised lest someone be sent who would affect this esteem adversely. By October of 1580 Parsons had established contact with Bernardino de Mendoza, Spanish ambassador in England. Through him Parsons established a relatively secure means of communication with Rome.¹⁰³ Mendoza promised Parsons full assistance and asked that a Spanish Jesuit be attached to his household. Parsons concurred with the suggestion and forwarded it to Mannaerts.¹⁰⁴ After Parsons received Acquaviva's letter of 27 March, he was more explicit. "Because your liberal promise about giving the help and the helpers we need emboldens us," Parsons suggested Ferdinando Capeci, Antonio Maria Parenticelli, and Fabricio Pallavicino, and asked that the first two be sent as soon as possible and the third later. Among the English, Parsons thought that John Castell was the best qualified if still alive.¹⁰⁵ Meanwhile he was making arrangements for the arrival of Jasper Heywood and Christopher Perkins.¹⁰⁶

Parsons may have expected Heywood and Perkins, but the General dispatched Heywood and William Holt. Holt was a last-minute replacement for Perkins, who did eventually come to England but not as a member of the Society. Acquaviva did not send any foreign Jesuits but continued to look for possible candidates. A Spaniard, unnamed in the correspondence, was already studying controversial theology in preparation for his departure. An Italian had not yet been found. Some had volunteered but the General had reservations about each. A few months later the General questioned the wisdom of sending foreign Jesuits into England:

> much as I favour that mission, as your Reverence knows, yet two facts made me doubt, at this time especially when the persecution waxes so hot; firstly because he did not see how there could be much assistance from men who were ignorant of the language, and who, separated from the rest of Ours, by

---

¹⁰² [Campion] to [Acquaviva], n.p. n.d. [England November 1580], ARSI, Fondo Gesuitico 651/612 (translated in Edwards, *Elizabethan Jesuits*, p. 89). Compare William Holt's recommendation: "There is one thing that has often come into my mind since my entrance into England, and which not without reason I have resolved to make known to your Reverence [Father General], if ever I had the chance, as I have now. I mean, in your 'missions' there is not so much need of speed as of the ripeness of prudence, learning and fervour of spirit in those that are sent. . . . I advise for the good of both, and for the good of all Catholics who are to profit by your aid, and I say that for your 'missions' there is need of devotion, prudence and ripeness of learning rather than of hurry" (Cited in Parsons, "Punti," p. 95).
¹⁰³ Edwards, *Robert Persons*, p. 40.
¹⁰⁴ London 20 October 1580, ARSI, Fondo Gesuitico 651/640.
¹⁰⁵ Unbeknownst to Parsons he died sometime in 1580 (*Mon. Ang.*, II, 260).
¹⁰⁶ [Parsons] to [Acquaviva], London 16 June 1581, ARSI, Fondo Gesuitico 651/596.

whom they might be helped, would have to manage each his own affairs; secondly, because for the same reason, they would be much more exposed to danger, as they would be much more easily taken up as foreigners, having no knowledge of places or persons, and being ignorant of whom they ought to shun, or to whom they might trust themselves.

Dangers and other demands led Acquaviva not to send any foreign Jesuits.[107] In fact there were sufficient virtuous and learned English Jesuits so that the General thought it better that the mission be carried out by the native born. There were many Englishmen eager to serve. William Allen continued to recommend young men to the Society and consistently urged that the Society not close its door to Englishmen. But the Society could accept only so many and others had to be turned away.[108] But if the mission failed, it would not be from lack of volunteers.

IV

In June of 1581 Jasper Heywood and William Holt disembarked at Newcastle, apparently under the protection of Henry Percy, Earl of Northumberland.[109] After a night at an inn, they journeyed to London and met Parsons at the Bellamy house at Harrow. The son of the epigrammatist John Heywood and uncle of the poet John Donne, Jasper Heywood had been educated with Princess Elizabeth by the same tutor. Later he began a promising academic career at Oxford and became a fellow of All Souls before he left England to become a Catholic priest. He joined the Society in Rome on 21 May 1562 and studied theology at Dillingen, where he remained as a successful lecturer and a popular preacher.

Sometime during 1570/71 Heywood began to endure nocturnal conflicts with the devil that left him too exhausted during the day for any work. He left Dillingen for an unnamed spa, where the waters proved slightly more beneficial than the sundry exorcisms. Sent to Augsburg, he immediately became involved in a raging theological controversy over the morality of a 5% rate of interest. Adhering to the traditional prohibition of usury, Heywood preached and argued that even a reasonable rate such as 5% was

---

[107] Acquaviva to Allen, Rome 28 May 1581, in Ryan, "Correspondence of Allen," pp. 79, 81; same to same, Rome 14 October 1581, *ibid.*, p. 85.

[108] See e.g. [Mannaerts] to Allen, Rome 27 October 1580, in Ryan, "Correspondence of Allen," p. 75.

[109] For this exposition of Heywood's mission I am indebted to Dennis Flynn, "The English Mission of Jasper Heywood, S.J.," *AHSI* 54 (1985) 45-76 and "'Out of Step': Six Supplementary Notes on Jasper Heywood," in *The Reckoned Expense: Edmund Campion and the Early English Jesuits. Essays in Celebration of the First Centenary of Campion Hall, Oxford (1896-1996)*, ed. Thomas M. McCoog, S.J. (Woodbridge, 1996) pp. 179-92; and to John Hungerford Pollen's unfinished history of the Elizabethan Jesuits, preserved in ABSI, 46/5A/1.

forbidden. In 1575 he went so far as to persuade Bishop Johann Egolph von Knöringen to forbid absolution to anyone who charged interest. The consequent uproar was so loud that the German Provincial Paul Hoffaeus intervened. To quell the storm, Hoffaeus forbade Heywood any more involvement in the controversy. But Heywood had a strong case and many supporters.[110] Heywood appealed to Pope Gregory XIII and to Duke William V of Bavaria. Throughout the dispute, relations between Heywood and Hoffaeus, his religious superior and theological opponent, deteriorated.[111] The Provincial begged the General and the German assistant that Heywood be recalled from his province and sent elsewhere. His prayers were answered in May of 1581.

Lest Heywood's patron, Duke William, perceive the new mission as punishment, Pope Gregory XIII wrote to him on 27 May. In England, the Pope told the Duke, the harvest was great and the labourers few. The few Jesuits there anxiously sought more men and had specifically asked for Heywood because "they hope that his authority, which is not slight there, will stand him in good stead." The Pope knew that the Duke would consent to Heywood's involvement in this important mission.[112] A day later, Father General Acquaviva wrote to William Allen that he had dispatched Holt and Heywood, who had been in Rome since the end of 1580 and for whom Parsons had asked, Jesuits "who in my judgement and that of all were men of tried virtue."[113] One wonders if the General informed Parsons and Allen of the conflicts in which Heywood had been involved, and the sufferings he had endured. After all that had transpired in Germany was he still the calibre of man the English desired?

Like Heywood, Holt was an Oxford man but less controversial. A native of Lancashire, he studied rhetoric, philosophy, and theology first at Brasenose College and then at Oriel. Crossing to Douai sometime after 1573, he studied theology for three more years and was ordained priest. On 8 November 1578 he entered the Society in Rome. He had barely completed his novitiate when he was sent to England.[114]

After the meeting in Harrow, Heywood and Holt separated to visit their

---

[110] One supporter was Peter Canisius. For an exposition of their friendship and Canisius's role in this controversy see James Brodrick, S.J., *Saint Peter Canisius, S.J. 1521-1597* (London, 1935) *passim*.
[111] Hoffaeus's account of the debate over usury can be found in ARSI, Opp. N.N. 158, ff. 2^r-83^v.
[112] Edwards, *Elizabethan Jesuits*, pp. 170-71.
[113] Acquaviva to Allen, Rome 28 May 1581, in Ryan, "Correspondence of Allen," p. 79. Although there was a comparable debate raging in England about usury (see Norman Jones, *God and the Moneylenders* [Oxford, 1989]), there is no evidence that Heywood was involved.
[114] Edwards, *Elizabethan Jesuits*, pp. 338-39; Godfrey Anstruther, O.P., *The Seminary Priests*, Vol. 1 (Ware/Durham, n.d. [1968]) pp. 174-75; *Mon. Ang.*, II, 359.

families and friends. They met again in Staffordshire, where they began their work among the recusants. While they were in the north of England, Parsons, who had been somewhere along the south coast, slipped across the channel to France to transact his urgent business with greater freedom. Although Heywood had been designated Parsons's deputy while the latter was out of London, he was not informed of his superior's plans to cross to France. Indeed, the letter in which Parsons delegated his authority to Heywood was marked "from the north." For six months Heywood did not know the whereabouts of his superior, and he was angry when he discovered that Parsons had left the kingdom. Parsons's hope to return to England was shattered when his name was inserted in the indictment against Campion. A return to England now would mean life in a hiding hole. Consequently Heywood's temporary appointment became permanent.[115]

By October Heywood had followed up Parsons's earlier contact with Bernardino de Mendoza, Spanish ambassador to England. For years the ambassador had been doing what he could to help the English Catholics. In the instructions given him by the King in 1578, Mendoza was permitted to receive the English Catholics kindly, to console them and encourage them to persevere in their faith, but he was forbidden to enter any negotiations with them against the Queen.[116] With the renewal of persecution during the summer of 1580, Philip II had asked Mendoza to ascertain the reasons for the renewal and to discover whether the persecution was calculated to create or to prevent disturbances. Fifteen months later Philip replied that it grieved him to think of the sufferings endured by English Catholics and of his own inability to do anything to help them. The King could do nothing because he

---

[115] Parsons told the General in an important letter of 21 October 1581 that no one in England knew that he had left the country and that no one knew that he was in Rouen except Allen, James Beaton, Archbishop of Glasgow, and Monsignor Michel de Monsi, Archdeacon of Rouen. In order to keep his location secret, Parsons had sent his servant to England with many letters sent, as it were, "from somewhere in the North" (Hicks, *Letters of Persons*, p. 107).

[116] Royal instructions to Mendoza, Madrid 8 and 26 January 1578, CSP Simancas (1568-79) 553-58, 558-60. Unfortunately there has not been a study of Mendoza's involvement in English affairs. Until it appears, De Lamar Jensen's *Diplomacy and Dogmatism: Bernardino de Mendoza and the French Catholic League* (Cambridge, Mass., 1964) is useful. In a letter to the rector of the English College written in London on 17 November 1580, Parsons described the ambassador as "most friendly to us" (Hicks, *Letters of Persons*, p. 60). A year later, on 4 July 1581, Parsons wrote to Allen that "the zeal of this man [Mendoza], too, in promoting the faith is almost incredible; and added to this is the fact that he knows me and the other members of our Order more intimately than does anyone else, and that he knows how and when to do things; so that if he were to remain in Paris there is no doubt that he would become a wonderful support to us and our cause, and that by his aid in a short time (with the help of God) we should do great things in the cause of the faith" (*Letters of Persons*, p. 72). Apparently Parsons thought when he wrote this letter that Mendoza was going to be removed from London and stationed in Paris. That transfer did not come for another few years and, as we shall see, under rather inauspicious conditions.

was certain that any intervention on his part would only add to the persecution of the Catholics. Meanwhile the King insisted that Mendoza continue his quiet support and encouragement.[117]

Although Heywood was but one of many clergy and leading Catholics who sought the ambassador's assistance, the ambassador was so impressed with him and his ability that he revised an earlier judgement: he now argued that Parsons, upon his imminent return from France, should oversee the English mission while Heywood tackled the extremely delicate visit to Scotland.[118] We shall consider the mission to Scotland in the next chapter. Here it is sufficient to note that William Holt was sent to Scotland and that Jasper Heywood was left to his own devices in England while Parsons remained in France, negotiating financial and military support for the Catholic cause in Scotland.

In 1581 and 1582 Heywood was active throughout the north of England, where Catholicism remained strong. He converted many and collected considerable alms from wealthy Catholics for those imprisoned for their faith. In Oxford and Cambridge he recruited candidates for the English colleges on the continent: twenty crossed in November of 1582 and fifty more in the following August.[119] Because of Heywood's background, a visit to Oxford was not surprising; a visit to Cambridge might have been prompted by Parsons's concern that the area had been neglected by the clergy and, as a result, Protestantism was rampant.[120] Heywood's family and background facilitated access to Philip Howard, Earl of Arundel, and to Henry Percy, Earl of Northumberland. On both he had significant influence. Heywood's success was duly acknowledged by William Allen: "Father Gaspar is a distinguished and prudent worker who has captured some large fish this year."[121]

---

[117] Philip II to Mendoza, Bardajoz 15 August 1580, CSP Simancas (1580-86) 49; same to same, Lisbon 19 November 1581, *ibid.*, 219. The King, however, was anxious to assist the English Catholics in their desire to have at least one of their countrymen (either Dr. Sander or William Allen) elevated to the cardinalate (Philip II to Mendoza, La Cardiga 28 May 1581, *ibid.*, 118; Juan de Idiáquez to Mendoza, La Cardiga 28 May 1581, *ibid.*, 118-19; Mendoza to Philip II, London 4 July 1581, *ibid.*, 139-40). In the last, Mendoza claims that it would be tremendously beneficial to the English to see one of their compatriots in such an exalted position.

[118] Mendoza to Philip II, London 20 October 1581, CSP Simancas (1580-86) 194-97.

[119] See Flynn, "'Out of Step'" for more details.

[120] Parsons to Acquaviva, 21 October 1581, in Hicks, *Letters of Persons*, p. 108.

[121] Allen to Agazzari, Reims on 14 March 1583, in Knox, *Letters of Allen*, p. 182. In the same letter Allen explained his conviction that the missionaries were making progress: "All that part of the country where we were born is catholic, though the common people sometimes go to the churches of the heretics through fear of the iniquitous laws. Nay, he [Allen's brother Gabriel] says that throughout all England up and down the hearts of almost every one are ours, while the outward actions of many persons are the Queen's. And in this respect we seem to have had no small success, since the minds of men, as we see, are imbued with the right

More ambivalent in his esteem was John Southcote, a secular priest who died in 1637. Writing years later, Southcote claimed that Heywood was a good scholar and "much honoured and loved by the secular priests" but he "carried a haughty mind and a stirring head, not in state matters as Father Parsons but other profane and ecclesiastical affairs." It is not known if Southcote referred to a specific incident or if his comment was simply a personal conclusion based on Heywood's style of life because, again according to Southcote, he "rode much in a coach accompanied with many and costly apparel. His carriage seemed to be as of a legate *a latere* and he took upon him to assemble a great number of priests as it were in a provincial council."[122] At a time when many priests were lurking in shadows, such a public display was unique. Nonetheless it may be a sign not of ecclesiastical ambition but of Heywood's return to the style to which he was accustomed before he joined the Society.

The Society of Jesus made its second appearance in a royal proclamation on 1 April 1582. The proclamation repeated charges that would be heard again and again over the next two centuries: Jesuits and seminary priests have

> persuaded [her Majesty's subjects] from the acknowledgement of their natural duties and allegiance unto her majesty as their natural prince and only sovereign, and by special direction from the pope and his delegates have been made instruments in sundry wicked traitorous practices, tending not only to the moving and stirring up of rebellion within their natural countries (which through the goodness of Almighty God and her majesty's provident government hath always been foreseen and prevented) but also to the endangering of her majesty's most royal person. . . .

Anyone, the proclamation continued, discovered assisting and harbouring these priests would be charged with misprision of treason and punished according to the laws of the realm.[123]

The proclamation intensified the persecution that continued throughout the spring of 1582.[124] The persecution, however, did not deter either Heywood

---

doctrine, though fear, which is not a lasting keeper, prevents them from confessing it with the mouth" (English translation from Thomas Francis Knox, ed., *The First and Second Diaries of the English College, Douay* [London, 1878] lxix).

[122] John Morris, S.J., ed., "The Note-Book of John Southcote, D.D.," in *Miscellanea I* (London, 1905) pp. 111-12.

[123] Hughes and Larkin, *Tudor Royal Proclamations*, II, 488-91. See also the proclamation of c. 6 May 1586, *ibid.*, 518-21.

[124] A year earlier Allen had attacked the government's claim that the persecution was the result of treason against the government and not of religious differences. "What hath Masse, Matins, Confession, Absolution, beades, Agnusdeies, and other consecrated tokens of our communion with al the Churches of Christ through al ages, what affinitie have they in nature with treason?" Allen asked. "Why do they reduce our offense rather to Treason, then to

or Parsons[125] from asking for more Jesuits.[126] Indeed, Parsons contended that the persecution would rebound on the government because the sympathies of more moderate Protestants had been aroused by the suffering that the Catholics endured.[127] Nonetheless hard-liners such as the Earl of Leicester thought the government was not doing enough to stop the spread of Catholicism.[128]

Sometime in 1582 Ralph Emerson, who at some unspecified time had left England to escort William Crichton to Scotland, returned to London as a companion to Heywood. Parsons claimed that Emerson's presence was a

---

Heresie? If our doctrine be wicked, our actions superstitious, our worship of God sacrilegious, idololatrical, or anywise untrue or unlawful: why are we not condemned of such crimes, rather then of treason or unduetifulness to our Prince? for if they be faultes, they are directly against Gods honour, and but indirectly and consequently against the Prince" (*An apologie and true declaration*, ff. 74^r, 76^{r-v}). On 12 October 1582 a royal proclamation summarized the government's attitude to these accusations: these books "in a secret manner dispersed through this realm by divers seditious and traitorous persons, tending not only to the defacing of true religion now established within these her highness' dominions but also most traitorously and injuriously to slander the present most happy and quiet government with cruelty and extraordinary manner of proceedings in the due execution of justice. . ." (Hughes and Larkin, *Tudor Royal Proclamations*, II, 506-08). Christopher Haigh contends if Elizabeth believed that Catholics were not executed for religion "it was because she allowed herself to be deceived by officials who framed Catholics, and because the definition of treason had been extended to include actions which Catholics could hardly avoid" (*Elizabeth I*, p. 38).

[125] Parsons asked Agazzari on 6 April 1582 to "prepare for us men who will face racks fearlessly, and for other points we do not care. Yet it is God alone who makes such men, and not human industry or will. Therefore I pray get us commended to God, and this is the chief aid that we can ask of you" (Hicks, *Letters of Persons*, p. 143). Petitions for prayers for England appear frequently in the Society. On 4 June 1581 the General instructed all fathers and brothers to pray for the English mission for the next three months. Three years later, on 15 July 1584, the General directed the Jesuits in France, Germany, and Italy to offer one Mass each month for the next two months for the English mission (ARSI, Hist. Soc. 42, f. 133^r). In his "Punti" Parsons cited a letter written by Allen on 29 March [1583]: "I have written more than once to Father Jasper to know whether he desires and thinks fit that some Fathers of the Society should be sent to England at this time, and whether he would rather have foreigners or Englishmen, and how many of both sorts or of one sort he wishes. I take this precaution not to err, especially in the prolonged absence of Reverend Father Robert, with whom I could easily settle the matter" (p. 89).

[126] In November of 1582 five Portuguese Jesuits unexpectedly arrived in England. The men had been exiled from the Jesuit college on the island of Terceira in the Azores when it was captured by Don Antonio in his struggle with Philip of Spain for the Portuguese crown. Their ship went off course in a storm and they landed in Southampton, where they were arrested. The Spanish ambassador interceded for them and asked for passports so that they could return to Portugal. Four, however, died during their imprisonment in Southampton, and the fifth shortly after his return to Lisbon (PRO, SP 12/155/94; Mendoza to Walsingham, London 15 November 1582, SP 94/1/107; same to Philip II, London 15 November 1582, CSP Simancas [1580-86] 414-16 and same to same, London 29 November 1582, *ibid.*, 418-20; Francisco Rodrigues, S.J., *História da Companhia de Jesus na assistencia de Portugal*, 4 vols. in 7 [Oporto, 1931-50] II/2, 432-35; *Mon. Ang.*, II, 442 and references).

[127] London [*vere* France] 1 March 1582, in Hicks, *Letters of Persons*, p. 133.

[128] See his letter of 5 September 1582 to Sir Francis Walsingham cited in Neale, *Elizabeth I and Her Parliaments*, II, 13.

great comfort to Heywood "as much on account of his holiness, which was very great, as for his knowledge of the places and houses which Father Campion used to frequent."[129] A consolation he may have been, but Emerson, as a lay brother, was unable to perform the spiritual ministries that were so desperately needed. Thus Heywood's pleas for further Jesuit assistance continued, but they remained unheeded.

It seems that these were not the only petitions that went unheeded. By 16 April 1583 Heywood complained to Allen that, although he had written several letters to Parsons and to the General on important matters, he had received no reply. Indeed, he had even sent John Curry, a secular priest but a future Jesuit, to deliver personally a letter to Parsons. Again there was no answer. The only assistance within the foreseeable future was the priests being sent by Allen, and they would not arrive until midsummer at the earliest.[130] As we shall see, Parsons was much involved in Scottish affairs at this time. Perhaps that preoccupation prevented his reply. Heywood was not aware of Parsons's activities and movements. Even if Heywood had been, it is doubtful that his anger would have been less.

One Jesuit did appear in England sometime in late 1582 or early 1583 and quickly offered his assistance to Heywood. His offer was unsolicited and his presence proved very embarrassing. A Yorkshire native, Thomas Langdale entered the Society of Jesus in Rome on the same day as Heywood, 21 May 1562. Ordained sometime in the 1560s, he was professed of the three vows on 21 May 1569. Over the next decade he worked as English penitentiary in Rome and at Loreto and as confessor to the Sicilian Duke of Terranova. During a brief meeting with Campion and Parsons on their way to England, Langdale expressed his interest in the mission and his willingness to help.

In late 1582 he was summoned to Rome by Father General Acquaviva for unspecified reasons. Apparently on the spur of the moment, or perhaps fearing what awaited him in Rome—Langdale boarded an English ship in Genoa and returned home. There, although he publicly proclaimed himself a Catholic and a Jesuit and even wore his habit, Langdale gave considerable scandal by attending Protestant services. Heywood prudently avoided any contact with Langdale despite the latter's attempts to arrange a meeting. In a letter to Allen Heywood reported how Langdale had offered his aid to the Privy Council and to Richard Barnes, Bishop of Durham. He claimed that he was a papal Nuncio sent to England to correct the errors of seminary priests, to free Catholic consciences unjustly bound by the Jesuits, and to

---

[129] "Punti," p. 55; ABSI, 46/5A/1, Chapter VI p. 39.
[130] Heywood to Allen, London 16 April 1583, in Foley, *Records*, IV, 678-80. This letter was cited in Parsons, "Punti," p. 91.

report to the Pope the state of the kingdom. Eventually he returned to Yorkshire, where he and other apostates worked for the Council of the North in the discovery and apprehension of Catholic clergy.[131]

Langdale was a harbinger of ill times. Tension between the older Marian clergy and the Tridentine attitudes of the new arrivals, both the Jesuits and the seminary priests, again threatened disruption of the mission. The peace that resulted from the meeting at Southwark in 1580 was proving to be temporary. And again the issue was the preservation of England's unique religious and ecclesiastical traditions against the Tridentine reform's stress on uniformity. Acting on his own authority, at a time when his letters to Acquaviva and Parsons went unanswered, Heywood arranged for another meeting of representatives of the clergy to discuss the issues.[132] The precise date and location are unknown, but we do know that the meeting was somewhere in East Anglia during the spring of 1583.[133]

The result was an agreement on eighteen points, almost all of which concerned fasting and abstinence. These regulations, like those of the earlier Southwark meeting, generally relaxed more strict English traditions in favour of the Tridentine norms. Intermingled with these points are exhortations that "all would follow the Romane use in their office and service, as a thing commended to all the world by the whole concell of Trent;" that "the going to the protestants church, in such sorte, as it is nowe required, is unlawfull and a schismaticall deed, notwithstandinge all obedience pretended or protestation of the contrarie religion;" and that "they have noe special jurisdiction given them to minister the sacrament of pennance [the Marian priests], examine better their authoritie, and in the meane tyme abstayne from the act."[134] Apparently the Marian priests saw

---

[131] Heywood to Allen, London 16 April 1583, in Foley, *Records*, IV, 678-80; ABSI, 46/5A/1, Chapter VI p. 66; Parsons, "Punti," pp. 100-05; *Mon. Ang.*, II, 386. In ARSI, Angl. 30/I, f. 177ʳ, there is an unsigned, undated account of Langdale's views and activities.

Langdale was not the first English Jesuit apostate. We have already noted Christopher Perkins, who returned to England sometime in 1581/82. Subsequently involved in a number of diplomatic missions, he was named Dean of Carlisle in 1596. Held responsible for the formulation of the Jacobean Oath of Allegiance, Perkins died in 1622. For more on his diplomatic missions see R.B. Wernham, *After the Armada* (Oxford, 1984) pp. 258-59; and "Queen Elizabeth I, the Emperor Rudolph II, and Archduke Ernest, 1593-94," in *Politics and Society in Reformation Europe*, eds. E.I. Kouri and Tom Scott (New York, 1987) pp. 437-51.

[132] See Parsons, "Punti," pp. 104-7.

[133] Interestingly the reception given by English Catholics to the Irish Dr. Thomas Strong, Bishop of Ossory, on his way from Rome to Ireland receives little mention in the correspondence. We know of his activities through a report to Allen by his brother Gabriel, a report that was relayed to Agazzari in Rome on 16 March 1583 (see Knox, *Letters of Allen*, pp. 183-84).

[134] AAW, II, 53 "The poynts agreed upon from Fath. Heywood" were printed in Knox, *First and Second Douay Diaries*, pp. 353-55 and Foley, *Records*, IV, 680-81. An Italian version, probably translated for the Roman authorities, can be found in ARSI, Angl. 31/II, ff. 218ʳ⁻ᵛ.

this agreement not as a negotiated compromise but as a dictated settlement. The entire statement was a reassertion of the ecclesiastical authority of the Jesuits and the seminary priests and a repudiation of traditional uses of the country. What must have been especially provocative was the suggestion that the Marian priests were without faculties to hear confession. It was this issue that exploded into a full-scale controversy in the seventeenth century when Richard Smith, Bishop of Chalcedon, questioned the faculties of the regular clergy. And it may well have been this problem that caused the subsequent storm.

In early May of 1583, shortly after the synod, Heywood was staying in London with was the Syminges.[135] The husband had conformed to secure their social position; the wife was Heywood's sister Elizabeth; one of the children was John Donne. On one of the Rogation days that preceded the feast of the Ascension (9 May 1583), a number of priests had been invited to dine. Because of the disagreement on fasts, two dishes had been prepared: Heywood, the husband, and some priests ate meat; the wife and the other priests ate fish. In the ensuing discussion, Heywood in some way annoyed his brother-in-law, who threatened the Jesuit with arrest.

This incident seems to have been but one of many. On 6 August Allen wrote to the General that "Heywood has sciatica and pains in his joints, he is unnerved. He cannot restrain himself and is a source of danger and a burden to the rest; he lives for the most part in common inns on account of the peril. Certain gentry have sent a message to Allen about recalling him, when Father Parsons shall come."[136] On 11 August Dr. Richard Barret, upon his return to Reims, wrote similarly to Father Agazzari: "Let me add a secret, dear Father, and I cannot write it without great grief. Father Heywood is not prudent enough in England. He gives too much opportunities to those who miss no occasion they can get for reprehending one of your fathers."[137] John Curry, the priest whom Heywood had sent to France in 1582 and who had become a Jesuit,[138] interrupted his novitiate and returned to England to moderate the dispute and to pacify those angered by Heywood. Apparently he succeeded, and he remained in England until the arrival of William Weston in September of 1584.[139]

Heywood meanwhile was ordered to leave England for a conference with Parsons in Rouen.[140] In early December he took ship from Rye to France.

---

[135] Flynn, "English Mission of Heywood," 59.
[136] Ryan, "Correspondence of Allen," p. 101.
[137] Knox, *First and Second Douay Diaries*, p. 332.
[138] See *Mon. Ang.*, II, 282.
[139] ABSI, 46/5A/1, Chapter VI, p. 59.
[140] [Acquaviva] to Allen, Rome 10 October 1583, in Ryan, "Correspondence of Allen," p. 93.

Just off the French coast the ship was driven back by a violent squall. Compelled to take shelter in an English harbour, the ship was searched, perhaps as a result of the closer surveillance because of the Throckmorton Plot, and Heywood was discovered. Arrested and sent to London, he was committed to the Clink on 9 December 1583. Although he was interrogated three times, Heywood was not tortured.[141] In company with five other priests, George Haydock, Thomas Hemerford, James Fenn, John Mundyn, and John Nutter, Heywood was arraigned for high treason on the 5th or 6th of February. On 12 February the other five priests were executed at Tyburn: Heywood remained in the Tower, presumably protected by influential family friends. There he remained until he was exiled in January of 1585.[142] Despite his willingness to return, he was never to see England again.

In March of 1585, Allen wrote to Acquaviva that Heywood should not go back "because he does not walk in step with Fr. Parsons, nor according to the same rules as ourselves."[143] In a later letter, Allen claimed that Heywood was "a good man, but not altogether suitable for work connected with the English mission."[144] Acquaviva decided that Heywood would be sent elsewhere.[145] In later years Heywood worked at the professed house in Naples, where he died on 9 January 1598.[146]

After Heywood's capture John Curry was the only Jesuit in England not in prison. Yet, according to Allen, men were eager to join the mission despite persistent doubts about the mission's future.[147] After the General's doubts were resolved,[148] William Weston and Thomas Marshall were selected for the mission.

---

[141] On this interrogation see [Allen] to [Agazzari?], [Reims] 6 March 1584, in Renold, *Letters of Allen and Barret*, pp. 77-78.

[142] A commission from Elizabeth to the Lord Chancellor on 15 January banished Heywood, James Bosgrave, John Hart, and others. They were told that they could stay in England if they obeyed the law. If they refused, they were permanently exiled (PRO, SP 12/176/9; CSP Venice [1581-91] 108). For Acquaviva's letter to Heywood upon his release (Rome 9 April 1585) see ARSI, Franc. 1/I, f. 221ᵛ. Acquaviva accepted Hart into the Society upon his arrival on the continent. See his letter dated Rome 9 April 1585, ARSI, Franc. 1/I, ff. 226ᵛ-227ʳ.

[143] Reims 8 March [1585], in Renold, *Letters of Allen and Barret*, p. 142.

[144] Allen to [Acquaviva], [Reims] 4 April 1585, in Renold, *Letters of Allen and Barret*, p. 148.

[145] "Wherefore, so far as this business is concerned, your Reverence may rest in peace and tranquillity. But still, to secure this end better and more securely, we have judged in our Lord that Father Jasper himself should be summoned to Rome, not to stay here, but be sent from hence elsewhither wherever shall seem most suitable," [Acquaviva] to Allen, Rome 9 April 1585, in Ryan "Correspondence of Allen," pp. 97-99.

[146] For his subsequent career see *Mon. Ang.*, II, 351-52.

[147] [Acquaviva] to Allen, Rome 22 March 1584, in Ryan, "Correspondence of Allen," p. 95.

[148] At the end of the chapter we shall return to the General's hesitation.

CHAPTER FOUR

V

William Weston was unanimous choice as the next missionary.[149] Another Oxford man, he entered the Society in Rome on 5 November 1575. He was in Spain when he received a summons from the General to report to Paris to discuss with Allen and Parsons the possibility of his working in England. Because his superiors in Spain would not allow him to make the trip during the winter, Weston did not arrive in Paris until June of 1584.[150] On the 12th he wrote to the General and volunteered for the mission. Weston admitted that his offer was "not without some anxiety and fear at the manifest danger of death, and of what is even worse than death. My mind often turns in silence to the prisons, the many kinds of torture, the gallows, the quartering, and the thought inspires me with bodily fear and horror." Nonetheless, he thanked God that he had been called to this service.[151]

Neither Allen nor Parsons nor Acquaviva doubted that Weston would be an exceptional missionary. No unanimity could be reached on his companion. Parsons had asked for either William Good, former missionary to Ireland, Sweden, and Poland, or Shakespeare's old teacher Simon Hunt,[152] or Richard Engham, or Robert Southwell. Nothing was said about Good and Southwell, but Engham was ill[153] and the General did not think that Hunt had the skills necessary for the mission.[154] Thomas Marshall was recommended by Acquaviva, and he too was summoned to Paris. Parsons, however, did not find him suitable.[155] John Gibbons was another candidate, but he frankly confessed that he did not have the courage required for the mission. Instead he volunteered to serve the mission with his pen from the

---

[149] Acquaviva to Allen, Rome 15 July 1584, in Ryan, "Correspondence of Allen," p. 97. See also Hicks, *Letters of Persons*, lxv-lxvi. Rumours that the Society intended to abandon the mission persisted. In a letter to Father Agazzari written in England on 22 December 1586, Robert Southwell complained of the reports still current that "by the Pope's direction no more of ours are to come, but we hope that this report is either false or portends something great for the advantage of the Catholic cause" (John H. Pollen, S.J., ed., *Unpublished Documents Relating to the English Martyrs 1584-1603* [London, 1908] p. 318).

[150] *Mon. Ang.*, II, 525.

[151] Weston to Acquaviva, Paris 12 June 1584, ARSI, Gall. 91, ff. 155^r-156^v.

[152] See *Mon. Ang.*, II, 363.

[153] He died in 1583 (*Mon. Ang.*, II, 297).

[154] Parsons to Agazzari, Paris 15 September 1584, in Hicks, *Letters of Persons*, p. 244; same to same, [Paris] 15 or 25 September 1584, *ibid.*, p. 245.

[155] Clancy, "First Generation," 155. See also Parsons to the General, Paris 20 August 1584, ARSI, Fondo Gesuitico 651/640; same to same, Paris 15 September 1584, in Hicks, *Letters of Persons*, p. 243; same to same, Paris 14 October 1584, *ibid.*, p. 254; same to same, Rouen 12 November 1584, *ibid.*, p. 258; same to same, Paris 25 November 1584, *ibid.*, p. 262; Parsons to Agazzari, Paris 25 November 1584, *ibid.*, p. 264; same to same, Rouen 22 December 1584, *ibid.*, p. 269; [Acquaviva] to Allen, Rome 15 July 1584, in Ryan, "Correspondence of Allen," p. 97; same to same, Rome 9 March 1585, ARSI, Franc. 1/I, ff. 218^v-219^r. On Marshall see *Mon. Ang.*, II, 403.

continent.¹⁵⁶ All agreed that Henry Garnet would be an exceptional missionary. The General, however, was extremely reluctant to send him on the mission because there were plans for him to work in Rome. He was, thus, unavailable and would not be sent until the following year.¹⁵⁷

Weston eventually went on his own, accompanied only by Ralph Emerson and a layman Henry Hubert (or Hubbard), who was returning to England. Surveillance was especially vigilant, and their risks were increased by a consignment of Catholic books they brought in with them. The two landed on the Norfolk coast on 10 September 1584. Shortly after their landing Emerson was arrested after a search revealed in his possession Catholic books, including the slanderous *Leicester's Commonwealth*. He was to spend the next twenty years in prisons—Poultry, the Clink, Wisbech, and finally Framlingham Castle—then to be exiled on the accession of James I. Without Emerson there was no one to introduce Weston to the Catholics. He went to London by himself and there—whether by chance or design, we do not know—he met John Curry, the only Jesuit in England not in prison. Shortly after their meeting Curry returned to Rome to complete his novitiate, leaving Weston without a companion.¹⁵⁸

Sometime before the end of 1584 Weston established contact with the imprisoned Heywood through the latter's sister. Through her he learned that a visit could be arranged without much danger. Accompanied by John Donne, Weston approached the Tower "with a feeling of great trepidation" and spent the day there. During the conversation Weston learned that, despite all attempts to keep his arrival a secret, Heywood had heard of it from the Earl of Northumberland and was confident that the Queen's Council also had been informed.¹⁵⁹ Probably as a result of this meeting, Weston was given the names of the leading English Catholics who would later provide the basis of his network.¹⁶⁰ It is likely that it was through

---

¹⁵⁶ ABSI, 45/5A/1, Chapter VI, p. 61. On Gibbons see *Mon. Ang.*, II, 328.

¹⁵⁷ Allen to Acquaviva, Reims 5 June 1584, in Renold, *Letters of Allen and Barret*, p. 101; Parsons to Acquaviva, n.p. 12 February 1585, same to same, Paris 28 May 1585, ARSI, Fondo Gesuitico 651/640. About Garnet, the General said: "we must give more careful thought to Father Henry Garnet, for not to mention a certain need for him here (because we usually rank these needs second to the work in England), there are also other reasons currently emerging that make us wonder if he is more suited to the quiet life rather than the unsure and worrisome one that must be lived in England" (Rome 12 July 1585, ARSI, Fl. Belg. 1/I, p. 262).

¹⁵⁸ ABSI, 45/5A/1, Chapter VI, p. 59.

¹⁵⁹ Philip Caraman, S.J., ed., *William Weston: The Autobiography of an Elizabethan* (London, 1955) pp. 10-15. See also Flynn, "'Out of Step'."

¹⁶⁰ In a letter to Agazzari from Reims on 14 January 1585, Allen wrote "Heywood behaves well and constantly, and even in prison bears himself well for his own salvation and that of others: but his other son [i.e. William Weston] who up to now is free, makes incredible progress and has caught many fishes, and those very big ones, who for good reasons I do not wish to name. He is said to behave in all matters with great prudence and piety" (Renold,

Heywood that Weston gained access to the Earl of Arundel, whom he later received into the Church.

At liberty for only two years, Weston achieved considerable fame as an exorcist.[161] More important for the continuation of the mission, he laid the foundations for an organization to support and protect the clergy within the country.[162] In April of 1585 a meeting between Weston and some wealthy Catholic laymen, perhaps friends and supporters of Heywood, was held at Mr. Wyford's house in Hoxton. The gathering presumably was caused by the recent act against Jesuits and seminary priests. A clause was directed against anyone who received and protected priests. Henceforth such assistance could result in death and forfeiture. Because of these new dangers to the laity, an alternative had to be found. William, Lord Vaux, Sir Thomas Tresham, Sir William Catesby, and Mr. Wyford agreed to donate 100 marks annually to a common fund. An appeal for more money would be made to other Catholics in the country. This fund would be administered by Lord Vaux.[163] The creation of this endowment, however, seems to have been the price the nobles and gentry were willing to pay to keep Jesuits and seminary priests away from their residences. Because of the new penalties for harbouring Jesuits, the conference agreed that the priests should take care of themselves and stay at inns. Unless the priests were specifically sent for, they were not to visit any Catholics, especially the gentlemen at Hoxton.[164] According to Parsons, Weston was "doing wonders and is affording great edification to every one" in his travels throughout England.[165] Although he was but one Jesuit and the persecution continued, his hope in the ultimate success of the mission was strong. A few years later he wrote:

Letters of Allen and Barret, p. 121).

[161] See Caraman, *William Weston*, pp. 22-30.

[162] Patrick McGrath and Joy Rowe argue that Weston is given too much credit for the establishment of this network and that previous systems have been ignored ("Elizabethan Priests: Their Harbourers and Helpers," 232 n. 39). I suspect that they are right, but before we can prove it we need to know more about the organization of the Marian priests, and of the seminary priests before the arrival of Heywood and the Jesuits.

[163] For the financial needs of the Jesuit mission see McCoog, "'Slightest Suspicion of Avarice.'" Tresham's continued support of the Jesuits is especially significant as his political sympathies differed considerably from the dominant Allen/Parsons party.

[164] Caraman, *William Weston*, p. 28 n. 3; Philip Caraman, S.J., *Henry Garnet (1555-1606) and the Gunpowder Plot* (London, 1964) pp. 45-46. Walsingham knew of the conference within a month from a spy (PRO, SP 12/178/39; SP 12/178/72 both of which are printed in John Morris, S.J., ed., *The Troubles of Our Catholic Forefathers Related by Themselves*, 3 vols. [London, 1872-77] II, 155-56, 158-59). As we have noted, one of the complaints against Heywood was his staying at inns. One wonders if he did so in order to avoid compromising the Catholic laity.

[165] Parsons to Agazzari, St. Omers 12 July 1585, in Hicks, *Letters of Persons*, p. 271. See also his letter to Agazzari from Rouen on 6 December 1584, *ibid*., p. 265. It was at this time that Weston became especially noted for his exorcisms.

> Peter's ship is as safe as ever. She may be tossed by the waves but never can she become a wreck. Buffeted and beaten by the surge, she is never broken. Hell can open wide its jaws, belch forth fire, shroud her in clouds of black smoke, but God's promise stands unaltered. . . . From the day the storm first struck her the Church has gathered great increase. Wherever she is brought to rest, she conquers. When persecution strikes her she is there all the firmer for it. Violently oppressed, she reigns in glory. . . . Prisons are full of priests, but God's Word is not in chains. In the midst of the tribulation, sorrow and weariness our mother Jerusalem is not sterile, and ceases not to bear her children. One day she shall see peace.[166]

Catholicism was the only hope for his countrymen. Since the accession of Elizabeth, religion had fallen into neglect. Unsatisfied by the established Church, many longed for something better. "If only," a sentiment that echoed the earlier optimism of Campion and Parsons, "we were given freedom to preach and teach publicly, I believe we would hardly see a thousand heretics left within a year. Weston saw tremendous opportunity in England and pleaded for more men to take advantage of it."[167] Perhaps as a reply to Weston's petition, the Jesuits Henry Garnet and Robert Southwell arrived in England in late July of 1586.[168] In a letter to the General on 25 July, Southwell told of their welcome:

> Our arrival has wonderfully cheered and inspired the Catholics, for they had previously been complaining that they were practically abandoned by the Society, and were full of misgiving, thinking that their pastors, dismayed by difficulties, were abandoning the flock that never stood in greater need of their care.[169]

Weston met the two Jesuits at a London inn on the 13th and went with them to Harlesford (or Hurleyford), home of Richard Bold, a recent convert of Weston and a former favourite of the Earl of Leicester. There they remained for eight days of prayer and consultation.[170] For the three it was "as if we were celebrating an interrupted octave of some great feast" as they

---

[166] Weston to Acquaviva, 10 May 1587, ARSI, Fondo Gesuitico 651/661. I use the translation in Caraman, *William Weston*, xxii.

[167] E[dmund] H[unt] to Parsons, [April 1586], SC, Anglia I, 28. I use the translation in Caraman, *William Weston*, xxiii.

[168] The government was alerted to their arrival almost immediately. See PRO, SP 12/191/35. Shortly before his departure for England, on 15 July, Southwell wrote a touching account of his anxieties to an unspecified Jesuit priest: "Stay me up, therefore, my Father with the flowers of prayer, which ascend in the odour of sweetness; encompass me with the apples of works, that if I must needs faint, it may not be from fear, but love" (printed in Foley, *Records*, I, 319).

[169] Printed in Pollen, *Unpublished Documents*, p. 308. For Garnet's account of their arrival see his letter to the General of 30 July 1586, ARSI, Fondo Gesuitico 651/624.

[170] On Hurleyford see Michael Hodgetts, *Secret Hiding Places* (Dublin, 1989) pp. 1-20.

preached, heard confessions, and sang Masses, some possibly written by the recusant composer William Byrd. Weston introduced the newcomers to the network that he had created. He gave them the names of Catholic houses to which they could resort and where they could reside. He arranged for guides to take them there. It was decided, probably in an attempt to implement the General's original instructions to Campion and Parsons, that the Jesuits would meet semi-annually for confession and consultation. The meetings, originally scheduled for February and August, were later changed to Easter and autumn. When the meeting ended on the 23rd, Garnet was conducted either to Harrowden, Lord Vaux's residence in Northamptonshire, or to Vaux's daughter's, Mrs. Brooksby's, at Shoby in Leicestershire. Southwell returned to London, to Lord Vaux's house at Hackney, to receive incoming priests. There, "hemmed in by daily perils, never safe for even the smallest amount of time," he devoted himself to hearing confessions, preparing sermons, and "other priestly duties."[171] Weston went first to Oxford to take care of a pressing problem and then to London. There, outside Bishopsgate, on 3 August, he was arrested.[172] Garnet and Southwell, in England less than a month, were on their own.

* * * * *

The English mission was fortunate that Mercurian died soon after he approved its initiation; it is extremely doubtful that he would have sanctioned its continuation. Everything that Mercurian had feared was happening. In his argument against the mission the General stressed the conditions under which Jesuits would be forced to work. After the arrival of Campion and Parsons the situation became even more dangerous with the passing of new legislation. One man had been executed and others imprisoned. Priests lived in hiding and in disguise. The English government's propaganda proclaimed Jesuits traitors, as Mercurian had prophesied. With no hierarchy, disputes regarding liturgical and ecclesiastical matters went unresolved. Matters became so bad that the initial enthusiasm of Mercurian's successor Acquaviva waned.

Campion's capture and execution clearly demonstrated the mission's dangers. Yet there was disagreement regarding its significance. In a letter to Agazzari on 12 October 1581 Allen confessed that he was "convinced that nothing has happened more happy or more wonderful than it [the capture of

---

[171] Southwell to Acquaviva, [England] 25 July 1586, in Pollen, *Unpublished Documents*, p. 309.
[172] Caraman, *William Weston*, pp. 69-79. See also Caraman, *Garnet and the Gunpowder Plot*, pp. 32-37, 42.

Campion] for the advancement of religion."[173] After Campion's execution Parsons emphasized the numerous benefits: "Both our adversaries and our own people cry aloud in one voice, that not though the lives of these men had been lengthened out to the hundredth year could they have done such good to their cause as has been effected by their brief but glorious death-agony."[174] Their death strengthened the fortitude of many Catholics who were now more willing to follow his example. The blood of the martyrs strengthened the faith of the recusants.

Claudio Acquaviva did not share Parsons's and Allen's elation. Mercurian had worried about Jesuits working in such hostile conditions, but Acquaviva and Oliver Mannaerts convinced him to authorise the mission. We do not know the arguments they advanced. Perhaps they maintained that the Jesuits could work effectively if they worked discreetly and prudently among the Catholics. As General, Acquaviva had been consoled by the fruits of Campion's ministry, but he had expected it to last more than a year. "Inasmuch as there is more merit in enduring torture rather than toil," Acquaviva conceded to Allen, "Father Campion will have greater influence in prison or being racked, than on the platform or by preaching, or any of his former occupations." Yet Acquaviva was disappointed. Campion had been sent to England to "toil" not to endure "torture"; he was to influence "on the platform or by preaching" and not "in prison and being racked." Martyrdom was indeed more meritorious, but Jesuits were sent to England not to be martyrs but missionaries. Hence future missionaries were to be more cautious and concerned about their own safety. Because Acquaviva doubted that foreign Jesuits could do so, he decided against sending any until Allen explained how they could actively participate in the mission without endangering themselves. Many might volunteer for the mission out of a desire for martyrdom, but the mission needed workers, not martyrs.[175]

By implication Acquaviva disapproved of Campion's and Parsons's high-profile challenge because it antagonised the government and sharpened the search for the Jesuits. Martyrs might be attracted to the mission, but could missionaries survive. As a result Acquaviva was beginning to doubt the

---

[173] Ryan, "Correspondence of Allen," p. 39. See Eamon Duffy, "William, Cardinal Allen, 1532-1594," *RH* 22 (1995) 278-79.
[174] "Punti," p. 45. See also his letter to Agazzari, 6 April 1582, in Hicks, *Letters of Persons*, p. 143.
[175] Acquaviva to Allen, Rome 14 October 1581, in Ryan, "Correspondence of Allen," p. 85. On this issue see John Bossy, "The Society of Jesus in the Wars of Religion," in *Monastic Studies: The Continuity of Tradition*, ed. Judith Loades (Bangor, 1990) p. 234, and "The Heart of Robert Persons," in *The Reckoned Expense: Edmund Campion and the Early English Jesuits. Essays in Celebration of the First Centenary of Campion Hall, Oxford (1896-1996)*, ed. Thomas M. McCoog, S.J. (Woodbridge, 1996) pp. 141-58, and Michael Williams, "Campion and the English Continental Seminaries," pp. 285-99 in the same volume.

feasibility of the mission. Despite his reservations the General promised to send Jesuits.[176]

The arrest of Jasper Heywood in December of 1583 placed the mission's future in greater jeopardy. In early 1584 some of the General's consultors advised against sending more men into England because of the severity of the persecution brought on by the discovery of the Throckmorton Plot.[177] It was commonly expected that the persecution would become even more intense. According to a letter about English affairs then circulating in France, the Queen herself had said "Hitherto we have washed our hands, as it were in milk; henceforward, however, we shall steep not only our hands, but our arms, in the brightest and best blood that is in the hearts of Papists."[178]

For different reasons French Jesuit Provincial Odo Pigenat complained to the General about the mission's continuation. Interestingly Pigenat was also sending frequent letters to the General about the political activities of Jesuits too intimately involved with the Catholic League.[179] Pigenat was concerned that the Society, albeit unjustifiably, was gaining a bad reputation because of the close association of some Jesuits with princes. Such association, he believed, was the reason for false rumours that the Society was involved in the assassination of William (the Silent) of Orange.[180] Perhaps Parsons's political activities and his association with the Guises were the real reasons for Pigenat's opposition to the mission's continuation. Nonetheless even such a strong supporter of the mission and the Guises as Claude Matthieu questioned the wisdom of sending more men to England during such persecution.[181] Indeed, Parsons himself had doubts because of

---

[176] Rome 14 October 1581, in Ryan, "Correspondence of Allen," pp. 81, 83.

[177] Details of the intensified persecution can be found in a letter of Robert Southwell to the Jesuit Provincial in Naples, Rome 3 February 1584, in Pollen, *Unpublished Documents*, pp. 305-6. See also Renold, *Letters of Allen and Barret*, p. 101 n. 1.

[178] [Allen] to [Agazzari?], [Reims] 6 March 1584, in Renold, *Letters of Allen and Barret*, p. 75.

[179] On the importance of leagues for French Catholicism see John Bossy, "Leagues and Associations in Sixteenth-Century French Catholicism," in *Voluntary Religion*, eds. W.J. Sheils and Diana Wood (Oxford, 1986) pp. 171-89.

[180] On Pigenat's protest see A. Lynn Martin, *Henry III and Jesuit Politicians* (Geneva, 1973) pp. 122-23. Parsons explained the Provincial's disapproval thus: "because he is of a good temperament, withdrawn, and a little timid, and thus has neither been informed of, nor involved in these negotiations. In general he does not manifest much favour . . . and has told me that much about the mission did not please him and that he would not continue it" (Paris 20 August 1584, ARSI, Fondo Gesuitico 651/640). In another letter to the General, written on 23 July 1584, Parsons claimed that Pigenat "is generally away from here, and when he was here there were many who did not think it right to weary him about our affairs, therefore His Reverence had not much chance of knowing all the particulars and circumstances of the work. Moreover he has a tender heart, which is quickly moved by the trials and persecutions of which he hears" ("Punti," p. 149).

[181] Parsons, "Punti," p. 147.

the fury of persecution and the disturbances caused by Heywood, and he advised against sending more men.[182] Temporarily at least there was a consensus. Pigenat, Matthieu, and Parsons agreed that no more Jesuits should be sent to England.. Acquaviva, therefore, decided that no more would be sent and Matthieu relayed the decision to Parsons.

Parsons, however, soon changed his mind because of "very satisfactory" developments in Scotland. Now he contended that the mission must be continued and that more men were required "for now more than ever is there need of one or two men in London to steer the barque and keep the others to the course." By June of 1584 Parsons was pleading with the General to reconsider. The General still hesitated. In his reply he asked for more information on the manner in which Jesuits were sent into England, their living conditions there, and their chances of ministering to the Catholics without discovery. It was not sensible, Acquaviva argued, to send more men into England to edify the faithful by their martyrdom, especially when their very presence seemed to intensify the persecution.[183]

In his efforts to persuade the General to continue the mission, Parsons stressed the slackening of persecution. Some English Protestants even said that persecution would eventually pass away completely and that no one would again be put to death because of religion. On his part Parsons believed that the English government would make peace with the Catholics if it knew how to do this honourably. The reason for the change in the government's attitude was the realization that its own demise was close.[184]

Such pleas swayed the General. In early July Acquaviva met the Pope "so that, not only through the grace of his blessing but also with the added light of his direction, I might be assured as to the will of God." Acquaviva relayed to him Parsons's and Allen's advice and their desire for more Jesuits. Papal approval assuaged Acquaviva's doubts.[185]

---

[182] "Punti," p. 129.
[183] Parsons to Acquaviva, Paris 11 [June] 1584, in Hicks, *Letters of Persons*, p. 204; Acquaviva to Parsons, Rome 3 July 1584, quoted in Pollen, "Politics of English Catholics," 402.
[184] Parsons to Acquaviva, 23 July 1584, in Parsons, "Punti," p. 149. Unfortunately Parsons did not explain what he meant by this. Was it simply a fear that the succession of the Stuarts would reverse everything? Or was there a fear that an invasion would topple the government?
[185] Acquaviva to Allen, Rome 15 July 1584, in Ryan, "Correspondence of Allen," p. 97.

CHAPTER FIVE

"ON THE CONVERSION OF SCOTLAND"

Hitherto ignored by English Jesuits, Scotland assumed a prominent position in the Society's plans in mid-1581. The appearance of the King's cousin Esmé Stuart, Sieur d'Aubigny, ended the domination of the pro-English Earl of Morton, James Douglas. His execution in June of 1581 and the reemergence of many old Marian supporters fanned the hopes of Catholics in Scotland and England.[1] Informed of these developments, Robert Parsons became interested in Scotland as a refuge for persecuted English Catholics.[2] He sent William Watts, a secular priest working in the north of England, to Scotland to investigate. Parsons urged him, if he could gain access to James, to impress upon the King the importance of his personal conversion and of his tolerance of Scottish Catholics and any English who might flee to Scotland.

Among the reasons why James should become Catholic were his reverence for his mother currently imprisoned in England; the establishment of better relations with neighbouring Catholic princes; the appreciation of previous Catholic assistance in the discovery of plots against his life; and, most important, his hope to succeed to the English throne, a feat that could be accomplished only with the aid of English Catholics.[3] Watts crossed the

---

[1] According to Spanish ambassador in France, Juan Bautista de Tassis, Mary Queen of Scots was extremely hopeful that her son would convert to Catholicism. Once James converted, she would be eager to assist English Catholics in their work for a restoration of Catholicism. Tassis obviously did not fully explain Mary's intentions, but he did insist that this whole affair would require considerable secrecy (Tassis to Philip II, Blois 10 April 1581, CSP Simancas [1580-86] 98-100).

[2] Michael L. Carrafiello argues that "the forcible conversion of England" through Scotland was among the original intentions of the English mission ("English Catholicism and the Jesuit Mission of 1580-81," *Historical Journal* 37 [1994] 761-74). Dr. Carrafiello, however, fails to note Mercurian's reluctance to approve the mission and his strong aversion to political involvement. He also fails to explain how Scotland could have been considered a secure base for Catholic intrigues while the Earl of Morton was alive.

[3] Parsons to Acquaviva, [Rouen] 21 October 1581, in Leo Hicks, S.J., ed., *Letters and Memorials of Father Robert Persons, S.J.* (London, 1942) pp. 108-10. Bernardino de Mendoza explained Watts's mission differently. According to the Spanish ambassador, six principal Catholic nobles met with him and he pointed out to them the advantages of a Catholic Scotland. Once converted, James could lead an army into the north of England to be joined by the six nobles and their retainers. Together they would demand the restoration of Catholicism, the recognition of James as Elizabeth's heir, and the release of Mary. If the Queen resisted or

border into Scotland on 26 August and was warmly received. Indeed he was even introduced to the King. In a report sent to Parsons, Watts told of many nobles favourable to Catholicism who promised to protect any English priest who fled across the border. Moreover the nobles requested that some learned priests be sent to work within Scotland. But, lest said priests prove a financial burden, they must have their own source of income. Finally, Watts had arranged a meeting, scheduled for 26 September, between Parsons and some of the nobles. To facilitate negotiations, Watts suggested that Parsons bring to this meeting a letter of introduction from Mary Queen of Scots.[4]

Watts's report provided detailed instructions for a Mr. Redman, an alias for Parsons.[5] To the rendezvous Redman was asked to bring Jasper Heywood, Mr. Reynold (presumably the secular priest William Reynolds), and an Italian priest. If these men were not available, Watts's informant insisted that plans be aborted: "either we must wait until they are available—and this is risky because the devil is busily at work—or we must desist because it is better to retreat than to advance without profit." Two letters from the imprisoned Scottish Queen to her friends should be brought. One letter should identify Redman; another should ask her son to place Catholics in important positions: specifically George, Lord Seton should be named governor of Edinburgh. The instructions concluded with aliases to be used, names of Scottish nobles that should be contacted, and most secure way of passing into Scotland. Unbeknownst to Watts, Parsons was no longer in England. Hence Parsons did not receive the report until 15 September, too late to attend the meeting. Parsons missed the meeting, but he hoped that he had not lost a unique opportunity.

The effect of Watts's report on Parsons must not be underestimated. In his letter to the General on 21 October Parsons explained why he had travelled to France. One reason was a meeting with James Beaton, Archbishop of Glasgow and Mary's ambassador to France. Presumably Parsons became interested in Mary and her party after the fall of Morton opened Scotland as a possible refuge for English Catholics. After Watts's journey, Scotland assumed a greater role in Parsons's missionary strategy. It was no longer a simple refuge for persecuted English Catholics; now "on the conversion of Scotland depends every hope, humanly speaking, of the

---

refused, they would depose her. The nobles agreed with this plan and pledged themselves to its observance. It was then decided to send a priest into Scotland to ascertain the situation (Mendoza to Philip II, London 7 September 1581, CSP Simancas [1580-86] 169-71).

[4] Watts's report was included in Parsons's letter to the General from Rouen on 21 October 1581, in Hicks, *Letters of Persons*, pp. 110-12.

[5] These instructions were not included in the copy used by Leo Hicks in his edition and were not known until another copy of the letter was discovered among manuscripts in ARSI, Fondo Gesuitico 651/640. I am currently preparing an edition of these letters for *AHSI*.

conversion of England." The heir to the English throne was the Queen of Scotland and then her son, and "some hopes have now begun to be conceived of this son of hers."[6]

Now Parsons focused his attention on the winning of Scotland. The venture would be expensive, and so Parsons sought assistance from both the General and the Pope.[7] Equally important was the choice of a Jesuit. Apparently the Scots had asked for an Italian or a Spaniard. Because Parsons would not dare ask for Robert Bellarmine, he suggested Achille Gagliardi, professor of theology at the Roman College, or Ferdinando Capeci, *repetitor* at the English College, whom he had earlier requested for the English mission. A Spaniard, Diego Sánchez, had already volunteered for the English mission but Parsons did not think him suited for Scotland. Instead he recommended Pedro Jiménez, professor of theology at Vienna, or Manuel de Vega, professor of theology at Vilnius.[8] Until one or two were available for the mission, Parsons would arrange for an English Jesuit to serve temporarily. His inability to return to England and Heywood's bout with sciatica left William Holt the only immediate candidate. It is unclear whether at this stage Parsons knew of the military plans for an invasion from Scotland suggested by Bernardino de Mendoza or, indeed, whether Mendoza was behind Parsons's meeting with Beaton.[9]

Holt travelled to Scotland with William Watts in late December of 1581. Again there was a warm reception from the Scottish Catholics. In one interview the Duke of Lennox and other Catholic nobles promised to work for King James's conversion. Their efforts would meet considerable Protestant opposition. In fact, Lennox argued, any Catholic settlement could be maintained against the combined resistance of Scottish Protestants and the English government only through the presence of loyal foreign troops. When

---

[6] Parsons to Acquaviva, [Rouen] 21 October 1581, in Hicks, *Letters of Persons*, pp. 108, 109.

[7] For unspecified reasons, Acquaviva did not think it advisable to approach the Pope for money at this time. Instead he raised 200 crowns and forwarded a draft for that amount to Michel de Monsi (Acquaviva to Parsons, Rome 23 December 1581, ARSI, Franc. 1/I, f. 115^v; same to de Monsi, Rome 23 December 1581, ARSI, Franc. 1/I, f. 116^r). Interestingly Mendoza sought Philip's aid for the same mission (Mendoza to Philip II, London 20 October 1581, CSP Simancas [1580-86] 194-97; same to same, London 9 February 1582, *ibid.*, 289-94; same to same, London 19 March 1582, *ibid.*, 319-20; and Philip II to Mendoza, Lisbon 18 December 1581, *ibid.*, 242). Philip contributed 2000 crowns.

[8] In a footnote to Parsons's letter, Hicks noted that "it is not altogether clear from the text whether these men were demanded for the English or the Scottish mission" (*Letters of Persons*, pp. 105-06, n. 30). Although Parsons did not specifically state the mission, the context in which the foreign Jesuits were discussed was the proposed Scots mission. It is more likely, therefore, that Scotland was their destination.

[9] In a letter to King Philip from London on 11 December 1581, Mendoza recounted that Heywood was sick and that Parsons had just been declared a rebel (CSP Simancas [1580-86] 235-37).

Holt returned to London in February of 1582, he was surprised to discover that the person to whom he was to report was the Spanish ambassador. Until that time he had not been aware of Mendoza's involvement in the negotiations.[10]

Holt wrote a glowingly optimistic account of his mission. According to him the majority of the nobles were inclined towards Catholicism and eager to work for its restoration. But without foreign support their efforts would be temporary because of English intervention. Well aware of the influence that a strong Catholic monarch in Scotland would have over England's foreign policy and for the succession to the English throne, Elizabeth would do all she could to prevent it.

The nobles proposed to hold public disputations between Catholic priests and ministers of the Kirk in order to expose the errors of the latter until their heresies were eradicated with the full restoration of Catholicism. Moreover the nobles were prepared to receive any English priests, not just to provide them with temporary refuge but also because of "a desire to be present at Mass and hear their sermons, as the difference between the two languages is very slight." Indeed English priests were preferred because they were not subject to Scottish laws. Because of the importance of the proposed disputations, any priest sent should be learned and experienced in controversy. William Reynolds of the English College (as we have seen, he was asked for in the instructions to Mr. Redman) and Richard Barret of the Roman College were specifically named.[11] Because the Duke of Lennox, through whom much business must be transacted, knew no other language, one priest must speak French.[12]

The prospect of James's conversion and requests from Scottish nobles influenced the Society's policy towards Scotland. Father General Mercurian, as we have seen, resisted pressure from Scottish Jesuits and the Archbishop of Glasgow, James Beaton, to inaugurate a Jesuit mission. On 12 January 1580 he had written to Claude Matthieu that the time was not ripe because neither the Pope nor Mary Stuart thought it opportune.[13] Acquaviva, however, was different. Even before he heard from Parsons about Watts's activities, Acquaviva considered the possibility.[14] Throughout the summer

---

[10] Mendoza to Philip II, London 9 February 1582, CSP Simancas (1580-86) 289-94.

[11] On Reynolds and Barret see Godfrey Anstruther, O.P, *The Seminary Priests*, Vol. 1 (Ware/Durham, n.d. [1968]) pp. 24-25, 287.

[12] This report was published in William Forbes-Leith, S.J., ed., *Narratives of Scottish Catholics under Mary Stuart and James VI* (Edinburgh, 1885) pp. 175-80. Mendoza wrote to Philip II from London on 9 February 1582 about Holt's return from Scotland and included with his letter a summary of the report (CSP Simancas [1580-86] 285-89).

[13] ARSI, Franc. 1/I, f. 68^r.

[14] Acquaviva to James Beaton, Archbishop of Glasgow, Rome 6 August 1581, ARSI, Franc. 1/I, f. 104^v.

Acquaviva received numerous petitions from Paris that the Society initiate a mission to Scotland. Presumably the requests came from Scottish exiles and French supporters of Henry, Duke of Guise after Morton's execution.[15] Progress nevertheless was slow despite Parsons's enthusiastic support.

By the end of November a decision still had not been made. Acquaviva asked John Leslie, Bishop of Ross, for more information about conditions in Scotland. The General—or at least someone involved in the decision—doubted whether the mission was compatible with the Society's Institute.[16] Papal approval was needed for a venture this great.[17] By the end of December Acquaviva decided in favour of a mission. Not surprisingly, he chose William Crichton[18] and Edmund Hay to investigate prospects in their native land.[19] On their journey they called on Parsons in Rouen to discuss the mission. At the time Parsons was still planning to travel to Scotland to discuss the situation with the Catholic nobles. At the meeting, however, it was decided that the two Scots should return to ascertain exactly what was happening and that Parsons would postpone his departure until their report.[20] Before Crichton continued the journey with Ralph Emerson as his companion, he and Parsons consulted the Duke of Guise. For Parsons, this was the beginning of a fruitful relationship.

William Holt, who returned to Scotland almost immediately after his first mission, and Crichton arrived in Scotland independently and almost simultaneously. On 7 March 1582 the two Jesuits met the Duke of Lennox.

---

[15] Acquaviva to William Crichton, Rome 17 September 1581, ARSI, Aquit. 1/I, f. 91ᵛ.

[16] Concerns regarding the Society's "way of proceeding" and a Scottish mission are interesting. Why did he and/or his consultors worry about the mission's legitimacy? Was there fear of Jesuit involvement in the political implications of the King's conversion? Or had news of Campion's capture made the General's staff more cautious?

[17] Rome 25 November 1581, ARSI, Franc. 1/I, f. 112ʳ.

[18] While in Rome as delegate to the general congregation that elected Claudio Acquaviva in 1581, Crichton spoke to the Pope about a mission to Scotland. In a letter to the papal Nuncio in France, written in Rome on 4 April 1581, Crichton urged that everything be done to aid James. If the King succeeded in his attempt to reestablish Catholicism without Roman support, Crichton feared an anti-papal backlash because the Pope had not provided any aid. If, on the other hand, the Pope rendered some assistance, the King would be grateful and obedient (HMC, *The Manuscripts of J. Eliot Hodgkin* [London, 1897] p. 263).

[19] Acquaviva to Archbishop of Glasgow, Rome 22 December 1581, ARSI, Franc. 1/I, ff. 114ʳ⁻ᵛ; same to Edmund Hay, Rome 23 December 1581, ARSI, Franc. 1/I, f. 114ᵛ; same to Robert Parsons, Rome 23 December 1581, ARSI, Franc. 1/I, f. 115ᵛ; same to William Crichton, Rome 22 December 1581, ARSI, Aquit. 1/I, f. 98ᵛ.

[20] Apparently Crichton went alone because there was not enough money to cover the expenses of both. On 19 March Mendoza wrote to Philip II from London to ask his advice on the Scottish negotiations. He relayed the information that Parsons would send another priest to Scotland as soon as he, Parsons, had received the money the ambassador sent him (CSP Simancas [1580-86] 319-20). Francis Edwards thinks, however, that Hay did accompany Crichton and that he later withdrew from negotiations because "he was unwilling to be associated with the use of armed force" (*Robert Persons: The Biography of an Elizabethan Jesuit 1546-1610* [St. Louis, 1995] pp. 64, 68).

At this important meeting at Dalkeith, according to A. Lynn Martin, "various plots and aspirations merged."[21] Holt relayed Mendoza's relatively noncommittal assurances of Spanish assistance,[22] and Crichton reported that the Pope promised enough money to support 15,000 troops.

Lennox was overjoyed at the offers. He had been desperate and on the verge of abandoning the King to the Protestants by returning to France. Now, encouraged by the assistance promised, he believed that the King and the Catholics would win. He therefore drafted a proposal with three aims: the restoration of the Catholic religion in Scotland, England, and Ireland; the deliverance of the Queen of Scotland;[23] and the return of those banished for their faith. To do this he required 15,000 foreign soldiers, specifically 3000 Spaniards, 2000 Italians, 2000 Swiss, 2000 Germans, and 6000 French, with equipment, artillery, and money. To ensure full cooperation, the army was to be paid for eighteen months. Because James was to be the head of the enterprise with Lennox as lieutenant general, negotiations must be carried out with Mary to ensure that James would succeed to her title.[24] Once

---

[21] This and subsequent manoeuvres receive their best treatment in A. Lynn Martin, *Henry III and the Jesuit Politicians* (Geneva, 1973) pp. 68-74 and in Edwards, *Robert Persons*, pp. 63-82. Martin's comment can be found on p. 71.

[22] In a letter to Philip II from London on 9 February 1582, Mendoza reported that he had listened attentively to plans that the Scots were resolved to execute. In his reply he assured them that Philip "would not fail to help and support them to attain their object." The ambassador pursued this matter very discreetly, under the "cloak of the English Catholics," so there would be no sign that Philip was involved. Mendoza moreover claimed that there was no proof that English Catholics would rise on their own without foreign assistance (CSP Simancas [1580-86] 289-94).

[23] Even before the ascendancy of the Duke of Lennox and the possibility of the King's conversion, the Duke of Guise had plotted an invasion of England. His object was the rescue of his imprisoned cousin Mary Queen of Scots. Only lack of money prevented the venture. But by 1579 he had obtained pledges of Spanish aid (we have noted Mendoza's proposal to the six English nobles) and in 1582 the rescue of Mary became part of a larger project. Not surprisingly, Mary's religion and her association with the Guise faction made her the object of a heated Protestant attack. The Huguenots saw her as the centre of a concerted Catholic attempt to destroy Protestantism totally. To prevent this, her downfall was essential. On this see Robert M. Kingdon, *Myths about the St. Bartholomew's Day Massacres, 1572-1576* (Cambridge, Mass., 1988) pp. 129-35. In late 1581 or early 1582 Henri Samier, an ardent Jesuit supporter of the Guises, visited Mary in England. Although we know little about the nature of this first visit, I do not think that it was a coincidence that it occurred while an enterprise was under discussion. Samier returned to France in September of 1582. For the next year he travelled throughout the continent in an attempt to gain support for Mary's cause. On Samier and his relations with the League see J.H. Pollen, S.J., "Mary Stuart's Jesuit Chaplain," *The Month* 117 (1911) 11-24, 136-49; A. Lynn Martin, "The Jesuit Mystique," *SCJ* 4 (1973) 31-40 and his *Henry III and the Jesuit Politicians*.

[24] Throughout these intrigues, attempts were made to work out an arrangement between Mary and James regarding the crown. Mary proposed an association whereby James would be granted the title of king and appointed to rule Scotland in their joint names. Discussions foundered on the terms of the association. See James's letter to his mother, Dalkeith 28 May 1582, in *Letters of King James VI & I*, ed. G.P.V. Akrigg (Berkeley, 1984) pp. 45-47 and D. Harris Willson, *King James VI and I* (London, 1956) p. 40.

arrangements were made, an insurrection in Ireland would be fomented to divert Elizabeth's attention. The Duke of Guise would then lead a small force across the channel, while James and Lennox commanded a Scottish-Spanish attack from the north. Charles Nevill, Earl of Westmorland, and other exiles would return to England and raise their retainers. Gregory XIII would encourage English Catholics to assist the invasion by renewing the Queen's excommunication. It was hoped that the rebellion and invasion would topple Elizabeth and liberate Mary.[25] When Crichton expressed some surprise at such excessive demands, Lennox conceded that he would accept any modifications made by the Duke of Guise.[26]

Lennox's suggestion redirected the negotiations. Instead of a consolidation of James's hold on Scotland against the Anglophile Protestant lords, the overthrow of Elizabeth became the goal. But an enterprise of this magnitude would require close cooperation among, and great support from, the Catholic powers. A new phase in the history of the English Catholics had begun. Attempts to secure the conversion of James VI and a restoration of Catholicism in Scotland as prelude to a similar restoration in England led Parsons and William Allen ever more deeply into the world of diplomacy.

At this crucial phase in the negotiations Parsons, having considered travelling to Scotland as the Scottish nobles had asked for some time, now made definite plans based on an intervention by Mary Queen of Scots. In a letter to Parsons via Mendoza, Mary begged the Jesuit to assume direction of the mission to Scotland. He must not, she said, waste his time in writing books while the salvation of Scotland was at stake.[27] But he delayed his departure after he received a letter from Crichton and Holt. Both were optimistic and asked that he wait until one or both returned. Meanwhile the Queen of Scotland had written to her son to promote the cause of Catholicism and commended Parsons by name to him. To further the cause utmost secrecy was required. Thus Parsons was reluctant to confide much

---

[25] Mary's potential danger to the Elizabethan reign caused renewed attempts at this time to reach an agreement with the Queen of Scots. In return for Elizabethan assistance and/or recognition, Mary was consistently asked to avoid any contact with Jesuits or seminary priests (and to reveal any overtures made by either), to maintain the religion as established in Scotland, and to work for the suppression of the seminary at Reims and the new college at Eu (CSP Scotland [1581-83] 116-17, 384-94, 426-27).

[26] Lennox's proposal and its subsequent adaptation can be found in Johannes Kretzschmar, *Die Invasionsprojekte der katholischen Mächte gegen England zur Zeit Elisabeths* (Leipzig, 1892) pp. 123-28, 135-46.

[27] Forbes-Leith, *Narratives of Scottish Catholics*, pp. 180-81. The historian Arnold Oskar Meyer did not agree with Mary's insistence. Regarding Parsons's flight from England, Meyer said that Parsons "was not shirking his duty, rather he was following his true vocation. Persons the mission priest could easily be replaced by another, but the works of Persons the author could only be written by few, and no one could equal him in his power of organization" (*England and the Catholic Church under Queen Elizabeth* [London, 1916] p. 199).

in a letter and promised to explain more when they met. In any case it must not become known that he had any dealings with Mendoza and that Mary Stuart was involved. If either became public knowledge, it would destroy the negotiations.[28]

Holt and Crichton arrived in France on 14 April 1582. With Parsons they went to Eu to consult the Duke of Guise.[29] Lennox's proposal was debated throughout May by Guise, Parsons, Allen, Crichton, Beaton, Claude Matthieu, Jesuit Provincial of France, and Juan Bautista de Tassis, new Spanish ambassador to France.[30] During the discussion all agreed that the time was ripe for action, even though they modified Lennox's proposals. Not everyone, however, was satisfied with the strategy. In a letter to Mendoza on 6 April the Queen of Scots complained about the diplomatic inexperience of the Jesuits (at the very time that Father Samier was in attendance at her court). They must be given very explicit instructions "for these good people may blunder seriously unless they have wise counsel and advice." Meanwhile she would not allow any negotiations to be carried out in her name.[31]

It is not clear why she was so annoyed. Perhaps the Queen was angry that Parsons had not made the trip. Mendoza too was unhappy. He had been instructed by his King not to go beyond generalities in the negotiations and not to pledge more than was necessary.[32] But Crichton altered that strategy. Angered by Crichton's commitment, the ambassador claimed that the Jesuit had made the assurances of Spanish aid entirely on his own initiative without proper authorization. Mendoza still hoped to persuade Parsons to visit Scotland, where he would preach and work quietly for the King's conver-

---

[28] Eusebius [*vere* Parsons] to Claudio Acquaviva, 11 April [1582], ARSI, Fondo Gesuitico 651/640.

[29] Holt claimed that he went to France instead of returning to England because increased vigilance along the borders made the journey especially dangerous. Instead the Jesuit suggested that Mendoza come to France for the debriefing (Mendoza to Philip II, London 1 April 1582, CSP Simancas [1580-86] 322-24).

[30] From Paris on 18 May Tassis informed Philip II of Lennox's requests (CSP Simancas [1580-86] 370-73). Two men from the meetings were Charles Paget and Thomas Morgan; according to Parsons, "the Duke of Guise and the Archbishop of Glasgow did not consider these two men as trustworthy, fearing lest they might hold secret correspondence with some of the Council in England, though said Queen of Scots trusted greatly in them contrary to the wish and opinion of the said Duke and Archbishop, her ambassadors" ("Punti per la Missione d'Inghilterra," ed. John H. Pollen, S.J., in *Miscellanea IV* [London, 1907] pp. 64-65). For this antagonism see Leo Hicks, S.J., *An Elizabethan Problem: Some Aspects of the Careers of Two Exile Adventurers* (London, 1964) p. 7. This exclusion caused hostility between Allen and Parsons, on the one hand, and Paget and Morgan on the other.

[31] CSP Simancas (1580-86) 330-33. Francis Edwards suggests that this letter was a forgery (*Robert Persons*, p. 73).

[32] Mendoza to Philip II, London 26 April 1582, CSP Simancas (1580-86) 349-52 and London 15 May 1582, *ibid.*, 362-64.

sion. Apparently the Spanish were worried that the enterprise was proceeding too rapidly and that they were becoming too much involved. Moreover they feared discovery. Conversion was easier and less costly than invasion. Unaware of Mary's and Mendoza's dissatisfaction, the intriguers pursued their goals. Holt returned to Scotland, and by the end of the month, Parsons[33] with William Tresham,[34] was on his way to Portugal, and Crichton, to Rome.[35]

A few days before his departure for Portugal, Parsons again wrote to Acquaviva. Since Crichton would explain all the details, Parsons said nothing about the reasons for the trip or the matters to be discussed. But Parsons desperately wanted to discuss the entire matter with the General. If by chance Acquaviva planned to be in Spain during June, Parsons would visit him.[36] All letters should be sent to the Society's college in Lisbon and addressed to Richard Millins.[37]

Parsons played an important role in the diplomatic negotiations.[38] In May of 1582 he delivered a memorandum to the papal Nuncio in France,

---

[33] According to Tassis, Parsons was "so ardent and confident in favour of the proposal so far as regards England, that encouragement must be given to a man so full of divine zeal for the restoration of religion" (Tassis to Philip II, Paris 29 May 1582, CSP Simancas [1580-86] 377-79).

[34] According to Mendoza, Tresham had long been involved in the Scottish intrigues (Mendoza to Philip II, London 15 May 1582, CSP Simancas [1580-86] 362-64).

[35] The English ambassador in France watched these proceedings and passed his apprehensions to Walsingham. From Paris on 1 August 1582 he wrote "that the Duke of Lennox has had waiting on him as a suitor a Scotch Jesuit, who passed from Scotland towards Rome and is to return to the Duke" (PRO, SP 78/8/2). His facts may be wrong but his suspicions were warranted. Among the manuscripts in the Jesuit archives in Rome are two undated papers written by Crichton (ARSI, Angl. 42, ff. 32^r-33^v, and ff. 56^{r-v}). The first deals with plans for an invasion of England and the second with the Scottish colleges and seminaries. They presumably date from this visit.

[36] There had been tension within the Society in Spain for a number of years. In the early 1580s some dissidents aroused the Inquisition's suspicions against the Society. Further aggravation was caused by serious criticism levelled by four Dominicans (see William V. Bangert, S.J., *A History of the Society of Jesus* [St. Louis, 1972] pp. 110-12). Acquaviva once considered going to Spain to deal with the problems, but by October he had decided against it (Acquaviva to Allen, Rome 23 October 1582, in "Some Correspondence of Cardinal Allen, 1579-85," ed. Patrick Ryan, S.J., in *Miscellanea VII* [London, 1911] p. 89).

[37] Robert Parsons to Acquaviva, [Rouen] 3 May [1582], ARSI, Fondo Gesuitico 651/640.

[38] In a judicious treatment of Parsons's role in political intrigues, T.G. Law conceded that the Jesuits "may fairly plead that political action was practically forced upon them in aid of their missionary enterprise, and that rebellion was justifiable, or even a duty, for the Catholic body. . . ." He requested a comparable allowance for Elizabeth's behaviour: "The Jesuit leaders lapsed into conspiracy as inevitably as the Queen lapsed step by step into the sanguinary act of 1585. But it is unjust and untrue to history to conceal or disguise these dangerous and formidable conspiracies, with the view of fixing more deeply upon Queen Elizabeth the stigma of religious persecution" ("English Jesuits and Scottish Intrigues, 1581-82," in *Collected Essays and Reviews*, ed. P. Hume Brown [Edinburgh, 1904] p. 243). Francis Edwards acknowledges Parsons's role but claims that he was only "a contributor, cooperator, or approver rather than the one who instigated the scheme" (*Robert Persons*, p. 72).

Giovanni Battista Castelli, in which he urged that a Catholic, preferably William Allen, be secretly designated Bishop of Durham because of the diocese's strategic position and because of the influence that the bishop wields in the area.[39] Despite the role that Owen Lewis had played in the struggles surrounding the establishment of the English College, Parsons suggested that he, although "not in too good odour with the majority of the English, still . . . a man of gravity and discretion," be in some way associated with Allen so that he could stir up the great lords in his native Wales to aid the invasion.

Because the English government was always suspicious of the allegiance of the Roman Catholic clergy, one last suggestion by Parsons must be noted. Once a date was established for the invasion, that information must be relayed to the principal Catholics within the country. Lest the secret be disclosed, it should be done just shortly before the invasion and by means of priests within England.[40] Apparently Parsons did not consider the possibility that not all the English clergy would be as enthusiastic in support of the invasion as he was.

Another memorial prepared at the same time and often attributed to Parsons, but more likely a program adopted by all interested parties in Paris, even claimed that "all the Catholics [within England] without any exception favour such an enterprise—indeed, they eagerly long for it." This memorial, sent to Gregory XIII and Philip II via Crichton and Parsons, detailed the goals of the enterprise and the reasons for immediate action. The situation in Scotland, upon which all depended, was already precarious and a delay could be fatal. The Duke of Lennox and his friends are in control of Scotland but "a few months hence God knows what will happen; for the Duke remains there at great risk to his own life, both from the ministers and also from the Queen of England and other heretics and enemies he has in Scotland."[41]

Armed with the memorial, Crichton and Parsons hoped that King Philip and Pope Gregory would deliver on their promises. That was unlikely.

---

[39] It had not been decided where Parsons would be during the invasion. He wanted to stay in France. Acquaviva discussed this with the Pope, who decided that Allen and Parsons were in a better position to judge. Acquaviva wrote to Allen that "in sending him and keeping him there the sole end I proposed was the greater glory of God; and as I fear so much that it is his presence that excites the fury of our enemies, not merely against him in person but also against the whole body of Catholics, they perhaps will slacken somewhat their persecution, when it becomes known that he is out of England" (Rome 5 November 1582, in Ryan "Correspondence of Allen," p. 89).

[40] The Nuncio in France to the Cardinal of Como, 22 May [1582], in Hicks, *Letters of Persons*, pp. 146-48.

[41] The full memorial is printed in Hicks, *Letters of Persons*, pp. 158-66.

Although Mary, informed of what had transpired in France, urged Spain to assume leadership of the enterprise and to execute the plans quickly, Philip was hesitant. In a letter to Tassis on 11 June 1582, the King confessed that he was afraid that the scheme would soon become public knowledge because too many were involved in it. He ordered Tassis to take no action until he received the King's approval. Two months later Mendoza informed the King that he continued to encourage the project by holding out hope of success while he explained that the King's preoccupation with affairs in France and England prevented his active participation[42]

According to Parsons, Philip and Gregory listened attentively to the proposals. The King promised 12,000 crowns and the Pope offered 4000 for the armies.[43] Parsons took advantage of his audience with the King to present the needs of the English Catholics, especially of the college now at Reims. Although Gregory assigned 2000 crowns annually for support, it was not sufficient. The King then promised to give the same amount.[44]

While Parsons and Crichton were negotiating with the King and the Pope, the Protestant lords, led by William Ruthven, Earl of Gowrie, with the encouragement of Queen Elizabeth, captured James VI at Ruthven on 22 August 1582.[45] The Duke of Lennox's power was curtailed, but not destroyed. Among the charges levelled against him was his tolerance of Jesuits in Scotland, some of whom were enemies of both the King of Scotland and the Queen of England.[46] Prospects now were not as auspicious as in the spring but, as Lord Seton wrote to the Jesuit General on 4 November, hope must not be abandoned, for the situation could improve.[47] Lennox's influence remained strong until he was banished in January of 1583.

Without Lennox's protection William Holt was arrested at Leith at the instigation of the English ambassador Sir Robert Bowes in March of 1583.

---

[42] Mary Queen of Scots to Mendoza, 29 July 1582, CSP Simancas (1580-86) 392-94; Philip II to Tassis, Lisbon 11 June 1582, *ibid.*, 379; Mendoza to Philip II, London 14 August 1582, *ibid.*, 395-97.

[43] In a letter to the Cardinal of Como in October, the papal Nuncio in Spain summarized Parsons's report. The King would not make any commitment until he was informed of the size of the papal subsidy: he would not and could not support the project alone. Eventually the Pope offered only 50,000 crowns, whereas the entire enterprise would cost approximately 400,000. The King was not pleased (Hicks, *Letters of Persons*, p. 170). He wanted the Pope to assume more of the financial burden, because Spain was already involved in a battle with the French in the Azores, where they supported Philip's rival for the Portuguese throne.

[44] Parsons, "Punti," pp. 60-63.

[45] A month before the raid, Mendoza informed Philip that Elizabeth was plotting with Archibald Douglas, Earl of Angus, to expel Lennox (Mendoza to Philip II, London 25 July 1582, CSP Simancas [1580-86] 387-89).

[46] The charges against Lennox can be found in CSP Scotland (1581-83) 152.

[47] CSP Scotland (1581-83) 197-98.

Over the next four months the English government tried to persuade James to hand Holt over to them so that he could be taken to England for trial and possible execution. When that failed, the ambassador asked that Holt be "intensely" examined in his presence, with torture if Holt was reluctant to confess. Holt told little, but he did mention something about Spain's involvement. On 21 July the King finally granted permission for Holt's examination in the presence of Bowes and for the use of torture if needed. Holt was given twenty-four hours to decide whether he would speak freely or under duress. With the connivance of the King, Holt escaped the next day. From then until his departure from Scotland in the spring of 1586, he spent most of his time in the southwest section of the country.[48]

Despite James's capture, the Duke of Guise insisted that the enterprise still be carried out. Indeed, according to the Spanish ambassador in France, news from Scotland simply reemphasized the need for such drastic action. But Philip hesitated as usual. On 24 September he instructed Tassis to tell Guise that he, the King, had been enthusiastic about the enterprise since its initiation and remained so, but before he committed anything he wanted good reasons for anticipating success, and assurances that the Pope would contribute as much money as the affair demanded. The King wanted Tassis to make it quite clear to the Duke that it was the Pope's failure to provide the financial support that was behind the collapse of the enterprise: the King was not to blame.[49] Guise meanwhile investigated other possibilities.

During his return from Lisbon Parsons was seriously ill. Nonetheless he followed Philip's instructions and stopped in Madrid to see the Nuncio. By Bilbao he was so ill that he could not continue his journey. A Jesuit brother sent by Gil González Dávila escorted Parsons to the Jesuit college in Oñate, where he cared for him until spring of 1583. Before he returned to France, he again consulted Philip II in Madrid, presumably about the new proposals that the Duke of Guise had formulated after the fall of Lennox. Parsons

---

[48] William Davison to Walsingham, Edinburgh 4 March 1583, CSP Scotland (1581-83) 317-19; Sir Robert Bowes and William Davison to Walsingham, Edinburgh 4 March 1583, ibid., 320-23; Walsingham to Bowes and Davison, [London] 14 March 1583, ibid., 330-31; Walsingham to Bowes, [London] 16 April 1583, ibid., 378-79; Bowes to Walsingham, Edinburgh 23 April 1583, ibid., 405; [William Fowler] to [Walsingham], [Edinburgh April 1583], ibid., 433-34; "Request from the Queen of England to the King of Scotland," May, ibid., 455-56; Bowes to Walsingham, Edinburgh 29 June 1583, ibid., 515; same to [Walsingham], Edinburgh 21 July 1583, ibid., 548-53; Mendoza to Philip II, London 4 April 1583, CSP Simancas (1580-86) 458; same to same, London 15 April 1583, ibid., 460-61; James VI to the Duke of Guise, Falkland 19 August 1583, ibid., 502-3; "Examination of Holt after his capture," Bodleian Library, Tanner MS 79, ff. 183^r-187^v; Hubert Chadwick, S.J., "A Memoir of Fr. Edmund Hay S.J.," AHSI 8 (1939) 73-74.

[49] Tassis to Philip II, Paris 5 September 1582, CSP Simancas (1580-86) 400-01; Philip II to Tassis, Lisbon 24 September 1582, ibid., 401-03.

arrived back in Paris at the end of May.[50] The first attempt to secure James's conversion had failed.

II

After Parsons crossed to France, he resided with Michel de Monsi (or de Monchy), Archdeacon of Rouen and Vicar-General of the non-resident Archbishop, Charles, Cardinal of Bourbon. One of the most powerful clerical figures in the city, de Monsi would later be the head of the Catholic League's *Conseil de l'Union* in Normandy. We do not know how the two met, but a likely possibility was through the Mendoza-Guise network. Through Monsi Parsons played a role in advancing the Catholic cause in France. Rouen had recovered from a brief period of Huguenot domination with a stronger, more fervent Catholicism. Throughout 1581 and 1582 there were special prayers in Rouen cathedral that God would bless Henry III with an heir. As long as Catholic succession depended solely on Henry's brother, Francis, Duke of Alençon, the possibility of a Protestant King was too great. Catholic fears were acerbated by stories of persecution and execution spread by Parsons and other English Catholics residing in Rouen. Persecution was not unique to England but endemic in Protestantism.[51]

Throughout the early negotiations about Scotland, Rouen remained Parsons's base. There he found time to write and publish a number of books. The Queen of Scots may have been dismayed by Parsons's interest in writing, but this was one of his reasons for leaving England. A printing press was established in Rouen. An Englishman, George Flinton, managed it, and George L'Oyselet was the printer.[52] In light of Parsons's contact with de Monsi, perhaps it is not surprising that the first book off the press was *De persecutione Anglicana*.[53] Within a year this exposition of the sufferings endured by English Catholics was translated into English, French, Italian, and German besides four more editions in Latin. Distributed widely throughout Europe, this small book was used not only to gain financial

---

[50] Parsons, "Punti," pp. 62-63; Edwards, *Robert Persons*, p. 79.

[51] On the religious state of Rouen at this time and de Monsi see Philip Benedict, *Rouen during the Wars of Religion* (Cambridge, 1981) pp. 167-70, 179, 195. John Bossy is one of the few historians who notes Parsons's involvement with the League. See his "The Society of Jesus in the Wars of Religion," in *Monastic Studies: The Continuity of Tradition*, ed. Judith Loades (Bangor, 1990) pp. 229-44 and "The Heart of Robert Persons," in *The Reckoned Expense: Edmund Campion and the Early English Jesuits. Essays in Celebration of the First Centenary of Campion Hall, Oxford (1896-1996)*, ed. Thomas M. McCoog, S.J. (Woodbridge, 1996) pp. 141-58.

[52] On the press and the books published see Hicks, *Letters of Persons*, xlii-xlv; A.C. Southern, *Elizabethan Recusant Prose 1559-1582* (London, n.d. [1950]) pp. 359-63.

[53] (Bononia [Rouen], 1581) ARCR, I, no. 874. Other editions and translations are nos. 875-84.

assistance for the impoverished English but to provide grounds for political action against Elizabeth.[54] Parsons centred his exposition on the treatment of Edmund Campion.[55] Such was the detestable pestilence of heresy that a man learned and loved was racked and tortured for religion. Contrary to the consistent claim of the English government that men such as Campion were not religious martyrs but political traitors, Parsons clearly showed the religious nature of the legislation through a careful delineation of various laws and their penalties. With hindsight we could reasonably conclude that the book implicitly argued that the political and diplomatic negotiations were justified because of the persecution engineered by the government against the recusants.

The second book, *A defence of the Censure, gyven upon two bookes of William Charke and Meredith Hanmer mynysters, which they wrote against M. Edmond Campian*,[56] was started in England but finished in France. The work did not just continue the controversy caused by Campion's *Rationes Decem* but contained Parsons's indignant onslaught on the treatment accorded Campion during his disputation and his trial, and on Charke's part in it. Besides castigating Charke, Parsons refuted various Lutheran and Calvinist errors he espoused. The third book, and the most important, was *The first booke of the Christian exercise, appertayning to resolution* generally known as *The Christian Directory*.[57] Although the planned second and third parts never appeared, this became Parsons's most popular and influential work, and one that was even expurgated and published in a pirated Protestant version in 1584.[58] In a letter to Acquaviva, Parsons

---

[54] On the part played by *De persecutione Anglicana* in collecting alms for the English see Thomas M. McCoog, S.J., "'The Slightest Suspicion of Avarice': The Finances of the English Jesuit Mission," *RH* 19 (1988) 104-05. Catholics were not the only Church to take up a collection for their troubled co-religionists. In the early 1580s there were national collections in England to aid the besieged city of Geneva "to helpe these godlie people, trobled for the gospel of Jesus Christ." See Patrick Collinson, *Archbishop Grindal: 1519-1583* (London, 1979) p. 270, and *The Religion of Protestants: The Church in English Society 1559-1625* (Oxford, 1982) pp. 126-27. Grindal himself gave £66.13s.4d in 1583 (*Grindal*, p. 345 n. 25).

[55] On the role that Campion played in the religious propaganda of the day see Thomas M. McCoog, S.J., "'The Flower of Oxford': The Role of Edmund Campion in Early Recusant Polemics," *SCJ* 24 (1993) 891-905.

[56] (n.p. [Rouen], 1582) STC 19401, ARCR, II, no. 624.

[57] (n.p. [Rouen], 1582) STC 19353, ARCR, II, no. 616. For the significance of this book in recusant spiritual tradition and in confrontation with Puritanism see Elizabeth K. Hudson, "The Catholic Challenge to Puritan Piety, 1580-1620," *CHR* 77 (1991) 1-20.

[58] On changes made in various editions see Ernest A. Strathmann, "Robert Parsons' Essay on Atheism," in *Jos. Quincy Adams Memorial Studies* (Washington, D.C., 1948) pp. 665-81. On Parsons's reaction to Bunny see Victor Houliston, "Why Robert Persons Would not be Pacified: Edmund Bunny's Theft of *The Book of Resolution*," in *The Reckoned Expense: Edmund Campion and the Early English Jesuits. Essays in Celebration of the First Centenary of Campion Hall, Oxford (1896-1996)*, ed. Thomas M. McCoog, S.J. (Woodbridge, 1996) pp. 159-77.

described this as a work "on resolution, suited to our needs. In the first part, reasons are set forth to stir up resolution; in the second, impediments to resolution are refuted."[59]

Like the Italian Jesuit Gaspar Loarte's *Essercitatio della vita christiana* (Venice, 1561), of which it is a very free adaptation, *The Christian Directory* is rooted in Ignatian spirituality.[60] In this life there are three essential things for every Christian: firm resolution to serve God, clear knowledge of how to begin this service, and strong perseverance till the end. Written for English Catholics, the book sought to root their desire to serve God so firmly that they could withstand any punishment and any persecution. If they persevered in God's service, they would be able to resist any temptation to conformity. Unlike *De persecutione Anglicana*, there was little talk of martyrs and martyrdom.[61] Discussion of this theme in Parsons's work was in the context of resolution. Here Parsons's goal was not making martyrs but making dedicated Christians.[62]

During Parsons's stay in Rouen, his relations with the Duke of Guise deepened. A common concern for the conversion of James as a precondition for Mary's liberation and for the reestablishment of Catholicism had brought the two together. With Guise as his ally, perhaps even his tutor, Parsons embarked on a political course that would have far-reaching consequences. One non-political consequence of Parsons's association with Guise was the establishment of an English college at Eu, the first of many colleges and seminaries for whose foundation Parsons was responsible. Apparently the Duke agreed to the college when Parsons and Crichton met him in April. By 14 May 1582 the English ambassador to France, Sir Henry Cobham, was writing from Paris to Sir Francis Walsingham of the Duke's promise; two

---

[59] 11 April [1582], ARSI, Fondo Gesuitico 651/640.

[60] I stress "very free adaptation" because Thomas H. Clancy, S.J. warns us that this is very much Parsons's book and not simply an adaptation of Loarte ("Spiritual Publications of English Jesuits, 1615-1640," *RH* 19 [1989] 438). See also Houliston, "Why Robert Parsons Would not be Pacified."

[61] After Parsons abandoned the field of martyrology, Allen entered it. His *A brief historie of the glorious martyrdom of xii. reverend priests, executed within these twelve monthes for confession and defence of the Catholike Faith* [(n.p. [Douai], 1582) STC 369.5, ARCR, II, no. 7] extolled these men as true martyrs for their faith, unjustly called traitors by the government. Like Parsons, Allen centred his history around Campion, "a sacred man so honorable in all nations for his learning and of so innocent a life," and it was a sad commentary on the state of the kingdom that it rewarded such a man with abuse, ridicule, and death.

[62] In "Society of Jesus and the Wars of Religion," John Bossy argues that Claudio Acquaviva convinced Parsons that "living missioners and not dead martyrs" were wanted in England (p. 240). I think the interpretation given to martyrdom in *The Christian Directory* demonstrates that Parsons did not exalt martyrdom as a goal but simply as a possible consequence of resolution. At this time Acquaviva wanted Parsons to write a life of Campion, not simply an account of his martyrdom. For references to this correspondence see Bossy, "Society of Jesus and the Wars of Religion," p. 234 and "Heart of Persons."

months later the ambassador was informed that a house had been erected for that purpose.⁶³ The Duke of Guise provided the building and an annual payment of £100 to cover costs for what was to become a preparatory school for the English college at Reims. Within two years the college was in full operation and the Duke faithfully paid the promised sum. Founded and subsidized by the Duke, the college practically died with him. After his assassination on 23 December 1588, despite attempts by Parsons to obtain Spanish support, the college began to contract. Any chance of its survival vanished when Spanish and French armies clashed throughout Normandy in the Catholic League's final attempt to prevent the accession of the Protestant Henry IV.⁶⁴

III

The Raid of Ruthven in August of 1582 destroyed prospects for an invasion of England through Scotland. The departure of the Duke of Lennox in late 1582 left the pro-English party in control but in disarray. To prevent foreign intrigues that would affect England's stability, the government persisted with its suggestion that some type of association regarding the government of Scotland be formed between James and Mary. Because the anti-English faction remained strong, schemes were still hatched even though Mary was often kept in the dark.⁶⁵ As we have seen, Guise, perhaps aware of the strength of the anti-English party, remained hopeful throughout.

Philip's Portuguese venture had ended successfully. Don Antonio, evicted from his one base in the Azores in the summer of 1582, had fled to England. His other trouble spot, the Netherlands, was quiet. In March of 1580 Philip had outlawed William (the Silent) of Orange and declared him a traitor. Orange retaliated by labelling Philip a tyrant and a murderer. He and his agents argued throughout the United Provinces that they should repudiate Philip totally. The Estates General sought a strong candidate as Philip's replacement.

---

⁶³ PRO, SP 78/7/74; Cobham to Walsingham, Paris 12 July 1582, SP 78/7/125.

⁶⁴ See Frédéric Fabre, "The English College at Eu—1582-1592," *CHR* 37 (1950) 257-80; Hubert Chadwick, S.J., *St. Omers to Stonyhurst* (London, 1962) pp. 5-6.

⁶⁵ In a letter to Mendoza on 28 February 1583, Mary complained that she had not heard anything about the enterprise in more than five months. Had it been abandoned? She blamed the Archbishop of Glasgow and claimed that he was so ambitious that he wanted to do everything himself. As a result she was going to open another line of communication through Thomas Morgan (CSP Simancas [1580-86] 446-49). Mary's rebuff of the Archbishop was but the first sign of discontent among the exiles. By the end of June Tassis was reporting growing antagonism between the English and the Scots exiles, between those whose first concern was the restoration of Catholicism and those who major preoccupation was the release of Mary, and between those who favoured Spain and those who endorsed France (Tassis to Philip II, Paris 24 June 1583, *ibid.*, 479-86).

Francis, Duke of Alençon (again we shall retain his older title although he was now Duke of Anjou) agreed to recognize all traditional rights, privileges, and liberties of the provinces; in return he became "prince and lord of the Netherlands" on 23 January 1581. The need for English support to resist Philip's efforts to reassert his authority was a factor in Alençon's pursuit of Elizabeth. On 26 July 1581, in the Act of Abjuration, the northern provinces rejected Philip's authority. Independence, however, was easier to declare than to maintain. Without full English support and without the full promised subsidy from the Estates General, Alençon's forces were no match for the army of the Prince of Parma.[66]

Confident of a successful outcome of the struggles in the Netherlands, Philip instructed his ambassador to provide Guise with money, 12,000 crowns in all (including 2000 crowns intended for the seminary at Reims), and the King promised to send 10,000 more in January of 1583. The Spanish King and the Duke of Guise were ready to act, but by May Guise concluded that the original plan must be altered because Scotland was safely in the hands of the Protestants. Therefore England would have to be invaded directly. This proposal was more expensive and hence he asked Philip for 100,000 more crowns. Once more the enterprise foundered on the shoals of finances. Philip contended that he could not afford more because of other commitments, and that Gregory XIII, since he was financially better off, should supply most of the money.

Papal promises must have been forthcoming, for plans were finalized by the end of May. Albert V, Duke of Bavaria, won over to the Scottish Queen by her Jesuit chaplain Henri Samier, was willing to help. Fearful of a French reaction to a Spanish-led enterprise, it was decided that the Duke of Guise, as Mary's kinsman, would command it. According to the plan, Guise would attack England through Sussex, and Bavaria through Norfolk. At the same time the Spanish would send their fleet to create a diversion in Ireland. English Catholics would, of course, rise to support the invaders.[67]

Besides the enterprise a more clandestine conspiracy was hatched in May. Ambassadors favourable to the enterprise whispered that the Guises were plotting to assassinate the Queen. The assassin was to be a member of the Queen's household, George Gifford, a crypto-Catholic disturbed by the

---

[66] Peter Limm, *The Dutch Revolt 1559-1648* (London, 1989) pp. 53-55.

[67] Philip II to Tassis, Lisbon 24 January 1583, CSP Simancas (1580-86) 436; Tassis to Philip II, Paris 4 May 1583, *ibid.*, 463-64; Philip II to Tassis, San Lorenzo 6 June 1583, *ibid.*, 475-76; Tassis to Philip II, Paris 24 June 1583, *ibid.*, 479-86. In M.A. Tierney, ed., *Dodd's Church History of England*, 5 vols. (London, 1839-43) III, xxviii-xxxi, there is an undated memorial recommending that the armies land in the county of Durham. It is followed (xxxi-xxxiii) by a letter written by Charles Nevill, Earl of Westmorland, and Edward, Lord Dacre on 5 March 1583 at Tournai to William Allen on the same topic.

Queen's execution of his relatives. According to Giovanni Battista Castelli, papal Nuncio in Paris, the Duke did not seek papal support in this matter. He simply asked that Gregory XIII provide the money for a military expedition to England if the plot was successful. Although Tassis relayed news of Guise's preparations for the invasion, he was afraid to mention one development lest the letter be intercepted. If this ploy was successful, it would be well known so quickly that the King would recognize it. By the end of the month, however, it was clear to the Nuncio and the ambassador that nothing would come of the conspiracy, and in a letter to Philip on 24 June Tassis clearly stated that this mysterious design was "a violent attempt" against Elizabeth. These machinations provided a partial basis for the Babington Plot.[68]

Throughout Guise's careful arrangements Philip was undecided about his role. Did he wish to remain in the background and simply provide money for the invasion? Or should he take a more active and obvious role? Because of reports the King had received from Mendoza that the English Catholics were quite paralysed with fear, that there were no associations among the English Catholic gentry for self-defence and no common plans for a revolt against the Protestant Queen, and that the ambassador had no knowledge of a league between principal Catholics and Guise, he finally decided to remain in the wings. He did not share the Duke's confidence and opted for discretion in case of failure.[69]

While plans for the enterprise were being modified, Robert Parsons was recuperating in Spain. On a visit to Madrid in late April, Parsons received the King's assurance that the invasion would be launched that year. He arrived in Paris in late May and informed Castelli of Philip's continued interest in the proposals.[70] Before his departure from Spain on 25 April, Parsons wrote to Acquaviva; the General's reply of 5 June was addressed to Paris.[71] Unfortunately Parsons's letter is not extant but it said something about his travels and about many kindnesses shown to him by other Jesuits. Without this letter, Acquaviva's elliptical response is even more difficult. Concerning the enterprise, Acquaviva told Parsons that he would receive specific details from Crichton upon his return from Rome. In brief, Gregory XIII favoured the project and would promote it "to the extent that he thought

---

[68] The relevant letters were published in John H. Pollen, S.J., ed., *Mary Queen of Scots and the Babington Plot* (Edinburgh, 1922) pp. 169-75.

[69] Mendoza to Philip II, London 28 March 1583, CSP Simancas (1580-86) 456-57; Mendoza to Mary, London 6[?] May 1583, *ibid.*, 467-70; Mendoza to Philip II, London 16 July 1583, *ibid.*, pp. 492-95. See also John H. Pollen, S.J., "The Politics of the English Catholics during the Reign of Elizabeth," *The Month* 99 (1902) 409.

[70] Edwards, *Robert Persons*, pp. 84-85.

[71] Acquaviva to Parsons, Rome 5 June 1583, ARSI, Gal. 44, ff. 9^v-10^r.

it lawful," i.e. by supplying financial assistance. It was impossible to persuade the Pope to provide anything more.

Now that this matter was concluded, the General thought that the Society could do no more than commend the affair to God in prayer. Therefore he dismissed two proposals advanced by Parsons: establishing a papal representative in England or in Spain to work on such matters, and placing a Spanish Jesuit at the embassy in London. If the enterprise was successful, the Society would take advantage of opportunities provided. Regarding the "business of the Cardinal," Acquaviva sounded a note of caution: "it will behoove the Society to be very careful about becoming mixed up in that matter; it will be fitting rather for the Society to keep out if it, since it little becomes our Institute. . . ." In light of Professor Bossy's careful exegesis of this letter, and especially of this passage, it seems that Parsons had informed Acquaviva of George Gifford's proposal to assassinate Elizabeth.[72] The General was shocked by the proposal itself and by Parsons's involvement. Such plots "little become our Institute." There was a limit, and assassination exceeded it. At this point, Acquaviva began to consider withdrawing Parsons from France for work in Rome.[73]

James VI's escape from his captors in June of 1583 once more altered plans and revived hopes of some Scottish involvement.[74] In July Father Samier was again dispatched to Sheffield to visit Mary after he called on the Spanish ambassador. One of his tasks was to gain assurances that Mary's Catholic supporters in Scotland would support the enterprise. In the instructions given Samier by Mary, the Queen promised those with whom the Jesuit was commissioned to deal, "both with Christian Princes, her relatives and friends, and with the Pope," that she still held "the silent sympathy of thousands." Besides many Protestant and Catholic nobles, the greater part of the common people supported Mary. So confident was she of such support that there was no need to test it before any invasion. Mary was convinced that once her adherents heard of the invasion "they would not be able to restrain themselves, but would betray themselves or the undertaking by their joy, their gestures, or their words." If the invasion came by way of Scotland, as she preferred, the whole north of England would be on her side. Mary concluded her instructions with a prayer for speed. Action must be taken

---

[72] If Bossy's interpretation is accurate, then Edwards's judgement may need revision: "While the Jesuit had little regard left for Elizabeth, the murderess of esteemed and innocent colleagues, and fully supported military intervention to set the record straight, at no time did he approve of assassination attempts" (*Robert Persons*, p. 85).
[73] For Bossy's exegesis see "Heart of Persons."
[74] Even before his liberation, James had written to the French King on 27 April 1583 through the intermediary William Holt. A copy of this letter can be found in ARSI, Epp. Ext. 28, f. 224.

now: she "may die, James may be married to a Protestant, or confirmed in heresy . . . . If Elizabeth dies, some worse heretics may seize the throne . . . ." She hoped that the Duke of Guise would command the enterprise and that he would have the support of Spain and Rome. Money was needed to prepare loyal Scots for the attack, and "some Englishman of repute" should be created a cardinal.[75]

In August the Duke of Guise sent an envoy, Richard Melino (*vere* Parsons) to inform the Pope of the new plans.[76] Everyone, including the Queen of Scots, again agreed that the time was ripe. Parsons was to bear a request that the Pope do more than simply pledge financial support: he must renew the excommunication of Elizabeth, appoint Allen to the bishopric of Durham (chosen because there were more Catholics in northern England), and promulgate a bull that the invasion was undertaken by the papacy and delegated to Spain and the Duke of Guise. Besides receiving a bishopric, Allen was to be accredited as Nuncio to Mary Stuart with powers of a legate *a latere*. After the invasion succeeded, Allen was to receive Queen Mary's solemn promise that she would remain faithful to Rome and a strong ally to Philip of Spain, would restore Catholicism, and would see to it that her son was raised a Catholic.[77] Interestingly Acquaviva, although delighted with the news of James's escape, was not enthusiastic about a proposal to send more Jesuits to Scotland. At that moment he thought the presence of Jesuits in the country would do more harm than good.[78] Acquaviva's reluctance was, I think, a result of his misgivings at Parsons's increased political involvement.

Because of James's escape and Scotland's consequent involvement, the strategy was changed yet again: According to the new plans Spain would invade Lancashire with the expectation that all of northern England and the Scottish borders would rise in support.[79] Other English nobles inclined to Mary: Edward Manners, Earl of Rutland, William Somerset, Earl of Worcester, George Talbot, Earl of Shrewsbury, Philip Howard, Earl of Arundel and Anthony Browne, Viscount Montague, would lead an uprising in the Midlands. Meanwhile the Duke of Guise would lead an invasion of southern England. A few days later Charles Paget was sent into southern

---

[75] Pollen, "Mary Stuart's Jesuit Chaplain," 18-19; Mendoza to Philip II, London 19 August 1583, CSP Simancas (1580-86) 499-500.

[76] Parsons informed the General that he would be setting out for Rome very shortly for reasons that he would explain upon his arrival (Paris 22 August 1583, ARSI, Fondo Gesuitico 651/640).

[77] Briefs from Pope Gregory XIII to many of those involved were published in Hicks, *Letters of Persons*, pp. 348-55.

[78] Acquaviva to Edmund Hay, Rome 20 October 1583, ARSI, Franc. 1/I, f. 224^v.

[79] The instructions given to Melino (Parsons) and Paget can be found in CSP Simancas (1580-86) 503-05 and 505-06. See also Meyer, *England and the Catholic Church under Elizabeth*, pp. 284-87.

England to discuss the plans with some Catholics and to ascertain the precise ports where the Duke of Guise could land. For some reason, perhaps the insistence of Mary Stuart, Thomas Morgan and Charles Paget, excluded from similar discussions in 1582, were again involved.[80]

Gregory XIII granted most of the requests relayed to him by Parsons. Allen was appointed papal Nuncio for the expedition and Bishop of Durham upon arrival. Parsons was given a bill of exchange to pay for James's bodyguard. Finally the bull of excommunication was to be renewed. In Rome Parsons met Acquaviva. Unfortunately there is no record of their conversation, but the General must have been very forthright in his criticism of Parsons's activities, because almost immediately a rumour was circulating that the General did not want Parsons to return to France.[81] But Parsons did return. He was in Paris in October; perhaps his current role as a papal courier extricated him from Rome. Even though he did leave Rome, we can discern effects of Parsons's meeting with the General in his subsequent career. Parsons was much less frequently employed on such diplomatic missions. Acquaviva probably would have preferred no involvement and whenever Parsons was obliged to embark on such missions, he explained to the General how he had no choice because of the insistence of others. Acquaviva realised that only withdrawal from France would totally extricate Parsons from such activities. Parsons, however, did abandon his residence in Rouen (where he was scheduled to meet Jasper Heywood in late 1583 to discuss the problems caused by Heywood in England) and returned to a Jesuit community, albeit the professed house of St. Louis in Paris, a hothouse of Guise supporters with Claude Matthieu as superior.

Parsons was confident. According to Tassis, Parsons was so consumed with a desire to see the plans executed that he persuaded himself that the business was more feasible than it actually was. Paget returned from his mission with news that English Catholic reaction to the enterprise was

---

[80] These two played major roles in the Throckmorton, the Parry, and the Babington Plots. In *An Elizabethan Problem*, Father Hicks critically examined those plots and concluded that Morgan and Paget were "agents of the Elizabethan Government," agents-provocateurs to disrupt the English Catholic cause. Their status does not concern us: we are not interested in establishing or denying the authenticity of the plots. Whether this specific plot was an expression of the frustrations of English Catholics or a creation of Walsingham and Cecil to destroy Mary and the Catholic nobles has little bearing on the issue: various efforts were made by the Allen-Parsons party to forge an enterprise against Elizabeth. On the possible connection between Giordano Bruno and Morgan's arrest see John Bossy, *Giordano Bruno and the Embassy Affair* (New Haven, 1991).

[81] These rumours the General denied. There was no doubt, the General explained to Claude Matthieu, that Parsons would be more useful in France than if he remained in Rome. Nor was there any suggestion that he stay in Rome except for a period of three or four months so that various negotiations could be worked out (Rome 20 October 1583, ARSI, Franc. 1/I, f. 224r).

unfavourable and that Mary Stuart was opposed.[82] The venture was delayed; the responsibility for delay, according to Tassis, must be placed at the feet of the Pope, not the Spanish King.[83] In fact the delay seems to have been a consequence of Philip's extreme caution and of others' fear to act once Philip decided against involvement. In early 1584 Parsons and Allen urged the Pope to do what he could to expedite the invasion before an opportunity was again missed.[84]

IV

These continental intrigues did not escape the attention of the English government. Sir Francis Walsingham learned about the King of Spain's support of an invasion from the interrogation of William Holt in Scotland in spring of 1583. Increased surveillance of the French ambassador's London residence led to the arrest of Francis Throckmorton around 20 November 1583.[85] From him Walsingham learned of the Duke of Guise's plan for an invasion of the Sussex coast and of the Duke's expectation of Catholic support. To Walsingham's surprise, Throckmorton confessed that he had no dealings with the French ambassador.[86] Instead he claimed that his main contact had been Mendoza, a disclosure that led to the Spanish ambassador's expulsion in the following January.

Mendoza, although he had come to doubt the wisdom of depending on the support of English Catholics, was a vital link between the princes and exiles on the continent, and between Mary and the Catholics within England. His expulsion removed the centre of this network.[87] Mendoza moved to Paris, where he replaced Tassis as Philip's ambassador. Before Tassis handed over English affairs, he wrote two memorials about England. If the enterprise was to be pursued, its goals should be the subjection of England

---

[82] Edwards, *Robert Persons*, p. 91. Paget was accused of deliberately setting Catholics against the proposal and of alienating Mary Stuart.

[83] Tassis to Philip II, Paris 15 November 1583, CSP Simancas (1580-86) 507-10.

[84] See the memorial drafted by Allen and Parsons to the Pope on 16 January 1584, in Hicks, *Letters of Persons*, pp. 193-97.

[85] John Bossy argues that the major source of information about this conspiracy was Giordano Bruno. See his *Bruno*.

[86] This does not seem to be quite accurate. The French ambassador, Michel de Castelnau, Seigneur de Mauvissière, had built a network for corresponding with Mary Stuart and had been visited by Throckmorton. He barely avoided expulsion because of the affair. See Bossy, *Bruno*, pp. 12-13, 15, 20, 28.

[87] Mendoza informed Philip on 26 January 1584 of Elizabeth's desire that he leave the country. In a more detailed letter of the 30th, an episode related by the ambassador reveals his Spanish pride. Told that he was being asked to leave the country for creating disturbances within it, Mendoza replied that he "was not born to disturb countries but to conquer them" (CSP Simancas [1580-86] 513-15, 515-16).

and the liberation of Mary. Hence England, not Scotland, should be invaded. The latter was too far from Mary's prison, and its invasion would give Elizabeth ample time to prepare a defence. If Charles Nevill, Earl of Westmorland, and others returned to England to raise their partisans, and if Catholic nobles within England did the same, Mary could be freed with the assistance of an invading army. Although Guise and his faction would urge Philip to invade Scotland, overthrow the Protestant nobles there, and permit James VI to lead an invasion from the north, all attention instead must be focused on Mary.[88]

In his second memorial Tassis discussed the increasing division among the English exiles. The Allen/Parsons party looked only to Spain for support and insisted that the enterprise be directed at England. The Scottish party, presumably the Paget/Morgan faction, were disappointed and frustrated and were looking elsewhere for support for an invasion of Scotland.[89] It seemed that the new ambassador Mendoza supported the Scottish party, and that his predecessor favoured Allen and Parsons. As the potential allies argued among themselves, Throckmorton was tried on 21 May and executed on 10 July 1584. The Throckmorton Plot was but the first of many plots real and imagined that damaged the Catholic cause and consolidated Cecil's control.[90]

As news of the arrest and imprisonment of Throckmorton echoed through the courts of Europe, William Allen and Robert Parsons sought to quell any fear that the government had real knowledge of the conspiracy to invade England. In a joint letter to Gregory XIII and Philip II, they assured both that the harm done by Throckmorton was limited, and that none of the actions taken against Catholics proceeded from any knowledge of a plot against the realm.[91] Nonetheless, during the spring of 1584 the confederacy collapsed.[92]

From Madrid on 10 February, Philip explained to his ambassador in Rome, Enrique de Guzmán, Count of Olivares, how he should justify his King's behaviour. Philip knew that he would be blamed for failing to act, but Olivares was to deflect such criticism by pointing out that the proper

---

[88] Tassis to Philip II, Paris 18 April 1584, CSP Simancas (1580-86) 521-25.
[89] Tassis to Philip II, Paris 27 May 1584, CSP Simancas (1580-86) 526.
[90] See Pollen, "Politics of the English Catholics," 99 (1902) 600-18, 100 (1902) 71-87 for a discussion of "plots and sham plots." Pollen offers Throckmorton as an example of one "torn in two ways by the loyalty due to religion, and the loyalty due to the monarch who persecutes religion" (617).
[91] 16 January 1584, in Hicks, *Letters of Persons*, pp. 196-97.
[92] In a letter to the Pope from Holyrood on 19 February 1584, James VI begged for financial assistance against "my greatest enemies and yours" (CSP Simancas [1580-86] 518-19). Two months later in a letter to Philip II from Paris on 18 April 1584, Tassis commented that "the king of Scots undoubtedly shows a good tendency to return to the right road" (CSP Simancas [1580-86] 521-25). Nothing was done.

foundations still had not been prepared within England. Without these preparations, more English Catholics would have been killed if Spain had acted. If anyone should be blamed for the collapse of the invasion, it was those within England who so carelessly prepared for the invasion and so rashly discussed the affair in advance.[93] In June the Duke of Alençon, last male heir of the house of Valois, died. His death not only left the Protestant Henry of Navarre as heir to the throne and made a war of succession inevitable, but it left the United Provinces of the Netherlands without a leader. The assassination of William the Silent on 10 July 1584 intensified the problem. Any lingering hope for an invasion of England died because the Duke of Guise hesitated to leave France at such a critical time.

V

William Holt remained in Scotland after his escape from prison, convinced that the King could be converted. On 20 March 1584 he wrote from Edinburgh that the "King of Scotland has the best disposition towards us [Catholics], and remains firm in these sentiments, but complains of your delay in sending to him." As evidence of the King's continued goodwill Holt explained that the King had exiled two principal ministers, one of whom was from Edinburgh. For those who remained he made life as difficult as he could. James did not conceal his preference for Catholics, whom he considered more loyal than Protestants. Furthermore the King approved Holt's continued presence in the kingdom and showed him favour. He sought the Jesuit's assistance "in some important matters, but this he wishes to remain a profound secret, for the present, in order to prevent any risk to himself from the outcries of the ministers, until circumstances shall allow of his declaring himself more openly." Holt was sure that James had decided to grant full liberty of worship as soon as he could do so without risking the peace of the kingdom and his own safety.[94]

Aware of James's disposition, the Archbishop of Glasgow pleaded with Pope Gregory XIII that more Jesuits, specifically Fathers Edmund Hay, James Tyrie, James Gordon, and William Crichton, be sent to Scotland.[95]

---

[93] CSP Simancas (1580-86) 517.

[94] Parsons to Acquaviva, Tournai 24 March 1584, ARSI, Fondo Gesuitico 651/640. See also Holt's letters from Edinburgh, 20 March [1584], 1 April 1584, 7 April 1584, and 8 April 1584, ARSI, Angl. 42, ff. 49^r-50^v (translated in Forbes-Leith, *Narratives of Scottish Catholics*, pp. 188-94). We do not know to whom these letters were addressed.

[95] See the two letters from James Beaton, Archbishop of Glasgow, to Father Acquaviva, Paris 13 November 1583 and 16 April 1584, ARSI, Epp. Ext. 14, ff. 157^r, 186^{r-v}. The Archbishop asked the Pope to encourage the Jesuit General to send some of his Scottish men into the kingdom because "they write from Scotland that the harvest is great, the laborers few, and that it is desirable to send some to them for the purpose of keeping the Catholics firm, and

The General, however, was not willing to approve a new mission to Scotland since he was considering cancelling the English mission. Acquaviva had explained to Hay in October of 1583 that the presence of Jesuits in Scotland would not benefit the Catholics. He was still reluctant, and the Pope concurred.[96] Their presence would probably do the King more harm than good. Around the same time, James VI turned against the invasion. Influenced by Patrick, Master of Gray, who was allegedly refused absolution by William Holt because the nobleman would not tell the Jesuit everything he knew about the political affairs of Mary Queen of Scots, James repudiated the enterprise.[97]

Frustrated by the consistent failure of Philip, the Duke of Guise, and the Pope to come to his assistance, and seeking some form of reconciliation with England, James now regretted any involvement in their political machinations and refused henceforth to have any dealings with the Jesuits.[98] But as long as James relied on the advice of James Stuart, Earl of Arran, there was still some hope for the Catholic cause, especially after the failure of another attempt to capture the King in April.[99] In the summer of 1584 Henri Samier made his third and last visit to Mary. Presumably he conveyed the sad news of the collapse of the alliance, for Mary realized at least by the end of the year that she could expect no support from Spain, Scotland, or France. Once again she began to explore other solutions.[100]

In early 1584 Parsons travelled to the Low Countries at the request of the Prince of Parma, who wished to consult him about English affairs. At first Parsons did not want to go, since he was expecting Heywood for the summit in Rouen. Parma insisted and wrote to ask Oliver Mannaerts, then Jesuit Visitor in Flanders, to intercede. Having left orders that Heywood should

---

assisting those who are ready to return, and might be easily reclaimed" (Paris 25 June 1584, translated in Forbes-Leith, *Narratives of Scottish Catholics*, pp. 196-97).

[96] According to Parsons, James "manifested great inclination towards the Catholic religion and great reverence for his mother . . . ." Parsons argued that such a predisposition was dangerous and that many Protestants were suspicious ("Punti," p. 135).

[97] In Scotland Holt was protected by the Setons, with whom he resided. By January of 1584 he had moved to Edinburgh to be closer to the King. In so doing he became less dependent on the Setons, who in turn were angered by this turn of events. On this see Parsons, "Punti," pp. 142-47; Francis Edwards, S.J., *The Jesuits in England* (London, 1985) pp. 273-74.

[98] Monsieur Fontenay to Mary Queen of Scots, Edinburgh 15 August 1584, CSP Scotland (1584-85) 260-73; Martin, *Henry III and Jesuit Politicians*, pp. 105-8. Yet as late as 19 February 1584 James was still writing to the Duke of Guise and to the Pope from Holyrood in an attempt to gain their assistance. He promised that, once he freed himself, he would follow Guise's advice in matters of religion (CSP Simancas [1580-86] 517-18, 518-19).

[99] As a result William Ruthven, Earl of Gowrie, was executed on 4 May. Archibald Douglas, Earl of Angus, John Erskine, Earl of Mar, and Andrew Leslie, Earl of Rothes, fled across the border into England.

[100] Pollen, "Mary Stuart's Jesuit Chaplain," 20-21. After this last visit to Mary, Samier became even more involved in the political affairs of the League. For his later life see 136-49.

wait in Rouen or travel to Flanders, Parsons left for Tournai. Parma was concerned about the increasing number of Catholic exiles. The previous year, a regiment of English soldiers had defected to Philip's service. But many had since returned to England because there was no way to incorporate them into the Spanish army. To prevent recurrences Parma wanted to place an English gentleman over the regiment and to create a few more companies from the English young men who daily fled to the continent. On this he wanted Parsons's advice. The Earl of Westmorland was given command of the English regiment, and the secular priests, William Watts and Joseph Pullen,[101] were assigned as chaplains to provide the new soldiers with religious instruction. Once a pension was received from Philip and more companies were established, Parsons was sure "many more would leave England . . . and the Queen of England will be more afraid of a few English Catholic soldiers than of many soldiers from other nations and, as a result, would not risk persecuting the Catholics within the country."[102]

Parsons returned to the professed house in Paris in May. He was barely back when Claude Matthieu and William Crichton pressed him to go to Scotland. Although James was no longer favourably disposed in public towards Catholicism, William Holt remained sanguine.[103] Unnamed Scottish lords thought that Parsons could prevent King James from abandoning the Catholic cause and from coming to some sort of agreement with Elizabeth. Matthieu and Crichton agreed. Parsons discussed the prospect with Allen even though he was not eager to make the trip. Besides the usual difficulties with such a journey, Parsons feared capture by the English.[104] But if the General ordered him, he would go. Regarding Scotland, Parsons seemed reluctant to become more involved (perhaps because of Acquaviva's earlier restrictions on his activities). Therefore he suggested that Claude Matthieu, who knew about all the negotiations pertaining to that mission, be appointed superior with power to dispatch Scotsmen.[105]

Despite Parsons's nomination of Matthieu, Father Acquaviva decided that Parsons should be placed in charge of the Scots mission.[106] Parsons warned

---

[101] Pullen later joined the Society (*Mon. Ang.*, II, 440-41, see under Polonus).

[102] Parsons to Acquaviva, Tournai 2 May 1584, ARSI, Fondo Gesuitico 651/640. Parsons explained this at greater length in "Punti," pp. 124-27. There, however, he mistakenly gave the date as 1583. See also Hicks, *Letters of Persons*, lxiii.

[103] In a letter to Father Agazzari from Paris on 12 June 1584, Parsons wrote that Holt was certain the King was "fired with hatred against the ministers, who every day preach and conspire against him [the King]" and that Holt believed a royal conversion was still possible (Hicks, *Letters of Persons*, p. 213).

[104] He was nearly captured on his way back to Paris (Edwards, *Robert Persons*, p. 105).

[105] Parsons to Acquaviva, Paris 29 May [1584], ARSI, Fondo Gesuitico 651/640.

[106] Acquaviva to Matthieu, Rome 4 June 1584, ARSI, Franc. 1/I, f. 194ᵛ; Hicks, *Letters of Persons*, p. 218 n. 8 and p. 221 n. 21. See also Parsons, "Punti," pp. 142-47

the General of possible conflicts between the Scots and the English, but Acquaviva dismissed such anxieties because all the important men involved in the mission specifically asked that Parsons be placed in charge.

There is no record of any Scottish opposition to Parsons's appointment. The French Provincial Odo Pigenat, however, was not happy.[107] Because there were worthy Scots in the Society, men who had held high position, Pigenat could not understand why Parsons was chosen. A second objection was jurisdictional: he did not approve of someone, especially from outside the province, having authority over members of his province. That is, he did not like men such as Matthieu and Parsons selecting Scottish Jesuits for a mission to Scotland.[108] In his reply Acquaviva explained that the two missions had to be treated together because the affairs of one nation were so intertwined with those of the other. The reason why Pigenat had no jurisdiction over the missions was the general reluctance of the Catholic laity in both countries to deal with foreign superiors.[109]

In late spring 1584 Acquaviva considered cancelling the English mission because of complaints from Pigenat and others.[110] The Scottish mission was going to suffer a similar fate. Despite Matthieu's and Crichton's petitions, the General agreed with Parsons's and Allen's decision that Parsons should not go to Scotland. Indeed he had not decided whether he would send anyone. He had asked Archbishop Beaton to write to Gregory XIII but yet had no reply. The issue in this decision, Acquaviva advised, was whether the presence of Jesuits in Scotland would do more harm than good to the King in his current position. In this regard the General agreed with Pigenat that Holt should be recalled from Scotland, but the final decision he left to Allen, Parsons, and their associates.[111]

---

[107] It will be recalled that Pigenat was opposed to continuation of the English mission. Although it was not stated in his letter to Acquaviva, Pigenat disapproved of Parsons's relations with the Guises.

[108] Pigenat to Acquaviva, ARSI, Gal. 91, f. 197^r.

[109] Acquaviva to Pigenat, Rome 22 September 1584, ARSI, Franc. 1/I, ff. 202^v, 203^v.

[110] Apparently those who disapproved of the activities of the Allen/Parsons faction found a receptive ear in Pigenat. On 20 August 1584 Parsons complained from Paris that men such as Morgan and Paget "who do not approve and who do not understand the Lord's ways," were quick to disparage the Jesuits. He asked the General if, at an opportune moment, he would warn Pigenat that he should not believe Morgan and Paget without first consulting those who knew the facts (ARSI, Fondo Gesuitico 651/640). In April of 1585, Thomas Morgan wrote to Mary Queen of Scots about Crichton's capture and confession. Although there was nothing in the confession that compromised Mary, Morgan complained that Jesuits should not be employed in such negotiations because they communicated sensitive information to each other. Morgan also presented a copy of the confession to Pigenat with a stiff protest (CSP Scotland [1584-85] 617-18). See also same to same, 21 March 1586, CSP Scotland (1585-86) 262-78.

[111] Acquaviva to Parsons, Rome 2 July 1584, ARSI, Franc. 1/I, ff. 197^v-98^r.

By the end of August 1584 both the English and Scottish missions were secure. Acquaviva deferred to Parsons on both. William Crichton and James Gordon left Dieppe for Scotland in late August and were captured at sea by Dutch Calvinists.[112] Gordon was later freed because the merchants who had chartered the ship were afraid of the wrath of his nephew George Gordon, Earl of Huntly.[113] Crichton and Patrick Addie, a secular priest who accompanied the Jesuits, were imprisoned at Ostend, where Crichton was to be executed for the murder of William the Silent because it was alleged that the Jesuits were responsible for his assassination the previous July. Crichton was saved from the gibbet; he was turned over to the English in September.[114] Found on him were some invasion plans apparently dated from 1582. When interrogated in the Tower, where he remained for nearly three years, he admitted everything.[115]

Crichton's confession concluded another chapter in the enterprise. Catholic exiles were again left dissatisfied and discouraged. In a letter to Mary Queen of Scots in October, Parsons confessed that "Doctor Allen and I having had a meeting together had concluded upon consyderation of owr thwartes and oppositions that wee receaved daylye in all owr doings and [from] men of our owne side and of the small successe owr former labors had browght forth wee had resolved I say to leave cogitation of soch matters and to follow only owr spirituall cowrse wheruppon all dependeth thowgh in longer time . . . ."[116] Disconsolate and fearful for his life, Parsons left

---

[112] Sir Edward Stafford, new English ambassador to France, wrote to Walsingham from Paris on 24 August that two Scots Jesuits, Crichton and Gordon, were at Dieppe, where they waited for a favourable wind. These two were the right hands of "Glasgow and Seton, who go to Scotland with assured hope that the King will be a Roman Catholic before Christmas" (PRO, SP 78/12/49). In his reply from Oatlands on 2 October, Walsingham told Stafford that the two had been taken at sea and sent hither by the Admiral of Flushing (PRO, SP 78/12/83).

[113] William Davison wrote to Burghley from Edinburgh on 6 September that Gordon had redeemed his liberty for 100 crowns (CSP Scotland [1584-85] 318-20).

[114] Hicks, *Letters of Persons*, lxiv; J.H. Pollen, S.J., "Memoirs of Father William Crichton, S.J.: 1584 to 1589," *The Month* 139 (1922) 317-24.

[115] The examination can be found in PRO, SP 12/173/2, 3, 4, 5. It is printed in Thomas Francis Knox, ed., *The Letters and Memorials of William Cardinal Allen (1532-1594)* (London, 1882) pp. 425-34. In letters to Walsingham, written on 25 September and 31 October 1585, Crichton complained of conditions within the prison and asked to be released (PRO, SP 12/182/35; 12/183/68). The Italian document with the plans for the invasion is probably SP 12/153/79. Crichton was released in May of 1587 through the intercession of Sir Christopher Hatton, whom Crichton described as "a Catholic at heart" (Pollen, "Memoirs of Crichton," 324).

[116] Rouen 10 [October] 1584, in Hicks, *Letters of Persons*, p. 246. Parsons's distress had been building. In a letter to Englefield from Paris on 24 July, he complained that Mendoza promised much but delivered little, and that the Pope would do nothing unless Philip was involved in the enterprise. Parsons was worried that in pursuit of the enterprise Mary was being forgotten (CSP Scotland [1584-85] 234-36). In a letter to the Cardinal of Como on 16 April 1584, Allen feared that he would abandon all hope in man and would be bitter for the rest of his life if the invasion were not carried out that year (Knox, *Letters of Allen*, p. 233).

Paris for Rouen and delegated the Scottish mission to Edmund Hay.[117]

Parsons's frustration at the failure of the Catholic powers to act was not the only reason for his flight from Paris. The appearance of *The copie of a leter, wryten by a master of arte of Cambridge, to his friend in London*,[118] better know as *Leicester's Commonwealth*, led to rumours that Leicester had sent hired murderers to Paris to assassinate the author of this scurrilous attack on his reputation.[119] *Leicester's Commonwealth* further angered Pigenat, and he again complained to Acquaviva, presumably because he thought Parsons was involved. Such virulent anti-English propaganda embarrassed Henry III's ally. Once again the militant policies of Parsons and his French allies devoted to the Guise cause were harming the Society's reputation. Pigenat's protest prompted Acquaviva to suggest to Parsons in January of 1585 that he come to Rome to do the final year of his Jesuit formation.[120]

Parsons was on the verge of leaving France for Rome as the General requested when a few developments forced him to remain. After a consultation with Allen he concluded that his departure now would cause needless inconvenience for three reasons. First, the King of Spain had asked Allen and Parsons personally to discuss the enterprise with Parma. Parsons explained that Parma had made it clear that he would discuss the affair only with Allen and Parsons. Secondly, Parsons was entrusted by Mary Queen of Scots to negotiate with Parma concerning her escape. The new plan called for Mary's escape and subsequent marriage to Parma who would then command a Spanish invasion from the Netherlands.[121] Thirdly, after the success of the *Christian Directory*, he had begun writing the other two

---

[117] Edmund Hay to Claudio Acquaviva, Paris 29 October 1584, translated in Forbes-Leith, *Narratives of Scottish Catholics*, pp. 198-201. In this letter Hay discussed Crichton's capture.

[118] (n.p. 1584) STC 5742.9, ARCR, II, no. 31. Recently Dwight C. Peck prepared a critical edition of this often neglected but influential work: *Leicester's Commonwealth: "The Copy of a Letter Written by a Master of Art of Cambridge" (1584) and Related Documents* (Athens, Ohio, 1985).

[119] It is still not agreed who wrote the book. A.F. Allison and D.M. Rogers attribute it to Charles Arundell (see notes after entry in ARCR, II, no. 31). John Bossy ("Heart of Persons") and Peter Holmes (*Resistance and Compromise: The Political Thought of the English Catholics* [Cambridge, 1982] p. 131) think that Parsons wrote it. Victor Houliston argues that the authors were Arundell and his circle and that the subsequent attribution to Parsons was an attempt to destroy his reputation ("The Fabrication of the Myth of Father Parsons," *RH* 22 [1994] 145). For detailed arguments for and against Parsons see Leo Hicks, S.J., "The Growth of a Myth: Father Robert Persons, S.J., and Leicester's Commonwealth," *Studies* 46 (1957) 91-105, and Peter Holmes, "The Authorship of 'Leicester's Commonwealth'," *JEH* 33 (1982) 424-30.

[120] Pigenat to Acquaviva, Paris 25 November 1584, ARSI, Gal. 91, ff. 309^{r-v}; Acquaviva to Parsons, Rome 29 November 1584, ARSI, Franc. 1/I, f. 207^r; same to Pigenat, Rome 9 January 1585, *ibid.*, f. 209^v; same to Parsons, Rome 9 January 1585, *ibid.*, f. 210^v.

[121] See Hugh Owen to Mary, Bever 13 January 1585, CSP Scotland (1584-85) 536-38.

promised volumes and editing the first volume, already corrupted and published by Protestants. He estimated that he would finish this work by summer. Afterwards he would depart for Rome. He hoped only that someone would be appointed to oversee the two missions during his absence. The work was not easy, and the temporary superior would have to do everything he could to prevent the English and Scots from being discouraged. The growth of the "faction which the devil stirred up against the Society, and Dr. Allen and myself particularly" [i.e. the Morgan and Paget faction],[122] would make this work more difficult.[123]

After the death of Alençon in June of 1584, Henry III invited Henry of Navarre to abjure Protestantism. He refused. In September, Henry, Duke of Guise and his brothers Charles, Duke of Mayenne, and Louis, Cardinal Guise, met other nobles in Nancy, where they founded a league with the declared aim of keeping Navarre from the French throne.[124] Pope Gregory XIII was reluctant to endorse the new league because he did not want to alienate Henry III. As we have seen, during these months Pigenat, a supporter of the King, criticized the policies of Matthieu and Parsons, supporters of the new league. On 31 December 1584 Spain decided to aid the Catholic League because the French monarchy had consistently aided the Dutch rebels. Spain and the Catholic League signed a treaty at Joinville that pledged both parties to the eradication of heresy within France and the Netherlands, and the exclusion of the house of Navarre from the French throne. Moreover Spain promised an annual subsidy and the Guises promised to restore Cambrai to Spanish control.[125]

Military operations quickly followed. The League controlled much of northern and central France. Initially the Catholic cause seemed almost

---

[122] Acquaviva was upset at the division and instructed Parsons to be more conciliatory. In a letter to Agazzari written at Mézières on the French border on 3 April 1585 (ARSI, Fondo Gesuitico 651/640), Parsons explained that he remembered Paget and his faction in his prayers and at Mass and that the tension had diminished because, using Bossy's translation ("Society of Jesus and the Wars of Religion," 238), "we attend solely to our own functions, and they to theirs, without getting mixed up with one another." Parsons was on his way to see Parma. The affairs in which he and Allen were now involved concerned Spain.

[123] Parsons to Acquaviva, n.p. [Rouen?] 12 February 1585, ARSI, Fondo Gesuitico 651/640. See also Parsons, "Punti," pp. 154-57. During these negotiations Parsons decided that the city of St. Omer was an ideal and easily accessible site for communication with the English and Scottish missions (Parsons to Acquaviva, Louvain 10 May 1585, ARSI, Fondo Gesuitico 651/640). Fewer than ten years later, a seminary/college founded and staffed by English Jesuits would be established there.

[124] The first league resisted the Huguenots; the second, the succession of a Protestant king. On the political theory and propaganda written by the League's supporters see Frederic J. Baumgartner, *Radical Reactionaries: The Political Thought of the French Catholic League* (Geneva, 1975).

[125] For a short survey of events leading to the treaty and its consequences see David Buisseret, *Henry IV* (London, 1984) pp. 15-18.

invincible in view of the success of the Guises in France and of Parma's army in the Netherlands. On 31 March 1585 the Duke of Guise published the Manifesto of Péronne, in which he emphasized the persecution of Catholics that would inevitably follow a Protestant succession. Graphic accounts of persecution suffered by Catholics in England played an important role in propaganda disseminated by the League. So strong was the power of the League that it forced Henry III to accept the humiliating Treaty of Nemours on 7 July and to support the League.[126]

Religious wars in France prevented Spain and the Catholic League from acting against England or for Scotland. Nothing could be done until the French Protestants had been defeated. Parsons meanwhile prepared to go to Rome, perhaps realizing that he could do nothing until the armies had finished their work. On 28 May 1585 Parsons told the General that he would be in Rome by September. Meanwhile he found his replacement as director of the missions. According to a report from a Spanish nobleman who had recently left Scotland, Holt was well and planned to cross to France to meet Parsons. He was to arrive in July or August. Parsons asked if Holt could oversee the missions until the end of Parsons's tertianship. Holt could return to Scotland after Parsons finished the programme.[127]

Preparations for the journey were disrupted by an unexpected emergency: Allen's near-fatal illness. On 27 July Allen suffered so seriously with a stone in either one of his kidneys or his bladder that many feared for his life. Anticipating the worst, Allen panicked and burned all his papers and ciphers. Parsons hastened to Allen's bed, concerned that if Allen died, his successor at Reims should continue his policies and not be one of the Paget/Morgan faction.[128] Allen survived and on 23 September he and Parsons travelled to Rome together;[129] Parsons was to begin his tertianship and Allen his search for further funding for the English College from the new Pope Sixtus V, elected on 24 April 1585.[130]

---

[126] R.J Knecht, *The French Wars of Religion 1559-1598* (London, 1989) pp. 59-60.

[127] Paris 28 May 1585, ARSI, Fondo Gesuitico 651/640.

[128] Parsons to Agazzari, Reims 12 August 1585, ARSI, Fondo Gesuitico 651/640. See also Barret to Agazzari, Reims 8 and 15 August 1585, SC, Anglia VI, 13 (printed in Penelope Renold, ed., *Letters of William Allen and Richard Barret 1572-1598* [London, 1967] pp. 167-72). Allen apparently wanted to transfer administration of the seminary to the Society of Jesus upon his death. This may explain Parsons's haste to ensure that a worthy successor be selected (see Renold, *Letters of Allen and Barret*, p. 175 n. 1). By October Sir Francis Englefield heard of Allen's serious illness; in a letter from Madrid on 19 October 1585 to Father Agazzari, he suggested that Agazzari use his influence to have either Parsons or Heywood [sic] appointed Allen's successor in Reims (ARSI, Fondo Gesuitico 647/241).

[129] On 30 September Thomas Rogers reported to Walsingham that Parsons had gone to Rome to discuss proposals for an invasion of England (PRO, SP 15/29/45).

[130] Renold, *Letters of Allen and Barret*, p. 165 n. 1.

The General's reply to Parsons's request for a substitute was ominous. Having heard from other Jesuits in Paris that Holt was not coming to France but intended to take advantage of improving conditions in Scotland, Acquaviva entrusted direction of the English and Scottish missions to Odo Pigenat, and in his absence James Tyrie.[131] The appointment of Pigenat was a reversal of a policy established by Acquaviva a year earlier. Was the change prompted by Pigenat's efforts to convince the General of the damage being done to the Society of Jesus by the League's supporters?[132] Acquaviva's selection of an extremely cautious Pigenat probably resulted from his desire to extricate Jesuits from diplomatic activities. The General realized that, regardless of who served under Pigenat, the French Provincial would not allow him to engage in the type of activities pursued by Parsons.

The Spanish/Guise alliance in France and Parma's victories in the Netherlands disturbed Elizabeth. Fearful of the coalition turning against her, Elizabeth sanctioned involvement in the Americas aimed at Spanish sovereignty: she approved attempts at colonization in Virginia, permitted Francis Drake to undertake a new expedition, and sent ships to interfere with Newfoundland fisheries. In an attempt to find allies Elizabeth even established contact with the Ottoman sultan and with North African states. More important Elizabeth finally shed her secret support and openly assisted the Dutch.

Once Henry III signed the Treaty of Nemours, the Dutch rebels lost their major protector. In August of 1585 England and the Estates-General of the United Provinces signed the Treaty of Nonsuch. Elizabeth offered the Dutch 6,400 infantry and 1,000 cavalry and an annual £126,000 for their support.

---

[131] Acquaviva to Parsons, Rome 12 July 1585, ARSI, Fl. Belg. 1/I, p. 262. Acquaviva explained the arrangements to Pigenat: "In Fr. Parsons's absence somebody must direct the two missions. I put you in charge. But possible inconvenience and suspicion . . . [occasioned by] a Provincial constantly dealing with Archbishop Beaton and the Nuncio, can be met by your operating through another, namely Fr. Tyrie [for Scotland] and perhaps another still for England" (Rome 1 July 1585, ARSI, Franc. 1/I, f. 230ᵛ). Years later Tyrie's death would be interpreted by Parsons as God's judgement: "[Tyrie] who albeit otherwise hee were a good and godly mann, yett in many pointes the factiouse had deceived him upon the difference of Nations, and indirectly his authoritie stoode them greatly in steede, for which it seemeth God tooke him so sodanely away to the admiration of all men" ("The observation of Certayne Aparent Judgements againste suche as have beene seditious [1598]," ed. John H. Pollen, S.J., in *Miscellanea II* [London, 1906] p. 208).

[132] The French Jesuits who supported the royal family were extremely apprehensive about political activities that attracted many members of the order. In December of 1586 the ArchBishop of Tuam, Milar O'Higgin, stayed at a Jesuit house in Paris. He was accosted by a layman who had come to Paris with a letter from the Spanish ambassador to negotiate with Matthieu. The superior was worried about the whole affair and feared either that the Archbishop was involved in some negotiations or that he would fall under suspicion because he stayed with Jesuits who were involved. He did not wish to offend the Archbishop, but he preferred that the Archbishop find accommodation elsewhere (Clement Patean to Acquaviva, Paris 21 December 1586, ARSI, Gal. 92, ff. 288ʳ-89ᵛ).

As security she was allowed to garrison the towns of Brielle and Flushing. The Earl of Leicester was placed in command of the English forces. His attempt to create a strong Protestant alliance as a counterweight to the Hispano-Guise coalition resulted in a conflict with his sovereign. There were limits to England's fears and to England's support, despite England's desperation.[133]

By royal edict in July, Henry III proclaimed Catholicism the only religion within France and gave Huguenots six months to convert or to go into exile. On 9 September, Pope Sixtus V excommunicated Henry of Navarre and Henry, Prince of Condé as lapsed heretics and declared them unable to succeed to the French throne.[134] The stage was set for renewed violence, but in France, not in the British Isles. Philip consistently resisted papal exhortations and pleas from the Guises for an expedition against Elizabeth. His resistance to their overtures began to crumble in October of 1585 when a combination of events, attacks by Drake on the Galician coast and in the Caribbean, the start of a new religious war in France, and the taking of Antwerp, convinced him that he should act.[135]

The two Jesuits working in Scotland, James Gordon and William Holt, were still convinced that James's sympathies were with his mother and the Catholic faith, even though the King and Elizabeth had reached an agreement that would be ratified the following year in a treaty. This agreement, the Jesuits argued, was imposed by the Protestant lords or was nothing more than diplomatic manoeuvring.

The Earl of Arran was still influential. Consequently Scottish Catholic nobles requested more Jesuits. Their request was forwarded to Acquaviva by the Archbishop of Glasgow, and the General directed Odo Pigenat to send Fathers Hay and Tyrie. Because Tyrie was Pigenat's delegate for Scottish and English affairs, he was indispensable in France. John Hay, proposed as a substitute, was rejected because his work at the college in Tournon was too important. On the other hand, Acquaviva was confident that the Duke of Guise would allow the withdrawal of John Drury from the

---

[133] John Guy, *Tudor England* (Oxford 1988) pp. 287-89; M.J. Rodríguez-Salgado, "The Anglo-Spanish War: The Final episode in 'The Wars of the Roses'?," in *England, Spain and the Gran Armada 1585-1604*, eds. M.J. Rodríguez-Salgado and Simon Adams (Edinburgh, 1991) pp. 5-6; Simon Adams, "The Outbreak of the Elizabethan Naval War against the Spanish Empire: The Embargo of May 1585 and Sir Francis Drake's West Indies Voyage," *ibid.*, pp. 45-69.

[134] De Lamar Jensen, *Diplomacy and Dogmatism: Bernardino de Mendoza and the French Catholic League* (Cambridge, Mass., 1964) p. 72. Since heretics could not hold property, this declaration in effect stripped both of their legal inheritance. See Kathleen A. Parrow, "Neither Treason nor Heresy: Use of Defense Arguments to Avoid Forfeiture during the French Wars of Religion," *SCJ* 22 (1991) 705-16.

[135] Rodríguez-Salgado, "The Anglo-Spanish War," pp. 7-9.

college in Angers for the Scottish mission. So Edmund Hay and John Drury travelled to Scotland in July of 1585 to reinforce James Gordon and William Holt.[136] Hay was appointed superior of the four.[137] According to Tyrie's report to Acquaviva in September, Hay and Gordon were in the north with the Earl of Huntly, Holt and Drury in the west with John Maxwell, Earl of Morton.

Edmund Magauran,[138] Irish Bishop of Ardagh, who had recently passed through Scotland on his way to the continent, affirmed the increase of Catholicism. The Bishop estimated that he administered the sacrament of confirmation to at least ten thousand persons during his stay in Scotland. Tyrie was informed that Elizabeth had written to James, strongly beseeching him to take action against the Jesuits. As a result the King published a proclamation requiring all Jesuits to leave the kingdom within one month and forbidding anyone, on pain of death, to receive Jesuits into their houses. Nonetheless no one felt threatened and no one "whose doors were open to us before, has closed them now." By October English reports to Walsingham heralded the Society's success. Sir Thomas Rogers related that the Jesuits had converted 10,000 and even expected to gain the King.[139]

Hopes were again shattered when another *coup d'etat* reversed policy: aided by the Earl of Morton who opposed Arran because he threatened the Earl's title, the exiled Protestant lords overthrew Arran in November of 1585 and assumed control of James. The Jesuit mission was affected. Through Catholic friends the four Jesuits had obtained royal letters granting

---

[136] Acquaviva to James Tyrie, Rome 1 July 1585, ARSI, Franc. 1/I, f. 230ʳ; same to Pigenat, Rome 1 July 1585, ARSI, Franc. 1/I, f. 230ᵛ; same to Parsons, Rome 12 July 1585, ARSI, Fl. Belg. 2, p. 262. After the General granted the request for two Scottish Jesuits, Archbishop Beaton was informed that Gordon and Holt preferred English Jesuits in case the King were compelled by Protestants to take some measures against them (Beaton to Acquaviva, Paris 15 February 1585, translated in Forbes-Leith, *Narratives of Scottish Catholics*, pp. 201-02).

[137] James Tyrie to Claudio Acquaviva, Paris 31 September 1585, translated in Forbes-Leith, *Narratives of Scottish Catholics*, pp. 206-07; Hubert Chadwick, S.J., "Father William Creichton, S.J., and a Recently Discovered Letter," *AHSI* 6 (1937) 264. In a report of 11 August, Thomas Rogers told Walsingham that Drury and Hay had just departed for Scotland, where many Catholics believed that the King had converted. A few days later, on 15 August, Walsingham wrote to the English ambassador to France that he had heard that Hay had gone to Scotland to deal with the King. Although James protested his devotion to England, Walsingham, with justification, doubted his sincerity: Hay was too wise a man to travel to Scotland unless he was confident that the King would overlook him (PRO, SP 15/29/39; SP 78/14/71).

[138] The letter does not name the bishop, but John H. Pollen, S.J., identified him as Magauran (*The Counter-Reformation in Scotland* [London, 1921] p. 59).

[139] James Tyrie to Acquaviva, Paris 30 September 1585, in Forbes-Leith, *Narratives of Scottish Catholics*, pp. 206-07; same to same, Paris 18 January 1586, *ibid.*, p. 208; Edward Wotton to Walsingham, Stirling 15 September 1585, CSP Scotland (1585-86) 104; Thomas Rogers to same, 18 October 1585, PRO, SP 15/29/47.

them the right to remain within the kingdom with complete freedom of action. The *coup d'etat* prevented their publication.[140] It was believed, however, that the imminent return of Claud, Lord Hamilton would result in the King's regaining his freedom.[141] Meanwhile the four Jesuits in Scotland asked for more financial assistance and for Scottish translations of the Bible, especially of the New Testament, which would do more than anything else to turn the people to Catholicism.[142]

Negotiations continued without Parsons. In January of 1586 Philip commissioned his ambassador in Rome, Count Olivares, to seek from Sixtus confirmation of Elizabeth's excommunication and a substantial contribution for military expenses. Once again the King was ready to embark on an expedition to restore Catholicism and to elevate Mary Queen of Scots to the English throne. At this juncture, however, Philip insisted that a suitable husband be chosen for Mary. Because Mary was too old to bear children, the choice of a husband would determine the government of England during her lifetime but would not guarantee the establishment of a secure dynasty. Philip feared that feigned conversion or maternal affection would result in James's designation as heir. Therefore a condition for Spanish participation was James's exclusion from the English throne. Sixtus, however, was not yet ready to abandon the Scottish King. Disagreement over the succession threatened the enterprise until Sixtus and Olivares reached a compromise in late February of 1586: decision over the succession would be postponed until Mary secured the throne, after which Sixtus promised to accept Philip's resolution.[143]

Parsons, who had barely finished tertianship, offered his views on the matter. On 20 May 1586 he reminded Don Juan de Idiáquez, Philip II's secretary of state, that Scotland, the Queen of Scots, the "most powerful section of the English nobility," and all English Catholics "owing to the great influence with them which he [Mr. Allen] possessed," were ready to

---

[140] Edmund Hay's memoir provides an account of the overthrow of Arran (Chadwick, "Memoir of Hay," 66-85). Although appointed to the Privy Council, Morton was called before the Council in 1586 to explain why he allowed Mass to be celebrated. Frequently warned and cautioned, he left Scotland in April of 1587 and was not to return without the King's licence. In July the Earl of Angus's claim to the earldom of Morton was recognised by Parliament.

[141] The fourth son of James Hamilton, second Earl of Arran, Claud, Lord Hamilton actively supported the restoration of Queen Mary. Involved in various plots and intrigues, he later sided with the pro-English lords because of his strong animosity towards James Stuart, recognised by James VI as Earl of Arran. Ordered abroad by the Earl in May of 1585, he went to Paris where he remained until Arran's downfall. Recalled by James, he returned to Scotland in January of 1586. He quickly became one of the leaders of the Catholic party.

[142] James Tyrie to Claudio Acquaviva, Paris 18 January 1586, translated in Forbes-Leith, *Narratives of Scottish Catholics*, pp. 207-9. The Archbishop of Glasgow contributed to their expenses (Pollen, *Counter-Reformation in Scotland*, pp. 60-61).

[143] Rodríguez-Salgado, "The Anglo-Spanish War," pp. 9-10.

support an invasion when he had first discussed the enterprise with the King in Lisbon. Now all had changed. Factions had developed among English Catholics "due partly to wiles of the heretics who are afraid of his [Allen's] influence, and partly to the envy of certain persons with little spirituality." The longer Philip waited, the less was his chance of success.[144]

Lingering hope of another *volte face* in Scotland died with the Anglo-Scottish League of 5 July 1586, in which Elizabeth agreed to provide an annual subsidy of £4000 and promised to do nothing to prevent James's succession, even though she would not explicitly recognize him as her heir. In return James pledged to maintain the religious settlement of both countries and to defend it against any adversary. The use of the English throne as bait eliminated James as a co-conspirator in any future intrigues. His accord with England also sealed the fate of his mother. James's capitulation left Parsons looking to Spain for a Catholic contender and successor.

VI

The assassination of the Prince of Nassau on 10 July 1584 sent shock waves throughout England. The Throckmorton Plot earlier had revealed that deposing Elizabeth was the objective of ever-changing, ever-failing, yet persistent Catholic conspiracies, and resulted in the total ruin, among others, of Henry Percy, Earl of Northumberland, who committed "suicide" in June of 1585. The Parry Plot in 1585, according to official propaganda, showed that the same powers would resort to assassination.[145] Regardless of their authenticity, the Throckmorton and Parry Plots proved very useful to the government's efforts in equating Catholicism with treason in the public mind. Fearful for the Queen's safety, the English rallied around her. Popular hysteria regarding invasion and assassination was turned neatly to political advantage. The identification of Protestantism with English nationalism, an identification developing for years, was now completely established.

In October of 1584 Lord Burghley and Sir Francis Walsingham, in an attempt to maintain the frenzied fanaticism, borrowed a type of oath more common to Scotland, and drafted the Bond of Association, whereby those who swore to it committed themselves to defend the Queen's life and to eliminate the assassins and those for whom the assassination was committed. When Parliament assembled in November, it acted quickly and decisively. The first act was "An Act for provision to be made for the surety of the

---

[144] Rome 20 May 1586, in Hicks, *Letters of Parsons*, p. 279.
[145] For detailed examination of this plot made see Leo Hicks, S.J., "The Strange Case of Dr. William Parry," *Studies* (1948) 343-62. Hicks argues that the plot not only lacked papal approval but actually was a governmental ploy to discredit the Catholics and to justify renewed persecution.

214   CHAPTER FIVE

Queen's most royal person" (27 Eliz. c. 1); the second was "An Act against Jesuits, seminary priests and such other like disobedient persons," (27 Eliz. c. 2).¹⁴⁶

The first act, modifying the Bond, specifically excluded from the throne any claimant found guilty of involvement in a plot or conspiracy against Elizabeth if she died a violent death. It directed all subjects "by all forcible and possible means [to] pursue to death every of such wicked person by whom or by whose means, assent or privity any such invasion or rebellion shall be in form aforesaid denounced to have been made, or such wicked act attempted . . . ." The second act declared traitors all Jesuits and seminary priests who remained within the kingdom forty days after the passing of the law.

Henceforth the mere establishment of their identity as Jesuits and seminary priests was sufficient for the charge of treason to be levelled against them, because they rejected the Queen's spiritual authority and recognised the authority of a foreign prince engaged in plots and conspiracies against her. The act commanded all English subjects in Jesuit colleges or seminaries to return to the kingdom within six months. Upon arrival they were to report to the bishop or to two justices of the peace and to pronounce the oath of supremacy. Failure to do so could result in a charge of treason. Anyone who contributed to the support of a priest in England or a student in a foreign seminary was guilty of *praemunire*.

To ensure more effective enforcement, common informers were again encouraged with threats of imprisonment and fines for not disclosing the location of Jesuits and seminary priests within the kingdom.¹⁴⁷ Some members of Parliament were not satisfied with such moderate measures and vehemently attacked the Jesuits. Thomas Digges condemned the act for its leniency. "These hellhounds," he said regarding the Jesuits,

> cladding themselves with the glorious name of Jesus, and such wretched souls as they bewitch with their wicked doctrine, are indeed the only dangerous persons to her Majesty . . . . They are fully persuaded her Majesty's life is the only stay why their Roman kingdom is not again established here. They also teach their disciples that it is not only lawful in this case to lay hands on God's anointed and to murder schismatic and excommunicate princes, but meritorious also: yea, they assure them Heaven for it . . . .¹⁴⁸

---

[146] On the bond see David Cressy, "Binding the nation: the Bonds of Association, 1584 and 1696," in *Tudor Rule and Revolution*, eds. Delloyd J. Guth and John W. McKenna (Cambridge, 1982) pp. 217-34.
[147] J.E. Neale, *Elizabeth I and Her Parliaments*, 2 vols. (London, 1953, 1957) II, 13-101; John LaRocca, S.J., "English Catholics and the Recusancy Laws 1558-1625: A Study in Religion and Politics," (unpublished Ph.D. thesis: Rutgers University, 1977) 104-18.
[148] Quoted in Neale, *Elizabeth and Her Parliaments*, II, 44.

Furthermore, anyone who knowingly assisted a Jesuit or a seminary priest, would "be adjudged a felon without benefit of clergy, and suffer death, lose and forfeit as in case of one attainted of felony."[149]

At this point the English government initiated a campaign to clear its reputation on the continent due to recusant martyrologies. Henry Brooke, Lord Cobham, English ambassador to France, testified in late winter of 1582 to the effectiveness of Catholic propaganda when he begged the French King to forbid sale of Catholic martyrologies. Cobham's fears were justified: French and later Italian Catholics were outraged by the accounts.[150]

An official English reply to charges of cruelty, *A declaration of the favorrable dealing of her maiesties commissioners*, appeared in 1583. A Latin translation soon followed.[151] William Cecil, Lord Burghley, published a fuller account, *The execution of justice in England*, which appeared in two English editions in 1583. It was translated into Latin, French, Dutch, and Italian for wider dissemination.[152] Cecil argued that the priests were treated with great leniency and that the torture they endured was extremely mild. He vehemently insisted that the Catholics were not martyrs but traitors to their legitimate sovereign.[153] William Allen's reply, *A true, sincere and modest Defence, of English Catholiques*, repudiated Cecil's claims and vindicated the martyrs' credentials.[154]

---

[149] On the dangers of and penalties for protecting priests see Patrick McGrath and Joy Rowe, "The Elizabethan Priests: Their Harbourers and Helpers," *RH* 19 (1989) 209-33.

[150] See McCoog, "'Flower of Oxford,'" 901.

[151] (London, 1583), STC 4901. The Latin translation is STC 4904. Traditionally the pamphlet was attributed to Cecil, but the editors of the STC and Michael A.R. Graves now claim that Thomas Norton was the author. See Graves's *Thomas Norton: The Parliament Man* (Oxford, 1994) pp. 276-78.

[152] (London, 1583), STC 4902, 4903. The other translations carry the STC nos. 4904-07. See Robert M. Kingdon, ed., *The Execution of Justice in England by William Cecil and A True, Sincere, and Modest Defense of English Catholics by William Allen* (Ithaca, N.Y., 1965) xvii-xviii.

[153] See Kingdon, *Execution of Justice*, xxiii-xxiv, and his "William Allen's Use of Protestant Argument," in *From the Renaissance to the Counter-Reformation*, ed. Charles H. Carter (London, 1964) pp. 164-78, and Thomas H. Clancy, S.J., "English Catholics and the Papal Deposing Power, 1570-1640," *RH* 6 (1961) 118-20. Traditionally Cecil has been considered a *politique* who persecuted Catholics for reasons of political expediency alone. Recently historians have stressed his apocalyptic understanding of politics and his depiction of the pope as Antichrist. See Malcolm R. Thorp, "William Cecil and the Antichrist: A Study in Anti-Catholic Ideology," in *Politics, Religion & Diplomacy in Early Modern Europe: Essays in Honor of De Lamar Jensen*, eds. Malcolm R. Thorp and Arthur J. Slavin (Kirksville, 1994) pp. 289-304.

Cecil's argument did not even convince all anti-Romanists. In 1590 Elizabeth ordered that an account of the trial and execution of Campion be cut from the 1587 edition of Holinshed's *Chronicles* because the author, Abraham Fleming, stated that Campion "died not for treason but for Religion." See Annabel Patterson, *Reading Holinshed's Chronicles* (Chicago, 1994) pp. 128-30.

[154] (n.p.d. [Reims, 1584]), STC 373, ARCR, II, no. 14.

The English government waged a propaganda campaign on the continent; at home it fought back with legislation and persecution. Catholics paid dearly for the intrigues of Parsons and Allen: their motives may have been laudable but their dreams were unrealistic, and the price paid by others horrendous. Although Elizabeth successfully resisted harsher parliamentary measures,[155] new laws and more severe implementation of older laws compelled more and more recusants to obey the Queen and attend her Church. Those who remained steadfast became a greater source of income.[156] Gentry such as Sir Thomas Tresham and Richard Shelley of Warminghurst could protest their innocence of any treasonous intent and could petition for toleration, but they would go unheeded.[157] Such attempts to separate religious and temporal concerns were not acceptable. Despite the effect of their machinations, Allen and Parsons continued in the hope that their eventual success would end all persecution.[158] Until the eventual restoration of Catholicism with the demise of the Tudor dynasty, they exhorted the Catholics in the kingdom to fidelity despite persecution.[159] To

---

[155] One of the many papers prepared for her consideration explicitly warned her against clemency. She was reminded that William the Silent never compelled any Catholic to conform to his Church. His only tactic was persuasion. Nonetheless, "his clemencie could nothinge mitigate ther develishe intentes" (PRO, SP 12/176/32).

[156] On the implementation of the laws during this period see LaRocca, "English Catholics and the Recusancy Laws," 102-18.

[157] See Roger B. Manning, "Richard Shelley of Warminghurst and the English Catholic Petition for Toleration of 1585," *RH* 6 (1962) 265-74. See also Arnold Pritchard, *Catholic Loyalism in Elizabethan England* (London, 1979) pp. 51-56. The petition can be found in HMC, Various Collections, III, 37-43. In it the authors condemn William Parry by name and protest their loyalty: "Lett suche diabolycall dissimulatyon, and trayterous thirst after hallowed blood, sinke both him and his confederates according to Gods Judgementes, to their deserved doome of deepe damnation. We for our partes utterlye denye that either Pope or Cardynall hath power or authoritie to commaunde or lycense any manne to consent to mortall Synne, or to committe or intend anye other Acte *Contra Ius divinum*. Muche lesse can this disloyall, wicked and unnatural purpose by any meanes be made lawfull, to wytt, That a native borne subject may seeke the effusion of the sacred blood of his annoynted Soveraigne. Whosoever he be therfore Spirituall or Temporall, that maynteyneth so apparent sacryledge, we therin doe renounce him and his conclusion, as false, develishe and abominable." On Tresham see Holmes, *Resistance and Compromise*, pp. 62, 177-79.

[158] In light of subsequent attempts by some to represent, in the words of Leo Hicks, Parsons "as the evil genius of Allen, drawing the good man into courses, especially those concerned with politics, which his own better judgement condemned," it is important to stress the very close working relation between the two. For a detailed exposition see Leo Hicks, S.J., "Cardinal Allen and the Society," *The Month* 160 (1932) 528-36. Eamon Duffy ("William, Cardinal Allen, 1532-1594," *RH* 22 [1995] 282) acknowledges Allen's involvement.

[159] In *An apologie and true declaration of the institution and endevours of the two English Colleges* ([Mons, 1581] STC 369 ARCR II, no. 6), Allen exhorted English Catholics: "Be humble, wise, meeke, peaceable, patient, and constant, in all your cogitations, wordes, answers, doings, and sufferings: that Christ Iesus whom you serve, may blesse and prosper your endevours, move her Majesties hart to have compassion, open her grave Counselers eies to see your innocencie, alter the enimies and il informers malice and malediction, unto love and good affection towards you . . ." (f. 105^r).

their troubled flock in England they offered martyrologies,[160] theologies of persecution, and works of controversy. In these endeavours there was no place for Jasper Heywood. He did not "walk in step" with Parsons, and was not suited for the mission. In subsequent years Heywood demonstrated just how different his gait was.

In 1590 Heywood submitted to Acquaviva a detailed criticism of Parsons and of his approach to the mission. Some complaints were at root Heywood's personal problems with Parsons. From the beginning Parsons and Heywood did not get along: even at their first meeting Heywood had become annoyed. Parsons's subsequent and sudden departure for France, Heywood's ignorance of Parsons's precise location, and lack of communication aggravated the predicament. Other grievances were more serious. Heywood protested bitterly about Parsons's antagonistic style. He accepted overzealous men into the Society; his controversial works and propaganda offended many and made the lives of Catholics in England more difficult. Indeed Heywood contended that the persistent challenge to debate simply intensified persecution. Other works insulted the Queen and her Councillors.

Heywood was especially upset by *Leicester's Commonwealth*[161] and believed Parsons responsible for Ralph Emerson's capture in September of 1584 as he smuggled copies of it and other Catholic books into the kingdom.[162] If it were not for these offensive publications, the predicament of the English Catholics would be nowhere near as dire. In fact, Mendoza himself had murmured against the books and thought that they had ruined any chances of interceding for Catholics and ameliorating their lot. Parsons was therefore culpable for the legislation and for the persecution of the Catholics.[163]

Parsons and Heywood diverged over policy. The quartering of Campion exploded unrealistic expectations for a quick conversion of England through the sheer irresistibility of Catholic truth. Because conversion would be more

---

[160] On martyrologies, and especially on the role of persecution within them see Thomas H. Clancy, S.J., *Papist Pamphleteers: The Allen-Persons Party and the Political Thought of the Counter-Reformation in England 1572-1615* (Chicago, 1964) pp. 124-58.

[161] One wonders if Heywood's anger at this book was the result of his friendship with the Dudley family. It was claimed that he was not executed but only exiled because Leicester's brother, Ambrose Dudley, Earl of Warwick, interceded for him (Parsons to Acquaviva, Paris 10 July 1584, ARSI, Fondo Gesuitico 651/640). One wonders what Allen though of this work. In *An apologie and true declaration* Allen criticized Puritans for writing "pestilent bookes" that undermined the social order: "It is no good, grave, nor Christian government, to suffer a ribald to open in booke or pulpit, to the people whose ears itch for such sport, against Superiors of al states, the particular faultes, either feyned (as they be commonly) or taken up by hearsay, or in deed committed, of Prelates, Princes, or peoples of other Nations" (f. 97^r).

[162] Many books were smuggled through the French embassy. On attempts to stop this route see Bossy, *Bruno, passim*.

[163] ARSI, Anglia 30/I, ff. 118^r-123^v.

arduous than the missionaries had anticipated, a new strategy had to be formulated. Safe on the continent, Parsons consorted with Catholic princes and relied more and more on the secular arm. Heywood meanwhile sought the best means for the preservation of a Catholic remnant surrounded by a potentially hostile government whose wrath was not to be aroused. Enmity was the inevitable result of the publication of controversial works. Persecution naturally followed conspiracies and plots. Temperance and moderation must be the watchwords, not zeal and fervour.

This was especially true of Heywood's associates, the Catholic nobility with traditional power and prestige, faithful to their religion but loyal to their Queen.[164] Heywood sought accommodation; Parsons sought confrontation. Parsons, however, gained and maintained the confidence of the General, who, despite his attempt to control some of Parsons's activities, ordinarily favoured him. Father Pollen accurately summarized the issue:

> Heywood has not, I think, received the praise that is his due, for his prudence, and this because he seems to have urged his measures in some wrong way, perhaps with nervous emphasis, or in excited words, or personal innuendoes, that robbed his wisdom of its true mead [sic] of praise.[165]

Heywood would spend the rest of his at times tortured Jesuit life in relative obscurity, but his charges would become an essential element in the traditional criticism of the Society. His quest for a more peaceful solution would be a recurring dream.

Criticism of the Society was becoming more frequent. Differences were dividing the English mission, disagreements in tactics and in strategies. Parsons and Allen looked more and more towards Spain for English Catholic relief while the Thomas Morgan and Charles Paget faction remained loyal to the Scottish cause. The rift would grow. In Parsons's "Punti" the existence of "factions" is mentioned frequently. Many of his opponents would later reappear in Parsons's "The observation of Certayne Aparent Judgements againste suche as have beene seditious" where Parsons recorded God's vindication of Parsons's cause through his treatment of Parsons's opponents. They were not simply Morgan and Paget but fellow Jesuits James Tyrie and Francisco, Cardinal Toledo. When Allen and Parsons arrived in Rome in the late summer of 1586 they found that they had opponents even in the English College.

---

[164] On this point see Dennis Flynn, "Donne and the Ancient Catholic Nobility," *English Literary Renaissance* 19 (1989) 307-11.
[165] ABSI, 46/5A/1, Chapter VI, pp. 51-52. See also Flynn, "English Mission," 68-75 for a thoughtful evaluation of Heywood.

VII

Despite the excitement generated by the possibility of James's conversion, the number of Jesuits sent to Scotland was small; rarely during this period were there more than three or four. On the continent, however, the Society of Jesus became further involved in Scottish affairs when it assumed the administration of a new Scots College.

With an endowment provided by Mary Stuart, James Beaton, and possibly John Leslie, a college was established in Paris in 1580 to train priests for work in Scotland.[166] The first president was Dr. James Cheyne, a secular priest. In September of 1581 the college was transferred to Pont-à-Mousson, where Charles Guise, Cardinal of Lorraine, had founded a college in 1574 for the express purpose of combatting heresy. Within a few years this college was elevated to university status; it was placed under the administration of Jesuits in 1580. Persuaded by Jesuits Antonio Possevino and William Crichton, Pope Gregory XIII granted an endowment of 600 crowns to the Scots College for fifteen years from August of 1581. In 1584 he was persuaded to add another 400, eventually increased to 600, with the stipulation that at least six Irish students be admitted. By the end of 1584 there were thirty-six Scots and seven Irish seminarians. Apparently the Society assumed control of the college around the date of its transfer.[167] Perhaps the Scots hoped that history would repeat itself: the Society became involved in England only after the English College was placed under its direction.

The Jesuit mission in Ireland was practically nonexistent in the early 1580s. The only Jesuit on the island, Charles Lee, remained in prison. Petitions by others, such as Richard Fleming, to return to their homeland were denied. Because of the political situation, Acquaviva explained to Fleming, he did not see what good would come from sending more Jesuits.[168] Despite the Society's absence, Irishmen continued to seek

---

[166] In the late 1570s John Leslie, Bishop of Ross, on instructions from Mary, sought papal approval to convert the "Scottish" monasteries in Germany into seminaries. Pope Gregory XIII wrote to Emperor Rudolph about this on 23 July 1578. In October the Emperor ordered the "Scottish" monasteries then occupied by German monks to be restored to their original owners, but little seems to have been done. In April of 1580 the Emperor confessed that he could not hand over the "Scottish" monastery in Vienna because the Scots had earlier relinquished possession and Popes Nicholas V and Paul II had given it to German monks. See Alphons Bellesheim, *History of the Catholic Church of Scotland*, 4 vols. (Edinburgh/London, 1887-90) III, 245-47.

[167] See Crichton's history of the foundation and early development of the Scots College, ABSI, 46/4/2; J.H. Baxter, "The Scots College at Douai," *Scottish Historical Review* 24 (1927) 251-57; and Hubert Chadwick, S.J., "The Scots College, Douai, 1580-1613," *EHR* 56 (1941) 571-80.

[168] Rome 3 September 1582, ARSI, Franc. 1/I, f. 139^r.

admission. Because the mission did not have its own novitiate, positions for Irish candidates had to be found in novitiates throughout Europe. Richard Fleming was worried that many good vocations were lost because of the shortage of spaces. He therefore urged Acquaviva to appeal to all provincials that they accept a few Irishmen into their novitiates. Acquaviva hesitated. All provinces, he contended, were so overburdened that they lacked either facilities or money to accept and train candidates for Ireland. Austria was the exception: its Provincial accepted two novices. Acquaviva was slightly disappointed that the two candidates were not well educated, but hoped that their piety and virtue would compensate.[169] Not only was Acquaviva unable to find places for Irish novices; he also failed to obtain for the Irish the faculties earlier obtained for the English.[170] Finally, when Irish Jesuits requested Robert Rochford's appointment as mission procurator in Paris, Acquaviva refused. He argued that their spiritual affairs could be well supervised by a non-Irish Jesuit; involvement in temporal affairs was alien to the Society's Institute.[171]

Acquaviva's difficulties with the English mission in general and with the activities of Robert Parsons in particular affected his relations with the Irish mission. He refused to send more Jesuits on this mission because of the persecution, and he was unwilling to appoint an Irish Jesuit to a position comparable to that of Parsons and possibly of Crichton. As a result the Irish mission was in a state of limbo. Apprehensive of another Jesuit involved in diplomatic matters, Acquaviva had no Irish Jesuit to keep him informed of political and religious developments. With no one to correct misunderstandings, the General wrongly concluded that the absence of rebellions signified English domination. There were no rebellions against English authority, but that authority never extended over the entire island and was never without some opposition. The O'Neills and O'Donnells still dominated the north and in 1584 demonstrated their loyalty to Rome by adopting the new Gregorian calendar. Catholicism remained strong throughout Ulster.

In Dublin persecution was sporadic.[172] Dermot O'Hurley, Archbishop of Cashel, was charged with supporting the revolts against the Queen in 1583. Because Irish law did not punish treasons committed abroad, he was not tried. But he was executed on 19 June 1584 under the Queen's warrant.

---

[169] Acquaviva to Fleming, Rome 22 June 1581, ARSI, Franc. 1/I, f. 102^v; same to same, Rome 31 August 1581, *ibid.*, f. 106^r; same to same, Rome 22 December 1581, *ibid.*, f. 113^v; Acquaviva to Heinrich Blyssem, Rome 1 July 1581, ARSI, Austr. 1/I, p. 95.

[170] Acquaviva to Claude Matthieu, Rome 11 February 1582, ARSI, Franc. 1/I, f. 120^r.

[171] Acquaviva to Odo Pigenat, Rome 8 April 1585, ARSI, Franc. 1/I, f. 226^r.

[172] The anonymous *Discourse for the Reformation of Ireland* (1583) proposed that martial law be invoked for the execution of Jesuits, priests, and nuns (Thomas S. Flynn, O.P., *The Irish Dominicans 1536-1641* [Dublin, 1993] p. 86).

Sir John Perrot, appointed Lord Deputy in 1584, summoned the third and last Elizabethan Irish Parliament in 1585. The Catholic opposition, surprisingly strong among members from the Pale, resisted requests for political concessions, and countered with a demand for religious toleration. An attempt by Perrot to pass a bill that would introduce into Ireland all post-1559 English religious legislation was defeated. This defeat so angered the Lord Deputy that he demanded that the English government punish his opponents. Without the English anti-Catholic legislation, persecution in Ireland would have to rely on extralegal means such as martial law and warrants.[173]

* * * * *

In a recent article John Bossy confessed a residual unease with Edmund Campion: "His angelism, his rhetorical mode, his way of turning a mission into a melodrama, all seem unattractive."[174] Robert Parsons, on the other hand, "was no angel, he got his hands dirty, he was touched with the sin of the world; but if he had kept himself as clean as Campion perhaps nothing would have been done at all." Campion and Parsons have been traditionally portrayed as conflicting types. Campion was attractive and sympathetic, Parsons calculating and cold. Both achieved legendary status, but it is Parsons that casts the darkest shadow over the history of the English Jesuits. His plunge into the political world of the Counter-Reformation helped create the popular myth of a Jesuit.

When Parsons crossed the channel in the summer of 1581 political schemes and diplomatic intrigues were not among the reasons. Although Parsons had established contact with the Spanish ambassador in London, there is no evidence that their dealings concerned sensitive political matters involving the Queen: instructions from the General forbade discussion of such matters. Indeed, according to Parsons, Jesuit authorities in Rome resisted all attempts by Catholic powers to elicit Jesuit involvement in secular affairs. References to the Queen in the works published by Parsons in England were gracious and conciliatory. Their sincerity should not be denied because of Parsons's later writings. It was not the aim of Catholics,

---

[173] Robert Dudley Edwards, *Church and State in Tudor Ireland* (London, 1935) pp. 263, 268-73; Steven G. Ellis, *Tudor Ireland: Crown, Community and the Conflict of Cultures 1470-1603* (London, 1985) pp. 284-88; Colm Lennon, *Sixteenth Century Ireland: The Incomplete Conquest* (Dublin, 1994) pp. 316-18; Ciaran Brady, *The Chief Governors: The Rise and Fall of Reform Government in Tudor Ireland 1536-1588* (Cambridge, 1994) pp. 293-97; and William Palmer, *The Problem of Ireland in Tudor Foreign Policy 1485-1603* (Woodbridge, 1994) pp. 115-16. On O'Hurley see Benignus Millet, O.F.M., "The ordination of Dermot O'Hurley, 1581," *Collectanea Hibernica* 25 (1983) 12-21.

[174] "Heart of Persons."

Parsons protested, to form unholy plots and stir up rebellion. That was the *modus procendi* of Protestantism. Catholicism taught obedience. There is no reason to believe that Parsons had changed his views before the summer of 1581.

Because of the Duke of Lennox's ascendancy, Scotland had potential as a place of refuge from intensified persecution. William Watts's initial report led to further investigation, during which the scenario changed. Instead of providing temporary sanctuary Scotland became the principal means for a termination of persecution within England and for the restoration of Catholicism. England's hope lay in Scotland. The new objective may have been Lennox's, Mendoza's, and Guise's goal from the start, but there is no evidence that Parsons was privy to their machinations. Nevertheless, once he was informed of the enterprise he supported it enthusiastically. Why did Parsons abandon his earlier declaration of loyalty for a course of action generally favoured by Protestants?

The effect of the execution of Campion must not be underestimated. Bossy warns that we must not see Parsons's enthusiasm for an enterprise simply as "a passion to avenge Campion." Yet Campion's trial and execution did reveal that the government would resort to any tactic in its campaign to destroy Catholicism. Even those like Campion who consciously avoided political discussions would be destroyed through concocted conspiracies espoused by paid liars. As long as Elizabeth was on the throne, Catholics would remain victims of oppression.

Moreover in France Parsons resided with the Archdeacon of Rouen, a strong partisan of the Duke of Guise. Their militant anti-Protestant fervour would have confirmed Parsons's doubts. Campion's execution proved what the zealous French Catholics proclaimed: Protestants could not be trusted either in England or in France and must therefore be resisted. Unless French Catholics wanted to suffer comparable persecution, they must rally around the Guises to prevent a monarchy "soft" on Protestants. If English Catholics truly wanted to end their suffering, they would have to work for Elizabeth's deposition and for the succession of the legitimate Queen Mary Stuart. That was the only real solution to England's religious difficulties.

As Parsons was drawn farther and farther into a political wilderness in his pursuit of James Stuart, Acquaviva watched warily. Unfortunately there is no study of Acquaviva, and so we cannot readily situate his concern for Parsons in a wider context.[175] A decade earlier Everard Mercurian ordered

---

[175] Mario Scaduto began researching a volume a few years ago, but age and illness prevented its continuation. Even at an early stage of research, he was intrigued by Acquaviva's relations with Parsons. In private conversations he contended that Acquaviva's consistent support for Parsons and the English mission was crucial for understanding his generalate.

David Wolfe to abandon similar activities. Wolfe did not comply, and he was dismissed from the Society. Was Acquaviva more flexible in his interpretation of the Institute? We know from Bossy's analysis that Acquaviva took a strong stand on assassination. The enterprise might be an acceptable feature of the Society's "way of proceeding," but assassination definitely was not. But how tolerant was Acquaviva? Apparently he placed some restrictions on Parsons's activities. We shall never know what was discussed at their meeting in Rome, but Parsons's gradual withdrawal from direct military negotiations shortly thereafter was not, I think, coincidental. Henceforth Parsons was out of the fray. In Rome he wrote letters and memorials in favour of the enterprise, but did not serve as an ambassador empowered to discuss military and financial arrangements. Like Wolfe, Parsons presumably was given a choice. Unlike Wolfe, he remained in the Society. Ironically when Parsons returned to royal corridors of power in 1588, he did so at the General's request. His task was to defend Acquaviva, now under attack from a coterie of Spanish Jesuits.

CHAPTER SIX

"THE WINTER IN THE SOUL"

In a letter to Father Alfonso Agazzari in August of 1581, Robert Parsons explained that the mission was going well despite the persecution. He stressed that the Catholics remained united and that quarrels were almost non-existent.[1] Parsons's evaluation may have been true in 1581, but by 1585 the lauded harmony was crumbling on the continent and in England. Factions were forming, and each party blamed the other for political intrigues that intensified persecution. Discord surfaced in the English College in Rome. Some students complained they were being treated as children by the Jesuits. They protested that the more intelligent seminarians were being seduced into the Society, thus depriving the mission of needed priests. Jesuits, the malcontents continued, were more interested in the welfare of their order than they were in the preservation of Catholicism in England. Consequently they should be removed from the government of the college. The majority of students, however, praised the Society and opposed the dismissal of the Jesuits. The disturbances occasioned an official visitation by Filippo, Cardinal Sega.[2]

Michael Williams, the historian of the English College, does not deny the problems, but places the visitation in its proper context. Elected pope on 24 April 1585, Sixtus V reduced the subsidies given by his more extravagant predecessor, and sought to replenish the depleted papal treasury.[3] Concerned too with the reform of clerical life in Rome, he ordered a visitation of all churches and colleges. A dispute with the Society of Jesus over the nature of their vows resulted in an inquiry into the four seminaries in Rome under

---

[1] Leo Hicks, S.J., ed., *Letters and Memorials of Father Robert Persons, S.J.* (London, 1942) p. 86.

[2] Arnold Pritchard, *Catholic Loyalism in Elizabethan England* (London, 1979) pp. 102-03, 107. On the issue of vocations to the Society from the English College see Leo Hicks, S.J., "The English College, Rome and Vocations to the Society of Jesus, March, 1579—July, 1595," *AHSI* 3 (1934) 1-36. Complaints can be found in Cardinal Sega's report in Arnold Oskar Meyer, *England and the Catholic Church under Queen Elizabeth* (London, 1916) pp. 492-519. See also ARSI, Rom. 156, ff. 42^r-82^v for the official account of this visitation. Memorials from provincial visitations in 1582 and 1585 can be found in ARSI, Rom. 52, ff. 19^v-20^r; Rom. 78, ff. 19^v-20^r; Rom. 51/I, ff. 338^r-340^v.

[3] Sixtus, a Franciscan, was, according to J.N.D. Kelly, "cool towards the Jesuits" (*The Oxford Dictionary of Popes* [Oxford, 1986] p. 272).

their direction. Thus the English College was not unusual in the attention it received from the new pontiff. The report submitted by Cardinal Sega was generally favourable to the Jesuits and their government.[4] One change, however, was the replacement of Agazzari as rector by William Holt, recently recalled from Scotland.[5] The presence of William Allen in Rome may have been a factor in quelling difficulties. Although they were stilled with relative ease, the troubles were nonetheless a portent of future tension.

II

Robert Parsons warned Don Juan de Idiáquez of the rift that was splitting English Catholics.[6] Concern over succession to the English throne caused the rupture. Two years earlier, in 1584, Parsons sang the praises of James.[7] Then he assured Claudio Acquaviva that "if we were able to win this young King to God it would be the greatest disaster for heresy that ever happened, because he is so zealous in all he undertakes, diligent, courageous and resolute, and therefore we ought not to shrink from offering many lives to God in order to purchase such a treasure for the Church." Lives had since been sacrificed and schemes devised, but the purchase had not been made.

---

[4] It is important to note, as Pritchard carefully does, that Sega was well known as a supporter of Spanish military intervention in support of English Catholicism and even suggested that the assassination of Elizabeth might be morally permissible. In his report Sega thinks that missionary priests can play a major role in preparing English Catholics for possible rebellion against Elizabeth. See Meyer, *England and the Catholic Church under Elizabeth*, pp. 276-77, 490-91, 497; Pritchard, *Catholic Loyalism*, pp. 107, 220 n. 17. Suggestions such as these, if known, substantiated Elizabethan fears about Catholics. Sega's reputation may explain why no mention was made of student opposition to increasingly pro-Spanish sentiment among the Jesuits. From Paris on 10 July 1584, Parsons wrote to Father Agazzari, the college's rector, of his approval of the latter's governance. However, the number of malcontents in Paris, who "all hail from you in Rome," was so great that "they are infecting the greater part of the young men who come from England with unfavourable opinions of the Society and malicious judgements in its regard" (Hicks, *Letters of Persons*, p. 216). What were these opinions and malicious judgements? Could they be a repudiation of Allen's and Parsons's political programme?

[5] Michael Williams, *The Venerable English College Rome* (London, 1979) pp. 13-16. Because Robert Southwell was at the English College at this time see Christopher Devlin, S.J., *The Life of Robert Southwell: Poet and Martyr* (London, 1956) pp. 64-78. In a letter to Agazzari on 22 December 1586, Southwell wrote of periodic troubles in the English College: "I recall at times the troubles you have had in the College, and in recalling them, I marvel that the devil should be able to stir up dissension among those, who here live in perfect harmony both with us and amongst themselves. Here, forsooth, we have so many enemies in common that there is no time for internal factions. Rather our great concern is how to consult for the safety of our lives and to advance Catholic interests" (printed in John H. Pollen, S.J., ed., *Unpublished Documents Relating to the English Martyrs 1584-1603* [London, 1908] pp. 317-18).

[6] Rome 20 May 1586, in Hicks, *Letters of Persons*, p. 279.

[7] Parsons to Acquaviva, Paris 23 July 1584, in Hicks, *Letters of Persons*, p. 222.

Some began to propose an alternative. The joint Guise-Spanish enterprise now foundered over plans for the succession to the English throne. As we noted in the last chapter, Olivares and King Philip seriously considered an invasion of England in February of 1586 that would have installed Mary as queen with the stipulation that her successor not be her heretical son James. In his efforts to eliminate James as a contender, the ambassador suggested that William Allen be cultivated, since he would have great influence with the Pope in settling the question of succession.[8] As for the Guises, James's supporters, they entreated the Pope to have nothing to do with an enterprise unless they were involved.[9]

But the Pope, confident that the Spanish King did not himself aspire to the English throne, agreed with Olivares that it would be unwise to allow James to succeed because of his religious vacillation, and that he would accept Philip's candidate. If the French King attempted to interfere in any way in Philip's mission, Sixtus promised to make his displeasure known as openly as necessary.[10] Privately Philip argued that the most suitable successor to the English crown was the one who would restore the country to the Catholic faith: i.e. himself. But instead of adding another country to his worldwide empire, Philip proposed to transfer his claim to his daughter Isabella, who would be safely married to an Austrian cousin (she eventually married her cousin Albert in 1598). A few months later, Spanish designs were furthered by Mary Stuart. In a letter to Mendoza she promised to cede and make over to King Philip by will her right of succession to the English crown if her son James did not convert to Catholicism before her death.[11]

Reports that the Spanish King intended the English throne for his daughter alarmed many English Catholics. Some exiles abroad contacted their countrymen and pleaded that they must not assist Philip's army in any way. Although Philip planned to conquer the country under the pretext of

---

[8] Eamon Duffy argues that Olivares's realization of Allen's importance resulted in Allen's detention in Rome, where he became "to all intents and purposes, a Spanish servant, receiving detailed briefings from the maladroit on the management of the Pope" ("William, Cardinal Allen, 1532-1594," *RH* 22 [1995] 283).

[9] On continued attempts of the Guises and of Scottish Catholics, especially Robert Bruce, to remain a part of the enterprise and to secure a Stuart succession see Hubert Chadwick, S.J., "Father William Creichton, S.J., and a Recently Discovered Letter," *AHSI* 6 (1937) 267-69.

[10] Olivares to Philip II, Rome 24 February 1586, CSP Simancas (1580-86) 560-69. See also Thomas Francis Knox, ed., *The Letters and Memorials of William Cardinal Allen (1532-1594)* (London, 1882) lxxv-lxxxv.

[11] Mary to Mendoza, Chartley 20 May 1586, CSP Simancas (1580-86) 581-82. De Lamar Jensen rightly argues that this "phantom will," although it almost certainly never existed, was not a Spanish invention to justify Philip's claims to the English throne but a final attempt by Mary to end Philip's hesitation ("The Phantom Will of Mary Queen of Scots," *Scotia* 4 [1980] 1-15; *Diplomacy and Dogmatism: Bernardino de Mendoza and the French Catholic League* [Cambridge, Mass., 1964] pp. 83-85).

returning it to Catholicism, they claimed that he could neither be trusted nor depended on for aid.[12] The "Black Legend" successfully circulating for decades among the English warned of the horrifying consequences of a Spanish succession. A better candidate had to be found, and the only viable alternative was James. Even after James VI had apparently withdrawn from all foreign intrigues when he reached an agreement with Elizabeth on 5 July, his cause was not abandoned. Either unaware of revised Spanish plans or hopeful that the strategy could be altered again, the Duke of Guise continued to propose a new enterprise to liberate Mary and James. He asked Spain to provide money and troops.[13] Meanwhile Philip was writing to his ambassador in Rome to persuade the Pope to agree to Philip's naming Mary's successor.[14]

Despite their disagreement on Elizabeth's successor, Philip II and the Duke of Guise pursued a common policy in France. Together they proclaimed Charles, Cardinal of Bourbon their candidate for the French throne. The success of the Catholic League throughout 1586 and 1587 led Henry III to fear that the Parisian reception of the Duke of Guise would be more rapturous than his own. Thus Henry would not allow him to attend a solemn *Te Deum* at Notre Dame shortly after Christmas of 1587.[15] Guise's preoccupation with the "War of the Three Henries" left him unable to do anything but watch and listen as his ally Philip II planned an English enterprise and advanced the cause of a Spanish successor.

Although it does not seem that Parsons was aware of Philip's ambition to nominate Mary's successor, the Jesuit was involved in the continuing saga of the enterprise. Others continued to campaign for James VI and to work for his conversion, but Parsons was no longer enthusiastic. In a letter to Alessandro, Cardinal Farnese, Parsons relayed the latest news from Scotland. The Earls of Huntly and Morton and Claud, Lord Hamilton resolved to extricate the King from the clutches of the heretics and to restore Catholicism in the realm. If their plans were to be successful, the English Queen must be distracted with a war or an invasion. If neither was possible, the Scottish lords needed a subsidy to maintain troops for restored Catholicism to survive.

Although Parsons did not have much hope in these plans, events in Scotland could provide an important distraction. The time was most opportune, Parsons suggested, if Philip had designs on either England or Ireland. According to reports from England, Catholics there preferred the

---

[12] Mendoza to Philip II, Paris 11 May 1586, CSP Simancas (1580-86) 574-77.
[13] Guise to Mendoza, 16 July 1586, CSP Simancas (1580-86) 589-90; Mendoza to Philip II, Paris 23 July 1586, *ibid.*, 595-96.
[14] Philip II to Olivares, San Lorenzo 22 July 1586, CSP Simancas (1580-86) 593-95.
[15] R.J. Knecht, *The French Wars of Religion 1559-1598* (London, 1989) pp. 59-63.

Prince of Parma to conduct the venture and offered him ports and other conveniences. Word had already reached Rome of the Parma's capture of the city of Neuss, in July and Parsons trusted "in God that one day we shall see the same thing happen in London."[16] Any possibility for success was destroyed by the discovery of yet another plot. Writing from Paris on 10 September 1586, Mendoza reported to Philip rumours of a plot to assassinate Elizabeth.[17] The Babington Plot succeeded in eliminating from the political stage the one person capable of holding the English Catholics together.

After the major conspirators were dealt with, a commission was sent to Fotheringay to try Mary for her complicity in the plot, according to provisions of the "Act for the Queen's Safety." The court judged that the government possessed conclusive evidence of Mary's complicity in her letter to Anthony Babington and condemned the Scottish Queen.

A new Parliament, summoned for 15 October 1586, convened on the 29th.[18] The safety of the Queen was the major topic. Diatribes against Mary were frequent. Sir Christopher Hatton called her "the hope of all idolatry"; Sir Walter Mildmay labelled her "the principal conspirator and the very root from which all the other lewd weeds do spring."[19] One after another members of Parliament recited Mary's involvement in various conspiracies against Elizabeth. Job Throckmorton, the newly elected representative from Warwick, strongly attacked Jesuits and all Roman Catholics for their machinations against the Gospel and the English Queen. About Mary Stuart he said:

> If I should term her the daughter of sedition, the mother of rebellion, the nurse of impiety, the handmaid of iniquity, the sister of unshamefastness; or if I should tell you that which you already know—that she is Scottish of nation, French of education, Papist of profession, a Guisan of blood, a Spaniard in practice, a libertine in life: as all this were not to flatter her, so yet this were nothing near to describe her.[20]

Elizabeth's leniency in 1572 towards Mary was recalled to demonstrate that the danger now must not be handed so kindly. Not one voice in either house of Parliament urged continued leniency. Since her arrival in England, Mary has been a problem. If she again escaped punishment, the parliamentary

---

[16] Rome 22 August 1586, in Hicks, *Letters of Persons*, pp. 283-85.

[17] CSP Simancas (1580-86) 623. See also the correspondence on pp. 603-16. The proclamation ordering the arrest of the Babington conspirators, dated 2 August 1586, can be found in Paul L. Hughes and James F. Larkin, C.S.V., eds., *Tudor Royal Proclamations*, 3 vols. (New Haven, 1964-69) II, 525-26.

[18] On the work of this Parliament see J.E. Neale, *Elizabeth I and Her Parliaments*, 2 vols. (London, 1953, 1957) II, 103-91.

[19] Quoted in Neale, *Elizabeth I and Her Parliaments*, II, 107, 108.

[20] Quoted in Neale, *Elizabeth I and Her Parliaments*, II, 110.

petition contended, Elizabeth would "be exposed to many more, and those more secret and dangerous conspiracies than before."[21]

Regardless of evidence against Mary, Elizabeth was averse to ordering the execution of a legitimate monarch. An added fear was the possible effect on James. Would it drive him into the welcoming arms of the Spaniards? But the campaign against Mary gained momentum. When it became clear that her son was more concerned with his right to succeed to the English throne than with the life of his mother, nothing could save her.

Parliament was adjourned on 2 December and was due to reconvene on 15 February. Mary's sentence was proclaimed on 4 December but Elizabeth still hesitated on its enforcement.[22] Elizabeth had ten and a half weeks to act. Under the skilful direction of Lord Burghley, Elizabeth was guided past various scruples into signing the warrant for Mary's execution.[23] She was executed on 8 February 1587.[24] Robert Southwell honoured the greatest victim of the plot with a poem "Decease release," which concludes:

> Rue not my death, rejoyce at my repose,
> It was no death to me but to my woe,
> The budd was opened to lett out the Rose,
> The cheynes unloo'sd to lett the captive goe.
>
> A prince by birth, a prisoner by mishappe,
> From Crowne to crosse, from throne to thrall I fell,
> My right my ruthe, my titles wrought my trapp,
> My weale my woe, my worldly heaven my hell.
>
> By death from prisoner to a prince enhaunc'd,
> From Crosse to Crowne, from thrall to throne againe,
> My ruth my right, my trapp my stile advaunc'd,
> From woe to weale, from hell to heavenly raigne.[25]

Mary's death moved one man to poetry; it moved others closer to the Spanish crown. On the day the news of her execution reached Rome, 24 March 1587, Parsons and Allen drafted a memorial on Philip's claim to the English title.

---

[21] Quoted in Neale, *Elizabeth I and Her Parliaments*, II, 113.

[22] See the royal proclamation in Hughes and Larkin, *Tudor Royal Proclamations*, II, 528-32.

[23] On Burghley's craft see Allison Heisch, "Arguments for an Execution: Queen Elizabeth's 'White Paper' and Lord Burghley's 'Blue Pencil,'" *Albion* 24 (1992) 591-604.

[24] On 6 February 1587 another royal proclamation ordered suppression of "sundry lewd and seditious bruits" recently spread throughout the realm. Although the precise nature of the rumours was not mentioned, apparently they dealt with stories about Mary's escape (Hughes and Larkin, *Tudor Royal Proclamations*, II, 534-35).

[25] *The Poems of Robert Southwell, S.J.*, eds. James H. McDonald and Nancy Pollard Brown (Oxford, 1967) pp. 47-48.

230   CHAPTER SIX

III

Shortly before Mary's execution an episode on the continent corroborated the government's fears of Catholics. English involvement in the Low Countries escalated consistently. When the Earl of Leicester was sent to Flushing to become Governor-General, there were 8000 English soldiers in Holland. His efforts to establish stronger centralized authority, originally hampered by Dutch disagreement on procedure, ended when Elizabeth recalled him to England to aid her deliberations on the fate of Mary Stuart. While Leicester was gone, two of his commanders betrayed the city of Deventer.[26]

In October of 1586 English forces commanded by Sir William Pelham and Sir William Stanley gained control of Deventer, a prosperous commercial centre. The garrison of mainly Irish soldiers recruited by Stanley was placed under his command. In late November Leicester returned to England; he delegated his executive authority to the Council of State and relinquished command of the English forces to Sir John Norris. He left Stanley independent of both. The garrison was not popular in the city. The soldiers were on edge and discontented, a situation that their lack of food, clothing, and money intensified. On 18/28 January 1587 Stanley freely yielded Deventer to the Spaniards and, with twelve hundred Irish soldiers, offered his services to Spain. The following day Sir Rowland Yorke handed over the Sconce of Zutphen, a fortress opposite the Spanish garrison in Zutphen.[27] Stanley forfeited a brilliant English career by his actions. He had already had the friendship and trust of the Earl of Leicester and some considered him the Earl's likely successor in the Netherlands and a possible candidate for Lord Deputy of Ireland. Nonetheless Stanley surrendered the city.[28]

Leo Hicks, S.J., claimed that Stanley was motivated by conscience: because Stanley and most of his soldiers were Catholics, he resented holding a city, most of whose inhabitants were Catholics, for Calvinist rebels. Albert Loomie, S.J., on the other hand, contended that Stanley's conversion to Catholicism and his surrender of the city would remain debated points

---

[26] Peter Limm, *The Dutch Revolt 1559-1648* (London, 1989) pp. 57, 60-61.

[27] Similar episodes followed. Within two years English troops at Gertruidenberg turned that city over to the Spanish because they had not been paid. Ghent was sold by some of the forces under the command of Sir John Norris, and Parma purchased Alost from the English captain William Pigot. But as Albert J. Loomie, S.J., points out, advantages to the Spanish were "more psychological than strategic" (*The Spanish Elizabethans: The English Exiles at the Court of Philip II* [New York, 1963] p. 140).

[28] For a biography of Stanley see Loomie, *Spanish Elizabethans*, pp. 129-81. The most recent analysis of Stanley's actions can be found in Simon Adams, "A Patriot For Whom?: Stanley, York and Elizabeth's Catholics," *History Today* 37 (July, 1987) 46-50.

because of Stanley's silence on these issues.[29] Although neither William Allen nor Robert Parsons had met Stanley before his surrender, Allen immediately came to his defence.[30]

The copie of a letter written by M. Doctor Allen: concerning the yeelding up, of the citie of Daventrie[31] was formulated in response to a query addressed by an unnamed English gentleman. The question, posed as a "case of conscience" was this: was Stanley's act treasonous or lawful? Could it be defended? Allen's reply was clear if not concise: "the rendering up of such townes, and places of the lowecountries as be in anie English menes custodie, is not onlie lawful, but necessarie to be done, under paine of mortal sinne, and damnation."[32] The fundamental reason was unlawful acquisition. The English government had no legal right to the towns, but had acquired them through aid furnished to rebels against their rightful monarch, a man who had not offended the English Queen.

Such involvement, however, was utterly consistent with the policies of the Queen: aid to heretics abroad and despoliation of the true Church at home. In both, the government endeavoured to use Catholics to destroy one another by testifying against one another at home and by fighting one another abroad. Catholics who knowingly participated in the destruction of other Catholics, Allen contends, incurred excommunication.[33] When wars were waged solely for religion and one party was an excommunicated prince, any Catholic aiding that prince was excommunicated.[34] At such times, a Catholic was freed from oaths of fidelity or of allegiance, because "those that breake with God" could not make any claim on their subjects. Allen, however, went a step farther. The surrender of Deventer was not

---

[29] Garrett Mattingly, *The Defeat of the Spanish Armada* (London, 1959) pp. 60-61; Leo Hicks, S.J., "Allen and Deventer (1587)," *The Month* 163 (1934) 505-17; Loomie, *Spanish Elizabethans*, pp. 129-47.

[30] Loomie notes that Allen did not meet Stanley until late 1589, and Parsons did not until the spring of 1590 (*Spanish Elizabethans*, p. 141). The second date is especially important because of attempts to blame Stanley's act on the influence of Parsons and the Jesuits. On this issue see Hicks, "Allen and Deventer," 508-10.

[31] (Antwerp, 1587) STC 370, ARCR, II, no. 8.

[32] *Copie of a letter*, p. 6.

[33] Allen's assertion that Stanley was morally bound to act as he did under pain of mortal sin is at variance with directions laid down by Acquaviva on 15 December 1582 for Jesuits in France. The occasion was the Duke of Alençon's attack on Netherlands. Could Catholics serve in his army? Could they fight in this war? Acquaviva instructed the fathers that they could not offer decisions regarding the quarrel, or refuse absolution to those who believed their prince was right. See John H. Pollen, S.J., "The Politics of the English Catholics during the Reign of Elizabeth," *The Month* 99 (1902) 404. In his autobiography (*William Weston: The Autobiography of an Elizabethan*, ed. Philip Caraman, S.J., [London, 1955] pp. 88-89), Weston told how he had persuaded a gentleman to "withdraw the military assistance he was giving to the Earl of Leicester in the unjust war he was waging with the heretics of Flanders against the King of Spain." One wonders how widespread this sentiment was.

[34] *Copie of a letter*, pp. 14-15, 19.

only justifiable, but exemplary. He encouraged other soldiers to do likewise: "al other of honour, conscience, and Religion, of our countrie, are bound to doe [the same that you have done]: as wel in this warre, as in al other, which either at home, or abrode, is waged for, or against Religion."

Praying that the example of Stanley would induce others to follow, Allen hoped that "when it shal please God to have mercie of our desolate countrie, [Catholic soldiers will be] not only restorers of old militare vertue, and discipline in the same: but be notable helpers by the valerous arme of your Christian Knighthoode, to reduce your people, to the obedience of Christes Church: & deliver our Catholike freindes, & brethren from the damnable, & untolerable yoke of Haeresie, and her most impure leaders."[35]

Although the surrender of Deventer did cause a stir, the small number of books about it published by the government and by Catholics is surprising.[36] Perhaps the incident was overtaken by subsequent events: the execution of Mary and the final preparations for the Armada. Three points, however, must not be overlooked. (1) The surrender of Deventer confirmed, and Allen's defense substantiated, government suspicions about the allegiance of the Catholics. (2) The surrender validated assertions of exiles such as Allen

---

[35] *Copie of a letter*, pp. 20, 21, 24, 28-29.

[36] According to Peter Milward in *Religious Controversies of the Elizabethan Age* ([London, 1977]) pp. 110-11), Allen's work was published in two different English editions in 1587 and translated into French in the following year. There was only one response: *A briefe discoverie of doctor Allens seditious drifts* ([London, 1588] STC 6166) by the anonymous G.D. Surprisingly moderate for a work of this type, the author in his rebuttal advanced now traditional arguments against papal usurpation of power and in favour of the legitimate authority of princes. The author was shrewd enough to perceive the main objective of the book: "wholy to prepare the mindes of the Romish Recusants (such as are apt hearers, and readie followers of his doctrine) for the furtherance and assistance of all seditious practises, that maie bee mooved and attempted against her Maiestie by the malicious Associates of that wicked confederacie" (p. 37). William Lightfoote's *The complaint of England* ([London, 1587] STC 15595), although it does not specifically treat Allen and Deventer, was an anti-Spanish diatribe that dismissed Jesuits as "Iscariots" and exhorted Catholics to obey their prince: "If I had [England is the speaker] consumed your wealth by the exactions of Naples, if I had disturbed your quiet by the Inquisition of Sevil, if I had tyrannized your lives by Spanish crueltyes, or inthralled your soules to Romish superstition, then might you have shaped out some shadow of reason, & pretended argument of probability, for the opposing of your selves, and the deposing of her, who had sought to torment you with such hellish miseries" (sig. B 2ᵛ), but one does not experience such treatment in England. In an undated letter to Father Acquaviva, Robert Southwell wrote of a reply to the defense of Stanley. Although many applauded the rejoinder, "in my judgement," wrote Southwell, "the pamphlet is insipid enough and most foreign to all sense of Christian justice, since in it a certain courtier—and he is either an atheist or plays the role of a theologian of uncertain faith—makes examples of war the foundations of his axioms" (ARSI, Fondo Gesuitico, 651/648 [in Thomas M. McCoog, S.J., ed., "The Letters of Robert Southwell, S.J.," *AHSI* 63 (1994) 110-11]). I do not know of any reply to Allen that fits this description. Interestingly Southwell was far more concerned about Protestant replies to the works of Robert Bellarmine. In this context see Robert W. Richgels, "The Pattern of Controversy In a Counter-Reformation Classic: The *Controversies* of Robert Bellarmine," *SCJ* 11 (1980) 3-15.

and Parsons that English Catholics would support a Spanish enterprise. (3) Finally, the surrender deepened division among English Catholics. Not every Catholic approved of Stanley's decision. A letter claiming to have been written by a Jesuit in England, but actually written by George Gifford, rejected Allen's explanation. The wars in the Netherlands were, according to Gifford, deemed necessary by the Queen and her Council for the welfare of the kingdom. That reason should be sufficient for a good subject. Moreover the Spanish fought not as Catholics but as enemies of England. When in the course of a discussion someone introduced the book recently written by Allen "or some other in his name,"[37] many were angered. They could not believe that Allen would write something so contradictory to his earlier works, and concluded that it was maliciously published in order to make "our cause odious to the world."[38] The rejoinder of these dissatisfied Catholics, who claim to represent the majority, is unfortunately only outlined, but its very composition does highlight the split among English Catholics over a subject's proper relations with a heretical monarch.

The anonymous letter that prompted *Copie of a letter* assured Allen that the two priests expected imminently would find "a verie ripe, and plentiful harvest to labour in, and be right welcome to manie hundreth soules, greedely expecting instruction to their salvation" if Allen could justify Stanley's act.[39] Allen hoped that a justification of Stanley's decision would prompt others to reconsider their involvement in these religious wars and eventually to defect to the Spanish cause. Thus the English army, spiritually fortified by its chaplains, could play a role in restoring Catholicism.

IV

In a letter to Rome shortly after his arrival in England on 25 July 1586, Robert Southwell complained of being "hemmed in by daily perils." A few days later, as the Babington Plot intensified persecution, increased surveillance in Bishopsgate, where Walsingham's agents lay in wait to catch

---

[37] Reluctance to accept Allen as author continued until this century. Ethelred Taunton (*History of the Jesuits in England* [London, 1901] pp. 120-21) has "no hesitation in saying it was the work of Robert Parsons and that Allen's name was used in accordance with the wish of those who reserved to themselves the right to decide under whose name political works should appear." See Hicks, "Allen and Deventer," 514-15.

[38] This letter can be found in SC, Coll. P, p. 329 (printed in Knox, *Letters of Allen*, pp. 299-301). On its authorship see Hicks, "Allen and Deventer," 515-17 and Devlin, *Robert Southwell*, pp. 154-56. Devlin suggests that Anthony Browne, Viscount Montague, had something to do with the publication because "it was always his earnest endeavour to combine his religious fidelity with a display of most meticulous loyalty" (p. 155). On Montague see Pritchard, *Catholic Loyalism*, pp. 44-49.

[39] [p. 4].

Babington, resulted in Weston's capture on 3 August.[40] Imprisoned in the Tower, Weston watched many Catholics personally known to him transported up the river:

> Catholics, tied hand and foot, were ferried along the river, up and down between the Tower of London and the tribunals . . . . It was easy to notice when these men were taken along the river in boats, for you could pick them out by the uniforms and weapons of the soldiers, and you could see the vast hustling mob of spectators and the countless people who took off in light boats and followed them the entire reach of the river.[41]

Wild rumours of an impending invasion to be followed by a general massacre spread throughout England.[42] The movements of Henry Garnet and Southwell were carefully watched; both were nearly captured. On 21 December Southwell listed the Jesuits then in prison: William Crichton, Ralph Emerson, Thomas Pounde, Thomas Metham, and now William Weston. Southwell castigated "the men who set on foot that wicked and ill-fated conspiracy, which did to the Catholic cause so great mischief, that even our enemies, had they had the choice, could never have chosen aught more mischievous to us or more to their mind."[43] Life was even more precarious and "yet the souls of Catholics are more precious than our

---

[40] On Weston and Babington see Caraman, *William Weston*, pp. 88-108.

[41] Caraman, *William Weston*, p. 83. Evidence of intensified surveillance can be seen in the number of papers from this period preserved in PRO that list names of priests and known Papists, and their places of residence. See SP 12/193/67; 12/195/30, 32, 34, 45, 46, 74, 77, 107, 115; 12/199/15, 91; 12/202/53, 61; 12/205/13, 14; 12/206/74, 75, 77 (many of which are published in John H. Pollen, S.J., "The Official Lists of Catholic Prisoners during the Reign of Queen Elizabeth, Part II, 1581-1602," in *Miscellanea II* [London, 1906] pp. 219-88). A new proclamation (ca. 6 May 1586) to explain the execution of seminary priests William Marsden and Robert Anderton claimed, again, that the priests "at the instigation of the pope and others favoring his pretended tyrannous authority over the crown of England and envying the happy and blessed state of her majesty's said government came daily into the realm to pervert and seduce her majesty's good subjects under color of religion, to draw them from their due and natural obedience towards her majesty and her crown, and to prepare their minds and bodies to assist such foreign invasion as was certainly discovered to be intended by the said pope and his adherents [the Babington Plot] . . ." (Hughes and Larkin, *Tudor Royal Proclamations*, II, 518-21).

[42] E.g. "Advices from Calais," [c. December 1586], CSP Foreign (1586-88) 174.

[43] Southwell to Acquaviva, 21 December 1586, in Pollen, *Unpublished Documents*, p. 314. See also the General's reply of 20 February 1587, ARSI, Franc. 1/I, ff. 290^v-291^r (printed in *Unpublished Documents*, pp. 319-21). In a letter written to Father Agazzari on the 22nd, Southwell warned that the men preparing for the mission "should gird themselves for heavier trials than their companions have hitherto suffered; for the sea is more boisterous than usual, and swept by fiercer storms. I do not say this to frighten them; for they know how securely those ride the waves who have Christ for pilot" (*ibid.*, p. 317). In the same letter Southwell told of rumours currently circulating that the Pope would send no more Jesuits but "whatever the case may be, we who are here have alone 'to bear the burden and heats of the day' till others arrive" (*ibid.*, p. 318).

bodies; and when one reckons the price at which they are brought, it should not seem much to endanger our lives for their salvation."

Effects of the plot on English Catholics continued into 1587. Mildmay and Throckmorton denounced the beleaguered nature of England and Protestantism. There was, according to Throckmorton, a "pestilent conspiracy against the Church of God and the professors of holy religion." The recent plot to assassinate Elizabeth and to establish Mary on the English throne was one aspect of what was alleged to be general Catholic policy: the destruction of Protestantism throughout Europe. According to Mildmay, "England, our native country, one of the most renowned monarchies in the world, against which the Pope beareth a special eye of envy and malice: envy for the wealth and peace that we enjoy through the goodness of Almighty God. . .; malice for the religion of the Gospel which we profess whereby the dignity of his triple crown is almost shaken in pieces."[44] To preserve the reformed religion against the intrigues of Catholic powers, new measures against recusants were needed. In March of 1587 the government amended a law of 1581 that imposed a fine of £20 per month for refusal to attend the established Church. According to the revised law (29 Eliz. c. 6) refusal to attend could result in the confiscation of two-thirds of recusants' property.[45]

On 26 August 1587 Garnet informed the General of the rigour with which these new laws were enforced.[46] He hoped that Catholics throughout the world would be informed of this new disaster, "for who could refrain from tears if he witnessed the worries of the widows, the orphaning of children, the dispersion of upright families, and finally the reduction of all Catholics to almost extreme beggary"? More and more frequently Catholics were cast into prisons built for punishment of the most criminal of men. More and more Catholics were hauled before judges, not to reply to alleged crimes but to answer questions about future possibilities. One obliged to answer such "Bloody Questions" was William Weston.[47] According to Garnet, the Jesuit handled himself well. When asked if he would take up arms should the papacy invade the kingdom, he replied that his vocation as

---

[44] Quoted in Neale, *Elizabeth I and Her Parliaments*, II, 168, 169.

[45] See John LaRocca, S.J., "English Catholics and the Recusancy Laws 1558-1625: A Study in Religion and Politics," (unpublished Ph.D. thesis: Rutgers University, 1977) 109-18.

[46] Garnet to Acquaviva, London 26 August 1587, ARSI, Fondo Gesuitico 651/624. See also the letter of 29 (o.s.) August 1587 in the same collection. On Weston's examination see his account in Caraman, *William Weston*, pp. 120-23. For Southwell's accounts of difficulties, see his letters to the General on 12 January and 26 and 28 August 1587, ARSI, Fondo Gesuitico 651/648 (in McCoog, "Southwell," 104-08).

[47] Patrick McGrath's study "The Bloody Questions Reconsidered" (*RH* 20 [1991] 305-19) is a much needed attempt to penetrate the confessional apologetic that has surrounded this issue to a more objective analysis of the nature and purpose of the questions.

a priest prevented him from fighting in a war. The government changed its approach and asked for which side he, as a priest, would pray. He answered that he "would simply ask that the will of God be done on earth as it is in heaven."

Despite the increased persecution, Garnet believed that there was a rich harvest that needed cultivation. Send more men! Garnet hoped that his description of life in England would not frighten potential recruits: "There is still life and spirit among the Catholics. Let the priests come dependent upon divine providence, armed with hope in the Lord, well instructed in virtue, and dead to the world and its affections." Southwell, although in a "most fruitful position" (i.e. with the Countess of Arundel) could not move around freely because it was not "to his advantage to desert the house in which he lives without someone to substitute for him." If there were more men, someone could live with him and they could take turns ministering to Catholics in London.

Garnet asked the General's advice on a number of pastoral problems that were arising. Was it licit for a priest, asked by a magistrate whether or not he was a priest, to deny it? Was this tantamount to denying Christ himself? Advice was needed on a number of irregular marriages contracted without dispensations, the possession of ecclesiastical furnishings from the suppressed monasteries and abbeys, and the lack of holy oil.

One achievement unmentioned by Garnet in his August letter was the establishment of a secret printing press in England. At the semi-annual meeting held in London in February, Garnet, taking advantage of his experience and of his contacts with the Stationers' Company, advised Southwell on the press. Its exact location remains unknown, but it seems that it was situated in the outskirts of London and was in operation by the spring of 1587.[48]

The successful erection of a press probably compounded Garnet's financial woes. The fund established by Weston's friends was not adequate, and Garnet had to find some way to supplement it. Sometime after the press was started, Garnet left London and travelled between Catholic houses in the provinces. He returned to London in February 1588 and remained there until

---

[48] Philip Caraman, S.J., *Henry Garnet (1555-1606) and the Gunpowder Plot* (London, 1964) pp. 42-44. See also Devlin, *Robert Southwell*, pp. 138-48. Nancy Pollard Brown argues that the press was established in a house owned by the Countess of Arundel within the precinct of the former Augustinian hospital near Spitalfields ("Paperchase: The Dissemination of Catholic Texts in Elizabethan England," in *English Manuscript Studies 1100-1700*, vol. 1, eds. Peter Beal and Jeremy Griffiths [Oxford, 1989] p. 123). On the importance of the printed word for the Society's mission see Brown's "Robert Southwell: The Mission of the Written Word," in *The Reckoned Expense: Edmund Campion and the Early English Jesuits. Essays in Celebration of the First Centenary of Campion Hall, Oxford (1896-1996)*, ed. Thomas M. McCoog, S.J., (Woodbridge, 1996) pp. 193-214.

July because "the rumours of war indicated that it was unsafe to travel around, and there is no better place to be than London for the assurance of good results."

The mission was making progress despite persecution: "Enclosed within private walls we are not reporting the fruit that would certainly be more abundant if we were able to preach from the roofs what we can now say into the ears of only a few." Because each priest was able to work with only a few persons, the mission was still in great need of men. Whether one worked with heretics, "and they cannot be converted in one conversation,"[49] or with schismatics, "and these you do not draw away from the meetings of the heretics with one disputation," or with Catholics, "it was not possible to cultivate a perfect piety in one day," more priests were needed. If the General sent more men, at least two could remain in London and the others could be given individual counties for their ministries.[50]

In 1586 Robert Southwell had met Anne Howard, Countess of Arundel, a fateful encounter for many reasons. In April of 1585 her husband Philip Howard, Earl of Arundel, had been arrested while trying to cross the channel to consult William Allen. Seized and thrown into the Tower, he never saw Anne again.[51] Deprived of Howard House and a considerable amount of her income, Anne lived in Arundel House on the Strand. The Countess's cautious desire to have a priest for the sacraments led to her introduction to Southwell in late 1586.[52] Anne provided shelter and support; she contributed money and what little protection she could to Jesuits and other Catholics. Because there had been no criminal charge levelled against the Earl, he might be released at any time. Southwell's efforts to console him during his period of imprisonment produced one of the gems of recusant literature, *An epistle of comfort*, written sometime between 1587 and 1588 and published by the secret press in London.[53]

In passages vibrant with imagery, Southwell consoles those who are unjustly persecuted for their faith. To suffer adversity for a good cause, the poet reminds his readers, "is not onlye the liverye and cognizance of Christ, but the very principall royal garment, which he chose to weare in this lyfe.

---

[49] Presumably the original prohibition against any dealings with heretics had been revoked.

[50] Garnet to Acquaviva, 9 June 1588, ARSI, Fondo Gesuitico 651/624. On Jesuit techniques for conversion see Michael Questier, "'Like Locusts over all the World': Conversion, Indoctrination and the Society of Jesus in late Elizabethan and Jacobean England," in *The Reckoned Expense: Edmund Campion and the Early English Jesuits. Essays in Celebration of the First Centenary of Campion Hall, Oxford (1896-1996)*, ed. Thomas M. McCoog, S.J., (Woodbridge, 1996) pp. 265-84.

[51] See Weston's account of Philip Howard in Caraman, *William Weston*, pp. 12-15.

[52] Devlin, *Robert Southwell*, pp. 131-35. See also C.A. Newdigate, "A New Chapter in the Life of B. Robert Southwell, S.J.," *The Month* 157 (1931) 246-54.

[53] (Paris [*vere* London], n.d. [1587-88]) STC 22946, ARCR, II, no. 714.

And thefore can it not be taken of a soldier but wel, to be cladd with his captaines harness, or of a disciple, to be like his maister." Our cause is the one, true Church, catholic and universal, untouched by theological novelties and consecrated by the blood of numerous martyrs. "Christianitie is a warfare, and Christians spiritual Soldiers, their conflictes continuall, though their enemies be divers." The Church was born in the suffering and death of Jesus and continues to grow through the "blood and slaughtered limmes of Gods Saincts." Those suffering now are thus playing a most important role in the Church.

Regardless of temptations, Southwell exhorts his readers to remain strong: "Let us hyde our heade in the helmett of salvation, that our eares yelde not to bloodye menacinges, our eyes detest heretycall bookes and service, our forehead always keepe the signe of the Croose, and our tongue be alwayes readye to professe our faythe." Even if our suffering should result in martyrdom, we can be consoled: "why should a dutyfull childe feare, to goe to his heavenly Father, a penitent soule to his sweete Saviour, an obedient member, to be ioyned with his head. If he came into this worlde to redeeme us, why should we doubte, but at our death he will receyve us, especiallye if we dye for him, as he dyed for us."

Unlike the deaths of Protestants, the executions of Catholics are true martyrdoms: "How is it possible for them to have the trueth of martirdome, that wante the trueth of Christe." Without the true faith, the executions of Protestants are "punishment for theyr perfidiousness." Martyrdom cannot be a just punishment for a crime, and so whoever is justly executed "Sainte he maye be, if he repente him of his faulte, and take his deathe as his iust deserte; But Martyre he can not be, though he endure never so manye deathes or tormentes." Therefore, Southwell concludes, "Rack us, torture us, condemne us, yea grinde us: youre iniquitye is a proofe of our fathe: You open us the waye to our desyred felycitye."

In a humble disclaimer in the introduction to the book, Southwell apologized for his work: "For as to the wayfaring pilgrim, wandering in the darke, and mistye night, every light, though never so litle, is comfortable: & to the stranger, that traveyleth in a land of divers language, any that can (though it but be brokenlye) speake his contrye tongue, doth not a litle reioyce: So peradventure in this foggye night of heresie, and the confusion of tongues, which it hath here in our land procured, this dime light, which I have set before you, and these my Catholicke, though broken speaches, which I shall use unto you will not be altogether unpleasant."[54] Catholics had found their most eloquent spokesman since Campion. In language as elevated, with sentiments as confident as Campion's "Brag," Southwell

---

[54] *Epistle of comfort*, ff. 24^v, 93^v, 130^v, 122^{r-v}, 182^v, 183^v, 186^v, 198^r, 3^v.

provided oppressed Catholics with a spirituality to sustain and encourage them.[55] As a result the government escalated its search for him.

V

Between Mary's trial and execution, Catholic exiles reformulated their strategy. It was imperative that someone be recognised as leader by all English Catholics. Unless that was done quickly, according to a memorial presented to Pope Sixtus V by Antonio, Cardinal Caraffa on 14 March 1587, English Catholics would abandon hope, and divisions among them would become even more pronounced. Of English Catholics, the memorial continued, the best qualified was William Allen. He was "unbiased, learned, of good manners, judicious, deeply versed in all English affairs, and the negotiations for the submission of the country to the church, all the instruments of which have been his pupils." Consequently Caraffa recommended that Allen be named cardinal. The Pope's reply was brief: as soon as Philip launched the enterprise, he would elevate Allen. For canonical reasons he did not wish to elevate Allen now unless the necessity of the enterprise "forced" him to do so.[56] Until the elevation, Parsons recommended that Philip persuade Sixtus to appoint Allen Archbishop of Canterbury as compensation.[57]

With Mary's execution imminent, the question of her successor became more urgent. Even before news of her death reached Rome, Allen entreated Philip to proceed with the enterprise. All English Catholics, according to Allen, clamoured for Philip to invade "to crown his glorious efforts in the holy cause of Christ by punishing this woman, hated of God and man, and restoring the country to its ancient glory and liberty." As a descendant of the House of Lancaster, Philip had a good claim to the English throne. Nonetheless this legitimate claim should not be the grounds for the invasion. Philip's war on England had two just causes "approved by divine and human laws and worthy of being declared just by a bull of the Apostolic See. These are to avenge the wrong done to religion and to obtain reparation for injuries received; the former of which will approve itself to every catholic, and the latter will not appear devoid of sound probability even to the heretics."[58]

Days later, when Mary's death was known in Rome, Allen and Parsons elaborated on Philip's claim to the English throne. They concluded their

---

[55] See Brown's "Robert Southwell" for a discussion of his adaptation of Ignatian spirituality for the Countess.
[56] CSP Simancas (1587-1603) 36-38. See also the note on 38.
[57] Olivares to Philip II, Rome 16 March 1587, CSP Simancas (1587-1603) 38-40.
[58] Allen to Philip II, Rome 19 March 1587, CSP Simancas (1587-1603) 41 (I use a translation from Knox, *Letters of Allen*, xc).

genealogical survey with a legitimation of Philip's title: no one within England and Scotland could base a claim on descent through the House of Lancaster; all claimants through descent from the House of York were unfit because of heresy or other defects; the only person outside the kingdom with a claim from the House of Lancaster was Philip; any other possible claimant had no means whereby he could enforce the claim; Philip was named as Mary's successor in her will;[59] with good grounds for going to war, the conquest of the kingdom would be just; it was fair that Philip have the kingdom as compensation for losses inflicted on him by English interference in the Netherlands; according to a decree of the Lateran Council, Catholics might retain all land taken from heretics if there was no Catholic heir; finally, Philip would be warmly welcomed and joyfully received by the English Catholics.[60]

Despite assurances that Catholics would eagerly accept Spanish succession, Parsons did not think it expedient to settle the issue definitively before the enterprise because public declaration of a Spanish succession would aid the heretics by widening divisions among Catholic exiles, and could result in loss of foreign support. The French and Scottish kings and the Pope might become suspicious. They might interpret Spain's efforts as an attempt to dominate Europe, undertaken "for reasons of state, and not for the sake of religion." At the moment the world believed that the enterprise was undertaken to restore Catholicism and to avenge insults against Philip and the faith. Nothing should be done that would make the world doubt these intentions. Once the enterprise was successfully concluded there would be no other Catholic claimant. Then Philip could present his credentials.[61]

Preparations moved into high gear with Mary's death. Immediately Olivares petitioned the Pope for Allen's elevation, and Allen and Parsons reiterated their conviction that something must be done in Scotland to distract Elizabeth or to prevent the Scots from assisting her during the enterprise.[62] Regarding the succession the two decided to say nothing: they would simply reply to any query that all Catholic hopes should be placed on

---

[59] We have noted Jensen's argument in his "Phantom Will of Mary Queen of Scots," that there never was such a will but it was simply a ploy devised by Mary to force the Spanish King into assisting her.

[60] Hicks, *Letters of Parsons*, pp. 299-303. See pp. 306-09 for another memorial of this period, and Knox, *Letters of Allen*, xcix-c.

[61] This memorial, dated 18 March, was written before Rome learned of Mary's death. It can be found in CSP Simancas (1587-1603) 41-43. A curious note has been added: "Melino [Parsons], although a servant of the Guises, had been won over to the Spanish side by Allen and Olivares, but it will be seen by the above document that he still had a leaning to the policy of his nominal master, Guise, who would have preferred to see his cousin James Catholic King of England."

[62] Olivares to Philip II, Rome 27 March 1587, CSP Simancas (1587-1603) 50-54; Allen to Philip II, Rome 30 March 1587, *ibid.*, 54.

the Spanish King. Allen denounced the Queen as an impious, traitorous usurper and begged Philip to act. Allen's role remained crucial.

Before Allen had an audience with the Pope, Olivares gave him a concise list of answers to be given to any possible papal question. Allen was to take this opportunity to encourage the Pope to support the Spanish enterprise by quelling papal doubts, and was to stress the nature of Mary's death: she died not just a Catholic but a martyr who did not, contrary to evil reports, recommend her son to the Queen of England.[63] Throughout Mary's distress, Allen would continue, France made no serious attempt to aid her, because the French King had an understanding with Elizabeth. The French remained undependable and consequently had better be excluded from any enterprise. In case the question of succession were raised, Allen must emphasize that English Catholics have avoided disputes on this subject, but they realize the hopelessness of converting James Stuart. If pressed further, Allen should add that the majority of English Catholics believed that the best claimant was the descendant of the Lancastrian/Portuguese line: the current King of Spain.[64]

VI

Despite James's vacillations and Parsons's and Allen's exhortations to support Spain, many in Scotland and England continued to regard the Scottish King as the preferred Catholic candidate. Once again from late 1586 into 1587, news regarding Catholic prospects in Scotland was bright, so bright that more Jesuits were demanded, and a better organized local administration requested. Among their successes Jesuits reported the conversions of three of Scotland's greatest nobles and many gentlemen. Only a shortage of priests prevented an even greater harvest. Two more Jesuits were sent in 1586: William Ogilvie and Robert Abercrombie.[65] Because of

---

[63] Mary Stuart assumed the central role in Richard Verstegan's martyrology, *Theatrum crudelitatum haereticorum nostri temporis* (Antwerp, 1587) ARCR, I, no. 1297. See A.G. Petti, "Richard Verstegan and Catholic Martyrologies of the Later Elizabethan Period," *RH* 5 (1959) 64-90.

[64] CSP Simancas (1587-1603) 55-56.

[65] Preserved in ARSI with a memorial requesting more Jesuits, a more definite structure, and marital dispensations (Angl. 42, ff. 33^r-34^r) is a list of cases of conscience submitted by Jesuits in Scotland to their colleagues on the continent for consideration (Angl. 42, ff. 225^{r-v}). One case I shall cite fully: "If Catholics are invited by the King himself and taken to the sermons of the heretics—sermons which are unaccompanied by heretical prayers and not dangerous to listen to—can they with safe conscience be present at such, when without serious loss they cannot avoid these sermons, and their presence would cause no scandal?"

"Reply: Such sermons are to be avoided, since it is almost incredible that men, uncultured and little versed in matters of religion, can be present at them without danger to their souls. But if it be certain, or extremely probable, that there is no scandal nor any danger to their souls, then, for the common good but not for any personal advantage, they can be present, provided no prayers be added." Crichton, in whose handwriting the above case is, later explained to

the increase in the number of Scottish Jesuits working in their homeland, Father Acquaviva asked that William Holt be recalled and released for a new assignment. Holt was then appointed rector of the English College in Rome.[66]

The conversions of such influential nobles strengthened hopes for the King's eventual conversion. William Crichton, recently released from the Tower and safe on the continent, insisted that the King could be converted and that his succession to the English throne should be secured. According to Crichton James should not be abandoned to the Protestant lords: he was Elizabeth's legitimate successor and more acceptable to the English than Philip. As long as James had champions, he remained a viable candidate, and the succession was a confused matter. Aware that public disagreement would create problems, Parsons and Allen temporized with the Scottish party by listening to proposals that included James, perhaps even married to the Spanish Infanta.[67] Once again an expedition was dispatched to convert the Scottish King. William Chisholm, Bishop of Dunblane, was accompanied by Crichton and another Jesuit, Alexander MacQuhirrie.[68] Olivares did all he

---

Acquaviva (Paris 4 June 1603) that the difference between Scottish and English Jesuits is this: Scottish Jesuits, although they do not allow Catholics to frequent heretical sermons, "don't hold those who occasionally go to the heretic's sermons to be schismatical or to need any other reconciliation to the Church than that of sacramental confession." On this issue see Hubert Chadwick, S.J., "Crypto-Catholicism, English and Scottish," *The Month* 178 (1942) 388-401.

[66] Mendoza to Philip II, Paris 20 October 1586, CSP Simancas (1580-86) 639-40; same to same, Paris 20 October 1586, *ibid.*, 641-42; same to same, Paris 28 November 1586, *ibid.*, 667-69; same to Idiáquez, Paris 6 March 1587, CSP Simancas (1587-1603) 34. On Holt see James Tyrie to Acquaviva, Paris 9 May 1586, ARSI, Gal. 92, ff. 121^{r-v}; Acquaviva to Tyrie, Rome 31 May 1586, ARSI, Franc. 1/II, f. 277^v. Pollen views Holt's recall as a possible ploy "to pacify the ever-suspicious ministers" (*Counter-Reformation in Scotland*, pp. 61-62).

[67] Without disclosing its candidate for the English throne, Spain continued to negotiate for Scottish support. In these discussions Jesuits Crichton and Parsons played roles. See Olivares to Philip II, Rome 3 July 1587, CSP Simancas (1587-1603) 119-20. Around the same time the Earl of Leicester became aware of Jesuit designs on the English throne through intercepted letters (Leicester to Privy Council, 1 August 1587, CSP Foreign [1587] 219).

[68] Pollen, *Counter-Reformation in Scotland*, p. 62. The two new Jesuits, however, did not augment numbers but simply replaced Drury and Ogilvie, both of whom died in late 1587. To gain his release from the Tower in May of 1587 Crichton presumably gave his word that he would never return to England or Scotland. But on 17 August 1587 he was dispatched once more to Scotland. In letters patent given by the Jesuit General on this occasion it is noted that Crichton was sent to Scotland "*non obstante promissione per eum Dominis Consilii Reginae Angliae de non redeundo in Scotiam facta, uti verum est ipsum nequaquam ut illuc remitteretur procurasse, per obedientiam*" (ARSI, Hist. Soc. 61, f. 45^r. See also f. 26^v). I am thankful to Father Francisco de Borja de Medina, S.J., for drawing my attention to this important instruction. On Crichton's subsequent activities see Borja de Medina's "Intrigues of a Scottish Jesuit at the Spanish Court: Unpublished Letters of William Crichton to Claudio Acquaviva (Madrid 1590-1592)," in *The Reckoned Expense: Edmund Campion and the Early English Jesuits. Essays in Celebration of the First Centenary of Campion Hall, Oxford (1896-1996)*, ed. Thomas M. McCoog, S.J., (Woodbridge, 1996) pp. 215-45. On MacQuhirrie see Peter J. Shearman, "Father Alexander McQuhirrie, S.J.," *IR* 6 (1955) 22-45.

could to sabotage the mission and thus frustrate the hopes of the Scots.[69] Allen, meanwhile, worked against the mission by writing books on the Spanish succession for circulation in England.[70]

Upon arrival in Leith, Dunblane's request for an audience with the King was consistently denied. Despite persistent efforts by Robert Bruce to convince the King that he should again seek Spanish support and ally himself with Philip, James had decided against this course of action by October of 1587, and opted to observe all developments from the sidelines. Instead of the requested meeting, the Bishop was given twenty days to leave the country, an order he was able to evade through influence of the friendly Earl of Bothwell, Francis Stuart. Dunblane's persistence was eventually rewarded: James finally granted an audience in March of 1588. In a preliminary interview with James's Vice-Chancellor, Sir John Maitland, Lord Thirlestane, the Bishop explained the wishes of Pope Sixtus and King Philip: both wanted to destroy Protestantism in England and offered James a chance to avenge all injuries done to him and his mother. Indeed they promised that they would even support his claim to the English throne. The wily Vice-Chancellor was sceptical and wanted some guarantees for his King. Would assurances be given that the King would not have to change his religion? Would he be guaranteed the English throne "in case the forces of the Spanish King were greater than his own?" No agreement was reached and no further efforts to gain Scottish support were attempted. Dunblane returned to Rome disappointed in July. Spain would have to act alone.[71]

Even Bruce's failure to induce James to support the Spanish cause did not

---

[69] Olivares to Philip II, Rome 16 March 1587, CSP Simancas (1587-1603) 38-40; same to same, Rome 27 March 1587, *ibid.*, 50-54. In a letter to Philip from Paris on 24 October, Mendoza compared these Scottish Catholics to "mothers, who, although they see their children do ill, continue to hope for their amendment" (*ibid.*, 155-57).

[70] Olivares to Idiáquez, Rome 10 July 1587, CSP Simancas (1587-1603) 122 (printed in Knox, *Letters of Allen*, p. 294). If Olivares was telling the truth, Allen and Parsons were consciously deceiving the Scottish faction: "finding in this William Cliton [Crichton], a Scotchman, this whim which is now current among his countrymen at Paris, that the King of Scotland can be converted and that it is fitting that the reduction of England, which his Holiness will have to make, should be to secure the succession of the said King, have thought it better for the present not to undeceive them with regard to this fancy, that they may not excogitate commotions; but they go on temporizing with them; and at the same time, knowing how much better his Majesty's rule will suit the English, and also of the inconveniences of being ruled by the Scotch, they employ themselves of their own movement in writing books in proof of this to be scattered through England when God shall cause the moment to arrive, assuming as they do from what Creighton has told them about Scotland being succoured that the whole enterprise cannot long be deferred" (translation in Knox, *Letters of Allen*, ciii).

[71] Chadwick, "Father William Creichton," 269-71. In February, during Dunblane's stay, James met the Jesuit James Gordon, uncle of the Earl of Huntly, to discuss matters of religion: the invocation of saints, communion under both species, predestination, and justification. To the King's astonishment, he and the Jesuit agreed on the last two (CSP Simancas [1587-1603] 260-61 and D. Harris Willson, *King James VI and I* [London, 1956] p. 82).

cause the Catholic earls to abandon all hope. Despite the evidence they insisted that James would convert and unite with the Spanish. In March of 1588, around the time of Dunblane's audience with the King, a Gordon, in flight after committing murder, sought the protection of the Earl of Huntly. The King ordered Huntly to hand him over on pain of death. Huntly refused. Many Catholic lords, e.g. Francis Hay, Earl of Erroll, David Lindsay, Earl of Crawford, and Claud, Lord Hamilton, aided by some Protestant but anti-English nobles, e.g. Francis Stuart, Earl of Bothwell, gathered in support of Huntly. The King's English supporters quickly withdrew him to Edinburgh for his protection. Huntly and his supporters did not follow.

Towards the end of April John Maxwell, Earl of Morton, and Colonel William Semple returned to Scotland in expectation of taking arms in defence of the Catholic cause. Both were keen partisans of Spain; in fact, Semple had anticipated Stanley's surrender of Deventer by his own surrender of Lierre in 1582.[72] They hoped to seize some port and at the proper time—perhaps in conjunction with the Armada—to cross the border into England. Morton launched a rebellion in southwest Scotland shortly after his arrival, but by the end of June it had been quelled by the King, who took Morton and Semple prisoner. Two months later Semple escaped from prison and left Scotland.[73]

VII

For years English Catholics and Spanish patriots had been clamouring for an invasion. Coalitions had been created and plans drawn, but each year brought another excuse. The Treaty of Nonsuch (20 August 1585) increased English financial aid and provided infantry and cavalry support to the Dutch. Despite Spanish protests, the English government did nothing to stop Francis Drake's pirating in the Caribbean. The final blow was Drake's raid on Cadiz in April of 1587. That spurred Philip into action.

Pope Sixtus V, always impatient with the King's procrastination, thought that the formal agreement reached on 29 July 1587 would finally goad the King. "If indeed our dearest son in Christ, Philip King of the Spaniards, inspired with zeal for Christian piety and love for the Catholic religion," the agreement ran, "is now girding to fight the battles of God, for instance, against the impious woman already stricken for her impure heresies and

---

[72] In his youth Semple was attached to the court of Mary Queen of Scots. He later joined a Scottish regiment fighting in Holland for William the Silent. After his betrayal of Lierre, Semple was involved in different political and diplomatic missions between Parma, Mendoza, King Philip, and the Catholic earls in Scotland.

[73] Chadwick, "Father William Creighton," 271-76.

notorious schism by the blade of anathema," the Pope promised a large financial contribution in two instalments, the first upon arrival of the fleet in England and the second after the capture of the island, if the Armada was launched that year. He promised to grant any reasonable favour the King considered important for the enterprise. The issue of confiscated ecclesiastical property would be dealt with in a method deemed most expedient by the Holy See and Spain. Finally, Sixtus granted Philip the right to name as ruler of the subdued kingdoms someone who would "stabilize and preserve the Catholic religion in those regions, and who will stand acceptable to the Holy Apostolic See, and accept investiture from it."[74]

As a prelude Allen was created a cardinal on 7 August 1587. On the same day Pope Sixtus V exhorted Philip to keep his promise: "This morning I have held a consistory and made Allen Cardinal to satisfy your Majesty, and though in proposing him I put forward a motive which was very far from being likely to excite suspicion, nevertheless it is reported that throughout all Rome there arose a universal cry—Now they are getting things into order for the war with England; and this supposition was current everywhere. Therefore your Majesty should not lose time, lest those poor Christians suffer greater injury; for if there be delay, that which you have judged to be good will turn out evil."[75]

Fear of Henry III's reaction to a Spanish Armada was quickly dismissed. He was under the control of the Catholic League, which, although in the ascendancy, could not risk a venture outside France. Tension between the Duke of Guise and the French King exploded in May of 1588 when the Duke visited Paris despite a royal prohibition. Royal attempts to round up Guise's supporters resulted in the "Day of the Barricades" (13 May 1588), whereby the League won complete control of the capital.

Henry III again capitulated, confirmed the Treaty of Nemours with the new Edict of Union, and recognised Charles, Cardinal Bourbon as heir presumptive. Henry, however, was playing for time: on 23 December 1588 he invited the Duke to his bedchamber in Blois, where the Duke was murdered by the royal bodyguard. On the following day Louis, Cardinal Guise was assassinated, and many leaders of the League were thrown into prison.

---

[74] "Terms of Agreement between the Pope and Spain for the Invasion of England," in Meyer, *England and the Catholic Church*, pp. 520-23.
[75] Thomas Francis Knox, ed., *The First and Second Diaries of the English College, Douay* (London, 1878) lxxxv. Regarding Parsons's role, Allen testified "for next under heaven F. Persons made me Cardinal" in a letter to Thomas Bailey ([Rome after 7 August 1587], in Penelope Renold, ed., *Letters of William Allen and Richard Barret 1572-1598* [London, 1967] p. 192). According to Eamon Duffy, "there is no doubt in all this that the Pope saw Allen as a Spanish stooge. . ." ("William, Cardinal Allen," 283).

Reaction was swift and loud. On 7 January 1589 the Sorbonne released all Frenchmen from loyalty to the King; in May, Sixtus summoned Henry to Rome to explain himself and threatened the French King with excommunication. The death of his mother Catherine de Medici on 5 January 1589 left Henry even more isolated. On 26 April Henry signed a treaty with Henry of Navarre against the Guises and the Catholic League. On 1 August Henry III was assassinated by Jacques Clément, a young friar. Before he died Henry recognised Henry of Navarre as his successor.[76] France's internal problems left Philip free to pursue the enterprise without fear of French intervention.

Philip tried in vain to meet the papal deadline to avoid losing a subsidy. Methods and goals were still debated and hopes, albeit dim, for an amicable settlement with Elizabeth were pursued in talks with English envoys. The longer the delay, the more the prospects for success diminished.[77] During the delays, concrete arrangements were made for reformation of the Church in England. Olivares and Cardinal Allen prepared for the restoration of Catholicism with a memorial in which specific persons were named to various dioceses and offices in England.[78] Allen also wrote two incriminating pamphlets. *An admonition to the nobility and people of England and Ireland* and its broadside summary *A declaration of the sentence and deposition of Elizabeth, the usurper and pretensed queen of Englande* were printed an Antwerp in 1588 for distribution after the Spanish invasions.[79]

Catholic relief was finally at hand and Allen recited the Queen's many evil acts that would have rendered even a legitimate monarch unworthy.[80] From the beginning Elizabeth was a usurper. Through various acts her father had declared her illegitimate and base. With "Luciferian pride" she gained the throne and retained possession "not by any dissent of inheritance or other lawful title, but only by enforced uniust lawes partly made by her

---

[76] Knecht, *French Wars of Religion*, pp. 62-65.

[77] See De Lamar Jensen, "The Spanish Armada: The Worst-Kept Secret in Europe," *SCJ* 19 (1988) 621-41 for an overview of the false starts and of the events that finally precipitated the Armada. On the often hostile relations between Philip and Sixtus see John Lynch, "Philip II and the Papacy," *Transactions of the Royal Historical Society*, series 5, 11 (1961) 23-42.

[78] Knox, *Letters of Allen*, pp. 303-05.

[79] *An Admonition*, STC 368, ARCR, II, no. 5; *A Declaration*, STC 22590, ARCR, II, no. 10. The broadside can be found in M. A. Tierney, ed., *Dodd's Church History of England*, 5 vols. (London, 1839-1843) III, xliv-xlviii. See also Leo Hicks's discussion in "Cardinal Allen's Admonition," *The Month* 185 (1948) 232-42; 186 (1948) 30-39.

[80] Compare Allen's portrait with the official cult of the Virgin Queen. On this cult see Carole Levin, "Power, Politics, and Sexuality: Images of Elizabeth I," in *The Politics of Gender in Early Modern Europe*, eds. Jean R. Brink, Allison P. Coudert, and Maryanne C. Horowitz (Kirksville, 1989) pp. 95-110, and *The Heart and Stomach of a King: Elizabeth I and the Politics of Sex and Power* (Philadelphia, 1994) pp.66-90; John N. King, "Queen Elizabeth I: Representations of the Virgin Queen," *Renaissance Quarterly* 43 (1990) 30-74.

supposed father beinge then an excommunicated person, and partly coacted by herself and her complices in the beginnninge of her pretended raigne."[81] From her exalted position she has committed the most grievous sins against God and his Church, and has opened her kingdom to heretics from throughout Europe.[82]

She has debased the country's ancient nobles, dismissed them from their traditional offices and honours, and promoted "base and unpure persons, inflamed with infinite avarice and ambition, men of great partialitie briberie and iniquity, to the highest honours and most proffitable offices of her courte and cuntrie."[83] Her personal life was no better than her rule. She "hathe abused her bodie, against Gods lawes, to the disgrace of princely maiestie & the whole nations reproche, by unspeakable and incredible variety of luste, which modesty suffereth not to be remembered."[84]

Her devious and faithless foreign policy has destroyed the kingdom's reputation. Her replacement of the suppressed feast of the Nativity of the Blessed Virgin with the celebration of her own birthday and the creation of a national holiday to commemorate her coronation were acts of pride and presumption.[85] Her inhuman cruelty climaxed with the execution of Mary Queen of Scots "by lawe and righte the true owner of the crowne of England."[86] Fear not, Allen advised his countrymen, the hour of retaliation is at hand: the wickedness shall end and the wicked be punished. The sentence of Pius V shall finally be enforced.[87]

The King of Spain, moved by his own zeal and piety, the exhortations of the Pope, and "also not a litle by my humble and continuall sute together with the afflicted and banished Catholikes of our nation,"[88] will direct the

---

[81] *An admonition*, p. XI.
[82] On Protestant refugees in England see Andrew Pettegree, *Foreign Protestant Communities in Sixteenth-Century London* (Oxford, 1986).
[83] *An admonition*, p. XV.
[84] *An admonition*, p. XIX.
[85] David Cressy has recently studied the successful creation of a national calendar around such events as the accession of Elizabeth and the defeat of the Armada. See *Bonfires & Bells: National Memory and the Protestant Calendar in Elizabethan and Stuart England* (London, 1989); "The Protestant Calendar and the Vocabulary of Celebration in Early Modern England," *The Journal of British Studies* 29 (1990) 31-52. On Elizabeth as "Virgin Mother" see Helen Hackett, *Virgin Mother, Maiden Queen* (London, 1995).
[86] *An admonition*, p. XXVIII.
[87] In Allen's political writings, the pope's deposing power plays an extremely important role. Thomas Clancy has argued that "the basic reason for Allen's insistence on the place of the Pope in the deposition machinery was probably that he considered the Pope's judgment an important safeguard against sedition." Without the pope there would have been no difference between the Catholic political arguments and those of Protestants who champion the right of a people to change its government at will. See "English Catholics and the Papal Deposing Power, 1570-1640," *RH* 6 (1961) 122.
[88] *An admonition*, p. XLIX.

crusade against Elizabeth. The Pope has discharged all Englishmen from their oaths of obedience and fidelity to the Queen,

> requiringe and desiringe in the bowels of Christ, and commaundinge under paine of excommunication and other penalties of the lawe, and as they looke for the favours and protection to them and theires, afore promised, and will avoide the Pope, kinges, and the other princes high indignation, that no man of what degree or condition so ever, obie, abetter, ayde, defend or acknowledge her for their prince, or superior, but that all and every one, according to their qualetie, callinge, and habillitie, immediately upon intelligence of his Holines will, by these my letters, or otherwise, or at the arivall of his Catholike Maiesties forces be ready, to ioine to the said army, with all the powers and aydes they can make, of men, munition, and victuals, to helpe towards the restoring of the Catholicke faithe, and actual deposinge of the usurper, in such sorte and place, as by the chefe manegers of this affare, and the Generall of this holye warr shall be appointed, for the best advancement of the cause.[89]

Catholics who do not heed Allen's advice but insist on taking arms against the Spanish "shall fieghte against God, & against his annointed, against your next lawfull kinge, against truthe, faithe, religion, conscience, and your deere cuntrie."[90] Such action would place not only their lives but their eternal salvation at risk. They should not aid the heretics and risk damnation. Be loyal to your God, your faith, and your ancestors.[91] Take courage! The Spanish army has shown itself to be invincible especially now that it is devoted to God's cause. Out of the spiritual treasures of the Church, the Holy Father will grant a plenary indulgence "and perdon of all their sinnes, beinge duely penitent, contrite, and confessed" to all who assist in this crusade.[92]

By 12 June a copy of Allen's work was in the hands of William Cecil. In a letter to Walsingham, Cecil noted how deceived Allen was if he thought that any nobleman or gentleman would favour an invasion. The book would simply result in more damage done to Catholics within the kingdom.[93] On

---

[89] *An admonition*, pp. LII-LIII.

[90] *An admonition*, p. LIIII.

[91] Allen, like John Knox and the majority of the religious figures of the period, "knew nothing of a 'watch-maker' God—a God who set the universe into motion and then merely let it run." They saw history as the exercise of God's sovereignty and interpreted historical events accordingly. See Richard Kyle, "John Knox's Concept of Divine Providence and its Influence on His Thought," *Albion* 18 (1986) 403; Peter Lake, "The Significance of the Elizabethan Identification of the Pope as Antichrist," *JEH* 31 (1980) 161-78.

[92] *A declaration*, xlviii.

[93] PRO, SP 12/211/15. Works such as these simply intensified English distrust of popery and cemented the identification of Protestantism with patriotism. On this see Anthony Fletcher, "The First Century of English Protestantism and the Growth of National Identity," in *Religion and National Identity*, ed. Stuart Mews (Oxford, 1982) pp. 309-17.

1 July a royal proclamation, after the now customary recitation of traditional charges against Jesuits and seminary priests, urged all good subjects to report "infamous slanderous bulls, libels, books, and pamphlets" and their distributors under pain of punishment.[94]

If some English Catholics found Allen's defence of Stanley offensive, they must have been scandalized by his vicious attack on the Queen and her reign. Elizabeth was unfit to rule not simply because of bad government and incompetence, but also because of illegitimacy and immorality. Moreover Cecil's predictions were fulfilled: Catholics within England suffered more because of the Armada.

Occasionally a historian, such as Father Pollen, seeks to exonerate Allen and the Catholic exiles. "It will be sufficient to say here," Pollen claims, "that it [*An admonition to the nobility and people of England*] was written to be published in case the Armada was victorious, and both Elizabeth and Protestantism defeated, and that, under these circumstances, he [Allen] was prepared to say the severest things of Elizabeth and her persecution." But the Armada failed and the proposals were not implemented. This, according to Pollen, reduces the treatise's value significantly: it is not a sure indicator of Catholic intentions.[95] But Allen miscalculated. His works were known by the government before the fiasco of the Armada. Their contents cannot be dismissed simply as an inconvenience and Allen cannot be considered innocent simply because his works were prematurely released.[96] Presumably Allen was not obliged to write either work and each is a reflection of his own position on Elizabeth and the English crown. Like Parsons, Allen had

---

[94] Hughes and Larkin, *Tudor Royal Proclamations*, III, 13-17. On the basis of this document and others, Robert M. Kingdon concluded that English Catholics were "engaged in treason, potentially if not actually, in intention if not in deed" (ed., *The Execution of Justice in England by William Cecil and A True, Sincere, and Modest Defense of English Catholics by William Allen* [Ithaca, N.Y., 1965] xxxvi-xxxvii).

[95] "The Politics of the English Catholics during the Reign of Elizabeth," *The Month* 99 (1902) 405.

[96] Albert J. Loomie, S.J., seems to exculpate Allen. There was "initial misapprehension of the English court over what the stolen copy of Cardinal Allen's *Declaration of the sentence and deposition of Elizabeth* actually meant to Spain. This proclamation was not in fact a significant symbol of a partnership of the Cardinal with Philip II. The document had been printed prematurely in anticipation of a bull of Sixtus V which in the end was never issued." In a different context Loomie asserted "that there was no moral duty imposed by Catholic theologians to support a Spanish force" ("The Armadas and the Catholics of England," *CHR* 59 [1973] 387). Regarding the first, a missed opportunity should not be mistaken for innocence. As to the second, our readings of the document differ. Francis Edwards's evaluation is more accurate. Parsons and Allen did encourage Philip because they believed that the English government would never grant tolerance to Catholics. "This is not to say," Edwards continues, "that they wished England to become simply a dependency of Spain, but it does mean that they were prepared to accept another dynasty, and even more readily foreign help, to do at this time what the English Protestants, or a party of them, were to accomplish successfully in 1688" (*The Jesuits in England* [London, 1985] p. 21).

250   CHAPTER SIX

earlier proclaimed Catholic loyalty. The pamphlets revealed his current position.[97]

But was Allen's *the* Catholic position or simply *a* Catholic position? Would most English Catholics have resisted the Spanish invaders? Or would they have emulated Sir William Stanley and heeded these exhortations? When the Armada was expected, Catholic prisoners were examined as to their allegiance, and the overwhelming majority professed themselves ready to fight for the Queen. Other observations confirm this. Sir Francis Englefield in February of 1589 wrote that there was no immediate hope for the reconversion of England because English Catholics themselves "are resolved to resist Spain." Years later, in 1602, the Venetian ambassador said "I am told that when Spain attacked England the last time all Catholics remained loyal to the Queen."[98]

As Philip prepared for war, Father Acquaviva marshalled the spiritual resources of the Society behind him. In September of 1587 the General asked that the usual monthly Mass said for the General's intentions "be offered for this purpose, namely, to ask the divine goodness for the success of whatever the Divine Majesty intends." The following April, the King ordered that prayers be said throughout Castile for the success of the Armada; the General approved. "This case," Acquaviva wrote, "is so just and universal, that we are all obliged to ask the Divine Majesty for its success, and this is what we are doing in our houses." He ordered the Roman houses to pray for the same intention.

Pedro de Ribadeneira, who, as we have seen, briefly visited England during the final months of Mary Tudor, justified the Spanish expedition.[99] His reasons were the usual ones: the restoration of Catholicism in England and just retaliation for English support of Dutch rebels and for English attacks on Spanish shipping and Iberian coastal towns. Ribadeneira argued that the honour of overthrowing English Protestantism rightly belonged to Spain: "it will be no less honor for Spain to throw the devil out of England, than it was to cast him out of the Indies, where he was worshipped and

---

[97]

[98] Pollen, "Politics of the English Catholics," 410-11.

[99] Francisco de Borja de Medina, S.J., "Jesuitas en la Armada contra Inglaterra (1588)," *AHSI* 58 (1989) 4-6. See also M.J. Rodríguez-Salgado, "The Anglo-Spanish War: The Final Episode in 'The Wars of the Roses'?," in *England, Spain and the Gran Armada 1585-1604*, eds. M.J. Rodríguez-Salgado and Simon Adams (Edinburgh, 1991) pp. 37-38, n. 65. On the priests and brothers that accompanied the Armada see Manuel Gracia Rivas, *La Sandidad en la Jornada de Inglaterra (1587-1588)* (Madrid, 1988) pp. 207-38; Thomas Flynn, O.P., *The Irish Dominicans 1536-1641* (Dublin, 1993) pp. 88-89. On the propaganda that appeared in Spain to justify the Armada see Carlos Gómez-Centurión Jiménez, "The New Crusade: Ideology and Religion in the Anglo-Spanish Conflict," in *England, Spain and the Gran Armada 1585-1604*, eds. M.J. Rodríguez-Salgado and Simon Adams (Edinburgh, 1991) pp. 264-99.

adored before the Word was preached there." Of all the reasons for the launching of the Armada, the most important was the restoration of Catholicism. The war against England was, according to Ribadeneira, a crusade "not only to ensure our defence, and to prevent English corsairs from infesting our seas and robbing our fleets—although these are just but less important aims—but to glorify God and to advance His holy church."[100]

Thirty years earlier Jerónimo Nadal, on an official visitation to the Spanish provinces, reminded Philip during an interview of the affection that Ignatius had for the young Prince, "in which affection he nurtured all us Jesuits."[101] Despite everything, the affection seems to have continued.

Once Philip chose a course of action, he ordered Alonso Pérez de Guzmán, Duke of Medina Sidonia, to follow instructions faithfully. The fleet was to avoid any encounter with the English and was to engage in combat only if attacked. In subsequent negotiations with the English Queen, the Prince of Parma and the Duke of Medina Sidonia were to insist on three things: religious freedom for English Catholics and amnesty for religious exiles; restitution of all cities and towns held by the English in the Netherlands; and compensation for damage done to Spanish subjects and dominions.[102]

Because these instructions contain no mention of Spanish claims to the English throne or, indeed, of the whole question of succession, apparently they should be interpreted as minimal demands made by a less than totally victorious Spanish force. If plans succeeded as efficiently as everyone expected there would be no need for negotiation. Even after the invincible Armada finally sailed from Lisbon on 30 May 1588, Allen and Parsons continued their diplomacy lest the Pope succumb to the French-Scottish faction that favoured James.[103]

The story of the defeat of the Armada is too well known to merit repetition.[104] The Spanish fleet was dispersed off Gravelines on 29 July, but

---

[100] Quoted in Gómez-Centurión Jiménez, "The New Crusade," p. 276.

[101] Nadal to Laínez, Toledo 18 March 1561, *Epp. Nadal*, I, 424-25.

[102] Philip specifically listed these objectives in a letter to the Duke of Parma, written in April of 1588 (printed in Geoffrey Woodward, *Philip II* [London, 1992] pp. 110-11). See also Jensen, "Worst-Kept Secret," 640-41. Geoffrey Parker discusses whether Philip would have attained these objectives: "If the Armada had Landed," in *Spain and the Netherlands 1559-1659* (London, 1990) pp. 135-47.

[103] Summary of letters from Olivares, Rome 27 June 1588, CSP Simancas (1587-1603) 324-25.

[104] Mattingly's *The Defeat of the Spanish Armada* remains definitive. An account promoted in celebration of the 400th anniversary of the event, Felipe Fernandez-Armesto, *The Spanish Armada* (Oxford, 1988) lacks the colour of Mattingly. The essays collected in Rodríguez-Salgado and Adams, *England, Spain and the Gran Armada* contain important contributions to the episode. John S. Nolan has corrected a serious underestimation of English preparedness for the invasion. See his "The Muster of 1588," *Albion* 23 (1991) 387-407. On the incorporation

a change of wind allowed Medina Sidonia to gather some of the scattered ships and to flee north. There were fears that he would regroup to land in Scotland for an assault from the north, or to invade Ireland.

Catholic earls in Scotland controlled nearly all the northern shires of Scotland and they welcomed the prospect of a Spanish invasion of England. The overthrow of Elizabeth would not only be a fitting punishment for her approval of the execution of Mary Stuart but would result in the destruction of the Protestant Church in Scotland. To them it was clear that, without the powerful support of Elizabeth, the Kirk could not survive. Many mourned the Armada's failure and would have joined Crichton's lament:

> For many a day did we await the fleet of the Catholic King, with a longing, a loyalty not less than that with which Christ's coming was looked for by those who cried: 'O that thou woudst rend the heavens and wouldst come down.' 'The mountains would melt away at thy presence.' But here there was no melting away of the mountains: they never even touched our shores, but fled, although none pursued.[105]

Once the threat from Spain had passed, Elizabeth exhorted James to take action against his powerful Catholic earls, and promised him greater financial assistance if he did so. In February of 1589 James was made aware of contact between the Catholic earls and Spain when the English ambassador presented him with intercepted letters.[106] In April James summoned his liegemen and marched north to face the earls. Neither side wished a violent confrontation, and so at Brig o' Dee near Aberdeen a compromise was reached. Huntly surrendered himself into James's hands; his life was spared and his lands were not forfeit. Bothwell, Crawford, and Erroll were tried and found guilty on 24 May; their punishment was left to the King. By autumn they were released. The leniency with which James treated his Catholic rebels angered Elizabeth and offered new encouragement to the Scottish exiles in their attempts to convince the continental powers that James's sympathies were Catholic.[107]

---

of the Spanish Armada into the myth of Gloriana see Susan Frye, "The Myth of Elizabeth at Tilbury," *SCJ* 23 (1993) 95-114. For the involvement of a number of Jesuits in the Armada, mostly Spanish and Portuguese see Borja de Medina, "Jesuitas en la Armada," 3-42. The instructions given to these Jesuits by the General can be found in ARSI, Instit. 117, ff. 510^r-511^v.

[105] Chadwick, "Father William Creighton," 259-60.

[106] For James's reaction see his letter to Huntly (February? 1589), in *Letters of King James VI & I*, ed. G.P.V. Akrigg (Berkeley, 1984) pp. 89-91.

[107] Helen Georgia Stafford, *James VI of Scotland and the Throne of England* (New York, 1940) pp. 41-50; William Forbes-Leith, S.J., ed., *Narratives of Scottish Catholics under Mary Stuart and James VI* (Edinburgh, 1885) p. 217.

Surprisingly Ireland played no role in pre-Armada schemes. G.A. Hayes-McCoy suggests that this demonstrates "what the [English] government had by that date accomplished and what still remained to be done." There were no plans for an invasion of Ireland, and those Spaniards who did come ashore were "castaways and not invaders." As Hayes-McCoy points out, the Spaniards who did land received assistance only in north Connacht and Ulster, the areas least affected by Tudor conquest and plantation. Immediately after the Armada there is little evidence of increased persecution.[108]

Ireland was without Jesuits. Irish Jesuits were dispersed widely and often dependent on the kindness of other provinces. Aspirations of Jesuits such as Robert Rochford that the Irish be gathered to form a college or a seminary went unheeded. Requests such as Richard Pembroke's to return to Ireland—with complaints that Ireland was ignored while Jesuits were sent to England and Scotland—were generally received with exhortations to self-mortification and acceptance of the Cross.[109]

VIII

Henry Garnet and Robert Southwell remained the only Jesuits in England outside prison. In January of 1588, as England awaited the Spanish invasion, the Privy Council ordered the more obstinate recusants to be placed under tight security and more moderate ones in the custody of private persons. In the following June some prominent recusants were imprisoned in the Tower of London or in castles throughout the realm. The government increased its surveillance of anyone suspected of aiding the invaders.[110] Despite the hardships Southwell remained optimistic. "For surely however much the squalls rage," Southwell wrote to Acquaviva, "the bark of Peter goes forward and advances." The only thing lacking was priests, and he prayed that more would be sent.[111]

---

[108] "The Completion of the Tudor Conquest and the Advance of the Counter-reformation, 1571-1603," in *A New History of Ireland: III Early Modern Ireland 1534-1691*, eds. T.W. Moody, F.X. Martin, and F.J. Byrne (Oxford, 1991) p. 115; Robert Dudley Edwards, *Church and State in Tudor Ireland* (London, 1935) pp. 274-75; Steven G. Ellis, *Tudor Ireland: Crown, Community and the Conflict of Cultures 1470-1603* (London, 1985) pp. 294-95.

[109] Robert Rochford to Claudio Acquaviva, Lisbon 31 December 1585 (transcript in ABSI, 46/23/8, p. 295); Acquaviva to Georg Bader, Rome 10 January 1587, ARSI, Austr. 1/II, pp. 314-20; Acquaviva to Richard Pembroke, Rome 7 December 1589, ARSI, Austr. 1/II, pp. 523-24; Richard Pembroke to Claudio Acquaviva, Vienna 24 November 1590, ARSI, Germ. 168, ff. 340^r-341^v.

[110] LaRocca, "English Catholics and the Recusancy Laws," 133-36. On the renewed persecution see the material collected in Pollen, *Unpublished Documents*, pp. 151-65.

[111] 12 January 1587 (o.s.), ARSI, Fondo Gesuitico 651/648 (in McCoog, "Southwell," 104-05).

Others were sent. William Holt and Joseph Creswell received instructions to proceed to England on 24 February 1588.[112] Acquaviva directed the two to call on the Prince of Parma if he was in Belgium, and to place themselves at his disposal.[113] No major decision was to be made without his advice and approval.[114]

Father Acquaviva instructed Holt and Creswell to behave modestly in Parma's presence and "on no account [to] obtrude themselves in affairs (of state)." If their advice was sought, they were not to make any proposal until it had been "well considered and commended to God and discussed between them." The same procedure, the General continued, was to be followed in England "should it happen that God gives us back that kingdom." Upon arrival in England, they were to devote themselves to "spiritual occupations." Regarding "help of other kinds," Rome would supply it.

In an attempt to improve the morals of his troops, Parma asked the Society of Jesus to establish a corps of chaplains for the army in Flanders in 1587.[115] Four years later, in 1592, Joseph Creswell explained to Philip II that he had been instructed at the insistence of Cardinal Allen to call on Parma and to assist the Armada.[116] Presumably Holt and Creswell would have crossed to England either with news of Parma's imminent departure or with the troops whom they would have served as chaplains.

According to the original plan the two Jesuits would separate: Holt to go to Scotland and Creswell to England. They were directed by the General to

---

[112] ARSI, Hist. Soc. 62, f. 45ᵛ; Rom. 156/II, ff. 158ʳ⁻ᵛ; Hicks, *Letters of Persons*, pp. 361-63. By 1 April William Brooke, Lord Cobham, received word that certain Jesuits would come from France and Rome to meet the Armada and accompany it to England (CSP Foreign [January-June 1588] 245). Two more Jesuits, William Murdoch and George Drury, were sent to Scotland sometime in 1588 (Pollen, *Counter-Reformation in Scotland*, p. 62).

[113] In a letter written to the General in early 1589, Garnet, aware of what the official reaction to the presence of two English Jesuits in this force would be, complained that "the two of ours who were in the army of Parma will be perhaps dangerous both to us and to all Catholics. But in this matter, your Paternity knows what is expedient" (ARSI, Fondo Gesuitico, 651/624).

[114] Hicks, *Letters of Persons*, pp. 362-63. See also Parsons's letter to Cosimo Massi, secretary to the Prince of Parma, Rome 24 February 1588, *ibid.*, p. 314. See also Claudio Acquaviva's letter to Parma, Rome 22 February 1588, ARSI, Fl. Belg. 1/I, p. 382.

[115] Fernandez-Armesto, *The Spanish Armada*, p. 62. Belgian Jesuit Thomas Sailly was the superior of these chaplains. On Sailly see Louis Brouwers, S.J., "L' 'Elogium' du Père Thomas Sailly S.I. (1553-1623) composé par le Père Charles Scribani S.I.," *AHSI* 48 (1979) 87-124. According to Thomas J. Morrissey, S.J., (*James Archer of Kilkenny: An Elizabethan Jesuit* [Dublin, 1979] p. 7), the chaplains "preached, catechised, heard confessions and celebrated Mass in the presence of the Army. On campaign they accompanied the soldiers, living under tent, following them onto the field of battle, animating them before combat, and thereafter comforting the wounded and dying under enemy fire. In times of peace and in winter quarters, they visited the hospitals, struggled against debauchery and blasphemy, appeased the quarrels and discords so prompt to break out amongst men of different nationalities, encouraged the men to frequent the sacraments and to become members of confraternities or sodalities."

[116] Hicks, *Letters of Persons*, lxxiii, lxxv; Hicks, "Cardinal Allen and the Society," 534.

ask Belgian Provincial, Frans DeCostere, if Francis Waferer and Henry Broy (or any of the English fathers then in Belgium) could accompany them.[117] Unless the Provincial had serious reservations, which he would later have to explain to Rome, the General wanted this request granted.[118] As members of other provinces, English Jesuits were subject to provincials who were not easily convinced that the needs of the Church and of the Society would be better met in the dangerous vineyards of England than in the proliferating colleges on the continent.[119] Until English Jesuits were able to receive and form their own novices and to direct their own mission, such problems would be frequent. In the case at hand, no one crossed.

Holt was removed as rector of the English College and assigned to the sensitive mission to Scotland because he was

> very much loved and trusted by them [the Scots] owing to his having been among them for five years more or less; and, because he is an Englishman who is known to be very devoted to Spanish interests, these Scottish lords, who are now tired of being dependent on France, and have very little hope of their own king becoming a Catholic, would unbosom themselves with greater freedom and confidence to him than to any one else of the Scottish nation.

Holt, moreover, was a discreet man capable of "any sort of negotiation with those [Scottish] lords if he were to go there with a certain amount of ready money and a guarantee of more when later on the time arrives to carry out the enterprise."[120] After the Armada's failure Holt remained in Belgium as a chaplain to the forces; Creswell was back in Rome by 26 August 1589 and was appointed rector of the English College.[121]

Two Jesuits did however arrive in England in 1588: John Gerard and Edward Oldcorne.[122] Both were admitted into the Society on 15 August 1588 and almost immediately dispatched to England. In November they landed in East Anglia. Garnet greatly looked forward to their arrival despite his

---

[117] See *Mon. Ang.*, II, 243-44, 516 for biographical information.
[118] Hicks, *Letters of Persons*, p. 363.
[119] There was occasional resentment that "foreign" Jesuits were depriving provinces of needed financial resources. Georg Bader, Austrian Provincial, complained that the acceptance of so many foreign Jesuits into his province burdened the province and restricted the number of Austrians. Acquaviva in reply reminded him that within the Society all must be received with charity and that nothing should be made of national differences (Rome 10 January 1587, ARSI, Austr. 1/II, pp. 314-20).
[120] [c. June 1587] "Some Points on Which His Majesty's Decision is Desired at the Earliest Moment, the Matters Themselves Demanding this Urgency," in Hicks, *Letters of Persons*, p. 307.
[121] Holt to Parsons, Brussels 17 April 1589, ARSI, Fondo Gesuitico 651/630; Creswell to Ludovico Masselli, Rome 26 August 1589, ARSI, Fondo Gesuitico 651/615. The principal topic of this letter is the assassination of Henry III.
[122] For biographical information see *Mon. Ang.*, II, 422-23, 503-04. *John Gerard: The Autobiography of an Elizabethan*, ed. Philip Caraman, S.J. (London, 1951) pp. 6-9.

apprehension over their lack of proper formation: "Although their arrival is of the greatest pleasure for us," Garnet wrote to the General, "we fear that it may not be a safe one, and because they are novices, we hardly think that they can be treated by us with that care which is necessary for novices. We hope that, having become perfect in such a short period of time, they know and can live immediately the ways of the Society and thus sustain the Society's esteem." This would be especially difficult in the post-Armada persecution.[123]

The defeat of the Armada unleashed a new fury on Catholics. "Now at last," Southwell lamented, "the asps' eggs have burst and with the most certain destruction of many, the poison has begun to be poured out and to spread violently far and wide."[124] Southwell complained that, now the peril of the Armada had passed, the hatred of the Spanish was redirected towards Catholics. Husbands and wives were separated. Many were dragged to courthouses for examination not only about their past deeds, but also about their future acts through the "Bloody Questions." Southwell lost friends in the persecution and as a result was slightly discouraged. He confessed to Acquaviva in December that, although storms instigated by heretics were much worse, worst of all was the "winter of the soul which we must at all costs avoid." He begged the General to pray that flowers would return in the spring. As a final comment on the passing of the Armada, Southwell concluded "the trouble of our time will not be calmed by the uproar of battle, but by the prayers and tears of faithful souls."[125]

Garnet too bordered on despair: "For when we thought that there was an end to these disasters by which we are already nearly destroyed, our hope was suddenly turned to sorrow, and now with redoubled effort the overseers are pressing upon us, and the masters among the Egyptians are burdening us with all the wrath conceived against Moses and Aaron." A month later Garnet wrote that some priests expected to be executed, and others now free anticipated prison "although nearly all of us can be said to be in prison because we dare not go around the city but at night and on urgent business."[126]

An important consequence of the defeat of the Armada was the govern-

---

[123] [early 1589], ARSI, Fondo Gesuitico, 651/624.
[124] Southwell to Acquaviva, 10 July 1588, ARSI, Fondo Gesuitico 651/648 (in McCoog, "Southwell," 112-13).
[125] Southwell to Acquaviva, 31 August 1588, in Pollen, *Unpublished Documents*, p. 325 (the original letter can be found in ARSI, Fondo Gesuitico 651/648 [in McCoog, "Southwell," 113-17]); same to same, 28 December 1588, ARSI, Fondo Gesuitico 651/648 (in McCoog, "Southwell," 121-23).
[126] Garnet to Acquaviva, London 29 October 1588, ARSI, Fondo Gesuitico 651/624; same to same, 24 November 1588, *ibid*. Similar sentiments can be seen in the letter written to the General in early 1589 in the same collection.

ment's attempt to formulate an oath to be submitted to all Catholics to ascertain their loyalty. Prominent recusants imprisoned before the Armada were allowed to leave after October if they conformed or demonstrated their loyalty to the Queen. Because each was asked to swear that he acknowledged Elizabeth as his Queen "notwithstanding any excommunication or past deposition of the pope, or any present or future such," he was obliged to deny the papal deposing power and, later in the oath, the spiritual power of the pope in England. Seeking a compromise, Catholics drafted a version that recognized Elizabeth as their lawful Queen. (In so doing "the Catholics have depended on the apostolic concession whereby it is licit to recognize her as queen and revere her until the public execution of the bull.") They offered her the obedience shown to any prince by a Catholic. Even in the revised form Catholics were willing to declare:

> that I have and ought to have that concern for her most royal person that I would wish with every effort to struggle to thwart and to fight to the death all those who will in any way endanger the life of her Highness, or lift a finger against her, or draw the least drop of her blood, or detract in the least from the above mentioned titles of Her Majesty within her dominions, be they persons of whatever state, condition, or grade.

Without comment Garnet submitted both versions of the oath to Acquaviva and asked his opinion.[127]

Southwell was not in London on 24 November 1588, and so he missed the triumphal display of thanksgiving. Perched in the window of a friend's house on Ludgate Hill, Henry Garnet viewed the entire spectacle. Interspersed in his description were comments on religious attire and services. "Most worthy of note," Garnet wrote to Acquaviva, "was the fact that the wives of the 'pseudo-bishops' made no appearance before the Queen, not so much because she hated married clerics but because she hated matrimony." Throughout the letter one senses an undercurrent of pride in England's achievement. For fear of the Queen's safety, orders were delivered to all households along the procession route to St. Paul's that no spectators were to be allowed to watch the proceedings from the window unless the owners would pledge their lives and their fortunes for the spectator's loyalty. Many would pledge for Garnet "because they are of the opinion that we are more interested in the safety of the queen than her Calvinist ministers are."[128]

---

[127] Garnet to Acquaviva, London 29 October 1588, ARSI, Fondo Gesuitico 651/624. Sir Thomas Tresham seems to have been behind the revision of the oath. See Caraman, *Garnet and the Gunpowder Plot*, pp. 74-78. See also Southwell's brief account of the issue in his letter to Acquaviva on 20 December 1588, ARSI, Fondo Gesuitico 651/648 (in McCoog, "Southwell," 119-21).

[128] Garnet to Acquaviva, London 5 December 1588, ARSI Fondo Gesuitico 651/624.

As Garnet watched the pageantry, he awaited the arrival of the two new Jesuits. By 24 November he knew that Gerard and Oldcorne had arrived safely.[129] John Gerard did not enter London until shortly before Christmas—much to Garnet's displeasure. In a letter to Acquaviva on 12 March 1589 Garnet praised the new men but complained of their imprudence in not reporting immediately to Garnet. Instead of contacting their superior, the new men went about their business alone and in so doing made some mistakes that had to be corrected.[130] With the new men, Garnet reconstructed a network of missions.

Parliament, originally scheduled to meet on 12 November 1588, was prorogued until 4 February 1589. National joy at deliverance from the Spanish foe permeated Sir Christopher Hatton's opening speech. Beginning with the conflict between Henry VIII and Pope Clement VII, Hatton recited the crimes committed by the papacy against an innocent country. The alliance between the Pope and the King of Spain was

> sufficient to show to all posterity the unchristian fury, both of the Pope (that wolfish bloodsucker) and of the Spaniard (that insatiable tyrant) in that they never bent themselves with such might and resolution against the very Turk or any other infidel, as they have done against a Virgin Queen, a famous lady, and a country which embraceth without corruption in doctrine the true and sincere religion of Christ. But yet, that which moveth her Majesty most is this: to think that ever any of her own subjects, mere Englishmen, born and brought up amongst us, should combine themselves—as some have done—with her so deadly enemies.

Some of these subjects, such as Cardinal Allen, Hatton attacked by name, but he did not forget that all enemies were not beyond the seas: "And here I may not forget those vile wretches, those bloody priests and false traitors, here in our bosoms, but beyond the seas especially. They will not cease to practise both at home and abroad."[131]

In light of such nationalistic attacks, it is surprising that more severe legislation did not follow. A reason, perhaps, was the realization by many on the Privy Council, including Cecil, that, regardless of what religious exiles did, Catholics within the kingdom were dependable. Two letters written by spies among the Catholics informed the government that it was obvious that the recusants were loyal and would not support any foreign invasion.[132] Nonetheless the laws were remained on the books.

---

[129] Garnet to Acquaviva, London 24 November 1588, ARSI, Fondo Gesuitico 651/624. On their arrival see Caraman, *John Gerard*, pp. 8-11.
[130] ARSI, Fondo Gesuitico 651/624.
[131] Quoted in Neale, *Elizabeth I and Her Parliaments*, II, 197, 199.
[132] See LaRocca, "English Catholics and the Recusancy Laws," 136-37.

To take full advantage of the failure of the Armada, William Cecil addressed a small booklet to the Catholics. Disguised as a letter written by the recently martyred Richard Leigh to the former Spanish ambassador, *The copie of a letter sent out of England to don Bernardin Mendoza* appealed for change in a policy that too strongly favoured Spain. The author complained that the Armada's failure and Allen's attacks on the Queen discredited Catholicism. The recent example of recusants imprisoned in Ely, who volunteered to fight for their country, clearly demonstrated that the persecution in England was not for religion but for treason. If all Catholics within England were as patriotic as these, there would be no problem.

A consequence of the Armada was a steadfast refusal of English people to accept Catholicism, and their virulent opposition to the pope. Both would persist regardless of Elizabeth's successor. The author therefore suggested that a more profitable way to work for Catholicism's growth would be to abandon force and to encourage sound teaching and virtuous example. To do so, greater care must be exercised so that only learned and temperate priests were sent into England. And, almost as an afterthought, Leigh/Cecil suggested that, perhaps out of charity, the pope should permit occasional conformity.[133] All agree that this "was an ingenious piece of propaganda designed to drive a wedge between the Jesuit missionaries and the main body of English Catholics."[134]

Cecil was eager to use the recent failure of the Armada to discredit the Spanish party and to widen the split developing among English Catholics not just abroad but within the kingdom. Joel Hurstfield, however, would like to interpret the work as more than just propaganda. According to him, Cecil thought that "Catholic Englishmen were loyal, as indeed Armada year *had* [italics Hurstfield's] shown, and, if the Jesuit spearhead were broken, internal religious peace would be in sight."[135] Although Hurstfield admits that Cecil did not believe in toleration, the historian argues that he was "groping towards some kind of *modus vivendi* with the Catholics." But was Cecil sincere? Or was he simply seeking to destroy English Catholicism by fomenting divisions within it? We have no solid evidence and must therefore depend on historical evaluation of the man. And here there is tremendous disagreement.

Before word of the disaster reached Rome, Olivares was formulating plans for Allen's and Parsons's new roles. In October Olivares advised Philip that Allen should be sent to the Netherlands, where he could advise

---

[133] (London, 1588) STC 15412, pp. 3, 4, 5, 9, 13, 33, 34.
[134] Joel Hurstfield, "Church and State, 1558-1612: The Task of the Cecils," in *Studies in Church History II*, ed. G.J. Cuming (London, 1965) p. 135.
[135] "Church and State," p. 135.

the Prince of Parma on any proposals submitted by the English. Because of earlier disasters, about which Rome had already been informed, Allen could "console and encourage the Catholics there [England] and keep them hopeful, as they would not then think that your Majesty had turned your back upon the undertaking."[136]

In another letter Olivares suggested that Parsons, a man in whom Olivares found "great fertility of resource and very good discretion," accompany Allen or, indeed, go alone if the Pope continued to oppose the sending of Allen.[137] Neither man was sent: Allen remained in Rome[138] and Parsons was sent to Spain to treat various matters with the King, one of which was the English mission and the King's continued involvement with it "in accordance with our Institute and without any interference in military matters." Before his departure, the General named Parsons superior of all Jesuits sent to England and of all English chaplains in the Spanish army.[139]

Of equal importance was Parsons's role in preserving the Society of Jesus as founded by Ignatius Loyola. Conflict between the Society and the Inquisition in Spain persisted. The Inquisition condemned one of the Society's liberties: the right to denounce heretics within the order only to their religious superior. In 1585, after the Inquisition learned that the heresies of some Jesuits at the college in Monterrey were being concealed, it arrested the Castilian Provincial and two fathers from the college. This case was remanded to Rome in 1587.[140]

---

[136] After Allen's death some English secular priests sought to disassociate him from the debacle of the Armada, and asserted that various writings published under his name had actually been written by the Jesuit Parsons. In their writings one is often left with the impression that the Cardinal was a naively spiritual man who was led and manipulated by the Jesuit. On this issue see Leo Hicks, S.J., "Cardinal Allen and the Society: III. Allen and Persons," *The Month* 160 (1932) 528-36. Garrett Mattingly concluded that Parsons was "deeper in the maze of intrigues and negotiations about the Enterprise than anyone except Allen himself" (*Defeat of the Armada*, p. 72).

[137] Olivares to Philip II, Rome 3 October 1588; same to Parma, Rome 3 October 1588, in Knox, *Letters of Allen*, cviii-cxiii; same to Philip II, Rome 9 October 1588; same to same, Rome 17 October 1588, CSP Simancas (1587-1603) 466, 471-72. The Pope was not happy with the proposal that Allen go to the Netherlands and "threw a series of spectacular tantrums" (Duffy, "William, Cardinal Allen," 283).

[138] Allen remained in Rome for the rest of his life. On 31 October 1588, because of complaints regarding discipline at the college still in Reims, he named Richard Barret president (Knox, *First and Second Douay Diaries*, xc).

[139] ARSI, Hist. Soc. 61, f. 45^v; Hist. Soc. 62, f. 28^v; Tolet. 4, ff. 41^{r-v}; Knox, *Letters of Allen*, cxiii.

[140] Henry Kamen, *Inquisition and Society in Spain in the Sixteenth and Seventeenth Centuries* (London, 1985) p. 155. According to Woodward, the incident that sparked the controversy was less heresy than morality. Woodward (*Philip II*, p. 56) claimed that the Jesuit Provincial Antonio Marceu was denounced by the Inquisition because he had not informed the Inquisition of improper advances made by a member of his province and, indeed, had dismissed the Jesuit who made this indiscretion public.

The conflict became more complex when Philip II, although a supporter of the Jesuits, was persuaded that the rules and practices of the Jesuits throughout his kingdom should be submitted to the Inquisition for examination, and that the term of the general should be reduced.[141] The Society's Institute, its "way of proceeding," was threatened. After frenzied negotiations the King decided to entrust the matter to two Jesuits, one nominated by himself, and the other selected by the General. José de Acosta and Robert Parsons were sent. In Francis Edwards's biography, Parsons finally receives due acknowledgement for his important role in this episode.[142]

Catholic writers were left with the theological significance of the Armada disaster. Why did God not favour his cause? Why had he revealed himself to be so Protestant? Pedro de Ribadeneira interpreted the defeat as an act of purification "in order to sanctify His Majesty and give him a chance to humble himself under his powerful arm, to make him acknowledge the very great power that God has given him, and to realize how little value his own power has without Him.[143]" It was now up to the King himself to examine and remedy the possible causes of "this scourge and universal chastisement," among which, Ribadeneira suggested, was the King's past attitude of complacency towards Queen Elizabeth to the detriment of the English Catholics.

Robert Parsons offered his explanation: "God did not wish that such ruin [that would befall all because Spanish ministers did not believe that there were Catholics in England] should be brought on his servants at the hands of our people, after having suffered as they have done from the heretics."[144] John Gerard, presumed author of a letter to Allen, was more practical. He sought some consolation from a realization that "the going of the Armada and the knowledge thus gained, have produced results that could not have

---

[141] In "The Religious Life in the Spain of Philip II and Philip III" (*Monks, Hermits and the Ascetic Tradition*, ed. W.J. Sheils [Oxford, 1985]), A.D. Wright claimed that problems with Philip resulted from "the royal aim of establishing peninsular organization and Castilian dominance within each religious order," and from "the early identification of the Jesuits with independent royal authority in Portugal" (267).

[142] ARSI, Hisp. 74, ff. 29ᵛ-30ʳ. According to Henry More, Parsons was chosen because he was "a man always acceptable to its [Spain's] monarch and one whom the General had always found good at persuasion" (Francis Edwards, S.J., ed., *The Elizabethan Jesuits* [London, 1981] p. 203). For more information on this conflict see William V. Bangert, S.J., *A History of the Society of Jesus* (St. Louis, 1986) pp. 98-100, 110-13; Edwards, *Robert Persons*, pp. 130-34.

[143] Borja de Medina, "Jesuitas en la Armada," 23. See also Gómez-Centurión Jiménez, "The New Crusade," pp. 278-90. Ribadeneira wanted to accompany the Armada but his health would not permit it (*ibid.*, p. 297 n. 74). On Ribadeneira's political philosophy in general see Robert Bireley, S.J., *The Counter-Reformation Prince: Anti-Machiavellianism or Catholic Statecraft in Early Modern Europe* (Chapel Hill, 1991) pp. 111-35.

[144] Parsons to Don Juan de Idiáquez, Seville 4 April 1591, SC, Coll P, f. 246 (printed in Knox, *Letters of Allen*, pp. 330-31).

been obtained otherwise; and that means have now been found by which the enterprise may be effected with greater ease and safety."[145]

The only published work in English to discuss this problem was the anonymous (but Richard Verstegan is the acknowledged author) *The copy of a letter lately written by a Spanishe gentleman*.[146] The author is willing to accept the disaster as punishment for sin, but he will not admit it as a cause for discouragement because "it was not donne by the puisance of man, but by the power of God." The crimes committed by England demand vengeance, and Spain will recover for another attempt. The Catholic exiles, "retayning the true love, and affection, that Christians oughte to cary to their country, preferring the soule before the body, do first desire the conversion of there dere countrymen, kindred, & friends, from a confused chaos of heresies, to the one only Catholique & Apostolique faith." Hence they will strive to ensure that "A Kyngdome is transferred from one people to another, because of iniustice, of iniuries, and contumelies, and divers deceyts" (Eccl. 10:8). Many times the children of Israel failed at first attempt, but like Julius Caesar in his conquest of Britain, they were eventually successful.[147] To all Catholic exiles who supported Spain, the setback was only temporary.

* * * * *

The political and military aspirations of Catholic exiles suffered other calamities after the Armada. Secret negotiations between Scottish Catholic earls and Spain, at times with tacit approval of James, ended with the surrender of the earls in the spring of 1589. Shortly thereafter the Jesuits Edmund Hay and William Crichton left Scotland with the Earl of Huntly.[148] Parma's army, long inactive as it awaited an invasion of England, was repulsed at Bergen-op-Zoom, a strategically important Dutch outpost, in autumn of 1588. Another spate of mutinies by unpaid Spanish troops followed. Parma therefore suggested that Philip open negotiations with the Dutch. Conflict continued because Philip was unwilling to consider possible toleration.[149] In France a series of assassinations left Huguenot Henry of Navarre as claimant to the French throne. Such developments in Holland and France, along with George Clifford, Earl of Cumberland's establishment of

---

[145] Allen forwarded this letter to Olivares, who quoted it to the King (Olivares to Philip II, Rome 9 October 1588, CSP Simancas [1587-1603] 466).
[146] ([Antwerp], 1589) STC 1038, ARCR, II, no. 759.
[147] *Copy of a letter*, pp. 4, 34.
[148] Chadwick, "William Creichton," 275-78.
[149] Limm, *Dutch Revolt*, p. 61.

a temporary base in the Azores, Francis Drake's raid on Cadiz in 1589, and the Sixtus's refusal to pay the promised subsidy after the Armada, prevented Spain from immediately taking further action.[150]

Fear of another Armada nonetheless swept England periodically, with tragic consequences for Catholics. In May of 1590 Garnet complained that whenever there were rumours of a Spanish invasion:

> It is we who are hauled before the magistrates, we who are subject to questioning, we who are tortured and torn apart, we who are not plotting but hiding at home, giving ourselves to prayer and devotions, we who are beaten about the head unless we swear that we will support the queen in a war, however unjust, unless we affirm that there is no authority in the pope to excommunicate or depose the queen, and that in any case we will take up arms against him.[151]

Can one detect in the desperation a hint of anger against the conspirators for whose crimes Catholics in England suffer? After the Armada more Catholics abandoned an aggressive, militant policy in favour of seeking some accommodation with the government. Opposition to the pro-Spanish policy of Parsons and Allen increased. Eventually it would converge with discontent in Rome and with the pro-Scottish faction in France and the Low Countries to form a powerful anti-Jesuit movement. But do Garnet's comments suggest that there was division even within the Society of Jesus over the best way to proceed?

Despite everything, Catholic religious practices persisted. Less than a year after the Armada, pilgrimages were still made to St. Winefrid's Well near Bangor, to the shock and derision of Protestants.[152] An active Catholicism continued, and an invasion did not occur. Militarily distracted

---

[150] For an analysis of these developments see R.B. Wernham, *After the Armada* (Oxford, 1984) and John Lynch, *Spain 1516-1598: From Nation State to World Empire* (Oxford, 1991) pp. 380, 459. Importantly Sixtus, probably out of a desire to free himself from dependence on Spain, appeared ready to accept Henry's conversion after his victory at Arques in September of 1589 (Michael Wolfe, *The Conversion of Henri IV: Politics, Power, and Religious Belief in Earl Modern France* [Cambridge, Mass., 1993] pp. 88-95).

[151] 25 May 1590, ARSI, Fondo Gesuitico 651/624. In a letter to Acquaviva on 16 January 1590, Southwell reported that "the condition of Catholic recusants here is the same as usual, deplorable and full of fears and dangers; more especially since our adversaries have looked for wars. As many of ours as are in chains, rejoice and are comforted in their prisons; and they that are at liberty, set not their hearts upon it, nor expect it to be of long continuance" (ARSI, Fondo Gesuitico 651/648 [in McCoog, "Southwell," 123-24, partially translated in Henry Foley, S.J., *Records of the English Province of the Society of Jesus*, 7 vols. in 8 (Roehampton/London, 1877-84) I, 324]). This outburst was occasioned by a false rumour that a strong Spanish force had landed in Ireland.

[152] William R. Trimble, *The Catholic Laity in Elizabethan England 1558-1603* (Cambridge, Mass., 1964) p. 140. One of the pilgrims was John Gerard (Caraman, *John Gerard*, pp. 46-48).

by France and Holland, Philip could do nothing for the English except promise assistance and financial support for the foundation of colleges in Spain. Financial support was greatly needed because English Catholics, especially Jesuits, had lost a generous benefactor with the assassination of the Duke of Guise. After his death and with renewal of the religious wars, the college at Eu collapsed, and the Douai college, protected by the Guises at Reims from 1578 to 1593, nearly did.[153] Now only Philip could provide needed assistance to the mission and the colleges.

The elimination of the Guises removed the only serious Catholic military opposition to Spanish succession in England. Without them there was no powerful prince to advance the Stuart King as a serious alternative to the Spanish Princess Isabella. John Bossy has shown that turmoil in France closed the traditional route from Rome to England. For clergy, especially Jesuits, the road to England was now through Spain physically and spiritually.[154] There preparations would continue. A curtain fell with the Armada, but it only ended the first act. The play continued, and "the play's the thing."

---

[153] The Scots College at Pont-à-Mousson was another casualty. The royal pension stopped with the death of Mary Queen of Scots, and Sixtus V cancelled the papal pension to save money. The Jesuit college provided some assistance for two years, but at the end of the academic year 1589-90 the seminary was closed. See Hubert Chadwick, S.J., "The Scots College, Douai, 1580-1613," *EHR* 56 (1941) 580.

[154] "Rome and the Elizabethan Catholics: A Question of Geography," *Historical Journal* 7 (1964) 135-42.

CONCLUSION

"OUR WAY OF PROCEEDING"

In the introduction I cited three historians whose observations or criticisms affected the orientation of this study. One, Hugh Trevor-Roper, lamented two techniques that he commonly found in the works of Jesuit historians. The first was a principle of "distorting background" whereby embarrassing or compromising details were conveniently omitted; the second was "the principle of unequal scholarship: the scrupulous straining at small historical gnats which diverts attention from the silent digestion of large and inconvenient camels."[1] Thankfully both are encountered less often now than they were forty years ago when Trevor-Roper wrote his article. Then language and images rather carelessly borrowed from the recent experience with Nazi Germany and the Holocaust were not uncommonly employed to characterise the Elizabethan government and to describe its treatment of Catholics. Heroes and villains dominated the historiography, but occasionally someone would question the confessional bias. Subsequent research has revealed a broad spectrum of English Catholicism, the gradual introduction of penal legislation, and the vast difference between passing such legislation and implementing it. Most historians would now agree with the view first proposed by T.G. Law. In "English Jesuits and Scottish Intrigues, 1581-82" written nearly a century ago, he argued that, once the full story of Catholic political intrigues has been revealed, then the Queen's lapse "step by step into the sanguinary act of 1585" becomes as understandable as David Wolfe's and Robert Parsons's progression from devoted subjects of the Queen to active supporters of an enterprise.[2]

From his arrival in Ireland, David Wolfe associated with the O'Neills and the FitzGeralds. Beyond the Pale, in areas under their influence, Catholicism flourished. Their independence, however, was threatened by new English proposals to extend the Pale and to subject them to their king. Wolfe eventually concluded that the Catholic Church's future depended on the repudiation of English rule. Thus, he supported the FitzGerald rebellion, which eventually led to his dismissal from the Society.

---

[1] "Twice Martyred: The English Jesuits and Their Historians," in *Historical Essays* (London, 1957) pp. 116-17.
[2] In *Collected Essays and Reviews*, ed. P. Hume Brown (Edinburgh, 1904) p. 243.

With the possible encouragement of Henry, Duke of Guise, Robert Parsons followed a similar path after his flight from England. English Catholicism could only be restored by means of the deposition of Elizabeth and her replacement by Mary Queen of Scots. Neither Wolfe nor Parsons entertained such radical notions when they first returned to their countries. In his early writing, Parsons professed loyalty to the Queen, a loyalty he gradually abandoned. Contrary to the assertions of some historians, e.g. Arnold Pritchard,[3] we cannot dismiss Parsons's sincerity because of his subsequent activities. Nor can we claim with Michael Carrafiello that Robert Parsons arrived in England with a clearly delineated political programme.[4] Parsons only became interested in more political means for the restoration of Catholicism after the failure of the original mission and the opening of Scotland. His desire to liberate his compatriots from religious persecution—and, indeed, from eternal damnation, the inevitable consequence, it was believed, of heresy—led Parsons to consider various strategies and, eventually, to play an important role in the formation of coalitions aimed at Elizabethan England. Because of his concern for the spiritual well-being and salvation of his compatriots, Parsons could have argued that his involvement in such enterprises was a spiritual pursuit harmonious with the Society's Institute.

Aware of coalitions directed against the Queen and of threats to her life, the English government tried to disrupt the enterprise in any way possible, i.e. aid to the Dutch rebels, encouragement of the Protestant lords in Scotland, proposals for a dynastic alliance with France. Within the kingdom the possible defection of Catholic nobles with their retainers to an invading army worried the government. Parsons and William Allen took it for granted that sympathetic Catholic nobles would support the enterprise. Indeed, in his defense of Sir William Stanley and his justification for the Armada, Allen dealt with any scruples about allegiance that may have plagued the Catholic nobility. The Elizabethan government was apprehensive that the exiles were right. Elizabeth's position would be secure only with the total submission of Catholics. Penal legislation, rarely enforced with full vigour, became more draconian with each threat of invasion. The earlier policy of attrition had failed because of the arrival of the seminary priests and Jesuits. Catholicism had not died a natural death. By means of the penal laws, it would, as Christopher Haigh noted, "be murdered."[5]

Catholics within the kingdom suffered as a result of a cycle of violence

---

[3] *Catholic Loyalism in Elizabethan England* (London, 1979) p. 10.
[4] "English Catholicism and the Jesuit Mission of 1580-81," *Historical Journal* 37 (1994) 761-74.
[5] *Elizabeth I* (London, 1988) p. 38.

generated by the interplay of official legislation and foreign intrigue. We shall never know how many would have followed the example of Charles Nevill, Earl of Westmorland, and Stanley and supported a Spanish invasion. If contemporary estimations, including William Cecil's who tended to exaggerate the Catholic menace, are correct, few would have assisted the Spaniards. Many would probably have professed their allegiance as Richard Shelley and Sir Thomas Tresham did in 1585, and would have preferred a settlement that would have permitted them to "render to Caesar the things that were Caesar's" and, in so doing, to acknowledge Elizabeth's temporal sovereignty fully.

Catholic exiles had gambled on an invasion, and after the failure of the Armada, it appeared that they had lost. They encouraged each other not to abandon hope, and they offered consoling explanations for the setback, but complains against such an active, pro-Spanish policy became more frequent. The Scottish party of Charles Paget and Thomas Morgan murmured about the activities of Allen and Parsons; anonymous students at the English College in Rome criticised their policies. Even within the Society, there was not unanimity. Odo Pigenat decried Parsons's involvement with the Guises. Jasper Heywood, exiled from England in 1585, played no further role in the English mission because he was "out of step" with the Allen/Parsons programme. We can even detect hints of anger in Robert Southwell's letters, and a touch of pride in Henry Garnet's account of the triumphal procession to St. Paul's. Nonetheless, disagreement and disapproval did not deter Parsons. With the approval of Father General Acquaviva, Parsons was certain that his course was the proper way for the Society to proceed in England.[6]

II

"Our way of proceeding" was a familiar refrain throughout this history. John O'Malley, S.J., the second historian, concentrated on the history of the Society of Jesus from its foundation in 1540 until the death of Diego Laínez in 1565, by which date the fundamental elements of the Society's "way of proceeding" had been established. O'Malley distinguished four phases in the early history of the Society. The fourth, lasting from 1558 or 1559 until 1565, was not only "a confirmation and consolidation of the stipulations of the *Formula* [of the Institute] and the *Constitutions* but also a routinizing of

---

[6] See his "The observation of Certayne Aparent Judgements againste suche as have beene seditious [1598]," ed. John H. Pollen, S.J., in *Miscellanea II* (London, 1906) pp. 202-11 for accounts of what happened to those who opposed Parsons.

the interpretation they had been given in the past decade."[7] Although the Society would continue to change after 1565, "it moved almost inexorably and ever more definitively into modalities characteristic of the Counter Reformation as such." But throughout there were tensions and inconsistencies.[8] The Irish, Scottish, and English missions were, generally speaking, initiated and developed during the fourth phase when the Society's "way of proceeding" was fairly well established and becoming routine. Can these missions, nonetheless, tell us something about the Society and its Institute?

Ignatius Loyola wrote one of his most famous letters to the Jesuits in Coimbra in May of 1547. Alarmed by reports of excessive penitential practices among the scholastics, Loyola reminded them of the life they had chosen:

> And yet God has called you to this, in which His glory and the salvation of the neighbor are set before you, not as a general end but one toward all your life and its various activities which must be made by you into a continuous sacrifice. This requires a cooperation from you that should not stop with example and earnest prayer, but includes all the exterior means which His divine providence has provided for the mutual help we should give one another. From this you can understand how noble and royal is the manner of life you have chosen. For not merely among men, but not even among the angels, is there a nobler work than glorifying the Creator and bringing His creatures to Him as far as their capacities permit.[9]

Other orders may serve the world through prayer and good example, but Jesuits strive to lead all persons to God by all possible exterior means. This was intrinsic to the Society. In the "General Examen," a summary of the Society's Institute presented to anyone seeking admission, Ignatius stressed that each Jesuit "save[s] and perfect[s] his own soul by helping other souls, his neighbors. . . ."[10]

Although Ignatian spirituality linked personal salvation and the salvation of the neighbour, there was often tension regarding their proper relationship. Jesuits who over-emphasised the first risked monasticisation of the Society by transforming it into an order that served through example and prayer. Those who placed too strong a stress on the second boded an unreflective activism that forgot "the greater glory of God"[11] in the quest for worldly

---

[7] *The First Jesuits* (Cambridge, Mass., 1993) p. 368. The "Formula of the Institute" is the essential characteristics of the Society of Jesus contained in the various papal bulls of approval. It can be found in Ganss's edition of the *Constitutions*.

[8] *First Jesuits*, pp. 368-69.

[9] *Letters of St. Ignatius of Loyola*, ed. William J. Young, S.J. (Chicago, 1959) pp. 122-23.

[10] The General Examen can be found in Ganss's edition of the *Constitutions*. The citation comes from paragraph 52, p. 91. See also *Cons*. no. 3.

[11] According to O'Malley, this expression, unofficially adopted as the Society's motto, can be found over a hundred times in the *Constitutions* (*First Jesuits*, p. 18).

goals. A balance was essential.[12] The Society of Jesus was conceived then as an apostolic religious order in which everything should be "essentially apostolic" with nothing directed exclusively to personal sanctification.[13] Freed from the monastic rhythm of common religious exercises, choral recitation of divine office, and regular corporal austerities, each Jesuit, on completion of his formation, is exhorted to follow "discreet charity"[14] and the counsel of his confessor. Ignatius, thus, did not consider it expedient to legislate general rules for "what pertains to prayer, meditation, and study and also in regard to the bodily practices of fasts, vigils, and other austerities or penances." He simply urged:

> . . . the members should keep themselves alert that the excessive use of these practices may not weaken the bodily energies and consume time to such an extent that these energies are insufficient for the spiritual help of one's fellowmen according to our Institute; and on the other hand, they should be vigilant that these practices may not be reduced to such an extent that the spiritual grows cool and the human and lower passions grow worse.[15]

Ignatius placed tremendous emphasis on mortified, discerning men capable of evaluating all ascetical and spiritual practices in light of their ministry, men of "discreet charity." Jesuits, therefore, ought to examine everything, including devotions and mortifications, in light of the goals of the Society, and indulge in nothing that would restrict their ability "to labour strenuously."

Antonio M. de Aldama, S.J., historian of the Society's Institute, argued that the fruit of "discreet charity" was adaptability.[16] Indeed this flexibility was at the very heart of Ignatian spirituality. Even the

> The Spiritual Exercises must be adapted to the condition of the one who is to

---

[12] See François Courel, S.J., "La fin unique de la Compagnie de Jésus," *AHSI* 35 (1966) 186-211, and the rebuttal by Michael C. McGuckian, S.J., "The One End of the Society of Jesus," *AHSI* 60 (1991) 91-111. In opposition to Courel, McGuckian insisted that a "double end" was of the very nature of religious life. The novelty of the Society lay not in the reduction of a double to a single end but "in the formulation of a rule which would integrate the apostolic thrust into the very heart of religious life, not as an added extra, but as an intrinsic and essential part of religious life itself. Ignatius achieved this by putting the emphasis on the salvation of souls without distinction, all souls, ours and our neighbours, seen as one" (110). I am not sure that the two interpretations are as far apart as McGuckian thinks.

[13] See Miguel A. Fiorito, S.J., "Ignatius' Own Legislation on Prayer," *Woodstock Letters* 97 (1968) 200.

[14] George Ganss describes "discreet charity" thus: it is "the charity exercised by a discreet person, one who exercises natural and supernatural prudence or judgment in his actions. This discreet charity impels him to choose the objectively better course after all the circumstances have been considered" (p. 261 n. 2 continued in his edition of the *Constitutions*).

[15] *Cons.* no. 582. See also *Cons.* nos. 300-02.

[16] *The Constitutions of the Society of Jesus: An Introductory Commentary on the Constitutions* (St. Louis, 1989) p. 15.

engage in them, that is, to his age, education, and talent. Thus exercises that he could not easily bear, or from which he would derive no profit, should not be given to one with little natural ability or of little physical strength.[17]

The same principle was enshrined in the Society's *Constitutions* by numerous escape clauses e.g. do such and such unless, in the given situation, something else seems better. All directions were to be adapted to times, places, persons, and circumstances. The superior exercised his prudence through the application of general norms to particular situations.[18]

In various exhortations Jerónimo Nadal stressed the mobility and flexibility necessary for Jesuit life. Explaining the three conventional types of Jesuit houses, he added a fourth:

> The principal and most characteristic dwelling for Jesuits is not the professed houses, but in journeyings, . . . I declare that the characteristic and most perfect houses of the Society is the journeys of the professed, by which they diligently seek to gain for Christ the sheep that are perishing.[19]

Nadal did not deny the importance of the other three, i.e. house of probation, college, and professed house.[20] Indeed he stressed their value as places for rest and reflection. But Jesuits found "their most peaceful house" in the world, in their mission.

Over the years many have studied the influence of the Society's colleges on education and culture. More recently, historians such as Louis Châtellier, A. Lynn Martin and David Gentilcore[21] have shifted attention to the

---

[17] *The Spiritual Exercises of St. Ignatius*, ed. Louis J. Puhl, S.J. (Chicago, 1951) no. 18.

[18] See John O'Malley, S.J., "The Ministries of the Early Jesuits: Social Disciplining or Discerning Accommodation?," *CIS: Review of Ignatian Spirituality* (forthcoming); Aldama, *Constitutions*, pp. 15-16.

[19] I use the translation found in John W. O'Malley, S.J., "To Travel to Any Part of the World: Jerónimo Nadal and the Jesuit Vocation," *Studies in the Spirituality of Jesuits* 16/2 (1984) 7. For a fuller discussion consult that article.

[20] A house of probation is a novitiate, where Jesuits normally spend their first two years and their final year (called "tertianship") of formation. Often the tertianship is done in a separate house. Professed houses are residences of formed Jesuits, i.e. those with final vows, who devote themselves to various apostolic activities. Professed houses are generally distinguished from other residences by their poverty: they are forbidden any source of regular income and rely on alms. Colleges, in the strict sense, are a group of Jesuits who together exercise the same office, e.g. the college of confessors at St. Peter's, Rome. Usually they are academic institutions, either halls of residence such as the English College, or centres of learning such as the Roman College or the colleges found throughout Europe. Using colleges as their base, Jesuits work throughout the surrounding countryside. All colleges are allowed regular income.

[21] *The Europe of the Devout: The Catholic Reformation and the Formation of a New Society* (Cambridge, 1989); *The Jesuit Mind: The Mentality of an Elite in Early Modern France* (Ithaca, N.Y., 1988); and *From Bishop to Witch: The System of the Sacred in Early Modern Terra d'Otranto* (Manchester, 1992).

college's role as an apostolic centre for evangelising the surrounding city or countryside. Further study is, however, needed of the effect of the colleges on the Society's "way of proceeding." Tied to an academic calendar, Jesuits lost their mobility. As colleges proliferated, fewer Jesuits "found their most peaceful house" throughout the world: more and more were required for the classroom. John O'Malley recognised the consequent tension "between the continuing insistence on the necessity of mobility and the long-term commitment required by the schools,"[22] but we must await further research before we can ascertain how influential this decision was on the "routinisation" of the Institute. Was the decision to administer colleges a factor in the simultaneous standardisation of Jesuit life?

Colleges stabilised Jesuit communal life which became more regularised. Throughout the period considered in this volume, the Institute became multi-volumed as congregational decrees and rules, communal and particular, created a uniform, distinctive Jesuit way of religious life.[23] Each province added its own modifications, but, in general, customs and practices were becoming universal.[24] Jesuit daily life followed a rhythm more harmonious with monastic practices than with Nadal's ideal.

We can see the gradual shift in the early Society's treatment of prayer and religious attire. The first General Congregation (1558) resisted demands for the introduction of required periods of daily prayer for all Jesuits. After the second General Congregation (1565) Francis Borgia, the newly elected General, prescribed for a few provinces an hour of prayer and two fifteen-minute periods for examination of conscience each day. The fourth General Congregation (1581) decreed a full hour of mental prayer for all.[25]

Regarding clerical dress, Ignatius refused to prescribe a habit for the Society. According to the "Formula of the Institute," in the matter of religious attire, Jesuits would "follow the common and approved usage of reputable priests."[26] In the *Constitutions* Jesuit attire was to have three characteristics:

---

[22] *First Jesuits*, p. 239.

[23] On Nadal's introduction to a residence in Augsburg of the regular daily routine common to Jesuit colleges see William V. Bangert, S.J., *Jerome Nadal, S.J. (1507-1580): Tracking the First Generation of Jesuits*, ed. Thomas M. McCoog, S.J. (Chicago, 1992) p. 319.

[24] On the rules see O'Malley, *First Jesuits*, pp. 337-39.

[25] John W. Padberg, S.J., Martin D. O'Keefe, S.J., and John L. McCarthy, S.J., eds., *For Matters of Greater Moment: The First Thirty Jesuit General Congregations* (St. Louis, 1994) First Congregation, decree no. 97; Second Congregation, decree no. 29; Fourth Congregation, decree no. 5, pp. 92-93, 120, 169. For a slightly dated but still useful introduction to the subject see Robert E. McNally, S.J., "St. Ignatius: Prayer and the Early Society of Jesus," *Woodstock Letters* 94 (1965) 109-34.

[26] This citation can be found in paragraph 6 in Ganss's edition of the *Constitutions*.

first, it should be proper; second, conformed to the usage of the region where one is living; and third, not contradictory to the poverty we profess. . . .[27]

Jesuits entering Germany wore the cassock of the Roman clergy. Nadal asked Father General Borgia if they could abandon that garb for the attire of the local clergy. Because of German dislike for foreigners, especially those from the south, the Roman soutane made Jesuit work more difficult. Borgia denied the request because there already was a great variety of clerical dress in the north, and because unity within the Society demanded standardisation.[28] By 1588 standardisation had progressed to such an extent that instructions to William Holt and Joseph Creswell referred to the "Society's dress" (*vestitum etiam Societatis*).

III

The early missions to Ireland and Scotland, brief and undertaken at the command of the pope, sparked no questions about the nature of the Society. Issues were first raised during David Wolfe's and William Good's sojourn. Wolfe was sent as a legate, Good as assistant to the Archbishop of Armagh who was given faculties to establish a university. In and around Limerick, Wolfe, Good, and later Edmund Daniel preached, established a school, and maintained good relations with the FitzGeralds. Neither Wolfe nor Good found the mission "their most peaceful house": both complained of spiritual desolation. Both wanted to leave, and Father General Mercurian eventually withdrew them. Their mission highlighted the possible consequences of life on the frontier without strong religious, communal support. Because of the dangers the men faced and the loneliness they endured, along with the risk of political involvement, Mercurian was extremely reluctant to continue the Irish mission. The style of religious life necessitated by Irish conditions, and not the qualities of the men sent on the mission, the General decided, was not compatible with the Institute.

Mercurian's anxiety about the proposed Jesuit mission to England stemmed from his experience with Ireland. Convinced of the value of the mission by his consultors, Mercurian addressed potential problems in his instructions.

As in Ireland, circumstances prevented the creation of Jesuit communities and full Jesuit observance. Jesuits in England were of necessity closer to the model proposed by Nadal. Each pursued his ministry without the support provided by communal life. His chief aid, according to Mercurian, was

---

[27] *Cons.* no. 577.
[28] Bangert, *Nadal*, p. 332.

"right intention, and a combination of distrust in them themselves with a firm confidence in God to whom alone they can look for grace and light."[29] Nonetheless, because of the realistic possibility of loneliness and desolation, the men should meet frequently for advice and spiritual assistance.[30] According to Mercurian, this was the custom of the Society.

Robert Parsons met his friend George Gilbert, a wealthy Catholic, upon arrival in England. A few years later Gilbert crossed to the continent and entered the Society. In England Gilbert arranged and financed the Jesuits' journeys at considerable personal risk and expense. In "A Way to Deal with Persons of all sorts so as to Convert them and Bring them back to a Better Way of Life—Based on the System and Method Used by Fr. Robert Persons and Fr. Edmund Campion,"[31] Gilbert explained his system. The majority of missionaries, both Jesuits and secular priests, travelled from house to house to minister to Catholics in the area; others were stationed in houses of some gentry as if they were a "relation, friend or steward, or in some office of dignity but little work, so as not to interfere with his own calling."[32] Besides caring for the family with whom they resided, these others undertook spiritual charge of an area around the residence. Although Gilbert does not mention it, there apparently was a third option: rooms rented for use of the priests. Throughout Parsons's letters from England there are references to such rooms. It is not clear, however, whether such rooms were lodgings or nothing more than storerooms for liturgical and devotional vestments, etc.

The first Jesuits in England resided either in a country house of a gentleman or travelled on a missionary circuit.. From our knowledge of the activities of Campion, Parsons, Holt, and Heywood, they had no stable residence. In 1584 Parsons suggested that one Jesuit reside in or around London so that he could receive incoming priests and arrange for their settlement.[33]

---

[29] Leo Hicks, S.J., ed., *Letters and Memorials of Father Robert Persons, S.J.* (London, 1942) p. 319.

[30] During semi-annual meetings the Jesuits followed the Jesuit daily order as it was well established in the continental colleges, discussed cases of conscience, heard each other's confessions, and exhorted one another to greater fervour. The meetings, generally held in or around London, brought considerable spiritual consolation to the men. In a letter to the General, Robert Southwell acknowledged that the confessions and renewal of vows remind the priests that "our small efforts are added to that mighty mountain which is being built up by the good deeds of all just men throughout the universe" (Southwell to Acquaviva, 20 December 1588, ARSI, Fondo Gesuitico 651/648 [in Thomas M. McCoog, S.J., "The Letters of Robert Southwell, S.J.," *AHSI* 63 (1994) 119-21]). See also Garnet to Acquaviva, 2 March 1590, SC, Coll P f. 555.

[31] Hicks, *Letters of Persons*, pp. 331-40.

[32] From our limited knowledge of activities of Jesuits in Ireland and Scotland, they seem to have travelled less frequently. At this time Jesuits in Ireland tended to avoid the Pale and to reside in areas generally controlled by sympathetic chieftains. Jesuits in Scotland usually resided with and were protected by one of the Catholic earls.

[33] Parsons to Acquaviva, Paris 23 July 1584, in Hicks, *Letters of Persons*, p. 223.

Persecution periodically destroyed the circuit. Campion's capture disrupted the system established by Gilbert. Because of new penal legislation directed against anyone who harboured a priest, Heywood when captured was erecting a new circuit less dangerous to lay Catholics. William Weston was apprehended while completing Heywood's work.

In 1589 Henry Garnet explained to Claudio Acquaviva the disorder that he had found in England upon his arrival. There was, he related, no adequate system for the reception and transfer of newly arrived priests. Indeed the situation was so bad that Garnet was not sure that any more secular priests should be sent. Because renewed persecution produced many clerical apostates, houses that had formerly welcomed the clergy were now closed. Consequently many priests wandered about the countryside.[34] Garnet and Southwell made the erection of a new network their top priority. Originally stationed at William, Lord Vaux's house in Hackney, Southwell welcomed the arriving priests. There Southwell lived relatively quietly and, as he testified to Father Acquaviva on 25 July 1586, was able to prepare sermons, to hear confessions, and to perform other priestly duties.[35] He later moved to Arundel House. Meanwhile Garnet, operating either from Lord Vaux's house in Northampton or his daughter's, Eleanor Brooksby's, in Leicester, established centres throughout the country where the new men could be sent.[36] Garnet's plan was this: experienced men established local centres where the newly arrived priests would live and work, and which they themselves would use as a base for their work throughout the countryside. From these centres, as from the Jesuit colleges on the continent, radiated apostolic activity.

Garnet wanted to set up his own house in London to reduce the risk of punishment for laity: harbouring clergy was a felony punishable by death. His first house was a small cottage in Finsbury Fields rented in 1588. Garnet described it to the General years later: it was a garden cottage accessible to clergy in London and to visiting priests. Because no one believed that anyone actually resided there, no one ever called on the house. For greater security, all food was cooked at night and all visitors were instructed to speak in a low voice. The house served as Garnet's refuge from the dangers and pressures of his work until it was discovered and raided in 1591.[37]

---

[34] Garnet to Acquaviva, [early 1589], ARSI, Fondo Gesuitico, 651/624; same to same, 12 September 1589, SC, Anglia I, 41.
[35] John H. Pollen, S.J., ed., *Unpublished Documents Relating to the English Martyrs 1584-1603* (London, 1908) p. 309. By August of 1587 Southwell was at Arundel House.
[36] Christopher Devlin, S.J., *The Life of Robert Southwell: Poet and Martyr* (London, 1956) p. 116.
[37] Garnet to Acquaviva, London 17 March 1593, SC, Anglia I, 73, translated in Philip Caraman, S.J., *Henry Garnet (1555-1606) and the Gunpowder Plot* (London, 1964) p. 68. See also pp. 122, 126.

Throughout the period under consideration there were few Jesuits in each mission: there were never more than four or five in Scotland and Ireland; in England, there were at most a half-dozen outside prison. In the Irish and Scottish missions one Jesuit was designated superior. The English mission developed a more sophisticated administration, one that resembled customary Jesuit governance. Its evolution can be traced through the instructions given to the Jesuits as they left for England.

Earlier in this study we examined the original instructions given to Campion and Parsons by Mercurian and subsequent ones given by Acquaviva to Heywood and Holt in 1581, to Weston in 1584, to Garnet and Southwell in 1586, and to Holt and Creswell in 1588.[38] A comparison reveals that instructions were modified or eliminated. In the original instructions, Father General Mercurian echoed a frequent Ignatian concern about poverty: the missionaries were forbidden to beg alms and, in case of emergency, they should turn only to trusted friends for assistance. Such prohibitions were lifted and Jesuits were permitted to gather and distribute money to subsidize their own and secular priests' activities, and to assist impoverished Catholics.[39] The General was drawing conclusions from the Society's experience in England. Prudent evaluation decided what assisted and what impeded the Society's work.

Dispensations from other religious and Jesuit obligations were granted. If penitents gave money to their confessors as restitution, the priests must forward it to those to whom it was owed. If there was doubt regarding the rightful recipient, Jesuits could spend the money on the poor and on works of charity. All Jesuit priests and brothers were authorised to dispense priests "in cases of irregularity and *defectus lenitatis*."[40] Living in secrecy and in constant danger, the priests could not always celebrate Mass. Therefore they were bound to offer only the weekly Mass for the General's intention. Moreover they could substitute other intentions if necessary. Indeed the Mass itself could be omitted if there was no convenient place. Paucity of Jesuits resulted in a dispensation from the obligation of having a fellow Jesuit as a confessor. In order to carry out their work more effectively, the fathers were given permission to publish dogmatic and spiritual pamphlets. Interestingly, Campion and Parsons had received papal permission to print books without

---

[38] Hicks, *Letters of Persons*, pp. 317 n. 6; 318 n. 19; 355-57; 361-63. The following discussion is based on these instructions.

[39] See Thomas M. McCoog, S.J., "The Finances of the English Province of the Society of Jesus in the Seventeenth Century: Introduction," *RH* 18 (1986) 14-33, and "'The Slightest Suspicion of Avarice': The Finances of the English Jesuit Mission," 19 *RH* (1988) 103-23 for more information on Jesuit poverty and the English mission.

[40] Leo Hicks interprets this curious phrase as referring to possible cooperation in shedding of blood by being present at a Catholic's execution (*Letters of Persons*, p. 356 n. 5).

specifying author, place, and publisher, but they had not received the general's authorization. That was first given to Garnet and Southwell. But, as we have seen, its lack did not silence the presses.[41]

On their journey Holt and Creswell were dispensed from the Society's regulation that they remain in Jesuit colleges en route and that they discuss their affairs with the community's superior. If they deemed it necessary, they were not required to "be seen everywhere in the Society's dress" but could "conform to the custom of respectable priests" or dress "entirely different[ly]," presumably in secular attire. Whenever they wore the Society's dress, they were to be concerned about edification. Thus they "would expose themselves to considerable comment" if they frequented public hostelries in cities where there were Jesuit colleges.

As superior of the mission, Parsons received all privileges, faculties, and favours that the General could grant "in the internal forum"; "in the external forum" he was granted all privileges and faculties first of a rector and later of a provincial. As rector Parsons would have been subject to the provincial of the province to which, if the General's wishes had been followed, the mission was attached. Once it became clear that the English mission would remain independent, the superior assumed the powers of a provincial. The precise date of the change is not known, but it occurred before Garnet's and Southwell's journey to England in 1586. Odo Pigenat's direction of the Scottish and English missions after Parsons's departure for tertianship in 1585 presumably ended with Parsons's completion of the programme in 1586. Apparently he persuaded Acquaviva to remove the English mission from Pigenat's administration. Beginning with the instructions to Garnet and Southwell, the superior assumed the powers of a provincial.

Within England the Jesuit superior was the only established ecclesiastical authority. Without him there was no church order. Because of omnipresent dangers of imprisonment and execution, exceptional but necessary arrangements were made to ensure its maintenance. Ordinarily the General named a successor upon death, resignation, or the completion of the incumbent's term. In the instructions to Holt and Creswell, Acquaviva not only named a successor to the superior but established a line of succession: Weston, Garnet, Holt (if he came to England), Southwell.

Parsons retained overall direction of the mission until his flight to France in 1581. From Rouen he delegated Heywood as his substitute but, as we have seen, the relation was not a cordial one. Heywood's authority and power had not been clearly defined and Parsons's prolonged absence and

---

[41] For other faculties granted see ARSI, Fondo Gesuitico 720/A/II/2; Acquaviva to William Allen, Rome 14 October 1581, in "Some Correspondence of Cardinal Allen, 1579-85," ed. Patrick Ryan, S.J., in *Miscellanea VII* (London, 1911) pp. 81-85.

silence compounded the problem. From a distance Parsons retained some authority, especially in the selection of missionaries. Weston became superior upon arrival, a position he retained despite his capture in 1586. With Weston's transfer on 21 January 1588 from the Clink to Wisbech in Cambridgeshire, where he remained until his exile in May of 1603, Garnet replaced him as superior.[42]

As in the missions in Ireland and Scotland, the superior was the only Jesuit official in the English mission until 1588. Garnet then introduced two other Jesuit positions on instructions from the General. From the more experienced missionaries, Garnet chose two consultors, the senior of whom became his admonitor.[43] In England an administration was evolving, but a major institutional problem still was not addressed: the precise relation between Parsons and the superior in England.

After Parsons's departure from England he retained the mission's superiorship with Heywood as his vicar. There is nothing, however, to indicate that Heywood's successor Weston was Parsons's delegate and not a superior in his own right. But Parsons's activities in France make it clear that he held some type of authority; apparently it was more personal than juridical. Jesuits in England were subject to their superior; Englishmen working in other areas, were subject to the local provincial. Neither group came under Parsons's jurisdiction. He served more as an intermediary advising the General on English affairs, and soliciting men and funds for the mission. Despite his reluctance he temporarily served in a similar role for the Scottish mission until his replacement by Pigenat and James Tyrie. Father Acquaviva vetoed a request from Irish Jesuits for a comparable official. Parsons's position was regularised in 1588 before his departure for Spain when Acquaviva named him superior of all Jesuits sent to England—and presumably after their arrival—and of English Jesuit chaplains in the Spanish army. He had no authority over other English Jesuits who remained subject to their provincial. Indeed, despite Parsons's authority over English Jesuit chaplains, foreign provincials occasionally claimed jurisdiction

---

[42] On the move see Philip Caraman, S.J., ed., *William Weston: The Autobiography of an Elizabethan* (London, 1955) pp. 161-63. At this time, and shortly thereafter, there were suggestions that Weston purchase his freedom: Weston himself rejected the proposals. See Caraman, *William Weston*, p. 118, and Caraman, *Garnet and the Gunpowder Plot*, pp. 67-68. In a letter to Acquaviva written the following day, 22 January, Southwell explained the incredible but true news that access would be given to the priests in Wisbech (ARSI, Fondo Gesuitico 651/648 [in McCoog, "Southwell," 108-10]).

[43] Within the Society each superior received advisors, consultors, appointed by his superior. Generally there were four. The superior was expected to listen to their views on important matters. The admonitor was one of the superior's subjects commissioned to report to the superior observations—either his own or those of other subjects—regarding the superior's governance and health.

over English Jesuit chaplains within their geographical boundaries, and resented the status of such Jesuits as quasi-ecclesiastical peculiars.

Subject directly to the General, the English mission was independent of the control of foreign provincials, yet extremely dependent on their goodwill. The English, like the Irish and Scots, relied on foreign provinces to make space for their candidates in the novitiates and houses of formation. There were more than occasional complaints that space was limited and money tight. Moreover there was no guarantee that a provincial would free the Jesuit after ordination for work in his native land. Problem cases such as Heywood were willingly conceded by provincials, but they were extremely reluctant to give up men such as Campion and Garnet; they did so only on the insistence of the General. Independent the mission might be but its future stability would be ensured only when it could accept and train its own candidates.[44]

* * * * *

John Bossy, the third historian, correctly contended that the Jesuits in England were spared many of the difficulties experienced by the secular clergy because of the flexibility of the Society's Institute. A distinctive Jesuit gown may be imposed throughout the continent; the amount of time to be devoted to daily prayer may be fixed; the daily order of the continental colleges may have acquired a monastic rhythm, but in these three missions such rules were not as important as the work. The Jesuit missions to Ireland, Scotland, and England demonstrate that the flexibility so highly prized by Loyola and had not been forgotten despite the proliferation of rules.

The absence of a thorough study of the generalate of Claudio Acquaviva makes an evaluation of his role in the development of the Society's Institute difficult. On the basis of the sheer volume of rules, regulations, and ordinances written during his long generalate, he is often blamed for the complete institutionalisation of Jesuit religious life. Yet if he is considered from the perspective of his support for the English mission, a different Acquaviva emerges. Acquaviva insisted that he did not send Jesuits to England to edify Catholics by their deaths but to strengthen Catholics by their lives of service. Candidates for the mission must be carefully screened. The life was difficult, and the Jesuits selected needed certain psychological and spiritual resources. Once the men were in England, Acquaviva insisted on certain practices such as the semi-annual meeting for their well-being. To ensure the success of Jesuit ministry, Acquaviva granted dispensations.

---

[44] See Thomas M. McCoog, S.J., "The Establishment of the English Province of the Society of Jesus," *RH* 17 (1984) 121-39.

Which is the authentic Acquaviva? Alas until further research is done, we can not say.

Of the three missions, Father General Claudio Acquaviva preferred the English. We do not know whether this preference was due to the larger number of Englishmen within the Society, or to a realisation that England's reconversion was strategically more important, or to his personal fondness for Robert Parsons. Whatever the motives, the English mission had a powerful champion whose support would rescue it periodically until Acquaviva's death in 1615. To the shock and anger of continental Jesuits, Acquaviva granted so many concessions to the English that continental Jesuits barely recognised them as members of the same religious order. Eventually Acquaviva liberated the English Jesuits from the jurisdiction of foreign provincials by introducing administrative novelties such as the prefecture in 1598. Resentment of such special privileges granted to the mission nearly resulted in its destruction after Acquaviva's death.[45]

During Acquaviva's generalate the Society of Jesus became more identified with the Counter-Reformation. Popes, kings, princes, and dukes, so carefully cultivated as friends and benefactors, now turned to Jesuits for advice and assistance in the struggle with Protestantism. Few Jesuits would have avoided the struggle with the disclaimer that priests should not meddle in politics. The struggle against Protestantism, it was argued, was not political but religious. It was a struggle that could not be ignored if Jesuits were sincerely interested in the salvation of their neighbour. Acquaviva probably shared Mercurian's apprehensions about over-involvement, and he steered Parsons from perilous shoals. There were limits to the Society's increasing alliance with Counter-Reformation popes and monarchs and Acquaviva strove to define them. Jesuits should not be involved in negotiations directly involved with military matters. This is made most explicit in Acquaviva's instructions to Parsons upon his departure for Spain in late 1588: Parsons should negotiate with the King "in accordance with our Institute and without any interference in military matters."

The issue of Jesuit involvement in secular affairs was discussed in several provincial congregations in the early 1590s. At least six drafted *postulata* on the subject for the fifth General Congregation (1593-94), which then decreed:

> Because our Society, called forth by the Lord for the spread of the faith and the harvest of souls, can happily attain the end it proposes through the ministries proper to its institute—spiritual armaments carried under the banner of the cross with benefit to the Church and the edification of our neighbors—that same Society would hinder the achievement of these goals and expose

---

[45] See McCoog, "Establishment of the English Province."

itself to extreme perils if it were to engage in what is secular and belongs to political affairs and the governance of states.[46]

A second decree stated:

> Special attention must be given to this warning: Ours are not to cultivate familiarity with princes to the detriment of spiritual welfare and religious discipline; and they should not become engaged in other secular affairs, even though connected with the particular affairs of relatives, friends, or anyone else, unless perchance in the judgment of superiors charity might occasionally dictate otherwise. . . . we must take special care that we make the effort to assist our neighbors within the limitations of our institute.[47]

Parsons worried that these decrees would curtail his activities. He protested that their complete observance was impossible for anyone concerned with the English mission because the "interests of the Catholic religion in England are so bound up and intermingled with those of the state that one cannot deal with the first without treating the second." Consequently, Parsons requested a dispensation.[48] Acquaviva replied that dispensations would not be easily conceded because the issue had so upset the universal Society. Nonetheless, Acquaviva continued, Parsons did not require a dispensation as long as he proceeded prudently and religiously. As regards England, the decree did not forbid Jesuits advising rulers on matters that pertained to the service of the Lord even if such matters were mingled with state affairs.[49]

In 1588 Acquaviva was under attack and on his fate depended the missions' future. He believed that the work undertaken by Jesuits in the three missions was important and thus justified concessions regarding finances, secular dress, communal life, and prayer. His understanding of the Institute, especially the recent congregational decrees, did not exclude but simply limited Parsons's activities. There was no guarantee that another general would be as sympathetic.

---

[46] Padberg, *For Matters of Greater Moment*, Fifth Congregation, decree 47, p. 200.
[47] Padberg, *For Matters of Greater Moment*, Fifth Congregation, decree 48, p. 200.
[48] Parsons to Acquaviva, Marchena 12 May 1595, ARSI, Hisp. 136, ff. 318^{r-v}.
[49] Acquaviva to Parsons, Rome 4 July 1594, ARSI, Tolet. 5/II, f. 348^r.

BIBLIOGRAPHY

ARCHIVES

LONDON

Archives of the Archdiocese of Westminster (AAW)

II. Collected letters and theological manuscripts, 1570-1581.

Archives of the British Province of the Society of Jesus (ABSI)

46/4/2. Hubert Chadwick's transcripts of documents pertaining to the Scots Colleges.
46/5A/1. John H. Pollen's manuscript history of the Jesuits in England.
46/23/8. Leo Hicks's copy of John MacErlean's transcripts of documents relating to 16th and 17th century Ireland, and to Irish Jesuits.

British Library (BL)

Harleian MS 422. Papers of John Foxe.
Add. MS 11055. Tresham Papers, vol. 1.
Add. MS 39828. Scudamore Papers, vol. 1.

Public Record Office (PRO)

SP 12/137. State Papers Domestic, Elizabeth April 1580.
SP 12/142. State Papers Domestic, Elizabeth September 1580.
SP 12/144. State Papers Domestic, Elizabeth November 1580.
SP 12/147. State Papers Domestic, Elizabeth January-February 1581.
SP 12/149. State Papers Domestic, Elizabeth May-June 1581.
SP 12/153. State Papers Domestic, Elizabeth April-May 1582.
SP 12/155. State Papers Domestic, Elizabeth August-September 1582.
SP 12/176. State Papers Domestic, Elizabeth January-February 1585.
SP 12/178. State Papers Domestic, Elizabeth April-May 1585.
SP 12/182. State Papers Domestic, Elizabeth September 1585.
SP 12/183. State Papers Domestic, Elizabeth October 1585.
SP 12/191. State Papers Domestic, Elizabeth July 1586.
SP 12/193. State Papers Domestic, Elizabeth September 1586.
SP 12/195. State Papers Domestic, Elizabeth November-December 1585.
SP 12/199. State Papers Domestic, Elizabeth March 1587.
SP 12/202. State Papers Domestic, Elizabeth June-July 1587.
SP 12/205. State Papers Domestic, Elizabeth November 1587.
SP 12/206. State Papers Domestic, Elizabeth December 1587.
SP 12/211. State Papers Domestic, Elizabeth June 1588.

SP 15/29. State Papers Domestic, Additional 1585, 1586.

SP 78/7. State Papers Foreign, France January-July 1582.
SP 78/8. State Papers Foreign, France August-December 1582.
SP 78/12. State Papers Foreign, France July-December 1584.
SP 78/14. State Papers Foreign, France June-December 1585.

SP 94/1. State Papers Foreign, Spain June 1577-May 1583.

OXFORD

Bodleian Library

Rawlinson MS D 353. Miscellaneous theological and historical papers, 16th and 17th centuries.
Tanner 79. Miscellaneous theological and historical papers, 16th and 17th centuries,

ROME

Archivio di Stato di Roma

Paesi Stranieri, busta 28, fasc. 1. Inghilterra.

Archivum Romanum Societatis Iesu (ARSI)

Angl. 14. Catalogi informationum prov. Angliae 1639-1649.
Angl. 30/I-II. Anglia historia I 1550-1589.
Angl. 31/I-II. Anglia historia II 1590-1615.
Angl. 41. Hibernia historia 1566, 1591-1692.
Angl. 42. Scotia historia: 1566-1634.
Aquit. 1/I-II. Epistolae generalium a 1571 ad 1612.
Austr. 1/I-II. Epistolae generalium 1573-1600.
Baet. 1a. Epistolae generalium a 1573 ad 1576.
Epp. Ext. 7/I-II. Epistolae cardinalium 1539-1569.
Epp. Ext. 10. Epistolae episcoporum 1555-1566.
Epp. Ext. 14. Epistolae episcoporum 1580-1586.
Epp. Ext. 28. Epistolae principum 1576-1585.
Epp. N.N. 1. Epistolae generalium ad diversas provinciae 1573-1590.
Epp. N.N. 51. Epistolae generalium 3 mart. 1556-1 apr. 1559.
Fl. Belg. 1/I-II. Epistolae generalium a 1573 ad 1576; a 1583 ad 1610.
Fl. Belg. 2. Epistolae generalium a 1576 ad 1582.
Franc. 1/I-II. Epistolae generalium a 1573 ad 1604.
Gal. 44. Registrum secretum epistolarum generalium a 1583 ad 1602.
Gal. 45. Epistolae generalium Franciae 1576-1580 et Aquitaniae 1575-1579.
Gal. 81. Epistolae Galliae 1565-1568.
Gal. 82. Epistolae Galliae 1569.
Gal. 90. Epistolae Galliae 1578-1579.
Gal. 91. Epistolae Galliae 1580-1584.
Gal. 92. Epistolae Galliae 1585-1587.
Germ. 105. Epistolae 1561-1565.
Germ. 106. Epistolae 1565-1567.
Germ. 108. Epistolae 14 Augusti 1569-26 Jul. 1573.
Germ. 141. Epistolae Germaniae Lit. Annuae 1572-1593.
Germ. 143. Epistolae Germaniae 1561.
Germ. 144. Epistolae Germaniae 1562-1563.
Germ. 145. Epistolae Germaniae 1564.
Germ. 147. Epistolae Germaniae 1566.
Germ. 148. Epistolae Germaniae 1567.
Germ. 149. Epistolae Germaniae 1568.
Germ. 150. Epistolae Germaniae 1569.
Germ. 151. Epistolae Germaniae 1570.
Germ. 152. Epistolae Germaniae 1571-1573.
Germ. 168. Epistolae Germaniae October 1587-December 1590.
Hisp. 68. Epistolae generalium Hispaniae 1567-1569.
Hisp. 74. Epistolae generalium Hispaniae Soli 1585-1599.
Hisp. 122. Epistolae Hispaniae August-December 1574.
Hisp. 123. Epistolae Hispaniae January-April 1575.

Hisp. 124. Epistolae Hispaniae May-August 1575.
Hisp. 136. Epistolae Hispaniae August 1593-June 1594.
Hist. Soc. 42. Catalogus defunctorum S.I. 1557-1623.
Hist. Soc. 61. Litterae patentes 1573-1601.
Hist. Soc. 62. Litterae patentes 1599-1640.
Instit. 117/I-II. Ordinationes et instructiones R.P. Generalium ab 1565 ad 1647.
Instit. 121. Epistolae aliquae pastorales praepositorum generalium ab 1556 ad 1600.
Instit. 187. Instructiones 1546-1582.
Instit. 188. Instructiones 1536-1596.
Ital. 58. Vota simplicia II 1548-1560.
Ital. 61. Epistolae generalium 1557-1559.
Ital. 65. Epistolae generalium 1564-1565.
Ital. 115. Epistolae Italiae 1560.
Ital. 122. Epistolae Italiae 1562-1563.
Ital. 146. Epistolae Italiae January-April 1575.
Ital. 148. Epistolae Italiae 1575.
Lus. 64. Epistolae Lusitaniae 1570-1572.
Lus. 65. Epistolae Lusitaniae 1572-1573.
Lus. 66. Epistolae Lusitaniae 1574.
Lus. 67. Epistolae Lusitaniae 1575.
Lus. 68. Epistolae Lusitaniae 1577-1584.
Opp. N.N. 158. Joannes Card. de Lugo, "Collectio tractatuum variorum moralium."
Rom. 12/I-II. Epistolae generalium ad Provinciam Romanam 1573-1584.
Rom. 51/I-II. Visitationes 1576-1589.
Rom. 52. Visitationes 1582-1665.
Rom. 78/I. Catalogi personarum et officiorum prov. Romanae 1604-1606, 1617, 1691.
Rom. 156/I-II. Romana historia collegiorum Anglorum, Scotorum, et Hibernicorum 1579-1783.
Tolet. 1. Epistolae generalium 1573-1584.
Tolet. 4. Epistolae generalium 1586-1594.
Tolet. 5/I-II. Epistolae generalium 1588-1600.
Fondo Gesuitico 647/241. Epistolae selectae, vol. 4 (Der-Gho).
Fondo Gesuitico 651. Epistolae selectae ex Anglia, fasc. 593-661.
Fondo Gesuitico 720/A. Missiones in Europa, fasc. 26.

Aldama, Antonio M. de, S.J. *Litterae Apostolicae ad Societatem Iesu pertinentes*. Unpublished compilation. Rome, 1953.

STONYHURST

Stonyhurst College (SC)

MS A, V, 1. Various papers concerning the history of the Society of Jesus.
Anglia I. Collected Manuscripts, 1554-1594.
Coll. P. Christopher Grene's 17th century collection of manuscripts and transcripts, section P.
Glover Transcripts II, B.I.16. Thomas Glover's transcripts of documents in the Roman archives, made in the late 18th or early 19th century.

VATICAN CITY

Archivio Segreto Vaticano (ASV)

Arm. 64, vol. 28. Anglia, Hibernia, et Scotia.

BOOKS

Published Documents

Akrigg, G.P.V., ed. *Letters of King James VI & I*. Berkeley, 1984.
Anderson, William James. "Narratives of the Scottish Reformation, I: Report of Father Robert Abercrombie, S.J. in the Year 1580," *IR* 7 (1956) 27-59; 8 (1957) 69.
———. "Narratives of the Scottish Reformation, II. Thomas Innes on Catholicism in Scotland 1560-1653," *IR* 7 (1956) 112-21.
Astudillo, E., S.J., ed. *Epistolae et Acta patris Iacobi Lainii secundi praepositi generalis Societatis Iesu*. 8 vols. Madrid, 1912-16. MHSI 44, 45, 47, 49, 50, 51, 53, 55.
Bain, Joseph, Boyd, William K., et. al., eds. *Calendar of State Papers Relating to Scotland and Mary, Queen of Scots, 1547-1603*. 13 vols. in 14. London, 1898-1969.
Brouwers, Louis, S.J. "L' 'Elogium' du Père Thomas Sailly S.I. (1553-1623) composé par le Père Charles Scribani S.I.," *AHSI* 48 (1979) 87-124.
Brown, Raydon et al., eds. *Calendar of State Papers and Manuscripts, Relating to English Affairs in the Archives and Collections of Venice*. 38 vols. in 40. London, 1864-1947.
Caraman, Philip, S.J., ed. *John Gerard: The Autobiography of an Elizabethan*. London, 1951.
——— ed. *William Weston: The Autobiography of an Elizabethan*. London, 1955.
Cervós, F., S.J., ed. *Epistolae P.P. Paschasii Broëti, Claudii Jayi, Joannis Codurii et Simonis Rodericii, S.I.* Madrid, 1903. MHSI 24.
——— and Nicolau, M., S.J., eds. *Epistolae et Monumenta P. Hieronymi Nadal*. 5 vols. Madrid-Rome, 1898-1964. MHSI 13, 15, 21, 27, 90.
Chadwick, Hubert, S.J. "Father William Creichton, S.J., and a Recently Discovered Letter," *AHSI* 6 (1937) 259-86.
———. "A Memoir of Fr. Edmund Hay S.J.," *AHSI* 8 (1939) 66-85.
Costa, M. Gonçalves da, ed. *Fontes inéditas Portuguesas para a história de Irlanda*. Braga, 1981.
Cross, Claire, ed. *The Letters of Sir Francis Hastings 1574-1609*. Frome, 1969. Somerset Record Society 69.
Edwards, Francis, S.J., ed. *The Elizabethan Jesuits*. London, 1981.
Ehler, Sidney Z. and Morrall, John B., eds. *Church and State Through the Centuries*. Westminster, Md., 1954.
Forbes-Leith, William, S.J., ed. *Narratives of Scottish Catholics under Mary Stuart and James VI*. Edinburgh, 1885.
Hartley, T.E., ed. *Proceedings in the Parliaments of Elizabeth I*. Leicester, 1981.
Hicks, Leo, S.J., ed. *Letters and Memorials of Father Robert Persons, S.J.* London, 1942. CRS 39.
HMC. *Various Collections*. 8 vols. London, 1901-14.
———. *The Manuscripts of J. Eliot Hodgkin*. London, 1897.
Hogan, Edmund, S.J., ed. *Ibernia Ignatiana*. Dublin, 1880.
Holmes, Peter, ed. *Elizabethan Casuistry*. London, 1981. CRS 67.
Hughes, Paul L. and Larkin, James F., C.S.V., eds. *Tudor Royal Proclamations*. 3 vols. New Haven, 1964-69.
Hume, Martin A.S., ed. *Calendar of letters and papers... preserved principally in the archives of Simancas*. 4 vols. London, 1892-99.
Ignatius Loyola. *Letters and Instructions of St. Ignatius Loyola*. Ed. Alban Goodier, S.J. London, 1914.
———. *Letters of St. Ignatius of Loyola*. Ed. William J. Young, S.J. Chicago, 1959.
———. *Saint Ignatius Loyola: Letters to Women*. Ed. Hugo Rahner, S.J. Edinburgh, 1960.
Knox, Thomas Francis, ed. *The First and Second Diaries of the English College, Douay*. London, 1878. Records of the English Catholics Under the Penal Laws I.
———. *The Letters and Memorials of William Cardinal Allen (1532-1594)*. London, 1882. Records of the English Catholics Under the Penal Laws II.
Law, Thomas Graves, ed. *Catholic Tractates of the Sixteenth Century (1573-1600)*. Edinburgh-London, 1901. Scottish Text Society 45.
Lecina, M., S.J., Agustí, V., S.J., and Restrepo, D., S.J., eds. *Sancti Ignatii de Loyola*

Societatis Iesu Fundatoris Epistolae et Instructiones. 12 vols. Madrid, 1903-11. MHSI 22, 26, 28, 29, 31, 33, 34, 36, 37, 39, 40, 42.
Lemon, Robert et al., eds. *Calendar of State Papers, Domestic Series of the Reigns of Edward VI. . . ..* 12 vols. London, 1856-72.
McCoog, Thomas M., S.J., ed. *Monumenta Angliae.* 2 vols. Rome, 1992. MHSI 142, 143.
—— ed. "The Letters of Robert Southwell, S.J.," *AHSI* 63 (1994) 101-24.
Moran, Patrick Francis. *Spicilegium Ossoriense.* Dublin, 1874.
Morris, John, S.J., ed. *The Troubles of Our Catholic Forefathers Related by Themselves.* 3 vols. London, 1872-77.
—— ed. "The Note-Book of John Southcote, D.D.," in *Miscellanea I.* London, 1905. CRS 1, pp. 97-116.
Parsons, Robert. "Of the Life and Martyrdom of Father Edmond Campian," *Letters and Notices* 11 (1877) 219-42, 308-39; 12 (1878) 1-68.
Peck, Dwight C., ed. *Leicester's Commonwealth: "The Copy of a Letter Written by a Master of Art of Cambridge" (1584) and Related Documents.* Athens, Ohio, 1985.
Petriburg., M. [Mandell Creighton]. "The Excommunication of Queen Elizabeth," *EHR* 7 (1892) 81-88.
Pollen, John Hungerford, S.J., ed. *Papal Negotiations with Mary Queen of Scots.* Edinburgh, 1901. Scottish History Society 37.
—— ed. *Unpublished Documents Relating to the English Martyrs 1584-1603.* London, 1908. CRS 5.
—— ed. *Mary Queen of Scots and the Babington Plot.* Edinburgh, 1922. Publications of the Scottish History Society, third series, Vol. 3.
—— ed. "Report to Cardinal Moroni on the change of religion in 1558-9 [1561]," in *Miscellanea I.* London, 1905. CRS 1, pp. 1-47.
—— ed. "The Official Lists of Catholic Prisoners during the Reign of Queen Elizabeth, Part II, 1581-1602," in *Miscellanea II.* London, 1906. CRS 2, pp. 219-88.
—— ed. "Father Persons' Autobiography," in *Miscellanea II.* London, 1906. CRS 2, pp. 12-47.
—— ed. [Robert Parsons] "A Storie of Domesticall Difficulties," in *Miscellanea II.* London, 1906. CRS 2, pp. 48-185.
—— ed. [Robert Parsons] "The First Entrance of the Fathers of the Society into England," in *Miscellanea II.* London, 1906. CRS 2, pp. 186-201.
—— ed. [Robert Parsons] "The observation of Certayne Aparent Judgements againste suche as have beene seditious [1598]," in *Miscellanea II.* London, 1906. CRS 2, pp. 202-11.
—— ed. [Robert Parsons] "Punti per la Missione d'Inghilterra," in *Miscellanea IV.* London, 1907. CRS 4, pp. 1-161.
—— ed. "Memoirs of Father William Crichton, S.J.: 1584 to 1589," *The Month* 139 (1922) 317-24.
Quirini, A.M., ed. *Epistolarum Reginaldi Poli S.R.E. Cardinalis et Aliorum ad Ipsum.* 5 vols. Brescia, 1744-57.
Renold, Penelope, ed. *Letters of William Allen and Richard Barret 1572-1598.* London, 1967. CRS 58.
Restrepo, D., S.J., ed. *Bobadillae Monumenta.* Madrid, 1913. MHSI 46.
—— and Fernández [Zapico], Dionysius, S.J., eds. *Polanci complementa, epistolae et commentaria P. Joannis Alphonsi de Polanco e Societate Jesu.* 2 vols. Madrid, 1916-17. MHSI 52, 54.
—— and Vilar, Joannes, S.J., eds. *Patris Petri de Ribadeneira, Societatis Iesu sacerdotis, confessiones, epistolae aliaque scripta inedita.* 2 vols. Madrid, 1920-23. MHSI 58, 60.
Rigg, J.M., ed., *Calendar of State Papers relating to English Affairs, preserved principally at Rome.* 2 vols. London, 1916-26.
Rodriguez, I., S.J., Agustí, V., S.J., and Cervós, F., S.J., eds. *Sanctus Franciscus Borgia.* 5 vols. Madrid, 1894-1911. MHSI 2, 23, 35, 38, 41.
Ryan, Patrick, S.J., ed. "Some Correspondence of Cardinal Allen, 1579-85," in *Miscellanea VII.* London, 1911. CRS 9, pp. 12-105.
Stevenson, Joseph et al, eds. *Calendar of State Papers Foreign Series of the Reign of Elizabeth.* 23 vols. in 26. London, 1863-1950.

Tyler, Royall et al., eds. *Calendar of State Papers Spanish*. 15 vols. in 20. London, 1862-1954.
Vélez, J.M., S.J. and Agustí, V., S.J., eds. *Vita Ignatii Loiolae et rerum Societatis Iesu historia auctore Joanne Alphonso de Polanco*. 6 vols. Madrid, 1894-98. MHSI 1, 3, 5, 7, 9, 11.
Vidaurre, Raimundus, S.J., and Cervós, F., S.J., eds. *Epistolae P. Alphonsi Salmeronis, Societatis Iesu*. 2 vols. Madrid, 1906-07. MHSI 30, 32.
Zapico, Dionysius Fernández, S.J., and de Dalmases, Cándido, S.J., eds. *Fontes Narrativi de S. Ignatio de Loyola et de Societatis Iesu initiis*. 4 vols. Rome, 1943-65. MHSI 66, 73, 85, 93.

Primary Printed Books

Acta Regia: or An account of the Treaties, Letters, and Instruments Between Monarchs of England and Foreign Powers. London, 1728.
Allen, William. *An apologie and true declaration of the institution and endevours of the two English Colleges*. Mons, 1581. STC 369; ARCR, II, no. 6.
———. *A brief historie of the glorious martyrdom of xii. reverend priests, executed within these twelve monthes for confession and defence of the Catholike Faith*. N.p. [Douai], 1582. STC 369.5; ARCR, II, no. 7.
———. *A true report of the late apprehension and imprisonnement of Iohn Nicols*. Reims, 1583. STC 18537; ARCR, II, no. 13.
———. *A true, sincere and modest Defence, of English Catholiques*. N.p. n. d. [Reims, 1584]. STC 373; ARCR, II, no. 14.
———. *The copie of a letter written by M. Doctor Allen: concerning the yeelding up, of the citie of Daventrie*. Antwerp, 1587. STC 370; ARCR, II, no. 8.
———. *An admonition to the nobility and people of England and Ireland*. Antwerp, 1588. STC 368; ARCR, II, no. 5.
———. *A declaration of the sentence and deposition of Elizabeth, the usurper and pretensed queen of Englande*. Antwerp, 1588. STC 22590; ARCR, II, no. 10.
Anonymous. *A Table gathered owt of a Booke named A Treatise of treasons*. N.p.n. d. [Louvain (?), 1573]. STC 23617.5. ARCR, II, no. 742.
———. *A Treatise of Treasons against Q. Elizabeth, and the Croune of England*. N.p [Louvain], 1572. STC 7601; ARCR, II, no. 502.
———. *A Warning for Englande Conteyning the horrible practises of the King of Spain in the Kingdom of Naples and the miseries whereunto that noble Realme is brought*. N.p. n.d. There were two editions of this work published probably in Strasbourg and Emden in 1555 (STC 10023.7, 10024).
[Arundell, Charles]. *The copie of a leter, wryten by a master of arte of Cambridge, to his friend in London [Leicester's Commonwealth]*. N.p., 1584. STC 5742.9; ARCR, II, no. 31.
Bartoli, Daniello. *Dell'Istoria della Compagnia di Giesu. L'Inghilterra*. Rome, 1667.
Boquin, Pierre. *A defence of the olde, and true profession of Christianitie, against the new, and counterfaite secte of Iesuites*. London, 1581. STC 3371.
Campion, Edmund. *Rationes Decem*. N.p. n.d. [Stonor Park, 1581]. STC 4536.5; ARCR, I, no. 135.1.
———. *Campion's Ten Reasons*. Ed. John H. Pollen, S.J. London, 1914.
Cecil, William. *The execution of justice in England*. London, 1583. STC 4902, 4903. Translations are STC 4904-07.
Charke, William. *An answere to a seditious pamphlet lately cast abroad by a jesuit, with a discoverie of that blasphemous sect*. London, 1580. STC 5005.
Donne, John. *Ignatius His Conclave*. Ed. T.S. Healy. Oxford, 1969.
Francken, Christian. *A conference or dialogue discovering the sect of Iesuites: most profitable for all Christendome rightly to know their religion*. London, 1580. STC 11325.
Fulke, William. *A confutation of a popishe and sclaunderous libelle, in forme of an apologie*. London, 1571. STC 11426.
G.D. *A briefe discoverie of doctor Allens seditious drifts*. London, 1588. STC 6166.
Hanmer, Meredith. *The great bragge and challenge of M. Champion a jesuite*. London, 1581. STC 12745.

Hay, John. *Certaine demandes concerning the Christian religion and discipline, proponed to the ministers of the new pretended kirk of Scotland*. Paris, 1580. STC 12969; ARCR, II, no. 410.
Ignatius Loyola. *A Pilgrim's Journey: The Autobiography of Ignatius of Loyola*. Ed. Joseph N. Tylenda, S.J. Wilmington, 1985.
———. *The Spiritual Exercises of St. Ignatius*. Ed. Louis J. Puhl, S.J. Chicago, 1951.
———. *The Constitutions of the Society of Jesus*. Ed. George E. Ganss, S.J. St. Louis, 1970.
Kingdon, Robert M., ed. *The Execution of Justice in England by William Cecil and A True, Sincere, and Modest Defense of English Catholics by William Allen*. Ithaca, N.Y., 1965.
Knox, John. *The first blast of the trumpet against the monstruous regiment of women*. N.p. [Geneva], 1558. STC 15070.
Leigh, Richard [*vere* Cecil, William]. *The copie of a letter sent out of England to don Bernardin Mendoza*. London, 1588. STC 15412.
Lightfoote, William. *The complaint of England*. London, 1587. STC 15595.
Martin, Gregory. *A Treatise of Schisme*. Douai, 1578. STC 17508; ARCR, II, 524.
More, Henry, S.J. *Historia Provinciae Anglicanae Societatis Iesu*. St. Omers, 1660.
[Norton, Thomas]. *A declaration of the favourable dealing of her maiesties commissioners*. London, 1583. STC 4901. The Latin translation is STC 4904.
Nowell, Alexander and Day, William. *A true report of the Disputation or rather private Conference had in the Tower of London, with Ed. Campion Iesuite, the last of August 1581* and *The three last dayes conferences had in the Tower with Edmund Campion Iesuite, the 18: 23 and 27 of September 1581*. London, 1583. STC 18744.
Padberg, John W., S.J., O'Keefe, Martin D., S.J., and McCarthy, John L., S.J., eds. *For Matters of Greater Moment: The First Thirty Jesuit General Congregations*. St. Louis, 1994.
Parsons, Robert. *A brief discours contayning certayne reasons why catholiques refuse to go to Church*. Doway [*vere* London], 1580. STC 19394; ARCR, II, no. 613.
———. *A brief censure uppon two bookes written in answere to M. Edmonde Campions offer of disputation*. Doway [*vere* London], 1581. STC 19393; ARCR, II, no. 612.
———. *A discoverie of I. Nicols Minister, misreported a Iesuite, latelye recanted in the Tower of London*. N.p. n.d. [*vere* London, 1581]. STC 19402; ARCR, II, no. 625.
———. *De persecutione Anglicana*. Bononia [Rouen], 1581. ARCR, I, no. 874.
———. *A defence of the Censure, gyven upon two bookes of William Charke and Meredith Hanmer mynysters, which they wrote against M. Edmond Campian*. N.p. [Rouen], 1582. STC 19401; ARCR, II, no. 624.
———. *The first booke of the Christian exercise, appertayning to resolution*. N.p. [Rouen], 1582. STC 19353; ARCR, II, no. 616.
Pocock, Nicholas, ed., *The History of the Reformation of the Church of England by Gilbert Burnet*. 7 vols. Oxford, 1865.
R.G. [William Cecil?]. *Salutem in Christo. Good men and evill delite in contraryes*. N.p. [London], 1571. STC 11504.
Rainolds, John. *The summe of the conference betwene J. Rainoldes and J. Hart*. London, 1584. STC 20626. Other editions can be found in STC 20627-20631.
de Ribadeneira, Pedro. *Historia ecclesiastica del scisma del reyno de Inglaterra*. Madrid, 1588. ARCR, I, no. 933.
Sander, Nicholas. *A treatise of the images of Christ, and of his saints*. Louvain, 1567. STC 21696; ARCR, II, no. 696.
———. *De origine et progressu schismatis anglicani*. Cologne, 1585. ARCR, I, no. 972.
———. *Rise and Growth of the Anglican Schism*. Trans. and ed. David Lewis. London, 1877.
[Society of Jesus]. *Annuae Litterae Societatis Iesu anni 1581*. Rome, 1583.
———. *Instructiones ad Provinciales et Superiores Societatis*. Antwerp, 1635.
Southwell Robert. *An epistle of comfort*. Paris [*vere* London], n.d. [1587-88]. STC 22946; ARCR, II, no. 714.
———. *The Poems of Robert Southwell, S.J.*. Eds. James H. McDonald and Nancy Pollard Brown. Oxford, 1967.
Stapleton, Thomas. *A counterblast to M. Hornes vayne blaste against M. Fekenham*. Louvain, 1567. STC 23231; ARCR, II, no. 729.

Tanner, Norman P., S.J., ed. *Decrees of the Ecumenical Councils*. 2 vols. London-Washington, D.C., 1990.
Tierney, M.A., ed. *Dodd's Church History of England*. 5 vols. London, 1839-43.
Tyrie, James. *The refutation of ane answer made be schir Iohne Knox, to ane letter, send be Iames Tyrie, to his umquhyle brother*. Paris, 1573. STC 24476; ARCR, II, no. 746.
Verstegan, Richard. *Theatrum crudelitatum haereticorum nostri temporis*. Antwerp, 1587. ARCR, I, no. 1297.
———. *The copy of a letter lately written by a Spanishe gentleman*. N.P. [Antwerp], 1589. STC 1038; ARCR, II, no. 759.

Secondary Literature

Adams, Simon. "The Release of Lord Darnley and the Failure of Amity," *IR* 38 (1987) 123-53.
———. "A Patriot For Whom?: Stanley, York and Elizabeth's Catholics," *History Today* 37 (July, 1987) 46-50.
———. "The Outbreak of the Elizabethan Naval War against the Spanish Empire: The Embargo of May 1585 and Sir Francis Drake's West Indies Voyage," in *England, Spain and the Gran Armada 1585-1604*, eds. M.J. Rodríguez-Salgado and Simon Adams. Edinburgh, 1991, pp. 45-69.
Aldama, Antonio M. de, S.J. *The Constitutions of the Society of Jesus: An Introductory Commentary on the Constitutions*. St. Louis, 1989.
Allison, A.F., and Rogers, D.M., eds. *The Contemporary Printed Literature of the English Counter-Reformation between 1558 and 1640*. 2 vols. Aldershot, 1989-94.
Anstruther, Godfrey, O.P. *The Seminary Priests*. Vol. 1. Ware-Durham, n.d. [1968].
———. "Owen Lewis," *The Venerabile* 21 (1962) 274-94.
Ashton, Robert. *Reformation and Revolution 1558-1660*. London, 1985.
Astraín, Antonio, S.J., *Historia de la Compañia de Jésus en la Asistencia de España*. 7 vols. Madrid, 1902-25.
Aveling, J.C.H. *The Handle and the Axe*. London, 1976.
Bangert, William V., S.J. *A History of the Society of Jesus*. St. Louis, 1972.
———. *Claude Jay and Alfonso Salmerón*. Chicago, 1985.
———. *Jerome Nadal, S.J. (1507-1580): Tracking the First Generation of Jesuits*. Ed. Thomas M. McCoog, S.J. Chicago, 1992.
Bartlett, Kenneth. "Papal Policy and the English Crown, 1563-1565: The Bertano Correspondence," *SCJ* 23 (1992) 643-59.
Basset, Bernard. *The English Jesuits*. London, 1967.
Baumgartner, Frederic J. *Radical Reactionaries: The Political Thought of the French Catholic League*. Geneva, 1975.
Baxter, J.H. "The Scots College at Douai," *Scottish Historical Review* 24 (1927) 251-57.
Bayne, C.G. *Anglo-Roman Relations 1558-1565*. Oxford, 1913.
Bellesheim, Alphons. *History of the Catholic Church of Scotland*. 4 vols. Edinburgh-London, 1887-90.
Benedict, Philip. *Rouen during the Wars of Religion*. Cambridge, 1981.
Bernard, G.W. *The Power of the Early Tudor Nobility: A Study of the Fourth and Fifth Earls of Shrewsbury*. Brighton, 1985.
Bireley, Robert, S.J. *The Counter-Reformation Prince: Anti-Machiavellianism or Catholic Statecraft in Early Modern Europe*. Chapel Hill, 1991.
Birt, Henry Norbert, O.S.B. *The Elizabethan Religious Settlement*. London, 1907.
Bitskey, István. "The Collegium Germanicum Hungaricum in Rome and the Beginning of the Counter-Reformation in Hungary," in *Crown, Church and Estates: Central European Politics in the Sixteenth and Seventeenth Centuries*. Eds. R.J.W. Evans and T.V. Thomas. London, 1991, pp. 110-22.
Blaisdell Charmarie J. "Calvin's and Loyola's Letters to Women: Politics and Spiritual Counsel in the Sixteenth Century," in *Calviniana: Ideas and Influence of Jean Calvin*. Ed. Robert V. Schnucker. Kirksville, 1988, pp. 235-53. Sixteenth Century Essays and Studies 10.
Booty, John E. *John Jewel as Apologist of the Church of England*. London, 1963.

Bossy, John. *Giordano Bruno and the Embassy Affair*. New Haven, 1991.
———. "English Catholics and the French Marriage, 1577-81," *RH* 5 (1959) 2-16.
———. "The Character of Elizabethan Catholicism," *Past and Present* 21 (1962) 39-59. Reprinted in Trevor Aston, ed., *Crisis in Europe, 1560-1660*. London, 1965, pp. 235-60.
———. "Rome and the Elizabethan Catholics: A Question of Geography," *Historical Journal* 7 (1964) 135-42.
———. "Leagues and Associations in Sixteenth-Century French Catholicism," in *Voluntary Religion*. Eds. W.J. Sheils and Diana Wood. Oxford, 1986, pp. 171-89. Studies in Church History 23.
———. "The Society of Jesus in the Wars of Religion," in *Monastic Studies: The Continuity of Tradition*. Ed. Judith Loades. Bangor, 1990, pp. 229-44.
———. "The Jesuits and the Reformation," in *Reconciliation: Essays in Honour of Michael Hurley*. Ed. Oliver Rafferty, S.J. Dublin, 1993, pp. 216-28.
———. "The Heart of Robert Persons," in *The Reckoned Expense: Edmund Campion and the Early English Jesuits. Essays in Celebration of the First Centenary of Campion Hall, Oxford (1896-1996)*. Ed. Thomas M. McCoog, S.J. Woodbridge, 1996, pp. 141-58.
Boyden, James M. *The Courtier and the King: Ruy Gómez de Silva, Philip II, and the Court of Spain*. Berkeley, 1995.
Bradshaw, Brendan. *The Dissolution of the Religious Orders in Ireland under Henry VIII* Cambridge, 1974.
Brady, Ciaran. *The Chief Governors: The Rise and Fall of Reform Government in Tudor Ireland 1536-1588*. Cambridge, 1994.
Brennan, Gillian E. "Papists and Patriotism in Elizabethan England," *RH* 19 (1988) 1-15.
Brigden, Susan. *London and the Reformation*. Oxford, 1989.
Brodrick, James. *Saint Peter Canisius, S.J. 1521-1597*. London, 1935.
———. *The Origin of the Jesuits*. London, 1940.
———. *The Progress of the Jesuits*. London, 1946.
———. *Saint Ignatius Loyola, The Pilgrim Years*. London, 1956.
Brown, Nancy Pollard. "Paperchase: The Dissemination of Catholic Texts in Elizabethan England," in *English Manuscript Studies 1100-1700*. Vol. 1. Eds. Peter Beal and Jeremy Griffiths. Oxford, 1989, pp. 120-43.
———. "Robert Southwell: The Mission of the Written Word," in *The Reckoned Expense: Edmund Campion and the Early English Jesuits. Essays in Celebration of the First Centenary of Campion Hall, Oxford (1896-1996)*. Ed. Thomas M. McCoog, S.J. Woodbridge, 1996, pp. 193-214.
Bucholtz, F.B. von *Geschichte der Regierung Ferdinand des Ersten*. 9 Vols. Vienna, 1831-38.
Buisseret, David. *Henry IV*. London, 1984.
Caraman, Philip, S.J. *Henry Garnet (1555-1606) and the Gunpowder Plot*. London, 1964.
———. *University of the Nations*. New York, 1981.
———. *Ignatius Loyola: A Biography of the Founder of the Jesuits*. San Francisco, 1990.
Carrafiello, Michael L. "*Rebus sic stantibus* and English Catholicism, 1606-1610," *RH* 22 (1994) 29-40.
———. "English Catholicism and the Jesuit Mission of 1580-81," *Historical Journal* 37 (1994) 761-74.
Cesareo, Francesco C. "The Collegium Germanicum and the Ignatian Vision of Education," *SCJ* 24 (1993) 829-41.
Chadwick, Hubert, S.J. *St. Omers to Stonyhurst*. London, 1962.
———. "The Scots College, Douai, 1580-1613," *EHR* 56 (1941) 571-85.
———. "Crypto-Catholicism, English and Scottish," *The Month* 178 (1942) 388-401.
Châtellier, Louis. *The Europe of the Devout: The Catholic Reformation and the Formation of a New Society*. Cambridge, 1989.
Clancy, Thomas H., S.J. *Papist Pamphleteers: The Allen-Persons Party and the Political Thought of the Counter-Reformation in England 1572-1615*. Chicago, 1964.
———. *An Introduction to Jesuit Life*. St. Louis, 1976.
———. *The Conversational Word of God*. St. Louis, 1978.
———. "English Catholics and the Papal Deposing Power, 1570-1640," *RH* 6 (1961-62) 114-40, 205-27; 7 (1963-64) 2-10.

———. "A Political Pamphlet: *The Treatise of Treasons* (1572)," in *Loyola Studies in the Humanities*. Ed. G. Eberle. New Orleans, 1962, pp. 15-30.
———. "The First Generation of English Jesuits 1555-1585," *AHSI* 57 (1988) 137-62.
———. "Spiritual Publications of English Jesuits, 1615-1640," *RH* 19 (1989) 426-46.
———. "Ignatius as Fund-Raiser," *Studies in the Spirituality of Jesuits* 25/1 (1993) 1-37.
Cleary, J.M. "Dr. Morys Clynnog's Invasion Projects of 1575-1576," *RH* 8 (1966) 300-22.
Collinson, Patrick. *Archbishop Grindal: 1519-1583*. London, 1979.
———. *The Religion of Protestants: The Church in English Society 1559-1625*. Oxford, 1982.
Costa, Manuel da. "The Last Years of a Confessor of the Faith: Father David Wolf," *AHSI* 15 (1946) 127-43.
Courel, François, S.J. "La fin unique de la Compagnie de Jésus," *AHSI* 35 (1966) 186-211.
Cowan, Ian B. "The Roman Connection: Prospects for Counter-Reformation during the Personal Reign of Mary, Queen of Scots," *IR* 38 (1987) 105-22.
Crehan, Joseph, S.J. "The Return to Obedience: New Judgment on Cardinal Pole," *The Month* 200 (1955) 221-29.
———. "Saint Ignatius and Cardinal Pole," *AHSI* 25 (1956) 72-98.
Cressy, David. *Bonfires & Bells: National Memory and the Protestant Calendar in Elizabethan and Stuart England*. London, 1989.
———. "Binding the nation: the Bonds of Association, 1584 and 1696," in *Tudor Rule and Revolution: Essays for G.R. Elton from his American friends*. Eds. Delloyd J. Guth and John W. McKenna. Cambridge, 1982, pp. 217-34.
———. "The Protestant Calendar and the Vocabulary of Celebration in Early Modern England," *The Journal of British Studies* 29 (1990) 31-52.
Cross, Claire. *The Puritan Earl: The Life of Henry Hastings Third Earl of Huntingdon 1536-1595*. London, 1966.
Dalmases, Cándido de, S.J. *Ignatius of Loyola*. St. Louis, 1985.
———. *Francis Borgia: Grandee of Spain, Jesuit, Saint*. St. Louis, 1991.
Delplace, Louis, S.J. "L'Angleterre et la Compagnie de Jésus avant le martyre du B. Edmond Campion," *Précis Historiques* 39 (1890) 269-88, 329-48, 417-35, 492-508.
Devlin, Christopher, S.J. *The Life of Robert Southwell: Poet and Martyr*. London, 1956.
Dickens, A.G. *The English Reformation*. 2nd edition. London, 1989.
———. "The Reformation in England," in A.G. Dickens, *Reformation Studies*. London, 1982, pp. 443-56.
———. "The Elizabethans and St. Bartholomew" in A.G. Dickens, *Reformation Studies*. London, 1982, pp. 471-89.
Diefendorf, Barbara B. *Beneath the Cross: Catholics and Huguenots in Sixteenth Century Paris*. Oxford, 1991.
Doran, Susan. *Monarchy and Matrimony: The Courtships of Elizabeth I*. London, 1996.
———."Religion and Politics at the Court of Elizabeth I: the Habsburg marriage negotiations of 1559-1567," *EHR* 104 (1989) 908-26.
——— and Durston, Christopher. *Princes, Pastors and People: The Church and Religion in England 1529-1689*. London, 1991.
Dudon, Paul. *St. Ignatius of Loyola*. Milwaukee, 1949.
Duffy, Eamon. *The Stripping of the Altars: Traditional Religion in England c. 1400-c. 1580*. New Haven, 1992.
———. "William, Cardinal Allen, 1532-1594," *RH* 22 (1995) 265-90.
Durkan, John. "Robert Wauchope, Archbishop of Armagh," *IR* 1 (1950) 48-65.
———. "William Murdoch and the Early Jesuit Mission in Scotland," *IR* 35 (1984) 3-11.
Edwards, Francis, S.J. *The Dangerous Queen*. London, 1964.
———. *The Marvellous Chance*. London, 1968.
———. *The Jesuits in England*. London, 1985.
———. *Robert Persons: The Biography of an Elizabethan Jesuit 1546-1610*. St. Louis, 1995.
Edwards, Robert Dudley. *Church and State in Tudor Ireland*. London, 1935.
Ellis, Steven G. *Tudor Ireland: Crown, Community and the Conflict of Cultures 1470-1603*. London, 1985.
Endean, Philip, S.J. "Who Do You Say Ignatius Is? Jesuit Fundamentalism and Beyond," *Studies in the Spirituality of Jesuits* 19/5 (1987) 1-53.

Evans, G.R. *Problems of Authority in the Reformation Debates*. Cambridge, 1992.
Fabre, Frédéric. "The English College at Eu—1582-1592," *CHR* 37 (1950) 257-80.
Fernandez-Armesto, Felipe. *The Spanish Armada*. Oxford, 1988.
Fiorito, Miguel A., S.J. "Ignatius' Own Legislation on Prayer," *Woodstock Letters* 97 (1968) 149-224.
Fisher, Arthur L. "A Study in Early Jesuit Government: The Nature and Origins of the Dissent of Nicolás Bobadilla," *Viator* 10 (1979) 397-431.
Fletcher, Anthony. "The First Century of English Protestantism and the Growth of National Identity," in *Religion and National Identity*. Ed. Stuart Mews. Oxford, 1982, pp. 309-17. Studies in Church History 18.
Flynn, Dennis. "The English Mission of Jasper Heywood, S.J.," *AHSI* 54 (1985) 45-76.
———. "Donne and the Ancient Catholic Nobility," *English Literary Renaissance* 19 (1989) 307-11.
———. "'Out of Step:' Six Supplementary Notes on Jasper Heywood," in *The Reckoned Expense: Edmund Campion and the Early English Jesuits. Essays in Celebration of the First Centenary of Campion Hall, Oxford (1896-1996)*. Ed. Thomas M. McCoog, S.J. Woodbridge, 1996, pp. 179-92.
Flynn, Thomas S., O.P. *The Irish Dominicans 1536-1641*. Dublin, 1993.
Foley, Henry, S.J. *Records of the English Province of the Society of Jesus*. 7 vols. in 8 Roehampton-London, 1877-84.
Frye, Susan. "The Myth of Elizabeth at Tilbury," *SCJ* 23 (1993) 95-114.
Garstein, Oskar. *Rome and the Counter-Reformation in Scandinavia*. Bergen, 1963.
———. *Rome and the Counter-Reformation in Scandinavia: Jesuit Educational Strategy 1553-1622*. Leiden, 1992.
Gee, Henry. *The Elizabethan Clergy and the Settlement of Religion*. Oxford, 1898.
Gentilcore, David. *From Bishop to Witch: The System of the Sacred in Early Modern Terra d'Otranto*. Manchester, 1992.
Gleason, Elisabeth G. *Gasparo Contarini: Venice, Rome and Reform*. Berkeley, 1993.
———. "On the Nature of Sixteenth-Century Italian Evangelism: Scholarship, 1953-1978," *SCJ* 9 (1978) 3-25.
———. "Who Was the First Counter-Reformation Pope?," *CHR* 81 (1995) 173-84.
Gómez-Centurión Jiménez, Carlos. "The New Crusade: Ideology and Religion in the Anglo-Spanish Conflict," in *England, Spain and the Gran Armada 1585-1604*. Eds. M.J. Rodríguez-Salgado and Simon Adams. Edinburgh, 1991, pp. 264-99.
Goodare, Julian. "Queen Mary's Catholic Interlude," *IR* 38 (1987) 154-70.
Gracia Rivas, Manuel. *La Sanidad en la Jornada de Inglaterra (1587-1588)*. Madrid, 1988.
Graves, Michael A.R. *The Tudor Parliaments: Crown, Lords and Commons, 1485-1603*. London, 1985.
———. *Thomas Norton: The Parliament Man*. Oxford, 1994.
de Guibert, Joseph, S.J. *The Jesuits: Their Spiritual Doctrine and Practice*. St. Louis, 1964.
Guy, John. *Tudor England*. Oxford, 1988.
Gwyn, Peter. *The King's Cardinal: The Rise and Fall of Thomas Wolsey*. London, 1990.
Gwynn, Aubrey. *The Medieval Province of Armagh 1470-1545*. Dundalk, 1946.
Hackett, Helen. *Virgin Mother, Maiden Queen*. London, 1995.
Hagan, J. "Miscellanea Vaticano-Hibernica, 1420-1631," *AH* 4 (1915) 215-318.
———. "Miscellanea Vaticano-Hibernica (1572-1585)," *AH* 7 (1918-22) 67-356.
Haigh, Christopher. *Reformation and Resistance in Tudor Lancashire*. Cambridge, 1975.
———. *Elizabeth I*. London, 1988.
———. *English Reformations: Religion, Politics, and Society under the Tudors*. Oxford, 1993.
———. "The Continuity of Catholicism in the English Reformation," in *The English Reformation Revised*. Ed. Christopher Haigh. Cambridge, 1987, pp. 176-208.
Hanson, Elizabeth. "Torture and Truth in Renaissance England," *Representations* 34 (1991) 53-84.
Hayes-McCoy, G.A. "The royal supremacy and ecclesiastical revolution, 1534-47," in *A New History of Ireland: III Early Modern Ireland 1534-1691*. Eds. T.W. Moody, F.X. Martin, and F.J. Byrne. Oxford, 1991, pp. 39-68.
———. "Conciliation, Coercion, and the Protestant Reformation, 1547-71," in *A New History of*

Ireland: III Early Modern Ireland 1534-1691. Eds. T.W. Moody, F.X. Martin, and F.J. Byrne. Oxford, 1991, pp. 69-93.

——. "The Completion of the Tudor Conquest and the Advance of the Counter-reformation, 1571-1603," in *A New History of Ireland: III Early Modern Ireland 1534-1691*. Eds. T.W. Moody, F.X. Martin, and F.J. Byrne. Oxford, 1991, pp. 94-141.

Hazlett, W. Ian P. "The Scots Confession 1560: Context, Complexion and Critique," *Archiv für Reformationsgeschichte* 78 (1987) 287-320.

Healey, Robert M. "Waiting for Deborah: John Knox and Four Ruling Queens," *SCJ* 25 (1994) 371-86.

Heisch, Allison. "Arguments for an Execution: Queen Elizabeth's 'White Paper' and Lord Burghley's 'Blue Pencil'," *Albion* 24 (1992) 591-604.

Hicks, Leo, S.J. *An Elizabethan Problem: Some Aspects of the Careers of Two Exile Adventurers*. London, 1964.

——. "Cardinal Allen and the Society," *The Month* 160 (1932) 342-53, 434-43, 528-36.

——. "The English College, Rome and Vocations to the Society of Jesus, March, 1579--July, 1595, *AHSI* 3 (1934) 1-36.

——. "Allen and Deventer (1587)," *The Month* 163 (1934) 505-17.

——. "The Catholic Exiles and the Elizabethan Religious Settlement," *CHR* 22 (1936) 129-48.

——. "The Strange Case of Dr. William Parry," *Studies* (1948) 343-62.

——. "Cardinal Allen's Admonition," *The Month* 185 (1948) 232-42; 186 (1948) 30-39.

——. "The Growth of a Myth: Father Robert Persons, S.J., and Leicester's Commonwealth," *Studies* 46 (1957) 91-105.

Hodgetts, Michael. *Secret Hiding Places*. Dublin, 1989.

Hogan, Edmund, S.J. *Distinguished Irishmen of the Sixteenth Century*. London, 1894.

Holmes, Peter. *Resistance and Compromise: The Political Thought of the English Catholics*. Cambridge, 1982.

——. "The Authorship of 'Leicester's Commonwealth'," *JEH* 33 (1982) 424-30.

Houliston, Victor. "The Fabrication of the Myth of Father Parsons," *RH* 22 (1994) 141-51.

——. "Why Robert Persons Would not be Pacified: Edmund Bunny's Theft of *The Book of Resolution*," in *The Reckoned Expense: Edmund Campion and the Early English Jesuits. Essays in Celebration of the First Centenary of Campion Hall, Oxford (1896-1996)*. Ed. Thomas M. McCoog, S.J. Woodbridge, 1996, pp. 159-77.

Hudon, William V. *Marcello Cervini and Ecclesiastical Government in Tridentine Italy*. DeKalb, Ill., 1992.

Hudson, Elizabeth K. "The Catholic Challenge to Puritan Piety, 1580-1620," *CHR* 77 (1991) 1-20.

Hudson, Winthrop S. *The Cambridge Connection and the Elizabethan Settlement of 1559*. Durham, N.C., 1980.

Hurstfield, Joel. "Church and State, 1558-1612: The Task of the Cecils," in *Studies in Church History II*. Ed. G.J. Cuming. London, 1965, pp. 119-40.

Hutton, Ronald. *The Rise and Fall of Merry England: The Ritual Year 1400-1700*. Oxford, 1994.

Jensen, De Lamar. *Diplomacy and Dogmatism: Bernardino de Mendoza and the French Catholic League*. Cambridge, Mass., 1964.

——. "The Phantom Will of Mary Queen of Scots," *Scotia* 4 (1980) 1-15.

——. "The Spanish Armada: The Worst-Kept Secret in Europe," *SCJ* 19 (1988) 621-41.

Jones, Norman. *Faith by Statute: Parliament and the Settlement of Religion, 1559*. London, 1982. Royal Historical Society Studies in History Series 32.

——. *God and the Moneylenders*. Oxford, 1989.

——. *The Birth of the Elizabethan Age: England in the 1560s*. Oxford, 1993.

Jordan, Constance. "Woman's Rule in Sixteenth-Century Political Thought," *Renaissance Quarterly* 40 (1987) 421-51.

Kamen, Henry. *Inquisition and Society in Spain in the Sixteenth and Seventeenth Centuries*. London, 1985.

——. *Spain 1469-1714: A Society of Conflict*. 2nd edition. London, 1991.

——. "Toleration and Dissent in Sixteenth-Century Spain: The Alternative Tradition," *SCJ* 19 (1988) 3-23.

Kelly, J.N.D. *The Oxford Dictionary of Popes*. Oxford, 1986.
Kenny, Anthony. "From Hospice to College," *The Venerabile* 19 (1958-60) 477-485; 20 (1960-62) 1-11, 89-103, 170-196.
King, John N. "Queen Elizabeth I: Representations of the Virgin Queen," *Renaissance Quarterly* 43 (1990) 30-74.
Kingdon, Robert M. *Myths about the St. Bartholomew's Day Massacres, 1572-1576*. Cambridge, Mass., 1988.
——. "William Allen's Use of Protestant Argument," in *From the Renaissance to the Counter-Reformation: Essays in Honor of Garrett Mattingly*. Ed. Charles H. Carter. London, 1964, pp. 164-78. Reprinted in *Church and Society in Reformation Europe*. London, 1985. Article XIII.
——. "Reactions to the St. Bartholomew Massacres in Geneva and Rome," in *The Massacre of St. Bartholomew*. Ed. Alfred Soman. The Hague, 1975, pp. 25-49.
Knecht, R.J. *The French Wars of Religion 1559-1598*. London, 1989. Seminar Studies in History.
Kretzschmar, Johannes. *Die Invasionsprojekte der katholischen Mächte gegen England zur Zeit Elisabeths*. Leipzig, 1892.
Kyle, Richard. "John Knox's Concept of Divine Providence and its Influence on His Thought," *Albion* 18 (1986) 395-410.
Lacouture, Jean. *Jesuits: A Multibiography*. Washington, D.C., 1995.
Lake, Peter. "The Significance of the Elizabethan Identification of the Pope as Antichrist," *JEH* 31 (1980) 161-78.
LaRocca, John, S.J. "Time, Death and the Next Generation: The Early Elizabethan Recusancy Policy," *Albion* 14 (1982) 103-17.
——. "Popery and Pounds: The Effect of the Jesuit Mission on Penal Legislation," in *The Reckoned Expense: Edmund Campion and the Early English Jesuits. Essays in Celebration of the First Centenary of Campion Hall, Oxford (1896-1996)*. Ed. Thomas M. McCoog, S.J. Woodbridge, 1996, pp. 249-63.
Law, Thomas Graves. "English Jesuits and Scottish Intrigues, 1581-82," in *Collected Essays and Reviews*. Ed. P. Hume Brown. Edinburgh, 1904. pp. 217-43.
Lennon, Colm. *Sixteenth Century Ireland: The Incomplete Conquest*. Dublin, 1994. New Gill History of Ireland 2.
——. "Edmund Campion's *Histories of Ireland* and Reform in Tudor Ireland," in *The Reckoned Expense: Edmund Campion and the Early English Jesuits. Essays in Celebration of the First Centenary of Campion Hall, Oxford (1896-1996)*. Ed. Thomas M. McCoog, S.J. Woodbridge, 1996, pp. 67-83.
Levin, Carole. *The Heart and Stomach of a King: Elizabeth I and the Politics of Sex and Power*. Philadelphia, 1994.
——. "Power, Politics, and Sexuality: Images of Elizabeth I," in *The Politics of Gender in Early Modern Europe*. Eds. Jean R. Brink, Allison P. Coudert, and Maryanne C. Horowitz. Kirksville, 1989, pp. 95-110. Sixteenth Century Essays and Studies 12.
——. "'Would I Could Give You Help and Succour': Elizabeth I and the Politics of Touch," *Albion* 21 (1989) 191-205.
Limm, Peter. *The Dutch Revolt 1559-1648*. London, 1989. Seminar Studies in History.
Loach, Jennifer. *Parliament and the Crown in the Reign of Mary Tudor*. Oxford, 1986.
Loades, David. *The Reign of Mary Tudor*. London, 1979.
——. "The Origins of English Protestant Nationalism," in *Religion and National Identity*. Ed. Stuart Mews. Oxford, 1982, pp. 297-307. Studies in Church History 18.
——. "Philip II and the Government of England," in *Law and Government under the Tudors: Essays presented to Sir Geoffrey Elton on his Retirement*. Eds. Claire Cross, David Loades, and J.J. Scarisbrick. Cambridge, 1988, pp. 177-94.
——. "The Spirituality of the Restored Catholic Church (1553-1558) in the Context of the Counter Reformation," in *The Reckoned Expense: Edmund Campion and the Early English Jesuits. Essays in Celebration of the First Centenary of Campion Hall, Oxford (1896-1996)*. Ed. Thomas M. McCoog, S.J. Woodbridge, 1996, pp. 3-20.
Loomie, Albert J., S.J. *The Spanish Elizabethans: The English Exiles at the Court of Philip II*. New York, 1963.

———. "Thomas James: the English Consul of Andalucia (1556-c.1613)," *RH* 11 (1972) 165-78.
———. "The Armadas and the Catholics of England," *CHR* 59 (1973) 385-403.
Lynch, John. *Spain 1516-1598: From Nation State to World Empire.* Oxford, 1991. A History of Spain.
———. "Philip II and the Papacy," *Transactions of the Royal Historical Society*, series 5, 11 (1961) 23-42.
Lutz, Heinrich. "Cardinal Reginald Pole and the Path to Anglo-Papal Mediation at the Peace Conference of Marcq, 1553-55," in *Politics and Society in Reformation Europe: Essays for Sir Geoffrey Elton on his Sixty-Fifth Birthday.* Eds. E.I. Kouri and Tom Scott. New York, 1987, pp. 329-52.
MacCulloch, Diarmaid. "The Myth of the English Reformation," *Journal of British Studies* 30 (1991) 1-19.
McCoog, Thomas M., S.J. *English and Welsh Jesuits 1555-1650.* 2 vols. London, 1994-95. CRS 74, 75.
———. "Campion's Plea for a Disputation," *The Month* 262 [n.s. 2 vol. 14] (1981) 414-17.
———. "The Establishment of the English Province of the Society of Jesus," *RH* 17 (1984) 121-39.
———. "The Finances of the English Province of the Society of Jesus in the Seventeenth Century: Introduction," *RH* 18 (1986) 14-33.
———. "'The Slightest Suspicion of Avarice': The Finances of the English Jesuit Mission," 19 *RH* (1988) 103-23.
———. "'The Flower of Oxford': The Role of Edmund Campion in Early Recusant Polemics," *SCJ* 24 (1993) 899-913.
———. "Ignatius Loyola and Reginald Pole: A Reconsideration," *JEH* (forthcoming).
———. "'Playing the Champion': The Role of Disputation in the Jesuit Mission," in *The Reckoned Expense: Edmund Campion and the Early English Jesuits. Essays in Celebration of the First Centenary of Campion Hall, Oxford (1896-1996).* Ed. Thomas M. McCoog, S.J. Woodbridge, 1996, pp. 119-39.
MacCaffrey, Wallace. *The Shaping of the Elizabethan Regime: Elizabethan Politics 1558-72.* London, 1969.
———. *Queen Elizabeth and the Making of Policy, 1572-1588.* Princeton, 1981.
———. "Parliament and Foreign Policy," in *The Parliaments of Elizabethan England.* Eds. D.M. Dean and N.L. Jones. Oxford, 1990, pp. 65-90.
MacErlean, John, S.J. "The Society of Jesus in Ireland [1540-1773])," *Irish Jesuit Directory* (1928) 166-80.
McGrath, Patrick. *Papists and Puritans under Elizabeth I.* London, 1967.
———. "Apostate and Naughty Priests in England under Elizabeth I," in *Opening the Scrolls: Essays in honour of Godfrey Anstruther.* Ed. Dominic Aidan Bellenger. Bath, 1987, pp. 50-85.
———. "The Elizabethan Priests: Their Harbourers and Helpers," *RH* 19 (1989) 209-33.
———. "The Bloody Questions Reconsidered," *RH* 20 (1991) 305-19.
———. "The Imprisonment of Catholics for Religion under Elizabeth I," *RH* 20 (1991) 415-35.
———. and Rowe, Joy. "The Marian Priests under Elizabeth I," *RH* 17 (1984) 103-20.
McGuckian, Michael C., S.J. "The One End of the Society of Jesus," *AHSI* 60 (1991) 91-111.
McNally, Robert E., S.J. "The Council of Trent, the 'Spiritual Exercises,' and the Catholic Reform," *Church History* 34 (1965) 36-49. Reprinted as Facet Book Historical Series--15. Philadelphia, 1970.
———. "St. Ignatius; Prayer and the Early Society of Jesus," *Woodstock Letters* 94 (1965) 109-34.
McRedmond, Louis. *To The Greater Glory: A History of the Irish Jesuits.* Dublin, 1991.
Maltby, William S. *The Black Legend in England: The Development of anti-Spanish Sentiment, 1558-1660.* Durham, N.C., 1971.
———. *Alba.* Berkeley, 1983.
Manning, Roger B. "Richard Shelley of Warminghurst and the English Catholic Petition for Toleration of 1585," *RH* 6 (1962) 265-74.
Marius, Richard. *Thomas More.* New York, 1984.
Martin, A. Lynn. *Henry III and the Jesuit Politicians.* Geneva, 1973.

——. *The Jesuit Mind: The Mentality of an Elite in Early Modern France*. Ithaca, N.Y., 1988.
——. "The Jesuit Mystique," *SCJ* 4 (1973) 31-40.
——. "The Jesuit Emond Auger and The Saint Bartholomew's Massacre at Bordeaux: The Final Word?," in *Regnum, Religio et Ratio: Essays Presented to Robert M. Kingdon*. Ed. Jerome Friedman. Kirksville, 1987, pp. 117-24. Sixteenth Century Essays and Studies 8.
Mathew, David. *Catholicism in England 1535-1935: Portrait of a Minority: Its Culture and Tradition*. London, 1936
Mattingly, Garrett. *Renaissance Diplomacy*. London, 1955.
——. *The Defeat of the Spanish Armada*. London, 1959.
Mayer, Thomas F. *Thomas Starkey and the Commonweal: Humanist Politics and Religion in the Reign of Henry VIII*. Cambridge, 1989.
——. "A Test of Wills: Cardinal Pole, Ignatius Loyola, and the Jesuits in England," in *The Reckoned Expense: Edmund Campion and the Early English Jesuits. Essays in Celebration of the First Centenary of Campion Hall, Oxford (1896-1996)*. Ed. Thomas M. McCoog, S.J. Woodbridge, 1996, pp. 21-37.
de Medina, Francisco de Borja, S.J. "Jesuitas en la Armada contra Inglaterra (1588)," *AHSI* 58 (1989) 3-42.
——. "Intrigues of a Scottish Jesuit at the Spanish Court: Unpublished Letters of William Crichton to Claudio Acquaviva (Madrid 1590-1592)," in *The Reckoned Expense: Edmund Campion and the Early English Jesuits. Essays in Celebration of the First Centenary of Campion Hall, Oxford (1896-1996)*. Ed. Thomas M. McCoog, S.J. Woodbridge, 1996, pp. 215-45.
Meyer, Arnold Oskar. *England and the Catholic Church under Queen Elizabeth*. London, 1916.
Millet, Benignus, O.F.M., "The ordination of Dermot O'Hurley, 1581," *Collectanea Hibernica* 25 (1983) 12-21.
Milward, Peter. *Religious Controversies of the Elizabethan Age*. London, 1977.
Morrissey, Thomas J., S.J. *James Archer of Kilkenny: An Elizabethan Jesuit*. Dublin, 1979.
Neale, J.E. *Elizabeth I and Her Parliaments*. 2 vols. London, 1953-57.
Newdigate, D.A., S.J. "A New Chapter in the Life of B. Robert Southwell, S.J.," *The Month* 157 (1931) 246-54.
Nolan, John S. "The Muster of 1588," *Albion* 23 (1991) 387-407.
Norman, Edward. *Roman Catholicism in England*. Oxford, 1985.
Nugent, Donald. *Ecumenism in the Age of the Reformation: The Colloquy of Poissy*. Cambridge, Mass., 1974.
Oberman, Heiko A. "Ignatius of Loyola and the Reformation: The Case of John Calvin," in *Ignacio de Loyola y su Tiempo*. Ed. Juan Plazaola. Bilbao, n.d. [1992], pp. 807-17.
O'Day, Rosemary. *The Debate on the English Reformation*. London-New York, 1986.
O'Donoghue, Fergus, S.J. "The Jesuits Come to Ireland," *Studies* 80 (1991) 15-21.
Ó Fionnagáin, Prionsias, S.J. *The Jesuit Missions to Ireland*. N.p. n.d. [privately printed].
Olin, John C. "Erasmus and St. Ignatius Loyola," in *Six Essays on Erasmus*. New York, 1979, pp. 75-92.
O'Malley, John W. *The First Jesuits*. Cambridge, Mass., 1993.
——. "The Jesuits, St. Ignatius, and the Counter-Reformation," *Studies in the Spirituality of Jesuits* 14/1 (1982) 1-28.
——. "To Travel to Any Part of the World: Jerónimo Nadal and the Jesuit Vocation," *Studies in the Spirituality of Jesuits* 16/2 (1984) 1-20.
——. "Early Jesuit Spirituality: Spain and Italy," in *Christian Spirituality: Post-Reformation and Modern*. Eds. Louis Dupré and Don E. Saliers. New York, 1989, pp. 3-27. Reprinted in John W. O'Malley, S.J., *Religious Culture in the Sixteenth Century*. Aldershot, 1993. Article IX.
——. "Renaissance Humanism and the Religious Culture of the First Jesuits," *Heythrop Journal* 31 (1990) 471-87. Reprinted in John W. O'Malley, S.J., *Religious Culture in the Sixteenth Century*. Aldershot, 1993. Article X.
——. "Renaissance Humanism and the First Jesuits," in *Ignacio de Loyola y Su Tiempo*. Ed. Juan Plazaola. Bilbao, n.d. [1992], pp. 381-403.
——. "The Society of Jesus," in *Religious Orders of the Catholic Reformation: In Honor of John C. Olin on His Seventy-Fifth Birthday*. Ed. Richard L. DeMolen. New York, 1994,

pp. 139-63.
——. "The Ministries of the Early Jesuits: Social Disciplining or Discerning Accommodation?," *CIS: Review of Ignatian Spirituality* (forthcoming).
Padberg, John W., S.J. "Ignatius and the Popes," in *Ignacio de Loyola y Su Tiempo*. Ed Juan Plazaola. Bilbao, n.d. [1992], pp. 683-99.
——. "Ignatius, the Popes, and Realistic Reverence," *Studies in the Spirituality of Jesuits* 25/3 (1993) 1-38.
Palmer, William. *The Problem of Ireland in Tudor Foreign Policy 1485-1603*. Woodbridge, 1994.
Palmer, William G. "Gender, Violence, and Rebellion in Tudor and Early Stuart Ireland," *SCJ* 23 (1992) 699-712.
——. "That 'Insolent Liberty': Honor, Rites of Power and Persuasion in Sixteenth Century Ireland," *Renaissance Quarterly* 46 (1993) 308-27.
Parker, Geoffrey. "If the Armada had Landed," in *Spain and the Netherlands 1559-1659*. London, 1990, pp. 135-47.
Parmiter, Geoffrey de C. "Edmund Plowden as Advocate for Mary Queen of Scots: Some Remarks upon Certain Elizabethan Succession Tracts," *IR* 30 (1970) 35-53.
——. "The Imprisonment of Papists in Private Castles," *RH* 19 (1988) 16-38.
Parrow, Kathleen A. "Neither Treason nor Heresy: Use of Defense Arguments to Avoid Forfeiture during the French Wars of Religion," *SCJ* 22 (1991) 705-16.
von Pastor, Ludwig Freiherr. *The History of the Popes From the Close of the Middle Ages*. Vol. XIX. London, 1930.
Patterson, Annabel. *Reading Holinshed's Chronicles*. Chicago, 1994.
Peters, Willem A.M, S.J.. "Richard Whitford and St. Ignatius' Visit to England," *AHSI* 25 (1956) 328-50.
Pettegree, Andrew. *Foreign Protestant Communities in Sixteenth-Century London*. Oxford, 1986.
Petti, A.G. "Richard Verstegan and Catholic Martyrologies of the Later Elizabethan Period," *RH* 5 (1959) 64-90.
Pogson, R.H. "Reginald Pole and the Priorities of Government," *Historical Journal* 18 (1975) 3-20.
——. "The Legacy of the Schism: Confusion, Continuity and Change in the Marian Clergy," in *The Mid-Tudor Polity c 1540-1560*. Eds. Jennifer Loach and Robert Tittler. London, 1980, pp. 116-36.
Pollard, A.W. & Redgrave, G.R. eds. *A Short Title Catalogue of Books Printed in England, Scotland, & Ireland and of English Books Printed Abroad, 1475-1640*. 2nd edition revised by W.A. Jackson, F.S. Ferguson and K.F. Pantzer. 3 vols. London, 1976-91.
Pollen, John Hungerford, S.J. *The English Catholics in the Reign of Queen Elizabeth: A Study of Their Politics Civil Life and Government*. London, 1920.
——. *The Counter-Reformation in Scotland*. London, 1921.
——. "The Rise of the Anglo-Benedictine Congregation," *The Month* 90 (1897) 581-600.
——. "Mary Stuart and the Opinions of her Catholic Contemporaries," *The Month* 91 (1898) 575-91.
——. "The Portrait of Father Robert Parsons," *The Month* 98 (1901) 113-26.
——. "A Curious and Original History of the Jesuits in England," *The Month* 97 (1901) 502-18; 98 (1901) 315-18.
——. "The Politics of the English Catholics during the Reign of Elizabeth," *The Month* 99 (1902) 43-60, 131-48, 290-305, 394-411; 100 (1902) 71-87, 176-88.
——. "The First Jesuits in Great Britain," *The Month* 102 (1903) 647-52.
——. "Mary Stuart's Jesuit Chaplain," *The Month* 117 (1911) 11-24, 136-49.
Prat, Joannes Marie. *Histoire du Pére Ribadeneyra*. Paris, 1862.
Pritchard, Arnold. *Catholic Loyalism in Elizabethan England*. London, 1979.
Questier, Michael. "'Like Locusts over all the World': Conversion, Indoctrination and the Society of Jesus in late Elizabethan and Jacobean England," in *The Reckoned Expense: Edmund Campion and the Early English Jesuits. Essays in Celebration of the First Centenary of Campion Hall, Oxford (1896-1996)*. Ed. Thomas M. McCoog, S.J. Woodbridge, 1996, pp. 265-84.

Quinn, D.B. and Nicholls, K.W. "Ireland in 1534," in *A New History of Ireland: III Early Modern Ireland 1534-1691*. Eds. T.W. Moody, F.X. Martin, and F.J. Byrne. Oxford, 1991, pp. 1-38.
Quinn, Peter A. "Ignatius Loyola and Gian Pietro Carafa: Catholic Reformers at Odds," *CHR* 67 (1981) 386-400.
Ravier, André, S.J. *Ignatius of Loyola and the Founding of the Society of Jesus*. San Francisco, 1987.
Reynolds, E.E. *Campion and Parsons*. London, 1980.
Richgels, Robert. W. "The Pattern of Controversy In a Counter-Reformation Classic: The *Controversies* of Robert Bellarmine," *SCJ* 11 (1980) 3-15.
Rodrigues, Francisco, S.J. *História da Companhia de Jesus na assistencia de Portugal*. 4 vols. in 7. Oporto, 1931-50.
Rodríguez-Salgado, M.J. *The Changing Face of Empire: Charles V, Philip II and Habsburg Authority, 1551-1559*. Cambridge, 1988.
———. "The Anglo-Spanish War: The Final episode in 'The Wars of the Roses'?," in *England, Spain and the Gran Armada 1585-1604*. Eds. M.J. Rodríguez-Salgado and Simon Adams. Edinburgh, 1991, pp. 1-44.
Rose, Stewart. *Saint Ignatius Loyola and the Early Jesuits*. 2nd edition. London, 1871.
Sanderson, Margaret H.B. *Cardinal of Scotland: David Beaton, c. 1494-1564*. Edinburgh, 1986.
Scaduto, Mario, S.J. *L'Epoca di Giacomo Lainez: Il Governo 1556-1565*. Rome, 1964.
———. *L'Opera di Francesco Borgia (1565-1572)*. Rome, 1992.
Scarisbrick, J.J. *The Reformation and the English People*. Oxford, 1984.
Schmidt, Peter. *Das Collegium Germanicum in Rom und die Germaniker*. Tübingen, 1984.
Schultenover, David G., S.J. *A View from Rome On the Eve of the Modernist Crisis*. New York, 1993.
Schurhammer, Georg, S.J. *Francis Xavier: His Life, His Times*. Trans. M. Joseph Costelloe, S.J. 4 vols. Rome, 1973-82.
Shearman, Peter J. "Father Alexander McQuhirrie, S.J.," *IR* 6 (1955) 22-45.
Simoncelli, Paolo. *Il Caso Reginald Pole: Eresia e Santità nelle Polemiche Religiose del Cinquecento*. Rome, 1977.
Simpson, Richard. *Edmund Campion*. 2nd. edition. London, 1896.
Skwarczynski, Paul. "Elsinore 1580: John Rogers and James Bosgrave," *RH* 16 (1982) 1-16.
Southern, A.C. *Elizabethan Recusant Prose 1559-1582*. London, n.d. [1950].
Stafford, Helen Georgia. *James VI of Scotland and the Throne of England*. New York-London, 1940.
Strathmann, Ernest A. "Robert Parsons' Essay on Atheism," in *Jos. Quincy Adams Memorial Studies*. Washington, D.C., 1948, pp. 665-81.
Sutherland, N.M. *The Massacre of St Bartholomew and the European Conflict 1559-1572*. London, 1973.
Swanson, R.N. *Church and Society in Late Medieval England*. Oxford, 1989.
Taunton, Ethelred. *The History of the Jesuits in England*. London, 1901.
Thorp, Malcolm R. "Catholic Conspiracy in Early Elizabethan Foreign Policy, *SCJ* 15 (1984) 431-48.
———. "William Cecil and the Antichrist: A Study in Anti-Catholic Ideology," in *Politics, Religion & Diplomacy in Early Modern Europe: Essays in Honor of De Lamar Jensen*. Eds. Malcolm R. Thorp and Arthur J. Slavin. Kirksville, 1994, pp. 289-304. Sixteenth Century Essays and Studies 27.
Trevor-Roper, Hugh. "Twice Martyred: The English Jesuits and Their Historians," in *Historical Essays*. London, 1957, pp. 113-18.
Trimble, W.R. *The Catholic Laity in Elizabethan England 1558-1603*. Cambridge, Mass., 1964.
Veech, Thomas McNevin. *Dr. Nicholas Sanders and the English Reformation*. Louvain, 1935.
Vercruysse, Jos E., S.J. "Nadal et la Contre-Réforme," *Gregorianum* 72 (1991) 289-315.
Walsh, Reginald, O.P. "Irish Manners and Customs in the Sixteenth Century," *AH* 5 (1916) 17-19.
Walsh, Walter. *The Jesuits in Great Britain*. London, 1903.
Walsham, Alexandra. *Church Papists: Catholicism, Conformity, and Confessional Polemic in*

Early Modern England. London, 1993. Royal Historical Society Studies in History Series 68.
Ward, Leslie. "The Treason Act of 1563: A Study of the Enforcement of Anti-Catholic Legislation," *Parliamentary History* 8 (1989) 289-308.
Waugh, Evelyn. *Edmund Campion*. London, 1935.
Wernham, R.B. *After the Armada*. Oxford, 1984.
———. "Queen Elizabeth I, the Emperor Rudolph II, and Archduke Ernest, 1593-94," in *Politics and Society in Reformation Europe: Essays for Sir Geoffrey Elton on his Sixty-Fifth Birthday*. Eds. E.I. Kouri and Tom Scott. New York, 1987, pp. 437-51.
Whiting, Robert. *The Blind Devotion of the People: Popular Religion and the English Reformation*. Cambridge, 1989.
Wiener, Carol Z. "The Beleaguered Isle. A Study of Elizabethan and Early Jacobean Anti-Catholicism," *Past and Present* 51 (1971) 27-62.
Williams, Michael. *The Venerable English College Rome*. London, 1979.
———. "William Allen: The Sixteenth Century Spanish Connection," *RH* 22 (1994) 123-40.
———. "Campion and the English Continental Seminaries," in *The Reckoned Expense: Edmund Campion and the Early English Jesuits. Essays in Celebration of the First Centenary of Campion Hall, Oxford (1896-1996)*. Ed. Thomas M. McCoog, S.J. Woodbridge, 1996, pp. 285-99.
Willson, D. Harris. *King James VI and I*. London, 1956.
Wolfe, Michael. *The Conversion of Henri IV: Politics, Power, and Religious Belief in Earl Modern France*. Cambridge, Mass., 1993.
Woodward, Geoffrey. *Philip II*. London, 1992. Seminar Studies in History.
Wormald, Jenny. *Court, Kirk and Community: Scotland 1470-1625*. Edinburgh, 1981. The New History of Scotland.
Wright, A.D. "The Religious Life in the Spain of Philip II and Philip III," in *Monks, Hermits and the Ascetic Tradition*. Ed. W.J. Sheils. Oxford, 1985, pp. 251-74. Studies in Church History 22.
Yellowless, Michael J. "The Ecclesiastical Establishment of the Diocese of Dunkeld at the Reformation," *IR* 36 (1985) 74-85.
———. "Dunkeld and Nicholas de Gouda's Mission to Scotland, 1562," *IR* 44 (1993) 48-57.
Younings, Joyce. *Sixteenth-Century England*. London, 1984. The Pelican Social History of Britain.

Theses

LaRocca, John, S.J. "English Catholics and the Recusancy Laws 1558-1625: A Study in Religion and Politics." Unpublished Ph.D. thesis: Rutgers University, 1977.
McCoog, Thomas M., S.J. "The Society of Jesus in England, 1623-1688: An Institutional Study." Unpublished Ph.D. thesis: University of Warwick, 1984.
Morrissey, Thomas J., S.J. "'Archdevil' and Jesuit: The Background, Life, and Times of James Archer from 1550 to 1604." Unpublished M.A. thesis: University College, Dublin, 1968.
Norris, Peter. "Robert Parsons, S.J. (1546-1610) and the Counter Reformation in England: A Study of his Actions within the Context of the Political and Religious Situation of the Times." Unpublished Ph.D. thesis: University of Notre Dame, 1984.
O'Donoghue, Fergus, S.J. "The Jesuit Mission in Ireland 1598-1651." Unpublished Ph.D. thesis: The Catholic University of America, 1981.
Pogson, R.H. "Cardinal Pole - Papal Legate to England in Mary Tudor's Reign." Unpublished D.Phil. thesis: Cambridge University, 1972.

INDEX OF NAMES, PLACES, AND SUBJECTS

Abercrombie, Robert, S.J., missionary, administrator (c. 1536-1613) 68, 120, 121, 241

Abingdon, Edward, Catholic layman (fl. 1580) 143

Acosta, José de, S.J., Provincial and General's representative in Spain (1539-1600) 261

Acquaviva, Claudio, S.J., General (1542-1615) 3, 121, 167, 169, 191, 195, 253, 256, 258, 278, 279; and Armada 250; and Campion 140; and English mission 132, 158, 159, 160, 169, 174, 175, 177, 204, 205, 217, 220, 260, 276-279; and French Jesuits 231; and Garnet 171; and Ireland 219, 220, 277; and Langdale 166; and Parsons 195, 196, 198, 203, 206, 222, 223, 267, 279-280; and Scottish mission 180, 181, 182, 186, 197, 202, 204, 205, 210, 225, 242; and Weston 170, 275-276; appoints Parsons superior of Scottish mission, 203; appoints Pigenat superior 209; elected General 158; instructions to Heywood and Holt 161, 275; instructions to Holt and Creswell 254-55, 272, 275-276; instructions to Garnet and Southwell 275-277; Institute 280; recommends Marshall for mission 170; sends Holt and Heywood to England 161

Act of Abjuration (1581) 194

Addie, Patrick, Scottish Catholic priest 205

Agazzari, Alfonso, S.J., Rector of English College, Rome (1549-1602) 107, 124, 129, 158, 168, 170, 174, 224, 225

Alba, Fernando Álvarez de Toledo, Count of Oropesa and Duke of (1507-1582) 39 74-77, 80, 82, 83, 90, 93, 116

Albert, Archduke of Austria (1559-1621) 226

Albert V, Duke of Bavaria (1550-1579) 194

Alcazar-Kebir (N.W. Africa), Battle of (1578) 115, 116

Aldama, Antonio M. de, S.J. 269

Alençon, Francis, Duke of (1555-1584) 89, 90, 114, 121, 122, 156, 190, 194, 201, 207, 231

Allen, Gabriel, William Allen's brother (+1597) 163, 167

Allen, William, Cardinal (1532-1594) 100, 103, 161, 166, 184, 194, 200, 208, 237, 259-261, 266; and Armada 246, 250, 251, 254, 259; and English Colleges 74, 124, 225; and Jesuit mission to England 103, 105, 123, 124, 129-131, 133, 134, 138, 158, 160, 165, 166, 169, 174-177; and Heywood 163, 166, 168, 169; and Parsons 156, 162, 203, 204, 206, 208; and Perkins 133; and persecution, 164, 216; and Scotland 185, 187; and Spanish claims to the English throne 218, 229, 239, 241, 242; and Stanley 231, 249, 266; and Throckmorton Plot 200; and various enterprises 90, 105, 197, 199, 205, 212, 226, 232, 239, 241, 249; and Weston 170; attacked by Cecil and Hatton 258, 259; created Cardinal 163, 245, 249, 250; proposed as Bishop of Durham 187, 197, 198; reactions against policies of 263; *A declaration of the sentence and deposition of Elizabeth, the usurper and pretensed queen of Englande* 246, 248; *A true, sincere and modest Defence, of English Catholiques* 215; *An admonition to the nobility and people of England and Ireland* 246, 249; *An apologie and true declaration of the institution and endevours of the two English Colleges* 216, 217; *The copie of a letter written by M. Doctor Allen: concerning the yeelding up, of the citie of Daventrie* 231- 233

Alost (Aalst, Flanders) 230

Alumbrados 126

Álvarez, Baltasar, S.J., spiritual writer (1535-1580) 125, 126

Anderton, Robert, Catholic priest (1560-1586) 234

Angers (France) 211

Anglo-Scottish League (1586) 213

Angus, Earl of. See Douglas, Archibald, Earl of Angus

Anjou, Duke of. See Henry III, King of France.

Anna of Austria, Emperor Maximilian's

daughter and Philip II's 4th wife (1549-1580) 74
Antonio, Prior of Crato, illegitimate son of Portuguese King Manuel I and pretender to Portuguese throne (+1595) 115, 116, 122, 165, 193
Antwerp (Belgium) 12, 58, 60, 64, 75, 83, 109, 114, 210, 246
Araoz, Antonio, S.J., Provincial (1516-1573) 29, 30, 34, 35
Argyll, Earl of. See Campbell, Archibald, Earl of Argyll
Armada (1588) 232, 244, 245, 249-256, 259, 261-263, 266, 267
Armagh (Ireland) 14, 17, 63
Arques (France) 263
Arran, Earl of. See Hamilton, James, Earl of Arran; and Stuart, James, Earl of Arran
Arras (France): Treaty of (1579) 114
Arundel, Earl of. See FitzAlan, Henry, Earl of Arundel
Arundell, Charles, Catholic layman, author of *Leicester's Commonwealth* (fl. 1585) 143, 206, 217
Atholl, Earl of. See Stuart, John, Earl of Atholl
Augsburg (Germany) 160; Diet of, 33; Interim of, 28
Aveling, J.C.H. 100, 102
Azores (Portugal) 122, 165, 188, 193, 263
Babington Plot (1586) 195, 198, 228, 233
Babington, Anthony, Catholic layman, (1561-1586) 143, 228, 234
Bacon, Nicholas, Lord Keeper (1509-1579) 89
Bader, Georg, S.J., Provincial (1540-1612) 255
Bailly, Charles, Scottish layman (1542-1625) 87
Bangert, William V., S.J., historian (1911-1985) 21, 22
Barnes, Richard, Bishop of Durham (1532-1587) 166
Barret, Richard, Catholic priest, President of English College, Reims/Douai (1544-1599) 181; complains about Heywood 168; named President of English College, Reims (1588) 260
Bartoli, Daniello, S.J., historian (1608-1685) 3, 4
Basset, Bernard, S.J., historian (1909-1988) 5
Basset, Charles, Catholic layman (fl. 1580) 143
Báthory, Stephen, King of Poland (1533-1586) 145

Bayne, C.G. 50
Bayonne (France) 94
Beaulieu (France): Edict of (1576) 90
Beaton, David, Cardinal (c. 1494-1564) 14, 19
Beaton, James, Archbishop of Glasgow (1517-1603) 61, 69, 119, 121, 162, 179-181, 185, 193, 201, 204, 210, 212, 219
Belgium 93, 254, 255 See also Flanders, Holland, Low Countries, Netherlands, Spanish Netherlands
Bellamy, Jerome, Catholic layman (+1586) 143
Bellarmine, Robert, Cardinal, S.J., theologian (1542-1621) 180, 232
Belost, Simon, S.J., confessor, administrator (1507-c. 1570) 101
Benoist, René, chaplain to Mary Stuart (fl. 1565) 68
Bergen-op-Zoom (Netherlands) 262
Bergerac (France): Peace of (1577) 122
Berkshire (England) 151, 154
Bernal, Pedro, S.J., Provincial (+1601) 97
Birt, Henry Norbert, O.S.B., historian (1861-1919) 44
Blois (France) 245; Treaty of (1572) 89
"Bloody Questions" 235, 256
Blount, Richard, S.J., Provincial (1565-1638) 6
Bobadilla, Nicolás, S.J., original member of the Society of Jesus (1509-1590) 14, 24, 26, 28, 40, 48, 57
Bodin, Jean, political philosopher (1520-1596) 156
Bold, Richard, Catholic layman (fl. 1585) 173
Boleyn, Anne, Queen of England (1507-1536) 18, 43, 49
Bond of Association (1584) 213
Bonner, Edmund, Bishop of London (1500-1569) 70
Boquin, Pierre, Huguenot minister (1500-1582) 149
Borgia, Francis, S.J., General (1518-1572) 30, 31, 34, 35, 62, 64, 66, 67, 69, 93-95, 101, 126, 271-272
Borgia, Juan, son of Francis Borgia (+1606) 95, 96, 113
Bosgrave, James, S.J., missionary, professor (c. 1548-1623) 145, 156, 169
Bossy, John 9, 126, 196, 221, 222, 264, 278
Bothwell, Earl of. See Hepburn, James, Earl of Bothwell; and Stuart, Francis, Earl of Bothwell

Bourbon, Charles de, Cardinal and pretender to French throne (1523-1590) 190, 227, 245
Bowes, Sir Robert, English ambassador to Scotland (1535-1597) 188, 189
Brabant (Belgium) 114
Broy, Henry, S.J., professor (1550-1598) 255
Briant, Alexander, S.J., missionary (1556-1581) 155, 156
Brielle (Netherlands) 210
Brig o' Dee near Aberdeen (Scotland) 252
Brill (Brielle, Netherlands) 83
Brinkley, Stephen, Catholic printer (fl. 1580) 143, 152
Broët, Paschase, S.J., original member of the Society of Jesus (c. 1500-1562) 14, 15-17, 20, 21, 23, 24, 26, 40, 61
Bromberg, Edward, Marian priest (fl. 1555-1580) 135
Brooke, Henry, Lord Cobham, English ambassador to France (1527-1597) 192, 215
Brooke, William, Lord Cobham (1564-1619) 254
Brooksby, Edward, Catholic layman (fl. 1585) 142, 143, 152
Brooksby, Eleanor, daughter of Henry, Lord Vaux, wife of Edward Brooksby (+ c.1625) 174, 274
Brooksby, Robert, Catholic layman, father of Edward (fl. 1585) 152
Brooksby, William, S.J. (c. 1559-1585) 143, 152
Browne, Anthony, Viscount Montague, Catholic peer (c. 1528-1592) 144, 153, 197, 233
Browne, Francis, Catholic brother of Viscount Montague (fl. 1580) 153
Bruce, Robert, Scottish agent of the Archbishop of Glasgow (+1602) 226, 243
Bruges (Belgium) 12
Bruno, Giordano, philosopher (1548-1600) 198
Bruscoe, Thomas, Catholic layman (fl. 1580) 136
Brussels (Belgium) 27, 28, 29, 34, 37, 38, 75, 83
Butler, Thomas, Earl of Ormond (1531-1614) 67
Butlers, Earls of Ormond 53, 67
Byrd, William, Catholic composer (c. 1538-1623) 174
Cadiz (Spain) 244, 263
Caithness, Earl of. See Sinclair, George, Earl of Caithness

Caligari, Giovanni Andrea, Bishop of Bertinoro and Nuncio in Portugal (+1613) 112
Cambrai (France) 207
Cambridge (England) 163, 277
Campbell, Agnes, wife of Turlough Luineach O'Neill 85
Campbell, Archibald, Earl of Argyll (+1573) 65, 85
Campbell, Finola, wife of Hugh O'Donnell 85
Campeggio, Lorenzo Cardinal (1474-1539) 11
Campion, Edmund, S.J., missionary, writer (1540-1581) 4, 6, 38, 103, 133, 134, 142, 143, 146, 152, 155, 156, 158, 162, 166, 173, 174, 175, 215, 217, 221, 222, 238, 273, 274, 278; and Jewel's challenge 46, 148; and Sir Henry Sidney 65; audience with Pope Gregory XIII 134; "Brag" 146, 147, 148, 149; condemnation of 145, 155; discussed in *De persecutione Anglicana* 191; disputations in the Tower of London 154, 155; execution of 155; instructions to 133; journey to England 134, 136, 143; *Rationes Decem* 152, 153-154, 191 requests more Jesuits 158; work in England 151-152
Candidus, Adrian (*vere* de Witte), S.J., preacher (+1558) 34
Canisius, Peter, S.J., Provincial, writer and missionary (1521-1597) 48, 56, 161
Capeci, Ferdinando, S.J., teacher (+1586) 106, 159, 180
Carafa, Carlo, Cardinal (1517-1561) 36
Carafa, Gian Pietro, Cardinal. See Paul IV, Pope
Caraffa, Antonio, Cardinal (+1591) 239
Carlos, Don, Prince of Spain (1545-1568) 29, 61, 74, 75
Carrafiello, Michael 266
Cashel (Ireland) 220
Cassilis, Earl of. See Kennedy, Gilbert, Earl of Cassilis
Castell, John, S.J. (c. 1546-1580) 159
Castelli, Giovanni Battista, Bishop of Rimini and Nuncio to France (c. 1517-1583) 187, 195
Castelnau Michel de, Seigneur de Mauvissière, French ambassador to England (1520-1592) 123, 199
Castile (Spain) 250
Câteau-Cambrésis (France): Treaty of (1559) 49, 53

Catesby, Sir William, Catholic layman (fl. 1575) 172
Catherine de Medici, Queen of France (1519-1589) 51, 52, 73, 74, 89, 114, 115, 246
Catherine of Aragon, Queen of England (1485-1536) 11
Catholic League 176, 190, 193, 202, 207, 208, 209, 227, 245, 246
Cecil, William, Lord Burghley (1520-1598) 6, 51, 76, 77, 87, 88, 198, 200, 213, 215, 229, 248, 249, 258, 259; and Ridolfi Plot 87, 88; attacked in *Treatise of Treasons* 89; *The copie of a letter sent out of England to don Bernardin Mendoza* 259, 267; *The execution of justice in England* 74, 215
Cervini, Marcello, Cardinal. See Marcellus II, Pope
Charke, William, Protestant writer (c. 1545-1617) 141, 149, 153, 155, 191
Charles, Archduke of Styria (1540-1590) 73
Charles IX, King of France (1550-1574) 51, 65, 74, 83, 85, 86, 90
Charles V, Holy Roman Emperor (1500-1558) 11, 27-30, 34
Châtellier, Louis 270
Chester (England) 63
Cheyne, Dr. James, Scottish Catholic priest (+1602) 219
Chisholm (I), William, Bishop of Dunblane (+1564) 59
Chisholm (II), William, Bishop of Dunblane (+1593) 59, 60, 61; mission to Rome 69; tries to convert James VI 242-244
Clancy, Thomas H., S.J. 25, 80, 102, 125
Clement VII, Pope (1478-1534) 11, 258
Clément, Jacques, O.P., assassin of King Henry III of France (+1589) 246
Clifford, George, Earl of Cumberland (1558-1605) 262
Clonmel (Ireland): Jesuit school in 65
Clynnog, Morys, Catholic priest, administrator (c. 1525-1581) 104, 106, 107, 108
Cobham, Sir Henry. See Brooke, Henry, Lord Cobham
Codure, Jean, S.J., original member of the Society of Jesus (1508-1541) 14, 15, 40
Cogordan, Ponce, S.J., Procurator (1500-1582) 57
Coimbra (Portugal): University of 95, 268
Cologne (Germany) 58

Colonna, Vittoria, supporter of *spirituali* (1490-1547) 26
Commendone, Gian Francesco, Cardinal (1524-1584) 56
Como, Cardinal of. See Galli, Tolomeo Cardinal of Como
Condé, Henry, Prince of (1552-1588) 122, 210
Condé, Louis, Prince of (1530-1569) 72
Congregation, First General (1558) 271; Second General (1565) 127, 271; Fourth General (1581) 271
Contarini, Gasparo, Cardinal (1483-1542) 26
Cordeses, Antonio, S.J., spiritual writer (1518-1601) 125, 126
Córdoba, Antonio de, S.J., administrator (+1567) 37, 39
Cork (Ireland) 55, 94
Cottam, Thomas, S.J., missionary (1549-1582) 136, 146, 156
Council of Troubles (Council of Blood) (1567-1576) 75, 83
Crane, Thomas, Marian priest (fl. 1555-1580) 135
Crawford, Earl of. See Lindsay, David, Earl of Crawford
Creagh, Richard, Archbishop of Armagh (+1585) 34, 62, 63, 64, 66, 79, 272
Creswell, Joseph, S.J., writer, missionary (c. 1557-1623) 143, 254; instructions to 272, 275-276; rector of English College, Rome 255
Crichton, Robert, Bishop of Dunkeld (+1585) 59
Crichton, William, S.J., writer, administrator (c. 1534-1617) 57, 68, 165, 195, 201, 203, 204, 220, 234; and occasional conformity 241; and Scots College 219; captured and confession (1584) 205; laments failure of the Armada 252; leaves Scotland (1589) 262; mission to Scotland (1582) 182, 183, 184, 185, 192; released from the Tower of London (1587) 242; returns to Scotland (1587) 242; sent to Rome (1582) 186, 187; sent to Scotland (1584) 205
Cromer, George, Archbishop of Armagh of the Established Church (+1543) 14, 19
Cromwell, Thomas, Earl of Essex (c. 1485-1540) 17
Curry, John, S.J., missionary (c. 1552-1596) 166, 168, 169, 171
Cusacke, Sir Thomas, Lord Chancellor of Ireland (1490-1571) 64, 78

Dacre, Edward, Lord, Catholic exile (+1584) 194
Dacre, Leonard, Lord, Catholic exile (+1573) 85, 91
Dalkeith (Scotland) 183
Daniel, Edmund, S.J., missionary (c. 1542-1572) 63, 64, 67, 78, 93, 94, 127, 272
Danzig (Gdansk, Poland) 120
Darbyshire, Thomas, S.J., administrator (c. 1520-1604) 78, 101, 102, 124, 142
Darnley, Henry, Lord. See Stuart, Henry, Lord Darnley
Davells, Henry, English agent in Ireland (+1579) 117
Dávila, Gil González, S.J., Provincial (+1596) 189
Day, William, Dean of Windsor (1529-1596) 155
De Costere, Frans, S.J., Provincial (+1619) 67, 79, 93, 101, 255
De Gouda, Nicholas, S.J., missionary (1515-1565) 56, 57, 68, 77, 78, 120, 131, 133; in Scotland 58-61
Derbyshire (England) 151, 152
Desmond, Earl of. See FitzGerald, Gerald FitzJames, Earl of Desmond
Deventer (Netherlands) 230-232, 244
Devereux, Walter, Earl of Essex (1539-1576) 84
Dieppe (France) 205
Digges, Thomas, M.P. (+1595) 214
Donne, John, poet (1573-1631) 160, 168, 171
Douai: English College in 74, 100, 103, 105, 106, 123, 124, 161, 264
Douglas, Archibald, Earl of Angus (c. 1554-1588) 188, 202, 212
Douglas, James, Earl of Morton (+1581) 88, 119, 120, 121, 178, 179, 182
Dover (England) 63, 87
Dowdall, George, Archbishop of Armagh (+1558) 14
Drake, Francis Sir (c. 1540-1596) 209, 210, 244, 263
Dress: the issue of religious attire 137, 151, 271-272, 276, 280,
Drogheda (Ireland) 63
Drury, George, S.J., missionary (c. 1548-c. 1590) 254
Drury, John, S.J., missionary (c. 1544-1588) 210, 211, 242
Dublin (Ireland) 63, 67, 85, 220; Dublin Castle 93, 119
Dudley, Ambrose, Earl of Warwick (c. 1528-1590) 217

Dudley, John, Duke of Northumberland (1502-1553) 25
Dudley, Robert, Earl of Leicester (c. 1532-1588) 51, 53, 65, 68, 71, 76, 87, 134, 154, 165, 173, 206, 210, 217, 230, 231, 242
Dumbarton (Scotland) 85, 86, 120
Dunbar, Gavin, Archbishop of Glasgow (+1547) 19
Dymus, David, S.J., missionary (c. 1540-1572) 118
East Anglia 255; synod in 167-168
Edict of Union (1588) 245
Edinburgh (Scotland) 16, 19, 20, 58, 59, 61, 70, 179, 201, 202, 244; Treaty of (1560) 50, 51, 53; Edinburgh Castle 119
Edward VI, King of England (1537-1553) 24
Edwards, Francis, S.J. 5, 6, 261
Eglinton, Earl of. See Montgomery, Hugh, Earl of Eglinton
Egolph von Knöringen, Johann, Bishop of Augsburg (+1575) 161
Eliano, Giambattista, S.J., missionary, writer (+1589) 127
Elizabeth I, Queen of England (1533-1603) 3, 28, 31, 43, 44, 46, 48-52, 54, 68-74, 76, 77, 89, 104, 105, 107, 122, 160, 169, 173, 178, 215, 259, 261; and Alençon 121, 156, 194; and Anjou 87, 88; and English Catholics 100, 103, 156, 157, 216, 222, 257, 265; and Ireland 52-54, 64, 65, 67, 84, 97, 110, 111, 117, 118; and James VI 203, 210, 211, 213, 227, 229, 252; and Mary Stuart 73, 76, 87-89, 228-230; and the Netherlands 83, 84, 114, 122, 209 and Philip II of Spain 75, 76, 82, 90, 93, 209, 246; and Scotland 68, 85, 86, 88, 119, 181, 187, 188, 252; attacked by William Allen 246, 248, 249; excommunication of 68, 71, 80-82, 99, 105, 134, 140, 141; plots against 6, 73, 87, 90, 91, 93, 100, 104, 115, 157, 184, 194-196, 197, 198, 200, 210, 212, 213, 222, 225, 227, 228, 229, 235, 240, 249, 252, 266
Elizabeth, Queen of Spain (+1568) 74, 75
Ely, Humphrey, Catholic priest (1539-1604) 136, 146
Emerson, Ralph, S.J., laybrother (1553-1604) 133, 136, 143, 156, 165, 171, 182, 217, 234
Engham, Richard, S.J. (c. 1556-1582) 170
England 1, 3-7, 11, 12, 19, 24, 25, 27,

28, 29-43, 46, 48-54, 63, 71, 73, 75-77, 80-82, 84-93, 98, 101-103, 106-112, 116, 117, 121, 122, 123, 124, 128, 129, 131-133, 136, 142, 145, 146, 148, 153, 156-163, 165, 166, 168-178, 180, 181, 183, 184, 187, 188, 190, 191, 193-202, 208, 209, 213, 217, 219, 221, 222, 224, 226, 227, 230, 233-236, 239-241, 243, 244, 245, 246, 250, 252-255, 259, 262, 263, 264, 267, 272-278

English Parliament 18, 43; (1559) 43, 44; (1562) 47; (1566) 71-73; (1571) 81; (1572) 88; (1576) 121, 122; (1581) 150; (1584-85) 213, 214, 215; (1586-1587) 228, 229, 235; (1589) 258

Englefield, Sir Francis, Marian Privy Councillor, Catholic exile in the service of Philip II (1522-1596) 105, 250

Erroll, Earl of. See Hay, Francis, Earl of Erroll and Hay, George, Earl of Erroll

Erskine, John, Earl of Mar (+1572) 88

Erskine, John, Earl of Mar (c. 1562-1634) 202

Eu (France) 185; English College in 192, 264

Eustace, James, Viscount of Baltinglass (+1585) 117

Eustace, Richard, S.J. (c. 1564-1597) 118

Évora (Portugal) 111, 112

Farnese, Alessandro, Cardinal (1520-1589) 227

Farnese, Alessandro Prince and later (15-86) Duke of Parma (1543-1592) 114, 115, 121, 122, 194 202, 203, 206, 208, 209, 228, 230, 244, 251, 254, 260, 262

Fasts and Fasting 135, 167-168

Favre, Pierre, S.J., original member of the Society of Jesus (1506-1546) 14, 25

Feckenham, John, O.S.B., Abbot of Westminster (c. 1517-1585) 98, 99

Felton, John, recusant layman (+ 1570) 81

Fenn, James, Catholic priest (+1584) 169

Ferdinand, King of the Romans and later Holy Roman Emperor (1503-1564) 35, 71

Fernando Álvarez de Toledo, Count of Oropesa and Duke of Alba. See Alba, Duke of

Fitton, Edward, Catholic layman (fl. 1580) 143

FitzAlan, Henry, Earl of Arundel (1512-1580) 76

FitzGerald, Gerald, Earl of Kildare and Lord Deputy of Ireland (1487-1534) 16

FitzGerald, Gerald, Earl of Kildare (1525-1585) 117

FitzGerald, Gerald FitzJames, Earl of Desmond (c. 1533-1583) 55, 67, 117

FitzGerald, James FitzMaurice (+1578) 67, 84, 94, 95, 97, 98, 111, 113, 115-119, 131, 136, 144

FitzGerald, Sir James (+1580) 117

FitzGerald, Sir John (fl. 1580) 117

FitzGerald, Thomas, Lord Offaly (Silken Thomas), Earl of Kildare (1513-1537) 16, 17

FitzGeralds, Earls of Desmond and Earls of Kildare 53, 67, 78, 265, 272

Fitzherbert, Thomas, S.J., administrator, writer (1552-1640) 143, 153

FitzMaurice, James. See FitzGerald, James FitzMaurice

Flanders 12, 13, 19, 28, 34-37, 50, 78, 84, 86, 92, 101, 103, 108, 109, 115, 202, 203, 231, 254 See Also Belgium, Holland, Low Countries, Netherlands, Spanish Netherlands

Fleming, Abraham, writer (c. 1552-1607) 215

Fleming, Richard, S.J., teacher (c. 1541-1590) 219

Flinton, George, printer (+c. 1584) 190

Floris, Nicholas. See De Gouda, Nicholas.

Flushing (Netherlands) 210, 230

Foley, Henry, S.J., historian (1811-1891) 4, 5

Fonseca, Pedro, Portuguese assistant, philosopher (1528-1599) 132

Forbes-Leith, William, S.J., historian (1833-1921) 7

Fotheringay Castle (England) 228

Framlingham Castle (England) 171

France 7, 19, 48-50, 56, 65, 67, 74, 80, 83, 84, 85-87, 89, 90, 92, 94, 99, 113, 116, 119-122, 156, 162, 163, 168, 176, 179, 183, 188, 190, 191, 196, 201, 202, 206-210, 215, 217, 222, 227, 241, 245, 246, 262-264, 266, 276, 277

Francis II, King of France (1544-1560) 49, 51, 52

Francken, Christian, ex-Jesuit, Protestant polemicist (1549-1600?) 141, 142

Frangipani, Fabio Mirto, Archbishop of Nazareth, Nuncio to France (+1587) 114

Freux, André des, S.J., Secretary to Loyola (+1556) 24
Fuljambe, Godfrey, Catholic layman (fl. 1580) 143
Fulke, William, Master of Pembroke College, Cambridge (1538-1589) 99, 155
G.D., *A briefe discoverie of doctor Allens seditious drifts* 232
Gagliardi, Achille, S.J., theologian (1537-1607) 180
Galli, Tolomeo, Cardinal of Como (c. 1525-1607) 91, 92, 97, 108, 110, 111, 112, 114-116, 118, 119, 127, 158, 188, 205
Gardiner, Stephen, Bishop of Winchester (c. 1483-1555) 25, 27
Garnet, Henry, S.J., missionary (1555-1606) 6, 171, 173-174, 234-237, 253, 255, 256-258, 263, 267, 274, 276-278; instructions to 275-277
Gembloux (Belgium) 114
Genoa (Italy) 166
Gentilcore, David 270
Gerard, John, S.J., missionary, administrator (1564-1637) 3, 110, 255, 258, 261, 262, 263
Germany 41, 75, 101, 161, 272
Ghent (Belgium) 109, 230; Pacification of (1576) 109, 111, 114
Gibbons, John, S.J., administrator, writer (c. 1544-1589) 170
Giberti, Gian Matteo, Bishop of Verona (+1543) 26
Giblet, William, Marian priest 135
Gifford, George, conspirator (fl. 1583) 194, 196, 233
Gilbert, George, S.J., benefactor (c. 1559-1583) 142, 143, 151, 153, 157, 273-274
Glasgow (Scotland) 20
Gleason, Elizabeth G. 128
Gloucestershire (England) 151
Goldwell, Thomas, Bishop of St. Asaph (c. 1500-1585) 133, 135, 136
Gómez de Silva, Rui, Prince of Éboli (1516-1573) 29
Gómez Suárez de Figueroa, Duke of Feria (+1571) 37, 39
González Dávila, Gil, S.J., administrator (+1596) 132
Good, William, S.J., missionary (1527-1586) 63-67, 78, 79, 93, 94, 101, 102, 121, 124, 125, 170, 272
Gordon, George, Earl of Huntly (c. 1510-1576) 61
Gordon, George, Earl of Huntly (1563-1636) 205, 211, 227, 244, 252, 262

Gordon, James, S.J., missionary, administrator (c. 1543-1620) 68, 201, 205, 210, 211, 243
Gordon, William, Bishop of Aberdeen (+1577) 59
Goudanus, Nicholas. See De Gouda, Nicholas
Gowrie, Earl of. See Ruthven, William, Earl of Gowrie
Graham, William, Earl of Montrose (c. 1492-1571) 61
Granada (Spain) 83
Granvelle, Antoine Perrenot de, Cardinal (1517-1586) 28, 30
Greenstreet Press 152, 153
Gregory XIII, Pope (1502-1585) 91, 128, 161, 184; and Catholic League 207; and England 90, 91, 99, 108, 111, 131, 194, 195, 198, 200; and English Colleges in Rome and Reims 105-107, 188; and excommunication of Elizabeth 140, 141; and Ireland 110, 112, 115, 116; and Jesuits 127, 128; and Jesuits in England 133, 144; and Scotland 121, 187, 201, 202, 204, 219; audience with Campion and Parsons before their departure for England 134, 135; faculties granted to Campion and Parsons 139-141
Grene, Christopher, S.J., missionary, writer (1629-1697) 3
Grey, Lady Jane (1537-1554) 25
Grey, Lady Elizabeth, 17
Grey, Leonard, Lord Deputy of Ireland (+1541) 17
Griffen, Richard, recusant layman (fl. 1580) 143
Griffen, William, recusant layman (fl. 1580) 143
Guerau de Spes, Spanish ambassador to England (fl. 1560-1570) 76, 93
Guibert, Joseph de, S.J., writer (1877-1942) 125
Guidiccioni, Bartholomeo, Cardinal (1470-1549) 22
Guise, Charles, Duke of Mayenne (1554-1611) 207
Guise, Charles, Cardinal of Lorraine, Archbishop of Reims (1524-1574) 19, 49, 92, 219
Guise, Francis, Duke of Guise (1519-1563) 49, 52, 72
Guise, Henry, Duke of (1550-1588) 119, 182, 184, 185, 189, 192, 194, 195, 197-202, 207, 208, 210, 222, 227, 245, 264, 266
Guise, Louis, Cardinal (+1578) 92, 119

INDEX

Guise, Louis, Cardinal (+1588) 207, 245
Guise, Mary, Queen of Scotland (+1560) 19, 49-50, 56
Guises 50-52, 73, 89, 90, 92, 119, 120, 176, 190, 193, 194, 198, 206, 207, 208, 210, 226, 240, 246, 264, 267
Guy, John 38
Guzmán, Enrique de, Count of Olivares, Spanish ambassador to Rome (+1607) 200, 212, 226, 240, 241, 242, 246, 259, 260
Hackney (England) 174, 274
Haigh, Christopher 99, 151, 266
Hall, James, recusant layman (fl. 1580) 143
Hamilton, Claude, Lord (c. 1543-1622) 212, 227, 244
Hamilton, James, Earl of Arran (c. 1537-1609) 212
Hamilton, John, Archbishop of St. Andrews (+1571) 59, 61
Hanmer, Meredith, Protestant theologian (1543-1604) 149, 153
Harding, Thomas, theologian (1516-1572) 46, 90, 148
Harlesford (or Hurleyford) (England) 173
Harrow (England) 160, 161
Harrowden (England) 174
Hart, John, S.J., missionary (+1586) 136, 146, 169
Hastings, Edward, brother of Henry Hastings, Earl of Huntingdon (fl. 1570) 110
Hastings, Francis, Earl of Huntingdon (1514-1560) 110
Hastings, Francis, brother of Henry Hastings, Earl of Huntingdon (+1610) 110
Hastings, George, Earl of Huntingdon (c. 1540-1604) 110
Hastings, Henry, Earl of Huntingdon (c. 1536-1595) 110
Hastings, Walter, Catholic brother of Henry Hastings, Earl of Huntingdon (fl. 1570) 110
Hatton, Sir Christopher, Lord Chancellor (1540-1591) 205, 228, 258
Hay, Edmund, missionary, administrator, Provincial (1548-1591) 57, 58, 60, 68, 182, 201, 206, 210, 211; missions to Scotland 69, 70, 77-78, 132; appointed superior in Scotland 211; leaves Scotland (1589) 262
Hay, Francis, Earl of Erroll (1564-1631) 244, 252
Hay, George, Earl of Erroll (1541-1574) 61
Hay, John, S.J., missionary, theologian (1547-1608) 68, 210; in Scotland (1579) 120, 121
Haydock, George, Catholic priest (+1584) 169
Hayes-McCoy, G.A. 253
Helyar, John, Catholic priest (c. 1503-c. 1540?) 25
Hemerford, Thomas, Catholic priest? (1554-1584) 169
Henry II, King of France (1519-1559) 27, 49
Henry III, King of France (1551-1589) 84, 87, 90, 114, 122, 190, 206-210, 227, 245, 246, 255; and English Catholics 156
Henry IV, King of France (1553-1610) 193, 201, 207, 210, 246, 262, 263
Henry of Navarre. See Henry IV, King of France
Henry VIII, King of England (1491-1547) 11, 15, 16, 18-21, 24, 39, 44, 48, 49, 104, 258
Henry, Cardinal King of Portugal (+1580) 115, 116
Henry Suso, German mystic (c. 1295-1366) 126
Henshaw, Henry, Catholic priest, Warden, English Hospice, Rome (fl. 1580) 106
Hepburn, James, Earl of Bothwell (c. 1535-1578) 70
Herbert, William, Earl of Pembroke (c. 1506-1570) 76
Herefordshire (England) 151
Heywood, Elizeus, S.J., administrator (1529-1578) 103
Heywood, Jasper, S.J., missionary (1535-1598) 101, 103, 159, 161, 164, 166, 168, 169, 172, 176, 177, 179, 180, 198, 202, 267, 273, 274, 278; and East Anglian synod 167-168; and Mendoza 162, 163; and Parsons 166, 217, 218, 276, 277; captured and imprisoned 169-171; complaints about 168, 169, 172; instructions to 275; sent to Naples 169; visited in the Tower by Weston 171, 172; work in England 160, 161, 163, 165, 168; work in Germany 160-161
Heywood, John, epigrammatist (c. 1497-1578) 160
Hicks, Leo, S.J., historian (1888-1968) 230
Hoffaeus, Paul, S.J., Provincial, German assistant (1525-1608) 161
Hogan, Edmund, S.J., historian (1831-1917) 7

Holland 230, 262, 264 See also Belgium, Flanders, Low Countries, Netherlands, Spanish Netherlands
Holt, William, S.J., missionary, chaplain, administrator (1545-1599) 159, 161, 273; and James VI 201; instructions to 272, 275-276; plans for his return to Scotland (1588) 254-255; proposed as temporary superior of English and Scottish missions 208-209; rector of English College, Rome 225, 242, 255; work in England 160, 161; work in Scotland 163, 180-182, 184-186, 188-189, 199, 201-204, 210, 211, 242
Holy Roman Empire 41, 56
Horne, Robert, Bishop of Winchester (c. 1519-1580) 1
Hornes, Philip de Montmorency, Count of (1524-1568) 75
Howard, Anne, Countess of Arundel (1557-1630) 236, 237
Howard, Philip, Earl of Arundel (1557-1595) 163, 172, 197, 237
Howard, Thomas, Duke of Norfolk (1538-1572) 76, 80, 85, 88; and Mary Stuart 86-88; execution of 88, 89
Hoxton (England) 146, 172
Hubert (or Hubbard), Henry, Catholic layman 171
Hunt, Simon, S.J. (1548-1585) 170
Huntly, Earl of. See Gordon, George, Earl of Huntly
Hurstfield, Joel 259
Idiáquez, Juan de, Secretary to Philip II (1540-1614) 212, 225
Ignatius Loyola, founder of the Society of Jesus (c. 1491-1556) 2, 9, 12, 14, 28, 30, 36, 39-41, 57, 137, 153, 260, 271, 278; and *Constitutions* 6, 8, 127, 130, 267, 271; "General Examen" 268; "Formula of the Institute" 267, 271; and England 12, 13, 24, 25, 27, 29-35, 38, 40, 41, 42, 129, 269-271; and elites 22, 23; and Ireland 15, 20, 24; and Philip II of Spain 29, 34, 251; and Pole 25, 26, 32, 33, 39; and *Spiritual Exercises* 8, 13, 16, 20, 22, 25, 126, 137, 269; letter to Jesuits in Coimbra 268
India 102, 118, 131
Ingolstadt (Germany): University of 23
Inquisition 260, 261
Institute: definition of 8, 9; affairs alien to 111-113, 118, 127, 128, 220, 266, 268, 271, 272, 278; and Acquaviva 223; and Mercurian 126; and Irish, English and Scottish missions 38-39, 41, 78-79, 131-133, 141, 182, 275-277; and Parsons's activities 196; attacked by Inquisition 186, 260-261; Pole's work for 26; poverty 275; problems with 40, 41
Ireland 1, 6-8, 14-21, 23, 24, 40, 50-52, 54-56, 61-67, 78, 79, 84, 85, 91, 93-99, 101, 108, 110-113, 115, 116, 117-119, 121, 126, 127, 131, 136, 144, 157, 167, 170, 183, 184, 194, 219, 220, 227, 230, 252, 253, 263, 265, 272, 273, 275, 277, 278
Irish Parliament (1536-1537) 17, 18; (1560) 53-54; (1569) 84; (1585) 221
Irvine (Scotland) 20
Isabella, Princess of Spain (1566-1633) 226, 242, 264
Isabella of Portugal, Holy Roman Empress (1503-1539) 115
James V, King of Scotland (1512-1542) 19, 20, 70
James VI, King of Scotland (1566-1625) 69, 92, 119, 121, 171, 180, 188, 189, 196-198, 212, 225; and Catholic earls 252, 262; and enterprise 178, 183-184, 200, 202, 203, 222, 227, 243; and Queen Elizabeth 203, 210, 211, 213, 252; and Queen Mary Stuart 183, 193, 213; and succession to English throne 212, 226-227, 241-242, 251; and William Holt, S.J. 189, 201; plans for his conversion to Catholicism 119, 178, 181, 190, 192, 201, 210, 219, 227, 241-244; theological discussion with James Gordon, S.J. 243
James, Thomas, Catholic layman (1556-c.1613) 143
Jay, Claude, S.J., original member of the Society of Jesus (c. 1500-1552) 14
Jewel, John, Bishop of Salisbury (1522-1571) 45, 46, 148, 154
Jiménez, Pedro, S.J., theologian (fl. 1580) 180
Joinville (France): Treaty of (1584) 207
John Casimir, Count Palatine (+1592) 114
Jones, Norman 43
Juan of Austria, Don, Governor of the Netherlands (1547-1578) 93, 97, 98, 109, 111, 114
Juana, Princess of Spain (1535-1573) 30
Julius III, Pope (1487-1555) 26, 27, 32, 33, 40; *Exposcit debitum* (1550) 26, 40; *Praeclara* (1555) 32
Kemp, William, Marian priest (fl. 1555-

1580) 135
Kennedy, Gilbert, Earl of Cassilis (c. 1541-1576) 61
Kenny, Anthony 104
Kerry (Ireland) 116
Kessel, Leonard, S.J., administrator (+ 1574) 57
Kilmallock 55; Jesuit school in 64, 65
King, Thomas, S.J., missionary (c. 1537-1565) 78, 101
Kirby, Luke, Catholic priest (1548-1582) 136
Knox, John, reformer (c.1513-1572) 49, 55, 58, 86
La Rochelle (France) 75
Laínez, Diego, S.J., original member of the Society of Jesus, Father General (1512-1565) 14, 35-39, 42, 48, 54-57, 60, 62, 77, 101, 104, 267
Lamoral, Count of Egmont (1523-1568) 75
Lancashire (England) 152, 161, 197
Langdale, Alban, Archdeacon of Chichester (+c. 1584) 144, 152
Langdale, Thomas, ex-Jesuit (1541-post 1580) 166, 167
LaRocca, John, S.J. 48
Laureo, Vincenzo, Bishop of Mondovì (+1592) 69
Law, T.G., historian (1838-1904) 265
Le Havre (France) 72, 73
Lee, Charles, S.J., missionary (c. 1546-1586) 94, 118, 119, 127, 219
Leicester, Earl of. See Dudley, Robert, Earl of Leicester
Leicester's Commonwealth 171, 206
Leicestershire (England) 174, 274
Leigh, Richard, Catholic priest (1561-1588). See Cecil, William, Lord Burghley
Leith (Scotland) 49, 58, 188, 243
Lennon, Colm 67
Lennox, Duke of. See Stuart, Esmé Sieur d'Aubigny and Stuart, Matthew 86
Lepanto: Battle of (1571) 83, 91
Leslie, Andrew, Earl of Rothes (c. 1528-1611) 202
Leslie, John, Bishop of Ross (1527-1596) 182, 219
Lewis, Owen, priest later Bishop of Cassano (1533-1595) 104-107, 187
Lightfoote, William, writer (fl. 1585) 232
Limerick (Ireland) 34, 54, 55, 63, 77, 94; Jesuit school in 34, 64, 65, 272
Lindsay, David, Earl of Crawford (c. 1552-1607) 244, 252
Lisbon (Portugal) 93-97, 111-113, 115, 165, 186, 189, 213, 251; Jesuit college in 95; São Roque 95
Loarte, Gaspar, S.J., spiritual writer (+1578) 192
London 12, 53, 63, 70, 76, 103, 142, 143, 146, 151, 152, 155, 160, 162, 165, 169, 171, 173, 174, 196, 221, 228, 236, 237, 257, 273, 274; Arundel House 237, 274; Bishopsgate 174, 233; Clink 169, 171, 277; Holborn 155; Howard House 237; Inns of Court 103, 142; Ludgate Hill 257; Marshalsea 142, 145; Poultry 171; St. Paul's 257, 267; Smithfield 143; Spitalfields 236; Tower 64, 76, 88, 145, 153-155, 169, 171, 205, 234, 242, 253
Longjumeau (France): Peace of (1568) 75
Loomie, Albert, S.J. 230
Louvain 28, 94, 103, 104, 114, 123; English Catholic exiles in 46, 71, 91, 92, 98; University of 28, 34, 35
Low Countries 7, 29, 30, 57, 83, 86, 87, 91, 122, 202, 230, 263 See also Belgium, Flanders, Holland, Netherlands, Spanish Netherlands
Loyola, Beltrán, relative of Ignatius (fl. 1540) 15
Luther, Martin, reformer (1483-1546) 2
Lyford Grange (England) 154
MacCaffrey, Wallace 122
MacDonald, James, Scottish leader (fl. 1560) 85
MacDonnell, Alexander Óg, Scottish leader (fl. 1567) 66
MacGibbon, Maurice, Archbishop of Cashel (+1578) 67
MacQuhirrie, Alexander, S.J., missionary (+c. 1605) 242
Madrid (Spain) 97, 98, 111, 115, 118, 189, 195, 200
Magauran, Edmund, Bishop of Ardagh (+1593) 211
Maitland, Sir John, Lord Thirlestane, Vice-Chancellor (c. 1545-1595) 243
Mannaerts, Oliver, S.J., Provincial, German assistant, Visitor (c. 1526-1614) 69, 132, 134, 145, 159, 175, 202
Manners, Edward, Earl of Rutland (1549-1587) 197
Manuel I, King of Portugal (+1521) 115
Mar, Earl of. See Erskine, John, Earl of Mar
Marcellus II, Pope (1501-1555) 24, 33
Marceu, Antonio, S.J., Provincial (+1603) 260
Marsden, William, secular priest? (+1586

234
Marshall, Thomas, S.J. (1545-1589) 169, 170
Marsupino, Francesco, Catholic priest (fl. 1540) 15
Martin, A. Lynn 183, 270
Martin, Gregory, Catholic priest, theologian (+1582) 99
Martinengo, Jerónimo, Abbot, Nuncio (fl. 1560) 51
Mary of Hungary, Regent of the Netherlands (1505-1558) 28, 30
Mary [Stuart], Queen of Scots (1542-1587) 6, 49-52, 57, 61, 65, 76, 82, 85-87, 90, 99, 108, 119, 122, 178-179, 181, 183, 196, 202, 204, 212, 242, 264, 266; and enterprises or plans for liberation 111, 157, 184, 188, 192-193, 196, 197, 199, 200, 202, 205, 212, 226-229, 235; and Don Juan of Austria 109; and Duke of Norfolk 86-87; and James VI 183, 193; and Jesuits 121, 128, 156, 185-186; and Parsons 184, 190, 206; and Scots College 219; and the crown of England 44, 48, 49, 51, 52, 68, 71, 73, 76-77, 82, 87-89, 93, 104, 121, 180, 222; execution of 229, 232, 239, 247, 252; flight into England 70; her reign in Scotland 55, 56, 58, 61, 68-70, 73, 74; life in England 71, 73, 76, 80, 86, 87, 110; reconciliation with Roman Church 70; will of 226
Mary Tudor, Queen of England (1516-1558) 24, 27-31, 34, 37, 38, 49, 101, 104, 105, 250
Mascarenhas, Dona Leonor, Lady-in-Waiting to Empress Isabella (1503-1584) 29
Matthias, Archduke of Austria (1557-1619) 109, 114
Matthieu, Claude, S.J., Provincial (1537-1587) 176, 177, 181, 185, 198, 203, 204, 207, 209
Maxwell, John, Earl of Morton (+1593) 211, 227, 244
Mayne, Cuthbert, Catholic priest (1544-1577) 123
McRedmond, Louis 8
Meléndez, Gonzalo, S.J., Procurator (fl. 1575) 98
Melino, Richard (*vere* Robert Parsons) 197, 240
Mendoza, Bernardino de, Spanish ambassador to England (c. 1540-1604) 93, 162-163, 178, 180, 181, 183-186, 188, 190, 195, 199, 200, 205, 217, 222, 226, 228, 244; and Parsons and Heywood 159, 162
Mendoza, Juan de, custodian of Castel Nuovo, Naples and later a Jesuit (+1556) 34
Mercurian, Everard, S.J., General (c. 1515-1580) 56, 125-128, 133, 142; and a Jesuit mission to England 123--125, 128-129, 131-134, 138, 272; and a Jesuit mission to Scotland 121; and England 92, 93, 101, 103, 105, 107; and English College, Rome 106, 107, 124; and Ireland 62, 63, 116, 118, 119, 272; and Scotland 56, 57, 69, 77, 181; and the Society's Institute 125-128, 131-132, 174, 175, 273, 279; and Wolfe 96, 97, 111-113, 126-128, 222; death of 133, 158, 159; instructions to Campion and Parsons 133, 136-141, 272, 275
Metham, Thomas, S.J., missionary (c. 1532-1592) 142, 156, 234
Mildmay, Sir Walter, M.P., founder of Emmanuel College, Cambridge (c. 1520-1589) 150, 228, 235
Millins, Richard (*vere* Robert Parsons) 186
Modena (Italy) 54
Mons (Belgium) 83, 114
Monsi, Michel de, Archdeacon of Rouen (fl. 1580-1593) 162, 180, 190, 222
Monterrey (Spain): Jesuit college in 260
Montgomery, Hugh, Earl of Eglinton (c. 1533-1585) 61
Montmorency, Anne de, Constable of France (1493-1567) 52
Montrose, Earl of. See Graham, William, Earl of Montrose
Moray, Earl of. See Stuart, James, Earl of Moray
More, Henry, S.J., Provincial, historian (c. 1587-1661) 3-5, 102, 136
More, Sir Thomas, Lord Chancellor (1478-1535) 12, 13
Morgan, Thomas, Catholic layman and opponent of Parsons (c. 1542-1606) 185, 193, 198, 200, 204, 207, 208, 218, 267
Moriscos 83, 87
Morone, Giovanni, Cardinal (c. 1508-1580) 32, 33, 36, 37, 54, 90, 104, 106, 107
Morrissey, Thomas J., S.J. 7
Morton, Earl of. See Douglas, James, Earl of Morton; and Maxwell, John, Earl of Morton
Morton, Nicholas, Catholic priest (fl. 1580) 135, 136
Morviller, Jean de, French ambassador to

Scotland and later Bishop of Orléans (1506-1577) 19
Mundyn, John, Catholic priest (1543-1584) 169
Munster (Ireland) 53, 62, 67, 84, 117
Murdoch, William, S.J., missionary, administrator (c. 1539-1616) 68, 254
Nadal, Jerónimo, S.J., administrator, Visitor, writer (1507-1580) 9, 12, 29-31, 33, 41, 131, 251, 270, 271-272
Namur (Belgium) 109
Nancy (France) 207
Naples (Italy) 34, 176
Natale, Thomas, ex-Jesuit (fl. 1555) 39
Neale, Sir John E., historian (1890-1975) 43
Nelson, John, S.J., missionary (c. 1534-1578) 123
Nemours (France): Treaty of (1585) 208, 209, 245
Nérac (France): Treaty of (1579) 122
Netherlands 74, 75, 77, 80, 83-85, 91, 109, 110, 113, 114, 121, 122, 193, 194, 201, 206-209, 230, 231, 233, 240, 251 See also Belgium, Flanders, Holland, Low Countries, Spanish Netherlands
Neuss (Germany) 228
Nevill, Charles, Earl of Westmorland (c. 1542-1601) 76, 77, 85, 184, 194, 200, 203, 267
Nicholas V, Pope (1397-1455) 219
Nicholls, K.W. 16, 17
Nijmegen: Convention of (1573) 90
Nonsuch (England): Treaty of (1585) 209, 244
Norfolk (England) 171, 194
Norfolk, Duke of. See Howard, Thomas Duke of Norfolk
Northumberland, Duke of. See Dudley, John, Duke of Northumberland
Normandy (France) 190, 193
Norris, Sir John, military commander (c. 1547-1597) 230
Northamptonshire 151, 174, 274
Northumberland, Earl of. See Percy, Henry and Percy, Thomas, Earl of Northumberland
Norton, Thomas, writer, M.P. (1532-1584) 215
Nottinghamshire (England) 152
Novarola, Giovanni Paolo, S.J. (fl. 1580) 106
Nowell, Alexander, Dean of St. Paul's (c. 1507-1602) 154
Nutter, John, Catholic priest (+1584) 169
Oath of allegiance (1588) 256, 257

Ó Fionnagáin, Prionsias, S.J. 113
O'Donnell, Calvagh, Lord of Tyrconnel (+1566) 65, 66
O'Donnell, Hugh, Lord of Tyrconnel (+1600) 66, 85
O'Donnell, Manus, Lord of Tyrconnel (+1564) 17, 18, 20
O'Donnells 65, 66, 220
O'Donoghue, Fergus, S.J. 7
O'Friel, Arthur, Archbishop of Tuam (+c. 1573) 20
O'Gallagher, Redmond, Irish Catholic priest 17
O'Healy, Patrick, O.F.M, Bishop of Mayo (+c. 1579) 111, 117
O'Higgin, Milar, Archbishop of Tuam (+c. 1590) 209
O'Hurley, Dermot, Archbishop of Cashel (+1584) 220
O'Malley, John W., S.J. 8, 9, 40, 267, 271
O'Neill, Brian, Earl of Tyrone (c. 1535-1562) 52, 53
O'Neill, Conn Bacach, Earl of Tyrone (c. 1484-1559) 17-18, 20, 52
O'Neill, Matthew (+1558) 52
O'Neill, Shane, Lord of Tyrone and Earl of Tyrone (c. 1530-1567) 51-54, 63, 65-67, 84
O'Neill, Turlough Luineach, Lord of Tyrone (c. 1530-1595) 84, 117
O'Neills 62, 66, 78, 220, 265
Oberman, Heiko A. 2, 8
Occasional conformity 47, 72, 98-100, 135, 242; and synod of Southwark 144-145; suggested by Cecil 259
Ogilvie, William, S.J., missionary (c. 1560-1594) 241, 242
Oldcorne, Edward, S.J., missionary (c. 1561-1606) 255, 258
Olivares, Count of. See Guzmán, Enrique de, Count of Olivares
Olivier, Bernard, S.J., (+1556) 29, 34, 36
Oñate (Spain) 189
Oporto (Portugal) 95
Ormanetto, Nicholas, Bishop of Padua and Nuncio in Spain (+1577) 92, 93, 97, 108, 110, 111
Ostend (Belgium) 205
Ottoman Empire 83, 84, 121, 209
Oxford (England) 35, 45, 103, 106, 153, 160, 163, 170, 174
Oxfordshire (England) 151, 153
Paget, Charles, Catholic exile and opponent of Parsons (+1612) 185, 197-200, 204, 207, 208, 218, 267
Paget, Thomas, Lord, Catholic exile

(+1590) 143, 144
Paget, William, Lord (1505-1563) 27, 28
Pallavicino, Fabricio, S.J., professor (1555-1600) 159
Palmio, Benedetto, S.J., Provincial and Italian assistant (1523-1598) 132
Parenticelli, Antonio Maria, S.J., professor of philosophy (1552-1589) 159
Paris (France) 12-14, 25, 61, 75, 119, 162, 170, 182, 190, 195, 198, 203, 206, 209, 219, 220, 245
Parma, Prince/Duke of. See Farnese, Alessandro, Prince and later Duke of Parma
Parpaglia, Vincenzo, Abbot, Nuncio to England (fl. 1560) 50, 54
Parry Plot (1585) 198, 213
Parry, William (+1585) 216
Parsons, Robert, missionary, administrator, writer (1546-1610) 3, 4, 6, 27, 38, 46, 100, 102, 105, 123, 132, 142, 143, 148, 153, 156, 161, 163-167, 170, 173-176, 200, 212, 221, 222, 227, 260, 265, 267, 273, 276, 277; and Acquaviva 195, 198, 205, 206, 220, 223, 266, 279-280; and Allen 206, 208, 239; and Henry, Duke of Guise 192, 207, 209; and Heywood 160, 168, 169, 217, 218; and James VI 213, 225, 227; and Mendoza 159, 162, 163; and Parma 202-203; and Perkins 133; and Sir William Stanley 231; and Throckmorton Plot 200; and Weston 170, 172; appointed superior of Scottish mission 203; audience with Gregory XIII 134; calls a synod at Southwark 143-145; Campion's capture and death 154, 175; debates the continuation of English mission 158-159, 176-177; defends Acquaviva in Spain 260, 261; designates Heywood his deputy 162; disavows knowledge of FitzMaurice rebellion in Ireland 136, 144; discouraged by repeated failure 205; explains defeat of Armada 261; evaluation of Pigenat 176; flight from England and work in France 155-156, 162-163, 190, 192, 198, 203, 276; founds a college at Eu 192-193; goes to Rome (1585) 208; instructions to 133; interest in Scotland 166, 177-182, 184, 185, 187, 203, 204; involvement with plans for an enterprise 199, 212, 222, 227, 233; journey to and work in England 136, 142-143, 146, 151, 152; knowledge of an assassination plot 196; laments the persecution of Catholics 157-158, 164-165, 216, 224; missions to Philip II 186-187, 189, 195, 260; named superior of all Jesuits sent to England and of English chaplains 260, 279; named superior of English mission 133, 139; on disunity among Catholics 225; operates a printing press in England 152; opposes occasional conformity 144, 145, 152; reaction against policies of 263; requests more Jesuits 158-159, 165, 170; sent to Rome (1583) 197-198; supports Armada 251, 259; supports Philip's claim to determine succession to the throne of England 218, 229, 239-242; won over to Spanish side 240; works for a Jesuit mission to England 102, 124, 125, 129-131, 133, 134; *Leicester's Commonwealth* 206; "A Confession of Faith" 146-147; *A brief censure uppon two bookes written in answere to M. Edmonde Campions offer of disputation* 153; *A brief discours contayning certayne reasons why catholiques refuse to go to Church* 152; *A defence of the Censure, gyven upon two bookes of William Charke and Meredith Hanmer mynysters, which they wrote against M. Edmond Campian* 191; *A discoverie of I. Nicols Minister, misreported a Iesuite, latelye recanted in the Tower of London* 153; *De persecutione Anglicana* 190-192; *The first booke of the Christian exercise, appertayning to resolution* 191, 192, 206
Pascal, John, Catholic layman (fl. 1580) 136
Patrick, Master of Gray (c. 1560-1612) 202
Paul II, Pope (1417-1471) 219
Paul III, Pope (1468-1549) 14, 15, 20, 21, 26, 40, 51, 128; *Regimini militantis Ecclesiae* (1540) 14, 40
Paul IV, Pope (1476-1559) 18, 24, 33, 36, 48
Paulet, Sir Amias, English ambassador in France (c. 1536-1588) 115
Pelham, Sir William, (+1587) 117, 230
Pembroke, Earl of. See Herbert, William

Earl of Pembroke
Pembroke, Richard, S.J. (c. 1561-1594) 253
Percy, Henry, Earl of Northumberland (c. 1532-1585) 160, 163, 171, 213
Percy, Thomas, Earl of Northumberland (1528-1572) 76, 77
Pérez de Guzmán, Alonso, Duke of Medina Sidonia (+1617) 251, 252
Pérez, Antonio, Secretary to Philip II (1534 or 1540-1607) 110
Perkins (or Parkins), Christopher, ex-Jesuit and Dean of Carlisle (1547-1622) 133, 159, 167
Péronne (France): Manifesto of (1585) 208
Perrot, Sir John, Lord Deputy of Ireland (c. 1527-1592) 84, 221
Persecution 157-160, 163-164 176, 177, 216, 217, 222, 233, 235-237, 249, 256, 263, 266, 274
Perth (Scotland) 49
Peter Martyr [Vermigli], reformer (1500-1562) 45
Peters, Willem A.M., S.J. 13
Philip II, King of Spain (1527-1598) 50, 67, 75, 75, 80, 91, 98, 121, 199, 212, 243, 254; and English Catholic exiles 76, 92, 162, 203, 264; and English College, Reims 188; and Loyola 29, 34, 38, 42, 251; and Mary Stuart 61, 68, 82, 90, 197; the Armada 244-246, 250, 251, 259; conflict in the Netherlands 84, 109, 193, 231, 262; dismissal of Alba 83; King of England 27-32, 34, 35; opposed to Elizabeth's excommunication 82; plans involving Ireland 67, 90, 91, 95-98, 112, 115; plans involving Scotland 180, 182, 187, 189, 202, 243, 244; proposals for an enterprise against England 205, 210, 212, 213, 227, 239; relations with Parsons and Allen 189, 206; relations with Elizabeth and England 48, 51, 52, 71, 75-77, 82-83, 90, 93, 103, 104, 108, 110, 111, 114, 195, 199, 200, 226, 228, 264; relations with the Guises 194, 195, 227; relations with the Jesuits 112, 261; right of succession to the English throne 226, 227, 229, 239, 240, 241, 245; struggle for the Portuguese crown 115, 116, 121, 122, 165, 193
Pierrepoint, Gervase, Catholic layman (fl. 1580) 143
Pigenat, Odo, S.J., Provincial (c. 1538-1608) 176-177, 204, 206, 207, 209, 210, 267, 276, 277
Pigot, William, English captain (fl. 1580) 230
Pius IV, Pope (1499-1565) 48, 51, 66, 77; and Council of Trent 50; and England 71; and Ireland 54, 62; and Scotland 56, 57, 61 and the Society of Jesus 77, 78
Pius V, Pope (1504-1572) 75, 80, 247; and England 76, 77, 80, 87, 99; excommunication of Elizabeth 134, 141: and Scotland 68-70; *Regnans in Excelsis* 71, 74, 80, 94, 99-100, 105
Poissy (France): Colloquy of 56, 77
Poitiers (France): Edict of (1577) 122
Polanco, Juan de, S.J., Secretary to Loyola (1516-1576) 12, 29, 38, 67, 101
Poland 102, 170
Pole, Henry, Lord Montague (c. 1492-1539) 110
Pole, Lady Catherine, wife of Francis Hastings, Earl of Huntingdon (+1576) 110
Pole, Reginald, Cardinal (1500-1558) 14, 19, 24, 25, 26, 28, 29, 31, 33, 37, 50, 104; and the Society of Jesus 26, 28, 32, 35, 37, 38, 40, 100; conflict with Paul IV 36, 37; friendship with Bobadilla 26; legatine mission 27; opposition to a Jesuit mission to England 129; opposition to a Spanish marriage 27; relations with Loyola 25-27, 32-33, 35-36, 38-39, 42; restoration of Catholicism in England 31, 33, 38, 39; supports the German College, Rome 32
Pollen, John Hungerford, S.J., historian (1858-1925) 4, 5, 7, 13, 249
Porte, Dorothy, wife of George Hastings, Earl of Huntingdon (+1607) 110
Portugal 7, 95-98, 111, 112, 115, 116, 165, 186
Portuguese Jesuits in England 165
Possevino, Antonio, S.J., author, diplomat (1534-1611) 126, 127, 134, 219
Pounde, Thomas, S.J., laybrother (1538-1615) 101, 142, 146, 148, 156, 234; "Six Reasons" 146
Prince of Orange. See William (the Silent) of Orange
Pritchard, Arnold 266
Pullen, Joseph, S.J., military chaplain (c. 1543-1607) 203
Quadra, Alvaro, de la, Bishop of Aquila (fl. 1560) 50

Quinn, D.B. 16, 17
Quinn, John, O.P., Bishop of Limerick (+ c. 1555) 34
Radcliffe, Thomas, Earl of Sussex, Lord Deputy of Ireland (c. 1525-1583) 53, 55, 63, 65, 85, 86
Raggio, Tommaso, S.J., scholar and diplomat (+1599) 127
Rainolds, John, theologian, President of Corpus Christi, Oxford (1549-1607) 146
Rastall, John, S.J., theologian (c. 1530-1577) 45
Recusancy 47, 99, 123, 135, 144, 150
Redman, Mr. (*vere* Robert Parsons) 179
Reims 123, 136, 144, 168; English college in 188, 194, 260, 264
Requesens, Luis de, Governor of the Netherlands (1528-1576) 83, 84, 109
Reynolds, Thady, Bishop of Kildare who later conformed (fl. 1540) 20
Reynolds, William, Catholic priest, theologian (1543-1594) 179, 181
Ribadeneira, Pedo de, S.J., theologian, diplomat (1526-1611) 3, 34-38, 250; and Elizabethan settlement 48; explains defeat of Armada 261
Ridolfi Plot (1571) 87, 93
Rishton, Edward, Catholic priest (1550-c. 1585) 3, 72, 130, 136, 155
Rivat, Jean, S.J. (+1610?) 57
Rizzio, David, Secretary to Mary Queen of Scots (c. 1533-1566) 69
Rochford, Robert, S.J., missionary (c. 1541-1588) 94, 118, 119, 127, 220, 253
Rodrigues, Manuel, S.J., Provincial (+1596) 111, 112
Rodrigues, Simão, original member of the Society of Jesus (1510-1579) 14
Rogers, John, diplomat and administrator (c. 1540-c. 1603) 145
Rogers, Sir Thomas, diplomat (fl. 1585) 211
Rojas, Francisco, S.J. (fl. 1555) 34
Rome (Italy) 2, 11, 20, 24-26, 30-32, 36-39, 41, 48, 51, 54, 58, 61, 62, 69, 72, 77, 78, 81, 92, 97, 98, 100, 101, 105, 110, 113, 115, 123-125, 129, 134, 136, 142, 143, 145, 148, 156, 158, 160, 161, 166, 167, 170, 171, 186, 195-198, 200, 206-208, 218, 220, 221, 223, 224, 228, 233, 239, 245, 255, 259, 260, 263, 264
English (Hospice) College 101, 104-107, 123-125, 129-132, 135, 153, 180, 181, 187, 218, 219, 224, 225, 242, 255, 267; *Exigit saepenumero* (1578) 108; *Quoniam Divinae Bonitati* (1579) 108, 131
German College 32, 34, 37, 39, 41 107
Roman College 32, 34, 41, 180, 181
Roscarock, Nicholas, Catholic layman (c. 1549-c. 1634) 143
Rose, Stewart 13
Rothes, Earl of. See Leslie, Andrew, Earl of Rothes
Rouen (France) 72, 162, 168, 182, 190, 198, 202, 203, 206, 276
Rudolph, Holy Roman Emperor (1552-1612) 219
Ruthven (Scotland): Raid of (1582) 193
Ruthven, William, Earl of Gowrie (c. 1541-1584) 188, 202
Rutland, Earl of. See Manners, Edward, Earl of Rutland
Ruysbroeck, Jan Van, Flemish mystic (1293-1381) 126
Rye (England) 168
Sadler, Sir Ralph, diplomat (1507-1587) 73
Sailly, Thomas, S.J., military chaplain (1558-1623) 254
Saint-André, D'Albon, Jacques, Marshal (c. 1505-1562) 52
St. Bartholomew's Day massacres (1572) 89, 91
St. Germain (France): Peace of (1570) 75, 87
St. Leger, Sir Anthony, Lord Deputy of Ireland (c. 1496-1559) 17, 18
St. Malo (France) 113
St. Omer (France) 207; Jesuit college in 136
St. Winefrid's Well (near Bangor, Wales) 263
Salisbury, Thomas, Catholic layman (c. 1555-1623) 143
Salmerón, Alfonso, S.J., original member of the Society of Jesus (1515-1585) 14; and Scotland 77; mission to Ireland 15-17, 20-24, 26, 40, 61; relations with Cardinal Morone 33, 37, 104; Vicar-General 56, 57
Salviati, Antonio Maria, Nuncio in France and later Cardinal (1507-1602) 119
Samier, Henri, S.J., secret envoy from the Guises to Mary Queen of Scots, preacher, diplomat (1540-1610) 183, 185, 194, 196, 202
Sánchez, Diego, S.J. (fl. 1580) 180
Sander, Nicholas, Catholic priest, theologian, Nuncio (c. 1530-1581) 3, 25, 43, 72, 92, 93, 98, 103, 105, 108,

115, 128; attacks occasional conformity 99; in Ireland 116, 117, 136; proposed candidate for the red hat 163
Sanlúcar de Barrameda (Spain) 97, 98
Santa Cruz, Alvaro de Bazán, Marquis of, naval commander at Lepanto and during the Armada (1526-1588) 116
Santiago de Compostela (Spain) 94
Sarum use: synod of Southwark and 144
Sconce of Zutphen (Netherlands) 230
Scotland 1, 7, 8, 19-21, 40, 49-52, 55-57, 59-61, 65, 68, 69, 73, 77, 78, 84, 85-88, 92, 99, 101, 108, 117, 119, 120, 121, 128, 131-133, 163, 165, 177-179, 181-185, 187, 188, 190, 193, 194, 196, 197, 199-205, 208-213, 219, 222, 225, 227, 240, 241, 244, 252-255, 262, 266, 272, 273, 275, 277, 278
  Scottish Parliament (1560) 50; (1567) 86; (1571) 86, 87
Scots College: administered by Jesuits (1580) 219; in Pont-à-Mousson (1581) 219, 264; in Paris (1580) 219
Scott, Sir Thomas, M.P. (fl. 1570) 88
Sea-Beggars 83
Sebastian, King of Portugal (+1578) 115, 121, 122
Sega, Filippo, Cardinal, Bishop of Riga and Nuncio in Spain (+1596) 115, 116, 188, 189, 224, 225
Semple, Colonel William, Spanish agent in Scotland (1546-1633) 244
Serrão, Jorge, S.J., Provincial (1528-1590) 97
Seton, George, Lord (c. 1530-1585) 179, 188
Setons 202
Shakespeare, William, playwright (1564-1616) 170
Sheldon, Henry, S.J., theologian, administrator (1652-1714) 3-4
Sheldon, Ralph, Catholic layman (fl. 1580) 144
Shelley, Richard of Warminghurst, Catholic layman (+1586) 216, 267
Shelley, Sir Richard, Prior of the Knights of St. John (c. 1513-c. 1589) 105
Sherwin, Ralph, Catholic priest, missionary (1549-1581) 136, 155
Shoby (Leicestershire) 174
Shrewsbury, Earl of. See Talbot, George, Earl of Shrewsbury
Sidney, Sir Henry, Lord Deputy of Ireland (1529-1586) 53, 65, 66, 84

Sinclair, George, Earl of Caithness (c. 1527-1582) 61
Sinclair, Henry, Bishop of Ross (+1565) 59
Sixtus V, Pope (1520-1590) 208, 210, 212, 224, 226, 239; and Armada 239, 244-245, 263; and France 246; and Scotland 243; and Scots College 264
Skeffington, Sir William, Lord Deputy of Ireland (+1534) 17
Smerwick (Ireland) 116, 117
Smith, Nicholas, S.J., missionary, administrator (1558-1630) 142
Smith, Richard, Bishop of Chalcedon (1567-1655) 168
Somerset, William, Earl of Worcester (c. 1527-1589) 197
Soto, Pedro de, O.P. theologian (1500-1563) 39
Southampton (England) 75, 165
Southcote, John, Catholic priest (1587-1637) 164
Southwark (England): synod of 143-146, 152, 167
Southwell, Robert, S.J., missionary, writer (1561-1595) 6, 170, 173-174, 225, 229, 232, 233, 234, 238, 253, 257, 267, 274-276; comments on Armada 256; complains about persecution 176, 256, 263; and Anne, Countess of Arundel 236, 237; printing press 236; *An epistle of comfort* 237-238
Spain 1, 2, 6, 7, 19, 29, 30, 48-52, 75, 83, 84-87, 89, 92, 93, 97, 99, 105, 108, 109, 111, 121-123, 156, 170, 186, 188, 195-197, 200-202, 207, 208, 213, 218, 227, 230, 241, 243, 244, 245, 250, 252, 259, 260, 262, 263, 264, 277, 279
Spanish Netherlands 29, 48 See also Belgium, Flanders, Holland, Low Countries, Netherlands
Spirituali 26, 36
Stackpole, David, S.J., missionary (c. 1548-1586) 118
Stafford, Sir Edward, English ambassador to France (c. 1552-1605) 205
Staffordshire (England) 162
Stanihurst, Richard, Catholic layman, writer (1547-1618) 143
Stanley, Sir William, Catholic military commander (1548-1630) 230, 233, 244, 249, 250, 266, 267
Stapleton, Thomas, Catholic priest, theologian (1536-1598) 1, 90
Stephens, Thomas, S.J. missionary in India

(1550-1619) 102, 142
Stirling (Scotland) 86
Stokesley, John, Bishop of London (c. 1496-1539) 11, 13
Stonor Park (Berkshire) 153
Stonor, John, Catholic layman (+1616?) 143
Strong, Thomas, Bishop of Ossory (+1602) 167
Stuart, Esmé, Sieur d'Aubigny, Duke of Lennox (c. 1542-1583) 86, 119-121 178, 180-182, 184, 185, 187-189, 193, 222
Stuart, Francis, Earl of Bothwell (c. 1563-1611/14?) 243, 244, 252
Stuart, Henry, Lord Darnley, King of Scotland (1545-1567) 68, 70
Stuart, James, Earl of Moray (c. 1531-1570) 70, 85, 86
Stuart, James, Earl of Arran (+1595) 202, 210-212
Stuart, John, Earl of Atholl (+1579) 61
Stuart, Mary. See Mary Queen of Scots
Stuart, Matthew, Earl of Lennox, Regent (1516-1571) 61, 86, 88
Stucley, Sir Thomas, Catholic soldier of fortune (c. 1525-1578) 91, 92, 98, 100, 105, 108, 115
Suso, Henry. See Henry Suso.
Sussex (England) 194, 199
Sweden 126, 127, 170
Syminges family: Dr. John Syminges, second husband of Elizabeth Heywood Dunne, daughter of John, sister of Jasper and Elizeus Heywood and mother of John Dunne 168
Tablares, Pedro, S.J. (+1565) 34, 35
Talbot, George, Earl of Shrewsbury (c. 1522-1590) 197
Tanner, Edmund, ex-Jesuit, Bishop of Cork (1527-1579) 67, 94, 118
Tassis, Juan Bautista de, Spanish ambassador to France (1530-1610) 178, 185, 188, 189, 195, 198, 199
Tauler, John, O.P., German mystic (c. 1300-1361) 126
Taunton, Ethelred, Catholic priest, historian (1857-1907) 4, 5
Terceira (Azores) 165
Throckmorton Plot (1584) 169, 176, 198, 200, 213
Throckmorton, Edward, Catholic layman (fl. 1580) 143
Throckmorton, Francis, Catholic layman (1554-1584) 143, 199, 200
Throckmorton, Job, M.P., Puritan controversialist (1545-1601) 228, 235

Throckmorton, Thomas, Catholic layman (fl. 1580) 143
Tilney, Charles, Catholic layman (fl. 1580) 143
Titchbourne, Chideock, Catholic layman (+1586) 143
Toledo, Francisco, S.J. theologian, later Cardinal (1532-1596) 218; and occasional conformity 145
Tournai (Belgium) 101, 203
Tournon (France) 210
Trent (Italy): Council of (1545-1563) 56, 58, 61, 68, 140, 167; excommunication of Elizabeth considered 71
Tresham, Sir Thomas, Catholic peer (c. 1543-1605) 172, 216, 257, 267
Tresham, William, Catholic layman, brother of Sir Thomas (fl. 1580-1595) 143, 186
Trevor-Roper, Hugh, Baron Dacre of Glanton 6, 7, 9, 265
Trimble, W.R. 23
Troyes (France): Treaty of (1564) 73
Tyrie, James, S.J., missionary, General's assistant (c. 1543-1597) 68, 201, 209-211, 218, 277; and John Knox 86
Tyrone (Ireland) 66
Ulster (Ireland) 17, 18, 20, 22, 52, 62, 63, 65, 85, 220, 253; proposed site for a Jesuit novitiate 62, 78
Utrecht (Netherlands): Union of (1579) 114
Vallareggio, Alexandro, S.J., missionary, procurator (1530-1580) 96, 97, 112
Valois, Marguerite (+1615), Queen Consort of Henry IV 74
Varia, Francisco de, S.J. (fl. 1575) 96
Vassy (France): massacre at (1562) 72
Vaux, Henry, Catholic layman, entered Jesuits on his deathbed (c. 1559-1587) 143
Vaux, William, Lord, Catholic peer (-+1595) 172, 174, 274
Vega, Manuel de, S.J., missionary (1540-1608) 180
Venice (Italy) 83
Verstegan, Richard, Catholic printer (c. 1565-1620) 262
Vienna (Austria) 41, 180, 219; Jesuit college in 35
Vilnius (Lithuania) 180
Viola, Giambattista, S.J., administrator (c. 1517-1589) 24
Vives, Juan Luis, humanist (1492-1540) 12
Waferer, Francis, S.J., (1541-1588) 255
Wales 103, 187

Walker, John, Archdeacon of Essex (+1588) 155
Walsh, Walter 4, 5
Walsingham, Sir Francis, Secretary (c. 1530-1590) 155, 192, 198, 199, 211, 213, 233, 248
Warwick (England) 228
Warwick, Earl of. See Dudley, Ambrose, Earl of Warwick
Watts, William, Catholic priest, missionary, military chaplain (c. 1560-c. 1582) 178-181, 203, 222
Wauchope, Robert, Archbishop of Armagh (+1551) 14, 19, 24, 40
Westminster (England): disputations at (1559) 43
Westmorland, Earl of. See Nevill, Charles, Earl of Westmorland
Weston, William, S.J., missionary (1550-1615) 3, 169, 170, 231, 274, 277; answers "Bloody Questions" 235; captured and imprisoned 174, 234; establishment of a missionary system and a financial fund 172, 236; instructions to 275-276; meeting with Allen and Parsons in Paris 170; requests more Jesuits 173; work in England 168, 171-174
Wexford (Ireland): Jesuit school in 94
Whitford, Richard, spiritual writer (c. 1495-c. 1555) 13
William IV, Duke of Bavaria (+1550) 22
William V, Duke of Bavaria (+1626) 161
William (the Silent) of Orange, Prince of Nassau (1533-1584) 75, 84, 109, 114, 176, 193, 201, 205, 213, 216, 244
Wilson, Stephen, servant of Mary Queen of Scots (fl. 1560) 58
Winzet, Ninian, Catholic priest, controversialist (1518-1592) 68
Wolfe, David, ex-Jesuit, missionary, Nuncio (c. 1528-c. 1578) 34, 39, 51, 54, 65, 77, 93, 94, 105, 113, 118, 126-128, 131, 265-266, 272; accusations against 95, 96; activities in Spain and Portugal 94-98, 111-113; and Mercurian 223; capture of (1567) 66; consults James FitzMaurice FitzGerald in France 113; diplomatic activities of 112; dismissal and death 113; mission to and work in Ireland 55, 61-66, 78, 79; proposal for an enterprise 93, 96-98, 108; released from prison 94; replies to accusations 96, 97
Wolsey, Thomas, Cardinal (c. 1474-1530) 11
Woodhouse, Thomas, S.J., missionary (+1573) 101
Worcester, Earl of. See Somerset, William, Earl of Worcester
Worcestershire (England) 151
Wyford, Mr., Catholic layman 172
Xavier, Francis, S.J., original member of the Society of Jesus (1506-1552) 14, 24
Yorke, Sir Rowland, military officer (fl. 1585) 230
Yorkshire (England) 152, 166, 167
Youghal (Ireland) 55; Jesuit school in 65, 67, 118
Zapata, Francesco, ex-Jesuit (fl. 1540) 15
Zornoza, Martín de, Spanish consul in Venice (fl. 1530) 26
Zutphen (Netherlands) 230
Viglius van Aytta, jurist, Secretary to Mary of Hungary (1507-1577) 28, 30

STUDIES IN MEDIEVAL
AND REFORMATION THOUGHT
EDITED BY HEIKO A. OBERMAN

1. DOUGLASS, E. J. D. *Justification in Late Medieval Preaching.* 2nd ed. 1989
2. WILLIS, E. D. *Calvin's Catholic Christology.* 1966 *out of print*
3. POST, R. R. *The Modern Devotion.* 1968 *out of print*
4. STEINMETZ, D. C. *Misericordia Dei.* The Theology of Johannes von Staupitz. 1968 *out of print*
5. O'MALLEY, J. W. *Giles of Viterbo on Church and Reform.* 1968 *out of print*
6. OZMENT, S. E. *Homo Spiritualis.* The Anthropology of Tauler, Gerson and Luther. 1969
7. PASCOE, L. B. *Jean Gerson: Principles of Church Reform.* 1973 *out of print*
8. HENDRIX, S. H. *Ecclesia in Via.* Medieval Psalms Exegesis and the *Dictata super Psalterium* (1513-1515) of Martin Luther. 1974
9. TREXLER, R. C. *The Spiritual Power.* Republican Florence under Interdict. 1974
10. TRINKAUS, Ch. with OBERMAN, H. A. (eds.) *The Pursuit of Holiness.* 1974 *out of print*
11. SIDER, R. J. *Andreas Bodenstein von Karlstadt.* 1974
12. HAGEN, K. *A Theology of Testament in the Young Luther.* 1974
13. MOORE, Jr., W. L. *Annotatiunculae D. Iohanne Eckio Praelectore.* 1976
14. OBERMAN, H. A. with BRADY, Jr., Th. A. (eds.) *Itinerarium Italicum.* Dedicated to Paul Oskar Kristeller. 1975
15. KEMPFF, D. *A Bibliography of Calviniana.* 1959-1974. 1975 *out of print*
16. WINDHORST, C. *Täuferisches Taufverständnis.* 1976
17. KITTELSON, J. M. *Wolfgang Capito.* 1975
18. DONNELLY, J. P. *Calvinism and Scholasticism in Vermigli's Doctrine of Man and Grace.* 1976
19. LAMPING, A. J. *Ulrichus Velenus (Oldřich Velenský) and his Treatise against the Papacy.* 1976
20. BAYLOR, M. G. *Action and Person.* Conscience in Late Scholasticism and the Young Luther. 1977
21. COURTENAY, W. J. *Adam Wodeham.* 1978
22. BRADY, Jr., Th. A. *Ruling Class, Regime and Reformation at Strasbourg, 1520-1555.* 1978
23. KLAASSEN, W. *Michael Gaismair.* 1978
24. BERNSTEIN, A. E. *Pierre d'Ailly and the Blanchard Affair.* 1978
25. BUCER, Martin. *Correspondance.* Tome I (Jusqu'en 1524). Publié par J. Rott. 1979
26. POSTHUMUS MEYJES, G. H. M. *Jean Gerson et l'Assemblée de Vincennes (1329).* 1978
27. VIVES, Juan Luis. *In Pseudodialecticos.* Ed. by Ch. Fantazzi. 1979
28. BORNERT, R. *La Réforme Protestante du Culte à Strasbourg au XVIe siècle (1523-1598).* 1981
29. SEBASTIAN CASTELLIO. *De Arte Dubitandi.* Ed. by E. Feist Hirsch. 1981
30. BUCER, Martin. *Opera Latina.* Vol I. Publié par C. Augustijn, P. Fraenkel, M. Lienhard. 1982
31. BÜSSER, F. *Wurzeln der Reformation in Zürich.* 1985 *out of print*
32. FARGE, J. K. *Orthodoxy and Reform in Early Reformation France.* 1985
33, 34. BUCER, Martin. *Etudes sur les relations de Bucer avec les Pays-Bas.* I. Etudes; II. Documents. Par J. V. Pollet. 1985
35. HELLER, H. *The Conquest of Poverty.* The Calvinist Revolt in Sixteenth Century France. 1986

36. MEERHOFF, K. *Rhétorique et poétique au XVIᵉ siècle en France.* 1986
37. GERRITS, G. H. *Inter timorem et spem.* Gerard Zerbolt of Zutphen. 1986
38. ANGELO POLIZIANO. *Lamia.* Ed. by A. Wesseling. 1986
39. BRAW, C. *Bücher im Staube.* Die Theologie Johann Arndts in ihrem Verhältnis zur Mystik. 1986
40. BUCER, Martin. *Opera Latina.* Vol. II. Enarratio in Evangelion Iohannis (1528, 1530, 1536). Publié par I. Backus. 1988
41. BUCER, Martin. *Opera Latina.* Vol. III. Martin Bucer and Matthew Parker: Florilegium Patristicum. Edition critique. Publié par P. Fraenkel. 1988
42. BUCER, Martin. *Opera Latina.* Vol. IV. Consilium Theologicum Privatim Conscriptum. Publié par P. Fraenkel. 1988
43. BUCER, Martin. *Correspondance.* Tome II (1524-1526). Publié par J. Rott. 1989
44. RASMUSSEN, T. *Inimici Ecclesiae.* Das ekklesiologische Feindbild in Luthers "Dictata super Psalterium" (1513-1515) im Horizont der theologischen Tradition. 1989
45. POLLET, J. *Julius Pflug et la crise religieuse dans l'Allemagne du XVIᵉ siècle.* Essai de synthèse biographique et théologique. 1990
46. BUBENHEIMER, U. *Thomas Müntzer.* Herkunft und Bildung. 1989
47. BAUMAN, C. *The Spiritual Legacy of Hans Denck.* Interpretation and Translation of Key Texts. 1991
48. OBERMAN, H. A. and JAMES, F. A., III (eds.) in cooperation with SAAK, E. L. *Via Augustini.* Augustine in the Later Middle Ages, Renaissance and Reformation: Essays in Honor of Damasus Trapp. 1991 *out of print*
49. SEIDEL MENCHI, S. *Erasmus als Ketzer.* Reformation und Inquisition im Italien des 16. Jahrhunderts. 1993
50. SCHILLING, H. *Religion, Political Culture, and the Emergence of Early Modern Society.* Essays in German and Dutch History. 1992
51. DYKEMA, P. A. and OBERMAN, H. A. (eds.) *Anticlericalism in Late Medieval and Early Modern Europe.* 1993
52, 53. KRIEGER, Chr. and LIENHARD, M. (eds.) *Martin Bucer and Sixteenth Century Europe.* Actes du colloque de Strasbourg (28-31 août 1991). 1993
54. SCREECH, M. A. *Clément Marot: A Renaissance Poet discovers the World.* Lutheranism, Fabrism and Calvinism in the Royal Courts of France and of Navarre and in the Ducal Court of Ferrara. 1994
55. GOW, A. C. *The Red Jews: Antisemitism in an Apocalyptic Age, 1200-1600.* 1995
56. BUCER, Martin. *Correspondance.* Tome III (1527-1529). Publié par Chr. Krieger et J. Rott. 1989
57. SPIJKER, W. VAN 'T. *The Ecclesiastical Offices in the Thought of Martin Bucer.* Translated by J. Vriend (text) and L.D. Bierma (notes). 1996
58. GRAHAM, M.F. *The Uses of Reform.* 'Godly Discipline' and Popular Behavior in Scotland and Beyond, 1560-1610. 1996
59. AUGUSTIJN, C. *Erasmus. Der Humanist als Theologe und Kirchenreformer.* 1996
60. McCOOG SJ, T. M. *The Society of Jesus in Ireland, Scotland, and England 1541-1588.* 'Our Way of Proceeding?' 1996